THE NAVAL HISTORY
GREAT BRITAIN

VOLUME THE FIRST

Mr WILLIAM JAMES.

ENGRAVED BY W. READ, FROM A PAINTING BY W. M?CALL.

THE
NAVAL HISTORY
OF
GREAT BRITAIN

FROM THE DECLARATION OF WAR BY FRANCE
IN 1793
TO THE ACCESSION OF GEORGE IV.

BY

WILLIAM JAMES

*A NEW EDITION, WITH ADDITIONS AND NOTES
BRINGING THE WORK DOWN TO 1827*

VÉRITÉ SANS PEUR

IN SIX VOLUMES
VOL. I.

London
MACMILLAN AND CO., Limited
NEW YORK: THE MACMILLAN COMPANY
1902

All rights reserved

First Edition, 5 vols., 8vo, and 2 4to vols. of Abstracts. 1822.
Second Edition, with additions and notes. 1826.
Third Edition, with a continuation by CAPTAIN CHAMIER, R.N.; in ten monthly parts 5*s*. each, or fifty weekly parts 1*s*. each, beginning May, 1836; in 6 vols., demy 8vo, with portraits, 54*s*. April 17, 1837.
Fourth Edition, in 6 vols., 8vo, with portraits, and index by C. T. WILSON. 1847.
Fifth Edition, in 6 vols., crown 8vo, with preface by T. W. COLE, stereotyped. 1859. *Reprinted*, 1864.
Sixth Edition, with corrigenda. December 5, 1877.
Seventh Edition, with addition by Professor YORK POWELL. April 19, 1886.
Transferred to Macmillan & Co., August, 1898. *Reprinted*, November, 1902.

TO THE

BRITISH NATION,

THIS

FAITHFUL HISTORY OF ITS NAVY,

OF THE SERVICES OF HIS MAJESTY'S FLEETS, SQUADRONS,
AND SINGLE SHIPS,

BY THE LATE

WILLIAM JAMES, Esq.,

IS RESPECTFULLY DEDICATED BY

THE EDITOR.

In Memoriam. William James.

Died 1827.

VÉRITÉ SANS PEUR.

"JAMES, one of the most pertinacious of investigators, set a new example. He honestly did his utmost to satisfy himself of the absolute truth of every statement which he submitted to his readers. He wrote hundreds of letters to the surviving actors in the events which he purposed to describe. He read and digested all the despatches, logs, gazettes, previous histories, foreign reports, and private narratives on which he could lay hands. He carefully balanced conflicting accounts, and arrived in the majority of instances at conclusions, the correctness of which has never yet been successfully attacked. He went to immense pains to give the exact Christian names of all officers whom he had occasion to mention, and to analyse the true force of every ship, the exploits of which he recounted. Never was there a man more painstaking, more indefatigable, more scrupulously conscientious."—THE FORTNIGHTLY REVIEW.

"This book is one of which it is not too high praise to assert that it approaches as nearly to perfection in its own line as any historical work, perhaps, ever did. The research and the labour must have been so great that they alone may be considered a striking monument of industry. With a candour almost as uncommon as his accuracy, Mr. James never fails to notice any variations of consequence in the statements of the hostile party, and either to refute it by argument or fairly to balance it with the opposing testimony. We cannot contemplate without admiration the impartial and unwearied zeal for historical truth which alone could have supported him through his tedious and thankless labours."—THE EDINBURGH REVIEW.

"The best Naval History of England. Its impartial statement of facts is so well established that it was constantly referred to by French naval officers visiting my ship in the Mediterranean, to decide any question in discussion."—ADMIRAL SIR PULTENEY MALCOLM,

"One of the most valuable works in the English language."—THE UNITED SERVICE GAZETTE.

PREFACE TO THE NEW EDITION.

A NEW edition of "James's Naval History" demands a few prefatory remarks. Since the Battle of Navarino (fought on the 20th of October, 1827), with which the work concludes, an element in nautical science unknown to our forefathers has passed into universal adoption, rendering the evolutions of fleets and single ships almost entirely independent of the fluctuations of wind and weather; and setting aside the most approved systems of attack and defence, as hitherto practised by the ablest commanders.

The introduction of steam must produce another change in maritime warfare, equal to that occasioned by the invention of gunpowder. History and past experience will cease to be referred to as practical teachers. The best lessons they can now supply are confined to the examples of skill, courage, and patriotic devotion, never to be surpassed, from which future Nelsons may learn how the battles of that great admiral and his contemporaries were fought and won. But while naval students admire these glorious records, they will see at once that the tactics of the last generation will cease to be available in future. They will learn to understand fully the difficulties and deficiencies inseparable from the manœuvres of sailing-fleets, with all the casual impediments of storms, or calms, of baffling or contrary winds, of lee shores, tides, currents, shoals, or breakers; and they will also rejoice while they wonder, at finding these obstacles comparatively negatived by the absolute power of steam propulsion,—a power which can be exercised and regulated with almost mathematical certainty.

Steam may be considered the most important agent in mechanics that man's ingenuity has yet brought into action. Its early development was slow—unlike printing, which reached perfection in infancy; but the progress of steam, as practically exercised within the last thirty years, is a tissue of marvels, opening prospects that baffle theory, and set the calculations of reason at defiance.

The idea of motion produced by steam-pressure appears to have originated with an Italian, named Brancas, residing at Rome, in 1628. The first real steam-engine is described by the Marquis of Worcester, a faithful royalist, in a small pamphlet published three years after the restoration of Charles the Second, in 1663, entitled "A Century of Inventions." He calls it, "a way to drive up water by fire;" but neither the public nor the government appeared to be much attracted by the discovery. Had the Starchamber not been abolished, the noble inventor would have incurred the risk of being brought before that righteous tribunal for an unholy alliance with the powers of darkness.

In 1769, James Watt, then a mathematical instrument-maker in Glasgow, obtained a patent for his great invention of performing condensation in a separate vessel from the cylinder. To this he made many subsequent improvements, and acquired additional patents. In 1778, the notorious Thomas Paine proposed the application of steam in America; and in 1807, Robert Fulton, a native of Pennsylvania, started a small steam-boat on the Hudson river. The progress of this vessel through the water scarcely exceeded five miles an hour. Fulton had meditated on the experiment since 1793; but although he claimed to be the first who applied water-wheels to the purposes of steam-navigation, most assuredly he was not the inventor. Yet he has often been so called, as in naming the new world, Amerigo Vespucci has supplanted Columbus to whom the lawful parentage belongs.

Mr. Millar, of Dalswinton, in Dumfriesshire, a Scotch gentleman of good family and fortune, and with a mind devoted to mechanical inquiry, expended many years, and many thousands by which his patrimonial estate became involved, in the construction of a steam-ship propelled by paddles.[1] This vessel was launched and tried on some water in the neighbourhood of Dalswinton, nineteen years anterior to the assumed discovery of Fulton. Mr. Millar offered his ship to the consideration of the government of the day. As usual, he was treated with indifference, and his proposal rejected. He was even unable to obtain a trial at his own expense. Surprised and disheartened at this repulse, he took his steamer to Stockholm, and offered it as a free gift to the Swedish sovereign Gustavus the Third, an enterprising, enlightened monarch, with ideas far in advance of his people and their resources. He had a mind active in improvement, but his exchequer was empty. Though he fully appreciated and understood the value of the offering, he had nothing to bestow in return but a gold snuff-box, with his portrait set in brilliants, valued at about 3000*l*.: a modern parallel of the unequal interchange of civilities between Sarpedon and Glaucus, in the Iliad. Gustavus promised great results, in case the principle of steam should be found applicable to general use. But soon afterwards, he fell by the hand of Ankerströem, and no time was allowed him to profit by the valuable acquisition so disinterestedly placed in his hands. With the king of Sweden's assassination ended the dream of Mr. Millar's life. He returned home a disappointed and impoverished man, adding one more to the list of those who have lived to see their reputations filched from them, and their claims appropriated by undeservers. The writer of this notice learned the facts here stated from Major Millar of Dumfries (eldest son of Mr. Millar), in whose possession he saw the snuff-box and portrait alluded to above—the only beneficial advantage the family ever derived from the persevering energy of their ancestor. It is hard to waste time and money in the enthusiam of scientific pursuit; but it cuts deeper still to be defrauded of well-earned fame. There is reason to suppose that the double vexation preyed on the mind and health of Mr. Millar, and hastened his death.

In 1819, the "Savannah," a vessel of only 350 tons burthen,

[1] See the "Scots Magazine," for 1788.

steamed across the Atlantic in twenty-six days from New York to Liverpool. She then proceeded to St. Petersburg, and subsequently recrossed the Atlantic, using steam during the three passages.

In 1825, Captain Johnston received a reward of 10,000*l*., for making the first steam-voyage to India, in the "Enterprise," which sailed from Falmouth on the 16th of August in that year. This, we believe, was the same skilful and fortunate navigator of whom it is recorded that, up to November, 1828, he had traversed the Atlantic in sailing-vessels one hundred and seventy-two times, without wreck, or capture, or a single accident of any kind which incurred a loss to the underwriters on the ships he commanded.

The "Great Western" arrived at New York, from Bristol, on the 17th of June, 1828, making the transit in eighteen days, which is now usually accomplished in half the time. War-steamers began to be built in England in 1838; and in 1840, the "Nemesis," and "Phlegethon"—"devil-ships," as they were called by the enemy—did good service during the Chinese war.

The loss of the "President," on her home passage, in the dreadful gale of March, 1841, for the moment produced a feeling of mistrust as to the permanent efficacy of steam navigation in situations of extreme peril, and for distant voyages on stormy seas; but the evil impression rapidly passed away. It was remembered that the "British Queen" and the Halifax mail-steamers weathered the hurricane to which the "President" had succumbed, and that many of the finest sailing-vessels in the royal navy and merchant-service had been lost by foundering at sea. The instance of the "President" was an isolated casualty, and not a test upon which to establish a general rule. Gigantic as that steamer was considered at the time, she bore no comparison to the dimensions of the "Himalaya," and the latter sinks into a dwarf by the side of the "Great Eastern."

Between the years 1842 and 1845, her Majesty's steam-sloop, "Driver," commanded by Captains Harmer and Hayes, performed the circumnavigation of the globe. While we are writing, in 1859, the navies of all the leading nations of the civilized world are principally composed of steamers on the most improved principles. Iron and the screw are rapidly superseding the old ribs of oak and the recent paddle.

It was expected that the late Russian quarrel would afford an opportunity of testing steam tactics in a general engagement; but the foe of the moment was too wary to risk the result. He preferred sinking his own ships at the eleventh hour to the chances of battle. For himself he took, perhaps, the wisest course; but when our hands were in, our blood warmed, and heavy war expenses incurred, it would have been more satisfactory for England if the problem had then been decided.

Sir Howard Douglas, in an able and scientific work, "On Naval Warfare with Steam," published shortly before the close of 1858, has, in addition to much valuable information, suggested some admirable rules for the future movements of fleets. His theory, that military manœuvres and principles will come largely into play in future naval operations, is soundly based, and so clearly demonstrated, that he must be a hardy casuist who would undertake to refute it. The same view had been previously taken by a distinguished naval officer, Admiral Bowles, in a tract published in 1846, entitled an "Essay on Naval Tactics." To these high authorities may be added that of Captain Dalgren of the United States Navy. Several French writers, amongst others, Labrouse, Paixhans, and De La Graviere, as early as 1843, delivered very explicit opinions that the employment of steam as a moving power would be attended with results beneficial to the nations of the Continent, while it will operate to the disadvantage of Great Britain—a hasty inference which Englishmen will not be disposed to admit. The wealth, population, and resources of England, her national spirit, her enterprise, her nautical science, and mechanical ingenuity, have neither remained stationary nor declined while those of other nations have gone on improving. On the contrary, they have advanced in more than an equal ratio. Why then is it to be supposed that the superior tactical skill of our commanders, so eminently displayed before the adoption of steam, should suddenly fail them under the influence of a newly-discovered and more manageable implement of warfare? The conclusion is "a thing devised by the enemy."

Lord Nelson, in his two splendid victories of the Nile and Trafalgar, won both by doubling upon his adversaries, and by bringing, without aggregate superiority of force, a concentrated power upon a given point, thus dividing the strength opposed to him, and beating it in detail. He could have executed these brilliant manœuvres with more precision had steam been used in his day; but it is unlikely that such advantages will again be offered to an attacking fleet. At the Nile, the French remained passively at anchor: at Trafalgar, the Franco-Spanish fleet, was drawn up in a double line, slightly verging towards a curve; so that when that formation was trisected by the two advancing columns of the English, the rear ships were placed out of condition to succour those in the van and centre within the required time. The wind was light, and the speed of Lord Nelson's fleet scarcely exceeded a mile and a half in the hour. This tardy pace subjected them to a long and heavy fire before they could get into action, which steam would have prevented. The "Victory," Nelson's flag-ship, leading the weather-column, was exposed to some hundreds of heavy guns during forty minutes before she reached the opposing line, or returned a shot. Steam also has another important advantage: it liberates the greater portion of the crew for the exclusive service of the guns. The old system of ships ranging up alongside of each other and exchanging broadsides at close quarters is not likely to happen again. It is more than probable that they would go down reciprocally, if at all equal in force, under a single discharge. The oblique, and not the direct order of battle must be substituted. The effect of such a mode of attack will depend much on the speed of the ships, and more on the talent of the commanding admiral. This plan requires a perfect knowledge of the most effective military manœuvres which the annals of war supply for study and practical application. The oblique order, as already stated, consists in concentrating a superior force, at the critical moment, against the flank or centre of the enemy, and throwing him into confusion, from which time must never be given to him to recover. This decisive movement was first practised by Epaminondas, the Theban general, at Leuctra and Mantinea; and thus he overthrew the best troops of ancient

Greece, the disciplined and, until then, invincible Spartans. Alexander, upon the same principle, won his conclusive victory at Arbela, against Darius; and in modern times Gustavus Adolphus, Frederick the Great, and Napoleon the First, illustrated its overpowering efficacy on many brilliant fields.

With the aid of steam, this system becomes even more available at sea than on shore, for where there is no inequality of ground or natural impediment, and speed is open to certain calculation, the incidental difficulties are diminished in proportion. But, again, the success of steam warfare must depend quite as much upon the relative abilities of the contending commanders as upon the courage or discipline of the men. Sir Howard Douglas's remarks on this particular point are worthy of repetition.[1]—"It may appear to some that in future naval battles there will be no attacks by fleets advancing directly in divisions of ships arrayed in line ahead on the broadside batteries of an enemy's fleet, as at Trafalgar, and that there will be no repetition of such a battle as that in Aboukir Bay. This would tend to show that the new system of naval warfare will put an end to that bold, resolute, and audacious mode of action, which was the wont of the British navy. But this will not be the case. It is true that in the present very improved state of naval gunnery, such a mode of attack as that adopted at Trafalgar could not be made without seriously crippling the attacking fleet, before it could close with the enemy; and it is not probable that so faulty a formation as that of the French fleet in Aboukir Bay will again occur. But our officers, imbued with the resources of tactical science and nautical skill, and our men able and ardent to carry out, with unflinching courage, their commands, will nevertheless find in steam warfare ample opportunities for acting in that vigorous and bold manner which has ever been congenial to the spirit of British seamen."

The peace advocates, who hailed the Great Exhibition of 1851 as the inauguration of universal harmony, a shutting of the temple of Janus, never to be reopened, are sadly mistaken in their

---

See "Naval Warfare with Steam," p. 114.

anticipations. At this moment continental Europe bristles with bayonets, and the anvil of the armourer smothers up the gentler cadence of the loom, the shuttle, and the spinning-wheel. In trade-loving America, the thirst for annexation has inspired a rabid appetite for glory not likely to be quenched until they find what a heavy outlay is inseparably attached to the commodity they covet. With the French, the love of glory is indigenous; it is the breath of their nostrils, the essence of their being. An army of 500,000 men, rusting in country-quarters—baited, but not fed, with field-days and reviews, with small pay, less promotion, and no prize-money—are not likely to be satisfied long in their profitless inactivity. Italy, for choice, is their secret aspiration; but England, rather than no war at all. How long will the Emperor Napoleon, supposing him to be wise and honourable, faithful to his treaties and just to his people, be able to restrain the army on whom he depends? Or how long will he be restrained by the force of European opinion? These are delicate questions not easily answered.

"The navies of Europe and America," says Sir Howard Douglas (Introduction, pp. 11 and 12,) "have so increased in the number and strength of the ships, and their *personnel*—in all that relates to the service and practice of war—that in a future contest, the sea will become the theatre of events more important and decisive than have ever yet been witnessed.

"The efforts of our nearest continental neighbours have been particularly directed, during the last nine years, to the reattainment of that rank and consideration which their nation formerly held among the naval powers of the world; and admitting this to be a just and laudable policy for France to pursue, Great Britain should at the same time keep steadily in view the measures now being carried out in that country conformably to the recommendation of the Commission of Inquiry of 1849, and must take corresponding measures to increase in due proportion the power, efficiency, and numerical strength of her naval forces, in order to maintain her present position. Thus the naval arsenals of two great nations in alliance with each other, one of them compelled by a necessity of the first and highest order,—that of providing effectually for its own security,—are resounding with the din of warlike preparations, while both might be participating in the financial advantages and social benefits of a sound and lasting peace."

The position is unpleasant, but inevitable. With a restless neighbour armed to the teeth, and within a few hours' sail of our shores, we have no certain security but in preparation; and however expensive the alternative may be, preparation is a thousand times better than surprise. Let England be on the alert, and she has no occasion to fear attack from any power or powers that may unite against her. At the commencement of the Crimean campaign we suffered fearfully for want of foresight. Before the fall of Sebastopol, we had gained our second wind, and could have gone on for ever. But why should we strain our quality of endurance by such unnecessary trials? May our statesmen profit by example, and avoid such costly mistakes in future! A strong Channel fleet, equal to any that can be equipped against us, and in constant exercise, with an ample reserve of gun-boats and mortar-vessels, will constitute a better chain of coast-defences than a triple wall of fortifications, if such could be erected, from the mouth of the Thames to the Lizard Point. Much has appeared from time to time, in responsible print, as to three formidable divisions of fifty thousand men each, convoyed by fleets of corresponding power, simultaneously collected and thrown at the same moment on distinct points of England, Scotland, and Ireland. A comprehensive plan of invasion, which supposes every possible contingency in the chapter of accidents to be combined against us, and not one to operate in our favour. The argument, like Touchstone's ill-roasted egg, is "all on one side;" the enterprise clearly impossible. Let the French expend millions upon millions on the fortifications of Cherbourg, either as a haven of refuge, or a hostile rendezvous. Cherbourg cannot cross the channel on a foggy night, to take Portsmouth by a *coup-de-main*; while Alderney is a well-placed outpost, an eye looking into the hostile camp to warn us of collecting danger.

If an army destined to invade another country escapes the opposing fleet, a landing can be effected at any chosen point. The history of all ages establishes this fact. But in the case of a descent on England, the enemy should be met at once in the confusion of disembarkation, before he has time to land his *matériel* of war, and to take up an inland position. It might then be more difficult to dislodge him: but with the sea close to his back, he fights without a base. Datis and Artaphernes found this to their cost when routed by Miltiades at Marathon, and William the Norman would in all probability have supplied another example at Hastings, but for the untimely arrow which deprived the English army of the generalship of Harold.

In the present edition of the Naval History, a few changes will be found in the arrangement of the sections into which the work is divided. These have been made for the purpose of equalizing the volumes; but there are no alterations whatever either in the series of events or in the substance of the original text.

London, April, 1859.

CONTENTS.

VOL. 1
1488 to 1792.

INTRODUCTION—First ship of war—Cannon, 1—Portholes, 2—Two important improvements in ships of war, 3—Origin of ships' rates, 5—The unrated classes, 6—Old MS. list of the navy, 7—Calibers of guns, 8—Ancient and modern shot, 9—Improved classification of the ships, 11—Decks of a ship of war, 11—First decks armed with guns, 13—Decks of a ship of war, 14—Origin of the term gangway, 16—Meaning of the term flush-decked, 17—Ambiguity in other naval terms, 18—Flush and quarter-decked ships, 21—Line-of-battle ships, 21—Frigates, 22—British frigates modelled from the French, 23—Constant-Warwick, the first British frigate, 24—Made a two-decker, 26—The classification of foreign navies, 28—English frigate-classes, 30—First genuine English frigate, 31—English and foreign 18-pounder frigates, 33—The post-ship classes, 34—Invention of the carronade, 36—Establishment of carronades for each class, 37—Dispute between the Ordnance and Navy Boards, 39—Advantages of the carronade shown, 40—Distinction between "guns" and "carronades," 42—Large and small calibers compared, 44—Calibers of English and foreign guns, 45—Remarks on the tonnage of ships of war, 47—Cause of variety of size in British navy, 48.

1792-3.

FIRST FRENCH REVOLUTIONARY WAR, 49—War declared against England, &c., 50.

BRITISH AND FRENCH FLEETS—State of the British navy, 51—Captains and commanders, 53—Dutch, Spanish, Russian, and other navies, 54—Comparative state of the French navy, 57—French seamen, 58—Armament of French ships, 59—First republican fleet at sea, 60—Lord Howe's first cruise, 61—Lord Howe and M. Morard-de-Galles, 62—Description of Brest, 65—Lord Howe and M. Vanstabel, 66—Description of Toulon, 69—Lord Hood at Toulon, 73—Commodore Linzee at Forneilli, 94—French frigates at Genoa and Spezzia, 97.

LIGHT SQUADRONS AND SINGLE SHIPS, 97—Scourge and Sans-Culotte, 98-Lieutenant Western, ibid.—Bedford and Leopard, 99—Re-capture of the St Iago, 100—Iris and Citoyenne-Française, 101—Venus and Sémillante, 103-Hyæna and Concorde, 105—Nymphe and Cléopâtre, 106—Boston and Er buscade, 110—Crescent and Réunion, 115—Agamemnon and French frigate 117—Thames and Uranie, 118—Capture of the Inconstante, 122—Captu of a privateer by a packet, 123.

COLONIAL EXPEDITIONS, 124—Colonies of the different powers, 125.

NORTH AMERICA, 125—Surrender of St. Pierre and Miquelon, 126.

WEST INDIES, capture of Tobago, 127—Ill success at Martinique, ibid.-Dreadful hurricane, 128—Surrender of Cape-Nicolas-Mole, St. Domingo, 13(

EAST INDIES 131—Attack upon the Résolue, ibid.—Capture of Pondicherr, 133.

1794.

BRITISH AND FRENCH FLEETS, 134—State of the British navy, 135—Violer proceedings at Brest, 136—Re-organization of the Brest fleet, 137—Sailir of Lord Howe, 138—Rear-admirals Montagu and Nielly, 140—Sailing M. Villaret-Joyeuse, 141—Chase of the Audacieux, 144—Lord Howe o the 28th of May, 145—Audacious and Révolutionnaire, 146—Lord How on the 29th of May, 149—Same on 31st of May, 160—M. Villaret joined k M. Nielly, 161—Lord Howe on the 1st of June, 162—Capture of the Ale: ander, 203—Mutiny on board the Culloden, 205—Lord Hood at Corsic 207—Lord Hood and M. Martin in Goujean bay, 214—Mutiny on boar the Windsor Castle, 215.

LIGHT SQUADRONS AND SINGLE SHIPS, 216—Extraordinary escape of ti Juno, 217—English Indiamen and French privateers, 219—Same and Frenc frigates, 221—Capture of the Pomone, 223—Capture of the Duguay-Trouin 225—Capture of the Atalante, 228—Carysfort and Castor, 229—Crescer and French squadron, 230—Romney and Sibylle, 233—Destruction of th Volontaire, 234—Capture of the Révolutionnaire, 235—Captains Osborr and Renaud off Isle-Ronde, 236.

COLONIAL EXPEDITIONS, WEST INDIES, 239—Capture of Martinique, 241-Capture of Sainte-Lucie, 245—Capture and re-capture of Guadaloupe, 24 —Commodore Ford at St. Domingo, 251—Capture of Tiburon, 253.

COAST OF AFRICA, 253—French spoliations at Sierra Léone, 254.

1795.

BRITISH AND FRENCH FLEETS, 255—State of the British navy, 256—Pic jected expedition from Brest, 257—Sir Sidney Smith's peep into Brest, 25 —Serious casualties to the Brest fleet, 262—Chase of M. Vence into Belle Isle, 263—Junction of Admirals Villaret and Vence, 264—Cornwallis' retreat, 269—Lord Bridport in the command of the Channel fleet, 272—Lord Bridport off Isle-Groix, 273—Expedition to Quiberon, 277—Dreadful gale in the Channel, 281—Capture of the Berwick, 283—Vice-admiral Hotham off Genoa, 285—Loss of the Illustrious, 294—Admiral Hotham off Hyères, 296—Re-capture of the Censeur, 303—Cruise of M. Ganteaume, 305—Nemesis at Smyrna, ibid.

BRITISH AND DUTCH FLEETS, 307—War between England and Holland, ibid.

LIGHT SQUADRONS AND SINGLE SHIPS, 308—Blanche and Pique, 309—Lively and Tourterelle, 313—Astræa and Gloire, 316—Burning of the Boyne, 317—Sir Richard Strachan and French convoys, 318—Captain Cochrane and French store-ships, 319—Thorn and Courier-National, 321—Capture of the Minerve, 323—Southampton and Vestale, 325—Rose and French privateers, 327—Mermaid and two corvettes, 329—Capture of the Eveillé, 330.

COLONIAL EXPEDITIONS, WEST INDIES, 331—Captain Wilson and a French squadron, 333—Victor Hugues and his successors, ibid.

EAST INDIES, 334—Capture of the Cape of Good Hope, 335—Capture of Trincomalé and Oostenburg, 337.

1796.

BRITISH AND FRENCH FLEETS, 339—State of the British navy, ibid.—New constitution in France, 341—Force in Toulon, 342—Recapture of the Nemesis, ibid.—Nelson at Laöna, &c., 343—Evacuation of Leghorn, 344—War between England and Spain, 346.

BRITISH AND SPANISH FLEETS, 346—Admiral Langara at Toulon, ibid.—Evacuation of Corsica, 347.

BRITISH AND FRANCO-SPANISH FLEETS, 349—Recapture of Corsica by France, ibid.—Sir John Jervis's retreat from the Mediterranean, 350.

BRITISH AND FRENCH FLEETS, 350—Loss of the Courageux, 351—Accident to the Gibraltar, ibid.

LIGHT SQUADRONS AND SINGLE SHIPS, 354—Sir Sidney Smith at Herqui, 355—Capture of the Etoile, 357—Capture of the Unité, ibid.—Capture of Sir Sidney Smith, 359—Capture of the Virginie, 361—Boats of Niger near the Penmarcks, ibid.—Spencer and Volcan, 363—Capture of the Argo, 364—Suffisante and Revanche, ibid.—Santa-Margarita and Tamise, 366—Unicorn and Tribune, 367—Dryad and Proserpine, 369—Southampton and Utile, 371—Glatton and French frigates, 375—Aimable and Pensée, 377—Mermaid and Vengeance, 379—Quebec and two French frigates, 380—Destruction of the Andromaque, 382—Raison and Vengeance, 385—Capture of the Elizabet, ibid.—Capture of the Bonne-Citoyenne, 387—Rear-admiral Sercey in the Indian seas, 389—M. Sercey and two British 74s, 391—Loss of the Amphion, 395—Pelican and Médée, 397—Terpsichore and Mahonesa, 399—

French privateers, 400—Lapwing at Anguilla, 401—Terpsichore and Vestale, 403—Minerve and Sabina, 407—Blanche and Ceres, ibid.

COLONIAL EXPEDITIONS, NORTH AMERICA, 408—Rear-admiral Richery at Newfoundland, 409.

WEST INDIES—Capture of Demerara, 410—Recapture of Sainte-Lucie, 411—Capture of St. Vincent and Grenada, ibid.—British at Léogane and at Bombarde, St. Domingo, 412.

EAST INDIES, 413—Capture of Columbo, Amboyna, and Banda, 414—Capture of Dutch squadron in Simon's bay, 416—Destruction of French settlement at Foul point, Madagascar, 417.

APPENDIX	419
Annual Abstracts	420
Notes to Annual Abstracts	449

DIAGRAMS.

Action of the Nymphe and Cléopâtre	108
Lord Howe cutting the French line on the 29th of May, 1794	152
Lord Howe cutting the French line on the 1st of June, 1794	165
Cornwallis's retreat; wearing of the Royal Sovereign to cover the Mars	267
Action of the Blanche and Pique	311

AUTHOR'S PREFACE.

THE flattering reception given to the first edition of this work again calls me before the public. Having no prepossessing adjunct to annex to my name in the title-page—no word, nor even letter, to denote the slightest connexion between that name and the professional subject treated of in these pages—I may be permitted to state my motives for undertaking a task of such apparent difficulty to a landman as a narrative of naval actions.

It is now upwards of thirteen years since the subject first engaged my attention. I was then a prisoner, or *détenu*, in the United States of America, and recollect, as if it were but yesterday, the impression made on my mind by the news of the Guerrière's capture. Having, during a few years' practice as a proctor in the island of Jamaica, learnt not to place implicit reliance upon what an American swore, much less upon what he loosely asserted, I expected, very naturally, to derive consolation from the result of an inquiry into the actual force—in guns, in men, and in size—of the contending frigates. My acquaintance, while professionally employed, with many matters relating to ships, facilitated my labours: and the degree of intercourse, which had necessarily subsisted between several officers of the British navy and myself, gave, I confess, a spur to my exertions.

I soon ascertained that official letter-writing, so far from being a fair representation of facts, was a political engine made use of by the Government to draw recruits to the army from the

Western States, to render the war popular throughout the Union, and to inspire the nations of Europe with a favourable opinion of the martial character of the United States. I found that, although the Republic was divided into two parties, democrats and federalists, the latter would only scrutinize or call in question the statements of the former when the deeds of the army were recounted; but that the most extravagant assertions, made by the Government or democratic party on behalf of the navy, received the stanch support of the federal or, misnamed, English party. As far, therefore, as related to the exploits of the American navy, the whole press of the Republic, from Maine to Florida, and from the Atlantic frontier to Louisiana, co-operated in furthering the views of the Government. Had these exaggerated accounts deluded the people of the United States only, the consequences would have been comparatively trifling; but, as if Buonaparte was the only potentate who could issue false bulletins, or that an official document, simply because it was drawn up in the English language, must be received as a truism by the English people, the press of this country unsuspectingly lent its aid in degrading the character of its own navy, and in exalting that of the United States.

While residing in an enemy's country, I could do little else in the matter on which my mind was bent than collect materials to be used at a future day. I did, however, manage to get inserted in some of the American journals a few paragraphs, setting right the comparative force in one or two of the actions, and had afterwards the pleasure to see those paragraphs copied into a London journal, as *admissions* extorted from the Americans themselves. At length my zeal nearly betrayed me; and I was on the eve of being sent to the interior, when I effected my escape, and arrived, in the latter end of the year 1813, at Halifax, Nova Scotia.

I there became a gratuitous contributor to the only newspaper of the three which could be called an English one, and published, from time to time, accounts of the different naval actions with the Americans; showing the exact force and dimensions of their ships, and communicating to the colonial public many novel and important facts. I also transmitted several letters on the subject to England; and they afterwards appeared in the Naval Chronicle. In March, 1816, I published a pamphlet, "An Inquiry into the merits of the principal Naval Actions between Great Britain and the United States, &c." and inscribed it as an "humble appeal to the understandings of the loyal inhabitants of his majesty's North-American provinces." In the succeeding June I arrived in England; and, in about a twelvemonth afterwards, I published a single octavo volume, entitled, "A Full and Correct Account of the Naval Occurrences of the late War between Great Britain and the United States." In June, 1818, I was induced to publish a work, in two volumes octavo, on the "Military Occurrences" of the same war; and in the latter end of that year, or the beginning of 1819, I formed the resolution, the presumptuous resolution, as I now think, of writing a narrative of the different naval actions fought between Great Britain and her enemies since the declaration of war by France in February, 1793.

Of that work, in its present amended state, I am now to speak. In the "Introduction," I have endeavoured to make the unprofessional reader acquainted with the rise and growth of the British navy; with the ancient as well as the modern armaments of the ships composing it; with the same respecting the ships of foreign navies; and, in short, with every other particular that I thought would assist him in understanding details, among which, to avoid too frequent a recurrence to paraphrase, I have been obliged to intersperse a great many technical terms. In order, however, to lessen the inconvenience arising from that circumstance, I have given a "Glossary of sea-terms," extracted chiefly from Falconer and Darcy Lever; and which Glossary, as it at present stands, is far more copious than it was in the old edition.

The main subject of the work I have divided into annual periods, and have subdivided each year's proceedings into three instead of, as formerly, four principal heads: BRITISH AND FRENCH OR OTHER FOREIGN FLEETS; LIGHT SQUADRONS AND SINGLE SHIPS; AND COLONIAL EXPEDITIONS.

Under the first head, the leading subject for the current year is invariably the state of the British navy. Some account of the navy of the opposite belligerent is then given; and, after that, the proceedings of the rival fleets. This head takes in all expeditions that are not of a colonial nature, the operations of

Buonaparte's invasion-flotilla, and a summary of such proceedings on shore, including measures of state and the movements of armies, as may contribute to throw a light upon naval history.

Under the second head, I have given an account of all actions between frigate-squadrons or single ships, boat-attacks, shipwrecks, and other naval proceedings not reducible under the fleet or the colonial head; and the third and last head takes in, as it specifies, all expeditions fitted out against the colonies of any of the belligerents. On first introducing this head, I have thought it requisite to enumerate the colonies possessed, at that period, by the different European powers.

It was in the "Naval Occurrences" that I first adopted the plan of exhibiting the comparative force of ships of war by a tabular statement. Before I introduced the plan into the present work, I consulted several naval officers; and they all agreed, that the statement conveyed to their minds the clearest idea of that which it was meant to express, the actual force of the combatants. A committee of the most scientific officers belonging to the American navy, having been ordered by the president to compute and report upon the relative strength of different classes of ships, compare them by the "weight of a ball in a round." M. Dupin, in the second, or naval part of his "Voyages dans la Grande-Bretange," a work of admitted science and research, wherever he has occasion to compare the force of two ships of war, adopts my mode, that of the broadside weight of metal. If it be the number and not the nature of the guns that decides the contest, what is to be understood by the frequent expression, "This ship is heavier than that?" Does it mean that the ship bears about her more wood and iron work, and is therefore heavier; or that her guns are of a larger caliber, and the balls she discharges from them heavier?

In reasoning upon the issue of any battle, I have found neither the talent nor the inclination to dwell on the consequences which might or did accrue to either nation from success or failure. The merits of the combat, considered as a combat, I have fully detailed, and freely discussed; and have left the field of politics open to those who know better how to traverse it. Disclaiming as I do all party-feeling, my task as an impartial narrator has sometimes forced me to make remarks which may be considered novel, if not, in an unprofessional writer, presumptuous. Where such strictures appear, the grounds of them also appear; and it would be as impossible for a rational mind to overlook, as it would be degrading for an independent one to withhold, the fair conclusion. If, notwithstanding my endeavours to be accurate, I have in any case argued from wrong data, and thus unintentionally committed injustice, I shall be ready to make the best atonement in my power. But who is so weak as to expect that, because among the attributes of a profession gallantry ranks as one, no member of that profession can be otherwise than gallant? Is it any reflection upon the army or the navy to say, that this general has nothing of the soldier about him but his gait; or that that admiral displays no trait of the genuine tar but his sea-phrases? I feel a satisfaction, however, in being able to declare, that no material misstatement has been charged to me in the first edition of this work; and yet, I neither spared the high, where facts told against them, nor refused my humble aid to the low, where their claims had been disregarded, and blustering assurance allowed to usurp the rights of modest merit.

There may be persons who consider, that a compilation of official letters from the "London Gazette," properly headed and arranged, would form the best Naval History that could be written. As I have not only omitted to give one of those letters entire, but have amended some, flatly contradicted others, and enlarged upon the remainder, it becomes me to show upon what grounds I, a private individual, have taken such liberties with documents that, as being official, are usually held too sacred to have their contents called in question. Beginning with the fleet actions, let the reader refer to Lord Howe's letter. It contains two misstatements: one, that a French ship of the line was captured in the night of the 28th of May; the other, that a French ship of the line was sunk during the engagement of the 1st of June. No doubt his lordship firmly believed what he stated, for a more honourable man did not exist. Lord Howe gives a sketch of the day's proceedings, and, for further information, refers to the bearer of his despatches, Captain Sir Roger Curtis. That sketch of the action may be comprised in three or four pages; while the details I have given fill 90 pages. Look, also, at the misstatements in Lord Collingwood's letter respecting the battle of Trafalgar. Compare that brief letter with my account, which occupies nearly 140 pages. I might refer, in a similar way, to every other general action of the two wars.

With respect to single-ship actions, the official accounts of them are also very imperfect. The letters are generally written an hour or so after the termination of the contest, and of course before the captain has well recovered from the fatigue and flurry it occasioned. Many captains are far more expert at the sword than at the pen, and would sooner fight an action than write the particulars of one. I know a case where, after an officer had written a clear and explicit account of an important operation he had been engaged in, his commander-in-chief sent him back his letter to shorten. In consequence of this, the gazette-letter was not only brief, but unintelligible If you are informed how long the action lasted, you seldom can learn at what hour it began or ended. As to the state of the wind, that is scarcely ever noticed. The name of the captured ship is given, and, now and then, the name of her commander; her numerical force in guns; also their calibers, generally when equal or superior, but less frequently when inferior, to those of the captor. The force of the British ship, being known to the Board of Admiralty, is left to be guessed at by the public, or partially gathered from Steel. Moreover, whatever may have been the mistakes or omissions in an official account, no supplementary account, unless it relates to a return of loss, is put forth to rectify or supply them.[1]

But even the minuteness of my accounts has given rise to objections. That trite maxim of expediency, "Truth is not at all times to be spoken," has been held up against me; and I have been blamed for removing the delusion, which the now no longer existing difference between the rated and the real force of a British ship of war had so long imposed upon the public. If, in showing that a certain frigate, instead of mounting, as was supposed, 38 guns, mounted 46, I leave to be inferred, that her captain did not deserve to be knighted for having captured a French frigate of 44 guns, I confer a benefit on the British

---

[1] Two exceptions occur to me: one, Captain Blackwood's letter, amending Lord Collingwood's respecting the prizes made at the battle of Trafalgar; the other, a letter from Vice-admiral Bertie, supplying the omission of the name of the Menelaus among the ships stated as present at the capture of the Isle of France.

navy; I assist to exalt, rather than to debase, the martial character of the nation. For instance, a French war breaks out to-morrow, and this same British frigate captures a French frigate of 44 guns. Is her captain knighted? No. Why? Because his ship is a 46, his opponent's only a 44, gun frigate. The nation at large, not knowing that the old 38 and the new 46 gun frigate were armed precisely alike, that, in fact, they were the same ship, exclaims, that the British navy is not what it was; that it now requires a 46-gun frigate to perform as much as, 25 years ago, was performed by a 38-gun frigate. It is the explanations I give which place the two actions upon a par; explanations due no less to truth than to the rising generation of Nelsons, who require but the opportunity to be afforded them to emulate, perhaps to outshine, the bravest of those that have gone before them.

Let not the reader imagine, because in the ensuing pages the veil may be drawn farther aside than has been customary, that he will find less to admire in the performances of the British navy. Far from it. Some hundreds of cases are here recorded, that are not to be found in any other publication of the kind; and even in many of those cases which have appeared before, my researches have enabled me to add particulars, calculated to raise the action to a still higher rank in the annals of the British navy.

I cannot recollect an instance where a British officer, of tried valour, has dissented from the opinion, that every justice ought to be done to the exertions of an enemy; and yet, I regret to say, there are officers, as well as others, who have objected to my work because it is too *Frenchified*. Such illiberal opinions I value as nought. Nay, in direct opposition to their spirit, I am gratified in reflecting, that I have shown an impartiality which will exonerate me from Hume's sweeping charge, that, " in relations of sea-fights, writers of the hostile nations take a pleasure in exalting their own advantages, and suppressing those of the enemy." I feel, also, a degree of pride in the proofs I have afforded, that a man may write an impartial naval history, and yet belong to the country the most conspicuous in it. I esteem the brave of every nation; but I glory in recounting the exploits, and in celebrating the renown, of the brave of my own. And I shall not, I trust, be considered less patriotic than the historian who says, "I confess, I love England," because I will not go the length of saying also with him, "and I hate her enemies."[1]

Could I have persuaded myself to make those "authentic and valuable works," the "Annual Registers,"[2] rather than the log-books of ships and the official accounts on both sides, the groundwork of my statements, I should have escaped both the troublesome task of seeking particulars, and the unpleasant one of passing censure. The fullness of my details would not have obliged me to violate historical unity, by dividing my subject into so many distinct heads; nor need I have run the risk of tiring the reader with the minuteness, nor of displeasing him with the technicality, of my descriptions. I should have cared less about the truth and originality, than about the easy flow and the "patriotic," which, in plain English, means the partial, tendency of my narrative; and, instead of employing five or six years, I should scarcely have taken twice as many months, to bring my labours to a conclusion. He who is best read on naval subjects can best appreciate the extent of my researches for matter that is novel. The accuracy of my statements, a yet more important point, can best be determined by those who were engaged in the services I profess to narrate. Of the many accounts of sea-fights to be found in these pages, there is not one but contains something original, something which has never before been in print, if it is only the state of the wind, the name of the foreign captain, or the particulars of the force mounted by the contending ships.

When I look upon the pile of letters, full 300 in number, the contents of which have so enriched these volumes, I cannot but feel grateful to the writers, many of whom are of the first rank and distinction in the navy; and I beg them individually to accept my acknowledgments. Several of the writers betray an unwillingness to disclose facts creditable to themselves, and others strictly enjoin me, rather to under, than to over, rate their performances. Much, too, as I had calculated upon voluntary communications (having in my Prospectus requested information of the profession at large), 20 or 30 unsolicited letters are all that I have received. Nor were the remaining letters replies to a circular requesting information generally, but

[1] Bisset.   [2] Preface to Brenton, p vi.

answers to a string of questions, leading directly to the point in doubt. In stating that upwards of 80 of my letters remain at this hour unanswered, I shall perhaps be excused for some of the omissions that may discover themselves in the work. A few of those letters have probably miscarried, and others may have given offence. One captain, indeed, was candid enough to tell me why he refused the least particle of information: he did not like the freedom of my remarks upon excessive flogging. Let me assure him that, on a review of my past labours, there is no part I would wish less to retract, or even soften down, than that which, to my regret, has provoked his anger.

The celebrated author of the "Decline and Fall of Rome," in the Preface to his first octavo edition, says: "Some alterations and improvements had presented themselves to my mind, but I was unwilling to injure or offend the purchasers of the preceding edition." This appears to me to be the excuse of an author who either is weary of his subject, or who feels that he is already seated upon the highest pinnacle of fame. As I am still fondly attached to my subject, and have yet my fame (such as it ever will be) to make, no cause exists to divert me from what I conceive to be my bounden duty to the public, to give the most full and accurate account in my power of the naval events of the period embraced by my work.

The improvements I have been enabled to make in this edition are, for the most part, highly important. Such of those improvements as relate to the heads under which the narrative is carried on have already been described. Nearly the whole of the tabular matter in each volume has been transferred to an Appendix at the end; where, also, the Annual Abstracts of the British navy are now placed, instead of being put up in a separate quarto volume. The notes have almost all been incorporated with the text; and subjects connected in interest, but disunited in the former mode of arrangement, have been brought together. All the accounts have been revised, and many of them greatly enlarged. Upwards of 200 cases, chiefly boat and shore attacks, have been added to this edition. Among the improvements, is an epitome, under the head of CONTENTS, of each year's proceedings, with a reference to the page at which the action or case is to be found.

In other naval histories, the name of the English captain is not always added to that of the ship he commands; and even when it is added, the christian name is seldom given. With respect to French captains, the omission of their names is generally preferable to the attempt to insert them; because almost invariably they are so misspelt, as to defeat every purpose of identity. In both these points, I was particularly careful in the first edition of this work; and I have in the present edition, at incalculable pains, inserted the christian and surname of every first-lieutenant in an action of note; of every officer killed and wounded in any action whatever; of every officer present (where obtainable) in any attack by boats, or in operations against the enemy on shore. When it is known that these names comprise some thousands, that the surnames of part only, and the christian names of scarcely any, are to be found in the gazette-letters, some idea may be formed of the difficulties I have experienced in consummating this part of my new plan. I will venture to say, that the Board of Admiralty themselves would have found considerable difficulty in adding the proper christian names to such a mass of surnames. A few christian names, and a few only, I have been obliged to leave in blank, and in others I may have erred; but I have used my utmost endeavours to be accurate in all. Let me here mention, that the London Gazette contains a great many misprinted names; and that its Index of "State Intelligence" is extremely imperfect and erroneous.

To render this new system of nomenclature of increased practical benefit, as well to the public at large as to the junior class of British naval officers, to do justice to whose gallant exertions was my chief motive in planning it, I have caused a list to be made of all the names, with the volume, year, and page in which they occur, and the progressive rank of the officer. Pardon me, reader, if I now descend, for a moment, from the station of the author, to give expression to feelings of rather a personal nature. To an affectionate partner, who has shared my anxiety in executing this arduous and protracted work, as well as incurred some of the *danger* consequent upon it, I am indebted for the Index of both the present and the preceding editions. The labour of the undertaking is manifest; and its accuracy will, I trust, be equally evident when there is occasion to refer to it.

In the Index to the last three volumes of the old edition, the names of the ships, as well as of the officers, appear; and, in my Prospectus of the new edition, I promised that the ships should form part of the Index to the present work. By the time, however, that the first three volumes had been gone over, the quantity of index matter was so great, that I decided to omit the ships; the rather, as no ship, no British ship at least, except in a single instance or so, is named in the work without her captain or commander being also named.

For their novelty as well as their utility, the Diagrams will perhaps be considered the most important improvement in the work. I wish they had been more numerous; but I found it impracticable to extend the number, and at the same time preserve that accuracy without which the diagram would obscure, rather than illustrate, the letter-press. Although, with one or two exceptions, not finished quite so well as I could desire, these woodcuts have greatly increased the cost, but without adding one shilling to the price, of the book.

The greater portion of the sixth volume is made up of the operations of the late American war, which, for the want of room, I was obliged to omit in the preceding edition. Here it is, I fear, that my zeal in the cause of truth, my wish, my determination to expose, as far as I am able, all counterfeit claims to renown in naval warfare, will subject me to the charge of national prejudice. Confident, however, that I have, in no instance, swerved from that impartiality which gives to these pages their principal value, I must console myself with the reflection, that those who charge me with being too severe in my strictures upon the officers and people of the United States, have never had an opportunity of forming a judgment of the American character. For the edification of such persons I subjoin a brief account of the frontispiece of an American naval work, published at that which is reputed to be the most Anglican of all the cities of the republic, Boston.

We are to suppose that the genius of America, having by some means got possession of old Neptune's car and trident, along with a pair of prancing sea-nags, is desirous to take an airing on the deep. Behold her, then, as she dashes through the waves, pointing with the trident, by her degraded into a staff for the national colours to some medallions of American worthies, fantastically stuck upon a monument, whose foundation, seemingly, is no other than the froth and foam which the lady herself has just kicked up. Wreaths of laurel, sea-gods, and a towering eagle, find appropriate places in the design. Upon the pedestal are the names of " MANLY, TRUXTON, JONES,[1] PREBLE, BARNEY, LITLLE, BARRY ;" and the pillar is ornamented with the medallions of " HULL, JONES,[2] DECATUR, BAINBRIDGE, STEWART, LAWRENCE, PERRY, MACDONOUGH ;" and at the top, with the names of " PORTER, BLAKELY, BIDDLE." Several other medallions present their backs to us: they probably represent " Warrington, Burrows, Chauncey, Elliott, Angus, Tarbell, Thomas ap Catesby Jones," &c. &c. Nor has our old friend Commodore Rodgers been entirely forgotten, although rather shabbily treated, by having only " GERS " of his name, and but one of his shoulders, thrust into view. In front of the car is a sort of raft, bearing pieces of cannon, mortars, shells, shot, &c.; but we search in vain for any of those chain and bar shot which the Americans employed with so much advantage in their warfare against the British. Upon the whole, no one, except an American, will consider as inapplicable to the design the following words of Mr. Addison: " One kind of burlesque represents mean persons in the accoutrements of heroes."

Previously to the late war with the United States, persons in this country were in the habit of exclaiming against " French boasting," " French misrepresentation," and " French impudence." My analysis of the American accounts has already, I trust, sufficiently shown that, in the art of boasting and misrepresenting, the French could never compete with the Americans; and I will now make it equally clear, that, in impudence also, our neighbours must yield up the palm.

Within this week or two, an American bookseller, domiciled in London, has been trying to serve the cause of his country by practising a trick upon the *gullible* portion of this. He has put forth, in a neat octavo volume, a " History of the United States, from their first settlement as colonies, to the close of the war with Great Britain, in 1815." Of that part of the work which relates to the late war I shall only speak, and I do pronounce it as barefaced a calumny against England as ever issued from the American press. The writer, whoever he is, for he seems to

[1] Paul.   [2] Jacob.

have been ashamed to tell his name, has found the misstatements in the American official accounts too moderate for his purpose: he has culled his choice collection of "facts" from the most violent party-papers in the United States; papers written when there was a fresh exciting cause to plead as some excuse for misrepresentation and invective; papers from which an American writer with a name would not, at this day, venture to draw his materials, even had he no other than an American public to please.

This genu*ine*, but anonymous American writer, comes, or probably sends, here to tell us (p. 385), that the attack by the President upon the Little Belt, was "insolence deservedly punished;" that (p. 397) "the Wasp, of 18 guns, captured the Frolic of 22," and that "in this action the Americans obtained a victory over force decidedly superior;" that (p. 405) " Admiral Cockburn, departing from the usual modes of honourable warfare, directed his efforts principally against unoffending citizens and peaceful villages," and that "the farm-houses and gentlemen's seats near the shore were plundered, and the cattle driven away or wantonly slaughtered;" that (p. 406) "the Hornet met and captured the British Peacock, of about equal force;" that (p. 411) Commodore Perry's victory on lake Erie "was achieved over a superior force;" that (p. 415) "Commodore Chauncey upon lake Ontario repeatedly offered battle to the enemy's squadron, which was superior in force; but Sir James Yeo, the British commander, intimidated by the result of the battle on lake Erie, retired before him;" that (p. 425) "Commodore Downie's squadron on lake Champlain carried 95 guns, and was manned with upwards of 1000 men, and that Commodore M'Donough's carried 86 guns, and was manned with 820 men;" that (p. 426) "the American sloop Peacock captured the Epervier, of equal force;" and that "the sloop Wasp captured the Reindeer, and afterwards in the same cruise sunk the Avon, each of superior force;" that (p. 437) "the Constitution captured the Cyane and Levant, whose forces united were superior to hers; and the sloop Hornet captured the brig Penguin, stronger in guns and men than the victor."

The worst is, that, for anything appearing to the contrary, these statements are contained in an *English* work; and I should not be surprised, if the "North-American Review" were by-

and-by to quote them, as admissions extorted from an English author of note, who had some special reason for concealing his name. It is to be hoped that the more influential of the English reviews will give a trimming to the only party whose name appears to this work, for his impudent attempt to palm upon the English public a book of lies and trash, for a book of "history." Unfortunately, the reprobation of the work may answer the publisher's purpose as effectually as the praise of it; and he is chuckling to himself as he reads this, to think that even I shall put into his pocket some "pretty considerable" amount in British coin for his libels upon British character.

Between the publication of the first and second parts of the former edition of my work, two volumes of another "Naval History" made their appearance before the British public. I discovered inaccuracies, but I abstained from noticing them, because the author had not completed his undertaking, and might, in his succeeding volumes, correct them himself. The whole work has since been published; and I have felt myself quite at liberty to discuss its merits: nay, I was bound to do so in my own justification, for who is there, when a naval occurrence is related differently by an unprofessional and a professional writer, that will not pin faith upon the latter? I am not such a hypocrite as to disown, that I derive a satisfaction from the comparison of Captain Brenton's work with my own, short as even that falls of what my wishes would have made it. And yet, how often have I longed for the experience of a post-captain of 20 years' standing, for some of those "great opportunities for obtaining the most correct information" enjoyed by my contemporary. Captain Brenton could go to the club-rooms and convivial meetings of his brother-officers, and collect his facts from among them; while for a single fact, often of dubious importance, I had to address myself to a stranger; one, perhaps, who thought so meanly of my abilities for the task I had undertaken, that he would not deign to send me a reply.

I hope, therefore, that those of the naval profession, who have felt, or who may feel, disposed to bear hard upon me for the inaccuracies they discover, or the strictures they dislike, will reflect upon the fallibilities of a naval historian of their own body. Let them consider, that any three of my six volumes contain more matter pertaining to naval history, than the five volumes of Captain Brenton. Let them make some allowance for the increased quantity of detail in my work, as well as for the increased liability to err, which I have thus brought upon myself. Let those, also, who may prefer the style of my contemporary to mine, reflect how much easier it is for a writer, who skims over the surfaces of things and finds little or nothing to start at, to construct well-turned periods, than a writer, who dips deeply into his subject, and stops every now and then to investigate a disputed fact. Finally, whatever literary aid Captain Brenton may have received, I can conscientiously say with Gibbon, " 1. My rough manuscript, without any intermediate copy, has been sent to press. 2. Not a sheet has been seen by any human eyes, excepting those of the author and the printer: the faults and merits are exclusively my own."

It is now upwards of eighteen months since I announced an intention of printing a new edition of my Naval History, and requested to have transmitted to me any corrections necessary to be made in the statements of the former edition. I expended upwards of fifty pounds in advertisements, urging naval officers to assist me in rendering my forthcoming work worthy of them and of the country. Consequently, I do not feel myself answerable for any misstatements which appeared in the old, and may reappear in the present edition. I trust, however, that there are very few of them. Two or three officers, who have never applied to me directly or indirectly, will find that I have corrected errors which had crept in respecting them, and have expressed my regret that those errors should have occurred. On the other hand, some of the most noisy claimants for redress will wish they had remained silent: justice, however, was all they could expect, and justice I hope I have done them.

I have still a trifling topic to touch upon. One evening at eight o'clock, my publishers sent me down two pretty little wide-printed volumes. The title of "Naval Sketch-book," and that by " An officer of rank," made me regret that the work had not appeared a twelvemonth earlier, in order that I might have profited by the naval information I expected to find within it. At the very first thumbful of leaves I turned over, my heart almost leaped into my mouth; for I read as follows: "Inconsistencies, Infidelities, and Fallacies of James." Here was a plurality of faults! I presently discovered that I, or my printer for me, had made use of *main* instead of *mizen*, but that the "officer of rank" had overlooked the circumstance of my having corrected the mistake in the ERRATA; and that, on another occasion, I had accidentally made an inappropriate use of the term *bear up*. As these little slips would not justify the heavy imputation cast upon me in the "Contents," I went through the work, and was pleased to find that, having no specific charge to bring forward, the author could only vent his spleen in general abuse of me and my work. I saw clearly, that the "officer of rank" was not what he pretended to be, any more than the sixpenny scribe noticed by him was "Capt. William Goldsmith, R.N." Before one o'clock the next afternoon, I traced the "officer of rank" through every ship he had served in, and found that, in 1793, when my work commences, he was just breeched; that seven years afterwards he entered the British navy; and that, at the battle of Algiers, in August, 1816, he had been not quite eight years a lieutenant. I may add, that, although many a boatswain's name does, the name of the "officer of rank" does not, appear in these pages.

The "officer of rank" made his virulent attack upon me a full twelvemonth after I had announced a new and improved edition as being in the press; but as regarded him, I staid my "corrective" pen, the moment I discovered that a new edition of the "Naval Sketch-book" was about to appear. I have seen it; and find that, as far as relates to me, the new work is a reprint of the old. I am therefore at liberty to proceed in "showing up" the "officer of rank." Will it be credited of a writer, who declares that he never presumes to give an opinion of a work until he has read it with attention, that he actually fathers upon me a "maxim," which I quote from another, for the express purpose of showing its objectionable tendency? Let the reader turn to p. 105 of the first volume of the "officer of rank's" book, and then to the passage at p. xxvi. of this Preface, beginning, "But even, &c."; which is a transcript of what appeared in my former edition. In another place, the "officer of rank" is disposed to be facetious with me, and that about a circumstance, which every British naval officer, possessed of feelings a little more refined than would fit him for excelling in a "galley story," must wish had never happened. But has not the "officer of rank" himself, in one alteration made by him, afforded a practical proof, that the *threat* of correction sometimes operates as beneficially as the actual infliction of it? The reader is requested to compare a sentence at the top of p. 174, vol. i., of the old, with a sentence at the top of p. 208, vol. i., of the new, edition of the " Naval Sketch-book." Nor is " Lyon," if it be so at all, the only name that will bear to be punned upon. " People," says the proverb, " who live in GLASS houses, should beware of throwing stones."—Pray, reader, do not, like this writer, condemn me without looking at the ERRATA;[1] and should you, then, in spite of my endeavours at accuracy, discover any misstatements, I request you will communicate them to me. If I say to an officer who may have a complaint to allege, send your statement in writing, it is because none but a written statement can serve his purpose or mine, and not because I fear him or any other man, or have the least expectation of a renewal of the disgraceful business that once occurred. I should be ill-fitted for the task I have undertaken, were I to found a charge against a whole profession upon the misconduct of one of its members.

In the Preface to the fourth volume of the old edition, I hinted at the probability of my undertaking an account of the principal naval actions of the first American war, or that commencing in 1775 and ending in 1783. I still think it probable that I shall make the attempt; and I would wish, also, to give a history of signal-making in the British and French navies, as exemplified in the different general actions fought between them. On this abstruse subject, I should be thankful to receive assistance from British officers; and I will undertake to return in safety any signal-books or other documents which they may please to send to me. Should I succeed in completing a volume of this description, a part of it will be devoted to CORRIGENDA AND ADDENDA connected with the present work; and it is to that end more especially that I solicit officers to apprise me of any inaccuracies they may discover. Diagrams applicable to actions detailed in these pages I would willingly insert in the supplementary volume; and I will thank officers to transmit me copies of any letters which they may have forwarded to the Admiralty, describing boat-attacks and other similar services

[1] In the present edition the erratas have, of course, been duly corrected in the page —*Editor.*

against the enemy; and which, not having appeared in the London Gazette, or only in the shape of abstracts, may not have been recorded in this work. When I state that my postage-account for the " Naval History," from first to last, has exceeded the sum of one hundred pounds, I shall be excused for requesting officers to endeavour to forward their communications free of charge.

   12, *Chapel Field, South Lambeth*,
      March 25, 1826.

GLOSSARY OF SEA-TERMS.

Aback, the situation of the sail of a ship, when its forward surface is pressed upon by the wind.

Abaft, the hinder part of a ship, or some point nearer to the stern than any given part; as, *abaft* the foremast.

Abeam, the point at right angles with the ship's mainmast: hence, *abaft* the beam, is a situation or position between the direct line abeam and the stern, and *before* the beam, is between the beam and the head.

Aboard, the inside of a ship: hence, any person who enters a ship is said to go aboard; but, when an enemy enters in time of battle, he is said to board. To *fall aboard*, is to strike against another ship. To *haul aboard* the main tack, is to bring the clew of the mainsail down to the chess-tree.

About, is the situation of a ship immediately after she has tacked, or changed her course, by going about, and standing on the other tack.

Abreast, synonymous with *Abeam*.

Adrift, the state of a ship or vessel broke loose from her moorings, and driven without control, at the mercy of the wind, sea, or current.

Afore, all that part of a ship which lies forward, or near the stem.

Aft, After, behind, or near the stern of a ship. See *Abaft*.

Aloft, up in the tops, at the mast-head, or anywhere about the higher yards or rigging.

Alongside, close to the ship.

Amidships, the middle of the ship, either with regard to her length or breadth; as, the enemy boarded us amidships, *i. e.* in the middle, between the stem and stern. Put the helm amidships; *i. e.* in the middle, between the two sides.

Anchor, best bower and *small bower*, the two stowed furthest forward or near to the bows; the *best bower* being the anchor on the starboard bow, the *small bower* tne one on the larboard bow; the *sheet anchor* is of the same size and weight as either of the bowers; *stream anchor* a smaller one; and *kedge anchor*, the smallest of all.

An-end, any spar or mast placed perpendicularly.

Astern, behind the ship.

Athwart hawse, the situation of a ship when she is driven by the wind, tide, or other accident, across the stem of another, whether they bear against, or are at a small distance from, each other, the transverse position of the former with respect to the latter being principally understood.

Athwart the fore-foot, is generally applied to the flight of a cannon-ball, as fired from one ship across the line of another's course, but ahead of her, as a signal for the latter to bring to.

Bar, a shoal running across the mouth of a harbour or river.

Bare poles, having no sail up.

Barricade, more commonly called *Bulwark*, the wooden parapet on each side of the forecastle, quarter-deck, or poop.

Beam;—On the beam, implies any distance from the ship on a line with the beams, or at right angles with the keel: thus, if the ship steers or points northward, any object lying east or west, is said to be on her starboard or larboard beam. See *Abeam*.

Bear up, or *bear away*, is to change the course of a ship, in order to make her run before the wind, after she has sailed some time with a side wind, or close hauled; and seems to have been derived from the motion of the helm, by which this is partly produced, as the helm is then borne up to windward or to the weather-side of the ship. Hence, *bear up* seems to have reference to the helm only; as, "Bear up the helm a-weather." With respect to any other thing, it is said, *Bear away*, or *bear down*; thus: "We bore away for Torbay;" "We bore down upon the ship, and engaged her."

Bearing, the point of the compass on which any object appears; or the situation of any object in reference to any given part of the ship.

Beating, the operation of making a progress at sea against the direction of the wind, in a zig-zag line, or traverse; *beating*, however, is generally understood to be turning to windward in a storm,[1] or fresh wind.

Belay, to make fast.

Bend the sails, is to affix them to the yards; *bend* the cable, to fasten it to the anchor, &c.

Bends, the streaks of thick stuff, or the strongest planks in a ship's side.

Bight, any part of a rope between the ends; also a collar or an eye formed by a rope.

---

[1] Ships cannot turn to windward in storms. Ships lie to in storms, under storm sails, and drift to leeward instead of turning to windward.—*Editor.*

Binnacle, the frame or box which contains the compass.

Birth, a place of anchorage; a cabin or apartment.

Bits, large upright pins of timber, with a cross-piece, over which the bight of the cable is put; also smaller pins to belay ropes, &c.

Board, the space comprehended between any two places where the ship changes her course by tacking; or it is the line over which she runs between tack and tack, when turning to windward, or sailing against the direction of the wind. Hence, *to make a good board,* or stretch, *to make short boards,* &c.—See also, *Aboard.*

Boarding-netting, network triced round the ship to prevent the boarders from entering.

Bow, is the rounding part of a ship's side forward, beginning where the planks arch inwards, and terminating where they close at the stem or prow. *On the bow,* an arch of the horizon, not exceeding 45 degrees, comprehended between some distant object and that point of the compass which is right ahead, or to which the ship's stem is directed.

Bowlines, ropes made fast to the leeches or sides of the sails, to pull them forward.

Box off, is, when a ship having got up in the wind or been taken with the wind ahead, the head-yards are braced round to counteract its effect, and prevent the ship from being turned round against your inclination.

Braces, ropes fastened to the yard-arms to brace them about.

Brails, ropes applied to the after-leeches of the driver, and some of the stay-sails, to draw them up.

Break ground, to weigh the anchor and quit a place.

Breeching, a stout rope fixed to the cascabel of a gun, and fastened to the ship's side, to prevent the gun from running too far in.

Bring to, to check the course of a ship by arranging the sails in such a manner that they shall counteract each other, and keep her nearly stationary; when she is said to *lie by* or *lie to,* having, according to the sea-phrase, some of her sails aback, to oppose the force of those which are full. *To come to* is sometimes used with the same meaning; although, more generally, it means to let go the anchor.

Bring up, to cast anchor.

Broach to, is when, by the violence of the wind, or a heavy sea upon the quarter, the ship is forced up to windward of her course or proper direction in defiance of the helm.

Bulkheads, partitions in the ship.

Bumkin, a short boom or beam of timber projecting from each bow of a ship, to extend the clew or lower edge of the foresail to windward.

Cable, a large rope by which the ship is secured to the anchor

GLOSSARY OF SEA-TERMS.

Cable's length, a measure of 120 fathoms, or 240 yards.

Cap, a thick block of elm, with a round hole in the fore part for the topmast to enter, and a square one abaft to receive the lowermast head.

Capstan, a machine by which the anchor is weighed.

Cat-head, a strong projection from the forecastle on each bow, furnished with sheaves or strong pulleys, and to which the anchor is lifted after it has been hove up to the bow by the capstan.

Cat's paw, a light air perceived by its effects on the water, but not durable.

Chains, or *channels*, of a ship, those strong projections from the sides below the quarter-deck and forecastle ports, in large ships, but above the guns in small ones, to which the shrouds or rigging of each of the lowermasts are secured, by means of wooden blocks, or *deadeyes*, strongly chained and bolted to the ship's side.

Chess-tree, a piece of wood bolted perpendicularly on each side of the ship near the gangway, to confine the clew of the mainsail; for which purpose there is a hole in the upper part, through which the tack passes, that extends the clew of the sail to windward.

Clew garnet, fore or main, is a rope running double from nearly the centre of the fore or main yard, to the clews or corners of the sail, where the tack and sheet are affixed, and is the principal means of clewing up or taking in the sail.

Close hauled, the arrangement or trim of a ship's sails when she endeavours to make a progress in the nearest direction possible towards that point of the compass from which the wind blows.

Club-hauling, tacking by means of an anchor.[1]

Coamings, the borders of the hatchway, which are raised above the deck.

Conning the ship, the directions given to the steersman by a superior seaman, termed the quartermaster, or by the captain, master, or pilot, as the case may be.

Courses, a name by which the fore and main sails, and driver, are usually distinguished.

Crank, the quality of a ship which, for want of a sufficient quantity of ballast or cargo, is rendered incapable of carrying sail, without being exposed to the danger of upsetting.

Cutwater, the knee of the head.

Davit, a piece of timber used as a crane to hoist the flooks of the anchor to the top of the bow; it is called fishing the anchor.

Driver, a large sail suspended to the mizen gaff: called also *spanker*.

[1] The very best description of this manœuvre is to be found in Captain Marryat's "Peter Simple."

GLOSSARY OF SEA-TERMS.   xliii

Edge away, as, when a ship changes her course, by sailing *larger,* or more afore the wind than she had done before.

Fill, is to fill the sail that has been shivered, or hove aback, to bring the ship to.

Fleet, an assemblage of ships of war, to the number of ten and upwards.

Flooks, the broad parts or palms of the anchors.

Flotilla, a fleet of small vessels of war.

Fore-and-aft, the lengthway of the ship.

Forging ahead, to be forced ahead by the wind.

Founder, to sink.

Furl, to wrap or roll a sail close to the yard, stay, or mast to which it belongs, and wind a gasket or cord about it to fasten it thereto.

Gaskets, a piece of plait to fasten the sails to the yards.

Grain,[1] to be in the, of another ship is immediately to precede her in the same direction.

Gripe, is when, by carrying too great a quantity of aftersail, a ship inclines too much to windward, and requires her helm to be kept a-weather, or to windward.

Gun-shot, implies, says Falconer, "the distance of the point-blank range of a cannon-shot." With submission, we take a gun-shot distance to mean *long,* and not *point-blank* range: if this be correct, a ship is within gun-shot of another when she is within a mile or a mile and a quarter of her.

Haul the wind, to direct the ship's course as near as possible to that point of the compass from which the wind arises.

Hawse-holes, the holes through which the cables pass.

Hawse, is generally understood to imply the situation of the cables before the ship's stem, when she is moored with two anchors out from the bows; *viz.,* one on the starboard, and the other on the larboard bow. It also denotes any small distance ahead of a ship, or between her head and the anchors by which she rides.

Hawser, a small cable.

Heave to, synonymous with *bring to. Heaving* to an anchor, is when all the cable is taken in until the ship is directly over her anchor, preparatory to its being weighed out of the ground.

Knot, synonymous with mile.

Labour, to pitch and roll heavily.

Larboard, a name given by seamen to the left side of the ship, when looking forward from the stern. *Port* is now generally used in place of *larboard.*

Large, a phrase applied to the wind, when it crosses the line of a ship's

---

[1] The term *grain* is obsolete.

course in a favourable direction; particularly on the beam or quarter hence, *to sail large*, is to advance with a large wind, so as that the sheets are slackened and flowing, &c. This phrase is generally opposed to sailing close hauled, or with a scant wind.

Lasking[1] course is when a ship steers in a slanting or oblique direction towards another.

Lie to, synonymous with *Bring to*, *Heave to*.

Looming, an indistinct appearance of any distant object, as ships, mountains, &c.

Luff, the order to the helmsman to put the tiller towards the lee-side of the ship, in order to make the ship sail nearer to the direction of the wind.

Main sheet, a large rope affixed to the lower corner or clew of the mainsail by which, when set, it is hauled aft into its place.

Main tack, another large rope affixed to the same corner of the sail, but to haul it on board or down to the chess-tree on the forepart of the gangway; when set upon a wind, or close hauled, the foresail is furnished with similar gear.

Musket-shot distance, from 300 to 400 yards.

Offing, implies out at sea, or at a good distance from the shore.

Overhaul, to examine; also to overtake a ship in chase.

Pay round off, is, when near the wind, to fall off from it against the helm, and in spite of every effort to prevent it.

Pistol-shot distance, about 50 yards.

Plying, turning to windward.

Port the helm, the order to put the helm over to the larboard side of the ship. Used instead of larboard, on account of the affinity of sound between the latter word and starboard.

Quarter, that part of a ship's side which lies towards the stern, or which is comprehended between the aftmost end of the main chains and the side of the stern, where it is terminated by the quarter-pieces.

Rake a ship, is when the broadside sweeps another's decks fore and aft, either by lying athwart her bows or her stern. *Rake* means also the inclination of the masts, bowsprit, stem, or sternpost.

Reef, to reduce a sail by tying a portion of it to the yards with points

Ride, to be held by the cable.

Round to, is when going *large* or before the wind, to come round towards the wind by the movement of the helm.

Ship the tiller, &c., is to fix it in its place.

Slipping the cable, unsplicing it within, a buoy and buoy-rope having been previously affixed to it, to show where the ship has left her anchor

[1] This term is obsolete

Splicing, the mode by which the broken strands of a rope are united.

Spring, to anchor with a, is, before letting go the anchor, to cause a smaller cable or hawser to be passed out of a stern or quarter port, and taken outside of the ship forward, in order to be bent or fastened to the ring of the anchor intended to be let go, for the purpose of bringing the ship's broadside to bear in any given direction.

Spring a mast, yard, or any other spar, is when it becomes rent or split by an overpress of sail, heavy pitch or jerk of the ship in a rough sea, or by too slack rigging.

Squadron, an assemblage of ships of war in number less than ten. See *Fleet*.

Stand on, to keep on the same course.

Starboard, the right side of the ship, when the eye of the spectator is directed forward, or towards the head.

Stay, to stay a ship, is to arrange the sails, and move the rudder, so as to bring the ship's head to the direction of the wind, in order to get her on the other tack.

Steer, to manage a ship by the movement of the helm.

Tack, is to change the course from one board to another, or to turn the ship about from the starboard to the larboard tack, or *vice versâ*, in a contrary wind.

Tant, or *taunt rigged*, means when a ship is very lofty in her masts. *All-a-tanto*, is said when a ship, having had some of her masts struck, has rehoisted them.

Taut, a corruption of *tight*.

Thrum a sail, is to insert in it, through small holes made by a bolt-rope-needle or a marline-spike, a number of short pieces of rope-yarn or spun-yarn, in order, by the sail's being drawn over a hole in the ship's bottom, to assist in stopping the leak.

Tow, to draw a ship or boat forward in the water, by means of a rope attached to another vessel or boat, which advances by the effort of rowing or sailing.

Turning to windward. See *Beating*.

Unmoor, is to reduce a ship to the state of riding by a single anchor and cable, after she has been moored or fastened by two or more cables.

Unship, is to remove any piece of timber, wood, &c., from the place in which it was fitted.

Wake of a ship, is to be immediately behind or in the track of her. It also means when a ship is hid from view by another ship.

Warp a ship, is to change her situation by pulling her from one part of a harbour, &c., to some other, by means of warps (ropes or hawsers), which are attached to buoys, to other ships, to anchors sunk in the bottom, or to certain stations on the shore, as posts, rings, trees, &c. The ship is then drawn forward to those stations, either by pulling on the warps by hand, or by the application of some purchase, as a tackle, windlass, or capstan.

Way, a ship is said to be *under way*, that is, to have way upon her, when she has weighed her anchor, and is exposed to the influence of the tide, current, or wind.

Weather a ship, headland, &c., is to sail to windward of it. The weather-gage implies the situation of one ship to windward of another when in action, &c.

Wear or *veer* ship, is to change her course from one board to the other by turning her stern to windward.

Weigh, is to heave up the anchor of a ship from the ground in order to prepare her for sailing.

Work a ship, is to direct her movements, by adapting the sails to the force and direction of the wind. To work to windward is a synonyme of beat, tack, turn to windward, &c.

PREFACE BY THE EDITOR.

THAT the British nation is greatly indebted to Mr. James, for the most faithful and unbiassed account of the different actions in which his majesty's ships and vessels have been engaged, does not admit of contradiction. It is true we have other naval histories. One indeed has been undertaken and compiled by an officer of high rank in his majesty's service, and although there is much ability in that history, yet it by no means enters into detail, either of the great actions, or those of single ships, with the accuracy, minutiæ, or impartiality which is to be found in the work of Mr. James.

In the first place, the Naval History alluded to above is most particularly inaccurate as to the different events which occurred during the Mutiny; and although the historian was himself present on that unfortunate occasion, as lieutenant of one of his majesty's ships at Spithead, in 1797, yet has he contrived to fall into errors, which Mr. James avoided; and has inadvertently stated as facts what most certainly never occurred. "A letter to Vice-admiral Sir Thomas Byam Martin, K.C.B., containing an account of the mutiny of the fleet at Spithead, in the year 1797, in correction of that given in Captain Brenton's Naval History of the last war," published in 1825, might have convinced the gallant officer of many very important mistakes, especially in regard to the London, the "letter" in question being from the pen of the captain of that ship during the mutiny. The reason given by Captain Colpoys for not having written his pamphlet previously to the appearance of the second edition of Brenton's Naval History, is not very flattering to that work.

"Discouraged" (he says, page 3) "by the general character of the work in question, for *incorrectness* and censorious stricture on the conduct of some officers of the highest rank and reputation in our service, I did not look into the book for I believe more than a year after it came out." Captain Colpoys remarks also, "I was greatly surprised at finding, from the pen of an officer professing to have been an *eye-witness*, and intimately acquainted with all the circumstances (see vol. i., page 411), so very erroneous a statement of the leading particulars of that event, and more especially of what took place on board the London, of which ship I was captain." If the reader will consult Mr. James on this point, he will see how inaccurate Captain Brenton has been.

For the second and third charges against the historian, not entering into sufficient detail, and being partial; one instance will suffice:—In the first edition of Brenton's Naval History, p. 338, vol. iii., a long account was given of the action between his majesty's ship Phœnix, and the French frigate Didon. In the present edition of Captain Brenton's History, the account of this brilliant action is given in the following words: "Between the battles of Ferrol and Trafalgar, the Phœnix of 36 guns, captured the Didon, a French frigate of about the same force. I purposely omit saying anything more on the subject of this action which is given at length in the first edition. *That account, which I believe to be correct, did not give satisfaction to some of the parties concerned.*"

Now it may be asked why, in the Preface to James's History, any remark concerning Captain Brenton's should be made? For this reason: in vol. i., p. 152, of the new edition, the following note is appended to some remarks arising from the delay in securing the prizes after the action of the 1st of June: "I perceive that I am very amply quoted in Mr. James's new edition. Whether it is quite fair to do so, is a question which I shall not pretend to decide. I can only say that my permission has never been obtained, and never will be; and that, at all events, it appears to me most unjustifiable to borrow so largely from a living author, and not to acknowledge the loan. I certainly cannot repay myself in kind. Mr. James's facts and statements I am not disposed either to borrow or to criticize. Mine are drawn from the best sources available in a long professional life, and from an acquaintance more or less intimate with most of the leading men of the period under discussion."

Now so correct did the editor of James's History find the account of the battle of the 1st of June in the former edition of Mr. James, that not one word was altered. It stands *now*, as it stood before, and in all probability will so remain to the end of time. Not one word has been borrowed from Captain Brenton, and although he is frequently quoted, as are many French historians, the quotation is always acknowledged, and is generally selected for the purpose of showing into what errors historians may fall. It would be, for instance, quite useless to borrow the account of the Phœnix and Didon: the gallant officers of the English ship may well complain of their historian, as not a name is mentioned. Baker and his brave associates find the whole description omitted, *because* "the account did not give satisfaction to *some* of the parties concerned." A complaint of that kind cannot be alleged against this work. Mr. James collected his materials with wonderful accuracy, and unceasing research. He published what he believed to be true, and cared very little whether it gave satisfaction or uneasiness. He wrote his history after years of toil and difficulty, and no other will ever displace it. He never altered his history, without proof was given him that he was in error, and had he believed a statement true, the words would have remained, in spite of all remonstrance from those who failed to disprove it.

The British nation may rest satisfied upon the general correctness of the present work; for, with the exception of about eight names being erroneously spelt, and ten christian names being omitted, only four objections to passages have been received by the editor. The principal error is as follows: In James's History it was stated that on the night of the 2nd of November, 1805, the Boadicea, Captain John Maitland, and Dryad, Captain Adam Drummond, after having chased the squadron under Monsieur Dumanoir, discovered to leeward the squadron under Sir Richard Strachan. Mr. James then says, "Having, without getting any answer to their signals, arrived within two miles of the Cæsar (Sir R. Strachan's ship), which was the weathermost ship of this squadron, and then standing close-hauled on the larboard tack, the Boadicea and Dryad, at about 10 h. 30 m. P.M., *tacked* to the north-east, and soon lost sight of friends and foes." The passage will be correct thus: "Having arrived within two miles of the Cæsar, which was the weathermost ship of this squadron, and then standing close hauled on the larboard tack, the Boadicea made the signal for an enemy being in sight, and although guns *shotted* were fired, and the lights kept up for more than half an hour, no notice whatever was taken of them. The Boadicea and Dryad with the wind at west-north-west, continued steering to the north-east, and soon lost sight of friends and foes, the enemy having bore up during the thick squally weather which came on about 11 P.M." It will be seen by this account, which is undoubtedly correct, that owing to the neglect on board the Cæsar, both the Boadicea and Dryad were unfortunately prevented from taking any part in the action which occurred on the 4th of November; the lights were seen by the Eolus, Lord William Fitzroy, who being farther off than the Cæsar, gave her credit for an equally proper look-out, and did not repeat the signal; and thus, owing to the delicacy of the one and the neglect of the other, both Captain John Maitland, and Captain Adam Drummond, were deprived the honour of participating in Sir R. Strachan's action.

Another error is relative to the affair between the Leopard and Chesapeake, on the 21st of March, 1807. James says, "It was these three men demanded at Washington, that on two accounts weakened the claim of the British. In the first place, the Melampus is not one of the ships named in the published copy of Vice-admiral Berkeley's order. Consequently the Leopard's captain, in taking away men who had deserted from the Melampus, exceeded, what appears to have been his written instructions." In justice to Captain Humphreys of the Leopard, we are bound to state, that he did in nowise exceed his orders. The reason assigned for taking the three men is, that they were clearly recognised as *deserters*. The other twelve Englishmen were subjects (but *not* deserters) of the King of England, and not being within the limits of the order, were not disturbed. These three men were sentenced to receive five hundred lashes, itself a sufficient proof that Captain Humphreys's brother officers approved his conduct. The late Hon. Sir George Berkeley, the commander-in chief, wrote to Captain Humphreys a letter, in which he strongly commends him for his judicious and spirited conduct. For this we refer our readers to that excellent work, Marshall's Naval Biography.

In continuing the Naval History to the present date, much information has been derived from Marshall's Account of the Burmese War, and from several pamphlets relative to that great and difficult undertaking. The Battle of Navarin is given from the best possible authority, and the work itself is brought up to the day after the last promotion, and finishes with the number of admirals, captains, commanders, &c, now on the naval list.

In conclusion it may be remarked, that not the slightest allusion made to Captain Brenton's Naval History, is meant in a tone of hostility to that production. It certainly becomes the editor of a work to clear the character of his principal from any allegation of pilfering other authors, and although it must be admitted that no great work of times past can be written without recourse to the pages of others, yet has James, wherever he has borrowed, most scrupulously acknowledged the debt. In launching this new edition, the editor feels convinced that every impartial naval officer, to whatsoever country he may belong, will admit that Mr. James executed the work with the honourable intention of doing justice to every man, of holding up the brave and meritorious to the admiration of the world, and fearlessly condemning the tyrant or the coward. That the work is true and just in all its dealings, there can be no doubt, for if any part has been unjust or untrue, it became the duty of those who saw the errors, to correct them.

Waltham Hall, Waltham Abbey.—*March* 1, 1837.

Since writing the above, Captain Brenton's last number has appeared, to which he has affixed "a Reply to some of the Statements in James's Naval History." This must be answered. I trust Captain Brenton will believe me sincere, when I say that no officer stands higher in the estimation of the public, for philanthropy, assiduity, and professional ability, than himself; and without flattery I add, that no man more richly deserves this eulogy than Captain Brenton. He has spent his youth in the service of his country, and his mature age for the benefit of the poor. With this opinion I trust it is impossible for any man to believe that I answer his Reply with the wish to detract from his character in the slightest possible degree, but merely that I am supporting the foundation (if I may use the term in reference to Captain Brenton's allusion), on which by building, I have according to him, misapplied my "talents."

The "Reply" commences with an expression of sorrow, "that neither Mr. James nor his Naval Editor should have steered a course through their literary labours without running foul of him or his book." Mr. James, in compiling his history, most assuredly referred to Captain Brenton's, and did certainly notice numerous errors in that work; that he quoted it where occasionally he found it correct, is likely enough; and how can history be compiled but by these means? But let us hope we are not like the silly beauty, who believed every word which detracted from an adversary was a compliment to herself. The two works in question are as different as night and day; one is a cursory history of modern Europe, lightly touching upon naval actions; the other is a naval *history*. The latter enters into every detail, and examines every question; it does not lightly skim over events, or give the account of a frigate action, such as the Nymphe and Cleopatra, in 14 lines and two words; nor does it because *some* of the parties concerned were dissatisfied, "blot out the written record," and veil the gallantry of the Phœnix, in her action with the Didon, by damning it into two lines and three words.

In all his general actions, with the exception of Trafalgar, Brenton is almost as concise. Individual praise is rarely bestowed, and merited censure seldom inflicted.

Captain Brenton's first fire in his "Reply," is directed against James and myself for misquoting him, calling a town, a tower. Admitted: for this, the printer's devil, who omitted to mark the correction made by myself, deserves to be chastised.

Captain Brenton's second shot, is in reference to a theft committed by James, in plundering certain parts of Brenton, from vol. i., p. 8, and never pleading guilty to the charge. I say, "not guilty." Let any person refer to the text, pp. 112 and 113 of James, and if they can condemn me, they must be like Jeffrey, "and sentence letters as he sentenced men."

3. If the Queen Charlotte's ports were four feet six out of the water, or five feet ten, I imagine no great harm is done to historic truth.

4. Diagrams, according to Captain Brenton's opinion, are of very little use. In this fourth shot, no accusation is brought against James or myself: it is merely a sort of apology on the part of Captain Brenton, for not having, in his work, given any diagrams excepting for fleets at anchor. The one of Navarin is recommended to the attention of Sir Edward Codrington.

5. In regard to the maintopmast of the Queen Charlotte going over the side, Captain Brenton says, "that we know nothing about it:" very likely not; but we give an extract from Lord Howe's despatch to prove that it *did go*. "The Queen

Charlotte had then lost her foretopmast, and the main topmast fell over the side very soon after.' (Brenton, vol. i., p. 136.) Now there seems some mystery, and some mysterious conversation, relative to this unfortunate maintopmast. All hands allow that it *did* go, and that is all which James states; but Captain Brenton says, "*you* know nothing at all about the matter; *I* know how the maintopmast was lost, and so do the gallant admirals, Sir Edward Codrington and Cochet. The conversation on the Queen Charlotte's quarter-deck at that moment was highly edifying. Let me say no more.—" This is particularly rich; we are all in the dark, and Captain Brenton, the *faithful historian*, will not show us a light. Now had Mr. James known of this conversation, which Sir Edward Codrington is thus called upon to give to the public, the reader might rest pretty certain he would have had it, word for word, without any regard to persons; do not, Captain Brenton, hide your light under a bushel, and allow the grave to put its extinguisher over so edifying a remark.

6. There is a note in James, vol. i., p. 153, relative to the guns of the prizes taken on the 1st of June, being Swedish manufacture and *chiefly* of brass. Captain Brenton has kindly corrected this statement, and begs to inform the public that the guns were *all* iron, and likewise, that for the word "*bursted*," (James, vol. i., p. 155) the public are to read "*burst*." This correction of a great historical fact, and of a typographical error is particularly useful and kind.

7. Captain Brenton begs to inform M. Jean Bon St. André, his heirs, his executors, and assigns, that he (M. Jean Bon St. André) is a special coward, and is not entitled to any praise, which by some "tortuosity of mind," might be twisted from the unqualified disgust expressed in the mention of him in James's Naval History.

8. The anecdote concerning Sir Thomas Troubridge is a matter of *taste*, it has nothing whatever to do with history. I think Captain Brenton quite right in endeavouring to enliven *his* work. Mr. James's not requiring that excitement, has omitted it.

9. Agreed: let us say no more about Lord Howe or the age of the prizes. I think there has been quite enough useless discussion on both sides.

10. Captain Brenton is at issue with James on the word "population" and "populace." We refer the public to Miss

Martineau and Malthus for the first, and to Cobbett's grammar for the second.

11. "The loss of the Ardent is copied from me," says Brenton. It is in these words in James: "While employed in this service, the Ardent unfortunately caught fire, blew up, and *left not a soul alive to relate the origin of the catastrophe.*" There's a theft!

12. As Captain Brenton has called me "a naval officer of taste and character," I am bound to explain why I retained James's method of calling "the lower deck, the first deck." By-the-by, Brenton is quite wrong in saying this method was borrowed from the Americans; the decks were so nominated in Henry the Eighth's time. An editor has no right to make such alterations; anything connected with history erroneously stated by Mr. James has been altered, but an editor's duty extends no further.

13. Lord St. Vincent was wrong. Sillaus remained on the French list for years after the capture of the Pégase.

14. For the affair of Captain Brown in Fort-Royal bay, see "Cooper Willyam's campaign, 1795, in the West Indies." Mr. James is much indebted to him.

15. "The *account* of the gale in Torbay, in which *I* was present, is copied from *me*." (Brenton.) James says, "On the 14th of February, after several days' detention in Torbay, by a heavy gale at south-east, in which nine of the 36 sail of the line in company parted their cables, but fortunately brought up again, Earl Howe," &c. There is an account of a gale of wind for you! no London pickpocket was half so adroit as James; he stole that in his hurry which was not worth stealing, and which is so scanty and threadbare, that I wonder the owner of the goods ever reclaimed them. Is it possible that a man of Captain Brenton's high feeling, and moral integrity, could bring this, as well as the loss of the Ardent, to detract from James's and to enhance the merit of *his* History?

16. "Neither Sir Charles Ekins, nor myself, is permitted to know anything." This is a great mistake of Captain Brenton; there is no naval writer in some respects more deserving of the highest praise than Sir Charles Ekins: his battle of the Nile is by far the best account extant. But both Sir Charles and Captain Brenton, may *occasionally* be wrong. There are spots on the sun; the proof that James duly appreciated Sir Charles Ekins, is by the manner he is quoted

17. Captain Brenton begs to inform any gentleman curious in old almanacks (and we recommend this meteorological remark to Mr. Moore), that on the night of the 20th of June, at Quiberon, it did not blow a gale of wind, although it rained; and the public are informed, that Puisaye slept on board the Pomone, at least until daylight. Captain Brenton adds, "but as I was present at this affair, I must of course be a 'disqualified' witness." Wait a moment.

18. There are 13 lines in James, vol. i., p. 252, claimed by Brenton, he is quite welcome to them.

19. Two more lines, claimed as original by Captain Brenton.

20. Now we come to something like an objection. Captain Brenton, upon the authority of his brother, the gallant Sir Jahleel Brenton, who was first-lieutenant of the Gibraltar in December, 1796, gives an animated account of the preservation of that ship, after she had struck on the Pearl rock, according to Brenton, and on a bank, according to James, near Cabrita point. The first objection started is, that Mr. James says, "the mainsail was set," and Sir Jahleel declares, "it was not set." Now I avail myself of this contradiction to prove to Captain Brenton that an eye-witness is not always correct. Mind, I do not say Sir Jahleel is not correct, but one of the eye-witnesses must be wrong. The log positively asserts that the mainsail *was set*. Sir Jahleel as positively states that it *never was set*. The log of a ship is its history, written by an eye-witness; the word of Sir Jahleel is unimpeachable, he was an eye-witness; who now shall pretend to say which is right? All the rest of the accounts nearly agree. But there is one question in James which Captain Brenton has not answered, and which, with his permission, I will ask again. "The Pearl rock, on which Sir Jahleel asserts the Gibraltar struck, lies about a mile and a half due south, and Cape Malabata, the north-east point of Tangier bay (on the opposite side of the strait), about 22 miles southwest of Cabrita point: how then with the wind at east-southeast, could the Gibraltar *want* 'to weather Cabrita point,' to get into Tangier bay?" Captain Brenton will find that eye-witnesses (we may refer him to Colpoys's remarks to Sir Byam Martin concerning the mutiny), are not always correct. I could bring Sir Walter Raleigh forward as an eye-witness, when he himself afterwards admitted that he was wrong.

The 20 different paragraphs given by Captain Brenton, having now been answered, I would ask, what would have been the sentence of a court-martial if such charges had been brought against an officer? "Frivolous and unfounded." It will be perceived that I have answered them in the light manner I thought they deserved. Had any accusation been brought forward which really affected Mr. James's character as an historian, I should have defended him in a more sober style, or have given him up as a pirate. But this is not all: Captain Brenton asserts that no landsman *can write* a Naval History, because he cannot comprehend the detail of nautical manœuvres, or understand the phraseology of a sailor. I defy Captain Brenton to point out *one*, only *one* nautical error in the whole of James's History, and this is perhaps the most wonderful part of the work. Every word is right, is strictly correct, and had Captain Brenton, who detected the grammatical error of the word "bursted," and seized with avidity on the typographical one of "tower," been able to discover an error, the eye which so scrupulously scanned the pages, and the hand which recorded the two trifling mistakes above, would not have been inactive on the very ground on which he states no landsman can write a naval history.

In defence of myself, if defence be necessary, let me say this much: I was censured by our best naval writer for having undertaken what he refused. I came to the task prepared to disarm every body. I erased many objectionable passages. I circulated a request that all officers would point out any errors in the former edition. I extracted the venom where the sting must remain, and in some cases, I infused a balm calculated to dispel the rancour. In no wise do I hold myself responsible for any of Mr. James's personal remarks, neither do I expect to enhance my literary reputation by "building on his foundation;" but I trust that if in the course of this publication I have inadvertently made an enemy, that Captain Brenton will receive me as a friend.

INTRODUCTION.

PREVIOUSLY to our entering upon the main subject of these pages, an inquiry into the origin and early progress of the British Navy, particularly as respects the constructing, arming, and classing of the ships, cannot fail to be useful, and will not, it is hoped, prove uninteresting. The Great-Harry, built in the third year of the reign of Henry VII. (1488), was, properly speaking, the first ship of the royal navy. The Great-Harry had three masts, and, as late as the year 1545, was the only ship of that description in the British fleet. She is represented to have been accidentally burnt at Woolwich in 1553. If so, she had run 65 years; which, according to the mean of modern terms of duration, was a very long period.

It is probable that the Great-Harry was the first ship belonging to the nation; but there is reason to believe that Richard III. owned a few of the ships which he employed. The remainder, as it appears, were either hired of the merchants, or supplied, under a law of the state, by the Cinque Ports. Whatever may be the doubts on these points, historians agree, that to Henry VIII. is due the honour of having, by his own prerogative, and at his sole expense, settled the constitution of the present royal navy. He instituted an admiralty and a navy-office, appointed commissioners, and fixed regular salaries, as well for them as for his admirals, officers, and sailors; and the sea-service, thenceforward, became a distinct profession.[1]

Cannons, or great guns, were used as early as the thirteenth century, in a naval engagement between the King of Tunis and the Moorish King of Seville.[2] They were also used by the

---

[1] Archæologia, vol vi., p. 202, and vol. xi., p. 158.

[2] James's Military Dictionary, tit. *Cannon*.

English on land at the battle of Cressy, fought in 1346; and by the Venetians at sea, in or about the year 1380.[1] According to some printed representations still extant, the English used them on board their ships in the reigns of Richard III. and Henry VII. The guns were not then, as now, pointed through embrasures, or portholes, but mounted *en barbette*, or so as to fire over the top-side, or bulwark, of the vessel.[2] The ships, therefore, could have had but one deck; and, when it is considered that they undoubtedly had but one mast,[3] we may conceive what puny "ships" they must have been.

The first appearance of portholes (invented, with some other improvements, by Descharges, a French builder at Brest) occurs in the representation of the Henri-Grace-à-Dieu, built at Erith in 1515, and said to have measured 1000 tons. No idea, however, can be formed of this ship's actual burden, unless we knew in what manner the tonnage was cast. The invention of portholes gave the power of adding a second tier of guns; and, accordingly, the Henri-Grace-à-Dieu appears with two whole battery-decks, besides additional short decks, or platforms, both ahead and astern.

The nature, or caliber, of great guns was not, as at present, designated by the weight of the shot which they discharged. One reason for this may have been, that the balls were not all made of the same materials, some being of iron, some of stone and some of lead,[4] three substances which differ greatly in specific gravity. It appears, also, that hollow iron shots, filled with combustible matter, were very early brought into use. Hence, the weight of the shot was of too fluctuating a nature to serve for the classification of the gun that discharged it. Among the different species of English ship-guns of former days, was the "cannon," with its varieties, the cannon-royal, cannon-serpentine, bastard-cannon, demi-cannon, and cannon-petro. The term "cannon" is a singular conversion of the generic into a specific term. Its ambiguity may have given rise to the occasional substitution of "carthoun."

The Henri-Grace-à-Dieu appears to have mounted, in the whole, 80 pieces, composed of almost every caliber in use. Of these 80 guns, not more than 54, according to the clumsy drawing which has been handed down to us,[5] were pointed through broadside ports. The remainder were mounted, either as bow

---

[1] Archæologia, vol. vi., p. 205.
[2] Ibid, p. 207.
[3] Ibid., p 202
[4] "Shottes of yron, shottes of stoen and leade."—*Charnock's Marine Architecture* vol. ii., p. 44.
[5] See the print in the 6th volume of the Archæologia.

or stern chasers, or as "murdering pieces," upon the afterpart of the forecastle; as, from its height and appearance, it then might truly be called. The use of these murdering pieces (the muzzles of which all point in the direction of the maintopmast head) is not easily discernible. The ship had four masts;[1] and, as the Great-Harry was the first two-decked,[2] so the Henri-Grace-à-Dieu was the first three-decked ship built in England. In a list of 1552, the latter appears as the Edward. Here all traces of her cease.

The next British ship of any note, and the largest of all that had preceded her, was the Soveraigne-of-the-Seas, built at Woolwich dockyard in 1637, by Mr. Phineas Pett.[3] Her tonnage has been variously stated. According to the account published by the designer of her decorations, Mr. Thomas Heywood, the Sovereign measured 1637 tons.[4] The exact agreement of this combination of figures with that denoting the year in which she was built, and its non-appearance in any tonnage-list of the time, render it likely that the figures, owing, perhaps, to the printer's mistake, were erroneously put together. In a list of the year 1652, the Sovereign, or, as subsequently named, Royal Sovereign, stands at 1141, in one of 1677, at 1543, and in one corrected up to 1740, at 1683 tons; a difference principally, if not wholly, attributable to the various methods of casting the tonnage in use at those several periods.

However, it is an account of the ship's armament which we most require, and that Mr. Heywood himself has been at the pains to record. "She has," says he, "three flush-deckes, and a forecastle, an halfe-decke, a quarter-decke, and a round-house. Her lower tyre hath thirty ports, which are to be furnished with demi-cannon and whole cannon throughout, being able to beare them. Her middle tyre hath also thirty ports, for demi-culverin and whole culverin. Her third tyre hath twenty-sixe ports for other ordnance. Her forecastle hath twelve ports, and her halfe-decke hath fourteen ports. She hath thirteen or fourteen ports more within-board for murdering pieces, besides a great many loopholes out of the cabins for musket-shot. She carried, moreover, ten pieces of chase-ordnance in her right forward, and ten right aft, that is, according to land-service, in the front and the reare."[5] Numbering the guns, we find 126 as the establishment of this first-rate of the seventeenth century.

[1] Derrick: Memoirs of the Royal Navy, p. 8
[2] Archæologia, vol. iii, p. 266.
[3] A Soveraigne, of 800 tons, occurs in a list of 1527.—See Pepys's Miscellanies, vol. viii.
[4] Charnock, vol. ii, p 283.
[5] Ibid.

Mr. Heywood, doubtless, had no intention to mislead his readers; but, it should be recollected, the Sovereign-of-the-Seas, when he and his men were employed upon the carved work and ornaments about her, did not mount a gun. The ship lay in dock; and all that he or they could know of her intended armament must have rested on hearsay. In the total number of ports, Mr. Heywood is apparently correct. The error lies in his having filled with guns the ten ports "right forward, and the ten right aft," as well as the six in-board ports on the forecastle. Reduce these, and there remain 100; the number of guns which the ship, when fitted for home-service, actually mounted. The pamphlet, containing Mr. Heywood's very elaborate account[1] of this "incomparable ship," has, for its frontispiece, an alleged representation of her. But the authenticity of the drawing is doubtful; chiefly because, in many important points, in the ports and guns especially, it is at complete variance with the letter-press.

It is probable that, about the middle of the seventeenth century, the practice of placing guns of a dissimilar caliber on the same deck ceased to prevail in the British navy.[2] This was a decided improvement. For a variety of calibers occasions delay and confusion in handing up and fitting the shot; especially where, as was the case here, the differently-sized balls were to be used on one deck. About coeval with this improvement was the removal of the greater part of that cumbrous pile of timber and iron-work, raised to so ridiculous a height at each extremity of the vessel. The ship found relief, also, in being no longer armed with "murdering," or in-board pieces; and, particularly, in having no standing bow and stern chasers, a portion of which were generally among the heaviest guns on board. Hence, from this time, an English ship of war could bring half the number of her guns into broadside action; an advantage which she had never before possessed.

The earliest list of the British navy, in which there is any classification of the ships, is probably that copied into Mr. Derrick's Appendix, (p. 303,) and bearing date in 1546. There King Henry's vessels, 58 in number, are classed, according to their "quality," thus:—"Shyppes;" "galleases;" "pynnaces;" "roo-baerges." Another list, bearing date in 1612, exhibits the classes following: "Shipps royal," measuring from 1200 to 800 tons; "middling shipps," from 800 to 600 tons; "small shipps,"

---

[1] It fills five quarto pages of Charnock.
[2] In the French, and some other navies, vessels so armed were occasionally captured during the eighteenth century.

350 tons; and "pinnaces," from 250 to 80 tons.[1] It will tend to clearness in our future inquiries, if we at once give an explanation of some of these terms.

A ship is defined to be " a large hollow building, made to pass over the sea with sails," without reference to the quantity, shape, or position of those sails; and, in this extended sense, the term appears to have been originally used. Hence, we are told that, before the days of the Great-Harry, all the ships of the royal navy had but one mast and one sail.[2] That ship is alleged to have had three masts,[3] and the Henri-Grace-à-Dieu, as already mentioned, four.[4] The galleas was probably a long, low, and sharp-built vessel, propelled by oars, as well as sails; the latter, perhaps, not fixed to the mast or any standing yard, but hoisted from the deck when required to be used. The lugger, or felucca, of modern days may serve for an example. The pinnace was a lesser description of galleas, and, most probably, had no mast, or, if any, a moveable one. The "roo-baerge," or row-barge, explains itself.

The division of the British navy into rates appears, for the first time, in a table drawn up by order of Charles I. in the year 1626, and styled, "The new rates for seamen's monthly wages, confirmed by the commissioners of his majesty's navy, according to his majesty's several rates of ships, and degrees of officers."[5] Those rates were, as now, in number six, and consisted each of two classes, to which different complements of men were assigned; but the armaments of the classes are not specified, they having probably been described in some preceding order, which has not been preserved. One fact is obvious, that the division into rates was adopted, rather to regulate the pay of the officers and seamen, than to mark any distinction in the force or construction of the ships. Hence, at this day, the captain of every rate is paid differently. The same is also the case with many of the subordinate officers.

The first appearance of a classification by guns occurs in what purports to be "A list of all shippes, frigats, and other vessels belonging to the State's navy, on 1st March, 1651,"[6] (new style) 1652. The number of classes, or subdivisions by guns, comprised within the six rates, amounts to 23, exclusive of two, which may be called, unrated classes. These were hulks and shallops. The latter were simply row-barges; the former,

---

[1] Charnock, vol. ii., p. 247.
[2] Archæologia, vol. vi, p. 202.
[3] Ibid., vol. iii., p. 266.
[4] See p. 2.
[5] Charnock, vol. ii., p 277.
[6] Pepys's Miscellanies, vol. v. p. 595.

stationary vessels, fitted with sheers to erect or remove masts, and also, it is probable, with accommodations to lodge the officers and crews of vessels under repair. Although the hulks were generally old and unseaworthy ships, one of them appears to have been "building at Portsmouth."

In the course of about 30 years several other unrated classes were added. Those only of which any notice need be taken are, sloops, bombs, fireships, and yachts. A list of November, 1658, shows that the sixth rate then comprised vessels mounting as few as two guns. Between that year and 1675, however, vessels of this small description appear to have been detached from the sixth rate, and to have been classed by themselves as sloops. The 13 individuals named in a list of the year 1675, mounted each four guns, and averaged in size 42 tons. In what way the latter were rigged cannot now be ascertained, because the mast and rigging books of the navy do not extend so far back; but it is probable, from their diminutive size, that they had only one mast, and were sloops in the proper sense, or that to which the term, in marine language, is restricted.[1]

Bombs, which are vessels carrying, besides six or eight light guns, one or two heavy mortars, from which shells are thrown into a town or fortification, appear, for the first time, in a list of 1688, and are said to have been invented by M. Reyneau, a Frenchman, and to have been first employed at the bombardment of Algiers, in 1681.[2]

Fireships and yachts first appear in a list of 1675. The use of the fireship, as the name implies, is, by means of ignited combustibles, to set fire to the vessels of an enemy. The yacht is simply a pleasure-vessel. According to Mr. Pepys, the Dutch, in the year 1660, gave Charles II. a yacht called the Mary; "until which time," he adds, "we had not heard of such a name in England."[3]

Although a certain number of guns is made the sign, or denomination, of every class within the six rates, the frequent occurrence of the same number of guns under different rates shows, that the classification by guns was, in some degree, subordinate to the classification by rates. A list, that gave the situation, or place of mounting, as well as the number of the guns on board the ships, would most probably show what it was that occasioned two classes, of the same apparent force, to be registered under different rates. It so happens, that no list or abstract that has been printed, or which is to be found among

[1] Falconer, p 485.   [2] See James's Military Dictionary, p 56.   [3] Derrick, p. 89.

the archives of the navy, contains any information on the subject. There is, however, in existence a curious manuscript-list, or rather set of lists, bearing date in 1677, and drawn up by the command, and for the private use of Charles II. The manuscript, which is elegantly written on vellum paper, and bound in gilt morocco, with silver clasps, afterwards belonged to the late Sir Thomas Slade, who was made a surveyor of the navy in 1755. Subsequently it came into the possession of the late Sir John Henslow, who was appointed to the same office in 1785; and at the decease of the latter, his executors presented it to Mr. John Knowles, of the Surveyor's Office, to whose kindness we are indebted for a perusal.

These lists exhibit the number, nature, and weight of the guns on every deck; the number of men assigned, as well for each caliber of gun, as for the ship's full complement; the number and specification of the officers; the tonnages; the years and places in and at which, and the persons by whom the ships were built; together with many other useful particulars. In or about the year 1650 a difference began to prevail, between the number of guns and men established upon the ships in "war at home," and in "peace at home, and peace and war abroad."

That difference, which is carefully noted in these lists, arose from an inability to carry a sufficiency of provisions for their crews. Hence, in the event of the ship's being ordered to a distance from home, both the men and the guns were partially reduced, in order to allow room for an additional supply of provisions; and that in time of war as well as of peace. Upon the whole, the information contained in these lists fills up what has hitherto been considered a chasm in the early history of the British navy; and so much of their contents as will elucidate our further inquiries respecting the armament and classification of the ships of the seventeenth century we have incorporated in an abstract.[1]

A single glance at the abstract referred to will show what it was, besides the number of guns, that governed the classification of several of the ships. For instance, No. 11 in the second, and No. 15 in the third rate, mount each 70 guns; but the one carries them on three, the other on two decks. Nos. 12 and 19 are similarly situated; and so are a few among the inferior classes. Hence, it is a difference in the number of battery-decks that, without reference to the number of guns, distinguishes the rates. The characteristic of a first-rate of 1677 seems to have been, to

[1] See Appendix, No. 1.

mount her guns on three whole decks, a quarter-deck, forecastle, and poop;[1] of a second-rate, to mount her guns on three whole decks and a quarter-deck;[2] of a third-rate, to mount hers on two whole decks, a quarter-deck, forecastle, and poop; of a fourth-rate, to mount hers on two whole decks and a quarter-deck; of a fifth-rate, to mount hers on her first gun-deck, from end to end, on her second, partially, with a few guns on the quarter-deck; and of a sixth-rate, to mount her guns on a single deck, with or without any on her quarter-deck. It is worthy of remark that there were, in these times, three-deckers of 64, and two-deckers of 30 guns; and that many single-decked ships of the present day exceed, nay, nearly double, even the former in tonnage.

Our attention is next called to the calibers of the guns, assigned to the different classes in the foregoing abstract. Considering the "VII" subjoined to cannon, to signify that the piece was that variety of the cannon whose cylinder was about seven inches in diameter, we at once identify the gun to be either the cannon-serpentine, or the bastard-cannon of Sir William Monson. Before we fix which of these two it was, it may be proper to state, that the 8½ and 8 inch cannon (cannon-royal and cannon) appear in no one list or abstract of the navy that we have seen. If they had been used previously to 1677, it could only have been for a short time, and then merely as bow or stern chasers on the lower deck. It is probable, too, that they were of brass, in order to be of diminished weight. Looking at the weight of the cannon VII, as expressed in the original list, we find it to range between 65 and 54 cwt.: whereas, the weight of the cannon-serpentine, Sir William states to have been 49 cwt., and that of the bastard-cannon 40 cwt. Now the caliber, or diameter of the bore, of the cannon-serpentine and bastard-cannon agrees not only with that of the cannon VII, but with that of the 42-pounder, the sea-service gun which has since been brought into use. Moreover, the last-named gun agrees in weight, if not with the cannon-serpentine and bastard-cannon, at least with the cannon VII.

With respect, also, to the shots severally thrown by the cannon-serpentine, bastard-cannon, cannon-VII, and 42-pound gun, we shall have no difficulty in showing, that they were all of nearly the same weight. For instance, the solid iron shot, that exactly fits a cylinder of seven inches diameter, weighs a trifle over 46½ lbs.; but, a small space being usually allowed to inter-

---

[1] No. 6 in the abstract is the only exception to this rule.   [2] Except No. 7.

vene between the circumference of the shot and that of the cylinder, denominated windage, (the expansion of the shot by a white heat, the incrustation of rust from damp, and the foulness of the cylinder after repeated firing, are the three chief considerations to be provided against by the windage,) the shot becomes reduced in diameter, until it weighs about 42 lbs. Or rather, the shot itself being the datum from which the caliber of the gun was originally determined, the latter was made to correspond with the former, allowing the customary windage. The shot of seven inches diameter cannot, as we have shown, weigh more than 46½ lbs. and a trifle : therefore, the 53½ lbs. assigned by Sir William Monson,[1] as the weight of the shot belonging to the cannon-serpentine, whose cylinder did not exceed seven inches, must be erroneous. It may have arisen from a typographical mistake, in substituting a 5 for a 4; and then 43½ lbs. would serve for the weight of a shot calculated for a seven-inch cylinder, only with less than the usual windage.[2] If any further proof were wanted, to show that the cannon VII and the 42-pounder were the same gun under different denominations, it might be found in the fact, that such first-rates in the list of 1677 as survived the first fifteen years of the new century, appear in the gun establishment of that time, with no other difference in their lower-deck armament than the substitution of " 42-pounders " for " cannons VII."

The demi-cannon, without doubt, was the 32-pounder of afterdays. The cannon-petro had, in the list of 1677, already changed its name to 24-pounder, and a 12-pounder (probably the ancient basilisk) also appears there. The whole-culverin and demi-culverin became subsequently the 18, and the 9-pounder. The saker, or sacer, both from its caliber and weight, was the 8½ feet, 22 cwt. 6-pounder; as was the light saker, the modern gun of the same nature, measuring six feet, and weighing 17 cwt. The minion was the 4-pounder: what name the 3-pounder of 1677 had previously taken does not appear.

It will be sufficient to say of the lesser calibers in Sir William's list, that they, or most of them, were afterwards called swivels; simply because, when again brought into use, they were mounted on stocks, or upright timbers, having a pivot on which the gun traversed. Upon the degree of credit due to Sir Willian Mon-

---

[1] See Appendix, No. 2.
[2] Different nations have different proportions for determining the windage. The English, for their long guns, divide the shot into 20, and the bore into 21 parts; the French, into 44 and 45, and, in some of their light pieces, 46 and 47. The English windage, except for carronades, is notoriously too great, and ought to be reduced.

son's account of the ancient sea-service ordnance, we are unable to pronounce; but the list certainly appears to have been drawn up without much care. At the same time, it must be owned, that great confusion prevails in all the accounts which have been published on the subject; as far, at least, as our researches have extended. The precise time at which the whole of the British sea-service guns dropped their names of beasts and birds of prey, to assume those designating the weight of the shot they respectively discharged, cannot well be ascertained; but the change certainly took place between the years 1685 and 1716, and that is sufficiently near for our purpose.

Soon after the commencement of the new century, a surprising diminution appears in the number of rated classes belonging to the British navy. In the abstract of 1677, a total of 129 ships divide into 31 classes, exclusive of 10 sub-classes, separated on account of a difference in the distribution or calibers of their guns, or in the amount of their complements of men; while, in an abstract taken in August, 1714, a total of 198 ships divide into only 10 classes. There is no great difficulty in explaining how this arose. A reference to the abstract of 1677 shows, that the 90, 70, 54, and 48, gun classes were the most numerous; the majority of the others comprising but one or two individuals each, and those among the earliest built in the abstract. Hence, the capture, wreck, or other disposal of a ship frequently annihilated a class; and we find that, between the years 1689 and 1697, the British navy actually lost, by capture alone, 50 vessels: it is probable, too, that at least an equal number fell by the perils of the sea.

King William, in the mean time, had built 30 large ships; (17 of 80, 3 of 70, and 10 of 60 guns;) and half that number of still finer ships had been captured from the French. Such ships of the 54-gun class, and of the classes between the 48 and 42 inclusive, as had not been lost or disposed of, appear to have been reduced, the first to 50, the latter to 40 gun ships. Besides which, some ships, constructed to mount 40 guns, had been built. Several 30 and 20 gun ships had been built, or taken from the enemy. Hence, the 10 rated classes of the year 1714 were, the 100, 90, 80, 70, 60, 50, 40, 30, 20, and 10, gun-ship class; the latter consisting of only one individual.

The rates themselves appear, about this time, to have also undergone a reorganization. The first-rate now descended no lower than the 100, and the second, no lower than the 90 gun class. The third admitted all classes below the 90, and above the 60. The fourth took for its limits the 60 and 50; and the fifth received all below the 50, down to the 30. The sixth-rate found room for every class below the 30, that had not, for its denomination, a term in which, as sloops, bombs, &c., the number of guns was not expressed. Desirous to show what, if any, progress in classification, armament, and size, half a century has produced, we will, by the aid of an abstract, investigate the state of the navy at the death of George I., in June 1727.

An Abstract of the British Navy in June 1727.[1]

No.	Rate.	Class.	Carriage-Guns. First or main Deck. No. Pds.	Second Deck. No. Pds.	Third Deck. No. Pds.	Quarter-deck and Forecastle. No. Pds.	Gross Weight of Guns. Tons.	Complement of Men. No.	Ships in each Class. No.	Burden. Tons.
		Gun-ships.								
1	First.	100	28 42	28 24	28 12	16 6	214	780	7	1869
2	Second.	90	26 32	26 18	26 9	12 ,,	175	680	13	1566
3	Third.	80	,, ,,	,, 12	24 6	4 ,,	147½	520	16	1350
4	,,	70	,, 24	,, ,,	-- --	18 ,,	126¼	480	24	1128
5	Fourth.	60	24 ,,	,, 9	-- --	10 ,,	104	365	18	195
6	,,	50	22 18	22 ,,	-- --	6 ,,	85½	280	46	755
7	Fifth.	40	20 12	20 6	-- --	-- --	57¼	190	24	594
8	,,	30	8 9	,, ,,	-- --	-- --	34	135	3	421
9	Sixth.	20	20 6	-- --	-- --	-- --	22¼	115	27	374

On the face of this abstract, there does not appear any greater increase in the size of the ships than the increased weight of the guns seems to authorize. One improvement, however, is evident: the poop or roundhouse deck is no longer armed. The two or four 3-pounders, formerly mounted there, now appear as 6-pounders on the quarter-deck and forecastle. We have here no clashing of classes on account of a similarity in the number of guns. On the other hand, that distinction between the rates, founded on the number of decks, and which so particularly characterizes the abstract of 1677, is destroyed.

The number of decks of a fighting-ship is generally considered to be a tolerable criterion of her force; and, if every ship of war notoriously mounted the same number and nature of guns upon a deck, the expression, single-decker, two-decker, or three-decker, would be thoroughly understood. By this a deal of

[1] The items of the table in the text have been carefully compiled from official and other documents. The guns are those established upon the several classes by an order of 1716; and which order continued in force until 1743. The complements are those borne between 1719 and 1733. The tonnage is that established in 1719, and which was not materially varied until 1743. The employment of swivel-guns in the navy, at or about this period (see page 13), renders necessary the distinction of carriage-guns. In the 30-gun class the complement was probably made up by two small pieces.

circumlocution, and of private, as well as of international bickering would be saved. As, however, ships' decks vary in length from 70 or 80, to upwards of 200 feet; and ships' guns, in caliber and weight, from the 3-pounder of 11, to the 42-pounder of 65 cwt., the simple term, one, two, or three-decker explains nothing. A strong instance, that occurs in the abstract of 1677, will illustrate this. There the three-decker, No. 12, is classed above the two-decker, No. 13;[1] and no one would imagine, that a second-rate, of three decks, was not of greater force than a third-rate, of two decks. The first discovery to the contrary is, that the two-decker mounts the greater number of guns; but that is only by a seventh: the next discovery is, that, in broadside-weight of metal, she is the more formidable ship by nearly a third; that of the 64 being 511, of the 74, 751 lbs.

Let us suppose, for argument-sake, that some such expressions as these were in use: "A 10-port two-decker," "A 13, or a 14-port two-decker." Any one of these three terms ought to enable us to get at the total number of guns in the ship, as readily as if, according to the former supposititious case, all ships' decks were armed alike. Take a person, wholly unacquainted with naval technicalities, and, pointing to the ship, No. 7,[2] as she lies on the water, ask him what number of decks she has. He replies, "Two." If he takes the pains to count her guns, he will agree with you, that she is a "10-port two-decker." Show him, next, No. 4, and ask him what she is. After a slight pause, he will say, "A 13-port *three*-decker, that seems to want four ports in the middle of her *upper* deck."

You smile at this double mistake of the landman's; and, as the best mode of convincing him of his error, carry him on board the ship. As he stands on the gangway, looking with wonder above, around, and below him, you, pointing down the waist, ask him what is the name of that deck. He answers you, "The lower;" or, if his eyes can penetrate the hatchway below, or his recollection furnish him with the number of tiers of cannon he counted when on shore, he may reply, "The middle deck." You assure him that the deck he is looking *down* upon is the *upper* deck. He raises his eyes towards the deck on which he is standing. You tell him that is the *quarter* deck. "Quarter!" he may think, if not exclaim, "why, it extends over more than half the ship, and only wants planking up in the middle to be the largest deck of the three." He may then be emboldened, on his part, to ask, "Why not call it the half-deck?" He is carried

[1] See Appendix, No. 1.   [2] See the short abstract at p. 11.

below, and shown a small space between the wardroom door and the break of the quarter-deck, and informed that *that* is the half-deck.

Although it would be a vain hope to expect to change names, which have stood their ground for ages, and are perfectly understood by the persons for whose use they were made; yet an endeavour to trace the origin of the terms by which the different decks of a fighting-ship are distinguished, may tend to elucidate many of the statements, and those by no means the least important, in the following pages. It is a remarkable fact, that the forecastle and quarter, or poop deck, although now the most insignificant, were once the only decks armed with guns. These were mounted, not as broadside, but as chase guns. Afterwards, a tier of them was placed on each side of the principal, or main deck; but, until the invention of portholes, all the guns were mounted, as formerly mentioned, *en barbette*.[1]

Almost the first use made of the power of pointing the guns through, instead of over, the ship's side, was to employ an additional tier of them. The deck, which sustained the lower and heavier tier, was named, by the English, the lower, or gun-deck; by foreigners in general, the first deck.[2] The deck next above the principal deck, the English called the upper,[3] foreigners the second deck. Hence, when a third deck was added, the latter had only to express it by that name; while the English had to change upper into middle, and apply the former term to the third deck.

Conformably to this arrangement, the English admiralty and navy boards call the single gun-deck, of what is commonly termed a one-decked ship, the upper deck, and the deck below it, upon which no guns are mounted, the lower, or gun-deck. With them, therefore, every reputed single-decked ship, except she be so small as to have no 'tween-decks, is, properly speaking, a two-decked ship: while foreigners, the French in particular, designate the upper as the second deck, when only any guns are mounted upon the lower. When otherwise, the upper deck is described as *the* deck,[4] and the guns placed upon it, as mounted in single battery;[5] the lower deck, as the English would call it, being named the false, or imperfect deck.[6] To

---

[1] See p. 1.
[2] Premier pont, *Fr.* Prima coperta, *It.* Primera cubierta, *Sp.* Primeira cuberta, *Portug.* Ver dek, *Dutch.* Forsta laget, *Swed.*, &c.
[3] Sailors frequently name this the main-deck; but shipwrights, when they use that term, apply it, very properly, to the lower, or principal deck.
[4] Le pont; la seule batterie.
[5] En batterie.
[6] "Faux-pont; pont au-dessous de la

call the lower, the gun-deck, when, as in the case of two, or three decked ships, guns are also mounted upon the deck or decks above it, tends to confuse, rather than to distinguish; but to call that the gun-deck, upon which no guns are mounted, is a gross absurdity. Yet, in official language, the lower deck of every ship is indiscriminately named the gun-deck, and the cabin at the after part of it the gun-room. So that the length of a modern frigate's "gun-deck," so frequently published for our information, is not the length of the deck whereon she mounts her guns, but of the deck beneath it, on which she lodges her men.

It is, however, in the storey erected above the upper deck, so called, that we must look for the most glaring, and as respects the armament of a ship, the most important, perversion of terms. The ancients were accustomed to build upon the short prow, or fore-deck of their galleys, a kind of turret, or small castle;[1] and the rudiments of this were plainly visible in the Venetian galleas, or greater war-galley, employed as late as 1571. The origin of the names, forecastle, with the English, castella di proa, with the Italians, gaillard d'avant, or, château de proa, with the French, as well as of the terms of similar import used by other nations,[2] is thus readily traced. The term "gaillards," taken alone, includes, apparently, all that part of a ship's upperworks intended for the accommodation of the principal officers. "Communément les logemens se pratiquent sur les ponts les plus élevés, pour avoir des jours dans l'accastillage : c'est cette combinaison d'ornement et de commodité qui forme ce que l'on appelle les châteaux ou gaillards."[3] The corresponding elevation at the after-part of the ship was designated by substituting, either *after* for *for*,[4] or *poop* for *prow*,[5] except in England, where, in one instance, the term half-deck was used;[6] but, in all others, quarter-deck, in reference, probably, to that portion of the ship's length over which it originally extended. The quarter of a ship is that part of the side which lies towards the stern, or which is comprehended between the aftmost end

première batterie." The Americans usually call this deck the *berth*-deck, meaning that on which the ship's company is lodged.

[1] As early as the twelfth century, "towers" in ships are recommended, from which to use the spears and other arms of the time. See Antiquarian Repository, vol. iii., p. 62.

[2] Castillo de proa, *Span.* Castillo du proa, *Portug.* Voor-kastreel, *Dutch.* Skents, *Swedish.*

[3] Traité Elémentaire de la Construction des Bâtimens de Mer; par M. Vial du Clairbois, &c., à Paris, 1805, tom. i., p. 148.

[4] Gaillard d'arrière, ou château de poupe.

[5] Castella di poppa, *Ital.* Castillo de popa, *Span.*, &c.

[6] See p. 3: also Charnock, vol. ii., p. 449: where Admiral Sir Cloudesley Shovel, as late as 1690, uses the term in the same way.

of the main-chains, and the sides of the stern where it is terminated by the quarter-pieces; but the quarter-*deck* is stated to extend all the way from the mainmast to the stern. This, however, applies to English ships only: the French usually make the extent of their "gaillard d'arrière" depend on the rate and class of the ship; in some it extends to about three feet ahead of the mainmast, in others to scarcely double that distance from the mizenmast. Most nations, as we have just shown, called the elevation above the quarter-deck the poop.[1] The French, however, named it *la dunette*.

The fallacy of the term *quarter*-deck betrayed itself as early, at least, as the year 1673; when the ship No. 16 in the first-given abstract,[2] was armed with seven guns of a side on her quarter-deck, while mounting only twelve of a side on either of her whole decks. It was but to add to these, the two guns of a side on the forecastle, and on the poop, to produce within one gun of a third complete tier; yet no one, but an unsophisticated landman, would think of calling the ship a three-decker. No, not although the great Mr. Pepys himself may be found denominating certain French ships, from one of which the two ships at No. 16 in the abstract were actually modelled, "ships with two decks and a half." These are Mr. Pepys's words:—" In 1672 and 1673, the French brought a squadron of about 35 ships to Spithead, to join our fleet. There were several excellent ships with *two decks and a half*, that carried from 60 to 74 guns; more especially one called the Superbe, which his majesty and royal highness went on board of: she was 40 feet broad, carried 74 guns, and six months' provisions. Our frigates, being narrower, could not stow so much provision, nor carry their guns so far from the water; which Sir Anthony Deane observing, measured the ship, and gave his majesty an account thereof, who was pleased to command Sir Anthony to build the Harwich,[3] as near as he could of the Superbe's dimensions; which was done accordingly, with such general satisfaction, as to be the pattern of the second and third rates built by the late act of parliament."[4]

In spite of so high an authority, however, the Harwich, and all ships built like her, were, and still continue to be, called two-decked ships.

[1] The elevation that, in former days, was frequently to be seen above the poop, was called by the English the poop-royal.
[2] See Appendix, No. 1.
[3] One ship of class No. 16 in the abstract of 1677, was the Harwich; the other, the Swiftsure.
[4] See Pepys's Miscellanies, p. 268. The second and third rates alluded to are those at Nos. 7 and 17 in the abstract.

The forecastle and quarter-deck, which, in their practical application as terms, have thus so violated precision, were originally detached elevations, that left the deck immediately below them, or so much of it as intervened between the fore and main masts, open and exposed. Hence ships so constructed were said to be deep-waisted. The French term analogous to this is *haut accastillé*, signifying a ship with high, or lofty upperworks; certainly a more intelligible expression. Afterwards it was found convenient, particularly in ships of war, to connect the two short decks by a boarded passage on each side, called the gangway; to support which were placed beams or rafters, that reached right across the ship. This gave to the whole such a continuous appearance that no person, not otherwise taught, would hesitate to call it, as our landman did,[1] the upper deck of the ship. And even a marine writer of France justifies the term:—"On peut regarder les gaillards comme *le pont le plus élevé* des vaisseaux, dont une partie est interrompue entre le grand mât et le mât de misaine; ce qui forme deux *demi-ponts* au niveau l'un de l'autre."[2]

Some advances have, however, since been made. The French, for instance, were accustomed occasionally to cover with a grating the open space between the two "half-decks;" and then it was no longer "les gaillards," or "les demi-ponts," but "le pont de cailbottis," the deck with a grating. "Je crois donc que les vaisseaux du second rang pourroient avoir trois ponts sans gaillards, ou plutôt les gaillards qui formeroient le troisième pont, seroient joints par des cailbottis, comme on l'a vû au Tonnant. De tels bâtimens, qu'on pourroit regarder comme n'ayant que deux ponts, seroient, au moyen du *pont de cailbottis*, &c."[3] In more modern times, each passage, or gangway, has in some cases been widened, so as to admit a gun to recoil; or, if necessary, as many guns as the passage, from its length, can receive. But even this, with the English, is not allowed to take from the deck that is underneath, and which is now almost covered from sight, its ancient name of *upper*. The ship, therefore, should particularity be requisite, not otherwise, has a new deck assigned to her, called the *spar*-deck, a name, of the origin or application of which every one seems ignorant. If it is because the ship's spare spars are stowed on that deck, so are they in the same place on board every ship; namely, on each side of

---

[1] See p. 12.
[2] Vocabulaire des Termes de Marine; par Cn Lescallier, Ordonnateur de Marine; à Paris l'an 6 (1798.)
[3] Elemens de l'Architecture Navale; par M. Duhamel du Monceau; à Paris, 1752.

the launch, between the fore and main masts. The French say, "Pont sur gueule," which may be rendered, "the deck built over the *mouth* of the upper deck," commonly called the waist. Why is this not as complete a deck as any in the ship? Hence, as no one ventures, in common utterance, to speak of a *spar-decked* one, two, or three decker, a ship of this construction may mount a whole tier of cannon beyond what her denomination expresses; and we shall, by-and-by, have to adduce some very formidable examples.

Not only the three and the two, but the single-decked ship feels, and that to a greater extent, the inconvenience of this ambiguous nomenclature. For instance, a ship that mounts 28 guns on a single deck, and 14 on the quarter-deck and forecastle, it is thought necessary to reduce, by cutting away the two latter short decks; thereby exposing to view her main battery-deck, from end to end, and disarming her, of course, of 14 out of her 42 guns. Yet this ship, materially altered as she is in her form, and stripped of a third part of her numerical force, undergoes no change of name: she is still a single-decked ship. It is true, that a similar operation performed upon the two, or the three-decker, would lead to a similar alteration in the form, and some, but not so great, a reduction in the force. A two, or three-decked ship, so cut down and reduced, would also retain her former name. But two, or three-decked ships, without quarter-decks, are of rare occurrence; while single-decked vessels of that form are very numerous. They descend to the lowest small-craft that has a deck upon which guns are, or may be mounted. It is likewise true, that the term flush-decked has been used to signify, that the single-decked ship of war, so named, is constructed without an over-built quarter-deck and forecastle.

Flush, in this its arbitrary signification, is synonymous with level. A flush-deck is, therefore, a level or even deck, throughout its extent.[1] In this sense is not every principal of fore-and-aft deck of a ship a flush-deck? Were not the three whole decks of the Sovereign-of-the-Seas called, by one who in that respect is no mean authority, "three-flushe-decks?" The term was evidently first used in the merchant-service, and stood opposed to that form of deck, which, as it runs aft, suddenly rises by a step or two, and then continuing in a line to the stern, becomes the quarter-deck of the vessel. Ships of this construction were described, properly enough, as *deep-waisted*; and the

---

[1] The French say, "Un pont entier, sans ravalement, ni interruptions."

generality of merchant-vessels are, to this day, built in that manner. Were *flush*, as meaning level, without fall or rising, to be used in reference to the upper edge of the gunwale, or planksheer, of the ship, instead of to her deck, it would serve perfectly well to distinguish an open-decked from a quarter-decked ship of war. For both the quarter-deck and the forecastle bulwarks cease at the extremities of the gangway; and the intermediate drop in the line (now perpendicular and abrupt, formerly softened down by a scroll or figure) is merely rendered less obvious, by the presence of the hammocks stowed in the waist nettings, or of the painted canvas that covers them. The French term corresponding with flush-ship, or flush-built ship, is, "Un bâtiment paré de long en long;" and that even a three-decked ship, according to the French application of the term, "les gaillards," or the quarter-deck and forecastle, may be without any decks of that description, is clear from the following example.

M. Clairbois informs us, that the French Ville-de-Paris, until subsequently raised upon so as to mount 12 or 14 guns more, was a 90-gun ship, "sans gaillards." Her original force we get from his book, and her dimensions and tonnage from the records in the navy office, the Ville-de-Paris having since (when a 104-gun ship) been captured by the British. To facilitate a comparison that we may afterwards have occasion to make, we subjoin the name, dimensions, and force of a British quarter-decked 90, built in 1756, which was about the time that the Ville-de-Paris herself was built.

Class.	Name	Length of Deck.	Breadth extreme.	Tons.	First Deck.	Second Deck.	Third Deck.	Quarter-Deck and Forecast.	Broadside weight of Metal
		Ft. In.	Ft. In.		No Pds	No Pds	No Pds	No. Pds.	lbs Eng.
Gunship. 90, Flush	Ville-de-Paris	187 ¼	53 8¼	2347	30 36	30 24	30 12	-- --	1170
,, Quarter-decked	Namur	174 11¼	48 7¼	1814	26 32	26 18	26 12	12 6	842

It may here be remarked, that flush-ships, whether single, two, or three deckers) for the term is equally applicable to all of them), have, according to the English seaman's phrase, a quarter-deck and forecastle; that is, two imaginary lines are drawn across the deck, one even with the foremast, the other with the after side of the gangway-entrance; and that portion of the deck which lies abaft the latter line is called the quarter-deck, that ahead of the former, the forecastle. The term gangway, like many others, is ambiguous in its meaning. It stands for the passage that leads from the quarter-deck to the forecastle, and, in that sense, is rendered in French by "passe-avant." It means also the entrance to the ship's deck from the top of the outside ladder; for which there appears no corresponding French term. The ladder nailed to the ship's side they call "échelle hors le bord."

Shipwrights know of no such ideal decks as quarter-deck and forecastle, in cases where the deck is continuous fore-and-aft; nor is the French term, "gaillards," at all applicable to them neither are we aware, whether or not the French naval people make a similar division of the upper deck of their flush ships. Still there are two terms, and those in general use, which, in a great degree, depend for their correctness upon the admission of the very terms, quarter-deck and forecastle, as divisional parts of a flush deck. For instance, flush vessels, of the smaller sorts especially, are seldom without a raised deck forward, that overhangs and covers nearly the whole of the imaginary forecastle; and that short deck is called the *topgallant* forecastle. Its use is, not to be a platform for guns, but to shelter the crew from the rain and the break of the sea. Corresponding with this, there is often, on board the larger flush ships, a short deck at the stern, named after, and every way resembling the poop. Its principal use is to be a roof to the captain's cabin. When confined to this office, the French call it "la petite teuge;" when extended forward to, or a little ahead of the mizenmast, they call it "le demi-gaillard." Their term "la dunette" seems applicable only, when this short deck is erected over "le gaillard d'arrière," or the proper quarter-deck. Both these short decks, the topgallant forecastle and poop, are usually without bulwarks, and therefore very slightly interrupt the continuous line, which, in our humble judgment, gives, or should give, the name to the flush ship. Although it is common for two, and three-deckers, except the lowest class of the former, to be constructed with poops, yet some ships are built without any, and others have them, for various reasons, cut away. If we take no account of these, it is because the slight operation they undergo causes no, or a very slight, reduction in their armament; and it is as it affects her armament only, that a ship's construction can claim any part of our attention

As these pages are not intended for the exclusive perusal of professional men, we shall be pardoned for qualifying some terms, and altering others, so as to render our expressions intelligible without the aid of a paraphrase. Accordingly, in this work, the several decks of a fighting-ship have been, and will be called, first, second, and third, instead of lower, middle, and upper. For example, we say, not *lower deck*, *middle deck*, *upper deck*, but as foreigners invariably do, *first deck*, *second deck*, *third deck*. Where a ship mounts the principal part of her guns on a single deck, we shall avoid saying, with the French and others, "the deck," by adjoining the word "main." Hence, a frigate's single battery-deck is her *main* deck; and so, indeed, it is generally called, for the reason that sailors are accustomed to call by that name the *upper* deck of every ship. Shipwrights, on the other hand, denominate the *lower* the main-deck; and to that, as a battery-deck, the term is every way the most applicable. We shall merely connect *main* with *first*, thus, first *or* main-deck, in order to its ready application, where wanted, to single-decked ships. To meet the term "faux-pont," as applied by the French to the deck that is below the main-deck of the latter class of vessels; and to avoid the paradoxical expression of lower deck, as applied to a reputed single-decked ship, we would say, with the Americans, the *berth*-deck, as being that on which the crew are lodged. However, the expression will be seldom required, and therefore less liable to offend those who may think it unwarrantably used.

As 99 out of every 100 two and three decked ships are constructed with a quarter-deck and forecastle, we may consider the latter as almost necessary appendages to the former; at least, we may venture to designate a ship, so constructed, as the common (adding, if necessary, or quarter-decked) two or three decker. No such adjunct, however, need be used, unless a flush two or three decker presents herself to notice. With respect to single-decked ships, commonly so called, the case is different. The flush ship has become a greater favourite than formerly; and the navy-lists of all countries now contain whole classes so constructed. Precision would therefore require, that we should mark well the distinction between the quarter-decked and the flush one-decker; and at the risk of frequently clogging our meaning with obscurity, we should be compelled to make the attempt, were it not that some other terms have stepped in, and, by narrowing the discussion, saved both the reader and ourselves from any embarrassment on the subject.

We have already shown that the term *ship* means any vessel that passes over the sea with sails.[1] But that is its general meaning: it has also a specific one, fully as well known. According to this, the term signifies a square-rigged vessel of at least three masts. The square-rigged vessel of two masts is denominated a brig; and the minor classes, that are not square-rigged, and which comprise sloops, cutters, schooners, &c., generally pass, among seafaring people at least, by the sweeping appellation of *fore-and-aft* vessels; an expression used in reference to the cut of their principal sails. Now, as the only quarter-decked brigs of war that we know of are a few belonging to the navy of Spain,[2] it may be taken for an axiom in naval affairs, that brigs of war, and all the small-craft below them, are flush-built: consequently the latter term, when they are mentioned, need not be used, but becomes applicable to one-decked *ship*-rigged vessels only, and is even still more restricted, as we shall presently show.

No sooner was anything like system adopted in the conduct of engagements between fleets than it became necessary that the line of battle should be composed of the larger and stronger ships, as being those the best able to bear the brunt of such encounters. The earliest list in which a separation of this kind appears is that of the British Channel fleet, under Admiral Russel, in 1691. There the honourable distinction of line-of-battle ship descends to the fourth-rate inclusive, and, with one exception to be noticed hereafter, has so continued ever since.[3] Exclusive of the ships destined to take their stations in the line of battle, there were attendant vessels, the duties of a portion of which were, to reconnoitre the enemy, to chase away stragglers, and to perform various other detached services: the remainder consisted of hospital-ships, bomb-vessels, and fire-ships. The reconnoitring or cruising portion usually comprised the fifth and sixth rates, and were denominated frigates. A navy was therefore composed of, line-of-battle ships, frigates, bomb-vessels, fire and hospital ships: the two first, as comprehending within the six rates the bulk of the fighting navy, constituted the two grand or principal divisions.

No one can dispute the propriety of the term line-of-battle ship, as above applied. We will now endeavour to ascertain

[1] See p. 5.
[2] The Port-Mahon and Vincejo, each of 277 tons, were so constructed.
[3] The first published abstract of the navy, in which the "line-of-battle" classes are separated from the others, is one of the year 1714.—See Derrick, p. 124.

how friggot,[1] frigat,[2] or in modern English, frigate, a term that in itself conveys no meaning, became invested with the extensive signification which we have also shown it to possess. The author of the "Dictionnaire de la Marine," published at Amsterdam in 1739, is the earliest writer we know of that treats on the frigate. He says, "The word *frégate* derives its origin from the Mediterranean, where it was usual to designate as frigates long vessels, that used both sails and oars, and carried a deck, of which the top-side, being higher than that of galleys in general, had openings resembling portholes, for the oars to pass through." —"Ce mot de frégate tire son origine de la Méditerranée, où l'on appeloit frégates de longs bâtimens à voile et à rame, qui portoient couverte, et dont le bord, qui étoit beaucoup plus haut que celui des galères, avoit des ouvertures, comme des sabords, pour passer les rames."[3] What occasioned these sailing galleys to be named frégata[4] is not very clear; but, at all events, we may safely conjecture, that the principal quality for which they were famed was swiftness of sailing.[5]

The contiguity of France, by her Mediterranean frontier, to the waters that gave birth to the "fregata," renders it easy to conceive that, ere many years had elapsed, vessels of a somewhat similar form, bearing the same name, appeared in the Channel. Augmented size and a bluffer body would diminish the rate of sailing, but were requisite, nevertheless, to counteract the storms and swells of a northern sea. Towards the middle of the sixteenth century, the generality of English merchant-ships were called frigates; some of which, towards the latter part of the century, were, as we are informed, hired from the merchant, to serve in the British navy. Accordingly, in a list of 1588, we find, among the "ships serving with Sir Francis Drake," the "frigat Elizabeth Fonnes," of 80 tons and 50 men; but how armed does not appear. A merchant-vessel, requiring the greater part of her hull for the stowage of her cargo, would carry her guns in a single tier: and there can be no doubt that the merchant-ships of those days were far better sea-boats than

---

[1] Fuller in his Worthies, Pepys, Raleigh, &c. Mr. Derrick, whenever he quotes passages from these and other English writers, alters the language to the modern standard. This is highly improper; as, were the reader not aware that such a liberty had been taken, he might justly doubt the authenticity of the quotations.

[2] Johnson. Mr. Todd also spells it in the same manner. We may here remark, that Johnson, or rather his printer, has misspelt the French word, calling it *Frigate* instead of *Frégate*. Both in Mr. Todd's edition and Mr. Chalmers's Abridgment the same error prevails.

[3] Dict. de la Marine, p. 498.

[4] "*Frégata;* Picciol navilo da remo." Baretti.

[5] The French give the name of *frégate* to a very swift-flying sea-gull.

the men-of-war; the tier-upon-tier of cannon and lofty upperworks of which rendered them fitter to be gazed upon in harbour, than to withstand the rough weather they must have been expected to encounter on the ocean.

Towards the close of the sixteenth century, Sir Robert Dudley, commonly called the Duke of Northumberland, prepared draughts of seven distinct classes of ships of war: the Galleon, Rambargo, Galizabra, Frigata, Gallerone, Galerata, and Passavolante. The accounts are not very satisfactory, as to the number and nature of guns which it was intended for each to mount.[1] Among them was a ship measuring 160 feet in length, and 24 in breadth, and constructed to carry a tier of guns on a single whole deck, besides other guns on two short decks, that resembled the quarter-deck and forecastle, or rather, not being united by gangways, the poop and topgallant-forecastle. Here the disposition of the guns is the same precisely as that which characterizes the modern frigate; and it is a singular fact, that this ingenious nobleman named his vessel, thus constructed and armed, *Frigata*. Sir Robert, early in the ensuing century, submitted his draughts to government; but, although some beneficial hints may have been taken, it does not appear that his proposition met a favourable reception. To prove his own confidence in his plan, Sir Robert, in the year 1594, caused a vessel to be built at Southampton, of a similar form to his intended Galleon, but measuring only 300 tons. With this vessel, which mounted 30 guns (of small calibers, no doubt), the inventor made a voyage to India; and, according to his report, the vessel fully answered his expectations.[2]

The author of the "Dictionnaire de la Marine" states, that the English were the first to name as frigates, upon the ocean,[3] long vessels, armed for war, having the deck much lower than that of galleons and ordinary ships.[4] This undoubtedly refers to single-decked vessels; but it is not clear whether, by "bâtimens armés en guerre," is meant regular king's ships, or armed ships hired of the merchants, and to which, as we have already shown, the name frigate was commonly applied. The probability, that the latter were those alluded to, is strengthened by the fact, that the first list of king's ships, one of 1604, in which any frigate appears, contains only "a French frigat."

---

[1] For the draughts, see Charnock, vol. ii, p. 177.
[2] See Charnock, vol. ii., p. 177.
[3] As distinguished from the Mediterranean sea.
[4] "Les Anglais sont les premiers qui aient appelé frégates, sur l'océan, les bâtimens longs, armés en guerre, qui ont le pont beaucoup plus bas que celui des galions et des navires ordinaires."—*Dict. de la Marine*, p. 498.

This vessel stands the last but one in the list, and, from her burden, 15 tons, must have been little better than a boat. The next list of king's ships, in which the frigate appears, is one of 1633. There the two last vessels are the "Swann frigat," and "Nicodemus frigat," each of 60 tons, 10 men, and 3 guns. In a subsequent list, they each appear with a different tonnage, number of men, and guns. One may conjecture that, as Charles I. made frequent visits of inspection to his different naval depôts, the Swan and Nicodemus were elegant, fast-sailing little ships, built to attend him thither; and it is not unlikely, that the diminutive French frigate of the former list had also been constructed for pleasurable purposes.

Fuller, who wrote in or about the year 1660, says, "We fetched the first model and pattern of our friggots from the Dunkirks, when, in the days of the Duke of Buckingham, then admiral, we took some friggots from them, two of which still survive in his Majestie's navy, by the names of the Providence and Expedition."[1] Now, the Duke of Buckingham appears to have filled the office of Lord High Admiral from 1619 to about 1636, and the names Providence and Expedition occur, both in the list of 1633, and in that of 1652, which is the next that appears in print. But the figures denoting the tonnages, men, and guns of the ships, in these early lists, are too contradictory to enable us to state more, than that the Providence and Expedition were small ships, mounting from 20 to 30 guns, the chief of them on a single deck. Mr. Pepys, also, whose authority in all matters respecting the ships of the British navy stands very high, says thus: "The Constant-Warwick was the first frigate built in England. She was built in 1649, by Mr. Peter Pett, for a privateer for the Earl of Warwick, and was sold by him to the States. Mr. Pett took his model of a frigate from a French frigate which he had seen in the Thames; as his son, Sir Phineas Pett, acknowledged to me."[2] Mr. Pepys, in his "Memoirs of the Navy," invariably, we observe, spells frigate *frigat;* but Mr. Derrick's correcting hand, and our inability to get a sight of the "Miscellanies" and "Naval Minutes" (stated by Mr. D. to be in Magdalen College, Cambridge), compels us, in quotations purporting to be from them, to spell the word, and indeed all the words, as if they had been written at the close of the eighteenth, rather than of the seventeenth century.

Mr. Pett may have taken his model some years before he was called upon to build a vessel from it; and there is no reason to

[1] Fuller's Worthies of England, vol. ii., p. 342.   [2] Derrick, p. 76.

suppose that the French frigate was a national frigate. She was, most probably, a privateer; and may have been one of the many that the enterprising "Dunkirks," as Fuller calls them, had fitted out. Both writers refer to a model, or pattern, as if there were something in their frigate to distinguish her from the generality of ships of war; and yet neither has taken the pains to give the faintest description of what that peculiarity, whether of form, or of armament, or of both, consisted. We may gather that the prototype, as she was a privateer, was a swift sailer, and not of very large dimensions or force. To arrive at any further particulars, we must grope a little deeper into the records of these early times.

The name of the Constant-Warwick occurs in several lists between 1652 and the end of the century; but in scarcely any two of those lists does the ship appear with the same tonnage and number of guns. Both the year in, and the place at which, and even the person by whom, she was built are differently stated; yet there was, undoubtedly, but one ship of the name in the British navy. Without quoting from so many contradictory authorities, we shall briefly state the result of our very careful researches on the subject.

The Constant-Warwick was built in 1646, at Ratcliffe, by Mr. Peter Pett the elder, for the use of the Earl of Warwick, as a privateer, or, in softer language, as a sort of private-armed cruising yacht. She measured, in the modern way of computing the tonnage, from 380 to 400 tons, and mounted 26 guns; consisting of 18 light demi-culverins, or short 9-pounders, on the main-deck, six light sakers, or short 6-pounders, on what was virtually the quarter-deck, and two minions on what, as being of no greater extent than was requisite for a roof to the chief officer's cabin, may be called the poop. We have seen several draughts of English fifth and sixth-rates, as they were constructed in the latter half of the seventeenth century, that correspond exactly with this arrangement of the guns. The deck on which the sakers are mounted is really a whole deck, reaching from stem to stern; but the bulwark, or barricade, commences only where that of the modern quarter-deck does, at the after side of the gangway-entrance. A ship, of the size and armament of the Constant-Warwick, well formed in her *carène*, or lower body, lightly but handsomely ornamented in her upper-works, and rigged according to the most approved plan of the day, did no discredit to the name of frigate, now first applied in England to any determinate form of vessel.

The earl subsequently disposed of his frigate to the commonwealth, but not, as it would appear, until she had afforded decided proofs of her superiority of sailing. At what precise time the transfer took place is uncertain; but the first list, in which the Constant-Warwick appears as a national ship, is one of 1652. There she classes as a fifth-rate, of 28 guns. In another list of the same year, her guns are stated at 32: a difference to be explained, perhaps, by one being the lowest, the other the highest, number of guns assigned to the ship in her new employ.[1]

The English were always fond of over-gunning their vessels; and it generally happened, when an English ship of war was taken by the French, that the latter, before they sent her forth as a cruiser, reduced, sometimes by a full sixth, the number of her guns. One instance may suffice. The Pembroke, when captured by the French, at the commencement of the eighteenth century, mounted 64 guns; but, when recaptured shortly afterwards, had on board only 50 guns, and these as the whole of her establishment.[2]

An addition of six guns to the Constant-Warwick's original number was, perhaps, no improvement; but what shall we say to an increase of 20, or, at all events, of 16 guns? Our suspicion that this had taken place was excited by seeing the name of the Constant-Warwick, as one of the six fourth-rate 42-gun ships, enumerated at No. 30 in the abstract of 1677.[3] There the ship, having her two bow-ports filled, carries 20, instead of 18 demi-culverins on what is now, in truth, the first gun-deck; and, having her quarter-deck bulwark continued forward on each side to her stem, readily finds room for a second whole tier of guns. The number first mounted on this second deck was probably 20, the same as on the deck below. Afterwards, 18 were considered enough; especially as the guns were not sakers, but demi-culverins, the same as on the first gun-deck. The poop, by this new operation, and, perhaps, by a little extension forward, becomes the quarter-deck, and is armed, at first probably with six, but afterwards with four minions; making 46 guns as the temporary, and 42 as the permanent, establishment of the ship.

When to the increased weight of the guns their carriages and shot is added the weight of wood and iron, consumed as well in the barricade to the second gun-deck as in strengthening the ship in every part, we may well give credit to a writer of 1665, who, in complaining that ships of the British navy are

---

[1] See this explained at p. 7. [2] See Charnock, vol. ii., p. 18.
[3] See Appendix, No. 1.

"over gunned," instances, among others, "the Constant-Warwick, from 26 gunns and an incomparable sayler, to 46 gunns and a slugg."[1] The worst is, that the Constant-Warwick, although thus changed in her form and qualifications, although, from an "incomparable sayler," converted to a "slugg," was allowed to retain her original appellation. So that, according to the loose accounts handed down to us, "the first frigate built in England" was an over-gunned, top-heavy, two-decker, instead of, as a little investigation now proves her to have been, a properly armed, snug one-decker.

There was, however, one part of the Constant-Warwick's peculiarity of construction that could not be altered, without a complete rebuild from the keel upwards: it was the sharpness of her lower body, or, as the naval draughtsman would call it, the fineness of her lines. This sharpness of form appears to have been the only characteristic of the frigate which the English builders thought worthy to be retained. It seemed to them a most convenient property, that suited all sizes and classes of ships; and, accordingly, between the years 1646 and 1653, upwards of 60 "frigates" were built, or building. One, among the latter, was to carry "from 50 to 80 guns." The remainder were variously classed, from 56 down to 12 guns; and the first was the only rate, from which they appear to have been excluded.

One natural effect of this extraordinary degree of sharpness, when applied to an overloaded ship carrying 60 or 70 guns, was so to increase the immersion of the vessel, that her lower battery approached too near to the water to be useful. This evil we shall explain in the words of Mr. Pepys. "In 1663 and 1664," says he, "the Dutch and French built ships with two decks, which carried from 60 to 70 guns, and so contrived that they carried their lower guns four feet from the water, and to stow four months' provisions; whereas, our frigates, from the Dunkirk-built, which were narrower and sharper, carried their guns but little more than three feet from the water, and but ten weeks' provisions."[2] Mr. Pepys then states, that five frigates (three of 70, one of 66, and one of 64 guns, according to the list of 1677[3]) were ordered to be built of such dimensions as to obviate those defects. In eight or ten years afterwards, we find Mr. Pepys still complaining of this want of buoyancy in the

---

[1] "Gibsons Observations on Military Management," as copied into Charnock's second volume.
[2] Derrick, p. 84.
[3] See Appendix, No. 1.

British frigates; as appears by another of his statements, already quoted to illustrate a point in our inquiries.[1]

Thus had the "first frigate," in less than 20 years, spread her name, if not her qualifications, over nearly the whole of the British navy. From the time, however, that the first and second-rates excluded all two-decked ships, as was certainly the case at the date of the abstract of 1677,[2] and may have been the case a year or two earlier, the frigate-classes were confined to the third and the three inferior rates. When, too, at the close of the seventeenth century, the classes within the first four rates assumed the name of line-of-battle ships,[3] the frigate became further restricted to the fifth and sixth rates; which, as the fifth-rate, by the new regulation, was confined to classes below the 50-gun ship, afforded but a very limited range. So that, by the year 1727, as already shown, the frigate-classes were reduced to three, the 40, the 30, and the 20 gun ship.

Our next object is to show, to a certain extent, what classes have emanated from these three; but as some foreign, particularly French, frigate-classes may occasionally come before us, it may render the subject more intelligible, if we here introduce a few general remarks on the system of classification adopted in the principal foreign navies.

It is difficult to say, whether the English or the French were the first to divide their navy into rates. We can only state, that in the year 1670, the French navy appears to have consisted of five *rangs*, or rates, each composed of several *ordres*, or classes; and that their first-class first-rates mounted 120 guns, and measured 1500 tons French; which, allowing for the difference both of weight and of casting the tonnage in the two countries, may be about equal to 1800 tons English. As a substitute for their sixth-rate, they had a class which they called *frégates légères*, or little frigates. Probably the name, without an adjunct, was applied to some ships of the fifth-rate, whose exterior form and manner of carrying their guns may have justified the appellation. Next to frégates légères were fire-ships; then barca-longas, and pinks. Of the composition of the Spanish navy, in these early times, we can say nothing: we can only remark upon their ships, as they appeared at sea, or in English ports.

The Dutch seem to have divided their navy into six (some accounts say, seven) rates. Their heaviest ships, of which there were but a few, are represented to have mounted 92 or 94 guns, of which a portion were probably swivels. The shallowness of

[1] See p. 15.   [2] See p. 8.   [3] See p. 21.

their waters cramped the Hollanders in the dimensions of their ships, and compelled them to adopt, in their larger vessels especially, a flatter floor and bluffer contour than characterized the vessels of other nations, of their southern neighbours in particular.

The great fault attributed to British men-of-war, at the latter part of the seventeenth, and early part of the eighteenth century, was their insufficient size, in reference to the guns they were forced to carry. Hence, their lower batteries could seldom be used in blowing weather; and they sailed and worked heavily. But even this had its advantages; for the British generally recaptured their ships, whenever they formed part of an enemy's chased fleet: and it is remarkable that, of the Comte de Forbin's fleet, which, in 1708, attempted a descent on Scotland, the only ships which perished in the gale that happened were such as had been taken from the English.

The foreign builders appear to have allowed a greater width to the portholes, and to the spaces between them. This, in a given number of portholes and spaces, necessarily added to the length of the vessel; and as that increased length required a proportionate breadth, a general increase of bulk, and thence of tonnage, became the consequence. The ship was thus rendered more buoyant, and her lower battery stood higher from the water; advantages which were sensibly felt by the British, in almost every encounter attended by a rough sea, or a wind fresher than common. In the form of the lower body of their ships, the French greatly surpassed the English; but, in point of materials and workmanship, the advantage was, and perhaps is to this day, on the side of the latter. To the British, however, is certainly due the merit of having been the first to introduce the curved form to that part of the stern against which the sea beats: on the other hand, they were among the last to abandon the immoderate contraction of the upper decks of their ships, and the consequent low position of their chain-plates.

The Spaniards appear to have taken the lead, even of the French, in the proportion between the size and the numerical force of their ships. As a sense of pride had induced Spain to build her ships higher, a sense of safety had impelled her to build them broader, than those of any other nation. When, therefore, the example of other states permitted her to ease her ships of a part of their cumbrous superstructure, Spain continued, for a while at least, to give them their former breadth. They undoubtedly possessed the advantages of greater stability, and of sides less penetrable by an enemy's shot. If the increased thickness of the sides added to the intrinsic weight of the ship, a counterbalancing property was found in the superior buoyancy derived from her increased width. One example will suffice to show the difference that prevailed between the builders of Spain and of England. The following are the dimensions of a Spanish and an English ship, of the same class or denomination; the one built, the other captured, in 1740 :—

Gun-ship.	Length of First Deck.		Breadth extreme.		Depth of Hold.		Tons.
	Ft.	In.	Ft.	In.	Ft.	In.	
Princessa .. 70	165	1	49	8	22	3	1709
Bedford ... ,,	150	10¼	43	7¼	17	10	1230

We may now resume our inquiries relative to the various frigate-classes that followed the three of 1727.[1] Two new classes were added in 1740: the one a 44-gun ship, averaging about 710 tons, and established with 40 guns on her two decks, similar to No. 7 in the short abstract at p. 11 but with 18 and 9, instead of 12 and 6 pounders; also with four 6-pounders on the quarter-deck. The other class was a 24-gun ship, averaging about 440 tons, and established with two 9-pounders only on the first deck, and twenty of the same caliber on the second deck, with two 3-pounders on the quarter-deck. Before nine years had elapsed, 38 individuals of the 44-gun class, several of them of increased dimensions, had been built, and such of the old 40s as could bear them, had been allowed four sixes for their quarter-decks; which made them also 44-gun ships, although of a weaker description. The remaining 40s were few in number; and, by the year 1755, the class became extinct. In 1748 a 28-gun ship was added, measuring about 585 tons, and constructed to carry twenty-four 9-pounders on the main-deck, and four 3-pounders on the quarter-deck. This was a decided improvement on the 24, as well as on the old 30 gun class: moreover, the 28 is the first ship that, in the arrangement of her guns, conveys any idea of the modern frigate.

In the year 1757 the following five frigates of the 28-gun class were built of fir instead of oak, as had hitherto been the general practice :—

See p. 28.

	Tons.		Year.
Actæon	585, sold as unserviceable	.	1766
Boreas	587, ditto ditto	. .	1770
Hussar	586, captured by the French		1762
Shannon	587, taken to pieces	. . .	1765
Trent	587, sold as unserviceable	.	1764

So that the four of these fir-built ships, not cut off by capture, lasted, upon an average, nine years.

In the year 1757, also, were added two classes, of no mean importance; one a 32, the other a 36 gun ship. The first of these merits a particular account. On the 29th of March, 1756, the Navy Board agreed with Mr. Robert Inwood, of Rotherhithe, at the rate of 9*l.* 17*s.* per ton, to build a fifth-rate ship, according to a draught proposed by Sir Thomas Slade, one of the surveyors of the navy. The ship was to measure 671 tons, and to mount twenty-six 12-pounders on the main-deck, four 6-pounders on the quarter-deck, and two 6-pounders on the forecastle. She began building in the succeeding April; and, after being named the Southampton, was launched on the 5th of May, 1757. Another ship from the same draught, named the Diana, and built by Messrs. Batsons, on the Thames, was launched in August of the same year: she was sold out of the service in 1793.

The Southampton may be considered as the first genuine frigate built in England; that is, as the first English ship, constructed to carry her guns on a single whole deck, a quarter-deck, and a forecastle, the characteristic, in the opinion of all the maritime nations, of the proper frigate. A naval writer of France, M. Lescallier, thus describes the frigate: "Frégate; navire de guerre, grée de même que les vaisseaux de ligne, qui leurs ressemble en tous dans ses manœuvres, et qui ne diffère d'eux qu'en ce qu'il est plus petit, et *qu'il n'a qu'une batterie de long en long.* Les frégates ont le plus souvent depuis vingt-six jusqu'à quarante canons, dont les calibres sont de 12 ou de 18, pour ceux en batterie, et du 6 ou du 8 sur les gaillards."[1] The frigates of the celebrated Chapman are all of the same form; and, indeed, no modern naval architect recommends any other. The Southampton always bore the character of a good sea-boat and a prime sailer, and reigned as such for 56 years; when a reef of rocks in the Crooked Island passage put a stop to her career. The 36-gun frigate carried the same number and nature of guns on the main-deck as the 32, with four additional 6-pounders on the quarter-deck. The class, which consisted but

[1] Vocabulaire des Termes de Marine.

of three individuals, averaged about 720 tons. The first launched was the Pallas. She was ordered in July, 1756, and launched August 30, 1757. The two others were the Brilliant and Venus.

We may notice, in passing, that it was upon one of the 32-gun class of frigates, the Alarm, that, in November, 1761, copper sheathing was first employed in the British navy. Like most other innovations, this seems to have had a weight of prejudice to remove. It was not until April, 1764, that a second ship, the Dolphin, of 24 guns, underwent the same operation. In nine months afterwards the Jason, of 32 guns, was coppered; and in March, 1776, the new ship, Daphne, of 20 guns. In that year four ships were coppered; in 1777, 10 or 12; and, before the termination of hostilities in 1783, there was scarcely a ship in the British navy that had not received the benefit of this highly-important invention. In November, 1783, after various vain attempts to counteract the effects of the copper sheathing upon the iron bolts, and in consequence of the success of several experiments made with 44-gun ships, and others of the smaller classes, it was ordered that copper bolts should in future be used, under the load-draught of water, in all the ships of the navy.

In the same year in which the above new classes, the 32 and 36 gun frigate, made their appearance, the British captured a French ship, the Bon-Acquis, of 946 tons, mounting eight 18-pounders on the first deck, twenty-eight 12-pounders on the second deck, and two 6-pounders on the forecastle; total, 38 guns. In 1758 the British also captured the French 36-gun frigate Mélampe, of 747 tons, and armed the same as the 36-gun class, already described; and, in the following year, the Southampton, assisted by the Mélampe, captured the French 36-gun frigate Danaé, of 941 tons, mounting twenty-eight 12-pounders on her main-deck, six 6-pounders on her quarter-deck, and two 6-pounders on her forecastle. Between 1759 and 1761 the British took three French 32-gun frigates, armed like the Southampton, and averaging about 700 tons. It appears, therefore, that the English, if not beforehand with, were very little behind, the French, in the construction of that justly-celebrated class of ship, the modern one-decked, or proper frigate.

In or about the year 1756 the British 50-gun ship, being found too weak to cope with any ship which the enemy usually admitted into his line of battle, was reduced to an under-line class. The ship, however, although armed much in the same way as the two-decked 44, was not considered as a frigate, but continued to be called, as formerly, 50-gun ship.

In 1744 some newly-discovered virtues in the British 44-gun ship caused 29 individuals to be added to a class, which would otherwise have been extinct in a third of the time. The ships, like the old ones, were complained of as crank, and as carrying their guns too near the water. Some attempts were made to render a few of the latter-built ships more stiff and buoyant; but all would not do, and the greater number being deprived of their lower-deck guns and fitted with poops, were converted into store-ships. A few individuals remained to attend convoys; but, although a provoking durability, common to the class, continued them for years in the service, they lost the appellation of frigates, and took that of the "old two-decked 44-gun ship;" a name, the very mention of which raises a smile among modern men-of-war's-men.

In 1780 the 38-gun frigate appeared, for the first time, as a British-built class. Before 1782 five individuals were launched, averaging 946 tons. These were named, Arethusa, Latona, Minerva, Phaëton, and Thetis. The Minerva appears to have been the first afloat. She was built at Woolwich dockyard, and launched June 3, 1780. The ships had ports for mounting, and were ordered to carry twenty-eight 18-pounders on the maindeck. The first admiralty order for establishing them with guns is dated September 30, 1779. There the quarter-deck and forecastle armament stands at ten 6-pounders, eight 18-pound carronades, and 14 swivels, and the complement of men at 270. On the 25th of the succeeding April 9-pounders were ordered in lieu of the sixes, and the complement was increased to 280 men. Subsequently the two forecastle 9-pounders were exchanged for twelves (afterwards again altered to nines), and the swivels ordered to be omitted. For these, carronades were substituted, a new kind of sea-service ordnance, of which we shall presently give an account. In 1780, also, the old 36-gun frigate was revived, but in an highly improved state, the average size of the ships being 880 tons, and the calibers of the guns changed from 12 and 6, to 18 and (first 6, then) 9 pounders. This increase of the main-deck calibers, from 12 to 18 pounders, was a very great improvement, and appears to have been adopted about the same time by the French; from whom were captured, in 1782, two 40-gun frigates, the Aigle and Hébé. The first measured 1003 tons, and mounted twenty-six, the second, 1063 tons, and mounted twenty-eight 18-pounders on the main-deck, with each of them 8-pounders on the quarter-deck and forecastle. The Spaniards, also, appear to have built, in 1781, one 40-gun

18-pounder frigate, the Santa-Sabina. Of 12-pounder 34s, they had built several, of very large dimensions. The Santa-Margarita, for instance, captured in 1779, measured 993 tons, and long proved herself a capital ship; and the Santa-Leocadia, captured in 1781, measured 952 tons. Indeed, such even still continued to be the difference of ideas in England and foreign countries, as to the due proportion to be observed between the size of the ship and the armament she was destined to carry, that all the French 12-pounder 32s, built since 1761, were about equal in tonnage to the British 18-pounder 38s.

Having already disencumbered the frigate classes of the 44-gun ship, we must now step a little back to clear them of some minor classes, which, owing to their insignificant size and force, in comparison with the frigates we have just been describing, were not worthy of so high a rank. Between 1757 and 1760 four ships were built, and four captured, by the British, averaging about 312 tons, and mounting from 14 to 18 guns on a single deck. In an abstract of 1760, and in another of 1762, these eight ships were classed by themselves as " frigates." Immediately afterwards, however, they were stripped of that name, and placed among the sloops; giving rise to a since well-known subclass, the ship-rigged sloop.

In the year 1775 a new 24-gun class commenced, averaging about 520 tons, and carrying twenty-two 9-pounders on the maindeck, with four 3-pounders (in 1780 exchanged for sixes) on the quarter-deck. In or about the year 1735 a 20-gun frigate-class was built, measuring about 430 tons, and mounting 9, instead of 6 pounders. This was undoubtedly an improvement upon No. 9 in the abstract of 1727; but, notwithstanding two successive proposals of increased dimensions (one of 1741, to measure 498, and the other of 1745, to measure 508 tons), no subsequent improvement was made in the class. The great difference in size and force, between the 20 and the 28 gun frigate, occasioned the former, at what precise time is uncertain, to take the name of 20-gun *post* ship; signifying, that she was of the lowest class to which a post-captain could be appointed. Subsequently, the 24-gun frigate became also called a post-ship.

The French adopted a somewhat similar plan; when we are unable to say, but probably about the year 1760. They called all their frigates, from 24 guns downwards, corvettes, a word derived from *corvettare*, to leap or bound. Lescallier, when treating on the frigate, says, "A vingt canons, ou au dessous, ce ne sont plus des frégates : on les appele *corvettes*, et leur calibre est ordinairement du 8 ou en dessous." In another place he says, "*Corvette;* espèce de bâtiment fait pour la guerre, de même forme à peu-pres, et portant le même grément qu'une frégate, à la réserve qu'il est plus petit. Les corvettes ont depuis six jusqu'à vingt canons."[1] Subsequently, the French applied the name to ships of 24 guns. In later times the French have constructed very large flush corvettes, and they certainly possess many advantages. To mount all their guns in a single tier, their dimensions require to be increased; and this enables them to carry heavier metal than ships of the same nominal force, that mount a part of their guns on a quarter-deck and forecastle.

So that the term *post-ship* was applied to ships of 24, 22, and 20 guns, and *ship-sloop,* to ships of 18, 16, 14, and any less number of guns; while the French term *corvette* comprehended both divisions of classes. The French named their armed brigs simply *brigs* (*bricks,* or *brigantines,* and commonly *avisos*), surprised, no doubt, that the British should apply the term *sloop* to any vessel, no matter how rigged or constructed, provided she was commanded by a master and commander. For instance, a 74-gun ship, if reduced in her armament, and a master and commander appointed to her, registers as a sloop; that is, unless fitted for, and expressly classed as, a hospital, prison, or store ship. It should be observed that the French, notwithstanding they commonly call their own men-of-war brigs of the largest class, *bricks* or *avisos,* do not hesitate to apply the term *corvette,* (although, as it has just appeared, originally restricted to ship-rigged vessels, or vessels "portant le même grément qu'une frégate") to British brigs-of-war of the smallest class. To meet this, we shall designate all French brigs-of-war above an acknowledged gun-vessel so rigged, *brig-corvettes.*

The proper frigate, therefore, is a ship that mounts 24 guns, at the least, on a single deck, besides other guns on a quarter-deck and forecastle. So long as this arrangement of the guns is adhered to, the denomination will, we conceive, apply to a ship of any force; but, when once the waist becomes barricaded and filled with guns, the vessel is no longer a frigate, but a flush two-decked ship. It may here be observed, that the term *flush* cannot with propriety be applied to a frigate, because, according to the above definition, a frigate must have a quarter-deck and forecastle. The term can only be used in reference to such real single-decked vessels as are to be found among the post-ship and

[1] Vocabulaire des Termes de Marine.

ship-sloop classes; and this is the restriction to which we alluded at a former page.[1]

We may gather from what has been stated, that the expression, one, two, or three decked ship is as vague in respect to the real number of battery-decks as it undoubtedly is in respect to the number of guns mounted on those decks; and that, when the number of decks and of guns is ascertained, no accurate judgment can be formed of the ship's force until the nature of those guns be also communicated; but, and a remarkable fact it is, let the number and nature of the guns once be known, and, owing to the long-established practice of mounting no guns of a dissimilar caliber on the same deck, the number of decks instantly presents itself; as, from the necessity of placing the heavier guns nearest to the water, does the manner in which all the guns are distributed.

So long as that species of ordnance, called *gun* by the English, and *canon* by the French, continued in exclusive possession of the decks of a fighting-ship, no difference existed between the number of carriage-pieces she actually mounted and the number which stood as the sign of her class in the published lists. In process of time, however, the nominal, or rated, and the real force of a ship lost their synonymous signification; and that in a manner and to an extent too important in every point of view to be slightly passed over.

In the early part of 1779 a piece of carriage-ordnance, the invention, by all accounts, of the late scientific General Robert Melville, was cast, for the first time, at the iron-works of the Carron Company, situated on the banks of the river Carron, in Scotland. Although shorter than the navy 4-pounder, and lighter by a trifle than the navy 12-pounder, this gun equalled in its cylinder the 8-inch howitzer. Its destructive effects, when tried against timber, induced its ingenious inventor to give it the name of *smasher*.

As the smasher was calculated chiefly, if not wholly, for a ship-gun, the Carron Company made early application to have it employed in the British navy, but, owing to some not well explained cause, were unsuccessful. Upon the supposition that the size and weight of the smasher, particularly of its shot, would operate against its general employment as a sea-service gun, the proprietors of the foundry ordered the casting of several smaller pieces, corresponding in their calibers with the 24, 18, and 12

---

[1] See p. 21.

pounder guns in use; or rather, being of a trifle less bore, on account of the reduced windage very judiciously adopted in carronades, and which might be extended to long guns with considerable advantage. These new pieces became readily disposed of among the captains and others, employed in fitting out private armed ships to cruise against America, and were introduced, about the same time, on board a few of the frigates and smaller vessels belonging to the royal navy.

The new gun had now taken the name of *Carronade*, and its several varieties became distinguished, like those of the old gun, by the weight of their respective shot. This occasioned the smasher to be called, irrevocably, a 68-pounder: whereas, repeated experiments had shown, that a hollow, or cored shot, weighing 50, or even 40 lbs., would range further in the first graze, or that at which the shot first strikes the surface of the water, and the only range worth attending to in naval gunnery. The hollow shot would, also, owing to its diminished velocity in passing through a ship's side, and the consequent enlargement of the hole and increased splintering of the timbers, produce more destructive effects than the shot in its solid form; one of the principal objections against which was, and still continues to be, its being so cumbrous to handle.

Before half the expiration of the year in which the first carronade had been cast, a scale was drawn up by the Navy Board, and sanctioned by the Lords of the Admiralty, for arming the different rates in the service with the 18 and 12 pounder calibers. In consequence of the first, second, and third rate ships having their quarter-decks as fully supplied with guns as there was room for ports on each side, no additional pieces could be placed there; but it was found that the forecastle would generally admit the opening of a pair of extra ports, and that the poop, which for nearly a century past had served chiefly as a roof to the captain's cabin, would, if timbered up on each side, afford space for three pairs of ports; making, in the whole, eight additional ports for the reception of carronades. The 50-gun ship was found to have room for a pair of additional ports on her quarter-deck, besides a pair on her forecastle, and three pairs on her poop, when the latter was barricaded; making altogether 10 ports. The 44-gun ship had no poop, and no armament on the quarter-deck :[1] by furnishing the latter with a barricade, and cutting through it four pairs of ports, besides an extra pair on the

[1] This refers to the latest establishment, or that of 1762, wherein two of the quarter-deck sixes are shifted to the forecastle, and the remaining two removed entirely to admit two additional 9-pounders on the main-deck.

forecastle, this ship might mount the same additional number of pieces as the 50. The three remaining classes of the fifth, and the first two classes of the sixth rate, would also admit of additional ports being cut through the sides of their forecastles and quarter-decks. The third class of the sixth-rate, and the quarter-decked ship-sloop class, being, in respect to their quarter-decks and forecastles, in a similar state to the 44, would require to be similarly built up, before they could mount the eight carronades assigned to them.[1]

Several captains complained of the carronade; some of its upsetting after being heated by successive discharges; others, that, owing to its shortness, its fire scarcely passed clear of the ship's side, and that its range was too confined to be useful. The captains of some of the 32-gun frigates, in particular, represented that one pair of their quarter-deck carronades was so much in the way of the rigging, as to endanger the laniards of the shrouds, and begged to have their established number reduced from six to four. As the principal objection to carronades appeared to have arisen from defects in the manner of mounting them, some additional instructions on that head were prepared and forwarded by Mr. Gascoigne, the chief proprietor of the Carron foundry. Some alterations were also made in the piece itself.[2] Still the Board of Ordnance, in repeated conferences with the Navy Board, maintained the superiority of the old gun, resting their arguments chiefly on the comparative length of

[1] The following is a copy of the document in question, with an additional column, showing to what amount the total of the carriage-guns of the different classes became augmented

Scale for Arming the different Rates in the British Navy with Carronades, as drawn up by Order of the Board of Admiralty, July 13, 1779.

Rate.	Class.	Quarter-deck. No.	Quarter-deck. Pdrs.	Forecastle. No.	Forecastle. Pdrs.	Poop. No.	Poop. Pdrs.	Total Number of Carriage-guns.
First . . .	100-gun-ship	--	--	2	12	8	12	110
Second . .	90 or 98 ,,	--	--	4	,,	6	,,	100 or 108
Third . . {	74 ,,	--	--	2	,,	,,	,,	82
	64 ,,	--	--	,,	,,	,,	,,	72
Fourth . . {	50 ,,	2	24	,,	24	,,	,,	60
	44 ,,	8	18	,,	18	--	--	54
Fifth . . {	38 ,,	6	,,	4	,,	--	--	48
	36 ,,	4	,,	,,	,,	--	--	44
	32 ,,	6	,,	2	,,	--	--	40
Sixth . . {	28 ,,	4	,,	,,	,,	--	--	34
	24 ,,	6	12	4	12	--	--	34
	20 ,,	,,	,,	2	,,	--	--	28
Sloops . . {	18, 16, and 14 ship-rigged.	,,	,,	,,	,,	--	--	{ 26, 24, and 22.

[2] One appears to have been the adding of two calibers to its length.

its range; while the Navy Board urged, that a vessel, able to carry 4-pounders of the common construction might, with equal ease, bear 18-pounders of the new; that the latter gun was worked with fewer men; that its shot was far more formidable and destructive; and that its range was quite sufficient for the purpose required. The commissioners adduced, as one instance, the case of the Flora frigate, whose boatswain, assisted only by a boy, made a surprising number of discharges from a forecastle 18-pounder, and caused great havoc and destruction on board the French frigate Nymphe, ultimately their prize.

Let us be permitted to remark that, with one single unimportant exception, the action between the British 36-gun frigate Flora and the French 32-gun frigate Nymphe is the first in which the mounted force of the combatants, as compared together in all the British accounts, was misstated; and that simply because it is, with the exception above alluded to, the first action in which a British ship-of-war mounting carronades was engaged. It was a long contest, and a sanguinary one, on the part of the Nymphe at least. Out of her complement of 291, the latter lost 136; the Flora, whose number of men on board was 259, but 36, in killed and wounded.

Captain William Peere Williams, having, in his official letter, stated that the Nymphe "mounted 32 guns, but was pierced for 40," says, in a postscript, "The Flora mounted 36 guns," and, he might have added, "was pierced for 44." According to the establishment of 1779, the Flora was entitled to mount four 18-pounder carronades on her quarter-deck and four on her forecastle, making her total of carriage-guns 44. That she did mount, and successfully use, one of a pair, at least, of carronades on her forecastle, appears by the Navy Board's report; and that she also mounted four carronades on her quarter-deck, we shall establish by a document which we shall presently lay before the reader. Hence the Flora mounted, not "36 guns," but 42, at the least. The French accounts say 44; thus: "La 10 Août, la frégate Française la Nymphe, de 32 canons, fut prise, après un combat opiniâtre, par la frégate la Flore, de 44 canons."[1] The following may be stated as the real mounted force of the two ships:—

	FLORA.		NYMPHE.	
	No.	Pdrs.	No.	Pdrs. Fr.
Main-deck	26 long	18	26 long	12
Quarter-deck and forecastle	10 "	9	6 "	6
	6 carr.	18		
Carriage-guns	42		32	

[1] Abrégé Chron. de l'Hist. de la Marine Française, 1804, p. 190.

Although pierced for, and mounting, the most guns, the Flora was the shorter vessel by six feet.

According to an official list, dated on the 9th of January, 1781,[1] there were then 429 ships in the navy mounting carronades; among which the 32-pounder carronade appears, and was the first of that caliber which had been used. The total of the carronades employed were 604; namely, eight 32-pounders, four 24-pounders, three hundred and six 18-pounders, and two hundred and eighty-six 12-pounders. In December of this year a recommendation to use 68-pounder carronades on the forecastle of large ships, and 42 and 32 pounders on the same deck of some of the smaller rates, induced the Navy Board to order the old Rainbow 44 to be fitted, by way of experiment, wholly with carronades of the largest description. Sir John Dalrymple proposed the casting of some that should carry a ball of 100 or 130 lbs. weight; but the Board resolved to confine themselves to the heaviest of the pieces already cast, the 68-pounder.

The necessary carronades were ordered from the foundry, and some of the foremen belonging to the works attended, to see them properly fitted: it was not, however, until February or March, 1782, that the Rainbow could be completed in her equipment. What additional force she acquired by this change in her armament, the following table will show: —

RAINBOW'S

	Old Armament.		New Armament.	
	Long Guns.	Broadside weight of Metal.	Carronades.	Broadside weight of Metal.
First deck	20 18-pdrs.		20 68-pdrs.	
Second deck	22 12	318 lbs.	22 42	1238 lbs.
Quarter-deck	— —		4 32	
Forecastle	2 6		2 32	
	44		48	

In the beginning of April the Rainbow, thus armed, and commanded by Captain (now Admiral Sir) Henry Trollope, who, with Captain Keith Elphinstone (the late Admiral Lord Keith), and the late Rear-admiral Macbride, were among the earliest patrons of the carronade, sailed on a cruise. All the well-known skill and enterprise of her captain failed, however, to bring him within gun-shot of a foe worth contending with, until the 4th of the succeeding September; when, being off Isle de Bas, he came suddenly upon a large French frigate. Owing to the latter's peculiar bearing, one of the Rainbow's forecastle 32-

---

[1] See Appendix, No. 3.

pounders was first discharged at her. Several of the shot fell on board, and discovered their size. The French captain, rationally concluding that, if such large shot came from the forecastle of the enemy's ship, much larger ones would follow from her lower batteries, fired his broadside "pour l'honneur de pavillon," and surrendered to the Rainbow. Although the capture of the Hébé had afforded no opportunity of trying the experiment contemplated by the Navy Board, and so ardently looked forward to by the officers and crew of the Rainbow, yet did the prize, in the end, prove a most valuable acquisition to the service, there being very few British frigates, even of the present day, which, in size and exterior form, are not copied from the Hébé. She measured 1063 tons, and mounted 40 guns, twenty-eight 18, and twelve 8 pounders.

In the course of 1782 a few of the larger sorts of the carronade were mounted on board some of the receiving-ships, in order that the seamen of such vessels as were in port refitting might be exercised at handling and firing this, to them, novel piece of ordnance. As one proof of many, that carronades were gaining ground in the navy, the captains of the few 38 and 36 gun frigates in commission applied for and obtained 24-pounder carronades, in lieu of the 18s with which their ships had been established. The termination of the war in January, 1783, put a stop to any further experiments with the carronade; but its merits were now too generally acknowledged to admit a doubt of its becoming a permanent favourite: in the British navy at least, where a short range is ever the chosen distance. The removal of the swivel-stocks invariably accompanied the cutting through of carronade portholes in the barricades of the quarter-deck and forecastle: and no one, aware of the difference in effect between a half and a 12-pound ball, could deny that the substitution of the latter was a surprising improvement in the art of attack and defence.

The most extraordinary circumstance connected with the employment of carronades in the British navy, is that, with all their alleged advantages, they should never have been thought worthy to be ranked among the guns of the ship that carried them. Whether they equalled in caliber the heaviest of those guns, added to their number a full third, or to their power a full half (in the 14-gun sloop class, the additional eight carronades made the numbers as 22 to 14, and the broadside weight of metal, in pounds, as 96 to 42), still they remained as mere a blank in the ship's nominal, or rated force, as the muskets in the arm-chest. On the other hand, the addition of a single pair of guns of the old construction, to a ship's armament, removed her at once to a higher class, and gave her, how novel or inconvenient soever, a new denomination. When, for instance, in 1740, the Admiralty ordered that the old 40-gun frigate should mount four 6-pounders on her quarter-deck, she became thenceforth a 44:[1] when also, in 1778, eight additional 6-pounders were placed upon the quarter-decks of the larger 90-gun ships, they were separated from their former companions, and promoted to a class by themselves, the 98.[2] When, in 1780, the Canada 74 received two additional 18-pounder long guns for her second deck, she became registered as a 76, and until the capture of the Hoche (afterwards named the Donegal), in 1798, was the only individual so registered: but when, in August 1794, the Canada received two 68-pounder carronades for her forecastle, she still remained as a 76. In 1780 the 50-gun ship Leander received on board two 6-pounder long guns, in exchange for two 24-pounder carronades:[3] what the latter, with their quadruple claim, had not interest to procure, was granted to the former unasked; and the Leander, for upwards of 30 years, continued to be the only 52-gun ship in the navy. In 1781 the 74-gun ship Goliath received on board two 68-pounder carronades; but, as they were not two 9-pounder "guns," she was not sent to keep company with the Canada. A dozen other instances might be adduced; but these will suffice.

So long as the word *gun* retains its signification, of a military engine which "forcibly discharges a ball, or other hard substance, by means of inflamed gunpowder," so long must a carronade be considered as a gun. Yet the distinction has usually been "guns and carronades;" in which sense, certainly, no ship in the British navy appears to have mounted more *guns* than were assigned to her by her rate. But why, when, at a subsequent day, the eight or ten "guns" upon the quarter-decks of ships became exchanged for carronades, was not the number of guns, as marked down in the list to denote the ship's class, reduced accordingly? What became of the gun classification, when some of the most numerous classes in the navy mounted all carronades, except for bow-chasers?

Among the excuses which may perhaps be offered for these seeming inconsistencies, are, that the classification of the ships was intended only as a guide for those who had the civil affairs

[1] See p. 30.
[2] Derrick, p. 178.
[3] See the Leander's name in the list, Appendix, No. 3.

of the navy to manage; that the employment of carronades, although ordered generally, was, as respected the actual use of them, too partial and fluctuating, during several years at least, to warrant the subversion of the old, or become the basis of a new system; that the addition of carronades to a ship's armament did not add one man to her complement, nor affect, in the slightest degree, the length and diameter of her masts and yards, or the proportion of boatswain's and carpenter's stores served out to her: in short, that the old classification, as far as the Navy Board was concerned, fully answered the purpose required. If the carronade innovation produced confusion anywhere, it must have been in the ordnance department, where the proportion of gunner's stores served out to a ship depends on the number and nature of her guns; and where, in truth, all the difficulties attendant upon the fitting of carronades, at their first employment, were sensibly felt.

With respect to the employment of carronades on board the armed ships of foreign powers, it may be sufficient to state, that, as far as the prize-lists are to be relied upon, no captured ship mounted any during the war which ended in 1783. Admitting, however, that carronades had begun to be used in any one foreign navy, and that they had also begun to disorganize, or render obscure, the national classification of that navy, still the English would have no reason to complain; inasmuch as, whatever might be the registered force of any contending ship of the enemy's, her actual mounted force is that alone which would appear upon the English records. Not so with the enemy; for he would at once discover that, how accurately soever his own guns stood enumerated, those of the ship he had fought with had been in part overlooked. He could, to be sure, and doubtless would, inform his countrymen what was the real number of guns opposed to him.[1] But, even then, one nation is left in the dark as to the true merits of the contest; while the other, attributing the discrepancy in the accounts to design rather than to accident, finds its animosity heightened to a pitch of rancour, as afflicting to humanity as it is repugnant to honourable warfare. So limited, however, had been the use, and, except in the Rainbow's case, so light the calibers of the carronade during the short period that intervened between its first employment in the British navy and the termination of hostilities with France, in 1783, that few if any of the published accounts require, on that account, to be recanvassed or disturbed. How the case

[1] See p. 39.

became altered in the succeeding war will be discovered, as the events of that war pass in order of detail.

There is another point in the armament of ships, requiring at present to be briefly noticed. Few persons but must know, that the destruction caused by discharges of cannon is, in a great degree, proportionate to the diameter and weight of the shot. Were it not for this, no ship's deck would be encumbered with guns, weighing each 56 hundredweight, when a tier that weighed one hundredweight each would answer as well. "Il est certain," says M. Duhamel, "que ce sont toujours les gros canons qui sont les plus avantageux dans un combat, et ainsi il est préférable de mettre sur un vaisseau un petit numbre de gros canons qu'un plus grand nombre de petits."[1] Nor would the expense of fitting the Rainbow with 68-pounders have been incurred when the same end could have been attained by arming her with 12-pounders. Carronades of the latter caliber were already in the arsenal at Woolwich, with their slides and carriages, ready to be placed on board: while those of the former caliber had to be cast at the foundry in Scotland; thence transmitted to Woolwich to be proved; thence to the port at which the ship was fitting; and, when there, were to be (an arduous task it was) properly and securely mounted. A 3 and a 32 pounder are equally guns; but he that would match them, because they *are* guns, might with the same propriety pit a man of three[2] against a man of six feet in height, simply because they are men. From this difficulty, attendant more or less upon all sea-fights, land-fights are wholly exempt. Every foot-soldier, in either army, enters the field with a musket on his shoulder; every cavalry-man wields either a pike or a broadsword, and is mounted on an animal of the same species and comparative strength, and every piece of artillery employed is within a trifle of the same caliber. Fix the number of each army, and mark the nature of the ground; and what more is generally required for coming to a conclusion on the relative strength of the combatants?

On the other hand, compare the account of the opposed forces in the case of the Rainbow and Hébé, as extracted from the work of an English naval chronologist, with the true state of the case, as exhibited in a preceding page. "On the 4th of September," says Schomberg, "Captain Trollope, in the Rain-

---

[1] Elemens de l'Architecture Navale; par M Duhamel du Monceau, p. 17.

[2] The only *man* three feet high was John Hauptman, who was exhibited in London in 1815.—*Ed.*

bow, of 44 guns, fell in with, and captured off the isle of Bas, la Hébé French frigate, of 40 guns, and 360 men, commanded by M. de Vigney, who was slightly wounded; her second captain and four men were killed, and several wounded. The Rainbow had one man killed."[1] Not another word is there on the subject. Who, then, with this account before him, but must censure Monsieur de Vigney for having submitted so tamely, as well as praise Captain Trollope for having conquered an enemy's ship so nearly his equal? Exhibit the nature, as well as number of the guns on each side, and an end is put to the delusion.

The several denominations, by which English guns in either service are identified with their respective calibers, are not applicable to foreign guns, every nation possessing, besides a scale of calibers, or natures, a standard of weights and measures, peculiar to itself. Until, therefore, the calibers, or pounders, of the several sea-service guns, in use by the different powers at war, can be reduced into English weight, it will be in vain to attempt any comparison between them. For instance, the gun with which the French arm the lower decks of their line-of-battle ships, above a 64 (a class that, with them, has long since been extinct), they denominate a 36-pounder; for the plain reason, that the shot suitable to its cylinder, and which shot measures in diameter 6·239 French inches and decimal parts, is assumed to weigh 36 French pounds. But the same shot measures 6·648 English inches and decimal parts, and weighs very little less than 39 English pounds. The following table, which has been drawn up with great care, is submitted as the only statement of the kind in print:—

Danish.		Dutch.		French.		Spanish.		Swedish.		Russian.	
Pdr.	English weight.	Pdr.	English weight.	Pdr.	[2]English weight.	Pdr.	English weight.	Pdr.	English weight.	Pdr.	English weight.
	lbs. oz.		lbs. oz.		lbs. oz.		lbs. oz.		lbs. oz.		lbs. oz.
--	--	--	--	--	--	--	--	48	44 15½	--	--
--	--	--	--	--	--	--	--	42	39 5½	42	37 14¼
36	39 11½	--	--	36	38 14	36	36 8	36	33 11½	36	32 7½
--	--	32	34 12¾	--	--	--	--	30	28 1¾	30	27 9½
24	26 7¾	24	26 2¼	24	25 14½	24	24 5½	24	22 7¾	24	21 10½
18	19 13½	18	19 9½	18	19 7	18	18 4	18	16 13¾	18	16 3¾
12	13 3½	12	13 1	12	12 15¼	12	12 2¾	12	11 3¾	12	10 13¼
8	8 13¼	8	8 10½	8	8 10	8[3]	8 1½	8	7 7¾	8	7 3¼
6	6 9¾	6	6 8½	6	6 7½	6	6 1¼	6	5 9½	6	5 6½

[1] Schomberg's Nav. Chron., vol. ii., p. 75.

[2] This, as well as the rest, is founded on a calculation; but practical experience has shown that French shots usually weigh an ounce or two more than is here assigned to them. It appears, indeed that the

Nothing can demonstrate the utility of such a table more clearly than the material difference observable between some of the calibers: the Danish 36-pound shot, for instance, weighs nearly two pounds more than the Russian 42; yet, nominally, the latter is the heavier by one-seventh. As it is for the gross, or broadside, and not for the individual calibers, that our calculations are chiefly wanted, that integral proportion, which comes nearest to the difference expressed in the table, will answer the purpose. Thus:

Add to the	{	Danish nominal weight,	5-48ths	}
		Dutch	"	1-11th	
		French[1]	"	1-12th	and it will produce the
		Spanish	"	1-72nd	English weight.[3]
Deduct from the	{	Swedish	"	1-16th	
		Russian	"	1-11th	

There is frequently between two ships a disparity of size, as denoted by the tonnage, not easily reconcilable with the number of guns mounted by each. Numerous instances might be adduced, but a few will suffice. The Rainbow measured 831 tons, and mounted 48 guns; while the Hébé measured 1063 tons, and mounted but 40 guns. Again, the old Blenheim measured 1827 tons, and mounted 98 guns; while the Triumph, built three years afterwards, measured 1825 tons, and mounted only 74 guns. In both pairs of cases, the disagreement of the force with the tonnage arises from the latter not being affected by the upper, or top-side construction of the ship. Had the Rainbow been built, as to her battery-decks, in the same manner as the Hébé, she would have mounted but 28 guns; and the Blenheim, at a subsequent day, had actually one of her decks

---

French 36-pound shot weigh nearly 37 pounds French. See "Voyages dans la Grand-Bretagne," par Charles Dupin, Force Navale, tome ii., p. 119. Admitting that the shots of the lesser French calibers are also exceeded in their real weights in the same proportion, the usual English weight assigned to the French shots, namely 40℔ for the 36, 28℔ for the 24, 20℔ for the 18, 14℔ for the 12, and 9℔ for the 8-pounder, are perhaps more correct than the weights specified in the above table. According to M. Dupin (Force Navale, tome ii., p. 97) the following are the weights of English shot in French pounds and decimals·

POUNDER.

42	32	24	18	12	9
38·92	29·682	22·24	16·68	11 12	8·34

Another French writer says, "le boulet de 6 Anglaise pèse un peu plus de cinq livres et demie, poids de marc."

[3] That highly useful little work, "The Bombardier, and Pocket Gunner," gives the Spaniards, instead of this gun, a 9-pounder, but in their own nomenclature it is invariably, as far as our discoveries have reached, an 8-pounder.

[1] According to the numbers in the table, it wants a 256th part of being so; but this difference may surely be passed over, if not for its insignificance, as some allowance for the more important difference mentioned in note [2] of the last page.

[2] All fractional parts may be given up thus: $1268 \div 12 = 105$ and a fraction, but 105 (without the fraction) $+ 1268 = 1373$.

removed, and then, without suffering the slightest decrease in her tonnage, mounted the same number of guns as the Triumph. A difference in size, however, is frequently observable between ships, that agree both in the number of their guns and in the manner of carrying them.

When it is considered that, proportionable to the size of the gun and its carriage, must be the port to which it is fitted, the space between that and the next port, and, as a necessary consequence, the whole range and extent of the deck, an increase in the principal dimensions and tonnage of the ship follows of course. Hence, one class of ship mounts twenty-six 12-pounders upon a deck 126 feet in length; another class mounts twenty-six 18-pounders upon a deck 145 feet in length; a third mounts twenty-six 24-pounders upon a deck 160 feet in length; and the tonnage of the several classes, estimated, upon an average, at 680, 1000, and 1370 tons, accords, very nearly, with the difference in the nature of the guns mounted by each.

When, therefore, two fighting-ships, numerically equal in guns and decks, but differing greatly in tonnage, meet at sea, the inference is, that the larger ship mounts the heavier metal. Moreover, as the more massive the gun and its carriage, the greater is the strength required to work it; so does the enlargement of the masts, yards, sails, rigging, anchors, and cables, require additional hands to manage and control them: hence, the larger ship is more numerously manned, and, on coming to close quarters, can present the most formidable show of boarders. Several other advantages attend the larger ship; among which may be reckoned her less liability, owing to her increased stoutness, to suffer from an enemy's guns, and the greater precision with which, owing to her increased stability, she can point her own.

The French and Spanish builders have certainly proceeded upon a more enlarged scale of dimensions than the builders of England; and the ports of their ships are, therefore, both wider and farther apart than the ports of those English ships which mount the same, or nearly the same, nature of guns. This, besides conferring many of the advantages already noticed, affords a greater space between and behind the guns, and so raises their line of fire, that they can act without risk from a troubled sea; an advantage, the want of which has often been felt by the old English two and three deckers.

A comparison of that class in the two rival navies, out of which, from the number of its individuals, the line of battle is chiefly composed, will show the different ideas that prevailed in

England and in France respecting the proportion that ought to exist between the armament and the size of a ship. The following is the result of a careful examination, and refers, in point of time, to the latter end of the year 1792, or just as the war with England was about to commence.

British 74.		French 74.	
Tons.	Proportion of Individuals to the Class.	Tons.	Proportion of Individuals to the Class.
From 1565 to 1665	8-10ths	From 1680 to 1720	1-10th
„ 1666 to 1720	1½-10th	„ 1720 to 1810	3-10ths
„ 1799 to 1836	½-10th	„ 1860 to 1900	6-10ths

Moreover, the smallest British 74 carried 32-pounders on the lower deck, while the smallest French 74, although upwards of 100 tons larger, carried only 24s. It is true that a French 24-pounder weighs a few pounds more than an English gun of the same nominal caliber; but that overplus is amply compensated by the difference in size between the two ships.

The gradual swell of the current of architectural improvement has, however, given increased size and buoyancy to the English modern-built ships of every class; many of which equal in dimensions and form, and surpass in strength and finish, the ships of any other power on the globe.[1] Still, those national navies, which, owing to frequent discomfitures, have been the oftenest renewed, are, in this respect, the most uniform; while that single navy, which has remained for ages unimpaired by defeats, and which has usually added to itself what the others have lost, exhibits in many of its classes the utmost variety of size. Its reduced scale of complements, ever its well-known characteristic, is owing, partly to the contracted size of its ships, and partly to a principle of pure native growth, a reliance upon the physical, rather than upon the numerical, strength of its seamen.

---

[1] It is but justice in regard to America, to mention that England has benefited by her example, and that the large classes of frigates now employed in the British service are modelled after those of the United States.—*Editor.*

FIRST FRENCH REVOLUTIONARY WAR.

On the 20th of April, 1792, that party in France, the self-constituted National Convention, in whose hands were the person of the king and the reins of the government, declared war against the Emperor of Austria, as King of Hungary and Bohemia. This was the first war (although from the situation of Austria not a naval one) in which France had been engaged since the peace of Amiens. Maritime hostility, however, if such it can be called, soon broke out, the National Convention, on the 16th of September, declaring war against the King of Sardinia. Ten days afterwards a French army entered the territory of Savoy, and a French squadron of nine sail of the line, commanded by Rear-Admiral Laurent-Jean-François Truguet (a young officer just promoted to that rank by the republican minister of marine, Bertrand), and having on board a strong body of troops, took possession of Nice, Montalban, Villa-Franca, and finally, after a destructive cannonade, and an assault by storm, with all its horrid military consequences, of the port of Oneglia.

On the 1st of October, according to an official return, the navy of France amounted to 246 vessels; of which 86, including 27 in commission, and 13 building and nearly ready, were of the line. The squadrons were designated according to the ports in which they had been built, or were laid up in ordinary; and, of the above 86 line-of-battle ships, 39 were at Brest, 10 at Lorient (afterwards united in designation with those at Brest), 13, including the only 64 in the French navy, at Rochefort, and 24, including a strong reinforcement recently arrived from the Biscayan ports, at Toulon. Of frigates at the different ports, there were 78, 18 of them mounting 18-pounders on the main deck, and none of them less than 12-pounders. Those, resembling in size and force the British 28-gun frigates, classed as 24-gun corvettes.[1]

On the 21st of of January, 1793, the French beheaded their king, Louis XVI.; and on the 24th the French ambassador, M. Chauvelin, as being now the representative of a regicide government, was ordered to quit England. A few weeks previous to this, a strong spirit of hostility on the part of the new republic had manifested itself against that country. On the 2nd of January the British 16-gun brig-sloop Childers, Captain Robert Barlow, was standing in towards Brest harbour, when one of the two batteries that guard the entrance, or goulet, and from which she was distant not more than three-quarters of a mile, fired a shot that passed over her. Captain Barlow, imagining that the national character of his vessel was doubted, hoisted the British ensign and pendant; whereupon the fort that had fired ran up the French ensign, with a red pendant over it, and the signal was answered by the forts at the opposite side of the entrance. By this time the flood tide, for the want of wind to counteract its force, had driven the Childers still nearer to the two batteries; both of which now opened a cross fire upon her. Fortunately a breeze soon sprang up, and Captain Barlow was enabled to make sail. Being a small object, the Childers was hit by only one shot, a French 48-pounder: it struck one of her guns, and then split into three pieces, but, providentially, did not injure a man.

The pertinacious refusal of the King of England, and of the stadtholder, to partake of the revolutionary benefits which had been so liberally tendered them, provoked the National Convention, on the 1st of February, to declare war against Great Britain and the United Netherlands. The announcement of this important event reached London on the 4th, and occasioned the immediate issue of orders to detain all French vessels in British ports. The French possessed here a decided advantage. When they embargoed their ports, which they did, of course, on declaring war, upwards of 70 British vessels were lying there; but now that a similar measure was adopted in the ports of England, not more than seven or eight French vessels could be found in them. On the 11th the King of England sent down to parliament a message on the subject of the declaration by France; and on the same day directed, that general reprisals should be made on the vessels, goods, and subjects of the

[1] See Appendix, No. 4.

French republic. Notwithstanding this, a French work, of some celebrity, accuses the English of having commenced the war. "Quand le gouvernement britannique nous déclara la guerre en 1793, son ambition, &c."[1]

The King of Spain having evinced, for the present at least, a similar disinclination to fraternize with democrats, was also doomed to feel the weight of republican wrath. War against Spain was formally declared on the 7th of March; but letters of marque against that nation had, it appears, issued since the 26th of the preceding month; and even previously to that, Spanish vessels had been both captured at sea and embargoed in port. The manifesto and counter-declaration of the Catholic king issued on the 23rd of March; and shortly afterwards Spain's neighbour, Portugal, declared herself a willing ally in the cause. The subsequent irruptions of the republican forces into the territories of the King of the Two Sicilies made him also a party in the war. With Austria, Prussia, and Sardinia, war had existed, as already in part stated, for some time previous to the declaration against England and the United Netherlands.

We are now arrived at an epoch that calls for a more particular account of the state of the British navy than we have hitherto deemed it necessary to give. It was this that suggested the formation of a series of annual abstracts, the first of the kind that have ever appeared in print; and which, being the result of a careful investigation of official and other records, are submitted, with some degree of confidence, to the public attention. The first abstract of the series shows not only the number of individuals, but the aggregate tonnage and established force in guns and men, of every class of ship belonging to the British navy at the commencement of the year 1793.[2] It also contains many other particulars, that will be found useful in drawing comparisons, as well between the British navy and the navy of any foreign power, as between the former itself at different periods. Were the "tons" not introduced, that acknowledged sign of improvement, the increasing size of the ships of any particular class would not discover itself; and we should be likely to form a very erroneous estimate of the comparative strength of the British navy at any two periods at which its numbers were summed up. The tonnages, it may be observed, are precisely those inserted in the official register; and, being

---

[1] Dict. Hist. des Batailles, par une Société de Militaires et de Marins; à Paris, 1818, tome ii., p. 56.

[2] See Appendix, Annual Abstract, No. 1.

all the product of one mode of casting, afford a tolerably fair criterion of the relative size of the ships.

The propriety of placing "cruisers" in a separate, and that the most conspicuous, compartment of the table will be evident, when it is considered, that they constitute the sole aggressing force of a navy. Of the "stationary harbour ships," some are usefully employed; but the generality have no existence as fighting-ships, and ought, strictly speaking, to have their names expunged from the published lists of the navy. So far, however, from sanctioning any curtailment, the monthly lists insert the name of every unseaworthy ship, as well as of every transport, yacht, and sheer-hulk. It does certainly seem very absurd, to consider a vessel, constructed solely for pleasurable purposes, as a ship of war; yet Steel ranks the large yachts with 20-gun post-ships, and that simply because the command of them devolves upon post-captains. In the official register their station, when in ordinary, is nearly at the bottom of the list; but, when in commission, they are removed to the rate, according to which the captain and officers receive their pay. The yachts, large and small, rank in the Abstracts with the hulks, hoys, and other excluded vessels. Every ship building, although her keel may not have been laid, or a single timber of her frame cut out, is also included in the published lists. One instance may suffice. In January, 1796, a 120-gun ship, to be named the Caledonia (in lieu of a ship of 100 guns, ordered in November, 1794,) was directed to be built, and appeared in Steel a few months afterwards; but the ship was not laid down until January, 1805, nor launched until June, 1808. After all this, as it may well be called, paper-force has been added, the total at the foot of such periodical list is taken to denote, in an unrestricted sense, the numerical strength of the British navy.

On the other hand, as no foreign power publishes any regular list of her navy, the British have generally to glean their information from multifarious sources; such as, among others, the hasty and imperfect views of reconnoitring officers, the obscure and often contradictory statements of prisoners, and the loose paragraphs, and, not unfrequently, studied misrepresentations, of the enemy's journals. And, after all, the sum-total of these driblets can have but a partial reference; not covering, as it should do, the swarm of brigs, schooners, and armed small-craft, whose depredations on British commerce are, nevertheless, too important to be slighted. Hence, the numbers usually brought forward, as objects of comparison between the British and

French navies, are wholly inadequate to the purpose, the one being greatly excessive, the other, to about an equal extent, deficient.

An expected rupture with Spain, respecting Nootka-Sound, in 1790, and with Russia, respecting Turkey, in the following year, had occasioned so unexampled an activity in the English dockyards, that, by the end of 1792, upwards of 60 of the 87 line-of-battle cruisers in the Abstract were in good condition. The excellent plan, which, at the recommendation of Sir Charles Middleton (afterwards Lord Barham), then comptroller of the navy, had been adopted since 1783, of setting apart for every sea-going ship a large proportion of the material articles of her furniture and stores, as well as of stocking the magazines at the several dockyards with every description of unperishable stores, displayed itself in the extraordinary despatch with which the ships at the different ports were equipped for sea-service: so that in a very few weeks after the order for arming had issued, the commissioned cruisers of the line became augmented from 26 to 54, and the total of the commissioned cruisers from 136 to upwards of 200.

The number of commissioned officers and masters belonging to the British navy at the commencement of the year was,

Admirals	17
Vice-admirals	19
Rear-admirals	19
,, superannuated	15
Post-captains	446
,, superannuated	20
Commanders, or sloop-captains	103
Lieutenants	1417
,, superannuated	29
Masters	297

and the number of seamen and marines, including officers of all ranks, voted by parliament for the service of the current year, was 45,000.[1]

To the uninitiated public, a nomenclature, in which "commander," *i. e.* he that commands, stands as a subordinate rank to "captain," must appear, to say the least of it, very extraordinary. The former rank was originally styled "master and commander;" probably to distinguish the merchant-master, hired to command a small ship of war, from the captain regularly brought up in the navy. In process of time, having a reference

[1] See Appendix, No. 5.

more to the sound than the sense of the term, the first two words were lopped off, and "commander" became both a generic term, signifying whoever possessed the command of a ship of war (hence, we frequently see, "Ships and their commanders," endorsed upon books and official records), and a specific term, denoting that rank next in subordination to a post-captain, or rather captain, as the rank is now more commonly called. The Americans use a term not quite so ambiguous as master and commander: they call their captains of the second order "masters-commandant," which means "masters-commanding;" and that, in many instances, is really the case, most of their present captains and commodores having originally been masters in the merchant-service. There is, however, a real distinction in naval language between a "captain" and a "commander;" inasmuch as the latter, besides receiving less pay, may remain a commander for a century if his life should last so long, while the former ascends progressively to the head of the list, as his seniors drop off, or are promoted to flag-officers. To show that there is a distinction between the two orders of captains, we have, as is seen above, added to "commanders" or "sloop-captains;" afraid to venture at lopping off the first term because so long used, and, among the profession at least, so well known, but sanctioned, in a great degree, in subjoining the latter term as an explicative, by the notorious fact, that every "commander" is officially styled (see the Admiralty lists), and officially as well as otherwise addressed, "captain."[1]

A slight sketch of the naval strength of England's maritime allies in the war may here with propriety be introduced. Holland, according to her published accounts, possessed a navy amounting to 119 vessels, from a 74-gun ship to a six-gun cutter. But this was on paper: when analyzed, the Dutch navy dwindles into comparative insignificance. For instance, of the 49 "ships of the line," the largest, owing to the local impediments formerly noticed,[2] was not superior to a second-class British third-rate; and of those there were but 10 in all. The remainder of the Dutch line was composed of 64 and 54 gun-ships; the latter a class expelled from the line of battle by all other navies, but retained by the Dutch as a handy description of two-decker for their shallow waters. Some of the Dutch frigates were fine vessels, but very few of them carried heavier metal than long

---

[1] This was an error which has been rectified. Although by courtesy commanders are called *captains*, yet they are never officially so addressed. The alteration took place when his late Majesty William the Fourth was Lord High Admiral.

[2] See p. 28.

12-pounders ; and the designation of frigate descended to ships of 500 tons, mounting twenty-four 8-pounders, including four in the 'tween decks amidships. We shall, however, for consistency sake, when having occasion to mention these vessels, call them corvettes. Upon the whole, the navy of Holland, especially as by far the greater proportion of the ships lay rotten, and rotting, in dock or at their moorings in the different harbours, was little more than a nominal advantage to England in the war she was about to commence.

Spain, according to a list given in Schomberg's fourth volume, possessed a navy which, in numerical amount, vied with that of France. Out of a total of 204 vessels, 76 were of the line, mounting from 112[1] to 60 guns; of which latter class, and of 64s, there were but 11. Of the 76 ships of the line, 56 appear to have been in commission, and, of the under-line vessels, 105; comprehending four-fifths of the whole Spanish navy. This was an extraordinarily large proportion, and out of which Spain might well stipulate to join the confederacy with 60 sail of vessels, great and small: a reinforcement, however, as the sequel will show, that proved of very little use. Portugal undertook to furnish six sail of the line and four frigates; which constituted nearly the whole amount of her navy. Her line-of-battle ships consisted chiefly of 74s, were fine vessels, and partly officered by Englishmen. The navy of Naples is represented to have been composed, including 74 gun-boats, of 102 vessels, mounting 618 guns, and manned by 8614 men. The principal part, if not the whole, of the line-of-battle force in this navy, consisted of four fine 74-gun ships, the Tancredi, Guiscardo, Samnita, and Parthenope; which four ships, in conjunction with a body of 6000 troops, the King of the Two Sicilies engaged to place at the disposal, when required, of the British commander-in-chief in the Mediterranean.

The principal maritime powers, which, when the war commenced, stood in the character of neutrals, were Russia, Denmark, and Sweden. The navy of the first power consisted of about 40 sail of the line, the second of about 24, and the last of about 18. Russia agreed so far to favour England in the war, as, with some restriction, to shut her ports against the vessels of republican France; but neither Denmark nor Sweden would confederate with their neighbour in a measure by which, as they conceived, and perhaps justly, their commerce would be lessened.

---

[1] The Santissima-Trinidad, until subsequently built upon and augmented in force, was so rated.

There was a fourth yclept neutral power, which, although possessing a navy of only a few frigates, and separated from Europe by the whole breadth of the Atlantic ocean, became in time, by her enterprising commercial spirit and expertness at concealing enemy's property, a more effective friend to France, and consequently a sharper thorn in the side of England, than if she had been at open war with her ; as, in the latter case, the numerous vessels of the United States, trading between France and her colonies, might, without any complaint, remonstrance, or quibble, have been legally detained by British cruisers.

At no previous period had France possessed so powerful a navy as was now ready to second her efforts to humble, if not overthrow, her great maritime rival. It amounted altogether to about 250 vessels, of which 82 were of the line ; and of these, nearly three-fourths were ready for sea, or in a serviceable state.[1] Moreover, the French government, shortly after the commencement of the war, in order to provide against those losses which, experience had shown, were likely to attend a contest with England, ordered to be laid on the stocks 71 ships, including 25 of the line ; and to be cast at the national foundries 3100 pieces of sea-service ordnance, including 400 brass 36-pounder carronades, the first of the kind, as it would appear, forged in France.

Among the French ships ordered to be built, were five to mount 100 guns, and eight frigates to carry 24-pounders on the main deck. Instead of the former, one ship to mount 130 guns, and be named Peuple, was laid down ; and, for the remaining four three-deckers, an equal number of 80s and 74s appear to have been substituted. Several of the old small-class 74s, or such as carried 24-pounders only on the lower deck, instead of being repaired to serve again in the line, or taken to pieces as unfit to serve at all, were cut down and converted into the most formidable frigates that had hitherto been seen. It is uncertain what was the exact armament of these "vaisseaux rasés ;" but they appear to have mounted 28 long 24-pounders on the main deck, 18 long 12-pounders, and four brass 36-pounder carronades, upon the quarter-deck and forecastle, making a total of 50 guns, with a complement of 500 men. It is believed that the first ship so fitted was named Expériment. Seven others were, Agricole, Brave, Brutus, Flibustier, Hercule, Robuste, and Scévola.

The strength of any navy, considered in a national point of

[1] See Appendix, No. 6.

view, is its line-of-battle, rather than its detached, or frigate force. The latter may cruise about, and interrupt trade, or levy contributions on some comparatively insignificant colonial territory; but it is the former that arrays itself before formidable batteries, and strikes dead into the heart of the parent state. According to the usual mode of comparing the British and French line-of-battle forces, we ought to be satisfied with the following statement:—

	No. of Ships.
British line	158
French line	82

The first, which is Steel's number for February, includes many ships for which there are no comparates in the number below. According to the first abstract in our series,[1] 113 is the proper number; but we shall add two of the ships in the building column, the Cæsar and Minotaur, because they were launched early in the present year; and, for the same reason, we shall not exclude more than two of the four French ships, described as nearly ready for launching. Hence, deducting the two French 74s declared to be unserviceable, and two other ships of the same class that were undoubtedly converted into frigates, the numbers will stand thus:—

	No. of Ships.
British line	115
French line	76

In the one case, the difference is as two to one, or nearly so; in the other, it is barely as three to two. Still, the comparison is imperfect; for, while the French line is possessed of as many as eight ships that mount from 110 to 120 guns each, the British line can produce no ship that mounts more than 100 guns; and, while upwards of a fourth of the latter's numerical strength is made up of 64-gun ships, the weakest ship belonging to the former mounts 74 guns.

There is no remedy here, unless we take the total number of guns mounted on each side, which would be 8718 and 6002; showing a difference of rather more than four to three. But, as every one of the lower-deck guns of any French line-of-battle ship is of greater nominal caliber, by one-ninth, than the heaviest long gun carried by any British ship:[2] and as a French gun of any given caliber is of greater power, by one-twelfth, than an

---

[1] See Appendix, Annual Abstract, No. 1.
[2] Should the Britannia, because she mounted 42-pounders on her lower deck, be deemed an exception, the Côte d'Or (afterwards Montagne), represented to have carried French 48-pounders on the same deck, may be set-off against her.

English gun of the same nominal caliber,[1] the mere number of guns on each side is still an inadequate criterion of force. It remains, then, to reduce the calibers of the 8718 English and 6002 French guns into English pounds; and, that being done, a very simple arithmetical operation produces the following statement:—

Ships.	No. of Ships.	No. of Guns.	Aggregate Broadside weight of Metal in English Pnds.
British line	115	8718	88,957
French line[2]	76	6002	73,957

Here is a difference, not as the loose unwarranted statements usually made public would have us infer, of more than a half, but of very little over a sixth; and it is this mode of comparison alone that can enable posterity duly to appreciate the efforts of the British navy, in the two long and eventful wars which succeeded and grew out of the French Revolution. Nor can the French themselves reasonably complain that this view of the relative strength of the two navies presents too slight a numerical difference; one of their conventional deputies, and no less a man than Jean-Bon Saint-André, having made the following public and uncontradicted assertion: "Avant la prise de Toulon, la France était la puissance maritime la plus redoubtable de l'Europe."

As soon as war was resolved upon, the seamen of France were called together, by addresses calculated to rouse their patriotism and invigorate their efforts. The most violent invectives were cast upon the king and government of England; and the latter's alleged hatred to France was painted in glowing colours. The sailors were promised that their pay should be augmented; that, during their absence at sea, their wives and children should be taken care of; that a considerable proportion of such prizes as they might capture should devolve on themselves; and then, an enticing picture was drawn of the richly-freighted ships of England, coming alone and unprotected from every quarter of the

---

[1] See p. 45.
[2] For the force of the different classes of French ships see page 59, and for the same of English ships the first annual abstract in the Appendix. The Gibraltar's guns, for the reasons stated at notes § and K* of that abstract, are not there specified. For the present it may suffice to state that the Gibraltar's broadside weight of metal was only 828 lbs., instead of 972, the quantum assigned to the generality of her class.

globe. But the most deadly blow that was aimed at British commerce was the animating call upon the French merchants and capitalists, to equip without delay strong and swift-sailing privateers. In short, the natural valour and enterprise of Frenchmen had never been raised to so high a pitch of enthusiasm as at the onset of this the first maritime war in which, with the slight exception of Sardinia, the republic was engaged.

As in the course of the details that are to follow frequent reference will be made to the force of French ships, a table, showing at one view the established armaments of the different classes, would tend to free the subject from much of its accustomed embarrassment. Fortunately the French navy, being composed wholly of French-built ships, a uniformity prevails that renders this mode practicable; and here follows, drawn up from authentic records, a tabular statement, which will afford the requisite information :—

Nos. for reference.	Class.	First or Main Deck. Number.	Pounders.	Second Deck. Number.	Pounders.	Third Deck. Number.	Pounders.	Quarter-deck. Number.	Pounders.	Brass carrs. No.Prs	Forecastle. Number.	Pounders.	Brass Carronades. No.Prs	Poop. No.Prs	Total No.	Complement.
1	120-gun ship	32	36	34	24	34	12	14	8	--	6	8	--	4 36	124	1098
2	110 ,,	30	,,	32	,,	32	,,	12	,,	--	4	,,	--	4 ,,	114	1037
3	80 ,,	30	,,	32	,,	--		12	12	--	6	12	--	6 ,,	86	840
4	74 ,,	28	,,	30	18	--		12	8	--	4	8	--	4 ,,	78	690
5	40-gun frig	28	18	--		--		10	,,	2 36	2	,,	2 36	--	44	330
6	38 ,,	26	,,	--		--		10	,,	2 ,,	2	,,	2 ,,	--	42	320
7	36 ,,	26	12	--		--		8	6	2 ,,	2	6	2 ,,	--	40	300
8	32 ,,	26	,,	--		--		4	,,	2 ,,	2	,,	2 ,,	--	36	275
9	28 ,,	24	8	--		--		--		6 ,,	2	,,	--	--	32	200

There is one remarkable peculiarity in the arrangement of the guns on board of French ships. So paramount to all other considerations is the comfort of the captain, that no guns are mounted in the cabin of a line-of-battle ship; and sometimes the aftermost port of the main deck of a frigate is left vacant, to answer a similar purpose. This is the reason that French ships of the line, and frigates occasionally when captured by the British, are established with a greater number of guns than they had previously carried; a British captain preferring the uniform appearance of his gun-deck to the greater comfort of domestic furniture.

In a week or two after the declaration of war against England,

Rear-admiral Pierre-César-Charles-Guillaume Sercey, with the 74-gun ships Eole, America, and Jupiter, and some frigates and corvettes, sailed from Brest bound to the West Indies; whither the Phocion 74 had previously gone. About the same time a squadron from Brest, Lorient, and Rochefort began to assemble in Quiberon Bay; and on the 4th of June Vice-admiral Morard-de-Galles, with all the line-of-battle ships then in the road, sailed from Brest for the same destination; having under his command, in the course of that and the following month, from 14 to 17 line-of-battle ships, and, by the latter end of August, a fleet composed of the 21 sail of the line and four frigates named in the following list:—

Gun-ship.

Guns	Ship	Officer	No.
120	Côte d'Or	Rear-adm. ——— Lelarge. Captain Touissant Duplassis-Grénédan.	2
110	Terrible	Vice-adm. ——— Morard-de-Galles. Commodore[1] ——— Bonnefoux.	1
110	Bretagne	Rear-adm. ——— Landais. Captain ——— Richery.	3
80	Auguste	Rear-adm. Yves-J. Kerguelen. Captain ——— ———.	4
80	Indomptable	Commodore Eustache Bruix.	
80	Juste	,, Jean-Elie Terrason.	
74	Trajan	,, Louis-Thos. Villaret-Joyeuse.	
74	Tigre	,, ——— Vanstabel.	
74	Audacieux	,, François-Joseph Bouvet.	
74	Téméraire	Captain Yves-François Doré.	
74	Suffren	,, Yves-Louis Obet.	
74	Impétueux	,, Jean-Pierre Lévêque.	
74	Aquilon	,, Jean-Baptiste Henry.	
74	Northumberland	,, Guillaume Thomas.	
74	Jean-Bart	,, Joseph-Marie Coetnempren.	
74	Tourville	,, Claude-Marie Langlois.	
74	Achille	,, ——— Keranguen.	
74	Convention	,, ——— Labatul.	
74	Neptune	,, ——— Tiphaigne.	
74	Révolution	,, ——— Tranquelléon.	
74	Superbe	,, ——— Bois-Sauveur.	

Frigates, Galathée, Engageante, Nymphe, and Sémillante.

[1] A word or two may be here usefully introduced on the comparative rank of French naval officers. The French have only two classes of flag-officers; "vice-amiral," vice-admiral, and "contre-amiral," rear-admiral. Their "grand-amiral," or, as recently styled, "amiral," is an honorary rank usually given to some prince of the blood, and was of course suspended during the republican dynasty. When a "vice-amiral" commands a fleet, he is usually styled "général," and sometimes "amiral." The French have, also, or rather had during the war, a rank of "chef de-division," or commodore, who hoisted his broad pendant even under a flag-officer. Their captains are divided into "capitaines de vaisseau de première classe," "capitaines de vaisseau de deuxième classe," and "capitaines de frégate." Of the first a portion bear, or rather bore during the war, the additional rank of "chefs-de-division," or commodores; and it is considered proper to give them that appellation in the list.

By a singular omission on the part of the French government, this formidable French fleet, instead of cruising in the ocean to harass British commerce, or speeding to the Antilles to strike a blow against one or more of the British colonies, was allowed to be at anchor in the road of Belle-Isle; with permission, however, to weigh occasionally, and stand across to the adjacent island of Groix. This was under an idea that England meant to make a descent upon that part of the French coast, in order to favour the cause of the royalists.

The necessity, on the part of England, of despatching squadrons, in the first instance, to the stations at a distance from home, occasioned some time to elapse ere a British fleet could be got ready, of sufficient strength to cope with the French fleet in Quiberon Bay, reinforced as that fleet was likely to be by ships from the neighbouring depôts of Lorient, Rochefort, and Brest. It was not, therefore, until the 14th of July that Admiral Lord Howe, with the Channel fleet, consisting of 15 ships of the line, besides a few frigates and sloops, set sail from St. Helen's. On the 18th, at 4 P.M, when about 20 leagues to the westward of Scilly, the fleet was taken aback in a squall from the northward, and the Majestic 74, in wearing, fell on board of her second astern, the Bellerophon: by which accident the last-named 74 had the head of her bowsprit, her foremast, and maintopmast carried away; but fortunately none of her crew were hurt. The Ramillies 74 was immediately ordered, by signal, to take the Bellerophon in tow. The former thereupon conducted her disabled companion to Plymouth, and on the 20th rejoined the fleet. On the 22nd Lord Howe was joined by the London 98, sent out to replace the Bellerophon in the line of battle; and on the next day, the 23rd, his lordship anchored with the fleet in Torbay.

On the 25th, having the day previous received intelligence that an American ship had passed through a French fleet, believed to consist of 17 sail of the line, about 10 leagues to the westward of Belle-Isle, Lord Howe again put to sea, with the wind at west, and on the same day fell in with the 24-gun ship Eurydice, Captain Francis Cole; who stated, that he had received a similar account from the master of an English privateer, with the addition, that the French were supposed to have stationed themselves off Belle-Isle, to be ready to protect a convoy daily expected from the West Indies. Lord Howe returned off Plymouth Sound, and was there joined by two ships, which he had requested to be sent to him: his force then consisting of the following 17 sail of the line, nine frigates, and five smaller vessels:—

Gun-ship.				
100 (D)	{ Queen Charlotte	{	Admiral (w.) Richard, Earl Howe.	1
			Captain Sir Roger Curtis.	
			„ Hugh Cloberry Christian.	
			„ John Hunter.	
	Royal George	{	Vice-adm. (r.) Sir Alex. Hood, K.B.	3
			Captain William Domett.	
„ (E)	Royal Sovereign	{	Vice-Adm. (r.) Thomas Graves.	2
			Captain Henry Nichols.	
98[1]	London . . .		„ Richard Goodwin Keats.	
	{ Cumberland .	}{	Rear-adm. (b.) John Macbride.	
			Captain Thomas Louis.	
	Montagu . . .		„ James Montagu.	
	Ramillies . .		„ Henry Harvey.	
	Audacious . .		„ William Parker.	
74	{ Brunswick . .		„ John Harvey.	
	Ganges . . .		„ Anthony Jas. Pye Molloy.	
	Suffolk . . .		„ Peter Rainier.	
	Majestic . . .		„ Charles Cotton.	
	Edgar . . .		„ Albermarle Bertie.	
	{ Veteran . . .		„ Charles Edmund Nugent.	
64	Sceptre . . .		„ Richard Dacres.	
	Sampson . .		„ Robert Montagu.	
	Intrepid . . .		„ Hon. Charles Carpenter.	

Frigates, Hebe, Latona, Phaëton, Phœnix, Inconstant, Southampton, Lapwing, Pegasus, and Niger.

Sloops, Incendiary (F.S.) and Ferret, two cutters, and one lugger.

Lord Howe then stood away to the westward, with the wind at north, and, having cleared Ushant, altered his course to the southward, and steered for the supposed station of the French fleet.

On the 31st, when the admiral had nearly reached the latitude of Belle-Isle, the wind, which had been blowing from the westward, veered suddenly back to north-north-east; and the fleet stood in towards the land, on the larboard tack. At 2 P.M. the British descried the island bearing east-north-east, and almost at the same moment the fleet of M. Morard-de-Galles, consisting of 17 sail of the line (all those in the list at p. 60. except the Côte-d'Or, Tigre, and two out of the three ships, Aquilon,

[1] In order to simplify these lists, we have omitted the letter referring to the class, or subdivision of the rate, in the annual abstracts, except where there is a difference of force. For instance, the Queen Charlotte and Royal George each mount 18-pounders on the third deck, but the Royal Sovereign mounts only 12-pounders. The figures after the names of the flag-officers refer to their relative seniority. The ships of each rate, or class, stand in the list according to the seniority of their respective captains. Were the rank of the officer not made subservient to the class of the ship, a degree of confusion would frequently ensue; thus, the Veteran, of 64, would rank above the Majestic and Edgar, of 74 guns. The letters r, w, b, enclosed in parentheses, stand for red, white, and blue, the colours of the flags worn by admirals, vice-admirals, and rear-admirals respectively, according to gradation of rank, as explained in the Glossary.

Impétueux, and Révolution), and several frigates, on the weather-beam.

Having been ordered to cruise off and on the coast, to be in readiness to protect a convoy from America, expected to arrive under the escort of M. Sercey and his three 74s, the French admiral, when first seen, was standing on the starboard tack close hauled. At 5 P.M. the French ships, then bearing from the centre of the British fleet north-west-by-west, and appearing from the masthead with their topsails just above the verge of the horizon, tacked to the eastward. Lord Howe, with his fleet formed in line of battle, continued standing in, with a very moderate breeze, until a little past 6 P.M ; when, being about three leagues from the north end of the island, he tacked to the northwest, and, after dark, each ship of the English fleet carried a light.

On the 1st of August, soon after daybreak, the wind being very light, 17 sail were seen, at a great distance, in the north-east. At 7 A.M. the British fleet put about on the larboard tack, but tacked again soon afterwards, an alteration of the wind favouring an endeavour to approach the enemy; many of whose ships, towards noon, were seen from the deck. Shortly afterwards it fell quite calm. As the evening came on, a light breeze sprang up from the north-west, of which the British fleet took advantage, and steered directly for the French fleet; but the wind again shifting to north-east, the British fleet hauled to the northward, in order to get in with the shore. The French fleet, when last seen in the evening, consisted of 21 sail, two of them reconnoitring frigates, whose hulls were visible from the deck.

On the 2nd not a French ship was to be seen; but the master of an American vessel from Lorient informed Lord Howe, that he had the day previous passed through the French fleet, which he also represented to consist of 17 sail of the line. On the succeeding day two French ships were chased by the British advanced frigates, but were too near the shore to be overtaken. The unsettled state of the weather, which subsequently became very tempestuous, rendered it necessary to disengage the fleet from the intricate navigation of this part of the French coast. The ships, accordingly, hauled their wind and stood off. On the 10th, the British admiral, after having, owing to the freshness of the wind, failed in an attempt to reconnoitre Brest, cast anchor in Torbay.

Having effected his escape from a fleet which, according to the intelligence derived from the English newspapers, and from prizes and neutrals brought in by his frigates, consisted, when it sailed, of a much greater force than 17 sail of the line, Vice-Admiral Morard-de-Galles returned to his anchorage in the road of Belle-Isle. Here, very soon, a spirit of mutiny began to show itself among the French sailors. The poor fellows were without shoes or shirts, and, although compelled by the orders of the government to be daily spectators of their own shore, had been feeding upon salt provisions until the greater part of them were infected with the scurvy. Add to this, that they were debarred, by their forced inactivity, from sharing the spoils of war with their more fortunate brother-tars in the open sea; and it will be acknowledged, that the crews of the French ships at Belle-Isle had ample cause for complaint.

In the commencement of September the sailors called upon the admiral to carry them to Brest; alleging, as a pretext for going thither, that the inhabitants were disposed to deliver up the port to the British, after the recent example of the Toulonese. To show that they were serious in their wish to repair to Brest, the crews of eight of the ships hoisted the topsails preparatory to weighing. In this emergency, after a council of officers had been holden, and delegates heard from the disaffected crews, the admiral found himself obliged to yield. Accordingly, on the 21st the French fleet got under weigh from Belle-Isle, and on the 29th anchored in the road of Brest.

The port of Brest will be so frequently alluded to in these pages, that a slight description of it may not be unacceptable. Brest lies a little to the southward of the most westerly point of France, and is in latitude 48° 22′ north, and longitude from Paris 6° 48′ west. It is considered to be one of the finest harbours in France, and perhaps in Europe. It possesses a safe roadstead, in which 500 ships of war may ride in 8, 10, and 15 fathoms, at low water. The entrance, called le goulet, is narrow and difficult, with two dangerous rocks, les Fillettes and le Mingan, nearly in mid-channel.

The coast is well fortified on both sides; and outside the entrance, or goulet, are two anchorages, where the men-of-war frequently lie: one to the northward, named Bertheaume Bay, sheltered from the north, north-east, and north-west winds; the other to the southward, named Camaret Bay, sheltered from the east-south-east, south, and south-west winds. There are three passages into these bays, and into Brest harbour, from the sea: one named, Passage du Four, between the main land and the island of Ushant; and which the British have since called the St. Vincent Channel; the second, Passage de l'Iroise, between

Ushant and the Isle des Saints; and the third, Passage du Raz, between the last-named isle and the Bec du Raz. The first and third passages are by far the most dangerous; and the Iroise, which is the centre or west passage, and of considerable width, is that off which the British fleet usually cruises. It is scarcely possible, however, to blockade the port of Brest, if the enemy inside is as vigilant as he ought to be. Brest contains the chief naval magazine of France, and is justly esteemed the key and bulwark of the country.

On the 23rd of August the Channel fleet again weighed from Torbay, and sailed to the westward, to escort the Newfoundland trade clear of danger, and afford protection to the homeward-bound West India convoy on its arrival in soundings. Having effected both objects, and cruised ten or twelve days to the north-west of Scilly, Lord Howe, on the 4th of September, re-anchored in Torbay. On the 27th of October, after detaching Commodore Pasley, with the Bellerophon and Suffolk 74s, and Hebe, Latona, and Venus frigates, to look after five French frigates that, two days before, had chased the Circe frigate into Falmouth, the British admiral once more put to sea, with his fleet augmented to 22 sail of the line, upon a cruise in the Bay of Biscay. On the 7th of November, when the fleet was close off Scilly, Commodore Pasley rejoined, without having seen anything of the squadron in pursuit of which he had been detached. On the 17th the Gibraltar of 80, and Suffolk of 74 guns, parted company; thus leaving still with Lord Howe 22 sail of the line, composed of all the ships (except the Suffolk and the four 64s) after mentioned, with the following ten ships in addition:—

Gun-ship.			
98	Prince		Rear-adm. (w.) George Bowyer.[1] Captain Cuthbert Collingwood.
74	Bellerophon	,,	Thomas Pasley.
	Tremendous	,,	James Pigott.
	Alfred	,,	John Bazely.
	Defence	,,	James Gambier.
	Vanguard	,,	John Stanhope.
	Bellona	,,	George Wilson.
	Invincible	,,	Hon. Thomas Pakenham.
	Russel	,,	John Willet Payne.
	Marlborough	,,	Hon. George Cranfield Berkeley.

On the 18th, at 9 A.M., latitude 48° 32' north, longitude

[1] Lord Howe, instead of the white, now carried the union flag at the main; and Rear-Admiral (w) Benjamin Caldwell had succeeded Rear-admiral Macbride in the command of the Cumberland.

1° 48' west, the 38-gun frigate Latona, Captain Edward Thornborough, descried from her masthead, at a great distance to windward, a strange squadron, which proved to be French, and consisted of the 74-gun ships, Tigre, Jean-Bart, Aquilon, Tourville, Impétueux, and Révolution, and frigates Insurgente and Sémillante, Espiègle brig, and Ballon schooner, under the command of chef-de-division Vanstabel, from Brest on the 13th, upon a cruise in Cancale Bay.

The French ships, mistaking, probably, Lord Howe's fleet for a merchant-convoy, bore down until their hulls were distinctly seen from the decks of the British ships. By signal from the commander-in-chief, the Russel, Audacious, Defence, Bellerophon, and Ganges, as the most advanced line-of-battle ships, went in chase. The French squadron had by this time hove to: but, perceiving that they were pursued by a superior force, the ships now filled, and made sail to get off, carrying, in a very fresh wind from south by east, accompanied by a heavy sea, whole topsails, with topgallantsails occasionally; while double-reefed topsails, with topgallantsails upon them, were all the sail which the British ships would bear. The Russel soon sprang her foretopmast; and at 11 A.M. the Defence, the weathermost line-of-battle ship, carried away her fore and main topmasts. The frigates were now ordered, by signal, to keep sight of the enemy and lead the fleet.

At a few minutes past noon the wind in a squall shifted a point or two to the southward. Thus favoured, the chasing ships tacked, and the Latona soon found herself so near to the two rearmost French frigates as to fire several shots at them. At 4 P.M. Captain Thornborough could have weathered and would have cut off one of them, the Sémillante, had not Commodore Vanstabel, in the Tigre, accompanied by his second, bore down to prevent him. The two French 74s passed so near to the Latona as to discharge their broadsides at her; but only two shots struck her, and they, fortunately, hurt no one. On receiving the fire of these ships, the British frigate gallantly luffed up and returned it; with so much effect, as to cut away the fore stay and main tack of the Tigre, besides doing some damage to her hull. No other ship of the British fleet was able to get near, although all the ships carried sail to that degree, that not only the fore and maintopmasts of the Defence, but the maintopmasts of the Vanguard and Montagu were carried away; and the ships were compelled, in consequence, to bear up for the Channel.

Towards evening the wind backed more round to the eastward, and, soon after midnight, shifted to east-south-east, and then east, the night being extremely dark. This alteration in the wind threw several of the advanced British ships as much to leeward, as they had previously been to windward; and, in expectation that the French ships would profit by the change and put about, or be restrained from bearing up, lest the leewardmost British ships should cut them off, Lord Howe kept his fleet upon a wind during the remainder of the night.

Towards 2 A.M. on the 19th, however, in the midst of a heavy squall of wind and rain, the French squadron bore away large to the west-south-west.[1] At 2 h. 30 m. A.M., on the weather clearing a little, the Bellerophon, who was now the most advanced, and quite out of sight of all her line companions, discovered two or three sail of the enemy right ahead, and some others on her lee or larboard bow: she immediately bore away, and steered to pass between the two divisions. The return of thick weather soon shut out all the ships from her view, and at daylight none were in sight but the Latona and the 36-gun frigate Phœnix, Captain Richard John Strachan. These frigates were at first supicious of each other, but in a little while came to a mutual recognition, and then bore up in company after an enemy's ship which had just hove in sight in the south-west, and was standing towards three others, that soon made their appearance in the west. On the Latona's making the signal, that these four ships, all of which were of the line, were superior to the chasing ships, Captain Pasley made the signal of recal; and the Bellerophon, accompanied by the Latona, Phœnix, and 38-gun frigate Phaëton, Captain the Honourable Robert Stopford, who had just joined company, bore away in search of the admiral, and, not finding him, steered for the Channel.

Having re-assembled the greater part of his ships, Lord Howe continued to cruise until towards the middle of December; when, no enemy appearing, he returned with the fleet to Spithead.

The squadron, which this time so narrowly escaped from Lord Howe, had been despatched upon a service that, if successful, would have redounded to the credit of France, and have caused a corresponding sensation on the opposite side of the Channel. The customary practice in England, of making expeditions,

---

[1] It is believed that some of the Queen Charlotte's officers, with their night-glasses, saw the French ships cross her bows, but found a difficulty in persuading Sir Roger Curtis of the fact.

whether great or small, the subject of newspaper paragraphs, having apprised the French government, that Vice-admiral Sir John Jervis, with four sail of the line, and a convoy, charged with provisions, naval stores, and troops, for the relief of Lord Hood at Toulon, was to sail from Portsmouth in the early part of November, a squadron, composed of six of the fastest sailing ships (the oldest of which, the Tourville, had not been launched a twelvemonth) of the Brest fleet, was detached to intercept the English vice-admiral.

On the 13th of November M. Vanstabel set sail from the road of Brest; and on the 19th, when Lord Howe's fleet hove in sight to leeward, the French commodore made sure that it was Sir John Jervis and his convoy, and bore down to endeavour to fulfil the object of his orders. Sir John was certainly to have sailed from Spithead in the beginning of the month, with one 98, one 74, and one 64 gun-ship, two 44s, and several frigates, sloops, and transports; destined to succour, not the royalists at Toulon, but those at Martinique and the adjacent French islands. M. Vanstabel, had he not fallen in with Lord Howe, would, however, have had to wait some days for his expected prey, Sir John Jervis, with his convoy of 39 vessels, not having been able, until the 26th, to get away from St. Helen's.[1] On the 30th M. Vanstabel returned to Brest, but not empty-handed; for, on the very day, or, as some of the French accounts say, on the very hour, on which he lost sight of the last ship of Lord Howe's fleet, he fell in with a British homeward-bound convoy (believed from Newfoundland), and took from it 17 ships and brigs, all deeply laden.

A battle between the two rival fleets had been so confidently predicted, that the nation was very ill prepared to receive the account of a bootless campaign. To suppose, however, that Lord Howe and his fleet had not, in both instances of his meeting the enemy, done all that was possible to bring on an engagement, betrayed a total unacquaintance with the subject. A fleet chasing in line of battle must not be expected to accomplish the best rate of sailing of the best sailer; for if one ship is inferior to the rest, the whole fleet must be detained, in order that the slowest ship should keep her station. The proverbial character of French ships renders it probable that the slowest sailer of the Brest fleet could have out-sailed the swiftest sailer of Lord Howe's; especially upon a wind, in a light breeze, as was the

[1] Captain Brenton, by mistake (Naval History, vol. ii., p. 14), states that Sir John Jervis sailed on the 6th.

case in the rencounter off Belle-Isle. In that of Cancale Bay, the French ships evidently got away by dint of superior sailing, aided by the thick and squally weather, and by the accidents which befel many of the leading British ships, and obliged them to discontinue the chase.

The refusal of M. Morard de Galles to come to an action with Lord Howe, where the forces were numerically equal, may have arisen from one or all of the following causes: an idea, founded on the reports of neutral and other vessels, met at sea, that the British admiral had upwards of 20, instead of 17 sail of the line; the orders of the French government, not to risk an engagement unless with such odds in his favour as would ensure success, or unless the expected provision-laden convoy from America, the object of solicitude to all France, should require his protection. Of this convoy we hear nothing during the present year; but Rear-admiral Sercey, who had been detached to escort it home, brought safe to the port of Brest, in the early part of November, his three 74s, the Eole, America, and Jupiter.

Having closed our year's account of the proceedings of the hostile fleets cruising in the Channel, we have next to attend to those stationed in the Mediterranean; on the northern coast of which is situated the second naval depôt belonging to France. Toulon lies about 10 French leagues east from Marseille, 24 south-west from Nice, and 125 in the same direction from Paris. The sea-front is well defended by batteries, that flank all the avenues. However, as this port is likely, in the course of our narrative, to become a very interesting spot, we shall borrow an able description of it from the work of a contemporary.

"The engineer who constructed the dock at Toulon had great difficulties to encounter; the ground was full of springs, and constantly undermined his foundation; he was therefore obliged to make an inverted arch of solid materials, which has answered the intended purpose: the French build their largest and best ships here. Besides the inner harbour which encloses the arsenal, they have an outer harbour and a road. The inner harbour is a work of art, formed by two jetties, hollow and bomb-proof, running off from the east and west sides of the town, and embracing a space large enough to hold thirty sail of the line, stowed in tiers very close together, as many frigates, and a proportion of small-craft, besides their mast-pond. The arsenal is on the west side, and the ships in ordinary or fitting, lie with their bowsprits or their sterns over the wharf; the storehouses, containing the various articles of equipment, are within fifteen yards of them; the rope-house, sail-loft, bakehouse, mast-house, ordnance, and other buildings, are capacious and good: the model-loft is worth the attention of strangers, but it is seldom they can obtain the indulgence of an admission. The water in the basin is, of course, sufficiently deep to receive a first-rate with all her stores. The east side is occupied by the victualling-department and the gun-boats: the north side is a fine capacious quay, on which stands the tower, extending from the dock-yard to the victualling-office; immediately in front of it is the mouth of the basin formed by the meeting of the two jetties to the distance of about sixty feet, on the easternmost one a pair of sheers is erected for masting the ships; a boom closes the entrance at night, and another runs from the jetty to the town, confining all the small-craft and timber on the west side of the harbour; the basin is never ruffled by any wind to occasion damage; the outer sides of the jetties present two tremendous batteries, à fleur d'eau, or nearly even with the water's edge, which we consider the very worst species of fort for a ship to encounter.

"The space for the anchorage of ships of war in the inner road is very confined, and probably not more than two or three sail of the line could lie there at a time; the ground is in general foul and rocky. The great road is a good anchorage, but neither extensive, nor secure from the effects of a Levanter, which throws in a heavy sea: it is defended on the south side by a peninsula, terminating at Cape Sepet: the bay of Toulon, which is eastward of this, is open, and the water deep, therefore not to be relied on as an anchorage in all weathers. The town, which, it has been observed, occupies the north side of the inner harbour, is fortified with great art, both on the land and sea approaches; but being commanded by the heights with which it is surrounded on all sides, must be dependent on them for protection. A semicircular chain of mountains on the north, extends from the Hieres-road on the east, to the pass of Oliol on the west; this pass might have bid defiance to any force, had it been guarded by British troops: it is five miles from the town. Strong batteries from the heights command also the arsenal and the anchorage. Fort la Malgue stands on a hill between the little and the great road; Fort Mulgrave occupies the tongue of land continued from this hill into the harbour: opposite to it, and on a point of land which forms the little road, at the distance of half a mile, stand the forts of Aiguillete and

Bellaguer; whence to Cape Sepet the shore is one continued chain of forts.

"The heights of Toulon are estimated at six hundred yards, and are of the most rugged and difficult ascent: the rocks crumbled under the feet of our daring countrymen as they mounted to the assault, and often precipitated huge masses on the heads of those beneath; the tops are guarded by the redoubts of St. Antoine, Artigues, St. Catherine's, and others · from the battery of La Croix, on the peninsula, to Cape Brun, the distance is two thousand yards, and this may be taken as the extreme breadth of the great road from north to south; westward of this may be about the same distance towards the grand tower and Bellaguer.

"The Mediterranean, though subject to strong and irregular currents, has no rise or fall of tide: this peculiarity of the inland sea subjects the port of Toulon to difficulties unknown to the rest of Europe, and its improvement, under such natural disadvantages, is highly creditable to the ingenuity and public spirit of the nation. They have but one large dock, which, when filled for the reception of a ship, is afterward pumped out by the convicts, who were formerly employed in working the galleys; but that species of force being now disused, these people are kept to such labours only as their crimes have deserved, and their strength will enable them to perform."[1]

France having assembled, at the time she declared war, a powerful fleet in the harbour of Toulon, it became necessary that an English fleet should be despatched, without delay, to the Mediterranean. Accordingly a fleet, in several divisions, proceeded for that destination. The first division, composed of one 98, and one 74 gun-ship, under the orders of Rear-admiral John Gell, in the St. George, sailed from Spithead early in April; and on the 15th of the month, was followed from the same anchorage by the second division, composed of two 98, and three 74 gun-ships, and two frigates, under Vice-admiral Philip Cosby, in the Windsor Castle. The third division, composed of one 100, three 74, and one 64 gun-ship, and two frigates, under Vice-admiral Hotham, in the Britannia, sailed also from Spithead early in May, and was followed, on the 22nd of the same month, by the fourth and last division, composed of one 100, five 74, and one 64 gun-ship, five frigates and sloops, two fire, and two hospital ships, under Vice-admiral Lord Hood, the commander-in-chief, in the Victory.

[1] Brenton's Naval History, vol. i., p. 200.

It was not until the middle of August that the vice-admiral arrived before the port of Toulon. His force then consisted of the following 21 sail of the line, besides frigates and sloops:—

Gun-ship			
100	{ Victory	{	Vice-adm. (r.) Lord Hood. Rear-adm. (w.) Sir Hyde Parker. Captain John Knight.
	Britannia	{	Vice-adm. (w.) William Hotham. Captain John Holloway.
98	Windsor Castle	{	Vice-adm. (b.) Philip Cosby. Captain Sir Thomas Byard.
	Princess Royal	{	Rear-adm. (r.) Charles Goodall. Captain John Child Purvis.
	St. George	{	Rear-adm. (b.) John Gell. Captain Thomas Foley.
74	Alcide	,,	Robert Linzee.
	Terrible	,,	Skeffington Lutwidge.
	Egmont	,,	Archibald Dickson.
	Robust	,,	Hon. Geo. Keith Elphinstone.
	Courageux	,,	Hon. William Waldegrave.
	Bedford	,,	Robert Mann.
	Berwick	,,	Sir John Collins.
	Captain	,,	Samuel Reeve.
	Fortitude	,,	William Young.
	Leviathan	,,	Hon. Hugh Seymour Conway.
	Colossus	,,	Charles Morice Pole.
	Illustrious	,,	Thomas Lennox Frederick.
64	Agamemnon	,,	Horatio Nelson.
	Ardent	,,	Robert Manners Sutton.
	Diadem	,,	Andrew Sutherland.
	Intrepid [1]	,,	Hon. Charles Carpenter.

The French had in Toulon ready for sea, exclusive of several frigates and corvettes, the following 17 sail of the line :—

Gun-ship			Gun-ship	
120	Commerce de Marseille.			Héros.
80	Tonnant.			Heureux.
74	{ Apollon.[2]			Lys.
	Centaure.		74	Orion.[2]
	Commerce de Bordeaux.			Patriote.[2]
	Destin.			Pompée.
	Duguay-Trouin.[2]			Scipion.
	Entreprenant.[2]			Themistocle.[2]
	Généreux.[2]			

There were also four sail of the line, Dauphin-Royal, 120, Triumphant 80, and Puissant and Suffisant 74s, refitting; nine

---

[1] It is doubtful if this ship joined before the latter end of August

[2] The seven ships thus marked had, since the commencement of the year arrived from the Biscayan ports.

ADMIRAL LORD HOOD.

FROM AN ORIGINAL PICTURE BY SIR JOSHUA REYNOLDS

repairing, or in want of repair, namely, Couronne and Languedoc 80s, and Alcide, Censeur, Conquérant, Dictateur, Guerrier, Mercure, and Souverain 74s; also one building, but not in a very forward state.[1] The fleet was commanded by Rear-admiral the Comte de Trogoff; who, even had the forces been more equally matched, was too sound a monarchist to fire a shot in the cause of republicanism. The spirit of disaffection existed, not only to a partial extent in the fleet, but very generally throughout the whole of the southern provinces; and the inhabitants, for their alleged disloyalty, were either feeling, or momentarily dreading, the full weight of republican rage.

Such being the posture of affairs, no surprise was excited when, on the 23rd of August, two commissioners came off to the Victory, Lord Hood's flag-ship, to treat for the conditional surrender of the port and shipping to the British. These commissioners represented themselves to be charged with full powers from the sections of the departments of the mouths of the Rhone, in which Marseille was situated, to treat for peace; expressly stating, that the leading object of their negotiation was to effect the re-establishment of a monarchical government in France. They expected, they said, the immediate arrival of deputies, similarly authorized, from the section of the department of Var, of which Toulon was the principal town.

To encourage the inhabitants of both departments to make a free avowal of their sentiments, Lord Hood issued, without delay, a preliminary declaration, in which he pledged himself, that, if a candid and explicit declaration of monarchy should be made

[1] The following table has been carefully drawn up, and may be relied upon as the most correct account of the kind that has appeared in print:—

State of the French Mediterranean Force, when Lord Hood was off Toulon, in August, 1793.

	120	80	74	40	38	36	32	28	Corvettes	Total
In Toulon — in the outer harbour, ready for sea	1	1	15	2	-	3	-	2	10	34
in the inner ditto, refitting	1	1	2	-	-	1	-	-	-	5
in ditto and the basin, repairing, or in want of repair	-	2	7	-	-	3	2	-	2	16
in ditto, building	-	-	1	2	-	-	-	-	-	3
Cruising in the Mediterranean	2	-	4	25	4	-	7	2	2	12	58
	-	-	-	1	3	2	5	-	2	4	17
Total	2	4	26	7	2	12	2	4	16	75

at Toulon, and Marseille, the standard of royalty hoisted, the ships in Toulon dismantled, and the harbour and forts placed provisionally at his disposal, so as to admit of egress and regress to the British fleet, the people of Provence should have all the assistance and support which that fleet could afford; that not an atom of private property should be touched; that a peace upon just, liberal, and honourable principles was the sole object of the treaty; and that, on such an event taking place, the port of Toulon, its batteries, and shipping, with the stores of every kind, as particularized in a schedule to be drawn up, should be restored to France. To this succeeded a very animated proclamation, addressed to the inhabitants of the towns and provinces in the south of France; wherein the miseries of the nation were forcibly, yet truly, depicted, and assurances given, that the coalesced powers would willingly co-operate with the well disposed, in putting down the odious faction that governed the country. As the republican forces, under General Carteau, were pressing hard upon Marseille, the British admiral was compelled to confine his assistance in that quarter to the granting of a passport, authorizing the inhabitants to import grain, of which the town stood greatly in need.

Toulon was not unanimous in the wish for a monarchical government. A republican party, although not very formidable, existed in the town, and the bulk of the fleet, with Rear-admiral St. Julien, the second in command, at its head, had avowed a similar sentiment; but the commander-in-chief, as already stated, was a stanch monarchist. It was this disunion that had prevented the expected junction of the deputies on board the Victory; and the admiral determined to send an officer to Toulon, to ascertain how matters stood. Accordingly, on the afternoon of the 24th, Lieutenant Edward Cooke, of the Victory, accompanied by a midshipman, and clothed with powers to treat with the royalists for the surrender of the port, departed on that perilous enterprise. He purposely delayed entering the harbour until 10 P.M. It was then dark and windy, and he kept close under a high shore until abreast of the French fleet; when, conceiving the boldest measure to be the safest, he pushed off to the ships, and, being taken for one of their own boats, passed unnoticed between them.

On reaching the dock yard, and escaping detention by a gunboat that had boarded him, Lieutenant Cooke received a deputation from the committee-general, but was not permitted to land until next morning. Finally, he was conducted to the chamber where the committee was sitting; and the latter signed a declaration, agreeing to Lord Hood's proposal. One of the articles of that declaration was: "The people of Toulon trust the English nation will furnish, speedily, a force sufficient to assist in repelling the attacks with which they are at this moment threatened, by the army of Italy, which is marching towards Toulon, and by that of General Carteau, who directs his forces against Marseille." In his way back to the fleet, Lieutenant Cooke was arrested, but liberated by the mob; and, on the same afternoon, reached the Victory in safety.

The same enterprising officer afterwards made a second trip; and the following extract from a private letter from Lieutenant Cooke gives an interesting account of one out of the many hairbreadth escapes he underwent:—"A French frigate lay very much in my way; therefore, to throw her off her guard, I stood directly towards her: till, having neared the shore so that her boat could not cut me off, I altered my course, and rowed for the shore as fast as possible. The frigate immediately manned and sent off her long-boat, who kept up a constant fire of swivels at me the whole way; but they were too late; the shot all passed over my head, and I landed safe, though by no means without some doubts: this, however, was not a time for reflection. From the nature of the shore, which is bounded by high rocks, it was absolutely necessary to pass the broadside of the frigate, who was anchored parallel to it: so stopping to take breath before I opened the vessel, I jumped from among the rocks and ran for it. As I expected, she fired instantly; but I had not far to go, so only received her first fire before I got to the path that led up the cliff. Here the looseness of the ground, with the sand and dirt that the shot threw up, bothered me very much. Having at length gained the top, which, though not high, was exceedingly steep, I hid myself in the bushes and fig-trees, till I again recovered my strength and breath; all which time the frigate kept up a constant fire, which, to be sure, made a confounded noise among the trees, but did me no harm. At length, quitting my post, I pushed forward for the city, and arrived about 10 o'clock, amidst the acclamations of the greatest multitude I ever beheld."

On the 26th, in the evening, Lieutenant Cooke returned, accompanied by Captain Imbert, of the French 74 Apollon, as a special commissioner from the committee-general, for the purpose of ratifying the treaty; and who assured Lord Hood, that Louis XVII. had been proclaimed by the sections, and that the latter had sworn to acknowledge him. On this, the vice-admiral resolved to land troops, and take possession of the forts that commanded the ships in the road. The unfortunate Marseillese had on the preceding day, the 25th, been compelled to open their gates to General Carteau and his army.

The French Rear-admiral St. Julien, to whom the seamen had intrusted the command of the fleet, in the room of Rear-admiral Trogoff, had, in the mean time, manned the forts on the left of the harbour, in order to oppose the British in their entry. Seeing this, Lord Hood, at noon on the 27th, ordered about 1500 troops, consisting of the greater portions of two regiments that had been embarked in the fleet, and about 200 marines and seamen to be landed near Fort Lamalgue. The service was promptly executed under the direction of Captain Elphinstone, of the Robust, and immediate possession taken of the fort; of which Captain Elphinstone was appointed governor. This fort, which was on the right of the harbour, commanded that occupied by St. Julien; who, on being informed by a flag of truce, that such of the ships as did not immediately proceed into the inner harbour and land their powder, would be treated as enemies, abandoned his position, and, with the crews of seven line-of-battle ships, amounting to 5000 officers and men, escaped into the interior. In the course of the morning, the remaining French ships removed into the inner harbour, in compliance with Captain Elphinstone's order; and in the afternoon, the British and Spanish fleets (the latter, composed of 17 sail of the line, having hove in sight just as the troops had effected a landing) anchored together in the outer harbour of Toulon.

On the same day, the 27th, Lord Hood issued a second proclamation, confirmatory of the assurances contained in his first; and, on the following day, received a satisfactory address from the united sections of the civil and military departments. On the 28th, also, the British at Lamalgue received a reinforcement of 1000 men from the Spanish fleet. Lord Hood appointed Rear-admiral Goodall governor of Toulon and its dependencies, and the Spanish Rear-admiral Gravina, commandant of the troops.

Having gained information that a detachment from Carteau's army, with ten pieces of cannon and some cavalry, was posted at Senary and Ollioules, two villages about five miles distant from Fort Lamalgue, Captain Elphinstone, on the 31st, sent directions to the committee of war at Toulon to forward to him a proportion of their best troops, with six pieces of artillery : he then marched at the head of 300 British, and the same number of Spanish troops, in the direction of Ollioules. The enemy was found very advantageously posted, with two pieces of cannon stationed on a bridge in his front; but, after a slight resistance, he abandoned his position, leaving in the hands of the conquerors his cannon, horses, ammunition, &c.

The French force consisted of between 700 and 800 men; and their commander, citizen Mouret, had received orders to possess himself of the heights that commanded the powder-magazine at Malaud. The British loss was Captain Douglas, of the 11th regiment, killed, and a sergeant and 12 privates wounded; the Spaniards lost three killed, and two wounded. On their way back to Lamalgue, the allied troops met the French royalist troops, who had been unavoidably delayed in their departure from Toulon. The success of Captain Elphinstone in this affair gained him many compliments on his knowledge of military tactics, so little expected in an officer of the navy.

During the early part of September, the increasing numbers of General Carteau's army on the west, and of General Lapoype's, or the army of Italy, on the east, kept the allied posts in a constant state of alarm. Nor was it at all lessened by the turbulent behaviour of the 5000 French seamen, lately belonging to the ships in port. Lord Hood, being determined to send these away as quickly as possible, gave orders that four of the most unserviceable of the French 74s, the Entreprenant, Orion, Patriote, and Trajan, should be got ready for their reception. Each ship's guns, except two 8-pounders, with 20 cartridges of powder for making signals, were sent on shore, as well as all the small arms. On the 14th the refractory seamen embarked, and the ships, being provided with passports, sailed under flags of truce; the Orion bound to Rochefort, the Aquilon to Lorient, and the Patriote and Entreprenant to Brest: the two latter ships reached their destination on the 13th of October; a day or two previously to that date, the two former arrived at their respective ports. The 16-gun brig-corvette Pluvier, at the same time, was sent to Bordeaux.

On the 18th of September, in the morning, the republicans opened two masked batteries, one of three, the other of two mortars, at the head of the north-west arm of the inner road, near La Petite-Garenne, upon the prize-frigate Aurore, carrying 12 and 6 pounders, Captain Henry Inman, and a gun-boat, or floating-battery, mounting four long 24-pounders and two brass mortars: which two vessels had been stationed near the Poudrière, for the defence of the head of the harbour, and to cover the fort of Malbousquet on the side next to the water.

On the 19th the republicans opened a fresh battery to the left of the above mentioned, mounted with several 24-pounders; and on the same day the British 98-gun ship the St. George, bearing the flag of Rear-admiral Gell, accompanied by a second floating-battery, under the command of Lieutenant Joseph Salvador Moriencourt, of the Princess Royal, 98, joined the Aurore. During the whole day a heavy fire was maintained between the 98-gun ship, frigate, and two floating-batteries, and the newly-erected works of the republicans: but at noon the two floating-batteries were forced to slip their cables, to get out of the reach of the enemy's fire. The works of the republicans, although partially destroyed by the fire of the British vessels, were quickly renewed, and the firing recommenced as briskly as ever.

On the 20th the floating-batteries returned to the attack; and the cannonade continued during that and the following day, but with so much increased disadvantage to the two floating-batteries, that one of them was sunk by the effects of the shot she had received. Among the wounded officers in one of the floats was Mr. Henry Vansittart, a midshipman of the Victory. A heavy oak splinter struck him on the head, cut through the skull to the thin membrane that covers the brain, and, passing on, took off the thigh of a Spanish bombardier, serving in company with the British seamen.[1]

On the 24th, Rear-admiral Gell having been appointed to command a small squadron of British, Spanish, and Royalist French ships, bound to Genoa, the Princess Royal 98, commanded by Captain John Child Purvis, in the absence of Rear-admiral Goodall, on shore as Governor of Toulon, took the place of the St. George before the republican batteries. A Spanish 74 now also formed part of the cannonading force. During the fire which was kept up at intervals every day, for some weeks, the Princess Royal (and not the St. George, as a contemporary states[2]) met with a serious accident. One of her lower-deck guns unfortunately burst: whereby three seamen were killed, the master, one master's mate, and 22 seamen and marines wounded. A piece of the upper part of the gun forced its way through both the second and third decks, overturning upon the former a gun and its carriage.

On the 24th, also, the Colossus 74 arrived, with 350 Sardinian

[1] Marshall's Royal Naval Biography vol. ii., p. 330. [2] Brenton, vol. i., p. 211

troops, from Cagliari. On the 28th 800 more arrived from Conti, in the Bedford and another 74, which had been detached to bring them; and on the same day, arrived Marshal Forteguerri from Naples, with the two 74-gun ships Guiscardo and Tancrédi, and four smaller vessels, having on board 2000 troops. On the 30th Rear-admiral Gell, having received his instructions from Lord Hood, sailed from Genoa with the St. George, Bedford, and Captain, British line-of-battle ships, two British frigates, and five sloops; one Royalist French, three Spanish sail of the line, and eight or nine French or Spanish frigates and corvettes formed part of his squadron.

During the night of the 30th the republicans, availing themselves of a thick fog, surprised a detachment of Spanish troops, and thereby got possession of the heights of Pharon, immediately over Toulon. On the next day, however, just as they had established themselves in their new position, the French were driven from it, with great slaughter, by a detachment of Spanish, Sardinian, Neapolitan, and British troops, under the command of Brigadier-general Lord Mulgrave (who had arrived on the 6th), assisted by Rear-admiral Gravina and Captain Elphinstone. The republican forces were stated to have amounted to 1800 or 2000 men, and to have lost nearly three-fourths of the number in killed, wounded, and missing. The loss of the combined forces consisted of 8 killed, 72 wounded, 2 missing, and 48 prisoners.

Napoleon Buonaparte was present in these attacks. The following anecdote of him is extracted from a French historical work: "Un jeune homme de vingt-trois ans fut jugé capable et digne du commandement de l'artillerie; on la lui confia. Ce jeune homme avait reçu une éducation toute militaire, et l'on remarquait déjà qu'un amour ardent pour la gloire enflammait le génie de Buonaparte. C'était lui-même. L'habileté et la hardiesse de ses dispositions se font remarquer. A l'attaque du fort Pharon, un commissaire de la convention critique et condamne la position d'une batterie. Buonaparte lui dit avec fierté: Melez-vous de votre métier de représentant; laissez-moi faire le mien d'artilleur: cette batterie restera là, et je réponds du succès."[1] The battery, it appears, did fully succeed, and Buonaparte received the applause of the generals present: shortly afterwards he was himself made a brigadier-general.

On the 5th of October a second division of 2000 Neapolitan troops, escorted by a Neapolitan 74, the Samnita, arrived at Tou

[1] Dictionnaire Historique, tome iv., p. 131.

lon. On the 8th it was resolved to attempt the destruction of three batteries which the enemy had recently erected, one on the height des Moulins, and two to the southward, on the height de Reinier; and all of which forts, particularly the two latter, menaced the shipping in the road. Accordingly, on the same night, a detachment of troops, composed of 50 Spaniards, 100 Piedmontese, 50 Neapolitans, 408 British, including 50 marines, and a party of seamen headed by Lieutenant Walter Serecold, of the navy, the whole under the command of Lieutenant-colonel Nugent, marched up the difficult ascent to the batteries, and stormed and carried them with a very trifling loss.

The French force in these batteries was said to consist of 300 men, and, at the heights a little above them, from 1200 to 1300 were concentrated. The narrow paths and rugged precipices by which the troops had to descend, in order to avoid the fire from two heavy batteries in the neighbourhood, rendered it impracticable to bring away the ordnance. The guns, therefore, consisting of one 4, one 6, two 16, and three 24 pounders, besides two 13-inch mortars, all of brass, were effectually destroyed, under the immediate direction of Lieutenant Serecold; and the combined forces returned to their quarters without molestation.

The city and suburbs of Toulon occupied a circumference of at least 15 miles, including eight principal, and several intermediate posts, between most of which there was only a water communication; the total amount of British troops, at this time in and about Toulon, amounted only to 1360 rank and file. Hence, the extended line of works necessary to defend the town on the land side, the small quantity of troops of which the garrison was composed, the strength, activity, and local experience of the besiegers; but, above all, the backwardness of some, and the jealousy and distrust of others, of the allied forces, were among the many difficulties under which Toulon was, even at this time, retained.

A Lieutenant-general Valdez having arrived, since the 18th, to succeed Rear-admiral Gravina, owing to the serious wound which the latter had received at the heights of Pharon, Admiral Langara, on the 23rd, wished Lord Hood to recognise the recent appointment by his catholic majesty of the lieutenant-general to the rank of "commander-in-chief of the combined forces at Toulon." This his lordship very properly resisted, averring, with truth, that Toulon and its dependencies had yielded to the British troops alone; and that, to command the latter, as well as the Sardinian and Sicilian troops, Major-general O'Hara, then off the port, had already been appointed.

By way of enforcing his demand, but under the pretence of shifting the berths of his ships, Don Juan de Langara placed his own three-decker alongside, and two other three-deckers, one on the bow, the other on the quarter, of the Victory, Lord Hood's flag-ship. At this time, be it known, the British fleet, by the departure of successive detachments, was reduced to ten sail of the line; while the Spanish fleet still consisted of its original number, seventeen. Lord Hood's firmness, however, was not to be shaken, and matters remained in their former state.

Finding the crews of his ship much weakened by the heavy draughts that had been made to assist in manning the various posts on shore, Lord Hood obtained from the grand master of Malta 1500 Maltese seamen, who stipulated, on being paid the usual wages of British seamen, to serve in the fleet during its continuance in the Mediterranean. On the 22nd Major-generals O'Hara and Dundas, the former with a commission to be governor of Toulon and its dependencies, arrived from Gibraltar: the governor of which had unfortunately sent but 750, instead of 1500 men, the number required of him.

Towards the end of October, or beginning of November, the third and last division of Neapolitan troops arrived at Toulon; and the combined forces amounted to 16,912 men, as the following details will show:—

	Rank and File.
French Royalists	1542
Piedmontese	1584
Neapolitans	4832
Spaniards	6840
British	2114
	16,912

Of this number, not more than about 12,000 were fit for duty; the remainder were sick in the hospitals; and of those fit for duty, 9000, or three-fourths, were necessarily distributed among the different posts on the extensive line of defence requisite to be maintained.

With respect to the republican troops that were menacing Toulon, although it is not easy to get at their exact amount, a little industry will enable us to show that they more than doubled the number of the combined troops by which it had hitherto been defended. The unfortunate Lyonaise had, since the 9th of October, surrendered to the republican General Kellerman, at the head of 60,000 troops; and the latter then marched away to co-operate with a part of the army of Italy in reducing Toulon. Thus: "Une armée de soixante mille hommes, composée des troupes que Kellerman a amenées des Alpes, des gardes nationales des villes et des campagnes voisines de Lyon, et de cinq cents canoniers destinés au service de cent pièces d'artillerie, est sous les murs, et n'attend que le signal pour foudroyer cette malheureuse ville."[1] "Le gouvernement envoya vers Toulon, pour le réduire, la même armée qui avait servi à soumettre Lyon: on y joignit plusieurs divisions de l'armée d'Italie."[2]

Supposing that, between the 9th of October and the beginning of November, half only of Kellerman's army had arrived, and estimating the divisions of the army of Italy at no more than 3000 men, there would be, before Toulon, at the last-mentioned date, 33,000 troops; and these, not composed of five different nations, but of Frenchmen wholly. Since some time in October, General Dugommier had arrived from Paris, to take charge of the besieging army; having under him Generals Laharpe, Garnier, Lapoype, Mouret, and, though last not least, Napoleon Buonaparte. General Carteau appears to have been superseded.

On the 15th of November, in the evening, a large corps of republican troops made a vigorous attack upon the British fort Mulgrave, situated on the heights of Balaguier, and one of the most essential posts around Toulon. The first assault was directed against the right, where the Spaniards were stationed: these retreated, firing their muskets in the air. At this moment Major-general O'Hara, having arrived from on board the Victory, directed a company of the Royals to advance. These instantly leaped the works, and put the enemy to the rout. The loss of the combined troops, in killed and wounded, amounted to 61; including, among the latter, Captain Duncan Campbell, of the Royals, who had commanded the detachment, and Lieutenant Lemoine, of the Royal Artillery. The loss of the French was supposed to amount to 600, in killed and wounded. In three days after this, Lord Hood received accounts that the 5000 Austrian troops, for whom, relying on the most positive assurances of the British minister at Turin, he had sent a squadron of ships and transports to Vado Bay, could not be spared. This was a sad blow upon the hopes of the Toulonese.

[1] Dictionnaire Historique, tome ii., p. 563.   [2] Ibid., tome iv., p. 130.

General Dugommier, having chosen a position on the heights of Arènes, directly opposite to the fort of Malbousquet, caused 20 pieces of cannon to be mounted upon it, and established his camp on the crest of another eminence, a short distance in the rear. These 20 pieces of cannon greatly annoyed the garrison of Malbousquet, endangered the arsenal that was contiguous to it, and threw some of their shells into the town: it was therefore resolved to try and bring away or destroy them.

For this service a corps of 400 royalist French, 600 Spaniards, 600 Neapolitans, 300 Sardinians, and 300 British, total 2200,[1] under the command of Major-general Dundas, on the morning of the 30th, marched from Toulon. With great difficulty the men ascended the heights, but, when there, succeeded at once in forcing the enemy to retire from his guns. Instead of forming on this summit, the troops, led on by their impetuosity, descended to the hollow in its rear, hoping to be able to carry the next eminence, it being that to which the enemy, on being driven from his battery, had precipitately fled. Here the combined forces encountered the main body of Dugommier's army, and were compelled, not only to fly in their turn, but to relinquish the battery which their valour had won, and which a moderate share of discretion would have enabled them to hold, until, at least, its guns were carried off or destroyed.

The loss of the combined forces in this unfortunate attack was severe; particularly on the part of the British, whose returns exhibited a list of 20 killed, 90 wounded, and 98 missing; more than two-thirds of the number which they had brought to the attack. Among the wounded prisoners was, unfortunately, the Governor of Toulon himself, according to whose excellent plan the attack had been made. General O'Hara did not, however, ascend to the battery until he knew it was in the possession of his friends; and, on witnessing the disorder of the troops, could not refrain from using his efforts to rally them. In attempting this he was wounded. Two soldiers supported him, until the bleeding of his wound, which otherwise was not dangerous, induced the general to order them to quit him, and save themselves. General Dugommier was himself wounded in the knee: what other loss the French sustained in this affair does not appear.

No sooner had the last-expected reinforcement joined the re-

---

[1] Yet, say the French writers, "Les assiégés firent une grande sortie le 30 Novembre. La rivière de l'As fut passée par *six mille hommes*, &c."—*Dict. Hist.* tome iv., p. 132.

publicans, than a council of war decided that a general attack should be forthwith made upon the fortifications and town of Toulon.[1] The report of deserters that the French force amounted, early in December, to between 40,000 and 50,000 men, was probably within, rather than beyond the truth: while, on the other hand, what with casualties and sickness, the combined forces could not assemble 11,000 firelocks; and two-thirds of these, as stated before, were distributed along a line of defence 15 miles in extent.

On the night of the 14th, in the midst of a storm, the French marched from their encampments in three columns, each column taking a route leading to a different point of the line of posts; so that their attacks might be simultaneous. By 2 A.M. on the 16th the besiegers had erected five batteries in front of Fort Mulgrave, and continued to bombard the works, with considerable effect, until 2 A.M. on the 17th; when, in the midst of dark and tempestuous weather, they succeeded in entering the fort by the Spanish side, and, after an obstinate but fruitless resistance on the part of the few surviving British, headed by Captain Conolly of the 18th regiment,[2] compelled the remnant of the garrison (originally not more than 700) to retire towards the shore of Balaguier.

While these operations were going on in this quarter, the column under General Lapoype succeeded in forcing all the posts upon the mountain of Pharon. Thus was the line of defence broken in upon in its two most essential points: and the ships in the harbour, and the town itself, overawed by the very cannon which had been mounted for their protection. Most of the ships, indeed, were compelled to unmoor, and retire to a safer position.

Things thus situated, a council of war was immediately held, composed of the following officers:—Lord Hood, Admiral Langara, Rear-admiral Gravina, Major-general Dundas, Lieutenant-general Valdez, Prince Pignatelli, Admiral Forteguerri, Sir Hyde Parker, Chevalier de Revel, and Sir Gilbert Elliot. At this council it was, after a most deliberate discussion, unanimously resolved that Toulon should be evacuated, as soon as proper arrangements could be made for that purpose; that orders should be sent to the troops occupying the redoubt, and the Lunette of Pharon, to retire to the posts of Artigues and St.

---

[1] Dictionnaire Historique, tome iv., p. 133.

[2] "La résistance des Anglais égale le courage opiniâtre des Français, quand ceux-ci, près de céder le fruit de tant de travaux, reçoivent un renfort."—*Dict. Hist.*, tome iv., p. 134.

Catherine's, and to maintain them as long as possible; that orders should also be sent to the posts of Great and Little Antoine, St. André, Pomet, and the Mills, to retire; that the posts of Malbousquet and Mississi should be held as long as possible; that the committee-general should make the necessary arrangements for informing the inhabitants of the intended evacuation, and that they should receive every possible assistance; that the sick and wounded should be embarked without delay; that the French ships of war which were armed, should sail out with the fleet; and that those which remained in the harbour, together with the magazines and the arsenal, should be destroyed; and finally, that measures should be taken on the same night (the 17th), if possible, for that purpose, but that such resolution was not to be put into execution till the last moment.

Admiral Langara undertook to deliver the necessary directions for destroying the ships in the basin; and also to scuttle or sink the two powder-vessels; which contained all the powder belonging, as well to the French ships as to the distant magazines, now within the enemy's reach.

The troops were withdrawn from the heights of Balaguier without much interruption from the enemy; as were likewise the troops from the other posts, deemed necessary to be at once evacuated. The purposed retention of the forts of Malbousquet and Mississi was, however, prevented, in consequence of the Neapolitans at the latter, which was the supporting-place, having abandoned it without orders. Such a panic, indeed, had seized the Neapolitan troops, during the sitting of the council, that they, one and all, deserted their posts, and were seen stealing on board their ships in great confusion and disorder In the course of the 18th the remaining troops were all concentrated in the town and at fort Lamalgue, ready to embark the moment the conflagration of the shipping should announce that it was time to complete the evacuation of the port.

The important service of destroying the ships and magazines was intrusted, at his own particular request, to Captain Sir William Sidney Smith; who, about a fortnight previous, had arrived from Smyrna in a small lateen-rigged vessel, which he had purchased and named the Swallow, and had manned with about 40 English seamen thrown out of employment at that port. Accordingly, on the same afternoon, taking with him the Swallow tender, three Spanish, and three English gun-boats, Sir Sidney proceeded to the arsenal, to prepare the combustible matter required for the occasion. The dock-yard gates had been judiciously closed and secured; but the people belonging to them had already substituted the three-coloured for the white cockade. The galley-slaves, in number 800, were, for the most part, unchained, and seemed to view with the eyes of freemen the devastation that was about to be committed on the national property. Upon these men the guns of the tender, and of a gun-boat, were forthwith pointed; and they remained quiet.

During this period, shot and shells, from Malbousquet and the neighbouring hills, were falling around; and, although occasioning no material interruption to Sir Sidney's little party, tended, very happily, to keep in subjection the slaves, as well as in their houses the republicans belonging to the town. As night approached, the enemy, in great numbers, descended the hill, and opened a fire, both of musketry and cannon upon the British: this was replied to, by discharges of grape-shot from a gun-boat, advantageously moored.

About 8 P.M. the Vulcan fireship, Captain Charles Hare, towed by the boats, entered the basin, and was placed, in a masterly manner, across the tier of men of war; her guns, which were all well shotted, being pointed in the direction best calculated to keep the enemy in check. At 10 P.M. the trains leading to the different magazines and storehouses, were, on a preconcerted signal, ignited; as was the fireship, although, by the accidental bursting of the priming, her commander nearly lost his life.

The flames ascended in terrific grandeur; and the Vulcan's guns, on being heated, discharged their contents, for the last time, against the enemies of their country. The rapid spread of the fire, while it almost overpowered, by its heat, some who knew no danger in their duty, laid open to view, by its light, all who were aiding in the doubly perilous service. The enemy, having now distinct objects to point at, opened his batteries from every quarter; when, suddenly, a tremendous explosion, unexpected by all, awed into silence both the besiegers and the attacked.

Again the heavy firing commenced, and the painful discovery was made that the Spaniards, in their premature retreat from a service which they had omitted to perform, had, instead of scuttling, set fire to, the Iris frigate, which contained several thousand barrels of powder. The explosion tore the Union gun-boat to atoms, and killed three of her crew, including the principal officer: a second gun-boat was blown into the air; but, very providentially, all the crew were picked up alive.

The business at the arsenal completed, Sir Sidney and his brave followers proceeded towards the basin, in front of the town, in order to effect what the Spaniards had reported impracticable; but, in the mean time, the bottom had been laid across the narrow entrance, and the British were received with such repeated volleys of musketry, as compelled them to abandon the enterprise. They then proceeded to destroy two 74s lying in the inner road, filled with French prisoners. These had hitherto evinced a disposition to resist; but the conflagration around them, and particularly the late awful explosion, induced them to accept, with thanks, Sir Sidney's offer to land them in a place of safety. This was rather a hazardous undertaking, as the prisoners were by far more numerous than the British: it was, however, effected; and the Héros and Thémistocle contributed their share to illumine the magnificent scene.

Having now effected as much as they were able, and more than, considering how ill they had been seconded, and how obstinately opposed, could possibly have been expected from them, Sir Sidney and his little party were preparing to rejoin their friends outside, when a second powder-vessel, the frigate Montreal, exploded close to them, with a concussion greater even than the first. The tender and the three boats, although within the sphere of the falling timber, which made the water foam around them, received, extraordinary as it may appear, not the slightest injury.

Exhausted in strength, so much so, indeed, that the men fell upon their oars, the British stood slowly out towards the fleet; heeding little, after their last narrow escape, the few ill-directed shot that were fired at them from forts Balaguier and Aiguilette.

As well as we can collect from the official accounts published on the subject, the following were the British naval officers who accompanied Sir Sidney Smith in his perilous undertaking. Captains Charles Hare and William Edge; Lieutenants Charles Tupper, John Gore, John Melhuish, Richard Holloway, Matthew Wrench, Thomas F. Richmond, Ralph Willett Miller, John Stiles; Charles Dudly Pater, Robert Gambier Middleton, Henry Hill, Joseph Priest, James Morgan, and Francis Cox; master, George Andrews; surgeon, William Jones; midshipmen, John Eales, Richard Hawkins, Thomas Cowan, William Knight, Henry Matson, Paul H. Valliant, and Mr. Young, who was killed. Among the officers wounded in Fort Mulgrave on the 17th, we find the name of Lieutenant Thomas Goddard and Midshipman John Wentworth Loring.

The commencement of the conflagration of the shipping had been the signal for evacuating the town; and, under the able management of Captains Elphinstone, of the Robust, late governor of Fort Lamalgue, Hallowell, of the Leviathan, and Matthews, of the Courageux, the whole of the troops embarked, and were on board the fleet by daylight on the morning of the 19th, without the loss of a man. What then must we think of an account which states thus?—" L'arrière-garde ennemie, taillée en pièces et poursuivie avant d'atteindre ses vaisseaux vers lesquels elle fuyait, tombe et périt dans la mer." [1] The Robust was the last ship that quitted the harbour; and, although fired at repeatedly, was not struck by a shot.

The Courageux having, in consequence of getting aground off Cape Corse, been hove down in the basin, was warped out without any rudder. The rudder, however, was afterwards brought off, slung alongside the launch and other boats, and was shipped in the road. The British fireship, Conflagration, which appears also to have been undergoing some repairs, could not be got away in time, and, in order that she might not fall into the hands of the enemy, was burnt.

Although the land is not the element on which seamen are expected to shine, the exigency of the case required that a great proportion of them should act on shore at Toulon. Whether as artillerists in the batteries, or musketeers in the field, they contributed their aid, always with cheerfulness, and never without effect. Their skill and bravery in action, not less than their strength and activity in the many laborious duties incident to a service so full of difficulties and dangers as the one they had engaged in, afforded a theme of praise and admiration to all who had seen their exertions and witnessed their undaunted courage.

Those who recollect (and who can forget?) the massacres that stained republican France will be gratified to learn, that 14,877 men, women, and children, of the loyal Toulonese, received an asylum on board the British ships. The Princess Royal, of 98 guns, bearing Rear-admiral Goodall's flag, had on board, at one time, 4000, and the Robust 3000, of these unhappy people.

But melancholy was the fate of those left behind. Many, in their way to the shore, were cut in two by the balls which were falling around them; others, overcome by their fears, fancied the hurried steps they heard behind were those of their pur-

[1] Dictionnaire Historique, tome iv., p.135.

suers; and some rushed, preferring instant death to infuriated vengeance, with their infants clinging to their breasts, into the waves and perished. Some thousands of others remained in the town, in the hopes that their age, sex, or political insignificance, would shield them from the bayonets of the soldiers, their *countrymen.* Vain hope!—a decree of the Committee of Public Safety had doomed the whole of them to destruction;[1] and the Toulonese deputies, Freron, and Moyse Bayle, worthy of such masters, were not to be moved by the entreaties even of Dugommier himself.

The speech of this general deserves to be recorded: " Deputies doubtless there were in this town, traitors who delivered it to the English; but the most criminal among them have fled. If there be any guilty men who have been so bold as to await the national vengeance, time will point them out; they will suffice to establish your justice as well as to appease the animosities which civil war produces. If you punish to-day, every passion will select its victims. Look at this town, deserted and laid waste! Whom would you immolate? Old people, women, and children, who never bore arms against us?"[2]

As a proof of the slight effect produced by this address of the French general, the monster Fréron, in a letter to his colleague, dated January 1, says: " We have required from the surrounding departments 12,000 masons to demolish and raze the city. Every day since our arrival we have cut off 200 heads." Of the total number of ill-fated Toulonese who were massacred by their republican countrymen no record has been preserved, or at least none has appeared in print. We are not, however, wholly without the means of judging, for the French writers say that when the British entered Toulon the town contained 28,000 souls, and that in a few weeks after the British quitted it there were but 7000 left.

Therefore, taking the number that escaped on board the British fleet at 15,000, we may consider that at and during a few weeks subsequent to the recapture of Toulon, nearly 6000

---

[1] "Ainsi les troupes républicaines entrèrent victorieuses dans Toulon, le 23 Décembre, 1793. La mort de tous ses habitans fut ordonnée par le comité de salut public, avec la démolition de la ville."—*Dict. Hist.,* tome iv., p. 136.

[2] "Représentans, sans doute il y eut dans cette ville des traîtres qui l'ont livrée aux Anglais; mais les plus grands coupables ont fui. S'il est des hommes criminels qui ayent osé attendre la vengeance nationale, le tems vous les fera connaître; lui seul peut éclairer votre justice, et calmer les haines qu'enfantent les guerres civiles. Si vous punissez aujourd'hui, toutes les passions choisiront leurs victimes. Voyez cette ville déserte et désolée! Qui allez-vous immoler? Des vieillards, des femmes, et des enfans, qui ne portèrent jamais les armes contre nous."—*Dict. Hist.,* tome iv., p. 136.

of the wretched inhabitants, men, women, and children, perished by the sword, musket, or guillotine, or plunged into the sea and were drowned in their endeavours to escape from the demoniac rage of an infuriated soldiery.[1]

It is now time to see what were the national advantages, in a military point of view, which were lost to France or gained to England by the seizure of Toulon. The French vessels that were in the port when the British entered were, according to the official accounts of the time, disposed of in the manner explained in the following table:—

Disposal of the Ships and Vessels that composed the French Force at Toulon, August 28, 1793.

	Ships or Vessels of, Guns,										
	120	80	74	40	32	26	24	20	18	16	14	Total.
Burnt, or otherwise destroyed	-	3	14	2	5	-	-	2	-	1	-	27
Brought away { by the British	1	-	2	2	3	2	1	3	-	-	1	15
{ by the Allies	-	-	-	-	1	-	-	1	1	-	-	3
Total { lost to the French	1	3	16	4	9	2	1	6	1	1	1	45
French { left to the { at Toulon	1	1	5	-	-	-	-	-	1	-	-	8
{ sent to Brest, &c.	-	-	4	-	-	-	-	1	-	-	-	5
Grand total	2	4	25	4	9	2	1	7	2	1	1	58

The fourteen 74s described in this table as burnt are meant to include one that was on the stocks; and the first two 40-gun frigates were also building. The five 74s represented as left to the French at Toulon include the Alcide, stated to be "unfit for service," but which ship was afterwards in an engagement at sea. The Alcide, and three of the four remaining 74s, namely, the Censeur, Guerrier, and Souverain, as well as the Dauphin-Royal (afterwards Sans-Culotte) 120, and Languedoc (afterwards Victoire) 80, had been intrusted to the Spaniards to burn; but the latter (treacherously as it would appear) left them untouched, and in possession of the French.

Information of a date subsequent to that of the official despatch lessened the number of vessels supposed to have been destroyed. The fire had not reached, or at least not materially injured, the 80-gun ship Tonnant, nor the Heureux, Commerce-

[1] That the rage of the troops was as indiscriminate as it was violent, will appear by the following anecdote: "Deux cents républicains de Toulon étant allés audevant de l'armée triomphante pour la féliciter, furent impitoyablement massacrés par l'avant-garde, et les soldats coupèrent les oreilles des morts, et les attachèrent à leurs chapeaux."—*Histoire Abrégée de la Révolution Francaise*, tome iii., p. 336.

de-Bordeaux, Mercure, and Conquérant, 74s; neither did the 74, nor either of the two frigates on the stocks, take the fire to any extent. Both these frigates, one named Minerve and the other Justice, were launched in September, 1794. The 74-gun ship was launched about the same time; her name was not, however, as generally supposed, Spartiate, but Barras. The frigates Sérieuse, Courageuse, and Iphigénie, and the brig Alerte also escaped unhurt. With respect to the buildings on shore, it was afterwards ascertained that the grand magazine had escaped the ravages of the flames, the smaller storehouses only having been consumed.

The powder-ships Iris and Montréal had been British frigates; the latter, of 681 tons, was captured by the French in 1779; the former, of 730 tons (originally an American frigate), in 1781. There had been at Toulon a third captured British frigate, the Richmond, of 664 tons; but she was sold or broken up a few months before the British entered the port.

In a French navy-list presented to the National Convention in the preceding March, many of the frigates at Toulon are described as old and unserviceable; their destruction or capture, therefore, was not of any material consequence to either party. Of the fifteen ships brought off by the English, few were worth much to their new masters. The Perle and Aréthuse were fine frigates, and so was the Topaze. Scarcely any of the smaller vessels reached a British port but to be condemned or laid up. Even the Puissant 74 did not quit Portsmouth after she arrived there; and that superb and powerful ship, the Commerce-de-Marseille, never sailed forth as a cruiser in the service of England.

This ship measured 2747 tons. As the Commerce-de-Marseille was the largest, so was she the most beautiful ship that had hitherto been seen; and, notwithstanding her immense size, sailed and worked like a frigate. Her force was precisely that of the 120-gun ship in the table at p. 59, except that none of the ships at Toulon appear to have yet received any carronades. Captain Brenton (vol. iii., p. 153) is therefore decidedly wrong in giving the Commerce-de-Marseille long 18-pounders on the upper deck, and long 12s on the quarter-deck and forecastle; her upper works, indeed, were almost too flimsy to bear 12s and 8s, the establishment of her class.

The Pompée 74 was a remarkably fine ship of 1901 tons, and long remained (she was not broken up until 1817) an ornament to the British navy. The Scipion, also, would have been an acquisition; but in November, while lying at anchor in Leghorn Roads, she caught fire and blew up; happily, however, no lives were lost. Most of the French ships brought off from Toulon were manned wholly (except as to having one British lieutenant) by French royalists. M. Farrand, who commanded the Puissant, received from the British government, for his gallant behaviour in defending his ship against the republican batteries, a pension of 200l. a year.

The following recapitulary table exhibits an amended account of the manner in which the 58 French vessels, which Lord Hood in his despatch states to have been in the road and harbour of Toulon when he arrived there in August, were disposed of at the evacuation of the port in the succeeding December:—

Amended Statement of the Toulon Force, at Lord Hood's Evacuation of the Port, December 18, 1793.

	120	80	74	40	36	32	28	Corvettes.	Total.
Burnt, or otherwise destroyed	-	1	8	1	-	2	-	2	14
Fitted out by the British { serviceable ships	-	-	2	2	1	-	1	3	9
{ unserviceable do.	1	-	1	-	2	-	1	2	7
by the Allies	-	-	-	-	1	-	-	2	3
Total { lost to the French	1	1	11	3	4	2	-	9	33
{ left to the French	1	3	14	1	3	-	-	3	25
Grand total	2	4	25	4	7	2	2	12	58

The frigate Alceste, the single one in the table described as fitted out by the allies, fell to the share of the Sardinians, by whom she was despatched on a cruise. In May, 1794, the Alceste encountered the French 36-gun frigate Boudeuse, and, after a long and well-fought action, was recaptured. The fourteen 74s left to the French include of course the four sent to the Atlantic ports with the refractory seamen.

Important as was the possession of Toulon, both to the commerce and the arms of Great Britain, the preceding details have shown that the place was not abandoned until every effort, on the part of the British at least, had been exerted for its preservation. The extended circumference of the works, their temporary and detached nature, the comparative paucity of the garrison, and its multifarious and discordant character, rendered the whole of the defensive operations peculiarly critical and hazardous. Yet, like other enterprises of fair promise but unfortunate issue, the proceedings at Toulon were found fault with in every stage. The port should have been entered by force of arms, and not by a convention with the disaffected inhabitants; the captured ships should have been manned and sent to England; the town garrisoned by troops upon whom a reliance could be placed; and such of the ships and stores as could not be brought away at the final abandonment of the port should have been wholly, not partially, destroyed.

What could 21 ships of the line with two regiments on board effect against a large and populous town guarded by 21 ships of the line in the port (the four that were fitting are included, as, although not ready to proceed to sea, they might have acted in defence of the harbour) and by formidable land-batteries at all the flanking points of a narrow entrance? The main object was to render the French ships useless to the republic, and that was done by the convention which agreed to their qualified surrender.

Was not Lord Hood, on the very day he was allowed to enter the road of Toulon, joined by a Spanish fleet as powerful as his own? And, admitting the Toulonese had, would Don Juan de Langara have consented that the French ships should be sent to England? Where were to be found men to navigate the prize ships? Lord Hood was compelled, as it was, to hire 1500 Maltese seamen to fill up the deficiencies in his own ships' companies; nor, with the King of Spain for an ally, would it have been politic in the British admiral to have reduced his force to any great extent below that of Don Juan de Langara. It was not possible to foresee the disgraceful defection of the Spanish and Neapolitan troops, nor the refusal on the part of the Emperor of Austria to send the promised 5000 men from Milan.

With respect to reinforcements from England, the capture of Toulon was not known until September; and then, such was the variety of expeditions on foot, and so remote the distance from Toulon, that a sufficient body of troops could scarcely have been assembled in time to have reached the spot previously to the evacuation. The destruction of the ships and magazines might certainly have been more complete; but here again the treachery of the Spaniards, and the pusillanimous flight of the Neapolitans, thwarted the plans of the British; and the only surprise is, that the latter, hurried and pressed as they were, effected as much as they did.

During the time that Toulon remained in possession of the allied forces, a very formidable insurrection existed in Corsica, and General Paoli, the leader of the insurgent party, sought the aid of the English, assuring Lord Hood that even the appearance of a few ships of force off the island would be of the most essential service to the popular cause.

Accordingly, in the month of September, a squadron, composed of the following line-of-battle ships and frigates, sailed from Toulon for Villa-Franca:—

Gun-ship.

74	Alcide	Commodore	Robert Linzee.
		Captain	John Woodley.
	Courageux	,,	John Matthews.
64	Ardent	,,	Robert Manners Sutton.

Gun-frigate.

32	Lowestoffe	,,	William Wolseley.
28	Nemesis	,,	Lord Amelius Beauclerk.

On his arrival off the latter port, Commodore Linzee, in conformity to the orders he had received, sent a letter on shore, containing the account of the restoration of monarchy at Toulon, as well as copies of the proclamations that had been addressed by Lord Hood to the inhabitants of the south of France. To this communication no answer was returned. The commodore then stood across to the island of Corsica, and showed his force off Calvi and San-Fiorenzo; meeting from the respective inhabitants no better reception than he had experienced at Villa-Franca, except that a few of the mountaineers came down and were supplied, at their request, with muskets and ammunition. His offers did not persuade, nor his force intimidate, the garrisons; although accompanied by an assurance that the latter, if desirous, should be conveyed to France.

The orders of the British commodore, in the event of a refusal on the part of the garrisons, were to attempt their reduction by force; or, should that appear too hazardous, to invest the places with his ships, and starve the inhabitants into a compliance. To blockade three such ports as Calvi, San-Fiorenzo, and Bastia, with three line-of-battle ships and two frigates, was impracticable; but Commodore Linzee, having been led to believe that the batteries of San-Fiorenzo could not, on account of the distance, co-operate with the tower and redoubt of Forneilli, situated about two miles in advance of the town, conceived he might make an advantageous attack by sea on that formidable post.

It being necessary, previously to an attack upon Forneilli, to get possession of a tower that commanded the only secure anchorage in the gulf of San-Fiorenzo, the Lowestoffe and Nemesis frigates were detached upon that service. As soon as the Lowestoffe, which in working up to Cape Mortella had got far to windward of her consort, arrived within gunshot of the tower, she opened a fire upon it; then stood out, and, on tacking in again, repeated the fire. Just as the third broadside was about to be bestowed, a boat was seen to quit the shore, and pull in the direction of the town of San-Fiorenzo. Captain Wolseley immediately despatched two boats, with Lieutenants John Gibbs and Francis Charles Annesley and 30 men, to take possession of the tower.

The British landed without opposition; and, although the ladder leading to the entrance, which was by an opening about 20 feet up the wall of the building, had been carried off by the fugitives, the seamen, by means of some spars found on the spot, managed to gain admission. Three long guns, one 24 and two 18 pounders, were found mounted at the top of this extraordinary tower (named Mortella, after its inventor), but the powder had all been thrown into the well. On observing the Lowestoffe's success, the Nemesis bore away to the commodore with the intelligence, and the squadron soon afterwards entered the bay and came to an anchor. Owing, however, to some unexplained cause, Commodore Linzee delayed his attack on Forneilli until the garrison had made such preparations as compelled him to submit to a defeat in the manner we shall proceed to relate.

After failing, owing to the variableness of the wind, in repeated attempts to near the shore, the Ardent, during the night, warped herself into a situation from which she could not only annoy the redoubt, but cover the remainder of the squadron in its approach. On the 1st of October, at 3 h. 30 m. A.M., the Ardent opened her fire. At 4 A.M. the Alcide advanced to her station, but getting too close to the Ardent, and being embarrassed by an unexpected flaw of wind, was with difficulty towed clear of some dangerous rocks. In the meanwhile, the Courageux pushed under the Alcide's stern, and covered her from the fire of the redoubt; against which, both the Courageux and Ardent kept up an unremitting fire. Soon afterwards the Alcide gained a station from which she could act; but, although the three ships continued their efforts until 8 h. 15 m. A.M., no visible effect was produced on the redoubt. The commodore therefore made the signal to discontinue the attack, and the three ships hauled out of gunshot

At this time the Courageux and Ardent, having been unexpectedly opposed to a raking fire from the town of San-Fiorenzo, had borne the brunt of the action (the former had been four times on fire by hot shot), were a good deal damaged, and had sustained a loss, the one, of her first-lieutenant (Ludlow Shiells) and one seaman (in the act of cutting a red-hot shot out of the ship's side) killed, and her second-lieutenant (William Henry Daniel) and 12 seamen wounded; the other, of one midshipman (John Martin) and 13 seamen killed, and 17 seamen wounded. The Alcide, having failed in her efforts to close, had sustained but a slight damage in hull, masts, or rigging. A 24-pound shot fell into the cutter as she was towing the ships clear of the rocks, and went through the bottom, but did not hurt a man. Soon afterwards, a red-hot shot struck the Alcide's ninth lower-deck port from forward, carried it away, came in on the lower deck, broke the sweep, and fell on the after-grating. One of the sailors, with a wet swab, took it up, and threw it overboard. The Alcide's loss amounted to only nine seamen wounded, three of them mortally. The enemy's force consisted of one 4, two 8, and thirteen 24-pounder guns, nine of which were mounted at the town, and six heavy mortars. The failure was attributed partly to a mistake as to the range of those nine 24-pounders, and to a want of co-operation on the part of General Paoli's adherents, who had undertaken, simultaneously with the attack from the sea, to storm the posts from the land; but the chief cause of the failure, undoubtedly, was the tardiness of Commodore Linzee in commencing the attack.

While the British fleet lay at Toulon, Lord Hood occasionally sent small detachments in quest of the remaining ships of the Toulon fleet, still, according to information received, cruising in the Mediterranean seas. On the morning of the 5th of October the British 74-gun ships Bedford, Captain Robert Mann, and Captain, Captain Samuel Reeve, with the 14-gun brig-sloop Speedy, Captain Charles Cunningham, arriving on this mission off the port of Genoa, discovered lying within the mole the French 36-gun frigate Modeste, likewise two armed tartans, vessels that generally carry two long 12-pounders as prow-guns, and two long 6-pounders abaft, with a complement of about 70 men.

The French factions at Leghorn and Genoa, by their sway over the inhabitants, having entirely changed the character of those ports, and repeated remonstrances on the subject having been made in vain by Lord Hervey, the British minister at

Leghorn, it was resolved, by a council of British naval officers, that, notwithstanding the assumed neutrality of the port, they would seize the French frigate and tartans.

Accordingly the ships stood in, and the Bedford warped herself close to the frigate. Early in the afternoon, she having veered her cable, dropped close alongside of, and boarded the Modeste. The crew, 275 in number, making some opposition to the striking of their colours, were fired on by the Bedford's marines, and lost, in consequence, one man killed, and eight wounded. Several of the French sailors leaped overboard, but were saved by the boats of the Captain, as she approached the frigate on the opposite side.

The Speedy's boats, in the meanwhile, boarded the two tartans, one of which, being strongly manned, slightly resisted; whereby her principal officer and one of her seamen were wounded. None of the British were hurt in either attack. The Modeste and tartans were brought safe off, and the frigate was purchased for the use of the British navy.

It being ascertained that another French ship, the 38-gun frigate Impérieuse, was lying in Spezzia bay, situated about a degree to the eastward of Genoa, the Captain 74 proceeded thither in search of her. On the afternoon of the 11th the Captain reached the entrance of the cove in which the Impérieuse had run for shelter, and, early on the following morning, the 12th, was towed in and moored close to the French frigate, as well as to the battery of Santa Maria. At 8 A.M. the Captain's boats, without any opposition from the fort, boarded and took possession of the frigate, which they found had been scuttled and abandoned by her crew. In the course of that and the following day, the British succeeded in weighing the Impérieuse; and the latter, under the name of Unité (there being an Impérieuse already in the service), became a fine 36-gun frigate in the service of her captors.

Light Squadrons and Single Ships.

Although Brest, Lorient, Rochefort, and Toulon, until the recent enlargement of Cherbourg, were the only ports in which France usually did, or perhaps conveniently could, construct and equip her ships of the line, yet there were many other ports, such as Havre, Cherbourg, St. Malo, Nantes, Bordeaux, and a few others, from which she sent out, singly, and in squadrons, frigates of a very superior class to make reprisals upon the commerce of her enemies, and prevent, if possible, any similar depredations upon her own. From those ports, also, issued forth innumerable private-armed vessels; some of which, belonging to Bordeaux, equalled frigates in size and force. It is under the head of "Light (that is, frigate) squadrons and single ships," that we purpose to notice, as far as our researches will enable us, every case, in which vessels, other than a fleet of line-of-battle ships (their movements falling under a preceding head), meet and engage; or between which, from the relative situation of the parties, as to force and other circumstances, an action might reasonably have been expected. Deeming it unnecessary that the locality, or site, of the different encounters should interfere with their chronological order, we shall, in this head of narrative, take the date only as our guide.

On the 13th of March, the British 16-gun brig-sloop Scourge, Captain George Brisac (but mounting then only eight 6-pounders, with a crew of 70 out of her complement of 90 men and boys), being a few leagues to the westward of Scilly, fell in with, and after a three hours' action captured, the French privateer Sans-Culotte, of 12 guns (eight long 8-pounders, and four English carronades, 12-pounders), with a complement of 81 men; of whom nine were killed, and 20 wounded, the Scourge escaping with only one man killed, and one wounded.

England herself appears to have been the first to commence active operations on shore, in the war declared against her by France. Early in the month of March, 3000 of the foot-guards, under the command of His Royal Highness the Duke of York, were sent to assist, conjointly with a large body of Hanoverians and Hessians, the loyal portion of the inhabitants of Holland in expelling the French from their country. Fortunately for our labours, we have only to record so much of the details as will exhibit a successful instance of the gallantry of British seamen.

On the night of the 15th of March, a detachment from the crew of the British 32-gun frigate Syren, Captain John Manley (who commanded the small squadron that formed the naval part of the expedition), lying at anchor at the Maese, off the Dyke, embarked, under the orders of Lieutenant John Western, on board of three gun-boats, and, taking advantage of the calm and fog that prevailed, pulled across to the French forts, five in number, which had been erected to bombard Willemstadt, a fortress situated on a small island in the Hollands Diep, about 30 miles east of Helvoetsluys. So animated and destructive a fire was kept up by the British, that their force became trebled in the eyes of the French, and the latter abandoned their works and fled.

The Governor of Willemstadt, the brave General Count Boetzelaer, having had no intimation of the intended attack in his behalf, was surprised at the firing, and received Lieutenant Western on his landing the next morning with heartfelt thanks. The latter, in the course of the day, was gratified at seeing the Dutch soldiers enter the town, with the cannon which he and his little party had compelled the French to abandon.

On the 21st, as this enterprising young officer was in the act of levelling one of the 12-pounders in his gun-boat, against the enemy's intrenched camp at the Noord post on the Moordyke, a musket-ball passed through his head. On the 24th the Duke of York attended the remains of Lieutenant Western (the first British officer, as it appears, who lost his life in the war) to the church of Dordrecht, and ordered a monument, with a suitable inscription, to be erected to his memory.

The subsequent events of the year, in Holland and the Netherlands, were wholly of a military nature; except that, on the 31st of October, a British squadron, composed of two frigates, a sloop, and a floating-battery (the Redoubt, mounting twenty 68-pounder carronades), under the orders of Rear-admiral John Macbride, in the 32-gun frigate Quebec, successfully co-operated with a detachment of the British army, commanded by General Sir Charles Grey, in expelling the French from the important posts of Ostende and Nieuport, and compelling them to retire upon Dunkerque.

Painful would be the task of recording an interchange of destructive firing between two ships of one and the same nation: it is not, however, to confirm, but to contradict, a statement of the kind, that the names of two English ships are here introduced. A work, which, being ostensibly written by a naval officer, ought to be of very high accreditation on naval subjects, contains the following statement: "On the night of the 11th of April (1793), the Bedford, of 74 guns, Captain Robert Mann, and Leopard, of 50 guns, Captain John Maude, fell in with each other off Scilly: the night being extremely dark, they either mistook or did not distinctly see each other's signals, and commenced a smart action. Unfortunately, the mistake was not discovered until several men were wounded on both sides."[1]

The fact is, that neither ship was off Scilly on the night in question; nor were the two ships within several hundred leagues

[1] Schomberg, vol. ii., p. 231.

of each other. Neither did they at any other time, or at any other place, exchange a shot. It is ascertained, also, that the Bedford, and it is believed that the Leopard, never had such an accident befal her. Moreover, no traces can be found of any two English ships of war having met and engaged, out of which a statement, so discreditable to both, could possibly have arisen.

On the 14th of April, in latitude 41° 43' north longitude 25° west, the British squadron under Rear-admiral Gell, already mentioned as bound to the Mediterranean, and which consisted of the

Gun-ship.
98 St. George . . { Rear-admiral (b.) John Gell, Captain Thomas Foley,
74 { Ganges . . „ Anth. Jas. Pye Molloy,
Edgar . . „ Albermarle Bertie,
Egmont . . „ Archibald Dickson,
Gun-frigate.
38 Phaëton . . „ Andrew Snape Douglas,

chased two sail in the north-west. The frigate soon overtook one of them, which proved to be the San-Iago, a large Spanish galleon, under French colours. Dropping a boat as she passed, the Phaëton left this vessel to be taken possession of by the Ganges, then coming up, and stood on in pursuit of the headmost enemy's ship. At the end of two hours the latter was also captured, and proved to be the French privateer General-Dumourier, of 22 long 6-pounders and 196 men, convoying to a port of France the richly-laden ship, which, eleven days before, her commander and crew had considered themselves so fortunate in having fallen in with.

For greater security, the Dumourier had since transhipped to herself 680 cases, containing each 3000 dollars, together with several packages, of the reputed value, in the whole, of upwards of 200,000*l.* sterling. The galleon was from Lima, bound to Spain, and had on board a cargo of an immense value. Both the Dumourier and San-Iago arrived, before the end of the month, in safety at Plymouth; and the latter ship and her precious lading, after a tedious litigation, were condemned as prize to the captors. This condemnation of a recaptured ship, however it might have been legally correct under the peculiar circumstances of the case, caused a great stir at Madrid, and was one of the principal causes of the war which afterwards broke out between Great Britain and Spain.

On the 13th of May, at 5 P.M., latitude 42° 34' north, and longitude 13° 12' west, the British 12-pounder 32-gun frigate

Iris[1] Captain George Lumsdaine, while standing to the southward, with the wind at north-north-east, discovered a strange sail in the north-east quarter. The Iris immediately hauled to the wind, and gave chase. At 6 P.M. she hove-to for the strange ship, which appeared to be a French national frigate. At 6 h. 30 m. P.M. an action commenced, and continued, without interruption, until 8 P.M.; when the Citoyenne-Française, as the stranger proved to be, hauled on board her fore and main tacks, and shot ahead, clear of her opponent's guns. At 8 h. 15 m. P.M., just as the Iris was about to make sail in pursuit, her foremast, main topmast, and mizenmast went over the side. On seeing this, the Citoyenne-Française, whose masts, though much cut by shot, were all standing, hauled to the wind, and escaped.

After a contest in which neither ship had been captured, each usually parts in uncertainty as to the name, if not the force, of her late antagonist. Such was the case here. On the arrival of the Iris, in five days afterwards, at Gibraltar, it was reported that the ship which she had engaged was the French 36-gun frigate Médée, belonging to Toulon. The plausibility of the statement having gained it credence at Gibraltar, sent it, stripped of every mark of doubt, to England. Here it appeared in the London journals as a positive fact, with the addition, that the Médée had arrived, in a shattered state, at Bordeaux.[2] Captain Schomberg, also, in his "Naval Chronology" (vol. ii.,

[1] Class *H* in the first Annual Abstract. As the force of British frigates will be frequently referred to, we have here drawn up a table of the long guns established upon the different classes, preserving the same letters of reference as are used in the Annual Abstracts.

Class in the Annual Abstracts.	Main Deck.	Qr. deck.	Forecastle.	Total Guns.	Net Complement.
		No. Pds.	No. Pds.	No. Pds.		
Z. and A.	38 gun frig.	28 18	6 9	4 9	38	277
B. and C.	36 ,,	26 ,,	6 ,,	4 ,,	36	257
D.	,, ,,	26 12	6 6	4 6	,,	247
E. and F.	32 ,,	26 18	4 9	2 9	32	257
G. and H.	,, ,,	26 12	4 6	2 6	,,	217
I.	28 ,,	24 9	4 ,,	- -	28	197

It will be remarked that classes Z. A. and C. have ten 9s upon their quarter-deck and forecastle, instead of eight 9s and two 12s, as in the first Annual Abstract. The fact is, the 12s were exchanged for 9s soon after they were ordered. This, however, is of little consequence, as the introduction of carronades effected an entire change in the quarter-deck and forecastle armament of almost every ship in the British navy.

[2] A large drawing in oil was made of the action, and one of the combatants is the French "frigate Médée." Had the picture not remained in the possession of the gentleman for whom it was taken, the windows of the different print-shops in the metropolis would have given additional currency to the mistake.

p. 253), has introduced the action of the Iris and Médée, as one about the existence of which there never had been the slightest doubt.

It nowhere appears in the French journals, that the Médée had any engagement in 1793, or ever anchored in the River Bordeaux: she was either in, or on her way to the West Indies. On the other hand, the letter of a citizen Vincent represents, that on the same day, hour, and place, as, according to the Iris's log, that ship engaged a French frigate, the Citoyenne-Française, a French frigate also, except as to ownership,[1] engaged an English frigate, mounting the same number of guns as the Iris. The two accounts agree tolerably well, as to the duration of the action, and the relative position in reference to the wind, of the combatants. Nor is it very difficult to conceive, that citizen Rigal should have mistaken the Iris's marines, in their red coats, for "troops;"[2] nor that citizen Vincent, when ready to commit to paper the oral communication of citizen Rigal, should write "beaupré" instead of "mât d'artimon." Moreover, the Citoyenne-Française did actually arrive at Bordeaux in a shattered state, as was said of the Iris's opponent. Under all the circumstances, therefore, we may consider it as proved, beyond a doubt, that the Citoyenne-Française, and not the Médée, was the ship engaged by the Iris.

Out of 217 men and boys (admitting her net complement to have been on board), the Iris lost four seamen killed, her first-lieutenant, master (Mr. Magee, mortally), and 30 seamen and marines wounded. The complement of the Citoyenne-Française could not have been less than 250 men and boys; of whom she appears to have lost Captain Dubedat, and 15 officers, seamen, and marines, killed, and 37 wounded. The ship, it is probable, had been one of the 32-gun frigates sold out of the French service at the reduction in 1783; several of which carried 12 and 8 pounders on the main deck, and measured from 800 to 850 tons: the Iris measured 688 tons.

Coupling, with so equal a force as evidently existed between these two frigates, the extent of the damage and loss sustained by the British frigate, we must admit that the officers and crew of the French ship deserve credit for the precision of their fire. Had they been as resolute in continuing, as they were bold in commencing, the action, the crippled state of the Iris renders it doubtful on which side victory would have ultimately perched

---

[1] The one belonging to the nation; the other to a private individual. [2] See Appendix, No. 7.

The affair not reaching that crisis, the Citoyenne-Française hauled up, singly, for the nearest French port, and the Iris resumed her course before the wind; the latter much indebted, no doubt, to a continuance of the favourable weather for arriving in safety at Gibraltar, the port of her destination.

On the 27th of May, at about 1 A.M., Cape Finisterre bearing south, 58° east, distant 125 leagues, the British 12-pounder 32-gun frigate Venus, Captain Jonathan Faulknor, and the French 36-gun frigate Sémillante, mounting 40 guns,[2] Captain Gaillard, descried each other. At 3 h. 30 m. A.M. the Venus tacked; and at 4 A.M. the Sémillante, having bore down to reconnoitre the stranger, passed to windward of her. The Sémillante soon afterwards hoisted a blue flag on the mizen-peak, and fired two guns to leeward, in quick succession. Upon this, the Venus hoisted her colours, and returned a shot to one which the Sémillante had just before fired to try her adversary's distance. At 4 h. 30 m. A.M. the Sémillante tacked for the Venus, who kept her wind, and carried sail to get the weathergage; but the former, unwilling to give up that advantage, also kept her wind. At 7 h. 30 m. A.M. the Sémillante fired a few random shot, and at 8 A.M. dropped nearer to the Venus; when the latter opened her fire, and a warm cannonade ensued. The two ships gradually neared each other until 10 A.M., when they were scarcely half a cable's length asunder.

The Sémillante, by this time, had lost her first and second officers, and had her masts, yards, sails, rigging, and hull much damaged by shot; and her guns, for the last half-hour had made no return to the vivid fire kept up by the Venus. In this state, the Sémillante, very naturally, strove to disengage herself from the combat. On observing her opponent's intention, the Venus trimmed her sails as well as she was able, and, ranging up alongside, gave the Sémillante a well-shotted broadside; then dropped a little astern, and was in the act of again shooting a-head to repeat her fire, when she discovered to leeward a large ship under French colours. The Sémillante, as if recognizing the stranger, bore up to join her; while the Venus, whose cross-jack yard,

---

[1] This ship's name does not again appear, except as having captured a British merchantman towards the end of 1794. She is then called "la frégate la Citoyenne Française." — *Moniteur*, 12 Dec. 1794. This strengthens the supposition that she had once belonged to the national marine.

[2] Armed precisely as No. 7 in the table at p. 59. In the first edition of this work we had classed all these ships as 32-gun frigates, according to their original denomination in the French service; but, finding that almost every one of them at the commencement of the war of 1793 took on board four additional 6-pounders, these ships here stand classed as 36s; in which we are borne out by most of the lists published in French works.

gaff, and main rigging, were entirely shot away, and whose masts, yards, sails, and rigging in general were much cut and injured, hauled as close to the wind as her crippled state would permit. Thus ended the action; and at that moment, according to the testimony of the master of an English merchantman, who was then on board the Sémillante, the latter had five feet water in her hold.

As a British 32-gun frigate, the Venus was an anomaly in point of armament, mounting 24 instead of 26 long 12-pounders on the main deck; which, with eight long 6-pounders and six carronades, 18-pounders, on the quarter-deck and forecastle, gave her a total of 38 guns. Her complement, excluding the Widow's men, was 231, fourteen more than the establishment of her class. Not having a marine on board, and being 20 seamen short, the Venus commenced action with only 192 men and boys. Of these she had two seamen killed, her master, and 19 seamen wounded. The loss on board the Sémillante (whose force has already been stated), out of a crew of at least 300, amounted to 12 officers, seamen, and marines, killed, and 20 wounded.

Some accounts represented the Venus's opponent to have been either the Engageant or the Proserpine; the one a 12, the other an 18 pounder frigate.[1] But such statements, however plausible, rested on no better foundation than rumour. A letter, extracted from the Moniteur of June 8, 1793, identifies the Sémillante, beyond all doubt, as the ship engaged by the Venus.[2]

Comparative Force of the Combatants.

		Venus.	Sémillante.
Broadside-guns	No.	19	20
	lbs.	222	279
Crew	No.	192	300
Size	tons	722	940

Making some allowance for the disparity in point of crew, we may consider these as a tolerably well-matched[3] pair of combatants; and it undoubtedly was a well-fought battle. Had the second French ship (for, although the French commander's letter mentions no strange vessel, yet the fact being noted in the log-book of the Venus, does not admit a doubt), and which ship was subsequently ascertained to have been the 36-gun frigate

---

[1] Schomberg's Naval Chronol., vol. ii., p. 232, and Gold's Naval Chronicle, vol. i., p 219.
[2] See Appendix, No. 8.
[3] In calling these ships *well-matched*, Mr. James does not do ample justice to Captain Faulknor or his brave crew, by the statement above; the French threw a heavier broadside by 57 lbs., had 108 men more than the English, and the Sémillante was the more powerful ship by 220 tons —*Editor*.

Cléopâtre, Captain Jean Mullon, delayed her appearance for about half an hour, the probability is, that the Sémillante, having suffered most in the action, would have become the prize of the Venus. The Cléopâtre crowded sail after the latter; but the Venus being far to windward, and having a smooth sea and a commanding breeze, got clear off; rejoining, at 3 P.M. on the 29th, her consort, the 36-gun frigate Nymphe, from whom, two days previous to the action, she had parted company in chase.

The following account of the meeting between the Hyæna and Concorde is extracted from Captain Schomberg's naval work: "In May, the Hyæna, of 24 guns, and 160 men, commanded by Captain William Hargood, being on a cruise off Hispaniola, fell in with La Concorde, French frigate, of 40 guns and 320 men. After a severe and spirited conflict, in which the Hyæna was dreadfully shattered, her first-lieutenant, and many of her crew, killed and wounded, Captain Hargood was obliged to surrender."[1]

The Hyæna being a ship of no more than 522 tons, mounting twenty-two long 9-pounders on her main deck, and two long 6-pounders, and six or eight ill-constructed useless carronades, 12-pounders, on her quarter-deck and forecastle, with a complement (she being on the peace establishment) of only 120 men and boys, while the Concorde was a regular French 40-gun frigate, mounting, like No. 5 in the table at p. 59, 44 guns in all, an obstinate resistance, on the part of the former, would have reflected the highest honour on the officers and crew of the British vessel; but, unfortunately, Captain Schomberg's account is erroneous in all the more important particulars. The circumstances of the case were these. On the 27th of May, early in the morning, when about two miles off Cape Tiburon, the Hyæna was discovered and chased by the Concorde, the advanced frigate of a French squadron, composed of the Eole and American 74s, and three or four frigates, some of which then, or very soon afterwards, were in sight from the Hyæna's masthead. As soon as she discovered the character of her pursuers, the Hyæna put before a light air of wind, but, being unable to make way against a heavy head sea, was rapidly gained upon. As the Concorde approached her on the quarter, the Hyæna fired a few of her main-deck guns, and then, without waiting, it would appear, to receive any fire in return, hauled down her colours to the French frigate.

[1] Schomberg, vol. ii., p. 257.

On the 11th of October, 1793, on board the Cambridge guardship, in Hamoaze, Captain Hargood and his officers were tried by a court-martial, and honourably acquitted; the sentence stating, that "every means had been used to prevent the Hyæna from being captured." In the first edition of this work, it was not mentioned that the Concorde was the advanced ship of a squadron. Two circumstances led to that omission: the neglect of Sir William Hargood to transmit the promised "particulars of the action and cause of the capture of his Majesty's ship Hyæna," and the very imperfect information furnished by a subordinate at a public office, even after he had received from his chief the most positive directions to make a full extract from the official document in his charge.

On the 17th of June the British 12-pounder 36-gun frigate Nymphe, Captain Edward Pellew, sailed from Falmouth on a cruise. Having, in his way up the Channel, arrived nearly abreast of the Start point, Captain Pellew ran out to the southward in the hope of falling in with one of the two French frigates which, a week or two before, the Nymphe and Venus had chased into Cherbourg, and which were known to be the Cléopâtre and Sémillante, already noticed in the action between the latter and the Venus. On the next day, the 18th, at 3 h. 30 m. A.M., the Start point bearing east by north, distant five or six leagues, a sail was discovered in the south-east quarter. At 4 A.M. the Nymphe bore up in chase under all sail; the stranger, which, by a singular coincidence, was the French frigate Cléopâtre, carrying a press of canvas, either to get away or to prepare for action.

At 5 A.M., finding that the Nymphe had the advantage in sailing, the Cléopâtre hauled up her foresail and lowered her topgallantsails, bravely awaiting the coming up of her opponent. At about 6 A.M., the Nymphe approaching near, the Cléopâtre hailed her; but Captain Pellew, not hearing distinctly what was said, replied only by the usual "Hoa! hoa!"[1] an exclamation instantaneously followed by three cheers from the crew of the Nymphe. Captain Mullon, upon this, came to the gangway, and, waving his hat, exclaimed, "Vive la nation!" and the crew

[1] Osler, in his Life of Captain Pellew (the first Lord Exmouth), gives the following account of this extraordinary rencontre: "At six o'clock the ships were so near that the captains mutually hailed. Not a shot had yet been fired. The crew of the Nymphe now shouted 'Long live King George,' and gave three hearty cheers. Captain Mullon was seen to address his crew briefly, holding a cap of liberty, which he waved before them. They answered with acclamation, shouting, 'Vive la république.' The cap of liberty was then given to a sailor, who ran up the main rigging and screwed it on the masthead."

of the Cléopâtre, at the same time, put forth a sound which was meant for an imitation of the cheers of the British.

At 6 h. 15 m. A.M., the Nymphe having reached a position from which her foremost guns would bear on the starboard quarter of the Cléopâtre, Captain Pellew, whose hat, like that of the French captain, was still in his hand, raised it to his head, the preconcerted signal for the Nymphe's artillery to open. A furious action now commenced, the two frigates still running before the wind, within rather less than hailing distance of each other. At about 6 h. 30 m. the Cléopâtre suddenly hauled up eight points from the wind; and, before 7 A.M., her mizenmast (about 12 feet above the deck) and her wheel were shot away.

In consequence of this double disaster the French frigate, at about 7 A.M., paid round off, and shortly afterwards fell on board of her antagonist, her jib-boom passing between the Nymphe's fore and main masts, and pressing so hard against the head of the already wounded mainmast, that it was expected every instant to fall; especially as the main and spring stays had both been shot away. Fortunately, however, for the Nymphe, the jib-boom of her adversary was carried away and her own mainmast preserved.

After this, the two frigates fell alongside, head and stern, but were still held fast, the Cléopâtre's larboard maintopmast-studdingsail boom-iron having hooked the larboard leech-rope of the Nymphe's maintopsail. Here again was danger to the mainmast. In an instant a maintopman named Burgess sprang aloft and cut away the leech-rope from the end of the main-yard; and, as an additional means of getting the ships apart, Lieutenant Pellowe, by Captain Pellew's orders, cut away the best bower anchor.

During these important operations no relaxation had occurred on the part of the British at least, in the main purpose for which the two ships had met. Soon after they had come in contact in the manner we have related, the Cléopâtre was gallantly boarded by a portion of the Nymphe's crew; one man of whom, at 7 h. 10 m. A.M., hauled down the republican colours, after the action had continued 50 minutes.[1] The firing now ceased, and it was just as the last of 150 prisoners had been removed into the Nymphe that the two ships separated.[2]

---

[1] Captain Pellew, in a letter to his brother, says, "We dished her up in 50 minutes."

[2] Mr. James has not given the account of this action with his accustomed accuracy, and leaves the reader to imagine that it was not till long after the Cléopâtre had run stern on to the Nymphe that she was boarded and carried by the English. Mr. Osler, whose work is compiled from

In order to render more intelligible our details of the manœuvres of the combatants in this celebrated frigate-action, we here subjoin an explanatory diagram:—

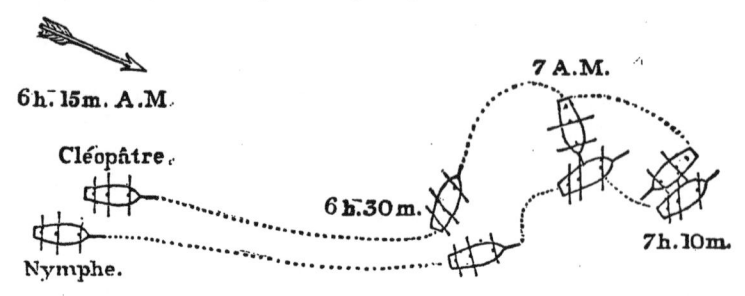

The Nymphe mounted the same main-deck guns as *D.* in the table at p. 101, with two long 6-pounders and eight carronades, 24-pounders, on the quarter-deck and forecastle; total, 40 guns.[1] The loss on board the Nymphe was tolerably severe. Out of a crew of 240, men and boys, she had her boatswain (Tobias James), one master's mate (Richard Pearse), three midshipmen (George Boyd, John Davie, and Samuel Edfall), 14 seamen, and four private marines killed, her second-lieutenant (George Luke), two midshipmen (John A. Norway and John Plaine), one lieutenant of marines (John Whittaker), 17 seamen, and 6 private marines wounded; total, 23 killed and 27 wounded.

The loss on board the Cléopâtre, in killed and wounded together, out of a crew, as certified by her surviving officers, of 320, men and boys, amounted to 63. Among the wounded were included the ship's three lieutenants, and among her killed was the truly gallant Captain Mullon. A round shot had torn open his back and carried away the greater part of his left hip. It is related that, having the list of coast-signals adopted by the

---

Lord Exmouth's own notes, gives the following account: "The Cléopâtre (from the loss of her mizen-mast and wheel) being thus rendered unmanageable, came round with her bow to the Nymphe's broadside, her jib-boom pressing hard against the main-mast. Captain Pellew, supposing that the enemy were going to board, ordered the boarders to be called to repel them; but the disabled state of the Cléopâtre was soon evident, and he at once gave orders to board her. *Immediately* the boarders rushed on the forecastle, a division of them, headed by Mr. Ball, boarding through the main-deck ports, fought their way along the gangways to the quarter-deck. The republicans, though much superior in numbers, could not resist the impetuosity of the attack. At 10 minutes past 7 they had all fled below or submitted, and the pendant of the Cléopâtre was hauled down." —*Osler's Life of Exmouth*, p. 85.

[1] [It is twice stated by James that the Nymphe had 40 guns, but he specifies only 36, viz. 26 + 2 + 8. Comparing her with other vessels of that size and date, it seems evident that her actual force was 26 twelves, 6 sixes, and 8 24-pounder carronades, total 40 guns; and 270 lbs., not 322 lbs., of broadside force.—H. Y. POWELL.]

French in one of his pockets,[1] Captain Mullon, during his short agonies, drew forth a paper, which he imagined was the right one (but which really was not), and died biting it to pieces. Here was a trait of heroism! And yet no French writer, as far as we can discover, has recorded the fact.

Comparative Force of the Combatants.

		Nymphe.	Cléopâtre.
Broadside-guns	No.	20	20
	lbs.	322	286
Crew	No.	240	320
Size	tons.	938	913

The Cléopâtre was armed the same as her classmate, No. 7, in the table at p. 59, except in having 28 instead of 26 long 12s, and eight instead of ten long 6-pounders.

The British vessel, according to this statement, possessed, in aggregate weight of metal, nearly the same force; but in number of men she was a fourth inferior. If length of service and nautical experience are to be taken into the account, the odds were in favour of the Cléopâtre, her crew having been upwards of a twelvemonth in commission, while the crew of the Nymphe had been very recently assembled, and that without any opportunity of selection. Still, the numbers 50 and 63 for the killed and wounded of the two crews show that in practical gunnery they were nearly upon a par; and both combatants displayed throughout the contest an equal share of bravery and determination.[2]

On the 21st the Nymphe arrived at Portsmouth with her prize, and on the 29th Captain Edward Pellew, along with his brother, Captain Israel Pellew, who happened to be on board the Nymphe during the action, were introduced by the Earl of Chatham to George III. His late majesty was thereupon pleased to confer on one brother the honour of knighthood, and on the other the rank of post-captain. The Nymphe's first-lieutenant, Amherst Morris, received also from the Board of Admiralty the step that was his due; and the second and third lieutenants, George Luke and Richard Pellowe, appear likewise to have distinguished themselves. The Cléopâtre, being a fine little frigate, was purchased by the British government; and, under the name of Oiseau (a Cleopatra being already in the service), became a cruising 36 of the 12-pounder class.

---

[1] Osler mentions that this gallant French officer took out his *commission* by mistake, and expired in the act of devouring it.

[2] It is seldom we read in a Paris newspaper a paragraph announcing the capture of a French ship of war, couched in such terms as these: "Les Anglais nous ont enlevé dernièrement la superbe frégate la Cléopâtre. Elle a été prise par une frégate d'égale force."—*Abréviateur Universel,* Juillet 16, 1793.

Towards the end of July the British 12-pounder 32-gun frigate Boston, Captain George William Augustus Courtenay, cruised off New York, in the hopes of intercepting the French 36-gun frigate Embuscade,[1] Captain (de vais.[2]) Jean-Baptiste-François Bompart, lying at anchor in that harbour; and who during her last cruise had captured or destroyed upwards of 60 British vessels. On the appearance of the Boston off the port, Captain Bomparte mistook her for the Concorde, a frigate under his orders then cruising in those seas. He accordingly sent his first-lieutenant (a Bostonian by birth) and a boat's crew of 12 men, with orders to the commander of the supposed Concorde to proceed immediately in quest of a certain pirate-ship, and, on capturing her, to hang the whole crew. As he approached the Boston, the American doubted, from the neat appearance of her rigging, whether or not she was a French ship: he lay on his oars awhile, until the master of a pilot-boat that had come alongside assured him she was a French man of war, he having passed under her stern and seen none but French sailors on board.

The fact is, that Captain Courtenay, desirous to deceive both the French captain and the Americans (whose communicativeness he knew) as to the national character of his ship, had placed upon the quarter-deck those among his officers and crew that spoke a little French; and the loud jabbering of these, as they hung over the taffrail, produced its full effect upon the Americans in the pilot-boat. Lieutenant Whitynow, satisfied that the ship in sight was the one he was in search of, pulled straight towards her, and, with his men, was made a prisoner.

On Captain Courtenay's expressing to the lieutenant of the Embuscade a desire to meet that ship at sea, the latter assured him of Captain Bompart's readiness to accede to his wishes, and promised that, if Captain Courtenay would allow him to write to his captain by the pilot-boat then in sight, the Embuscade, in the course of a few hours, should be outside the Hook. This was done, and Captain Courtenay sent at the same time a verbal

---

[1] Armed precisely as No. 7 in the table at p. 59, except in having two instead of four brass carronades. The Embuscade has been described (Brenton's Nav. Hist., vol. i., p. 460) as a "French frigate of the large class, or what was called an 18-pound ship." Captain Brenton's mistake, as we shall hereafter show, arose from the inaccuracy of an official despatch.

[2] It appears necessary to mark this distinction, it not being customary in the French as in the British navy, to assign one order of captains to the command of post-ships and another to the command of sloops of war. With the French, a "capitaine de vaisseau," or captain of a ship of the line, frequently, as in the case of M. Bompart, commands a frigate; but it is not the general practice (indeed we are not aware of an instance, except occasionally in a flag-ship) for a "capitaine de frégate" to command a ship of the line.

message to Captain Bompart, proposing to meet the Embuscade, and stating that the Boston would wait for her three days. The pilot-master, being scrupulous about delivering the message, caused a written copy of it to be posted up in one of the public coffee-rooms of the city. It soon reached the French captain; and the Embuscade, after a council of the officers had been called, got under weigh, and stood out to sea.

On the afternoon of the 30th, while the Boston was anxiously awaiting the expected rencontre, 12 sail appeared in the south-east; and which, according to the report of the Embuscade's lieutenant, were a French squadron of two 74-gun ships (Eole and America), four frigates, and six corvettes, bound to New York from Port-au-Prince, but last from the Chesapeake. At sunset they were distant about ten miles, and soon afterwards disappeared from the Boston, who at this time was about four leagues off the Long Island shore. The presence of a formidable French squadron was not very flattering to Captain Courtenay's hopes, let his combat end as it might; however, he stood pledged to give the meeting, and was resolved, as we shall presently see, not to degrade the flag under which he served.

On the 31st, at 3 A.M., a ship, apparently large, was descried coming down before the wind, in the direction of north-east by east. The Boston immediately cleared for action. At 3 h. 30 m. A.M. the strange ship passed about three miles and a half to windward, making signals with false fires. At 3h. 50 m. A.M. the ship was discovered to be a frigate, under French national colours. The Boston now hoisted the same colours; whereupon the stranger ran up at her peak a blue flag with a white cross, and thus made herself known as the Embuscade.

At 4 A.M. the latter wore to the eastward, and the Boston set her mainsail; as did also the Embuscade. At 4 h. 45 m. A.M. the Boston tacked, hauled up her mainsail, hauled down the French, and hoisted English colours; and was passed by the Embuscade, at about a mile and a half distance. At 5 A.M. the Boston again tacked; when the Embuscade bore up, and at 5 h. 5 m. A.M. ranged along the former's larboard and weather side. The Boston thereupon fired her larboard guns; which were promptly answered by the starboard ones of the Embuscade, as the latter lay with her main topsail to the mast. The Boston then wore, and, on coming to on the starboard tack, laid her main topsail to the mast also; and an animated fire was kept up by both ships. At this time the high land of Neversink, in the Jerseys, bore north-west, distant four leagues.

At 5 h. 20 m. A.M. the cross-jack yard of the Boston was shot away; and at 5 h. 45 m. A.M. her jib and foretopmast staysail, with the stays themselves, as well as all the braces and bowlines, met the same fate; consequently, she had no further command of those sails. At 6 h. 10 m. A.M. her maintopmast, and the yard with it, fell over on the larboard side, and the mizen derrick was shot away. At 6 h. 20 m. A.M. Captain Courtenay, and Lieutenant James Edward Butler, of the marines, while standing at the fore-part of the quarter-deck, were killed by the same cannon-ball. At this time, too, the mizen, mizen topmast, and mizen staysail were shot away; the mizen-mast was also expected, every moment, to go by the board, and the only two lieutenants, John Edwards and Alexander Robert Kerr, were below, wounded; the latter with the temporary loss of sight in one, and with total blindness in the other, of his eyes, and the former by a contusion in the head, which rendered him senseless. At 6 h. 40 m. A.M., finding that the crew were in some confusion for the want of officers to give orders, Lieutenant Edwards, although still suffering greatly from the stunning effects of his wound, came on deck, and took command of the ship.

At 6 h. 40 m. A.M. the Embuscade dropped a little astern, with the view of putting an end to the battle at once, by a raking fire; and which the Boston, having no use of her sails, with difficulty wore round in time to avoid. On coming to on the larboard tack, the Boston could not use many of her guns, because the wreck of the main topmast lay over them. Thus circumstanced, with her principal officers dead or disabled, the British frigate put before the wind, under all the sail she could set; and at 7 h. 7 m. A.M. the Embuscade, who, to all appearance, was nearly as crippled as herself, stood after her. At 8 A.M., however, when about four miles off, the French frigate brought to with her head to the eastward, and was soon lost sight of by the Boston.

Besides the long-gun establishment of her class, as particularised at *H.* in the table at p. 101, the Boston mounted six of those useless *monkey-tailed* 12-pounder carronades; making her guns in all 38. Her net complement was 217 men and boys; but, having sent away in a prize her third-lieutenant and 12 seamen, she had actually on board no more than 204. Out of this number, she lost her gallant commander, the lieutenant of marines, and eight seamen and marines killed, her two remaining lieutenants (already named), one master's mate, two midshipmen (whose names we are unable to give), and 19 seamen and marines (the chief of them badly) wounded ; total, 10 killed and 24 wounded.

The Embuscade was armed like her class-mate, No. 7, in the table at p. 59, except in having but two instead of four carronades. Her established complement was not above 280 or 300, but Captain Bompart, while lying in New York, had augmented the number to 340, and his ship's company, for effectiveness, far exceeded the generality of French crews of the same numerical strength. Deducting the 13 absentees on board the Boston, 327 remain : out of which number, according to the New York papers of the day, the Embuscade had 50 killed and wounded.

Comparative Force of the Combatants.

		Boston.	Embuscade.
Broadside-guns	No.	19	19
	lbs.	210	240
Crew	No.	204	327
Size	tons	676	906

This long and close-fought action was viewed, from beginning to end, by crowds of American citizens, standing on the Jersey beach. The superior size of the Embuscade attracted the notice of every one ; and few among the spectators, on observing the Boston haul off, were so prejudiced as not to admit that, to all appearance, the British frigate had no hopes left of bringing the combat to a favourable termination. That the Boston had not neglected any means of doing so, will appear by the following account of the quantity of powder and shot expended by her in the action :—

	No.		No.
Powder . . 36 half-barrels		Double-headed shot	50
Round shot, 12 and 6 pounders	842	Musket balls	500
Grape shot in cases	72	Pistol balls	150
Case shot	70	Cartridges, in all	474

Although none of the Embuscade's masts fell during the contest, on her arrival at New York the French frigate had to take all of them out; and her yards, rigging, and hull must also have been considerably injured, or the Embuscade, doubtless, would have continued the chase, in order to consummate her victory. The Embuscade lay at New York, from the 2nd of August to the 9th of October, getting in her lower masts, and repairing the damages she had sustained by the Boston's fire.

The Boston, after losing sight of the Embuscade, had a very

narrow escape. She was about entering the Delaware to refit in that river, when the pilot gave information, that two French frigates (believed to have been the Concorde and Inconstante) were lying at anchor opposite Mud Fort. No time was to be lost, and the British frigate, discharging the pilot, hauled up for St. John's, Newfoundland; where, on the 19th, the Boston arrived in safety.

On account of the acknowledged gallantry of Captain Courtenay in the engagement with the Embuscade, the late king was pleased to settle on his widow a pension of 500*l*. and on each of his two children 50*l*. per annum. Captain Bompart, some time after his return to New York, was also rewarded for his good conduct, by being appointed to the Jupiter 74, recently arrived from St. Domingo.

The following is the account of the death of Captain Courtenay, as it appears in a contemporary work: "The action soon began, and continued with great bravery on both sides, until the iron hammock-rail of the quarter-deck being struck by a shot, a part of it took Captain Courtenay on the back of the neck, and he fell, but no blood followed: the first-lieutenant caused the body to be immediately thrown overboard, lest, as he said, it should dishearten the people; and after this precaution, hauled away from the enemy, who had no inclination to follow him."[1] All we can say to this extraordinary statement is, that our account was taken chiefly from the Boston's log-book, and that we have not the least reason, from subsequent inquiries, to believe it to be incorrect. The officer, Lieutenant John Edwards, thus severely treated, after acting a short time in command of the Pluto sloop, whose commander, the present Vice-admiral Sir James Nicoll Morris, had been posted into the Boston, resumed his station on board of the latter, went to England in her in extreme ill-health from his contusion, was made a commander on the 22nd of June, 1795, and died as such, from the effects of his old wound, on the 15th of January, 1823; the very month, if not the very day, on which the book, containing this serious charge against him, both as an officer and a man, appeared before the public.

About the middle of October, the British 18-pounder 36-gun frigate, Crescent, Captain James Saumarez, sailed from Spithead on a cruise. Having received information that two French frigates, stationed at Cherbourg, had made several valuable captures, and that one of them usually quitted the port in the

[1] Brenton, vol. ii., p. 461.

evening, stood across the Channel during the night, and returned the next morning, with what prizes she had picked up, Captain Saumarez, on the night of the 19th, ran close off Cape Barfleur, and there awaited the frigate's return.

Just as the day dawned the Crescent, standing on the larboard tack, with the wind off shore, descried a ship and a large cutter coming in from the seaward: she immediately edged away for the two strangers, and, in a little while, ranged up on the larboard and weather side of the ship, which was the French 36-gun frigate Réunion, Captain François A. Dénian.

A close and spirited action now ensued, in the early part of which the Crescent lost her foretopsail yard, and soon afterwards her foretopmast; but, putting her helm hard a-starboard, she came suddenly round on the opposite tack, and brought her larboard guns to bear. The Réunion, by this time, had lost her foreyard and mizentopmast, and became exposed, in consequence, to several raking fires from the Crescent. After a brave resistance of two hours and ten minutes, by which time she was utterly defenceless, the Réunion struck her colours; a measure the more imperative, as the British 28-gun frigate Circe, Captain Joseph Sydney Yorke, which, during the greater part of the action, had laid becalmed about three leagues off, striving her utmost to get up, was now approaching. The cutter, which was believed to be the Espérance, mounting 12 or 14 guns, had made off as soon as the firing commenced, and escaped into Cherbourg.

Both ships were a good deal damaged in their sails and rigging; and the Réunion, besides losing her foreyard, mizentopmast, and maintopgallantmast, had several shots in her lower masts, and a still greater number in her hull. Almost the only shot that entered the Crescent's hull struck the apron, and set fire to the priming of the forecastle 9-pounder on the opposite, or unengaged side; which, going off, discharged its contents in the direction of some gun-boats coming out of Cherbourg.

The Crescent's main deck armament was that of her class, as given at *C.* in the table at p. 101, and her quarter-deck and forecastle guns were not, as we formerly stated, 14, but eight carronades, 18-pounders, and two long 9-pounders, total 36 guns. Out of her 257 men and boys in crew, the Crescent had not a man hurt by the enemy's shot; but, in the very first broadside, one of her seamen had his leg broken by the recoil of the gun he was fighting.

The Réunion, in her long guns, was armed the same as the

Embuscade,[1] except in having eight instead ten 6-pounders: she also had six brass 36-pounder carronades; making the total of her guns 40. The complement of the Réunion, according to the British official account, amounted to 320 men; but the number deposed to by the French officers, to entitle the captors to head-money, was 300.[2] Of these the French frigate, according to the letter of Captain Saumarez, lost 120 in killed and wounded; but, by another account, the loss on board the Réunion consisted of 33 officers, seamen, and marines killed, and 48 severely wounded.

Comparative Force of the Combatants.

		Crescent.	Réunion.
Broadside-guns	No.	18	20
	lbs.	315	310
Crew	No.	257	300
Size	tons.	888	951

Neither the Réunion's six heavy carronades, nor the Crescent's eight light ones, were very efficient pieces: hence the difference in the maindeck guns of the two frigates gave a decided advantage to the Crescent. Under all the circumstances, therefore, it must be owned that, if the officers and men of the Réunion lacked skill, they were by no means deficient in courage. Many persons on the French shore witnessed the combat; and the Réunion's consort in Cherbourg, believed to have been the Sémillante, made an attempt to go out to her assistance; but a contrary tide and the failure of wind, aided perhaps by the knowledge that a second enemy's frigate was in the offing, detained her in port.

As a reward for his services on this occasion, Captain Saumarez, soon after his arrival at Portsmouth, received the honour of knighthood; and, as a further proof how highly the Crescent's performance was rated, Sir James was presented by the city of London with a handsome piece of plate. In addition to the reward bestowed upon Captain Saumarez, the Crescent's first-lieutenant, George Parker, as he justly merited, was promoted to the rank of commander. The second and third lieutenants present in the action were Charles Otter and Peter Rye. The Réunion was purchased by the British government, and added

---

[1] See p. 113; also table at p. 59.
[2] This discrepancy commonly arises from an excess of numbers in the French ship's rôle d'équipage; a document to which the English captor naturally refers, in the first instance, for ascertaining the complement of his prize.

to the navy, under the same name as a cruising 12-pounder 36-gun frigate.

On the 22nd of October, at 2 A.M., the British 64-gun ship Agamemnon, Captain Horatio Nelson, while cruising off Sardinia, saw five sail standing across her to the westward, close upon a wind. These were a French squadron commanded by Commodore Perrée, and consisting of the

Gun-frig.		Gun frig.
40 Melpomène.		28 Mignonne.[1]
38 Minerve.		G.-bg.-corv.
36 Fortunée.		14 Hasard.

At 2 h. 10 m. A.M. the strangers tacked, by signal of rockets, and were then about three miles on the Agamemnon's weather bow. At 4 A.M. the Agamemnon got within hail of a frigate, but, lest the latter should prove to be a Neapolitan or Sardinian, with a convoy, was careful not to fire into her. Receiving no answer, however, to the hail, and observing the frigate to be making sail, the Agamemnon fired a shot ahead of her. On this, the frigate crowded sail to get off, steering two points from the wind; and the Agamemnon, to prevent the frigate from getting before it, kept her about two points on the bow, chasing under every stitch of canvas. The four other vessels were now seen on the Agamemnon's quarter, steering after her and the frigate.

At daylight the frigate ahead hoisted French national colours, and began firing her stern-chasers. Occasionally, too, the frigate's superiority in sailing enabled her to give a yaw and fire her broadside; in return for which the Agamemnon could bring only a few of her foremost guns now and then to bear. While the breeze continued fresh, the 64 and frigate left the other ships far behind; but at 9 A.M., the two former having run into nearly a calm, the four ships in the north-west came up fast. To these, now plainly discovered to be two large and one smaller frigate, and an armed brig, the chase, evidently in a shattered condition, made signals: on which her friends stood for her, and she, hauling more up, was presently in the midst of them.

The Agamemnon, having her maintopsail cut to pieces, main and mizenmasts, and fore-yard badly wounded, and a great quantity of rigging shot away, could not haul her wind; and these four French frigates and brig-corvette, with the option, at

---

[1] Named Fotchet in the published accounts.

any time before noon on that day, of bringing a British 64-gun ship to action, left her unmolested, and pursued their route.

The Agamemnon had only 345 men at quarters; and of these she lost one man killed and six wounded. The aggregate crews of the five French vessels amounted to at least 1100 men: what loss was sustained by the only ship among them that came within reach of the Agamemnon's shot cannot now be ascertained.

On the 24th the Agamemnon anchored in Cagliari Bay to repair her damages; and the French frigates proceeded to Mortella Bay. From this anchorage they might probably have been compelled to remove by the fire of the tower which, as is elsewhere stated, had been captured in the preceding month by the boats of the Lowestoffe;[1] but Commodore Linzee had since removed the guns into a tender which he chose to fit out. The consequence was, that the Corsicans, left in charge, had no alternative but to abandon the tower, and a party from the French squadron immediately landed and took possession of it.

On the 24th of October, at 9 h. 30 m. A.M., the British 12-pounder 32-gun frigate Thames, Captain James Cotes, being in latitude 47° 2' north, and longitude 7° 22' west, standing close-hauled to the southward, with the wind at west-south-west, saw a sail bearing south; which sail, after hoisting a blue flag at the fore by way of signal, as it afterwards proved, to a brig that accompanied her, bore away large. The weather soon came on very thick, and did not clear up until 10 h. 15 m. A.M.; when the stranger, now seen to be a frigate, appeared on a wind standing for the Thames. The latter immediately cleared for action, and at 10 h. 30 m. P.M. the French 40-gun frigate Uranie, the frigate in sight, fired a gun to windward, and hoisted French national colours.

The two ships, having the same object in view, soon passed very near to each other, on contrary tacks; at which time the Uranie fired her broadside, and wore round on the opposite tack. An action now commenced, and was continued, with great spirit on both sides, until 2 h. 20 m. P.M.; when the Uranie, getting under the stern of the Thames, gave her two or three raking broadsides, and then attempted to board on the starboard quarter; but, on receiving through her bows a well-directed fire from six or seven of the Thames's maindeck guns, double-shotted, the Uranie threw all her sails aback, and hauled off to the southward. The British crew, on seeing this, gave three

---

[1] See p. 95.

hearty cheers; but the Thames was in too crippled a condition to make sail in pursuit.

The Thames, whose force consisted only of her established long guns, 32 in number, had quitted England 30 men short of complement, and was obliged, in consequence, to take the marines from the 6-pounder to assist in working the 12s. Her loss in the action, out of a crew of 184 men and boys, amounted to 10 seamen and one private marine killed, her second-lieutenant (George Robinson), master (George Norris), one master's mate (David Valentine), one midshipman (James Dale), 14 seamen, and five private marines wounded.

The Uranie's force in guns was exactly that of the French 40-gun frigate, in the table at p. 59, and her complement was stated to have been from 320 to 350. The constant stream of musketry that poured from her during the whole of the action renders it probable that the highest of those numbers came nearest to the amount. The loss on board the Uranie does not appear; but it was believed to have been very severe, and to have included among the killed her captain, M. Tartue.

Comparative Force of the Combatants.

		Thames.	Uranie.
Broadside-guns	No.	16	22
	lbs.	174	403
Crew	No.	187	320
Size	tons.	656	1100

Opposed to so decided a superiority, it will not appear surprising that the Thames should have suffered to the extent now about to be detailed. Her three lower masts and bowsprit were shot through in several places; all her stays were shot away, as was all the main rigging, except a few shrouds, and they were rendered useless. The maintopmast rigging was even worse than the main rigging, and the topmast was shot through in three places. The maintopsail yard was shot away in the slings by a double-headed shot, and the yard-arms came down in front of the main yard; the slings, both iron and rope, and the geers of the main yard, were shot away, so that the yard hung by the trusses, about a third of the mast down; and the mainsail was cut to pieces, particularly the leech-ropes.

The foremast had received nearly the same damage as the mainmast, except that the slings of the fore yard were not all cut away, whereby the yard remained aloft: the foretopmast rigging, except a shroud or two, was all shot away; as were all the stays, back-stays, lifts, braces, ties, halliards, and other tackling. The bowsprit was shot through in several places; and all the bob-stays and bowsprit shrouds were cut by shot and langridge: the jib-stay and halliards had been shot away at the first broadside. The mizenmast was so injured, and the rigging so cut, that the gaff was obliged to be lowered, as soon as the action ended, to prevent the mast from going over the side; and the fore-part of the top was entirely shot away.

The hull of the Thames had received innumerable shots; the chief part of the gangways was shot away; the main deck in front of the mainmast was torn up from the waterway to the hatchways, and the bits were shot away and unshipped. Six shots had passed between wind and water on the starboard, and three on the larboard side. One gun on the quarter-deck, and two on the main deck, were dismounted; and almost all the tackles and breechings were cut away. The loss on board the Thames, as we have just seen, amounted to 11 men killed, and 23 (two of them mortally) wounded. The surprise is that, after being so terribly mauled by shot, her loss was not treble what it proved.

The condition of the Uranie can be taken only from her appearance as she lay to, about two miles from her opponent, repairing her damages. Her masts, though all were standing, seemed to be greatly injured, as did her rigging and sails. Several men were seen over her sides, stopping shot-holes; and it was evident that she was pumping, with all her remaining strength.

The Thames could steer but one course, and that was right before the wind. Judging that the Uranie would certainly renew the contest, as soon as she was in a state to bear down, Captain Cotes commenced refitting the Thames, in order to receive her. The British crew had been so busied in their various duties, that they had scarcely bestowed a glance beyond their own ship; and at 4 P.M., when inquiries were made after the Uranie, not a person, either on deck or in the tops, could see anything of her: and yet it did not appear possible that, under every advantage of sailing, she could have gained a distance to be completely out of sight.

Soon afterwards four sail made their appearance, and came up fast, under English colours. The wind had by this time freshened from the south-west; and the Thames, being without any after-sail, and having her runners all carried forward and crossed, to serve both as stays and shrouds, was not able to haul upon a wind. On this, one of the frigates ranged up under her stern, and gave her a broadside. The Thames then brought to, hailed that she was in a defenceless state from a previous action, and struck her colours to the French 40-gun frigate Carmagnole, Captain Zacharie-Jacques-Théodore Allemand, having in her company the 36-gun frigates Résolue and Sémillante, and 16-gun brig-corvette Espiègle. M. Allemand ordered Captain Cotes to send his boat on board the Carmagnole; but the Thames not having any boat fit to take the water, nor even the means of hoisting one out, the Carmagnole had to send one of her boats to take possession of the prize.

The French commodore inquired particularly the description of the Thames's late opponent: it was given to him as minutely as possible. He then said that she was the Uranie, a frigate of his squadron, which, two days before, had gone in chase of a yellow-sided brig. He was informed that such a vessel, apparently either a Spanish packet or small brig of war, had been seen in her company: whereupon he expressed himself highly indignant at the captain of the Uranie; declaring, that the latter ought to have annihilated the Thames in half the time.

The Thames, being taken in tow by the Carmagnole, was conducted to Brest, where she arrived on the following day. Her surgeon had been removed from her on the preceding evening, and the wounded of her crew remained unattended for three days; at the end of which time they were transported to the hospital. The British officers and men were completely pillaged by the French crew, over whom the French officers had little or no control: it is, however, but fair to state, that the latter did all in their power to mitigate the sufferings of their prisoners.

Several of the officers late belonging to the Thames resided two years at Brest, and, naturally enough, made the most diligent inquiries after the frigate that had engaged them, but never could hear the least tidings of her. Coupling this circumstance with the Uranie's sudden abandonment of the action, and with the visible effects of the repeated broadsides of the Thames upon her hull, as she lay pumping in their view, the British officers could not but consider that the efforts of their ship, although not crowned with victory, had sent to the bottom an enemy's ship of greatly superior force.

In this hope, however, they were deceived. The name of the Uranie, immediately or soon after she arrived in port, was changed to Tortue. Our suspicion that such had been the case, we recorded in the first edition of this work. By referring to the proceedings instituted in the Admiralty Prize-court against the French frigate Tortue, captured by the Polyphemus in January, 1797, we have since found it expressly deposed by Captain Magendie and his two senior lieutenants, that, previously to the capture of the British frigate Thames, the Tortue, represented by them as mounting 44 guns, had been named Uranie. In consequence of that, we believe, the British admiralty, on receiving the Tortue into the service, changed her name to Urania.

On the 25th of November, at 1 A.M., the British 12-pounder 32-gun frigates Penelope, Captain Bartholomew Samuel Rowley, and Iphigenia, Captain Patrick Sinclair, cruising in the bight of Leogane, island of St. Domingo, discovered on the west quarter, and immediately chased, the French 36-gun frigate Inconstante, from Port-au-Prince, bound to Petit-Trou. At 1 h. 30 m. A.M. the Penelope, who had far outrun her consort in the chase, got close alongside of the Inconstante, between whom and herself a smart cannonade commenced. In a short time the hammock-cloths of the Penelope on the engaged side caught fire, and 50 hammocks were destroyed before the flames could be extinguished. The action, nevertheless, still went on, and continued until the Iphigenia came ranging up on the French frigate's starboard quarter; when, at 2 A.M., the Inconstante hauled down her colours. The Penelope had one seaman killed, and one midshipman (John Allen) and six seamen wounded; the Iphigenia, no person hurt. The Inconstante, out of a crew of 300 men and boys, had her first-lieutenant and six seamen killed, and her captain and 20 men (including three mortally) wounded. The prize was purchased for the navy, and registered, under her French name, as a 12-pounder 36.

On the 1st of December his Britannic majesty's packet the Antelope, Captain Curtis, being off Cumberland harbour, in Cuba, on her way to England, from Port-Royal, Jamaica, which port she had quitted three days previous, fell in with two French schooner-privateers, of formidable appearance. The packet immediately bore up for Jamaica, and was followed, under all sail, by the privateers. The Atalante, one of the two, outsailing her consort, continued the chase alone. During that and the following day, until 4 P.M., the packet rather gained upon her pursuer; but the wind suddenly failing, the latter took to her sweeps, and soon swept up alongside of the Antelope. After the exchange of a few shots, the schooner sheered off. On the 2nd, at 5 A.M., it still being calm, the Atalante again swept up, and, on reaching her opponent, grappled her on the starboard side. The privateer then poured in a broadside, and attempted, under cover of the smoke, to carry the Antelope by boarding; but the crew of the latter drove back the assailants with great slaughter.

Among the sufferers by the privateer's broadside, was the packet's commander, Mr. Curtis, who fell to rise no more; as did also the steward, and a French gentleman, a passenger. The first-mate, too, was shot through the body, but survived. The second-mate having died of the fever soon after the packet had sailed from Port-Royal, the command now devolved upon Mr. Pasco, the boatswain, who, with the few brave men left, assisted by the passengers, repulsed repeated attempts to board, made, at intervals, during the long period that the vessels remained lashed together. At last, the privateersmen, finding they had caught a tartar, cut the grapplings, and attempted to sheer off. The boatswain, observing this, ran aloft, and lashed the schooner's square-sail yard to the Antelope's fore shrouds. Immediately a well-directed volley of small arms was poured into the privateer, and the crew called for quarter. This, notwithstanding the Atalante had fought with the red or bloody flag at her mast-head, to indicate that no quarter would be shown by her, was granted, and possession was forthwith taken of the prize.

The Antelope mounted six 3-pounders, and had sailed with 27 hands; but she had lost four by the fever, and two were ill in their hammocks, consequently the packet commenced the action with only 21 men, exclusive of the passengers. Her total loss in the action was three killed, and four wounded. The Atalante mounted eight 3-pounders; and her complement was 65 men, composed of French, Americans, and Irish. Of these the first and second captains and 30 men were killed,[1] and 17 officers and men wounded. The Atalante had been fitted out at Charleston, in the United States. The Antelope now carried her prize in triumph to Annotta Bay, Jamaica, where the two vessels arrived on the morning succeeding the action.

The unparalleled bravery of one of the Antelope's passengers, a M. Nodin, formerly a midshipman in the French navy, deserves to be recorded. It is related of this young man, that he stood by the helm and worked the ship, armed with a musket

[1] The number of dead lying on the deck, when the schooner was taken possession of, amounted to 20. It is probable that none had, as conjectured, been thrown overboard: hence, admitting 16 to have been, as is stated, the number of privateersmen found unhurt, the schooner's complement, or commencing the action, would be 12 fewer than appears in the text.

and a pike, which he alternately made use of: that, when he perceived the Atalante's men climbing the quarters of the Antelope, he quitted the helm, and with the pike despatched such as came within his reach, returning at proper intervals to right the vessel; that, with the pike and musket, he killed or disabled several men, and continued his astonishing exertions for upwards of an hour and a quarter.[1]

Colonial Expeditions.

An enumeration of the principal colonies possessed by the several powers at war, as well as by those far from disinterested lookers-on, the neutral nations, may usefully precede the accounts which, under this head of the work, we purpose to give, but only, except where the navy is exclusively concerned, in a summary manner.

There were possessed in

North America.

BY ENGLAND, { Upper and Lower Canada; Settlements in Hudson's Bay; Provinces in Nova-Scotia and New Brunswick; Islands of Cape Breton, Newfoundland, and St. John, or Prince Edward; the Magdalen islands, and the Bermudas or Somers islands.

FRANCE, { Small fishing islands of St. Pierre and Miquelon, on the coast of Newfoundland.

West Indies.

ENGLAND, { Island of Jamaica, Bahama islands, and the Bay of Honduras, to leeward; and, to windward, Barbadoes, Grenada, and the Grenadines, Antigua, St. Vincent, Dominique or Dominica, St. Kitt's, or St. Christopher's, Nevis, Montserrat, and the Virgin islands.

HOLLAND, { Islands of Curaçoa and St. Eustatia, and part of St. Martin; Dutch Guiana, on the coast of Terra Firma, contiguous to the river Oronoko, with the settlements of Surinam, Demerara, Berbice, and Essequibo.

SPAIN, { Islands of Cuba, Trinidad, Porto Rico, and the east part of St. Domingo; Mexico, Peru, East and West Florida, &c.; great part of the east coast of South America; the rich settlements of Monte Video and Buenos Ayres on the Rio de la Plata, and part of the coast from that river to Cape Horn.

PORTUGAL, { A large tract of country on the east coast of South America, including Pernambuco, Rio Janeiro, St. Salvador, and St. Sebastian; and from Para to the Rio de la Plata.

DENMARK, Islands of Santa Cruz, St. John, and St. Thomas.

[1] The Jamaica House of Assembly, with its wonted liberality, as soon as the gallant conduct of the Antelope's officers and crew was made known, voted the sum of 500 guineas to be distributed among them.

SWEDEN, Island of St. Bartholomew.

FRANCE, Islands of Martinique, Guadeloupe, the Saintes, Désirade, Ste. Lucie, Tobago, and Marie Galante; also part of St. Domingo and St. Martin; French Guiana, or Cayenne, on the coast of Terra Firma.

Coast of Africa.

ENGLAND, Fort James, on the river Gambia; Sierra Leone; Cape Coast Castle.

HOLLAND, Cape of Good Hope; settlements of Amsterdam, Acra, and Delmine, on the coast of Guinea.

PORTUGAL, Madeira; the Azores or Western islands; Cape de Verd islands; island of St. Thomas on the line; Loango, St. Paul, and a few other small trading forts.

DENMARK, A few small trading forts.

FRANCE, Sénégal, Gorée, &c.

East Indies.

ENGLAND, Greater part of the coasts of Malabar and Coromandel; island of Pulo Penang, and Bencoolen on the island of Sumatra; chief part of New Holland; Andamin islands, in the Bay of Bengal; St. Helena.

HOLLAND, Batavia and several other settlements in the island of Java; Samanap on the island of Madura, and Malacca on the peninsula of that name; Masulipatam on the coast of Coromandel, and Cochin on the coast of Malabar; Trincomalée, Pointe de Galle, and Columbo in the island of Ceylon; factories of Porca and Quilon in the Travancore country; Amboyana, Banda, Ternante, &c.

SPAIN, Philippine islands, and settlement of Manilla in the island of Leuconia.

PORTUGAL, Goa on the Malabar coast; Macao at the mouth of the Tigris on the coast of China.

DENMARK, Tranquebar, on the coast of Coromandel.

FRANCE, Fort Pondicherry on the coast of Coromandel; factories of Mahé on the coast of Malabar; of Chandernagore, up the Ganges, also of Karica, Yanam, and a few others; island of Mauritius, or Isle de France; Isle Bourbon; Foul Point on the island of Madagascar.

North America.

We shall now proceed in our narrative of colonial occurrences, taking the different stations in the order in which they have just been named; North America, West Indies, Coast of Africa, and East Indies. In the station of North America is included that of Newfoundland; at which island, or rather at St. John's, its principal port, the British naval force, on the breaking out of the war, consisted of the 64-gun ship Stately, Captain J. S. Smith, bearing the flag of Vice-admiral Sir Richard King, the 32-gun frigates Boston, Fox, and Cleopatra, and four or five small sloops. The first act of hostility in this quarter was the capture of the small fishing islands of St. Pierre and Miquelon, which had been taken from the French in 1778, and were injudiciously restored to them by the treaty of 1783.

Aware of the importance of these fishery islands, the British government, in a very few days after war had been declared, despatched orders to Halifax, Nova-Scotia, for their immediate seizure. In pursuance of those directions, Brigadier-general Ogilvie, with a detachment of the royal artillery, and 310 rank and file of the 4th and 65th regiments, embarked, on the 7th of May, in the British 28-gun frigate Alligator, Captain William Affleck, the Diligente armed schooner and three transports. On the 14th, at daybreak, the Alligator and convoy made the island of St. Pierre; and, it having been stated (although, as it proved, erroneously) that a French frigate was in the harbour, a division of the troops was landed about five miles to the westward of the town; after which, the ships made sail for the harbour. A summons for the surrender of the islands was sent to M. Danseville, the commandant, who demanded terms of capitulation, but, on these being refused, surrendered the islands of St. Pierre and Miquelon at discretion. The battery consisted of eight 24-pounders, the garrison of between 80 and 100 men, besides about 500 armed fishermen; and the whole population of the two islands, of 1502 souls, including 761 for Miquelon. Eighteen small vessels laden with fish and two American schooners containing provisions and naval stores, were taken in the harbour.

West Indies.

The distance between Barbadoes and Jamaica, aided by the violent and steady force of the trade-wind, as it blows from one island to the other, having rendered it necessary to divide the British West Indies into two commands, or stations, we shall find it most convenient to conform to the same arrangement; especially, as the naval operations carried on upon either station are usually conducted by the admiral in command there, or by a detachment from his squadron. When the news of the war reached Barbadoes, the commander-in-chief on the station was Vice-admiral Sir John Laforey, who had his flag on board the 50-gun ship Trusty, Captain John Drew; which, with a small frigate and two or three sloops, was all the British force in that quarter.

ILL SUCCESS AT MARTINIQUE.

The island of Tobago had been taken from the British in the late war, and the French were confirmed in the possession of it by the treaty of Amiens. It was therefore an object to retake it as speedily as possible. Accordingly, on the 12th of April, directions to that effect having been promptly forwarded, Major-general Cuyler, at the head of a detachment composed of 50 artillerymen, 418 of the 9th and 60th (4th battalion) regiments, and 32 marines, total 470 officers and men, embarked from Bridge-town, Barbadoes, on board the Trusty, 18-gun sloop Nautilus, Hind armed schooner, and Hero merchant-ship, and, on the 14th, arrived in Great Courland Bay, Tobago. On the same evening the troops were landed ; and, on their approaching within two miles of the enemy's fort at Scarborough, a summons was despatched to M. Monteil, Lieutenant-colonel of the 32nd regiment and commandant of the island. He refused to surrender, and an assault was resolved on.

On the 15th, at 1 A.M., the British proceeded to the attack, and under a heavy fire of round, grape, and musketry, succeeded, with their bayonets chiefly, in entering the enemy's works. The conquerors, then, in noble violation of custom, admitted their captives to the privileges of prisoners of war. The British loss was three killed and 25 wounded ; that of the enemy, as represented, 15 in killed and wounded. The force on the batteries appears to have been 21 guns, 11 of them 18-pounders. The amount of prisoners did not exceed 200; but it was conjectured, that full 100 armed inhabitants, besides several mulattoes and negroes, had, on the first rush of the British, escaped from the fort.

In consequence of representations made by the royalists of Martinique to Rear-admiral Gardner, who had recently succeeded Rear-admiral Laforey, and to Major-general Bruce, the military commander-in-chief at Barbadoes, intimating, that even the display of a small British force would occasion a great number of the inhabitants to declare for the monarchy, Rear-admiral Gardner's squadron, consisting of the Queen 98, Captain John Hutt, bearing his flag, the Duke, of the same force, Captain the Honourable George Murray, the Hector and Monarch 74s, Captains George Montagu and Sir James Wallace, with one or two others, and a division of transports, having on board about 1100 British and 800 French royalist troops, proceeded off the island.

Between the 14th and 17th the troops were disembarked, under cover of the British ships, assisted by a French royalist

74-gun ship and 36-gun frigate; the latter the Calypso, and the former, late the Phocion (both ships having belonged to the republican navy), but now newly named the Ferme.

On the 18th the united forces moved forward, in two columns, to attack the two batteries which defended the town of St. Pierre; and in which the governor of the island, General Rochambeau, was posted, with, as is alleged in the French accounts, only a few hundred troops. Unfortunately, some alarm having taken place among the royalists, the latter, in a mistake, fired on each other, and severely wounded their commander. This so disconcerted the men, that they turned upon their heels, and marched back to the post they had quitted. The British being, in point of numbers, as was conceived, considerably inferior to the republicans, marched back also, and, by the 21st, were again on board their ships. The knowledge of what treatment the royalists were likely to experience if they fell into the hands of the republicans, induced Major-general Bruce to hire vessels to bring them off; and Captain le Vicomte de la Rivière, putting himself and his 74 and frigate under the orders of the British admiral, saved a great number of his unfortunate countrymen. By this prompt measure, some hundreds of the loyal inhabitants, whites, browns, and blacks, escaped being massacred, and were afterwards distributed as settlers among the different islands. There were, however, as many as 2000 that remained. These were seized and confined as "aristocrats;" and, if there was a "committee of public safety" in the island, met, without doubt, a similar fate to that which had befallen many thousands of their royalist brethren in Europe. Soon after the unfortunate issue of this expedition, Rear-admiral Gardner sailed for England, and the Ferme and Calypso joined the Spaniards at the island of Trinidad.

Previously to our quitting the Windward Islands, we must not omit to mention that on the 12th and 13th of August a dreadful hurricane raged there; that the islands of St. Eustatia, St. Christopher, and St. Thomas experienced the utmost of its violence; and that, besides the numerous plantations laid waste, several vessels and lives were lost, both at sea and on the different coasts.

The British naval commander-in-chief at Jamaica, when the war broke out, was Commodore John Ford, having his broad pendant flying on board the 50-gun ship Europa, Captain George Gregory, which ship, along with a few 12-pounder frigates, and some smaller vessels, composed the whole British force on this station. The troubles of St. Domingo soon gave occasion for its employment. A Monsieur Charmilly, last from England, had succeeded in persuading his countrymen at Jérémie, in that fine island, to throw themselves upon British protection. Accordingly, M. Charmilly himself was deputed by the inhabitants of Grande-Anse, including the quarter at Jérémie, to carry to Major-general Williamson, the lieutenant-governor of Jamaica, the terms on which they were willing to capitulate. Among the articles, the whole of which were liberal, and many highly advantageous to the British, was one, that the mulattoes should have all the privileges enjoyed by that class of inhabitants in the British islands.

After the terms had been agreed to, and just as the expedition that was to see them enforced was on the eve of sailing, arrived a Major Carles, a French officer belonging to the town of Cape-Nicolas-Mole; and who, having been captured and carried into Nassau by a New-Providence privateer, had represented to Lord Dunmore, the governor, that the inhabitants of the Mole, if a certain number of troops could be landed for their support, would also surrender themselves to the arms of Great Britain. This representation had induced his lordship to send the major down to Jamaica; and the plan was considered by the governor and council as feasible.

With this double object in view, on the 9th of September, the British 50-gun ship Europa, Commodore Ford, and some of the smaller vessels on the station, took on board, at Port-Royal, along with Monsieur Charmilly and Major Carles, a detachment of British troops, composed of the 13th regiment, the flank companies of the 49th regiment, and a proportion of royal artillery, under the command of Lieutenant-colonel Whitelock, of the 13th; and the whole arrived, on the 19th of September, off Jérémie. The troops, on their landing, were received by the inhabitants with every demonstration of joy and fidelity, and the British colours were hoisted under a royal salute, accompanied by the other ceremonies usual on such occasions.

Commodore Ford, in order, by a diversion, to add to Colonel Whitelock's security, despatched Captain Rowley, of the 32-gun frigate Penelope, with the Iphigenia and Hermoine, of the same force, to the Bay des Flamands, near St. Louis, on the south side of the island, with orders to capture or destroy some French merchant-vessels that were stated to be lying there. Captain Rowley succeeded in bringing away ten, the chief of them laden with colonial produce. With respect to Major

Carles, it had been resolved that he should proceed in a flag of truce to the Mole, to sound the inhabitants, and then return to Jamaica, in order to digest the plan of the enterprise. But Commodore Ford, learning at Jérémie that a speedy attack on the Mole was meditated by the republican party, determined to proceed there himself, to frustrate, if possible, the attempt.

On arriving, on the 21st, near the harbour of Cape-Nicolas-Mole, the commodore landed Major Carles, who, on the next day, made the signal agreed upon between himself and the commodore; and the latter, with the Europa and small vessels, approached, under proper caution, the formidable battery at the entrance. It was now ascertained that the blacks and mulattoes at Jean-Rabel, to the amount of 800 or 1000, were hourly expected to attack the town, and that the inhabitants were in the utmost despondency. No time was therefore to be lost, and Commodore Ford sent on shore a copy of the same capitulation that had been acceded to at Jérémie.

Soon after daylight the next morning this was returned duly executed,[1] and the Europa proceeded to the anchorage, where, after the proper forms had been gone through, the town of Cape-Nicolas-Mole, and its extensive dependencies, were surrendered to the arms of his Britannic Majesty.

Thus was seen the extraordinary spectacle of a French port, confessedly one of the finest harbours in the West Indies, guarded by batteries mounted with upwards of 100 pieces of heavy cannon, in the quiet possession of a 50-gun ship.

The marines of the Europa, about 58 in number, with Brevet-major Robinson at their head, were all the British force that was on shore; but Commodore Ford, very judiciously, held 200 seamen ready to land at a moment's warning. This precautionary measure continued, without relaxation, until the arrival from Jérémie, on the 28th, of the grenadier company of the 13th; and was not wholly laid aside till the arrival, on the 12th of the succeeding month, of the Penelope and Iphigenia, from Jamaica, with five companies of the 49th regiment, under the command of Lieutenant-colonel Dansey, who succeeded Brevet-major Robinson as commandant of the district. The acquisition of these frigates enabled the commodore, by sending them off Port-au-Paix, to put a stop to an expedition, consisting of upwards of 5000 men, with which the republicans had intended to attempt the recapture of the town and batteries of the Mole.

[1] With an additional article, agreeing to take into British pay the officers and men in garrison, and to allow the former the same rank which they had before held.

Just at the close of the year, the parishes of Jean-Rabel, St. Marc, Arcahaye, and Boncassin, on the north, and the province of Léogane, on the south side of the bight, surrendered to the British, upon terms similar to those which had been granted to Jérémie and Cape-Nicolas-Mole.

East Indies.

The British naval force in the East Indies, at the beginning of the war, consisted of only a 64-gun ship, the Crown, lying at Madras, and one or two frigates and sloops at, or in the neighbourhood of, Calcutta, and was under the command of Commodore the Honourable William Cornwallis. An occurrence that happened in these seas, nearly a year and a half before the war became known there, must be cursorily noticed ere we commence upon the regular narrative.

During the prevalence of hostilities betweeen the East India Company and Tippoo Saib, in 1790 and 1791, the principal assistance which, owing to the internal nature of the campaign, the British navy could render, was to watch the port of Mangalore on the Malabar coast, and prevent the French, who rather favoured the cause of Tippoo, from throwing in supplies. In the beginning of November, 1791, while Commodore Cornwallis, who had then his broad pendant on board the 38-gun frigate Minerva, and was accompanied by the 36-gun frigate Phœnix, Captain Sir Richard John Strachan, and Perseverance, Captain Isaac Smith, lay at anchor in the road of Tellicherry, a fort and anchorage situated a few leagues to the southward of Mangalore, the French 36-gun frigate Résolue got under way from Mahé, a French factory, about seven miles to the southward of Tellicherry, and, in company with two country coasting-vessels, steered towards Mangalore.

As soon as the French frigate and her small convoy arrived abreast of Tellicherry, the British commodore detached the Phœnix and Perseverance to search the vessels for contraband of war. The Phœnix having run alongside the Résolue, Sir Richard informed the French captain of the nature of his orders, and of his determination to execute them, and despatched immediately a boat with an officer to board the two vessels; which, in the meanwhile, the Perseverance had brought to.

The captain of the Résolue resisted this insult to the French flag by firing first, as is alleged, at the boat, and then at the Phœnix. The latter, who must have expected and been prepared for this crisis in the affair, was not slow in returning the compliment, and a close and smart action ensued. At the end of twenty minutes, however, the Résolue, being much cut up in hull, spars, and sails, and having sustained a loss of 25 men killed and 40 wounded, struck her colours to the two British frigates in company, with a loss to the frigate that had engaged her of six men killed and 11 wounded.

Now, it can no more be denied that the French captain did his duty in resisting the search of his convoy than that he most gallantly supported the honour of his flag, in delaying to haul it down until his loss had become so severe, and his chance of escape so utterly hopeless. Hopeless, indeed, except perhaps by flight, it was from the first; for, in addition to the unprepared state of his frigate, the Résolue carried only 12 and 6 pounders, while all three British frigates, the one in action, the second within gun-shot, and the third in sight, carried 18 and 9 pounders.

The search having been made, and no contraband of war found, Sir Richard was about proceeding to rejoin his commanding officer at anchor in the road, but the French captain declined to continue in charge of his surrendered ship. The Résolue was therefore taken possession of by the British, towed into the road of Mahé, and there left with yards and topmasts struck.

M. Saint-Félix, the commodore of the French squadron, arrived soon afterwards, in the 40-gun frigate Cybèle; and a correspondence, conducted with much anger on one side, and with temper and firmness on the other, ensued between the French and British commodores. M. Saint-Félix threatened further resistance, if any vessels under his orders were attempted to be detained.

It appears, however, that the Cybèle and Résolue afterwards got under way and put to sea, attended by the Minerva and Phœnix; who cruised with them several days, and also brought to some vessels under French colours without interruption. M. Saint-Félix subsequently despatched the Résolue on another service; and Commodore Cornwallis did the same with the Phœnix. The Minerva and Cybèle were thus left cruising together; but, although the two commodores kept each other's company for some days, we hear of no further altercation between them. The attack upon the Résolue occasioned, as may be supposed, some stir in France; but matters were then in too disturbed a state for the nation to take that notice of the transaction which, in more settled times, would certainly have been the case.

Owing to the zeal and promptitude of Mr. Baldwin, his majesty's consul at Alexandria, information that war had been declared by France, and that all the British and Dutch vessels in the ports of the latter had been seized, reached Fort St. George in Calcutta, on the 1st, and Fort William in Bengal on the 11th of June. Measures were immediately adopted for taking possession of the different French factories in this quarter; and Chandernagore, Karica, Yanam, Mahé, and some others, yielded without resistance. Such was not the case, however, with Pondicherry. This important fortress, reputed to be in full as good a state of defence as when attacked at the breaking out of the last war, was, after every requisite preparation, besieged by Colonel Braithwaite, at the head of a powerful force.

On the 1st of August, the governor, Colonel Prosper de Clermont, was summoned to surrender, but refused: and the bombardment commenced, slightly on the 20th, and with full effect on the 22nd. In less than two days the enemy's guns were silenced, and he exhibited flags of truce on all the salient angles. Upon this the fire of the British ceased, and an officer from the fort presented himself, with a letter from Colonel Clermont, desiring to capitulate, and to be allowed 24 hours to reduce the terms into form. This was refused by Colonel Braithwaite, who demanded that the place should be surrendered at discretion by 8 A.M. on the 25th; until when, he replied, he would cease to fire, but not to work. A second deputation, however, disposed Colonel Braithwaite to accept of terms less rigorous, and, on the 23rd, a capitulation was signed, which, while it considered the garrison, amounting to 645 Europeans and 1014 sepoys, as prisoners of war, secured the lives and properties of the inhabitants.

The loss sustained by the British amounted, of the Europeans, to 37 killed and 49 wounded, and of the natives, to 56 killed and 82 wounded. While the siege was carrying on, the British 38-gun frigate Minerva, Rear-admiral the Honourable William Cornwallis, assisted by three Indiamen, effectually blocked up the place by sea, chasing entirely off the coast the French frigate Cybèle, now commanded (owing, we suppose, to the change of dynasty) by Captain Pierre-Julien Thréouart, and accompanied by three smaller vessels, supposed to have on board supplies and reinforcements for the garrison.

BRITISH AND FRENCH FLEETS.

The total number of ships at the foot of this year's abstract of the British navy[1] does not greatly exceed that at the foot of the last; but in commissioned cruisers, those of the line especially, the improvement has been great. The latter have increased from 26 to 85, and the commissioned total from 135 to 279. This rapid increase is attributable not so much to the accession of newly-built or newly-captured ships as to those precautionary measures which we commended at a former page.[2] It was not the want of ships but the want of men that was so sensibly felt. Every means, however, had been used, and with some effect, to invite the seamen to enter. Where those means failed, recourse was had to the sad alternative of pressing; and at length one or more very formidable fleets were enabled to put to sea.

During the year 1793 the British cruisers had effected the capture or destruction of 140 French armed vessels, including 52 belonging to the national navy. Of the national ships, but 35 were captured, and out of these 30 were added to the British navy, exclusive of six of the 88 captured privateers.[3] On the other hand, the loss sustained by the latter was comparatively slight, including but four vessels, and not one of these above a small 32-gun frigate.[4] Five of the ships building at the commencement of the war had been launched, as well as two out of the 22 under-line ships ordered since; and the remaining 20, among which were six 18-pounder frigates, having been laid down in the merchants' yards, were most of them in great forwardness. The chief reason of this was, that the king's yards

---

[1] See Appendix, Annual Abstract, No. 2.
[2] See p 53.
[3] See Appendix, No. 9.
[4] See Appendix, No. 10.

were filled with ships under repair: moreover, none of the ships alluded to as in such forwardness exceeded a frigate in size.

The consequence we have ventured to attach to the carronade as a standard gun in the British navy imposes upon us the task of watching its progress through the several classes of ships. During the year 1793 no order issued directing its general use; but several captains obtained leave for their ships to be fitted with carronades on the quarter-deck, forecastle, and poop. One ship, too, the Redoubt, fitted up as a floating battery, was armed wholly with carronades, and those of the highest caliber, 68-pounders.

The number of commissioned officers and masters belonging to the British navy at the commencement of this year was—

Admirals	17
Vice-admirals	16
Rear-admirals	22
,, superannuated 20	
Post-captains	276
,, superannuated 24	
Commanders, or sloop-captains	167
Lieutenants	1382
,, superannuated 29	
Masters	327

and the number of seamen and marines for which supplies were voted was 85,000.[1]

Soon after the return of the Brest fleet from Belle-Isle,[2] those officers and seamen who belonged, or were suspected to belong, to the disaffected party, were sacrificed to the jacobinical rage of Robespierre and his agents. The captain and two of the lieutenants of the Côte-d'Or and the captain of the Jean-Bart were condemned to suffer death. Rear-admiral Kerguelen and some other commanders were imprisoned. The captain of the Tourville was tried, and, for a wonder, acquitted.[3] Several petty officers and seamen suffered by the guillotine, and a great many others were imprisoned or sent away in small detach-

---

[1] See Appendix, No. 11.
[2] See p. 64.
[3] A writer in the Victoires et Conquêtes (tome iii, p. 8.) states, that the second in command to Vice-admiral Morard-de-Galles, "Contre-amiral Linois" (the name repeated two or three times, and proved to mean that able and enterprising officer), escaped the fate of Captain Coetnempren by affecting fatuity. Of the two rear-admirals, second and third in command, one was named Lelarge and the other Landais. M. Linois, or Durand-Linois (as his name stands in the Etat de la Marine), at this time commanded the Atalante frigate, on her way from Isle-de-France, and, in the month of February, accompanied by the Fidelle, of the same force, brought safe to Lorient, in defiance of the English fleets and cruisers, ten richly-laden East Indiamen; a service for which France, in the then exigency of her affairs, was greatly indebted to him.

ments to the armies. The loss which the fleet thus sustained was supplied partly by the 5000 men that had just arrived from Toulon and partly by levies of landmen dragged from the interior. With respect to officers, youth and ardour in the cause of republicanism were the chief requisites sought after; and a young chef de division, M. Villaret-Joyeuse (an officer, it must be acknowledged, of some merit), was made a rear-admiral, and appointed to succeed M. Morard-de-Galles in the command of the fleet. The flag of the new commander-in-chief was immediately hoisted on board the Côte-d'Or, or, as by the orders of the National Convention this fine three-decker was newly-named on this occasion, the Montagne.[1] The names of several other ships (see list, Appendix No. 6) were also changed, the tricoloured flag was formally adopted as the national colours, and the navy of republican France, in the vaunting language of the day, became "cleansed and regenerated."

In this state of renovation and excitement the destruction of the French ships and stores at Toulon, although it had considerably weakened the power of the republic in the Mediterranean, appeared scarcely to be felt at the great depôt on the Atlantic frontier. There the dockyards and arsenals resounded with the notes of war and preparation, and every republican breast was inspired with the hope of being able ere long to strike a decisive blow against the navy of England. The seamen of Brest and Lorient, in an address to them by the deputies of the Convention, Jean-Bon Saint-André and Bréard, were told, "You will conquer them: yes, you will conquer those eternal enemies of our nation. As to that, you have but to will it, and it is done." "Never before," says a French writer, "did there exist in Brest a fleet so formidable and well disciplined as that which is now lying there. Unanimity and discipline reign among officers and men; and all burn with desire to fight the enemies of their country, to the very banks of the Thames, and under the walls of London."

That this irrepressible ardour in the French navy would, however, effect more for the national advantage if aided by an extraneous stimulant, was evidently the opinion of Jean-Bon Saint-André; for he proposed to the National Convention, and actually had interest to get adopted, a decree, declaring that the captain and officers of any ship of the line belonging to the

---

[1] The Côte-d'Or was built from the draught of the celebrated Sané (the reputed designer of 48 French line-of-battle ships), and, in size, beauty, and force, surpassed every other ship in the world, except perhaps the Commerce-de-Marseille.

republic who should haul down the national colours to the vessels, however numerous, of an enemy, unless the French ship should be so shattered as to be in danger of sinking before the crew could be saved, should be pronounced traitors to their country, and suffer death; and that the captain and officers of any frigate, corvette, or smaller vessel, who should surrender to a force double their own, unless their ship was reduced to the before-mentioned extremity, should be punished in the same manner.[1] Notwithstanding this highly insulting decree, it is but justice to the French officers to declare that they never appear to have required to be thus stimulated to do their duty.

With respect to the newly-organized French seamen, their valour was to be roused into action by less rigorous means. The report of a citizen Thibaudot was made the subject of a decree of the National Convention, and, under the designation of "Instructions to the sailors of the French republic," was transmitted to the different seaport towns. These instructions contained, for the most part, fabulous accounts of the exploits of the French navy in former days; days so remote that the memory of no man could reach them, and the events of which, for that reason, were supposed to be unknown to the illiterate sailor. "Have not French sailors," it was asked, "acquired the habit of courage and victory? Often have they conquered with an inferior force; and if sometimes their enemies have gained the advantage, it has been owing to their superiority in number of ships and of men. It is a homage which truth has extorted from the admirals of the proudest maritime nation. Admiral Byng said in his defence, 'I defy any one to produce me a single example where the English have conquered on the sea with an equal force.'"[2]

This libel upon a brave but unfortunate officer[3] requires to be refuted. Admiral Byng, after having stated that the French fleet opposed to him was superior in the size of their ships, weight of metal, and number of men, besides their advantage in point of sailing, which enabled them to fight, or avoid fighting, as best suited their purpose, adds:—"I do not plead the superiority of the enemy as a reason for not attacking them, but only why such an attempt might, not only possibly, but most pro-

---

[1] Moniteurs of Nov. 5, 1793, Jan. 12, and Feb. 5, 1794.

[2] "Je défie qu'on me cite un seul exemple où les Anglais aient vaincu sur mer à force égale."—*Mon.* Feb. 5, 1794.

[3] Shot on board the Monarch in Portsmouth Harbour, March 14, 1757 by the sentence of a court-martial, for *an error in judgment* (having been acquitted of cowardice or disaffection), in an engagement with a French fleet, off Minorca, May 20, 1756.

bably, be unsuccessful; since it is evident that, notwithstanding my previous information of their strength, I did not hesitate to attack, and do the utmost in my power to defeat them."[1] This is the only passage in the admiral's defence that bears at all on the point, and surely no one but citizen Thibaudot could have perverted its meaning.

These addresses being read by the chief officers to the different ships' companies, their effects were soon manifest in the eagerness of the seamen to be led against their ancient foe, in order to prove by their prowess that they merited the eulogiums which their masters had so liberally bestowed upon them. Old ships were fitting and new ones constructing to add such a force to the already formidable fleet in Brest water as could not fail, it was thought, to make a serious impression upon the strongest fleet that England had in her power to send to sea.

The British Channel fleet, although it had lain at anchor during the winter months, was ready for a start, the moment intelligence should arrive from the numerous cruisers off the French coast, that the Brest fleet had put to sea. As the spring advanced, two objects, exclusive of fighting the latter, rendered it necessary that Lord Howe should quit port. One was to see the East and West India and Newfoundland convoys clear of the Channel; the other to intercept a French, or rather a Franco-American convoy, amounting, as was alleged, to 350 sail, and known to be returning from the ports of the United States of America, richly laden with the produce of the West India islands; particularly with provisions and stores, of which the republic stood greatly in need; so much so that the horrors of famine were beginning to be felt.

On the 2nd of May, the whole of the merchant-vessels being assembled at St. Helen's, and the wind having shifted from the southward to the north-east, the fleet and convoy, amounting together to 148 sail, including 49 ships of war, of which 34 were of the line, weighed, and by noon got clear of the anchorage. On the 4th Lord Howe, having arrived off the Lizard, directed the different convoys to part company, detaching Rear-admiral Montagu, with six 74s and two frigates, to protect them to the latitude of Cape Finisterre;[2] Captain Peter Rainier, with the

---

[1] See "Trial of Admiral the Hon. John Byng; published by order of the Admiralty."—P. 101.

[2] Captain Brenton (Nav. Hist., vol. i., p. 246) says, "Lord Howe, after seeing the convoys to the southward of Cape Finisterre, detached Rear-admiral Montagu, with six ships of the line, to protect the trade still further, while his lordship returned and cruised 100 leagues to the westward of Ushant." A singular mistake to be made by a writer who shows (p. 250) that he had the Queen Charlotte's log to refer to.

Suffolk 74, a 64-gun ship, and four or five frigates, having previously been ordered to see them safe through the remainder of the passage. This reduced the Channel fleet to 26 sail of the line, seven frigates (including one that joined afterwards), one hospital-ship, two fireships, one brig-sloop, and two cutters; of which the following are the names:—

Gun-ship.			
100 (D)	Queen Charlotte	Admiral (union) Richard Earl Howe.	1
		Captain Sir Roger Curtis.	
		,, Sir Andrew Snape Douglas.	
	Royal George	Vice-adm. (r.) Sir Alex. Hood, K.B.	3
		Captain William Domett.	
,, (E)	Royal Sovereign	Vice-adm. (r.) Thomas Graves.	2
		Captain Henry Nichols.	
98	Barfleur	Rear-adm. (w.) George Bowyer.	
		Captain Cuthbert Collingwood.	
	Impregnable	Rear-adm. (w.) Benj. Caldwell.	5
		Captain George Blagden Westcott.	
	Queen	Rear-adm. (w.) Alan Gardner.	
		Captain John Hutt.	
	Glory	,, John Elphinstone.	
80	Gibraltar	,, Thomas Mackenzie.	
	Cæsar	,, Anth. Jas. Pye Molloy.	
74	Bellerophon	Rear-adm. (w.) Thomas Pasley.	
		Captain William Hope.	
	Montagu	,, James Montagu.	
	Tremendous	,, James Pigott.	
	Valiant	,, Thomas Pringle.	
	Ramillies	,, Henry Harvey.	
74	Audacious	,, William Parker.	
	Brunswick	,, John Harvey.	
	Alfred	,, John Bazely.	
	Defence	,, James Gambier.	
	Leviathan	,, Lord Hugh Seymour.	
	Majestic	,, Charles Cotton.	
	Invincible	,, Hon. Thomas Pakenham.	
	Orion	, John Thomas Duckworth.	
	Russel	,, John Willet Payne.	
	Marlborough	,, Hon. G. Cranfield Berkeley.	
	Thunderer	,, Albemarle Bertie.	
	Culloden	,, Isaac Schomberg.	

Gun-frig.	Frigates.		
38	Phaëton	,, William Bentinck.	
	Latona	,, Edward Thornborough.	
32 (H)	Niger	,, Hon. Arthur Kaye Legge.	
	Southampton	,, Hon. Robert Forbes.	
	Venus	,, William Brown.	
	Aquilon	,, Hon. Robert Stopford.	
28	Pegasus	,, Robert Barlow.	
H. S.	Charon	,, George Countess.	

Gun frigate.	Frigates.		
F. S.	{ Comet . . .	Captain	William Bradley.
	{ Incendiary . .	„	John Cook.
Slp.	Kingfisher . .	„	Thomas Le Marchant Gosselyn.
Cut.	{ Rattler . . .	Lieut.	John Winne.
	{ Ranger . . .	„	Charles Cotgrave.

Lord Howe immediately steered for, and on the 5th, early in the morning, arrived off Ushant. The Phaëton and Latona frigates, covered by the Orion, then ran round the island, to ascertain whether or not the French fleet was in port. While standing in towards point St. Mathieu, the reconnoitring ships plainly saw the fleet at anchor in Brest-road, and returned to Lord Howe with the intelligence. The British admiral, well aware that, if the French fleet came out, it would be to afford protection to the convoy then hourly expected from America, steered straight for the latitude through which the latter would most probably pass. From the 5th to the 18th inclusive the fleet kept crossing the bay in various directions, without seeing an enemy's sail.

On the 19th Lord Howe, having returned off Ushant, again ordered the Phaëton and Latona, covered this time by the Cæsar and Leviathan, to look into the harbour. At 11 A. M. the four ships parted company. The service was executed, and the port found vacant; and at 8 P.M. the reconnoitring detachment rejoined the fleet. The Leviathan, on her way in, had spoken an American vessel, from whose master Lord Hugh Seymour learned, that the French fleet, of what force not exactly known, had sailed from Brest some days before.

We shall now proceed to furnish such particulars relative to the strength and object of the grand armament which France had equipped and sent to sea as the studied concealment and obscurity that pervade the French accounts will permit. Since early in May the convoy from the United States, under the protection of Rear-admiral Vanstabel, with the two 74-gun ships Jean-Bart and Tigre, two frigates and a brig, had been expected to make its appearance off the French coast. The above squadron, which had put to sea from Brest on the 26th of December, had arrived at Norfolk, Virginia, early in February, and sailed again on the 2nd of April, with a convoy numbering 117 sail, all deeply laden with provisions and West-Indian produce. On the 6th of May Rear-admiral Nielly, with the five following ships of the line,—

Gun-ship.
80	Sans-Pareil . . .	{ Rear-adm. Joseph-Marie Nielly,
		{ Captain Jean-François Courand,

Gun-ship.

74 {
Audacieux . . . Captain Jean-François Pilastre,
l'atriote . . . . ,, ———— Lucadore,
Téméraire . . . ,, ———— Morel,
Trajan . . . . ,, ———— Dumourier,
}

and several frigates and corvettes, sailed from Rochefort, with orders to form a junction with Rear-admiral Vanstabel and the convoy, in latitude 47° 48' north, and longitude 15° 17' west of Paris, because of the asserted knowledge, that a British squadron had been detached to intercept it.

On the 16th of May, at 5 h. 30 m P.M., the grand fleet of France, consisting of the following 25 ships of the line, besides 15 or 16 frigates and corvettes, under the joint command of Rear-admiral Villaret-Joyeuse and the Conventional deputy Jean-Bon Saint-André, who accompanied the admiral in the Montagne, sailed from the road of Brest, with a fair wind at north east :—

Gun-ship.

120 Montagne	Rear-adm.	Louis-Thomas Villaret-Joyeuse.
	Commod.	———— Bazire.
	Captain	Jean-François Vignot.
110 { Terrible	,,	Pierre-Jacques Longer.
Révolutionnaire	,,	———— Vandangel.
Républicain	Rear-adm.	François-Joseph Bouvet.
	Captain	Pierre-Mandé Lebeau.
80 { Indomptable	,,	———— Lamel.
Jacobin	,,	———— Gassin.
Juste	,,	———— Blavet.
Scipion	,,	———— Huguet.
74 { Achille	,,	Guil.-Jean-Noël La Villegris.
America	,,	Louis L'Héritier.
Conception	,,	Joseph-Allary.
Entreprenant	,,	———— Le Franc.
Eole	,,	Bertrand Keranguin.
Gasparin	,,	———— Tardy.
Jemmappes	,,	———— Desmartis.
Impétueux	,,	———— Douville.
Montagnard	,,	Jean-Baptiste-François Bompart.
Mont-Blanc	,,	Thévenard.
Mucius	,,	———— Larréguy.
Neptune	,,	———— Tiphaine.
Northumberland	,,	François-Pierre Etienne.
Pelletier	,,	———— Berard.
Tourville	,,	———— Langlois.
Tyrannicide	,,	Alain-Joseph Dordelin.
Vengeur	,,	———— Renaudin.

The object of this fleet being in part the same as that of the detachment which had quitted Rochefort, its course was nearly similar. It is a singular fact that, during the dense fog of the following day, the 17th, the French fleet passed so near to the British fleet, as to hear the latter's fog-signals, of ringing bells and beating drums; and yet, when the fog cleared away on the morning of the 18th, the two fleets had separated sufficiently to be out of each other's sight.

On the 19th M. Villaret was joined by the Patriote from M. Nielly's squadron, with information that he had been so lucky as to fall in with and capture the British 32-gun frigate Castor, Captain Thomas Troubridge, along with the chief part of a convoy from Newfoundland, which the frigate had in charge. On the same day M. Villaret himself had the good fortune to fall in with the Lisbon convoy, of 53 sail, chiefly Dutch vessels under the care of the Dutch frigate Alliance and corvette Waakzaamheid. The ships of war effected their escape, but 18 or 20 vessels of the fleet were captured. We will now quit M. Villaret for a while, and attend to the proceedings of the British admiral, who was so strenuously endeavouring to fall in with him.

On the 19th, in the evening, the Venus frigate, from Rear-admiral Montagu's squadron, joined Lord Howe. The rear-admiral, having on the 11th parted from the East-India fleet, cruised, as he had been directed, between Cape Ortugal and the latitude of Belle-Isle, for the purpose of endeavouring to intercept the French convoy daily expected from North America. On the 15th his squadron captured the French 20-gun ship-corvette Maire-Guiton, one of M. Nielly's squadron, and recaptured 10 sail of the Newfoundland convoy, recently taken by the latter, and which the corvette was escorting to a port of France. It was the intelligence obtained from the prisoners in the recaptured vessels, as well respecting the squadron of Rear-admiral Nielly, as respecting that on its way from the Chesapeake under Rear-admiral Vanstabel, consisting, it now appeared, of four, instead of two sail of the line, and thus making, should the two squadrons unite, a force of nine sail of the line and several frigates and corvettes, that induced Rear-admiral Montagu to detach the Venus to Lord Howe, requesting a reinforcement. He then, with his six two-deckers and remaining frigate, proceeded straight along the same parallel of longitude to the latitude (from 45° to 47° north) in which, according to the information of the prisoners, the Rochefort squadron had been directed to cruise; in the hope of being in time to intercept the convoy, before M. Nielly could effect his junction with it, or, should the latter have done so, of soon receiving the expected reinforcement, and still accomplishing the object of his instructions.

Considering, from the course which the French fleet would probably steer, that Rear-admiral Montagu was in jeopardy, Lord Howe, at 4 A.M. on the 20th, made all sail, to save the squadron, if possible, from the hands of M. Villaret. By noon on the 20th the British fleet was enabled to make good a course west by south. Nothing occurred worthy of notice until about 2 A.M. on the 21st, when the look-out ships made the signal for a strange fleet. This proved to be a part of the Lisbon convoy, taken by the Brest fleet, as already mentioned. Out of 15 or 16 ships, brigs, and schooners, which made their appearance, 10 were secured, and, on the removal of their crews, burnt; Lord Howe not wishing to weaken his crews by sending the prizes into port. The remainder of the convoy effected their escape.

The prisoners gave information that the French fleet, when they quitted it on the evening of the 19th, was between two and three degrees to the westward, and that it consisted of 26 sail of the line and four frigates. The additional sail of the line was, as we have stated, the Patriote from M. Nielly's division; and the reduction in the number of frigates arose, probably, from the frequent intercourse necessary to be maintained between the three French admirals, Villaret, Vanstabel, and Nielly. A careful comparison of the logs of the different merchant-ships placed the French fleet on the day mentioned in latitude 47° 46' north, and longitude 11° 22' west of Greenwich. Among other particulars gleaned from the prisoners were, the presence of Jean-Bon Saint-André, the intended employment of hot shot, and a piece of information peculiarly gratifying to the British sailors, the alleged determination of the French officers to engage at close quarters.

No sooner did Lord Howe receive the exhilarating intelligence of the French fleets being so near, than he gave up the idea of joining Rear-admiral Montagu, whom he now considered to be far enough to the southward to be out of danger, and pressed his fleet in pursuit of M. Villaret. At noon on the 21st a favourable change of wind enabled the fleet to make a great stretch to the northward and westward; but, at noon on the 22nd, the wind returned to its old quarter, and drove the fleet to the southward. On the 23rd, at 8 A.M., came into the fleet a Dutch dogger and two or three captured merchant-ships, which had parted from the French fleet two days before. At noon on the same day the wind again favoured the British; so that by noon on the next day, the 24th, according to the logs of the recaptured vessels, Lord Howe was within five miles of the same longitude, and within half a degree of the same latitude as that in which the French fleet had been left on the 21st; namely, in latitude 47° 34' north, and longitude 13° 55' west of Greenwich.

After this the British fleet again fell off to nearly a west-south-west course, and so continued without any occurrence of moment happening until the 25th, at 4 A.M.; when a French 74-gun ship, with a merchant-brig in tow, was discovered at a great distance to windward, and a strange ship and brig, evidently cruisers, to the eastward. Chase was given by the Audacious and the Niger frigate to the vessels to the eastward, and by the fleet in general to the line-of-battle ship to windward. The latter, casting off her prize, effected her escape, by manifest superiority of sailing. The merchant-brig proved to be an American, laden with wine, and the line-of-battle ship, the Audacieux, on her way to the Brest fleet from M. Nielly's squadron; from which she had, on the preceding evening, parted company: as had also the two vessels in sight; one, the 20-gun ship-corvette Républicaine, the other the 16-gun brig Inconnue. These, less fortunate than their consort, became the prizes of the ships that had chased them, and with the American brig, were committed to the flames.

Having tacked in chase, the fleet, on the 25th at noon, again hauled on the starboard-tack, with the wind at north by east. On the 26th, at daylight, the fleet once more tacked, and at noon, the wind having shifted to west by south, steered to the northward. On the 27th, at 9 A.M., having got a few leagues to the northward of the latitude in which he had reason to think M. Villaret was cruising, Lord Howe bore up and ran to the eastward, with the wind, which had drawn more to the southward, on the starboard quarter.

On the 28th, at 6 h. 30 m. A.M., latitude at noon 47° 34 north, longitude 13° 39' west, the wind fresh from south by west, with a very rough sea, the look-out frigates of the British fleet, then formed in the order of sailing, made the signal for a sail in the south-south-east, and immediately afterwards, for a strange fleet directly to windward. At 8 h. 15 m. A.M. Rear admiral Pasley, in the Bellerophon, which ship, with the Russel, Marlborough, and Thunderer, formed the weathermost division, was ordered to reconnoitre; and at 9 A.M. the strange fleet, having wore, was seen, with topgallant sails set, bearing down towards the fleet of the British. Lord Howe now made the signal to prepare for battle, and at 9 h. 45 m. A.M., having previously, for their safety, recalled the frigates, ordered the Bellerophon, by signal, to shorten sail. At 10 A.M. the French fleet, which consisted of 26 sail of the line[1] and five frigates, having approached within nine or ten miles, hauled to the wind on the larboard-tack, and lay to. Three of the ships were observed to be shifting their maintopsails, and one a maintopsail yard. After a considerable delay, during which a three-decker was seen to pass along the line as if to speak each ship, the French fleet formed an indifferent line ahead. At 10 h. 35 m. A.M. the British fleet, having, by signal from the Queen Charlotte, wore round in succession, came to on the same tack as the French, and pressed to windward, in two columns, having the weather division already named as a flying squadron. At 11 h. 10 m. A.M. the signal was made, that there would be time for the ship's companies to dine.

At 1 P.M., or a little after, the French ships filled and made sail, and soon afterwards commenced tacking. At 1 h. 30 m. P.M. the British flying squadron was ordered to harass the enemy's rear-ships; and in a quarter of an hour afterwards, it appearing that the French were inclined to make off, Lord Howe threw out the signal for a general chase. This was almost immediately followed by another, to engage the enemy on arriving up with him.

At 2 h. 30 m. P.M., the Russel, being nearly a mile to windward of the other ships of her division, discharged a few shots at the enemy's sternmost ships as they were hauling on the starboard tack, and the latter fired in return. At a little before 3 P.M. the Bellerophon, just as the enemy's rear-ship, a two-decker, was right abeam, tacked; as did, by signal, the whole of the British fleet, excepting the Russel, Marlborough, Thunderer, and frigates, which ships, for the purpose of getting into the wake of the French fleet, now close hauled in line ahead on the starboard tack, with the wind fresh and squally from the southward, stood on a little longer.

At a few minutes past 5 P.M. the French van and centre shortened sail, in order, as it appeared to the British, that the Révolutionnaire might exchange places with the rearmost two-decker.[2] At 6 P.M. the Bellerophon, notwithstanding that this

[1] The same that are named in p. 141, with the addition of the Patriote, as noticed in p. 142.

[2] According to M. Jean-Bon Saint-André's official report, this act of the French three-decker was not sanctioned by the

day, from some defect in her trim, she was the slowest sailor of her division, got near enough, by having embraced the proper moment for tacking, to open her fire upon the gallant French three-decker, now, of her own choice, the rearmost and most exposed ship of her fleet. At 6 h. 20 m. P.M. the Marlborough, then with the Russel and Thunderer on the Bellerophon's weather quarter, was ordered to engage the rear of the enemy, who had just made sail. The Bellerophon, having had her main cap upset and disabled by a shot, was now obliged to take in her maintopsail. In consequence of this accident and of the wounded state of her mainmast, Rear-admiral Pasley, after having, for upwards of an hour and a quarter, been unsupported in his very gallant engagement with the Révolutionnaire, made the signal of inability, and bore up.

By this time the Russel, Marlborough, and Thunderer had backed their maintopsails and opened a distant fire upon the Révolutionnaire, as well as upon the ship next ahead of her. Having just lost her mizenmast,[1] and being otherwise much disabled by the well-directed fire of the Bellerophon, the Révolutionnaire wore round on her heel, and put before the wind. Almost as soon as she had borne up, the crippled three-decker was intercepted and engaged by the Leviathan, who, with the Audacious, had passed to windward of the Bellerophon in the latter's disabled state.

At 7 h. 30 m. P.M. the Queen Charlotte made the signal, "to assist ships engaged," and in a minute or two afterwards repeated it, with the Russel and Marlborough's pendants. Meanwhile the Leviathan continued to engage the Révolutionnaire until the coming up of the Audacious. The Leviathan then passed on, fired a broadside at the next ship in the French line, but at 8 P.M., in compliance with the signals just made by the commander-in-chief (to form line ahead and astern as most convenient, and for the Bellerophon, Leviathan, Russel, and Marlborough to leave off chase), dropped down towards the main body of the fleet.

The Audacious, having placed herself on the Révolutionnaire's lee quarter, poured in a heavy fire; and, until recalled by signal,

---

admiral: "Un de nos vaisseaux, le Révolutionnaire, par des motifs que nous ignorons encore, avait diminué de voile à l'apparition de l'ennemi. Malgré les signaux que lui furent faits, il demeura sous le vent et de l'arrière de l'armée, en sorte qu'a l'entrée de la nuit, et lorsque nous ne pouvions plus l'observer, il fut engagé par plusieurs vaisseaux Anglais."

[1] She had caught fire in the top, and it may have been cut away, in order that it might not, in its crippled state, fall in board.

the Russel, who was at some distance to leeward, also fired at her. The Audacious and Révolutionnaire now became so closely engaged, and the latter so disabled in her masts and rigging, that it was with difficulty the former could prevent her huge opponent from falling on board of her. Towards 10 P.M. the Révolutionnaire having, besides the loss of her mizenmast, had her fore and main yards and maintopsail yard shot away, dropped across the hawse of the Audacious; but the latter quickly extricated herself, and the French ship, with her foretopsail full, but, owing to the sheets having been shot away, still flying, directed her course to leeward.

The men quartered forward in the Audacious, declared that the Révolutionnaire struck her colours just as she got clear of them; and the ship's company cheered in consequence. The people of the Russel declared, also, that the Révolutionnaire, as she passed under their stern, had no colours hoisted. That the latter was a beaten ship may be inferred from her having returned but three shots to the last broadside of the Audacious: moreover, her loss in killed and wounded amounted, if the French accounts are to be credited, to nearly 400 men. Still the Révolutionnaire became no prize to the British; owing partly to the disabled state of the Audacious, but chiefly because the Thunderer, on approaching the latter, and being hailed to take possession of the French ship, made sail after her own fleet.

Such was the crippled state of the Audacious, that it was some time before she was enabled to wear clear of the French line. Having effected this, she used every effort to repair her damages, in time to resume her station at daylight. The loss on board the ship (and the Audacious appears to have been the only ship that sustained any loss by the Révolutionnaire's fire) bore no proportion to the extent of the injuries done to her masts, yards, rigging, and sails. She had but three men killed, and 19 (including three mortally) wounded. Just as daylight arrived, nine sail of French ships[1] made their appearance about three miles to windward. The Audacious, who was now with her standing rigging very indifferently stoppered, her foresail and three topsails unbent, and her main topsail in the top, in

---

[1] It is doubtful what ships these were. The squadron of M. Vanstabel consisted, besides his prizes, stated to be 10 in number, of eight square-rigged vessels, and he was certainly within hearing of the firing on the 28th. The squadron of M. Nielly was also not far distant. Moreover, two small squadrons from Lorient and Rochefort were cruising in the bay, one under the command of Commodore Jean Joseph Castagnier.

the act of being bent, put before the wind, with the main and foretopmast staysails only, and those ill set from the stays having been shot away.

Fortunately, the prevailing haze brought down rain and thick weather, and screened the Audacious, in some degree, from the enemy's view. The greatest exertions were made by every officer and man to get the ship under sail; but before that could be accomplished, the haze cleared, and discovered two ships in chase, which, in all probability, were the Audacieux and a frigate, detached by M. Villaret in search of the Révolutionnaire. At this time the Audacious passed her old opponent, without any mast standing, at the distance of about a mile and a half. Just as the Audacious had set sail enough to maintain her distance ahead of her pursuers from the southward, the French 36-gun frigate Bellone, accompanied by a ship and brig-corvette, came rapidly up from the eastward.

These, observing the shattered condition of the Audacious, the state of whose masts would not admit of an alteration in her course, and encouraged by the proximity of their friends, whom they saw bearing down under all sail, stood athwart the crippled ship, and exchanged several shots with her. The two corvettes, however, soon dropped astern, but the Bellone, for upwards of an hour, hung on the quarter of the Audacious, harassing, but not materially injuring her.

Either feeling the effects of some of the 74's aftermost guns, or tired of a vain pursuit, the frigate, at about half an hour after noon, after making a signal to her consorts astern, left off chase, and hauled to the wind. In a little while afterwards the weather again became hazy, and the Audacious got once more out of sight of her pursuers. Having run 24 leagues directly to leeward, and being unable to haul to the wind, the Audacious deemed it best to proceed straight into port, and accordingly, on the morning of the 3rd of June, anchored in Plymouth Sound. Fortunately for the Révolutionnaire, she was soon found by the Audacieux; who, taking the dismasted three-decker in tow, conveyed her in safety to Rochefort.[1]

After the Audacious and Révolutionnaire had parted company from their respective fleets, both of the latter continued on the starboard tack during the remainder of the night, steering, under a press of sail, in a parallel direction. Every ship in the British fleet carried a light; but none was observed to be carried by

---

[1] The similarity of name in the ship that had fought, and the ship that now succoured, the Révolutionnaire, threw a great deal of confusion into the accounts.

any of the French ships.[1] On the 29th, at daylight, the wind still fresh from south by west, with a heavy head sea, the rival fleets were about six miles apart; the fleet of the French on the weather bow of that of the British. At a little after 4 A.M., a strange line-of-battle ship, on the larboard tack, was observed stretching into the French line. This was the Audacieux; which ship, however, did not, as represented in most of the accounts, remain with M. Villaret, but was presently detached, as already mentioned, with a frigate, in search of the Révolutionnaire.

At 7 A.M., when the chasing ships of the preceding night, in obedience to a signal made by the Queen Charlotte, had fallen into their stations in line ahead and astern of her, as most convenient, Lord Howe, with the view of making some impression on the enemy's rear, directed the ships of the fleet, formed thus: Cæsar, Queen, Russel, Valiant, Royal George, Invincible, Orion, Majestic, Leviathan, Queen Charlotte, Bellerophon, remainder uncertain, to tack in succession. At 7 h. 30 m. A.M., the fleet being now on the larboard tack, a signal was made to pass through the enemy's line, in order to obtain the weather-gage; and at 7 h. 35 m. A.M., another signal, giving permission to fire on the enemy in passing, but without the intention, on account of the distance, to bring on an immediate general action.[2] As the British van neared the French rear on the opposite tack, the latter fired, but at too great a distance to deserve a return, until about 20 minutes afterwards; when the ships of the British fleet having hoisted the red ensign, the commander-in-chief the union at the main, and the other admirals their respective flags, the Cæsar and Queen opened a fire in passing.

At 8 A.M. the van ships of the French began wearing in succession, to support their rear thus menaced, and, running to leeward of their line, edged down towards the centre and van of the British. Having passed the rear of her fleet, the leading French ship, then distant about three miles from the British centre, hauled close to the wind, as did successively the ships astern of her. At 9 A.M., or a few minutes after, the whole of

---

[1] And yet the following statement appears in a French account of this rencontre: "Il était nuit, et la flotte française avait hissé des fanaux à tous ses mâts d'artimon. Les Anglais finirent par imiter cet exemple, après avoir long-temps hésité à le faire, et les deux flottes purent enfin s'apercevoir." — *Victoires et Conquêtes*, tome iii., p. 15.

[2] It is evident that the naval historian has here fallen into an error. If the English fleet were to pass *through* the enemy's line, it is obvious that the fleets, during the operation of *passing through*, could not be at too great a distance to engage. The fact is, that in endeavouring to get the weather-gage, the van of the English fleet passed astern of the rear of the enemy's line.—*Note by the Editor*.

the French fleet being then on the larboard tack, the same as the British fleet, the van-ships of the former again bore away, and at 10 A.M. opened their fire, but without effect, upon the van-ships of the latter. Soon afterwards the distance between the two vans became lessened; and the Invincible (who gallantly luffed out of the line to get nearer to the enemy), Royal George, Valiant, Russel, Queen, and Cæsar, in succession, exchanged broadsides with the French van, and did an evident injury to the leading ship, the Montagnard. Nor did the British van escape with entire impunity, several of the ships having had their rigging and sails, and one or two their masts and yards, considerably damaged. At 11 h. 30 m. A.M., the signal was made to tack in succession, with the view of passing through the enemy's line. Finding, however, that the British van was not sufficiently advanced to cut off more than a few of the French rear ships, Lord Howe presently annulled the signal, and continued to stretch on upon the larboard tack. At half-past noon the signal to tack was repeated; but, owing to the smoke, it remained for awhile unseen, and, when seen, was only, as we shall proceed to show, partially obeyed.

The leading ship in the British line, the Cæsar, making the signal of "inability to tack," wore, and ran past the eighth ship of her own line (and which eighth ship, the Majestic, appears to have been at least three-quarters of a mile astern of her leader, the Orion), before she hauled close to the wind on the starboard tack, and cut through; and, even then, the Cæsar kept rather off, instead of close to the wind; or, in other words, from the enemy, instead of towards him. At a few minutes before 1 P.M., just as the Terrible, the third French ship from the rear, by heavy pitching, had carried away her foretopmast, the Queen wore, and, rounding to under her second astern, luffed up, so as to open a distant fire on the third ship of the French van. The Queen then passed along the French line, and, by the time she had reached the centre ship, became closely engaged.

The signal to engage and cut through the enemy's line, hoisted at 1 h 15 m. P.M., was then flying; but the Queen had sustained too much damage to haul up for that purpose, and at 2 h. 45 m. made the signal of disability. At 3 h. 25 m. P.M., having passed the last ship in the French line, the Queen ceased firing, and with difficulty wore round on the larboard tack. Neither the Russel nor the Valiant, both of which had wore, succeeded in getting very near to the enemy. The Royal

George was the first ship that tacked; and the Invincible took the earliest opportunity of wearing under her stern: they both luffed up on the starboard tack, but, on account of the progress then made by the French fleet, could only succeed in bringing to action the two rearmost French ships, the Tyrannicide and Indomptable.

It is now time to attend to the Queen Charlotte. The small quantity of sail carried by the Cæsar, namely, treble-reefed topsails and foresail, with the maintopsail part of the time unbent on account of a split in it (yet her signal to set more sail had been twice made), and some unexplained cause of delay in the Majestic, rendered it very difficult for the Queen Charlotte to keep astern of her leader, and drove her, in consequence of the small sail she was obliged to carry, considerably to leeward of the line; which line, from these causes, had become very loose and irregular.

In this state Lord Howe, observing that the Queen was suffering greatly from the enemy's fire, and apprehensive that, owing to the Cæsar's inattention to the signal to carry more sail, the French ships, all of which carried their mainsails, and the greater part of them single-reefed topsails, would pass so far ahead as to defeat his intended manœuvre, resolved himself to set the example of breaking through the enemy's line.

Accordingly, at 1 h. 30 m. P.M., carrying now double-reefed topsails, courses, jib, and maintopmast staysail, the Queen Charlotte tacked, and hauled up to east-south-east, passed astern and to windward of the Cæsar, then steering east by north, she passed astern and to leeward of the Orion, who had not yet gone about. Stretching boldly on, heedless of the fire opened upon her from the French line, the Queen Charlotte arrived abreast of the opening between the sixth and seventh ships from the rear; but, doubtful if she could pass through without getting foul, the Queen Charlotte kept away, and, pouring a broadside into the lee beam of the Eole, as was evidently the sixth ship's name, repeated it while luffing close round her stern: a manœuvre which we have endeavoured to illustrate by the Diagram in p. 152.

The Bellerophon and Leviathan, the Queen Charlotte's two seconds, quickly tacked after their gallant chief. The Bellerophon succeeded in passing ahead of the Terrible; who, from the leeward position of the Tyrannicide and Indomptable, was in reality the rearmost ship in the French line, and who, on account of the loss of her foretopmast, had herself dropped somewhat astern; thus leaving two ships between her, the Bellerophon, and the space through which the Queen Charlotte had passed. Having, previously to tacking, had her wheel shot away, the Leviathan could only fetch to windward of the two disabled French ships already named.

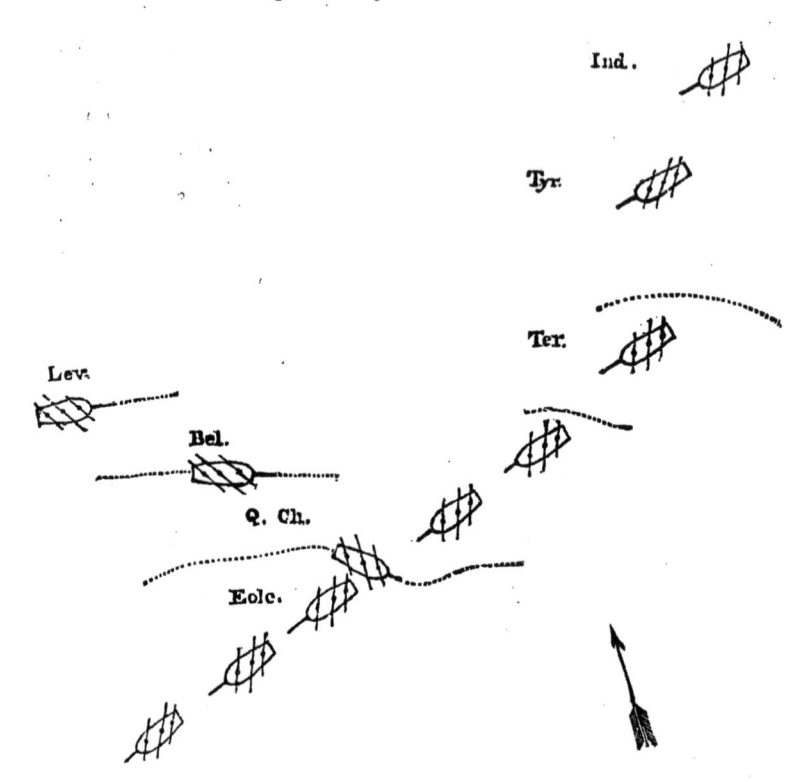

As soon as possible after she had gone through the French line, the Queen Charlotte put about on the larboard tack, and, hoisting the signal for a general chase, left the two disabled ships, Tyrannicide and Indomptable, to be brought to by her friends astern, and pursued the Terrible, then, using her utmost efforts to regain her station, with her foretopmast gone as already mentioned; and who, (the French van having by this time wore round on the starboard tack,) reached nearly the centre of her fleet before the Queen Charlotte could get near enough to open a fire upon her.

The Orion, who had wore next to the Invincible, passed

between the Tyrannicide and Indomptable, then at some distance apart. Being in too disabled a state to obey the signal to tack in chase, the Orion bore up, and on the Queen Charlotte's making her signal to engage, placed herself, with her maintopsail aback, upon the lee-quarter of the Indomptable. By the time the Orion had poured two broadsides into her disabled antagonist, her place alongside of the latter was taken by the Barfleur, who had come up under a press of sail, and a few of whose shot, as she commenced engaging, appear to have struck the Orion. Notwithstanding the additional fire thus poured upon her by the three-decker, the Indomptable bravely kept her colours flying. One of the other crippled French ships, however, appears to have struck hers; but, in a few minutes afterwards, receiving a rememorative broadside from one of her consorts, she quickly rehoisted them.

The conduct of the Cæsar, in running down her own line instead of hauling up towards that of the enemy, was considered by the French admiral, and very naturally, as the sole effect of the heavy fire opened by his van: hence, says Jean-Bon Saint-André, "the advanced ships of the enemy, being forced to give way, put about towards their rear." Whether animated by this apparent shyness in his opponent, and resolved to bring on an action, or apprehensive that his rear would be cut off unless he promptly gave it support, M. Villaret made the signal for his fleet to wear in succession. By an extraordinary coincidence in reference to what had occurred in the British fleet, the French van-ship, the Montagnard, with her masts all standing, but disabled, no doubt, in rigging and hull, continued in apparent contempt of the signal, to stand on upon the larboard tack.

Another strange coincidence it was, that the French admiral, finding his signal not obeyed, wore out of the line, and, as gallantly as judiciously, led his own fleet on the starboard tack to the rescue of his two disabled ships in the rear. Nor could Lord Howe, in the unsupported state of the Queen Charlotte, who had only near her the Bellerophon and Leviathan, and they in a crippled state upon her lee-quarter, prevent the complete success of the French admiral's well-designed, and, as acknowledged by many in the British fleet, prettily-executed manœuvre.

All the Queen Charlotte could do was to wear, and, with the other ships which, at 4 P.M., she called about her, run down to cover the Queen and Royal George, towards whom the French admiral now seemed to be bending his course. This movement again brought the two vans within random shot, and some firing was interchanged, in which the Glory had an opportunity of distinguishing herself: she passed three French ships in succession within pistol-shot, and, giving them a broadside apiece, succeeded in knocking away a topmast from each of two of them.

But even this did not bring on a general engagement; for the French admiral, satisfied apparently with having extricated his two disabled ships, wore round, and, standing away large on the larboard tack, rejoined his rear. The British fleet wore in the same direction, but kept the weather-gage; and at a few minutes after 5 P.M. all firing ceased. Each fleet now busied itself in forming a line on the larboard tack, and in repairing the damages occasioned by this smart, though partial contest.

The lower deck of the Queen Charlotte, owing to the lowness of her ports (four feet and a half) and the roughness of the sea, was full of water; and the pumps, during the greater part of the ensuing night, were kept constantly going. In other respects, the Queen Charlotte, considering her exposed situation, suffered very little. Of the 12 or 14 ships that had the good fortune to be engaged, the Queen, Royal George, Royal Sovereign, and Invincible, were those only whose casualties were of serious consequence.[1]

[1] The following is an account of the damages sustained by some of the ships, as extracted from their logs:—

Principal Damage in

Ships.	Hull.	Masts and Rigging.
Cæsar	Leaky from shot-holes: two 24-pounders split.	Fore-yard cut; also stays and rigging.
Queen	Struck repeatedly, but not so low as to occasion leaks.	Mizentopmast and fore-yard shot away: mainmast, bowsprit, and foretopmast shot through.
Russel	Leaky from shot-holes.	Bowsprit shot through; braces, &c.
Royal George	Ditto.	Mizentopsail yard shot away: shrouds, braces, &c.
Invincible	Hull not materially hurt.	Maintopmast shot away: main and fore masts and yards shot through.
Orion	Ditto.	Mizenyard shot in two: mainmast and maintopmast, mizentopmast, and spanker-boom shot through.
Majestic	Ditto.	Mizenmast cut through (between poop and quarter-deck) by a 36-pound shot.
Ramillies	Ditto, a gun dismounted.	Sails, rigging, &c., cut.
Queen Charlotte	Hull not materially hurt.	Mizenyard injured also rigging, &c.
Defence	Ditto.	Sails, rigging, &c.
Royal Sovereign	Ditto.	Mainmast, maintopmast bowsprit, and main-yard injured.

The Cæsar had three seamen and marines killed, and 19 wounded; the Queen, her master (William Mitchell), and 21 petty-officers, seamen, and marines or soldiers[1] killed, and her captain, who lost his leg at the same instant that the master fell, sixth lieutenant (Robert Lawrie), and 25 petty-officers, seamen and marines or soldiers wounded; the Royal George, including her eighth lieutenant, George Heighman, and one midshipman, 15 killed, and 23 wounded; the Invincible, 10 killed, and 21 wounded, including one midshipman, William Whithurst; the Royal Sovereign, eight killed, and 22 wounded; the Orion and Ramillies, three killed each; and the Defence, Majestic, and Queen Charlotte, each one killed, the latter her sixth lieutenant, Roger A. Rawlinson. The Defence and Majestic had also, one three and the other thirteen wounded: making a total loss to the British fleet, of 67 killed, and 128 wounded.

Such were the exertions on board the Queen, that, before dark, a maintopsail yard was got up for a fore-yard, a foretopgallantmast for a mizentopmast, a foretopgallant yard for a mizentopsail yard; new sails were also bent fore and aft, and the ship was again reported ready for service.

That several of the French ships were damaged in their masts, yards, and rigging, was evident to the British fleet; but what particular ships, exclusive of the Indomptable and Tyrannicide, had so suffered, cannot at this late day be ascertained.

From the moment that he gained sight of the British fleet on the morning of the 28th, until he wore on the afternoon of the 29th, the French admiral possessed the weather-gage of his opponent. M. Villaret, therefore, had it at his option to bring on a general action. His declining to do so may raise an inference, that he considered himself to be inferior in point of force. To ascertain in what relation as to strength the two parties really stood on the morning of the first skirmish, shall therefore be our next inquiry; and, as this is the first instance of a meeting between two hostile fleets, we shall be obliged, in describing the force on each side, to enter more into minutiæ than is likely to be necessary on any future occasion.

With one or two exceptions, the British ships mounted precisely the same number and nature of long guns as are assigned to their several classes in the abstract for the year 1793. The

---

[1] Detachments of the Queen's and 29th regiments were serving on board the British fleet as marines, and soldiers appear to have served in a similar manner on board the French fleet.

first exception is the Royal Sovereign; that ship having received on board two 24-pounders for her entrance-ports on the second deck, in lieu of two 12-pounders taken from her forecastle. The next exception is the Gibraltar, formerly a Spanish 80-gun ship: her first-deck ports, being found too small to receive 32-pounders, were fitted with 24s; of which she mounted 62 on her two principal decks, along with eighteen 9-pounders on her quarter-deck and forecastle.[1]

The carronades of such ships as mounted any appear, with two exceptions, to have been of no higher caliber than 18-pounders. The names of the Alfred and Ramillies occur in the list we referred to at a former page;[2] the one with four, the other with eight (two on the forecastle) 12-pounder carronades. The only ships in Lord Howe's fleet that appear, besides, to have mounted any carronades, are the Leviathan and Marlborough, and those carronades, two on board of each, were 68-pounders. Some of the ships, and among them the Cæsar, had no poop-bulwark; others were ordered poop-carronades on a subsequent day; which shows that, at this time, they had none. In order to make ample allowance for any ships that may have procured carronades without a special order (and no general order, as a peremptory one, then existed), we shall consider ten ships as having mounted six 18-pounder carronades each; making, with the Leviathan and Marlborough's four 68-pounders, 64 carronades for the whole British fleet.

As to the complements, although a slight reduction in the crews of British ships of war appears to have been ordered since the preceding April, and although there was notoriously, at this period, a scarcity of seamen in the British navy, we shall, meaning to make a corresponding allowance on the other side, assign to Lord Howe's ships the establishment ordered for each class at the commencement of the year 1793;[3] deducting, of course, the widow's men, and adding to the crews of several of the flag-ships the customary supernumeraries, namely, 50 men for the commander-in-chief, 25 for each of the two other full admirals, and 15 for every one of the four rear-admirals. This will make the aggregate complements of the British fleet amount to 17,241 men and boys. With respect to the size of the ships, having

---

[1] See Appendix, Annual Abstract, No. 1. For the guns of the two 18-pdr. 100s, as named with the other ships, in the list at p. 139, see D; for those of the single 12-pdr. 100s, (substituting two 24 for two 12 pounders) see E; of the four 98s, see H; of one of the 80s, see K; of two of the 74s (the Brunswick and Valiant), see M; and for the guns of the remaining fifteen 74s, see N, or O.
[2] See Appendix, No. 3.
[3] See Appendix, Annual Abstract, No. 1.

before us the registered tonnage of every one of them, we can, without any difficulty, state the aggregate amount.

Nor will there be so much difficulty in getting at the armament of the French ships as may at first sight appear. Of the many French line-of-battle ships captured by the British, none have been found to mount fewer, although some have occasionally more, long guns, than the number established upon their particular class by the ordinance of 1786; and which, with the brass carronades since established, are fully particularized in the small table given at a preceding page.

The French fleet, it will be remembered, consisted, on the morning of the 28th, of one 120, three 110, four 80, and eighteen 74-gun ships.[1] The two newest of the 80s, the Indomptable and Sans-Pareil, were armed precisely as the 80 in the table at p. 59: the other two appear to have mounted 8s instead of 12s on the quarter-deck and forecastle. The following, then, appear to have been the carriage long guns and carronades mounted on each side:—

	British.				*French.*		
Long guns.		No.	No.	Long guns.		No.	No.
32-pounders	.	. 706		36-pounders	.	. 746	
24	,,	. 180		24	,,	. 258	
18	,,	. 660		18	,,	. 540	
12	,,	. 244		12	,,	. 166	
9	,,	. 320		8	,,	. 392	
			2110				2102
Carronades.				Carronades.			
68	,,	. . 4		36	,, brass	. . .	112
12	,,	. . 60					
			64				
		Total	2174			Total	2214

In stating the complements of the French ships, we shall, with a certainty of not overrating them, follow the establishment of 1786, or that expressed in the table, at p. 59. The fact is, nearly all French ships carried a greater number of men than that regulation permits; and it is this assumed overplus that constitutes the allowance to which we referred.

The size of the French ships is a matter of minor importance compared with the guns and crews; but, even here, the number of French ships of all classes, which the British have captured, enables us to adopt an average that cannot be materially wrong. For instance; 2600 tons for the 120; 2350, for each of the 110s;

[1] See p. 141.

2220, for each of the 80s; and 1860, for each of the 74s. Having, in order to show in what manner our statements are grounded, premised these particulars, we present the following as the

Comparative Force of the Two Fleets, on the Morning of May 28.

			British.	French.
Ships	. . . .	No.	26	26
Broadside-guns	{	No.	1087	1107
	{	lbs.	22,976	28,126
Crews	Agg.	No.	17,241	19,989
Size	„	tons	46,962	52,010

On the morning of May 28, consequently, there was not much to deter the French admiral from engaging, unless he saw, with Jean-Bon Saint-André's eyes, "30 British sail of the line" instead of 26. It is true that there was, in Lord Howe's fleet, one two-decker more than we have named: the Charon, late a 44, now a hospital-ship. From being stationed in the rear of her own, and therefore at a proportionably greater distance from the French fleet, her two rows of ports must have been more evident than her size, and may have given rise to the supposition that she was a ship of the line in reserve.

We say not much to deter M. Villaret, because, under all the circumstances, no imputation of cowardice can attach, simply because a French fleet forbears to attack an English one numerically equal. Moreover, the French could plainly discern among the English ships seven three-deckers; while they themselves possessed but four. It was not probably known to them, that four of those seven three-deckers were of inferior force to four of their own two-deckers, and that the smallest of their four three-deckers was of superior force to the heaviest ship in the British fleet. For instance, a British 98-gun ship throws, in broadside weight of metal, 958 lbs.; a French second-class 80-gun ship (the 80 in the table at p. 59 throws 39 lbs. more,) 1079 lbs.; a French 110-gun ship, 1278 lbs.; while the Queen Charlotte (reckoning, as in all other cases, the long guns only) threw no more than 1158 lbs. One circumstance, if true, brings the two fleets a trifle nearer to an equality. It is stated in the French accounts, that the Patriote had on board 550 sick, being upwards of three-fourths in number of her proper crew.

The separation, on the evening of the 28th, of the Audacious and Révolutionnaire left the numbers still equal, but reduced the strength of M. Villaret's fleet, in the ratio of the difference in force between a British 74 and a French 110 gun ship. With respect to the battle of the following day, the 29th, Jean-Bon Saint-André attributed his failure, partly to the disobedience of his van-ship, the Montagnard, in not having tacked when ordered, whereby the weather-gage was lost; but principally, to the (most people will think extraordinary) circumstance, that the British, for all they had " 30 sail of the line," set sail and ran away.[1]

Having established, or, which was the same thing, asserted, these facts, the Conventional deputy assured the French people, that the battle of the 29th, although "not decisive," had been "eminently glorious." This rodomontade apart, Admiral Villaret, in recovering the Indomptable and Tyrannicide, at a time when they were all but captured, gave an undoubted proof of his skill and gallantry. On the other hand, some of the British ships, besides the Cæsar, were badly manœuvred. It was this apparent hesitation to follow their own admiral that encouraged the French admiral, when in the very act of abandoning his rearmost ships, to wear round and attempt their recovery; a plan in which, as we have seen, he but too well succeeded.

On the 29th, at sunset, the two fleets, each on the larboard tack, with the wind fresh at south-west, were about ten miles apart, that of the French bearing north-west from that of the British, or away on the latter's lee bow. As the evening advanced, the weather thickened, and remained foggy during the night. On the 30th, however, at about 9 A.M., it cleared a little, and discovered a part of the French fleet, still in the north-west, but on the starboard tack.

On perceiving the British, the French hauled round upon their former tack. The British admiral immediately made the signal for forming the line ahead and astern of him as most convenient, and upon the Invincible's signifying by signal that she had sprung a lower mast or yard, gave her permission to quit the line; out of which, being in a disabled state, she was towed by one of the frigates.

Soon after 10 A.M. the signal was made to form in two columns, and at 10 h. 15 m. A.M. for the starboard division to keep in the wake of the Queen Charlotte, who set her foresail and bore up towards the enemy. At 10 h. 30 m. A.M. the admiral asked the ships of the fleet, by signal, if they were in a condition to renew the action. The whole answered in the affirmative, except the Cæsar.

The weather beginning again to get very thick, Lord Howe made the signal for the fleet to come to the wind on the larboard

[1] Moniteur of July 5.

tack in succession; and, shortly afterwards, for the van to keep closer order. M. Villaret had now disappeared; and the fog became so dense that, at times during the remainder of the day, no ship of the British fleet could see her second ahead or astern. The ships, in consequence, became much scattered. It was, in all probability, the sight of six of these ships in a different direction from that in which the body of the British fleet was supposed to lie, that occasioned Jean-Bon Saint-André to state in his official report, that Rear-admiral Montagu, with his division, had joined Lord Howe during the fog.

On the 31st, at about 9 A.M., the weather again cleared, and the British ships hastened to get into their stations. At noon the French fleet was descried to the northward, and was plainly seen to consist of 32 sail, including 26 of the line; but, to the surprise of the British, nearly the whole of the ships appeared in a perfect state. At 2 P.M. Lord Howe bore up; and the French, having previously edged away a little, formed their line on the larboard tack.

At 3 h. 30 m. P.M. Lord Howe made the signal for the ships of the fleet to come to the wind together on the larboard tack, and, soon afterwards, to form the larboard line of bearing; the ships edging away together towards the enemy. Soon after 5 P.M., at which time the two fleets, estimating from the centre of each, were about five miles apart, successive signals were made for the British van, centre, and rear, to engage the van, centre, and rear of the enemy.

Several of the French ships, as if M. Villaret expected an immediate attack, were observed to exchange places in the line; and, although many of the heavy sailers among the British ships were a long way astern, a general action might probably have been brought on that evening. But the scene of confusion, that had occurred two days before, induced the British admiral to prefer a daylight contest, when there could be no difficulty in understanding the signals; and he accordingly, at a few minutes past 7 P.M., hauled to the wind on the larboard tack, to put that plan into operation.

Considering it likely that the French admiral, in order to weather the British fleet on the opposite or starboard tack, would make sail after dark, Lord Howe ordered that every ship should carry commanding sail all night, and judiciously stationed the Phaëton and Latona frigates about a mile to leeward of his own fleet, for the purpose of watching the motions of that of M. Villaret; to whom we shall now pay some attention, leaving Lord Howe to complete his arrangements for the awful business of the ensuing morn.

When the French admiral, in the battle of the 29th, wore round to support his rear, he was followed, as already stated, by every ship except the Montagnard: the latter stood on upon the larboard tack, and, keeping that course too long, parted company. The Seine frigate was sent to bring her back; but neither ship, owing, we may suppose, to the foggy state of the weather was able to rejoin the fleet. At 8 P.M. two ships, answering to the description of the Montagnard and Seine, were descried from the mast-heads of some of the British ships, at a great distance to windward, close hauled on the starboard tack, the French fleet then equally distant to leeward, and consequently out of sight of the former. At 8 h. 30 m. P.M. the 74-gun ship Trente-un-Mai, Captain Honoré Ganteaume, one of the Cancale squadron, joined Admiral Villaret; as, on the following day, did Rear-admiral Nielly, with the Sans-Pareil, Trajan, and Téméraire, formerly mentioned.[1] M. Villaret took this opportunity of sending home the crippled ship Indomptable, attended, as it would appear, by the Mont Blanc 74, to see her safe into port.

The French admiral was thus left with 26 sail of the line; and M. Villaret had certainly no reason to feel less confident in his strength from what he had witnessed at the last meeting. Nor was the bringing to of the English fleet, on the evening of the 31st, calculated to inspire the French officers and crews with any higher opinion of their adversaries. The French officers, indeed, having made sure of being attacked, too hastily attributed the sudden hauling up of the British to disinclination: Captain Courand, in particular, made a sneering remark on the subject to Captain Troubridge, who, with the Castor's purser and about 50 of her crew, was a prisoner on board the Sans-Pareil.

The British fleet continued, during the night, standing to the westward; and at daybreak on the 1st of June, latitude 47° 48' north, longitude 18° 30' west, the wind a moderate breeze from south by west, and the sea tolerably smooth, the French fleet, which, as wisely conjectured by Lord Howe, had carried a press of sail all night, was descried about six miles off, on the starboard or lee bow of the British fleet, and still steering in a line of battle upon the larboard tack.

In a very popular narrative, intended to illustrate a set of drawings of the action by Mr. Robert Cleverly, the French fleet is represented to have been on the starboard or lee *quarter* of

[1] See pp. 140, 141.

the British fleet ; and upon this the writer founds his assertion that Lord Howe was mistaken in supposing that M. Villaret intended carrying sail to weather him.[1] The fact is, the superior sailing of the French ships had enabled M. Villaret so to forereach upon the British fleet, that, had daylight been deferred a few hours, or another fog intervened, he would probably have weathered his on the contrary tack, and effected his escape.

At 5 A.M. the ships of the British fleet, by signal, bore up together and steered north-west, and at 6 h. 15 m. A.M., north. At about 7 h. 10 m. A.M. the fleet again hauled to the wind on the larboard tack. The French fleet was now plainly seen to consist of the same number of ships of the line as on the preceding evening ;[2] and the whole, except one or two, appeared complete in their masts and rigging.

At 7 h. 16 m. A.M. Lord Howe signalled that he should attack the centre of the enemy, and at 7 h. 25 m. A.M., that he should pass through the enemy's line, and engage to leeward. The two fleets being now about four miles apart, and the crews of the British ships, after the fatigue of sitting up three nights, needing some refreshment, Lord Howe hove to, and gave the men their breakfasts. This over, the British fleet, at 8 h. 12 m. A.M., filled and bore down on the enemy. In a few minutes afterwards a signal was thrown out for each ship to steer for, and independently engage, the ship opposed to her in the enemy's line.

Some changes now became requisite in the British line, in order that the French three-deckers (into one of which, the Républicain, M. Nielly, had shifted his flag) and other heavy ships might be suitably opposed. With this view, the Royal Sovereign exchanged places with the Marlborough, the Barfleur with the Invincible, and the Royal George with the Montagu; and, as soon as the several ships had got to their new stations, the British fleet was formed in line abreast, thus : Cæsar (van-ship), Bellerophon, Leviathan, Russel, Royal Sovereign, Marlborough, Defence, Impregnable, Tremendous, Barfleur, Invincible, Culloden, Gibraltar, Queen Charlotte, Brunswick, Valiant, Orion, Queen, Ramillies, Alfred, Montagu, Royal George, Majestic, Glory, Thunderer.[3] The frigates and smaller vessels were, as

---

[1] Narrative, &c. published by M. de Poggi, p. 14.

[2] "Counted 26 line-of-battle ships, six frigates and corvettes ; 13 ships ahead, and 12 ditto astern, of the French admiral." —*Queen Charlotte's log.* See also Lord Howe's letter in London Gazette of June 11, 1794. " La flotte de la république était composée de 26 vaisseaux."—*Moniteur* of July 5. Notwithstanding this concurrent testimony, no English writer has admitted the French fleet to have consisted of fewer than 27, and some have numbered it at 28, sail of the line.

[3] A contemporary, uninformed apparently of the changes that had taken place about an hour before the commencement of the battle, places the ships in line as they had previously been formed. See Brenton's Naval History, vol. i., p. 292.

usual, stationed in the rear: it may suffice to mention that the Pegasus was repeater of signals to the Queen Charlotte; the Niger, to the Royal Sovereign, and the Aquilon, to the Royal George.

The French fleet was drawn up in close head-and-stern line, bearing about east and west; and, as far as can be collected from the French accounts, the following is the order in which the ships were placed, beginning at the van, or west end of the line: Trajan, Eole, America, Téméraire, Terrible, Impétueux Mucius, Tourville, Gaspairn, Convention, Trente-un-Mai, Tyrannicide, Juste, Montagne, Jacobin, Achille, Vengeur, Patriote, Northumberland, Entreprenant, Jemmappes, Neptune, Pelletier, Républicain, Sans-Pareil, Scipion.[1] Of the French frigates we are not able to state more, than that the Tamise (late British Thames), Captain Jean-Marthe-Adrien L'Hermite, was the repeater of the Montagne. Both the English and the French ships were carrying single-reefed topsails: of the latter, some were lying to, and others backing and filling, to preserve their stations; and the former were steering about north-west, with a fresh breeze at south by west, and, from the reduced sail they were under, were going at the rate of very little more than five knots an hour.

At 9 h. 24 m. A.M. (Queen Charlotte's time) the French van opened a distant fire upon the British van, particularly upon the Defence, who was rather ahead of her line; which line, only a quarter of an hour before, had been as perfect as it could well be formed, and had inspired the veteran chief with the most sanguine hopes of success in his plan, that of each ship cutting through the line astern of her proper opponent, and engaging her to leeward. After having, at 8 h. 38 m. A.M., hauled down the preparative flag from the signal to engage (No. 36), Lord Howe emphatically shut his signal-book, as if he considered that, for the present at least, it would no more be wanted. Not many minutes afterwards, however, he had to reopen it, to call upon the Gibraltar, Culloden (who had backed both fore and main topsails), and Brunswick, to make more sail, and soon had the mortification to observe the Russel, and, above all, his vanship, the Cæsar, with their maintopsails aback, although neither was within gun-shot of the enemy.

[1] No two English accounts agree as to the disposition, or even the names, of the ships in the French line; but they all concur in so stationing the ships whose names *are* correctly given, that those dismasted, according to Jean-Bon Saint-Au- dré's report, did not lose a spar, and *vice versâ*. The line, as here given, reconciles those important differences, and, upon the whole, is as correct, we believe, as can anywhere be obtained.

Lord Howe's attention was presently called to a more interesting subject. At 9 h. 30 m. A.M. the Queen Charlotte, then, with the signal for close action at her mast-head, steering a slanting course direct for the larboard quarter of the Montagne, and being distant from her about a random shot, was cannonaded by the third ship in the French admiral's rear, the Vengeur, a portion of whose fire was necessarily intercepted by the Brunswick, the latter having obeyed the signal to make more sail, and become, in consequence, further advanced towards the enemy. Instead of returning the Vengeur's fire, the Queen Charlotte, desirous to be the first through the enemy's line, set topgallant-sails and let fall her foresail. This presently carried her past the Vengeur, and abreast of the next ship, the Achille, who now opened her broadside.

At 9 h. 52 m. A.M. the Queen Charlotte returned this fire; but, meaning it only as a mask to his principal object, a decisive attack upon the Montagne, Lord Howe gave orders that the guns upon the third and quarter-decks only should be fired. The officers stationed at the first and second decks, however, hearing the firing over their heads, supposed that they were at liberty to begin, and opened accordingly; but the seamen reloaded their guns with so much celerity, that no delay occurred in manning those on the opposite side ready for the crash they were intended to make in the stern of the Montagne.

Just as the Queen Charlotte, having arrived abreast, and within about two ships' length, of the larboard quarter of the Montagne, had put her helm up to pass astern of the latter, the Jacobin was seen stretching ahead under the Montagne's lee, as if afraid to encounter the broadside, which the Charlotte, in her passage through the line, would discharge into her bows. Passing close under the stern of the Montagne, so close that the fly of the French ensign, as it waved at her flagstaff, brushed the main and mizen shrouds of the Queen Charlotte, the latter poured into the French three-decker a tremendous broadside. By this time the Jacobin had got nearly abreast of the Montagne to leeward, the very position which the Queen Charlotte herself had intended to occupy. Scarcely, however, had Lord Howe expressed his regret at the circumstance, than Mr. Bowen, the master, observing by the motion of her rudder that the Jacobin was in the act of bearing up, ordered the helm of the Queen Charlotte to be put hard a-starboard; and so little room had the British three-decker to spare in luffing up, that her jib-boom grazed the larboard mizen shrouds of the Jacobin.

Directing her larboard guns at the starboard quarter of the Montagne, the Queen Charlotte discharged her opposite ones into the stern and larboard quarter of the Jacobin, now lying nearly becalmed under her lee. The Jacobin, as she dropped astern, returned this fire with such of her guns as would bear; and a shot from one of them cut away the Queen Charlotte's foretopmast. The movements of Lord Howe's ship, from the time she bore up to pass astern of the French admiral to the moment at which her topmast was shot away, the following diagram will more clearly exhibit.

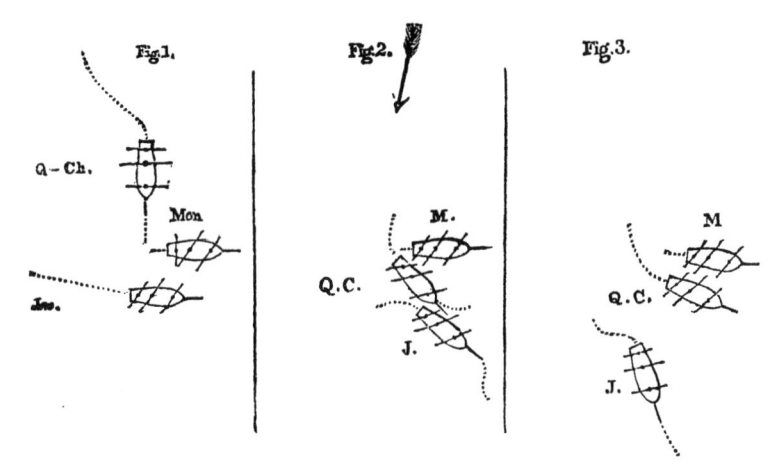

Frustrated thus in her attempt to reach the lee-bow of the Montagne, the Queen Charlotte could only continue to ply her larboard guns at the French three-decker, who, at about 10 h. 10 m. A.M., having her stern-frame and starboard quarter dreadfully shattered, and sustained a loss of upwards of 100 killed and nearly 200 wounded, set her maintopmast staysail, and without, incredible as it may appear, bestowing a single shot in return for the many she had received (her ports, indeed, on the starboard or lee side appear to have been shut), ranged a head clear of the Queen Charlotte's destructive fire.

Observing that the Jacobin had also made sail, and that several other French ships were preparing to follow the example of their admiral and his second, Lord Howe, at 10 h. 13 m. A.M., threw out the signal for a general chase. Meanwhile the Queen Charlotte, checked in her progress, lay between the Juste, the Montagne's second ahead, on her larboard bow, and the Jacobin, on her starboard quarter: the latter, however, soon disappeared in the smoke to leeward.

Let us here pause a moment to reflect upon the situation of the Queen Charlotte, thus opposed single-handed (for neither the Gibraltar nor the Brunswick, her two seconds, were near enough to aid her), to one French 120, and two 80 gun ships. Had M. Villaret, or rather the Conventional deputy, Jean-Bon Saint-André, who to all intents and purposes was the commanding officer of the French fleet, possessed firmness enough, at the moment the Queen Charlotte's foretopmast came down, to have bore up with the Montagne athwart the hawse of the British three-decker, the latter, without some extraordinary interposition in her favour, must either have sunk or surrendered.

Prevented by the hasty flight of the French admiral and his second astern, and the loss of her foretopmast at so critical a moment, from taking up with the antagonist of her choice, the Queen Charlotte could only continue, as she did, to pour her heavy broadsides into the Juste, still, with herself, making slow way to the westward, or towards the van of the two lines. In a very few minutes the Juste, who was distantly engaged on the opposite or windward side with the Invincible, lost first her foremast, and then her main and mizen masts. About the same time the Queen Charlotte's maintopmast came down. The loss of a second topmast, and the damaged state of her rigging and lower yards, rendered the ship wholly unmanageable; and although, having silenced the fire of the Juste, she was desirous to go ahead in quest of a fresh opponent, the Queen Charlotte could barely keep steerage-way.

The Juste still lay abreast of the latter ship to windward, with a French jack hoisted at her bowsprit-end, and a spritsail set, to carry her, if possible, clear of her foes. Owing to her being painted similarly to the Invincible, who now lay at a short distance ahead of her, but was concealed by the smoke, the Juste, seen but indistinctly from the same cause, escaped the attention of the Queen Charlotte, until, wearing round, she passed under the latter's stern, and gave her a raking broadside; one of the shots from which, a 36-pounder, passed through the British ship's wing-transom. At the same moment a French three-decker, close hauled, was seen on the Queen Charlotte's weather quarter, approaching under all sail, and evidently intending to weather the whole British line before she ran to leeward. Just, however, as the three-decker, which was the Républicain from the rear division, had advanced to a position from which her guns could bear on the Queen Charlotte, and just as the latter was expecting to receive, and preparing to return her fire, the main and mizen mast of the former, at whom the Gibraltar was then distantly firing from to windward, went by the board. The Républicain instantly bore up, and passed within gun-shot astern of the Charlotte; but such was the state of confusion on board, that the French three-decker let slip the favourable opportunity, and ran by without firing.

After having, as already stated, ranged ahead of the Queen Charlotte, the Montagne, setting her topgallantsails, continued to stand on, followed by the Jacobin, until nearly abreast of her own van; when, being joined by such of her friends as had no leeward opponents to keep them in check, she wore round on the starboard tack, and with eleven sail in her train, stood in the direction of the Queen, then lying about a point upon her starboard or weather bow in a crippled condition.

The perilous situation of the Queen attracted Lord Howe's attention; and having by signal ordered the ships of the fleet to close and form in line ahead or astern of her, the Queen Charlotte slowly and with difficulty wore round on the starboard tack. All the sail that could be set was presently spread, and, followed by the Barfleur, Thunderer (as fresh as when the action began), Royal Sovereign, Valiant, Leviathan, and a few others, the Queen Charlotte stood away, with the wind a little abaft the beam, to protect the disabled and gallant ship, that, on the present as on the former occasion, had performed so admirably. Seeing this, the French admiral relinquished his design on the Queen, merely cannonading her with a part of his line, as he stretched on to the support of five crippled French ships towing towards him in the east; two of which in particular, being wholly dismasted, ought previously to have been secured by those British ships, of which there were several that had taken but little part in the action.

The battle of the 1st of June may thus be summarily described. Between a quarter and half-past 9 A.M. the French van opened its fire upon the British van. In about a quarter of an hour the fire of the French became general, and Lord Howe and his divisional flag-officers, bearing the signal for close action at their mast-heads, commenced a heavy fire in return. A few of the British ships cut through the French line, and engaged their opponents to leeward; the remainder hauled up to windward, and opened their fire, some at a long, others at a shorter and more effectual distance. At 10 h. 10 m. A.M., when the action was at its height, the French admiral, in the Montagne, made sail ahead, followed by his second astern, and afterwards by such others of his ships as, like the Montagne, had suffered little in their rigging and sails. At about 11 h. 30 m. A.M. the heat of the action was over, and the British were left with 11, the French with 12, more or less dismasted ships. None of the French ships had at this time struck their colours; or, if they had struck, had since rehoisted them: they, for the most part, were striving to escape, under a spritsail, or some small sail set on the tallest stump left to them, and continued to fire at every British ship that passed within gun-shot.[1]

After failing, as already stated, in his attempt upon the Queen, Admiral Villaret stood on, and succeeded, contrary to all expectation, in covering and cutting off four of his dismasted ships, the Républicain, Mucius, Scipion, and Jemmappes; a fifth, the Terrible, having previously joined him, by fighting her way through the British fleet. At about 1 h. 15 m. P.M. the general firing ceased; but it was not until 2 h. 30 m. P.M. that the six dismasted French ships nearest at hand, the Sans-Pareil, Juste, America, Impétueux, Northumberland, and Achille, were secured: and some of these reopened their fire upon the ships that advanced to take possession of them. At a little after 6 P.M. a seventh French ship, the Vengeur, was taken possession of, but in so shattered a state, that in ten minutes afterwards she went down, with upwards of 200 of her crew on board, composed chiefly of the wounded.

Thus ended this memorable engagement; in which, and in the skirmishes of the 28th and 29th days of May, the British sustained a loss in gross, the details of which will appear pre-

[1] The following is a list of those dismasted ships, according to the best information now to be obtained:—

BRITISH.		FRENCH.	
Impregnable	Topgallantmasts.	Trente-un-Mai	Topgallantmasts, one or more.
Royal Sovereign			
Orion	Maintopmast.	Tyrannicide	Ditto, and probably a topmast.
Glory	Fore ditto, and topgallantmasts.	Terrible	Main and mizen masts.
Queen Charlotte	Fore and main topmasts.	Républicain	
Bellerophon		Scipion	
Brunswick	Mizenmast and foretopgallantmast.	Mucius	
		Jemmappes	
Royal George	Foremast and all three topmasts.	Achille	All three lower masts.
		America	
Queen	Mainmast, and mizentopmast.	Juste	
		Northumberland	
Defence	All three lower masts.	Sans-Pareil	
Marlborough		Impétueux	Ditto and bowsprit

The six last-named French ships became eventually prizes to the British.

sently, of 290 killed and 858 wounded; including among the killed, Captain Montagu, and among the wounded, Admiral Bowyer, and Rear-admiral Pasley, Captain Hutt, with the loss of a leg, and Captain John Harvey (mortally), of an arm. The total loss on the British side, 1148,[1] is less, however, than the loss in killed and wounded represented to have been sustained by the six French ships only which were carried into port.[2]

For the total loss sustained by the French, in this to them most disastrous engagement, we must trust to conjecture, unless we take the round number which they themselves have published. That number is 3000 for the killed and mortally wounded alone;[3] a full half of which loss fell to the share of the seven captured ships. Hence, reckoning the slightly wounded on board the 19 returned ships at 500, we may estimate the total loss of the French, in killed, wounded, and prisoners, at 7000 men.

As, when the action commenced, the French fleet was, within one ship, numerically equal to the British fleet opposed to it, we shall, without again entering into the particulars of the force on each side, consider the two fleets to have been fairly matched.

Having, to the best of our ability, presented a general view of the collective operations of the two fleets in this celebrated battle, we will now endeavour to give a description of the individual part performed by each British ship engaged in it. Difficult as the task may be, it is yet due to the officers and men, who shared with the gallant chief the fatigue and perils of the day, that the attempt should be made. Our attention will be directed to the ships, according to the order in which they successively ranked in the line.

[1] See Appendix, No. 12.
[2] The following statement will show the size in tons, complement, and loss of each of the six captured French ships:—

Ships.	Tons.	Actual Complements.	Alleged Loss. Killed.	Alleged Loss. Wounded.
Sans-Pareil	2242	814	260	120
Juste	2143	877	100	145
America	1884	720	134	110
Impétueux	1878	713	100	75
Northumberland	1811	700	60	100
Achille	1801	700	36	30

The guns of the prizes were all new, of Swedish manufacture, and chiefly of brass The Portuguese government made an offer for them; but the British government, in this instance, became the purchaser at 24,000l.; and many of these beautiful and highly finished guns now ornament the forts in and around Portsmouth.

[3] Victoires et Conquêtes, tome iii., p. 28.

The Cæsar, as the van or leading ship, claims our first attention. In bearing down to engage, the Cæsar appears to have dropped a little astern, and, as proved by Captain Molloy's own witnesses at the court-martial subsequently held upon him, to have brought to at a greater distance to windward, namely, upwards of 500 yards, than was consistent with the support she owed to her own fleet, and the impression which so formidable a two-decker was calculated to make upon the fleet of the enemy. It may naturally be asked, Why bring to to windward, when his admiral had signalled that *he* should pass through the enemy's line and engage to leeward? The fact is, the signal was not compulsory on any captain. It contained a qualifying N. B. in the following words: "The different captains and commanders, not being able to effect the specified intention in either case (the signal applying to the passage through a line to windward or to leeward), are at liberty to act as circumstances require:" a negativing, or, at least, neutralizing nota-bene, which, very properly, was omitted in the next new code of signals.

Captain Molloy's preference of the windward to the leeward mode of attack seems to have rested on a belief that had he run down under the stern of the enemy's van-ship, the Cæsar's proper opponent, his own ship would have had such fresh way that, in hauling up to get alongside, she would have shot far ahead, and thereby have done less execution than if the Cæsar had taken a position on the Trajan's weather quarter.[1]

Undoubtedly, the farther distant a ship is from an enemy's line, provided she is within shot of it, the more she exposes herself to damage, simply because two or more ships can then fire at her: whereas, by closing with one ship, that ship alone becomes her opponent, and no other, while the two lines remain parallel, can bring her broadside to bear. Unfortunately practical proof of this was wanted, and the state of the Cæsar's hull, masts, yards, and rigging soon afforded it. Anxious to retrieve his error, and act in obedience to the signal which had long been flying on board the Bellerophon, his flag-officer's ship, Captain Molloy now attempted to wear and make sail; but, a shot having driven a splinter and three parts of the fore-tackle fall into the starboard quarter-block of the tiller-rope, the latter had become jammed in the sheave, and the rudder would not move.[2] During half an hour the accident remained unremedied, and nearly the whole of the time undiscovered. It appears, also,

---

[1] Minutes of the Court-martial on Captain Molloy, published in 1796, p. 142.

Ibid., pp. 175, 193.

that the use of the relieving-tackles or of the rudder-pendants, as substitutes for the tiller, did not occur. All this while the ship was dropping further astern; and, when she did bear up to re-engage, her powerful battery, equal in weight of metal to a 98-gun ship's, came too late into play to be of any decided effect. In the mean time the French van-ship, the Trajan, with no other visible injury than a few shot-holes in her sails, and no other loss, as subsequently proved, than three men killed and about half a dozen wounded, had set her jib and wore out of the line.

The Cæsar had no spars shot away; but the mizenmast, mizenyard, cross-jack yard, and mizentopsail yard were much cut; and so were many of the shrouds, backstays, &c. She received 64 shot in the starboard side of her hull, and had seven guns disabled by shot, exclusive of one which burst. The disabled guns were, one 32-pounder, one 24-pounder, and five 12-pounders. The bursted gun was a 24-pounder; which, in exploding, killed two, and wounded three of her men. The loss which the Cæsar sustained by the enemy's fire appears to have been, 14 seamen killed, and about 52 or 53 wounded.

The next ship in the British line to the Cæsar was the Bellerophon, bearing the flag of Rear-admiral Pasley. This ship, with the signal for close action at her mast-head, bore down to within musket-shot of the weather quarter of the Eole, the second ship in the French line; and, at about 8 h. 45 m. A.M., opened her broadside with good effect. In her approach, the Bellerophon had received a very heavy and destructive fire from the three headmost French ships; and the van-ship, the Trajan, being, from the Cæsar's forbearing conduct, without an opponent, still continued to fire at her occasionally. At 10 h. 50 m. A.M., Rear-admiral Pasley lost his leg, and was carried off the deck.

The Bellerophon, now under the command of Captain William Hope, continued warmly engaged, until 11 h. 45 m. P.M.; when the Eole, having seemingly had enough of the action, wore round astern of her leader, then with topgallantsails set standing on upon the starboard tack. The two French ships, in passing, opened their starboard broadsides upon the Bellerophon; who, in the act of wearing after the Eole, lost her maintopmast, and shortly afterwards, her foretopmast. Having suffered greatly from her two opponents, the Bellerophon, at a little before noon, made the signal for the Latona to come to her assistance.

Captain Thornborough was not slow in obeying the summons; and the Latona, as she passed near the two French 74s, answered their fire with as smart a return as a frigate's battery could give. The Bellerophon, with her fore and main topmasts gone, and her mainmast dangerously wounded, and all her boats and spars upon the booms, as well as the greater part of her standing and running rigging cut to pieces, was unable to haul to the wind after the two fugitives; and the latter, being subsequently joined by a third ship, kept firing at every British vessel near to which they passed. The Bellerophon's loss amounted to only three seamen and one marine or soldier killed, the rear-admiral, captain of marines (Walter Smith), boatswain (Mr. Chapman), and 24 seamen and marines or soldiers wounded.

About the same time that the Bellerophon commenced action, the Leviathan opened her fire upon the America, bearing a commodore's broad pendant. A close and furious engagement ensued, and in about an hour the foremast of the America was shot away. At 11 h. 50 m. A.M. the Trajan and Eole, as they passed to leeward of the America and Leviathan, hove to on the latter's starboard quarter, and opened a very heavy and annoying fire. In a little while, however, they filled and stood to windward. The Leviathan and her opponent, in the mean time, had wore round together, so that the latter was now the weathermost ship. After a further interchange of broadsides, the America, finding that several British ships, some of which had already fired at her, were fast approaching, made an attempt to haul off; but such was the shattered state of her main and mizen masts from the Leviathan's shot, that they both fell, the latter by the board, leaving this gallant and well-defended ship a mere log on the water.

The America lost more than a third of her crew in killed and wounded. Two guns were dismounted, and one burst during the action, and killed seven men. One of the two French ships that fired at the Leviathan and America in passing struck the latter on the starboard quarter with a red-hot shot. Having completely disabled and silenced her opponent, the Leviathan left her with colours still hoisted upon one of her stumps, and made all sail to close with Lord Howe, in obedience to the signal then flying. The skill of the America's crew was not equal to their bravery; for the Leviathan had only one spar, her fore-topsail yard, shot away. Her masts, however, were injured her rigging and sails a good deal cut; and she lost 10 seamen killed, and one midshipman (Mr. Glen, mortally), 31 seamen, and one marine or soldier wounded.

The Russel hove to to windward of, and commenced cannonading her proper opponent, the Téméraire, about the same time that the Leviathan opened her fire. At 1 A.M., or thereabouts, the Russel's foretopmast came down; and at 11 A.M. the Téméraire, observing the ships of her van in the act of wearing, made sail to leeward, and was followed through the line by the Russel. The French ship, not being greatly damaged in her masts or rigging, was able to haul up a little to starboard; while the Russel, having her foretopmast hanging through the top, could not trim her sails in any other direction, and therefore brought to on the larboard tack, the same on which she had commenced the action.

The Russel now found herself to leeward of the three French van-ships. Of these, the America was fully employed with the Leviathan, and was also without any masts; but the Trajan and Eole, having no particular opponents, and being in a perfect state aloft, poured each her broadside into the Russel, and then hauled to the wind and got clear. After she had returned this salute, the Russel passed on to the assistance of the Leviathan, and fired two raking broadsides into the America; the fate of which ship, however, as far as effective opposition went, had already been decided by her first opponent. The Russel then accompanied the Leviathan to the new line forming astern of the admiral, and at about 2 h. 30 m. P.M., in compliance with the signal to stay by prizes, stood for and again fell in with the America; who then prudently hauled down her colours, and was quietly taken possession of by the Russel. The damages of the Russel, beyond what have been detailed, were not material; and her loss amounted to eight seamen and marines or soldiers killed and 26 wounded.

The Royal Sovereign became opposed to the Terrible, a three-decked ship like herself, and bearing the flag of Rear-admiral Bouvet. At 9 h. 23 m. A.M., after having been struck by several shots from the French van-ships, the Royal Sovereign commenced firing at the Terrible, whose battery promptly opened in return. The distance, however, at which the Royal Sovereign had brought to to engage was considered too great, and her signal to engage closer was made, and kept flying some time. At a few minutes before 10 A.M., Admiral Graves was badly wounded, and carried off the deck: the command, in consequence, devolved upon Captain Henry Nichols. At 10 h. 38 m. A.M., the Terrible had her main and mizen masts shot away, and immediately bore up; in doing which she yawed so much that the Royal Sovereign raked her repeatedly. Seeing the enemy's van ships preparing to run, the Royal Sovereign now hoisted the signal for a general chase, and set courses, spritsail, jib, and staysails, in pursuit of the Terrible; whereupon the Montagne and Jacobin, both apparently fresh and unhurt, came to the assistance of the latter.

At 11 h. 45 m. A.M., after having fired her larboard guns at one of the French van-ships while passing on the starboard tack, the Royal Sovereign commenced a close action with the Montagne, and was soon afterwards joined, but too far to windward to be of much effect, by the Valiant. In about half an hour the Montagne bore away, and was followed a short distance by the Royal Sovereign; who then hauled up, as well as the disabled state of her rigging and sails would permit. In obedience to the signal then flying, to stay by prizes, the Royal Sovereign, at 2 h. 40 m. P.M., not knowing that the America was in possession of the Russel, fired several shot at the prize, and, on taking possession of her, sent the Russel's people back to their ship. The Royal Sovereign had her three topgallantmasts shot away, and lost one midshipman (William Ivey), 10 seamen, and three marines or soldiers killed, Admiral Graves, one captain and one lieutenant of foot, and 41 seamen and marines or soldiers wounded.

At 9 h. 45 m. A.M., the Marlborough began firing at her proper opponent, the Impétueux, and, in five minutes afterwards, passed under the latter's stern, and ranged up alongside of her to leeward. In about a quarter of an hour the Impétueux fell on board the Marlborough, entangling herself in that ship's mizen shrouds, and a most destructive cannonade ensued. At 10 h. 15 m. A.M., the next ship in line astern of the Impétueux, the Mucius, to get clear of the Defence, who was pressing her hard, made sail ahead, and fell on board upon the bow of the Marlborough; the three ships thus forming a triangle, of which the Marlborough was the base.

Just as the Mucius got up, the Marlborough's mizenmast fell over the side, and, in a quarter of an hour afterwards, her fore and main masts followed. Still the Marlborough continued a very animated fire, and very soon shot away all the lower masts, as well as bowsprit, of the Impétueux: the masts of the Mucius met the same fate. Both ships are stated to have struck to the Marlborough; but, when masts fall, the dropping of the colours is not always to be taken as a sign of surrender. About this time the Montagne, in running by the Marlborough's stern, opened a fire that caused serious destruction on board of her. One shot entered the starboard quarter, and struck one of the guns exactly opposite the wheel, wounding three men stationed at it: it then wounded Captain Berkeley, a young midshipman, and several men. The Montagne, as indeed did all the other French ships, fired an immense quantity of langridge.

The command now devolved upon Lieutenant John Monkton, who evinced the utmost skill and bravery in defending the ship. At length the Marlborough made a signal for assistance, and was taken in tow by the Aquilon. Meanwhile the Mucius, being without an opponent, effected her escape; as would have done, also, the Impétueux, but that she was in too crippled a state to make sail. The latter was afterwards taken possession of by the Russel, whose people, as already stated, had quitted the America by the orders of Admiral Graves. The Impétueux was found to have sustained a loss of about 100 killed, and 75 badly wounded.

The Marlborough's loss, as might be expected, was extremely severe: she had one midshipman (Abraham Nelson), 23 seamen, and five marines or soldiers killed, her captain, second and fifth lieutenants (Alexander Rudduch and Michael Seymour, the latter with the loss of his left arm), one master's mate (Mr. Pardoe), four midshipmen (Messrs. Fitzgerald, Shortland, Linthorne, and Clarges), 68 seamen, and 14 marines or soldiers wounded.

The Defence, in bearing down, being rather in advance of her own line, had the good fortune to be the first in cutting through that of the enemy: she passed between the Mucius and Tourville, and, owing to some of the French ships astern not being properly attacked, was presently in the thickest of the fire. Her exposed situation soon caused the loss of her main and mizen masts. The Mucius, after a while, quitted the Defence, and stretched on to windward of the Marlborough; and the Tourville, also, taking advantage of the crippled state of her opponent, hauled up and made sail from her. The near approach of other French ships, and, among them, of the Républicain three-decker, with only her foremast standing, compelled the Defence, after the additional loss of her foremast, by engaging them, to make a signal for assistance. The Républicain soon afterwards set her foresail and ran to leeward; and at about 1 P.M. the Phaëton, by directions from the admiral, took the Defence in tow. The latter lost her master (William Webster), boatswain (John Fitzpatrick), 11 seamen, and four marines or soldiers killed, one master's mate (J. Elliot), one ensign of foot, 25 seamen, and nine marines or soldiers wounded.

On her way from her station in the rear, to speak the admiral as she had been ordered, the Phaëton passed, at about noon, four French 74s, standing on the starboard tack. These were, probably, the Trajan, Eole, Téméraire, and Tourville; but one of them must have subsequently separated and bore up, as three ships only were seen to windward in the afternoon. The Phaëton then ran under the stern of a fifth 74, the Impétueux, but, as the French ship was dismasted, did not fire at her. As soon, however, as the Phaëton came within range of the larboard guns of the Impétueux, the latter, contrary to the usual practice, which is that frigates, as they pass to and fro in a fleet without engaging, are not to be molested, opened a fire upon her. The frigate promptly returned the ungracious salute, and continued engaging the French 74 for ten minutes; during which the Phaëton sustained a loss of three men killed and five wounded. Captain Bentinck then made sail, and at 30 m. P.M. spoke Lord Howe, who ordered him to give aid to the Defence; which the Phaëton accordingly did.

The next ships of the British line, the Impregnable, Tremendous, Barfleur, Invincible, Culloden, and Gibraltar, having, with one exception, kept rather too much to windward to give full effect to their batteries, offer nothing in their proceedings of equal importance to the accounts we have been detailing.

The ship particularly excepted from the six above named, is the Invincible, who had conducted herself so honourably on the 29th of May. This ship, at 9 h. 45 m. P.M., began engaging the Juste, a ship far superior to her in force, and the proper opponent of the Gibraltar. In a short time the animated fire kept up by the Invincible so annoyed the Juste, that the latter bore up, and, there encountering the heavy broadsides of the Queen Charlotte, struck her colours.

The loss sustained by each of the above six ships was as follows: Impregnable, her master (David Caird) and six seamen killed, and her eighth lieutenant (William Buller), boatswain (Mr. Patterlo), and 22 seamen wounded; Tremendous, her first lieutenant (Francis Ross), one seaman, and one marine killed, and six seamen and two marines or soldiers wounded: Barfleur, eight seamen and one marine killed, and Rear-admiral Bowyer, her sixth lieutenant (William Prowse), two midshipmen (Messrs. Fogo and Clemons), 18 seamen, and three marines or soldiers wounded; Invincible, four seamen and marines or soldiers killed, and ten wounded: Culloden, two seamen killed, and her third lieutenant (Tristram Whitter), and four seamen wounded; and the Gibraltar, one seaman and one marine killed, and 12 seamen wounded

No one of these six ships appears to have had any spar shot away, except the Impregnable, who lost her three topgallant-masts, and had her fore-topsail yard shot away in the slings; but, owing to the promptitude and dexterity of two of her officers, Lieutenant Robert Waller Otway, and Midshipman Charles Dashwood, in going aloft and lashing the yard to the cap, the Impregnable was enabled to wear on the starboard tack, when, at 40 m. P.M., the signal to that effect was made by the Queen Charlotte.

Both the Barfleur and Invincible, the latter especially, had their masts wounded, and their sails and rigging much cut. So little, however, did Captain Pakenham think of his ship's casualties, that, on seeing the crippled state of the Queen Charlotte, he sent lieutenant Henry Blackwood to Lord Howe, expressly to say, that the Invincible was sufficiently manageable to bear his lordship's flag. The admiral did not, however, think it necessary to shift his flag, but immediately sent the lieutenant and his boat's crew to take possession of the Juste.

Having already detailed the proceedings of the Queen Charlotte and her opponent flag-ship, the Montagne, we have merely to describe the damage and loss which each sustained in the action. In addition to the loss of her fore and main topmasts and their yards, the Queen Charlotte had her fore and main yards and all three masts wounded in several places, and her standing and running rigging very much cut. Her loss amounted to her seventh lieutenant (Roger R. Rawlence), one lieutenant of foot, and 11 seamen killed, and Captain Douglas (by a shot from the Gibraltar, it is believed), one midshipman (J. Holland, badly), 22 seamen, and five marines or soldiers wounded; the whole of which loss, with a very slight exception, was incurred in bearing down to the attack.

According to the French accounts, the Montagne, although comparatively unhurt, as we have stated her to have been, in masts, rigging, and sails, was dreadfully battered in hull; her rudder was unhung by the shattered state of the sternpost, two of the gun-room ports on the starboard side were knocked into one, the binnacle and wheel were destroyed; also the second stern-gallery, a great portion of the starboard quarter-deck bulwarks, and all the boats as well on the booms as over the quarters. Several of her guns were dismounted, and more than 250 shot are represented to have struck and entered the ship along her starboard water-line: near the stern, in particular, the leaks occasioned by the shot-holes were very serious.

In this state of her matériel, the personnel of the Montagne could not but suffer extremely. Among the 300 killed and wounded, already mentioned as the amount of her loss in the action, the Montagne, from the stern and quarter fire to which she was exposed, lost a great proportion of officers. The "intendant" Russe and the flag-captain Bazire were killed by the same shot. Two or three lieutenants were also killed, and several enseignes or midshipmen. Among the wounded, also, were several lieutenants and inferior officers; and the French admiral himself had a narrow escape, the seat on which he stood during the action having been shot from under him. Jean-Bon Saint-André, likewise, might have been numbered among the sufferers, but that **his** fears, early in the action, prompted him to seek security below: " Frappé du spectacle dont ses yeux sont témoins, Jean-Bon Saint-André ne peut surmonter la frayeur qu'il éprouve, et, pour éviter le danger, il se hâte à descendre à la première batterie."[1]

The Brunswick, Lord Howe's second astern, is the next ship to which our attention is called. The slanting manner in which the British fleet bore down to the attack, and the forward position of the Brunswick just as it commenced, exposed her to much of the fire directed at the Queen Charlotte. This, besides damaging the Brunswick's rigging, killed several of her crew, and filled the cockpit with wounded, before the ship fired a shot. It was Captain Harvey's intention, as second to his admiral, to cut through the line astern of the Jacobin, the second to the French admiral; but, when the Jacobin ranged ahead, as already stated, the Achille closed upon her, so as not to have a sufficient space to pass through. The Brunswick thereupon bore up, and pushed for an opening between the Achille and Vengeur; but the latter, with the view of frustrating that design, gallantly shot ahead and closed the interval.

As the only alternative, the Brunswick kept her helm aport, and ran foul of the Vengeur; the Brunswick's three starboard anchors hooking in the Vengeur's larboard fore-shrouds and fore-channels.[2] The two ships immediately swung close to each other, and paying off before the wind, dropped out of the line. The British crew, unable to open the eight lowerdeck starboard ports from the third abaft, blew them off; and the Brunswick and Vengeur, with their heads pointing to the northward, and

---

[1] Victoires et Conquêtes, tome iii., p. 20.
[2] On the master, Mr. Stewart, asking Captain Harvey if he should cut the ship clear of the Vengeur, the latter is said to have replied, "No; we have got her, and we will keep her."

with some considerable way upon them, both ships having squared their yards on coming in contact, commenced a furious engagement. The Vengeur's musketry, and her 36-pounder poop-carronades loaded with langridge (old nails and pieces of iron), soon played havoc on the Brunswick's poop and quarter-deck, killing a captain of foot, and several officers and men, and wounding, among others, Captain Harvey himself, but not so severely as to occasion him to go below: the wound was by a musket-shot, which tore away three of the fingers from his right hand.

At about 11 A.M. a ship was discovered, through the smoke, bearing down on the Brunswick's larboard quarter; having her gangways and rigging crowded with men, as if with the intention of releasing the Vengeur by boarding the Brunswick. Instantly the men stationed at the five aftermost lowerdeck guns, on the starboard side, were turned over to those on the larboard side, and to each of the latter guns, already loaded with a single 32-pounder, was added a double-headed shot. Presently the Achille, for that was the ship, advanced to within musket-shot; when five or six rounds from the Brunswick's five after guns on each deck brought down, by the board, the former's only remaining mast, the foremast.[1] The wreck of this mast, falling, where the wreck of the main and mizen masts already lay, on the starboard side, prevented the Achille from making the slightest resistance; and, after a few unreturned broadsides from the Brunswick, the French ship struck her colours. It was, however, wholly out of the Brunswick's power to take possession, and the Achille very soon rehoisted her colours, and, setting her spritsail, endeavoured to escape.

In about half an hour after the dismasting of the Achille, and when the latter, by the aid of her spritsail, had got to some distance from the Brunswick and Vengeur, another ship was seen bearing down, in the direction in which the Achille had ap-

[1] It is stated in other works, and is still contended by one of the Brunswick's surviving officers (although the master's log, minute as it is in other respects, notices no other ship, English or French, than the Vengeur), that the Achille had all three of her masts shot away by the Brunswick's partial fire. In opposition to this, the log of the Valiant, the ship next in line to the Brunswick, states, that at a few minutes past 10 A.M. her opponent lost her main and mizen masts; and the log of the Ramillies says: "10 h. 45 m. saw one of the enemy's ships opposed to our centre with her main and mizen masts gone." That this must have been the Achille is clear, because all the other dismasted ships in the French line, except the Northumberland, and she lost all three masts together, lay at or near to the two extremities. Moreover, was not a broadside from the Queen Charlotte sufficient, even without the additional fire of the Valiant, to bring down the masts of a French 74? The end-on position, in which the Achille approached the Brunswick, in all probability led to what, from the most attentive review of the subject, we must still consider to be a mistake.

proached, and which ship, fortunately for the Brunswick, proved to be the Ramillies. Meanwhile the two fast-locked combatants continued in hot action; on the part of the Brunswick, the fire from her quarter-deck, forecastle, and poop, was but feebly maintained. From the destructive effects of the Vengeur's musketry, it became difficult to stand to the guns there situated; but the fire from the two principal decks of the Brunswick was maintained as vigorously as in the early part of this hard-contested action.

On the lower deck, the seamen, profiting by the rolling of the Vengeur, frequently drove home the coins, and depressed the muzzles of the guns, each of which was loaded with two round shot, and then again withdrew the coins, and pointed the muzzles upwards; thus, alternately, firing into their opponent's bottom, and ripping up her decks. During this deliberate and destructive operation, Captain Harvey was knocked down by a splinter; but, although seriously hurt, he was presently on his legs again. Soon afterwards, however, the crown of a double-headed shot, which had split, struck his right arm, and this gallant officer was compelled to go below.[1] The command of the Brunswick now devolved upon Lieutenant William Edward Cracraft.

At about 45 m. P.M. the two ships, having remained three hours entangled, swung off from each other, and, tearing away the three anchors from the Brunswick's bows, separated. It was now that the Ramillies, who had arrived up a few minutes before, and, having lost but two seamen killed and seven wounded, was quite a fresh ship, commenced her attack upon the Vengeur. While the Ramillies was waiting for the French ship to settle further from the Brunswick, in order to have room to fire at her without injuring the latter, the Brunswick, by a few well-directed shot, split the Vengeur's rudder, and shattered her stern-post; besides making a large hole in her counter, through which the water rushed in great quantity. At this spot the Ramillies, now only 40 yards distant, pointed her guns, and, assisted occasionally by her consort, reduced the gallant but at this time overpowered Vengeur, in a very few minutes, to a sinking state; when suddenly, as if perceiving the Achille making off in the distance, the Ramillies filled and made all sail from the two exhausted combatants, between whom, soon after 1 P.M., all firing ceased.

[1] On this occasion, Captain Harvey is reported to have addressed his crew in the following words: "Persevere, my brave lads, in your duty. Continue the action with spirit, for the honour of our king and country; and remember my last words,—The colours of the Brunswick shall never be struck."

It was about the same time that the Vengeur, who saw her fate approaching, displayed a union jack over the quarter, as a token of submission and of a desire to be relieved. But the Brunswick, having had all her boats destroyed, could afford her enemy no protection. At about 1 h. 30 m. P.M. the Brunswick lost her mizenmast, and, in consequence, became still less able to bestow any assistance upon the Vengeur, who had by this time removed the jack from her quarter to the larboard arm of her cross-jack yard.

The loss of the mizenmast, the wounded state of the other masts, and the damage done to the rigging, rendering it impossible to haul up for the British fleet, to leeward of which M. Villaret was now leading a fresh line on the starboard tack, to recover as many as he could of his dismasted ships, the Brunswick put her head to the northward, with the intention to make the best of her way into port, should the French fleet, as, fortunately for her, proved to be the case, forbear from molesting her.

All possible sail was therefore made upon the ship, and the effective survivors of the crew began immediately to repair the damaged rigging, fish the masts, and secure the lowerdeck ports, through which the water was rushing at every roll. About 3 P.M. the Brunswick fell in with the Jemmappes, wholly dismasted, and only under the influence of her spritsail. From this ship the Brunswick had received some annoying shot while engaged with the Vengeur. As the Brunswick luffed up under her lee within hail, the Jemmappes displayed a union jack over her quarter, and signified that she had struck to the English admiral, at the same time pointing to the Queen, then at a considerable distance in the south.

The extent of the damages sustained by the Brunswick will appear by the following detail of them. The mizenmast, as we have seen, was gone; the bowsprit was cut two-thirds through near the gammoning, the mainmast badly wounded, and the foremast also, which latter had received one very deep shot three feet below the trussel-trees. All the running and most of the standing rigging were shot away, all the yards in a shattered state, and all the sails shot to pieces. No fewer than 23 guns lay dismounted. The ship had been on fire three times from the Vengeur's wads; and her yards, rigging, and sails were all much injured by shot. Her starboard quarter-gallery had been entirely carried away, and her best bower-anchor, with the starboard cat-head, was towing under her bottom.

The loss on board the Brunswick was proportionably severe;

consisting of one captain of foot (Alexander Saunders), one master's mate (Thomas Dalton), one midshipman (James Lucas), 30 seamen, and 11 marines or soldiers killed, and her captain (mortally[1]), second lieutenant (Rowland Bevan), one midshipman (Mr. Hurdis), one ensign of foot, 91 seamen, and 19 marines or soldiers wounded.

The Achille, at about 4 h. 15 m. P.M. with colours rehoisted on one of her stumps, and a small sail or two set, was overtaken by the Ramillies and unopposedly secured; having sustained a loss in her different encounters, as alleged by her officers, of 36 killed and 30 badly wounded. As to the Vengeur, shortly after the Brunswick had quitted her, she lost her wounded fore and main masts, the latter, in its fall, carrying away the head of the mizenmast. Thus reduced to a complete wreck, the Vengeur rolled with her ports in the water, and, as the lids of most of those on the larboard side had been torn off or shot away in her board-and-board conflict, the Vengeur began filling faster than ever. Notwithstanding that the ship was literally sinking, the Vengeur, it is said, rehoisted her colours, and set a small sail on the stump of her foremast.

In this state, at about 6 h. 15 m. P.M., fortunately for her brave officers and crew, the ship was approached by the Alfred, Culloden, and Rattler cutter; who immediately lowered as many of their boats as would swim, and sent them to save the people. The boats of the Alfred took off 213, and those of the Culloden and the cutter (the zeal and activity of whose commander, Lieutenant John Winne, did him great credit) nearly as many more. Consequently, when the ship went down a few minutes after the last boat had pushed off from her, very few besides the badly wounded could have perished in her.

Among the 30 or 40 unhurt by wounds, doubtless there were several who, as British sailors frequently do in similar cases of despair, had flown to the spirit-room for relief. Thus inspired, it is not extraordinary that, when the ship was going down, some of them should exclaim, "Vive la nation!" "Vive la république!" or that one, more furiously patriotic than the rest of his drunken companions, should, at this painful moment to the spectators, (and something of the kind we believe did happen), wave to and fro the tri-coloured flag, under which he had so nobly fought.

---

[1] It was found necessary to amputate the arm above the elbow on the evening after the action; but Captain Harvey, owing, it is thought, to his splinter-wound did not survive beyond the 30th of June.

Among the survivors of the Vengeur's crew, were Captain Renaudin and his son, a boy of twelve years of age. These were accidentally taken off by different ships' boats; and each, until they met again at Portsmouth, imagined the other had perished. Affecting indeed must have been the interview to all who witnessed it; to the father and son rapturous in the extreme. Captain Renaudin was afterwards exchanged, and proved, as we shall by-and-by have occasion to show, as humane as he had already shown himself a gallant man.

The Valiant, the next ship claiming our attention, hove to, at 9 h. 30 m. A.M., to windward of her proper opponent (reckoning from the rear) the Patriote, and, as she well might, from the latter's sickly state, soon drove her to leeward. The Valiant then passed through the line ahead of the Patriote, and engaged the Achille soon after the Queen Charlotte had quitted her. At 10 h. 5 m. A.M. the Achille's main and mizen masts, disabled, no doubt, by the three-decker's previous fire, fell over the side; and the Valiant then stretched ahead, until she brought to to windward of the Royal Sovereign, as has already been related. The Valiant's loss of spars was confined to her maintopsail and cross-jack yards, and her loss of men to one seaman and one soldier or marine killed, and five seamen and four soldiers or marines wounded.

The Orion bore down upon and engaged the Northumberland, and fired a few shot, as they would bear, on the Patriote ahead of her. At about 10 h. 30 m. A.M. the two French ships bore up, and the masts of the Northumberland, which, previously to her attack by the Orion, had received several destructive shot from the foremost guns of the Queen, fell over the side; as, a few minutes before, had the main topmast of the Orion, carrying with it the main-top and main-yard. The Orion then hauled up, as well as she could, in support of the Queen Charlotte; and the Northumberland set her spritsail, and endeavoured to get off to leeward: the latter, however, was subsequently secured, and found to have sustained a loss in killed and wounded of 180, including a large proportion of officers. The Orion received no other damage of any consequence than what has been related; and her loss extended to only two seamen killed, and 20 seamen and four soldiers or marines wounded.

The Queen, in bearing down to engage, having suffered considerably in her sails and rigging, was unable to get abreast of her proper opponent, the Northumberland; who, with her fore and main tacks down, was running fast ahead. She therefore closed with the seventh French ship from the rear, the Jemmappes.[1] This ship also made sail ahead, and then ran to leeward; but the Queen kept close upon her starboard quarter, and annoyed her much. The Jemmappes, having had her colours twice shot away, rehoisted them at the mizen topgallant-mast head; but at 10 h. 45 m. A.M. her mizenmast went by the board.

At 11 A.M. the Queen's mainmast went over the lee side; springing, in its fall, the mizenmast, and carrying away the forepart of the poop, and part of the quarter-deck bulwark. In another quarter of an hour the mainmast of the Jemmappes fell, as did immediately afterwards, her foremast. At this time the Queen had fallen round off, and the crew of the Jemmappes, having been driven from their quarters with great slaughter, came upon deck, and waved submission with their hats; but the Queen was in too disabled a state to take possession. Her mizen topmast had been shot away since the fall of her mainmast; her foremast and bowsprit had been shot through in several places; and her mizenmast, from its wounds, was expected every instant to fall; her rigging had also been cut to pieces, and all her sails rendered useless.

After about an hour's exertions in repairing some of her principal damages, the Queen managed to get her head towards her own fleet, and was steering along to leeward of it when at about 30 m. P.M., she discovered, through the smoke to leeward, 12 sail of French ships standing towards her. The leading ship, the Montagne, passed without firing, and so did her second astern; but the third ship opened her fire, as did also every one of the remaining eight, the last of which was the Terrible, with only her foremast standing. The latter was towed into the line by three frigates; two of which cast off and hauled to windward, to engage the Queen. The Queen, however, soon convinced them that her guns were not so disabled as her masts; and the two frigates put up their helms and ran to leeward without returning a shot.

The appearance of the Queen Charlotte and the newly-formed line astern of her had caused the Montagne and her line to keep more away than M. Villaret had at first intended; the Queen, therefore, suffered but little from the distant cannonade to which she was exposed. On coming abreast of the Queen's late antagonist, the Jemmappes, the French admiral detached a frigate

[1] In the first edition, this ship, by mistake, was named the Scipion; but we have now the most positive proof, that the Scipion was the sternmost ship in the French line: other circumstances, also, have since made it clear, that the Jemmappes, a fine new 74 of the largest class was the Queen's opponent.

to tow the latter off, as well as two other dismasted two-deckers lying at no great distance from her. The damages which the Queen had previously sustained have already appeared: her loss amounted to 14 seamen and marines or soldiers killed, her second and an acting lieutenant (Richard Dawes and George Aimes), one midshipman (Mr. Kinneer), and 37 seamen and marines or soldiers wounded.

Of the remaining seven ships of the British line, two only require to have any account given of their proceedings; with respect to the rest, it will suffice to show what loss they each sustained. That of the Ramillies has already been stated. The Alfred had six seamen and two marines or soldiers wounded, but none killed; the Montagu, her captain, in the early part of the action, and three seamen killed, and two midshipmen (Hon. Mr. Bennett and John Moore), and 11 seamen wounded; the Majestic, two seamen killed, and five wounded; and the Thunderer, no killed nor wounded: a circumstance not difficult to be accounted for, if the following minute, which appears in the log-book of the Royal Sovereign, is correct: "11 h. 40 m., observed a ship lying a considerable distance to windward, which we supposed to be the Thunderer; threw out her pendant, the signal for chase and close action being flying."

The proceedings of the Royal George and Glory are all that remain to be detailed. At 9 h. 38 m. A.M. the Royal George, in bearing down, opened her fire chiefly upon the Sans-Pareil and Républicain, and in a short time passed through the French line between those ships, in hot action with both. It may here be remarked, that three French ships, the Entreprenant, Pelletier, and Neptune, intervene between the Républicain, the present opponent of the Royal George, and the Queen's brave antagonist, the Jemmappes. Two of the above three ships (for the Neptune, during a while, was smartly engaged by the Montagu), if they found opponents at all, suffered little or nothing from them; and, that the Ramillies and Alfred, their natural opponents in the British line, escaped with about equal impunity, has already been shown. At all events, two of the slowest sailing ships in the British rear, if not in the British line, had the honour of checking the way of the three rearmost French ships, and, as we shall presently show, of reducing two of them at least to so disabled a state, that, instead of one only, as was the case, both ships ought to have been secured by the four or five fresh ships belonging to the British at this extremity of their line.

From her indifferent sailing, the Glory had been a long time in getting down, but at length cut through the French line astern of the Scipion, and, engaging the latter close to leeward, soon brought down by the board all three of her masts; losing, by the return fire of the Scipion, her foretopmast and main and mizen topgallantmasts. Ranging ahead, the Glory found herself opposed to the Sans-Pareil, whose fore and mizen masts had just fallen under the heavy fire of the Royal George. The Républicain now came in for her share of the united fire of the two British three-deckers; one of which ahead, and the other astern, raked her with such effect as to compel her to retreat, with main and mizen masts reduced to a tottering state, and which, as we have elsewhere related, fell soon afterwards. In manœuvring to get away, however, the Républicain obtained the opportunity of returning the rake to each of her antagonists. The Sans-Pareil and Scipion, meanwhile, completely silenced in their fire, had dropped astern; but, the Royal George having lost her foremast and main and mizen topmasts, had her wheel rendered useless, and tiller-ropes shot away, and the Glory being also much disabled in her masts and rigging, neither French ships could be taken possession of by them.

The loss sustained by the Royal George amounted to one midshipman (John Hughes) and four seamen and marines killed, her second lieutenant (Thomas Ireland), master (John Bamborough), two midshipmen (Messieurs Boyce and Pearce), and 45 seamen and marines wounded. The Glory had her master (George Metcalfe), one midshipman (David Greig), and 11 seamen killed, and 31 seamen and eight marines or soldiers wounded.

The alleged loss sustained by the Sans-Pareil was as many as 260 killed, and 120 badly wounded: an overrating, probably, as to the killed, but it is now too late to clear up the point. On board the Sans-Pareil as a prisoner, was Captain Troubridge, late of the British frigate Castor, with a portion of her officers and crew. When, in the afternoon, the Majestic fell in with, and took possession of, this noble two-decker, Captain Troubridge remained on board, and, with his men, assisted in navigating the Sans-Pareil into port. Wherever we can, with propriety, introduce an anecdote creditable to the officer, and interesting to the public, we are ready to do so; but we should never have thought of inserting the vulgar and disgusting anecdote, which a contemporary, in a seeming laudatory manner too, has related of Captain Troubridge.[1]

[1] Brenton, vol. i., p. 308.

The fortunate possession of a French account of the proceedings of the Scipion, on this day of dreadful carnage, enables us to give a full and interesting account of the casualties that befel that ship. The loss of her three masts has already been mentioned. Seventeen of her guns were dismounted, her furnaces knocked down, and the hot shot in them scattered about the deck, to the great danger of setting fire to the ship. From her first and second batteries alone, the Scipion is represented to have discharged 1440 round shot; and her loss, by the enemy's fire, is stated at 64 men killed, and 151 wounded. In comparing this ship's aggregate loss with that of any of her companions in the action, it should be recollected, that the additional number of killed assigned to most of the prizes, and enumerated at a former page, is from doubtful authority, and indeed, from the over proportion to the wounded, in all probability exaggerated. The Scipion, notwithstanding she was in this deplorable state, and notwithstanding there were so many comparatively untouched ships yet remaining in the British fleet, managed to rig herself with jury-masts and join her admiral

After having, in this surprising manner, recovered four of his crippled ships, two of the number without a stick standing except the bowsprit, M. Villaret put away to the northward, and by 6 h. 15 m. P.M., with the whole of his remaining 19 line-of-battle ships, and all the rest of his fleet, except a frigate left to reconnoitre, was completely out of sight of the fleet which had been engaged with him. The state of many of the ships composing that fleet, and of the prizes in its possession, was such, that it took until 5 A.M. on the 3rd before Lord Howe could make sail. His lordship then steered to the north-east, and, without any further occurrence worth notice, anchored at Spithead at 11 A.M. on the 13th; having with him his six prizes, and the whole of his fleet, except nine sail of the line, which he had ordered to Plymouth.

Our attention is now called to Rear-admiral Montagu, whom, with six sail of the line and a frigate, we left cruising to intercept the French convoy from America; and which was escorted, not by four sail of the line, as the rear-admiral had been led to suppose, but by two, the Tigre and Jean-Bart, as already mentioned.[1] The Rear-admiral's orders were to cruise until the 20th, and then, if unsuccessful in his object, to rejoin the commander-in-chief; but, from the prospect held out by the intelligence he had received, the rear-admiral was induced to wait

See p. 140.

over the prescribed period some days, especially as the Venus had not returned to him. While thus waiting, Rear-admiral Montagu recaptured some vessels of the Lisbon convoy, that had escaped from the Channel fleet, and from them learnt that the Brest fleet was at sea, and, equally with himself, seeking the expected Franco-American convoy. Having exceeded, by four or five days, the time he had been directed to cruise to the northward of Cape Ortugal, and finding, by one of the recaptured ships, that Lord Howe, instead of being at the appointed rendezvous off Ushant, was as far to the westward as the longitude of 14°, and in probable pursuit of the French fleet, Rear-admiral Montagu, in compliance with the spirit of his orders, made the best of his way into port, and, on the 30th of May, anchored in Plymouth Sound.

The interception of a provision-laden convoy of upwards of 100 sail, in the present distressed state of France, being of the utmost importance to England, the British admiralty, on the very day, June 2nd, on which the board received the account of Rear-admiral Montagu's arrival in port, sent back orders for him to sail immediately, taking with him the four line-of-battle ships supposed to be ready for sea in the port. This reinforcement was ordered, in anticipation of the expected junction between MM. Nielly and Vanstabel, although the admiralty were still of opinion, correctly enough, that the latter had sailed from America with only two sail of the line. With his force thus augmented to 10 sail of the line, including two 64s, the rear-admiral was to hasten to the rendezvous off Ushant; there to await the arrival of intelligence from Lord Howe, and, in the event of an action between the fleets, was to be ready to protect any disabled British, or to capture any disabled French, ships. If, however, any certain intelligence should in the mean time reach the rear-admiral of the approach of the Franco-American convoy, he was to make all sail in that direction, and endeavour to intercept it.

On the 3rd of June, as has already been mentioned, the Audacious arrived in Plymouth Sound, with the intelligence that the two fleets had had a partial engagement, and were likely to have a decisive one. On the 4th, Rear-admiral Montagu, not having received any alteration of his orders, weighed and put to sea with the following nine sail of the line and two frigates, with every probability that he should have disabled ships either to succour or to capture.

Gun-ship.			
	Hector . . .	{	Rear-adm. (b.) George Montagu.
			Captain Lawrence William Halsted.
	Alexander . .	„	Richard Rodney Bligh.
	Ganges . . .	„	William Truscott.
74	Colossus[1] . .	„	Charles Morice Pole.
	Bellona . . .	,	George Wilson.
	Theseus . .	„	Robert Calder.
	Arrogant . .	„	Richard Lucas.
	Minotaur[1] . .	„	Thomas Louis.
64	Ruby[1] . . .	„	Sir Richard Bickerton.
Frigates,	Pallas[1] and Concorde.[1]		

On the 8th, in the morning, the rear-admiral reached his station, about thirteen leagues south-west by west of Ushant. At 3 h. 30 m. P.M., the wind a moderate breeze from north-north-east, 12 sail were descried and chased in the east-south-east. At 4 P.M., eight of the strangers being discovered to be French line-of-battle ships, the British squadron formed the line of battle ahead on the larboard tack, and stood on to meet them. At 6 P.M. the French squadron which consisted of the 110-gun ship Majestueux, and 74-gun ships Aquilon, Jupiter, Marat, Nestor, Rédoubtable, Révolution, and Superbe, also two frigates (one a rasé), a corvette, and a cutter, under the command of Rear-admiral Cornice, tacked from the British squadron, and, with all the sail the ships could carry, stood into the bay of Bertheaume. At 8 P.M., having chased the French close under the land and nearly into the road, where already lay, as seen by the advanced frigate, the Concorde, two ships apparently of the line, the British squadron tacked and stood off for the night under easy sail.

On the 9th, at 7 A.M., the wind still light from the northward, a fleet was seen bearing west, and at 9 A.M. was discovered to be French, and to consist of 19 sail of the line, three frigates, and two smaller vessels. This, as may be conjectured, was the remnant of the grand fleet, standing in for the land, then about 17 leagues distant. Immediately Rear-admiral Montagu, whose squadron was about three leagues nearer to the shore, formed in line of battle ahead on the starboard tack, and M. Villaret did the same on the opposite or larboard tack; forming in very compact order, with his five dismasted ships in tow: two of them three-deckers (Républicain and Terrible), and the remainder 74s. two only of which, the Mucius and Jemmappes, were wholly dismasted. It was the former's intention to keep the wind of

[1] These ships composed the reinforcement.

his enemy; but, fearing that the Ganges and Alexander, who were astern, and sailed very ill (the latter in particular), would not be able to weather the French fleet, then about six miles distant, Rear-admiral Montagu, at 9 h. 30 m. A.M., put about and formed his squadron in line on the larboard tack; the van-ships edging away to starboard, to enable the leewardmost ones to get into their stations.

Having thus, within him, in an enemy's port at no great distance, a force fully equal, and outside of him not more than six or seven miles off, preparing to attack him, a force (making every allowance) nearly double, Rear-admiral Montagu felt it necessary to continue standing on to the southward. The French admiral now detached two ships from his rear in chase; and at noon, when his van came into the wake of the British squadron, the whole French fleet bore up in pursuit. The effective ships soon gained rapidly in the chase, owing to the slow sailing of the Ganges and Alexander; for these two ships, although carrying all the canvas they could spread, the rear-admiral was obliged repeatedly to shorten sail, being determined not to abandon them: the Bellona, indeed, as a proof of her superiority of sailing, during the greater part of the time, had her topsails on the cap, her courses hauled up, and her yards braced by. At 5 P.M., notwithstanding that his headmost ships were then within four miles of the British rear, the French admiral, fearful of being drawn to leeward of his port with his crippled ships, hauled upon a wind to the eastward on the larboard tack. At 6 P.M., Rear-admiral Montagu hauled up in line of battle on the starboard tack, and, stretching on, soon lost sight of M. Villaret and his fleet. After standing to the northwest during the whole of the next day, in the vain endeavour to fall in with Lord Howe, the rear-admiral, at 4 P.M. on the 10th, bore away for the Channel, and on the 12th anchored in Cawsand bay, Plymouth; where he was the same day joined by nine ships of Lord Howe's fleet, the admiral, with the remainder and the prizes, having, as already stated, proceeded to Spithead.

On the 11th M. Villaret, or, rather, Jean-Bon Saint-André, cast anchor in Bertheaume Bay, in company with M. Cornice; and notwithstanding the comparative unsafety of that roadsted, and the pressing wants, as well of the wounded men to be sent to the hospital as of the disabled ships to be refitted in the dock-yard (the Montagne herself had actually to send her rudder to Brest to be repaired), M. Jean-Bon Saint-André preferred, for the present, the risk of remaining there, to the still greater risk, as he conceived it, of encountering the indignation of the people of Brest, at the loss of so many of their ships, and, in killed, wounded, and prisoners, of so many thousands of their countrymen. On the 12th, the same day that Rear-admiral Montagu anchored in Cawsand Bay, the long-expected, the critically-circumstanced Franco-American convoy, consisting of 116 sail, within one (a ship having foundered through bad weather) of its original number, under the escort of Rear-admiral Vanstable, with the three ships of the line, Tigre, Jean-Bart, and Montagnard (which latter, it is believed, with the Mont-Blanc, had joined him near the scene of action on the 29th of May), anchored in the road of Bertheaume; notwithstanding the promised sharp look-out which was to have been kept for it by British fleets and squadrons. This joyful event happened very opportunely for the discomfited admiral and deputy; and the French men-of-war fleet and merchant convoy entered Brest in triumph.

Having conducted both admirals and both fleets, after the great battle fought between them, to the respective ports from which they originally sailed, we shall take a cursory notice of some of the published accounts on each side connected with the subject. Jean-Bon Saint-André's official report to the National Convention contains, among many minor ones, two important mistakes: one, that the British fleet consisted of 28 sail of the line, drawn up for battle, besides a reserve of several others; and secondly, that two British ships sank in the action, one while engaged to windward with the Montagne, and the other in the rear, upon the authority of Rear-admiral Nielly, who is stated to have declared that he saw her go down. As a set-off to this, most of the English unofficial accounts gave the French 27, and some 28, sail of the line; and Lord Howe's letter expressly states, that one French ship "sank in the engagement." M. de Poggi, who published in England a "Narrative of the Proceedings" of Lord Howe's fleet, rectifies the mistake about the sinking of the Jacobin, but makes a much greater, by declaring, that the Audacieux, Montagnard, and Mont-Blanc, foundered: the last after the action of the 29th of May, and the two former in that of the 1st of June.

The conventional deputy blames several of the captains for not obeying signals, and scruples not to declare that, but for their gross neglect, "et notamment l'impéritie de celui du Jacobin," the French, instead of losing any of their dismasted ships, would have captured all those of the British. Jean-Bon Saint-André further declares, that he left his enemy in a worse condition than himself; that Lord Howe, had he possessed the means of attacking him, would have employed them, as the French did not attempt to escape; and that the British admiral took no steps to prevent the French frigates, and even the smallest of the corvettes, from towing away those ships which had been forced out of the line.

The charge against the captain of the Jacobin is both an unfounded and an ungrateful charge. Was it not a shot from that ship, which, by cutting away the foretopmast of the Queen Charlotte, enabled the Montagne to effect her escape? And had not Lord Howe good reason to attribute the paucity of his prizes, although seven in number, to the palpable remissness of several of his captains? There were, undoubtedly, at the close of the action, 12 or 14 English line-of-battle ships, without even a topgallantmast shot away; and some of these ought certainly to have secured two (the Scipion and Jemmappes), if not four (including the Républicain and Terrible), of the five more or less dismasted French ships. Of frigates and sloops of war, as on almost every similar occasion, the British had not only none to spare, but not enough to perform the services, for which, chiefly, vessels of that description are attached to a fleet.

So that, in untoward occurrences of this nature, as in number of line-of-battle ships, the British and French fleets were nearly upon a par. That Lord Howe should have preferred departing with his six prizes, to waiting the issue of another attack, may have surprised, whether joyfully or not, the French conventional deputy. But perhaps there were not a few among the admiral's countrymen who could appreciate his motive; who might consider that, although many of the British ships were in a condition for active service, those very ships had attained their effective state by their tardiness in engaging: while the ships that had evinced an eagerness for close combat lay disabled around the Charlotte, possessing, like her, all the spirit, but none of the means, again to distinguish themselves. In fact, had the 1st of June battle terminated similarly, in point of indecisiveness, to that of the 29th of May, there would have been many unpleasant courts-martial.

Let us now pay the attention that is due to a professed historical account of the battle, inserted in a French work of some celebrity. That account begins by adopting the rhapsodical speech of Barrère de Vieuzac respecting the sinking of the Vengeur. It is needless to repeat the account; but some allowance ought to be made for the credulity of the French, when their national self-love was so powerfully wrought upon by the flaming descriptions of the same event in all the London opposition journals. Suffice it, that a first-rate ship of war, then constructing at Brest, under the direction of the celebrated Sané, the largest (being 24 feet longer and three feet broader than the Commerce-de-Marseille), and pronounced to be the finest ship that had ever been launched, was to have her name changed from Peuple to Vengeur, in commemoration of the martyrized ship; the model of which latter was to be suspended under the arch of the Pantheon, and artists, painters, sculptors, and poets, were called upon to exert their several talents, in celebration of the glorious event.[1] However, according to the narrative of the proceedings of the Montagne, as given in the same work, wherein such pains have been taken to perpetuate the nonsense of which we have here afforded but a sample, that ship, although not reduced to such an extremity as to be a competitor for the crown of martyrdom, deserved fully as well of the nation as the Vengeur.

Having described the onset of the battle, the account states that the Queen Charlotte, " of 120 guns," attacked the Montagne, and was several times driven back by the latter and her two seconds. That the Jacobin, by manœuvring improperly, allowed Lord Howe, "towards noon," to cut the line, and get under the stern and upon the quarter of the Montagne, into whom the Jacobin herself, by mistake, had till then been firing. That, followed by two three-deckers, and three other ships of inferior force, the Queen Charlotte surrounded the Montagne and cut her up beyond example. That the latter remained two hours so engaged, and was all the while invisible to the rest of her fleet. That the Queen Charlotte ran foul of the Montagne and attempted to board her (at this moment Jean-Bon Saint-André went below, as we have already related[2]), but that Lord Howe, fearing the opposition he was likely to experience, prudently retired to leeward to the distance of several toises. That the Queen Charlotte, presently perceiving the damaged state of the Montagne, and that her fire had slackened, readvanced to the attack; when a young aspirant, Bouvet by name, who had received three wounds, and whose left arm was then suspended in a sling, requested M. Villaret to allow him to sweep the deck of the English admiral, "de balayer le pont de l'amiral Anglais." That was precisely what the French admiral most wished; and

[1] See Appendix, No. 13. [2] See p. 173.

accordingly young Bouvet, although fired at from the Queen Charlotte's tops, riddled with bullets in his clothes, his hat pierced in three places, and with five fresh wounds as the price of his temerity, discharged a carronade, a 36 (misprinted 56) pounder, and had the happiness to see his audacity crowned with complete success, "et a le bonheur de voir son audace couronnée d'un plein succès." The effect of this carronade, pointed at the quarter-deck of the Queen Charlotte, was so prompt, that immediately Lord Howe set all his sails, fled, made the signal for his ships to follow him, and quitted the immovable Montagne. "Ainsi," says the writer of this precious article, "la valeur d'un seul homme donnait la victoire au vaisseau amiral, et l'arrachait des mains des Anglais, fuyant à toutes voiles."[1] Lest even the credulous French reader should take all this for a hoax, the writer adds in a note, that on the 26th of February, 1795, the National Convention, upon the report of Desbourges, a member of the Committee of Safety, passed a decree, ordering to be paid to young Bouvet the sum of 300 francs (scarcely enough, one would think, to equip him with a new coat and hat), for his loss of time during the healing of his eight wounds, and as a "national recompense" for the courage he had displayed in the battle of the 1st of June.

The following more sober account is from the pen of an experienced French admiral. "The action began with great spirit on both sides. The English captains, more accustomed than ours to manage ships of war, cut through our line in several places. Meanwhile the republicans fought with infinite courage. Several ships were dismasted or disabled in the two fleets, and the action ceased before the victory was decided. One of our ships only, the Vengeur, disabled and sinking, had been," not yet, but this is a mistake of no great consequence, "taken possession of by the enemy. But, what is incomprehensible, is our abandonment, upon the field of battle, of six French ships, disabled but not subdued, which, lying together in a group, kept the tri-coloured flag flying, as if stretching forth their arms to the fleet, entreating to be succoured. To recover these six ships, and to take two disabled English ships," probably the Queen and Brunswick, "at no great distance from them, it sufficed simply to put about. It is to be wished we could blot out this disgraceful event." After alleging other complaints against the commanding officer of the French fleet, M. Kerguelen proceeds as follows: "We have thus sacrificed uselessly the

[1] Victoires et Conquêtes, tome iii., p. 22.

men, the ships, and the interests of the Republic. But ignorance and presumption then presided over its destinies upon the ocean, and the most disgraceful defeat was transformed into a genuine triumph. We proclaimed a victory, after having lost seven fine ships, that mounted upwards of 500 pieces of cannon. We gave to the commander-in-chief the rank of vice-admiral,[1] and threw flowers in the way of the representative that had embarked in the fleet, on his return to Brest,"[2]

Although none of the English accounts of this battle, and of the one or two skirmishes that preceded it, enter very minutely into particulars, yet all of them are more or less inaccurately drawn up; and two, as being the work of professional hands, claim a share of our attention. One account is rather tactical than historical, and may be dismissed in a few words. We naturally turned first to the plate (out of upwards of 70 that the work contains), which purports to give the relative position of the rival fleets at the time that the Cæsar, on the 29th of May, defeated Lord Howe's plan, by steering large from the enemy's line. Our mortification equalled our surprise, on finding this important, this easily-described point of the day's proceedings so, to say the least of it, unintelligibly represented.[3] The plate, purporting to describe the onset of the 1st of June battle, is also incorrect, inasmuch as it represents the attack to have been made "at right angles," or perpendicularly to the enemy's line: whereas, whatever may have been the intention of Lord Howe, the attacking force, the rear and a part of the centre of it especially, approached in an oblique manner. A French account accordingly says: " On vit cette flotte s'avancer à pleines voiles, dans un ordre parfait et sur une ligne *oblique*."[4] It was this oblique approach (caused, as is clear, by the forward movement

---

[1] The date of M. Villaret-Joyeuse's appointment as a vice-admiral is September, 28, 1794.

[2] Histoires des Evènements des Guerres Maritimes entre la France et l'Angleterre, depuis 1778 jusqu'en 1796: à Paris, per Y. J. Kerguelen ancien, contr' amiral, p. 362.* Another French work has just reached us, entitled, "Histoire de la Marine de tous les Peuples, depuis la plus haute antiquité jusqu'à nos jours; par A. J. B. Bouvet de Cressé, Professeur de Belles-Lettres: à Paris, 1824." We are disappointed. All that it contains in the way of novelty is the following liberal remark of the writer, in reference to the mutinous proceedings of the Brest fleet, see p. 64, in the summer of 1793: "Déclarons, avant tout, que, dans cette affaire, et dans toutes celles qui précédèrent et suiverent, soit à bord du *Censeur* ou du *Ca-ira*, soit à bord de la *Montagne*, soit à Aboukir, soit à Trafalgar, nul Français n'a à se reprocher un acte de félonie; déclarons encore que, sur aucun point, l'Anglais n'a jamais osé attaquer les émules des Duquesne, des d'Hector, des de Grasse, des la Motte-Piquet, etc., etc., sans une force d'un tiers en plus. Paris la sait; Londres, pleurent ses éternelles guinées, le sait mieux encore." tome ii., p. 450.

[3] Naval Battles, from 1744 to the Peace in 1814, critically reviewed and illustrated, by Charles Ekins, Rear-admiral, C.B., K.W.N., Part ii., plate iii., (25), fig. 6.

[4] Victoires et Conquêtes, tome iii., p. 17

* See Appendix, No. 14.

or head-way of the French fleet), and the neglect of the British van-ship, and, through her default, the inability of some of the ships near her, to make a close and impressive attack upon the French van, that occasioned the French also to say: "Les Anglais, qui avait parfaitement reconnu la position de l'escadre française, n'attaquèrent point l'avant-garde, mais ils s'attachèrent à combattre le centre et l'arrière-garde."[1] In direct opposition to this the tactical English writer says: "On the 1st of June, had Lord Howe attacked the centre and rear of the French line with his whole force, he would have gained a complete and easy victory; not to follow up his success, I hold to be a great and inexcusable error."[2]

The next plate in Admiral Ekins's work, or that meant to represent "the situation of the two fleets about 1 P.M. when the enemy was completely beaten,"[3] is so filled with blunders as to require nearly as many distinct explanations as there are ships scattered upon it. Let it suffice to state, that all the ships in both fleets have their masts standing except the Queen and two unnamed ships; neither of which, however, is meant for the Jemmappes, a ship so named appearing as fully masted and rigged as any ship upon the plate. "The French fleet," says the English writer whom we have next to attend to, "was no longer manned and officered as in the splendid times of Louis XVI. The high-spirited men who were the companions of De Grace (Grasse), Suffrien (Suffren), and D'Orvilliers, had fallen beneath the axe or the guillotine, or fled from their country to avoid it. Most of the seamen had been marched to the Rhine and the Moselle, to fill the ranks of the army, and their places were supplied by wretched conscripts and fishermen. The captains of the ships of the line were men totally unqualified, from their habits, for such a station: they had been, with few exceptions, masters of merchantmen, and knew nothing of the signal-book or the mode of conducting a ship of war."[4]—"The British fleet was remarkably well manned, but the officers were generally deficient from want of practice, the natural consequence of ten years' retirement: some of them had little idea of keeping a ship in her station, either in line of battle or order of sailing, during the night and in blowing weather. Habit, however, soon conquered this difficulty; so that, had the enemy been discovered at daylight in the morning, the commander-in-chief might have formed his line of battle with perfect facility from his three lines

---

[1] Victoires et Conquêtes, tome iii p. 17.
[2] Naval Battles, &c., p. 190.
[3] Naval Battles, &c.
[4] Brenton, vol. i., p. 246.

in the order of sailing. The exercise of great guns was not sufficiently attended to during the cruise."[1]

Now it is singular that the French, amidst all their excuses, should never have attributed the unfavourable issue of the battle to the inexperience or the cowardice of the crews. "Les marins français, jaloux de la gloire des guerriers de terre, combattaient avec enthousiasme. *La victoire ou la mort*: telle était la devise inscrite en lettres d'or sur les pavillons bleus arborés à bord de leurs vaisseaux. Toutes leurs actions montraient qu'ils ne voulaient pas être parjures. Ils se battaient avec la plus rare bravoure, et l'intrépidité des nouvelles recrues rivalisait avec celle des vieux marins."[2] It must be admitted that the French crews, those in the captured ships especially, did behave in a very gallant manner, and certainly betrayed no want of skill in manœuvring their ships. With respect to the sweeping charge against the French officers, and that charge in particular which accuses those captains who had been "masters of merchantmen" (and of which class, by-the-by, there were not so many as here represented) of knowing "nothing of the mode of conducting a ship of war," it meets an answer in the noble conduct of Captain Lamel, of the Indomptable, on the 29th of May,[3] who had very recently been promoted from the merchant service, in which he had acted as master during a number of years.

That Lord Howe did not consider his fleet to be very numerously manned may be inferred from his destroying so many valuable prizes and recaptures in preference to sending them in for adjudication; and, respecting the quality of his crews, there appears to be a diversity of opinion, even among naval men. "Much has been said by various writers on naval subjects, of the manner in which the French fleet was manned, but no mention has been made of the ineffective state of the British ships when they first put to sea to meet the republicans. An idea thereof may be formed by the Montagu having joined the grand fleet with only 13 men, including the quartermasters, able to take the helm; seven in one watch, six in the other. The captain of her foretop had only been 15 months at sea. The Ramillies was equally destitute of able seamen; and many others nearly so."[4] We have thus shown, as we trust, that the alleged disparity in the manning of the two fleets had no foundation in fact, not at least to the extent wished to be inferred by the post-captain in whose work the assertion is contained.

[1] Brenton, vol. i, p. 248.
[2] Victoires et Conquêtes, tome iii., p. 19
[3] See p. 152.
[4] Marshall, vol. i., p. 663.

The writer, who states also that five of the ships which the French carried off "required no more than a summons from a frigate"[1] to induce them to surrender, appears to have been as much misinformed of what befel the Phaëton while running past the dismasted, apparently silenced, and subsequently captured, Impétueux, as of the age of Lord Howe's prizes, which he designates as "a few old ships," and regrets were not destroyed. The fact is, two only of the seven captured ships, the Northumberland and Achille, could be called old, and they could find ships of equal if not greater age in the British fleet, but not one ship of their own rate, except the Brunswick, that equalled them in size. The Vengeur, Impétueux, and America had only been launched the preceding year; and the two latter were considered as the finest 74s that had ever been seen in a British port. But what shall we say of the Sans-Pareil? Here was a ship, also newly launched, nearly equalling in size the Queen Charlotte herself, and which subsequently proved to be so fast a sailer that her facility in overtaking French privateers, although dead in the wind's eye, and practising every possible manœuvre to escape, would scarcely be credited even of a frigate.

The same writer, who has laboured so hard to disparage the victory of the 1st of June, endeavours, or rather (for he has since in part retracted his words) did endeavour, to fix upon Rear-admiral Montagu a very serious imputation; because, having, on the night of the 8th, with nine two-deckers, including a 64, chased nine French sail of the line, one a three-decker, he did not, on the morning of the 9th, rush into battle with another French fleet, composed of one 120, one 80, and twelve 74-gun ships, in an effective state, besides two dismasted 110-gun ships and three dismasted 74s, towed by some of the former, and accompanied by a long train of frigates and corvettes. The best refutation of so extraordinary a charge is a reference to the numbers admitted to have been present on each side. But who, upon a mere midshipman's opinion, would have imputed a backwardness to fight to an officer whose professional life through a long course of service had been passed in honour, and who had already fought and conquered in two frigate actions, each time against an opponent of equal force?[2]

---

[1] Brenton, vol. i., p. 303.

[2] First action fought September 14, 1779, between the British frigate Pearl, of 32 guns, 12 and 6 pounders, 220 men (of whom 10 only, except the officers, had served in a ship of war), and 683 tons, and the Spanish frigate Santa-Monica, of 32 guns, 12 and 6 pounders Spanish, 280 men, and 956 tons. The engagement lasted two hours, during which the Santa-Monica had

ADMIRAL EARL HOWE.

FROM THE ORIGINAL BY GAINSBOROUGH.

IN THE TRINITY HOUSE, LONDON.

A summary of the honours and rewards which fell to the share of the conquerors in the 1st of June victory will conclude our long, but we trust not uninteresting, account of the first decisive meeting between the British and republican fleets. On his arrival at Spithead, the gallant veteran (his lordship was then 70 years of age) was greeted with joy and enthusiasm. On the 26th of June the royal family came down to Portsmouth, and immediately proceeded to pay a visit to Lord Howe, on board his ship at Spithead. His majesty, attended by his principal minister, there held a naval levee, and presented the admiral with a diamond-hilted sword, valued at 3000 guineas, also a valuable gold chain to be worn round the neck. The royal party then dined with Lord Howe on board the Queen Charlotte, and returned to the shore in the evening. The king would, it is understood, have invested Lord Howe with the riband of the garter, but was restrained from acting, according to the claims of justice and the dictates of his heart, by the strong political prejudices of the minister at his elbow.

Of the two admirals next in command to Lord Howe, one was created an Irish peer, by the title of Lord Graves, and the other Lord Viscount Bridport. Rear-admirals Bowyer, Gardner, Pasley, and Curtis were created baronets; and Sir George Bowyer and Sir Thomas Pasley had settled upon them a pension of 1000*l.* a year each for their wounds. The first-lieutenant of every line-of-battle ship in the action, and of the Audacious also, was made a commander; and several other lieutenants belonging to the different flag-ships, as has since been the general practice, were promoted to the same rank. It need scarcely be stated that the unanimous vote of thanks to Lord Howe, and to the officers, seamen, marines, and soldiers serving under him in the fleet passed both houses of the British parliament.

Happening to have it in our power, we here subjoin the names of all the first-lieutenants in Lord Howe's fleet; as also of the second-lieutenants, where the command of the ship devolved upon the first, or the first was killed during the engagement. John Whitby, Cæsar; George Burlton, Bellerophon; Robert Larkan, Leviathan; Henry Vaughan, Russel; Peter M'Kellar, Royal Sovereign; John Monkton, first, Alexander Ruddoch,

---

38 men killed and 45 wounded, and the Pearl 12 killed and 19 wounded.

Second action fought September 30, 1780, between the Pearl, as before, and the French frigate Espérance, of 32 guns, 12 and 6 pounders French, nearly 200 men, and about 850 tons: action also two hours; French ship's loss 20 killed and 24 wounded, Pearl's, 6 killed and 10 wounded.

second, Marlborough; John Larkan, Defence; William Burgess, Impregnable; Thomas W. Clayton, second (first killed), Tremendous; Adrian Renou, Barfleur; Henry Blackwood, Invincible; Edward Rotheram, Culloden; John Marsh, Gibraltar; John Cochet, Queen Charlotte; William Edward Cracraft, Brunswick; George Rice, Valiant: Roger Mears, Orion; William Bedford, acting captain on the 1st of June, and Richard Dawes, acting first, Queen; Joseph Eyles, Ramillies; John Chesshire, Alfred; Ross Donnelly, Montagu; John Draper, Royal George; Chapman Jacobs, Majestic; William Ogilvy, Glory; Joseph Larcom, Thunderer; and Joseph Bingham, Audacious.

The gallant master of the Queen Charlotte, whose skill and steadiness in conducting that ship, as well under the stern of the Eole on the 29th of May, as under that of the Montagne on the 1st of June, was the theme of praise of all in the fleet, and of none more than Lord Howe himself, could only, on account of the rules of the service, stand the chance of obtaining that promotion in his profession, which he coveted more than anything else, by being reduced as a master and appointed a lieutenant. Mr. Bowen (the present Captain James Bowen, one of the commissioners of the navy) was accordingly made a lieutenant; and the different captains of the fleet, to evince their high opinion of his worth, readily appointed him, at Lord Howe's suggestion, their agent for the prizes; thus affording to Lieutenant Bowen a handsome remuneration for his services, but not a jot more than he had most honourably earned.

As it could not be denied that several ships of the British fleet had misbehaved themselves, both in the action of the 29th of May and in that of the 1st of June, an indiscriminate praise of the captains would have been an act of extreme injustice towards those who, on both occasions, strove their utmost to fulfil the intentions of their gallant chief. The following, therefore, were the officers whom Lord Howe named as meriting a "particular claim to his attention." Admirals Graves and Sir Alexander Hood; Rear-admirals Bowyer, Gardner, and Pasley; Captains Lord Hugh Seymour, Pakenham, Berkeley, Gambier, John Harvey, Payne, Parker, Henry Harvey, Pringle, Duckworth, and Elphinstone; Captains Nichols of the Royal Sovereign and Hope of the Bellerophon, on the inability of their respective flag-officers to remain at their posts, and Lieutenants Monkton of the Marlborough and Donnelly of the Montagu, in similar situations.

If, as a contemporary observes, "the discretionary power given by the last part of the signal No. 39, on the 1st of June, places the conduct of those officers who did not go through the line, in a far more favourable point of view than it would otherwise have appeared,"[1] the same cause proportionably enhances the conduct of those officers who, scorning to shelter themselves behind such a plea, boldly dashed into the thickest of the fire.

The difficulty of a due discrimination was certainly very great, and Lord Howe did well to relieve himself from much of the responsibility, by transmitting to the Admiralty the logs of the several ships of the fleet, signed by their respective captains. With these documents before them, the Lords of the Admiralty restricted the delivery of medals to the flag-officers and captains of the ships that appear in italics in the following list: Cæsar, *Bellerophon*, *Leviathan*, *Russel*, *Royal Sovereign*, *Marlborough*, *Defence*, Impregnable, Tremendous, *Barfleur* (flag-officer only, until at a later day, when her gallant captain received one), *Invincible*, Culloden, Gibraltar, *Queen Charlotte*, Brunswick, *Valiant*, *Orion*, *Queen*, *Ramillies*, Alfred, Montagu, *Royal George*, Majestic, *Glory*, Thunderer; also the *Audacious*. The Montagu's captain was killed in the action, and the Brunswick's captain had since died of his wounds.

The captain of the Cæsar, one of the expected ships, felt displeased at the following paragraph in Lord Howe's letter, describing the partial engagement of the 29th of May: "But, as the smoke at intervals dispersed, it was observed that the Cæsar, the leading ship of the British van, after being about on the starboard tack and come abreast of the Queen Charlotte, had not kept to the wind; and that the appointed movement would consequently be liable to fail of the purposed effect."

Captain Molloy accordingly wrote to request a court-martial upon his conduct on that day. Lord Howe wished to include that on the 1st of June. The order was granted, and the court-martial sat on board the Glory in Portsmouth harbour, from the 25th of April to the 15th of May, 1795. The court pronounced Captain Molloy's personal courage unimpeachable, but, considering that he had not done his best to pass through the enemy's line on the 29th of May, nor taken a proper station for coming to action with the enemy on the 1st of June, dismissed him from the command of the Cæsar.

It is probable that this, as well as some other courts-martial,

[1] Brenton, vol. i., p. 371.

would have been spontaneously ordered by the Admiralty, but that such a proceeding was considered likely to detract from the éclat of the victory. In our humble opinion, no consideration of that kind ought to have been allowed to check the course of justice. Every officer virtually complained against should have been tried for his conduct: it is not improbable that, although some might have been found guilty, others would have cleared themselves from every shadow of blame.

We must not omit to add, that the corporation of the Trinity House, the merchants at Lloyd's, and the cities of London, Edinburgh, and Dublin, with the usual liberality of Britons on such occasions, opened a subscription for the relief of the wounded, as well as of the widows and children of those who had fallen in the action; whereby a considerable fund was raised.

On the 22nd of June Rear-admiral Cornwallis, in the Excellent 74, sailed from Plymouth Sound, with a fleet of 12 sail of the line (all 74s but one, a 64), to cruise in the Bay of Biscay, and escort the East India fleet clear of soundings; and, on the 7th of September, Lord Howe, in the Queen Charlotte, with a fleet of 34 ships of the line, including the five Portuguese 74s, Vasco-de-Gama, Maria Primeira, Rainha-de-Portugul, Condé-de-Henrique, and Princessa-de-Biera, sailed from Torbay, and stood over to the coast of France. On the 9th, having arrived off Ushant, the admiral detached the Leviathan, Russel, and two frigates, to look into Brest road; but, before the ships could put their orders into execution, Lord Howe recalled them, the wind having come too far to the northward to secure their safe return. The British fleet then took its departure from Ushant, and stood down Channel into the track (latitude 49° to 50° north, and about 25 leagues to the westward of Scilly) of the British, as well as the Dutch and Spanish, merchant-convoys; a few of which latter passed through and obtained the protection of the fleet. After having cruised eight days with pleasant easterly weather, a fresh breeze sprang up from the south-west, and, veering to north-west, with thick weather, set in to blow a very severe gale. A heavy sea arose in consequence, and the ships of the fleet were soon obliged to lie to, under their storm-stay-sails and close-reefed main topsails. The veteran admiral, however, persevered in keeping the sea until, on the 20th, the Invincible, Ramillies, Tremendous, and Arrogant, severally made the signal of distress. Lord Howe, on this, bore up; and, shortly after the fleet had wore, the Maria Primeira, Commodore

Marie, carried away her bowsprit and foremast. The fleet was immediately brought to on the larboard tack, and the admiral ordered the Orion to stay by the disabled ship. On the 21st the fleet again bore up, and, late the same evening, re-anchored in Torbay.

Early in November Lord Howe again sailed, and, occasionally putting into port to refit and water, cruised to the westward and in the Channel during the greater part of the remainder of the year. But the British admiral was not afforded a second opportunity of distinguishing himself, as the Brest fleet did not again quit port; not, at least, until almost the last day of the year.

In the latter end of October, or beginning of November, Rear-admiral Nielly, with the five 74-gun ships, Marat, Tigre, Droits-de-l'Homme, Pelletier, and Jean-Bart, the Charente, Fraternité, and Gentille frigates, and Papillon brig-corvette, sailed from Brest on a cruise to the westward, and, as it was understood, to endeavour to intercept the homeward-bound Lisbon and Oporto fleet. On the 6th of November, at 2 h. 30 m. A.M., latitude 48° 25' north, longitude (from Greenwich) 7° 53' west, this squadron fell in with the two British 74-gun ships Alexander, Captain Richard Rodney Bligh, and Canada, Captain Charles Powell Hamilton, returning to England after having escorted the Lisbon and Mediterranean convoys to a safe latitude.

The two British ships, when first seen, were to leeward of the French squadron, steering north-east, with the wind at west. The Alexander and Canada immediately hauled upon the wind, on the larboard tack, and, at a little before 4 A.M., passed the strange ships, the nearest distant about half a mile, but without being able to ascertain their national character. Shortly afterwards the two British ships kept a little free, letting out the reefs of their topsails, and setting studding-sails. At 5 A.M. it was discovered by the night-glasses that the strangers were standing after the British ships; whereupon the latter crowded all sail, and hauled more to the eastward. At about daybreak the Canada passed the Alexander, and, steering a more northerly course, brought herself on the latter's larboard bow. Two ships of the line, one bearing a rear-admiral's flag, and two frigates, now went in chase of the Canada; and the remaining three ships, one with a commodore's pendant, and one frigate, pursued the Alexander.

At 7 h. 30 m. A.M., the French squadron hoisted English colours, and at 8 h. 15 m. A.M., the Alexander and Canada did the same. On observing this, the French hauled down the English, and hoisted their own colours. The division in chase of the Alexander now drawing within gunshot, the latter discharged her stern-chasers at the van ship, and received in return a fire from her bow-guns. At 9 A.M. a similar interchange of firing took place between the Canada and the French admiral in the Marat; whose shot, passing over the former, produced no effect. The Canada's signal was now made to form ahead for mutual support; a signal which Captain Hamilton instantly answered, and strove his utmost to execute; but the French admiral, seeing the British ship's intentions, hauled more to the starboard, and, with the aid of his second, who now began firing at intervals, compelled the Canada to resume her course.

The Alexander continued firing her stern-chase guns until nearly 11 A.M.; when the advanced ship of the three in chase of her (believed to have been the Jean-Bart) ran up and brought the British ship to close action. So well-directed a fire in return was opened by the Alexander, that, in half an hour, the French 74 was compelled to sheer off and call a frigate to her assistance. The French commodore, in the Tigre, next advanced, but would not come fairly alongside: notwithstanding which, the Alexander, in about half an hour, shot away the head of the Tigre's main topmast, her main yard in the slings, and her mizen topmast. A third ship now took the latter's place, and used her endeavours to compel the Alexander to surrender.

This unequal conflict the British 74 sustained until some minutes past 1 P.M.; by which time she had her main yard, spanker-boom, and three topgallantyards shot away, her three lower masts shot through in many places, all the other masts and yards more or less wounded, nearly the whole of the standing and running rigging cut to pieces, her sails torn into ribands, her hull shattered, and on fire in several places, and her hold nearly filled with water. The other ships, also, which had quitted her consort, were rapidly advancing, and the French admiral already threw his shot over her. Captain Bligh, therefore, justly deemed any further efforts as a needless waste of lives, and ordered the colours of the Alexander to be hauled down.

As far as could be ascertained, the Alexander's loss amounted to about 40 men in killed and wounded; including, among the latter, one lieutenant of marines, the boatswain, and pilot. The Canada, owing to the high firing of the French, sustained very little damage and no loss, and reached a home-port in safety. According to the French papers, the Alexander's two principal opponents were very much disabled, and sustained between them a loss in killed and wounded amounting to 450 officers and men.

Escorted by the squadron of M. Nielly, the Alexander proceeded to Brest, and, as a proof that her damages were of the most serious kind, was with difficulty floated into the harbour. Captain, or rather Rear-admiral Bligh (for he had been promoted during his absence), in his letter to the Admiralty, of date November 23, states that he was treated by his captors with great kindness and humanity; but it would otherwise appear, that the acts of the French authorities at Brest toward the Alexander's late officers and crew were quite of an opposite character: "Here the population (populace) insulted the prisoners as they marched to the place of their confinement: officers and men shared the same lot; they were denied the commonest rations of provisions, and reduced to starvation. A wretched dog that crept into the cells was killed, and his head alone sold for a dollar, to satisfy the cravings of nature: a prisoner, in a state of delirium, threw himself into the well within the prison walls, and his dead body, after lying some time, was taken out, but no other water was allowed to the people to drink; an English lady and her daughters, confined with the men, had no separate apartment, and all their privacy was supplied by the generous commiseration of the British sailors, who, standing side by side close together, with their backs towards the fair captives, formed a temporary screen while they changed their garments. These facts were supplied to the author by the officers who were present."[1] At all events, Rear-admiral Bligh and his officers received the most marked attention from Captain Renaudin, the late commander of the Vengeur; and who, having been exchanged for Captain Cotes of the Thames, had recently returned to Brest.

On the 27th of May, 1795, Rear-admiral Bligh, having got back to his country, was tried by a court-martial for the loss of the Alexander, and, as may well be supposed, was most honourably acquitted.

A few weeks before the year closed, a ship of the Channel fleet, that had missed the opportunity of distinguishing herself in action with the French fleet, gave to her name some considerable degree of notoriety, by becoming the scene of a very

[1] Brenton, vol. i., p. 304.

disgraceful and by no means unalarming procedure. On the 3rd of December, at 10 P.M., as the 74-gun ship Culloden, Captain Thomas Troubridge, lay at Spithead, the greater part of her crew, bursting into open mutiny, unshipped the ladders, and barricaded themselves below. The officers having got the marines under arms, sent to acquaint the admiral of the Channel fleet, and the captain of the ship, who was then on shore. On the next morning, the 4th, at 7 A.M., the petty officers, who had been confined below by the mutineers, were allowed to come on deck; and several of the well-disposed among the people took the opportunity of effecting their escape. On calling a muster at a few minutes before noon, the well-disposed were found to consist, besides the commissioned and warrant officers, of the whole of the petty officers, all the marines but six, and 86 of the seamen; leaving about 250 for the number of the mutineers. In the course of the afternoon Admirals Bridport, Cornwallis, and Colpoys came on board, and endeavoured, but in vain, to persuade the men to return to their duty.

Matters continued in this alarming state during the whole of the 8th, 9th, and 10th; except that, on the latter day, the mutineers permitted the necessary water and provisions to be got up from below. On the 11th, Captain the Honourable Thomas Pakenham went on board, and succeeded, at last, in persuading the men to return to their duty. The ship's company were then mustered, and the ringleaders, ten in number, seized and sent on board different ships, there to await their trial. It was discovered that the mutineers had broken into the magazine, raised a barricade of hammocks across the deck between the bits, had loaded with grape and canister shot the two second guns from forward, and pointed them towards the hatchway, and had collected upwards of 50 muskets and several tomahawks. On the 15th of December a court-martial sat on the ten mutineers; two of whom were acquitted, and eight sentenced to be hanged. On the 13th of January five of the eight suffered on board the Culloden at Spithead, and the remaining three received the king's pardon.

The proceedings of the British Mediterranean fleet, which was still commanded by Admiral Lord Hood,[1] now demand our attention. Lord Hood, who soon after the evacuation of Toulon, the more conveniently to take on board provisions and wine from Gibraltar, Alicant, and Minorca, had remained with his fleet in the Bay of Hyères, an anchorage formed by a small group of

[1] See page 96.

islands of that name, situated in the vicinity of Toulon, having received intelligence that the republican forces at Corsica were much straitened for provisions, detached several cruisers, with orders to prevent any succours from being thrown into the island. Among the detached ships was the Ardent 64, Captain Robert Manners Sutton; who was stationed off the harbour of Villa-Franca, for the chief purpose of watching two French frigates, which, according to intelligence received, were preparing to conduct to Corsica a convoy of vessels, having on board a supply of troops and stores. While employed on this service, the Ardent unfortunately caught fire, blew up, and left not a soul alive to relate the origin of the catastrophe. The quarter-deck of the ship, with some of the gunlocks sticking in the beams, and the marks of the splinter-netting deeply impressed on the planks of the deck, was found floating not very far from the spot, and thus left no doubt of the manner in which the Ardent had been lost.

The great importance of Corsica to France in the present state of her ships and arsenals at Toulon, and the no less importance of the harbour of San Fiorenzo to Great Britain, as a point of rendezvous for her Mediterranean fleets, suggested to Lord Hood and Major-general Dundas the propriety, with the troops then on board the fleet, of assisting the loyal part of the inhabitants in an attempt to expel the French from the island. Accordingly, on the 24th of January, at 4 P.M., after two officers, sent to communicate with General Paoli, had returned with a favourable report, the British fleet amounting, including army-victuallers, horse and other transports, to 60 sail, got under way from the Bay of Hyères, and proceeded towards the Bay of San-Fiorenzo.

On the next day, the 25th, a gale of wind came on, and dispersed and endangered the fleet; the Victory, among other ships, having had two maintopsails blown to rags, and the yard itself rendered totally unserviceable. On the 29th the fleet, being driven greatly to leeward, gained, but not without difficulty, Porto-Ferrajo, in the island of Elba. As three-decked ships were not qualified to navigate narrow seas and rocky coasts, particularly in the winter season, the 74-gun ships, Alcide, Captain John Woodley, bearing the flag of Commodore Robert Linzee, Egmont, Captain Archibald Dickson, and Fortitude, Captain William Young, accompanied by two frigates, the Lowestoffe and Juno, and by several transports with troops, were detached, on the 5th of February, to a bay lying to the westward of Cape Mortella; where they arrived in safety on the

7th. On the same evening the troops, in number about 1400, and commanded by Major-general Dundas, disembarked, and immediately took possession of a height which overlooked the tower of Mortella, the first of several strong positions necessary to be reduced, before the anchorage at the west side of the gulf of San-Fiorenzo could be made properly secure; and which tower, it will be recollected, had been recaptured from the British, or rather from the Corsicans, in the October of the preceding year, by a squadron of French frigates.

An attack against the tower, by sea and land, was decided upon; and, on the 8th, the Fortitude and Juno anchored in the best manner for battering it with effect. The two ships kept up an unremitting fire for two hours and a half; without, however, making any material impression on the walls of the building. At the end of this time the Fortitude's mainmast was much wounded, many of the shrouds were cut away, three of her lower-deck guns dismounted, several hot shot in her hull, and a great many of her men had been blown up by an explosion of powder from a box which had been struck by a hot shot. The ship also was now so near to the tower and the rocks, that, should the wind die away, it would be difficult, and, should it blow on shore, might be impossible, to save her. Under these circumstances, the two vessels ceased firing, and hauled out of gun-shot. The Fortitude sustained a loss of six men killed, and 56 wounded, eight of them dangerously. No sooner had the ship got clear of the tower, than she was perceived to be on fire, from the second deck to the upper part of the quick-work on the quarter-deck, occasioned by a hot shot that had lodged in her side. After cutting out the shot, and opening the side in several places, the fire was extinguished; and that, fortunately, before it had produced any material damage. The Juno, although she had been admirably placed by her commander, came off with very little damage, and without any loss.

The battering from the height on shore had been as unsuccessful as that from the ships, till some additional pieces were mounted, and hot shot used; when one of the latter, falling among, and setting fire to, the bass-junk with which, to the depth of five feet, the immensely thick parapet was lined, induced the garrison, 33 only in number, and of whom two were mortally wounded, to call for quarter. The tower mounted one 6 and two 18 pounders; the carriage of one of which had been rendered unserviceable in the course of the cannonade. These guns had been brought on shore from the French frigates, when they retook the tower in October, 1793. There was a furnace for heating shot, and the garrison had about forty 6 and one hundred and thirty-five 18-pounder charges left at the time of surrender.[1] It is but justice to Ensign Thomas le Tellier and his men (four of whom were seamen) to acknowledge, that they proved themselves skilful artillerists, and maintained their post until it was no longer tenable.

The following detailed account of what damage the Fortitude suffered by the fire from the tower is, indeed, the best encomium that can be passed upon the little garrison within it. Two 18-pound shot through the centre of the mainmast, and nine main shrouds shot away. One of the lower-deck port-timbers cut through, and all the sill of the port carried away. One of the quarter-deck ports cut down to the deck. The heels of the fore-topgallantmasts and foretopmast, and the cap and cross-trees shot away. The spare maintopmast and jibboom cut through. Some shots in the hull, but none under water. A great part of the running rigging and blocks shot away, and most of the top-mast-backstays; also, as already stated, three lower-deck guns dismounted.

The next post to be attacked was the Convention redoubt, mounted with 21 pieces of heavy ordnance, and considered as the key of San-Fiorenzo. By the most surprising exertions of science and labour, on the part of the officers and men of the navy, several 18-pounders and other pieces were placed on an eminence of very difficult ascent, 700 feet above the level of the sea. This rocky elevation, owing to its perpendicularity near its summit, was deemed inaccessible; but the seamen, by means of blocks and ropes, contrived to haul up the guns, each of which weighed about 42 hundred weight. The path along which these dauntless fellows crept would, in most places, admit but one person at a time. On the right was a descent of many hundred feet; and one false step would have led to eternity; on the left were stupendous overhanging rocks, which occasionally served as fixed points for the tackle employed in raising the guns. From these 18-pounders, so admirably posted, a cannonade was unremittingly kept up during the whole of the 16th and 17th. On the latter evening, when the fire of the redoubt had become nearly overpowered, it was determined to storm the works; a service which was executed with vigour, and crowned with suc-

---

[1] A contemporary, in the very teeth of the official return, says: "The force was only one 24-pounder, mounted *en barbet* (*barbette*) on a sliding-carriage, and recoiling on an inclined plane." Brenton, vol. ii., p. 54.

cess. A part only of the garrison was made prisoners: the remainder retired to another stronghold, which was distant about 400 yards, and separated by a deep ravine, from the former. That post the republicans abandoned about midnight, then crossed over to the town of San-Fiorenzo with their two frigates, and left the British in quiet possession of the tower and batteries of Fornelli. On the next day, the 18th, the squadron anchored in perfect security, in Mortella bay. On the 19th the French, having set fire to one of their frigates, and left the other sunk, and to all appearance destroyed by the shot from the British, evacuated the town of San-Fiorenzo, retreating towards Bastia. On the same evening San-Fiorenzo, with its formidable batteries mounting 25 pieces of cannon, including two 12-inch mortars, two 36, and seven 24 pounders, was taken possession of by the British; and the seamen soon found means to weigh and carry off the Minerve, a fine French 38-gun frigate. The prize was taken into the British service, named (there being already a Minerve) San-Fiorenzo, and established as a first-class 36. The frigate which had been set on fire was the Fortunée, of the same force as the Prudente, and others of her class.

The loss sustained by the combined forces in these several attacks amounted to 17 privates killed, one lieutenant, and 35 non-commissioned officers and privates wounded. General Paoli, at the head of about 1200 Corsicans, was at hand, ready to assist the British, in case his services should be required. The active part taken by the navy, in all the operations on shore, none were more ready to acknowledge than Major-general Dundas, the commanding officer of the land-forces.

Lord Hood, having failed to convince Major-general Dundas of the practicability of reducing Bastia, the capital of Corsica, with the small force which had already effected so much, sailed from San-Fiorenzo bay on the evening of the 23rd, to try what effect the appearance of his fleet alone would produce. After cruising off the port for a fortnight, and gaining every intelligence necessary to facilitate his plans, the British admiral, with a part of his squadron, sailed back to San-Fiorenzo bay; where he arrived on the 5th of March. The major-general still declining to act, until the arrival of an expected reinforcement of 2000 men from Gibraltar, Lord Hood took on board that proportion of the land-forces which had originally been ordered to serve on board the fleet as marines, and obtained, also, two officers and 30 privates of artillery, with some ordnance-stores and intrenching tools.

With this force, on the 2nd of April, Lord Hood again set sail for, and on the 4th arrived at, the anchorage before Bastia. On the same evening the troops, commanded by Lieutenant-colonel Vilettes, with the guns, mortars, and ordnance-stores, and also a detachment of seamen commanded by Captain Horatio Nelson of the Agamemnon, were, under the able superintendence of the latter, disembarked at a spot a little to the northward of the town. The total of the combined forces, when landed, amounted to 1248 officers and men, exclusive of the Corsicans, under General Paoli, in number about the same; and the number of French and Corsican troops in garrison at Bastia was, as it afterwards appeared, 3000. Lord Hood moored his fleet, in the form of a crescent, just out of reach of the enemy's guns, the Fortitude, Captain Young, being stationed as the centre ship; while the harbour's mouth was effectually guarded by Captain Benjamin Hallowell, with a flotilla of gun-boats and armed launches. As the enemy had magazines of provisions and stores on the island of Capraïa, the recently-captured frigate Impérieuse, Captain William Wolseley, was despatched thither, and prevented the republicans from making any use of them.

On the 11th the British batteries, which had been erected on several commanding heights, being ready to be opened, Lord Hood sent a written summons to the town; but which the French general, Lacombe-Saint-Michel, would not even read. At the appointed signal, therefore, the batteries, consisting of five 24-pounders, two 13, and two 10-inch mortars, and two heavy carronades, commenced their fire upon the enemy's works, and were promptly answered by the numerous guns with which the latter were crowned. The Prosélyte, mounting 12-pounders (a frigate-bomb, brought away from Toulon), and commanded by Captain Walter Serocold, was directed to be placed as a floating-battery against a part of the town; but, on her coming to anchor, the swell cast her the wrong way, and she became exposed, in consequence, to a dreadful fire from the enemy's forts. The French fired nothing but hot shot at her; and several of these, lodging among the casks and other inflammable stuff in the hold, set the ship on fire. Captain Serocold, having made the signal of distress, continued firing upon the town, till the boats from the squadron were alongside; when he and his crew quitted the Prosélyte, and the latter, shortly afterwards, was consumed by the flames.

At length, on the 21st of May, after a siege of 37, and a negotiation of four days, the town and citadel of Bastia, with the several posts upon the neighbouring heights, surrendered, on terms highly honourable to the besieged; whose bravery in holding out so long excited the admiration of the conquerors.

The possession of this important post was accomplished with the slight loss, to the army, of seven privates killed and dead of their wounds, two captains and 19 privates wounded, and six privates missing; and, to the navy, of one lieutenant (Cary Tupper, of the Victory) and six seamen killed, and one lieutenant (George Andrews, of the Agamemnon) and 12 seamen wounded. The principal naval officers associated with Captain Nelson at the batteries, and to all of whom Lord Hood expressed himself greatly indebted, were, Captains Anthony Hunt, Joseph Bullen, and Walter Serocold; and Lieutenants John Gore, Henry Hotham, John Styles, George Andrews, and Charles Brisbane.

The few republican troops in the island being now completely invested by the British and loyal Corsicans, General Paoli, who commanded the latter, persuaded the inhabitants to withdraw their allegiance from France and transfer it to England. Accordingly, the assembly of the *general consult*, held at Corte on the 14th of June, declared unanimously the separation of Corsica from France; and, with the same unanimity, and with the strongest demonstrations of universal satisfaction and joy, voted the union of Corsica to the crown of Great Britain. On the 19th the formal surrender was made to Sir Gilbert Elliott, his majesty's viceroy, and the latter took an oath "to maintain the liberties of Corsica, according to the constitution and the laws;" the members of the assembly, on their part, taking the oath of allegiance and fidelity to the king of England.

The expected reinforcement of troops from Gibraltar having arrived, under the command of Lieutenant-general the Honourable Charles Stuart, immediate preparations were made for attacking the fortress of Calvi, which was still in the possession of a republican garrison. Captain Nelson, of the Agamemnon, the senior officer at Bastia in the absence of Lord Hood (who, with the bulk of the fleet, had returned to watch the Toulon squadron), carried the troops to Port-Agra, a small cove about three miles from Calvi. On the 19th of June the whole of the men disembarked, and on the same evening encamped in a strong position upon a neighbouring ridge. Lord Hood, returning on that day to Mortella bay, sent a detachment of the Victory's seamen, with some ordnance and other stores, under the orders of Captains Hallowell and Serocold, to Calvi. On the 27th he arrived himself before that place, in the Victory, and immediately landed seven of his first-deck guns, for the use of the batteries constructed to act against the town and its powerful defences. The British batteries were soon opened, but, not till the siege had lasted 51 days, could General Casa-Bianca be induced to capitulate. This he did on the 10th of August, upon terms highly flattering to the bravery of the garrison of Calvi.

The loss, on the part of the British army, amounted to one field-officer, two lieutenants, and 20 privates killed, and three captains, four lieutenants, and 46 non-commissioned officers and privates wounded; and, on the part of the British navy, to one captain (Walter Serocold, by a grape-shot at the principal battery, while getting the last gun into its place), one midshipman, and five seamen killed, and six seamen wounded. Among the non-reported wounded was Captain Nelson, who lost his eye, in consequence of a shot striking the battery near him, and driving some particles of sand with considerable force into it. The loss sustained by the enemy does not appear in the published accounts.

Among the vessels found in the port of Calvi, and delivered up to the British, were the French frigates Melpomène and Mignonne. The latter mounted 32 guns, 8 and 4 pounders, was small and of little value, and, after lying up for a year or two, was burnt as unserviceable at Porto-Ferrajo. The Melpomène, on the contrary, was a fine 40-gun frigate of 1014 tons, and was added to the British navy as a cruising frigate of the 38-gun class. A considerable quantity of naval stores also fell into the hands of the British.

The French in Toulon having succeeded in equipping most of the ships, which had been left to them by the British at its evacuation, put to sea, on the 5th of June, with the following seven sail of the line: 120-gun ship Sans-Culotte (late Dauphin Royal), 80-gun ships Bonnet Rouge (late Couronne) and Tonnant, and 74-gun ships Censeur, Duquesne, Généreux, and Heureux, with four or five frigates. Lord Hood, who, as already stated, then lay off Bastia, departed the moment he received the information, with 13 sail of the line and four frigates, consisting of the

Gun-ship.

100	Victory . .	Admiral (b.) Lord Hood. Captain John Nicholson Inglefield. ,, John Knight.
	Britannia . ,	Vice-adm. (w.) William Hotham. Captain John Holloway.

Gun-ship.

Guns	Ship	Officers
98	Princess Royal	Vice-adm. (b.) Sam. Cranston Goodall. Captain John Child Purvis.
98	Windsor Castle	Vice-adm. (w.) Philip Cosby. Captain Sir Thomas Byard.
98	St. George	Rear-adm. (b.) Sir Hyde Parker. Captain Thomas Foley.
74	Alcide	Rear-adm. (w.) Robert Linzee. Captain John Woodley.
74	Terrible	Rear-adm. (b.) Skeffington L. Captain George Campbell.
74	Egmont	Rear-adm. (b.) Archibald Dickson.[1] Captain John Sutton.
74	Bedford	,, Robert Mann.
74	Captain	,, Samuel Reeve.
74	Fortitude	,, William Young.
74	Ilustrious	,, Thomas Lennox Frederick.
74	Berwick	,, William Shield.

Frigates, Romulus, Juno, Meleager, and Dido.

On the 10th the two fleets gained sight of each other; the British immediately made all sail in chase. On the 11th, at daylight, the British and French admirals were between three and four leagues apart. To avoid an action with a force so superior, M. Martin pushed for the anchorage in Gourjean bay; which he reached with his fleet about 2 P.M. But none of the British ships were able to get near, except the 28-gun frigate Dido, Captain George Henry Towry; who received, and gallantly returned, the fire of some of the rear-ships, as well as of two forts that guarded the entrance to the anchorage. It was Lord Hood's intention to follow the French into the bay, and, from the judicious plan of attack which he had matured, little doubt was entertained that every ship of the squadron would have been either captured or destroyed, but the prevalence of calms and unfavourable winds occasioned the enterprise to be abandoned. The plan, as given out in orders, was, for the Britannia and St. George to engage the Sans-Culotte; the Victory and Princess Royal, the Bonnet-Rouge; the Windsor Castle and Alcide, the Généreux; the Bedford and Egmont, the Duquesne; and the Fortitude and Captain, the Tonnant. The Terrible was to draw off the attention of the battery on the east point of the bay, and the Berwick, of the battery on the west point; while the Illustrious, assisted by the four frigates, were to attack the five French frigates. The two French ships of the line, Heureux and Censeur, left out of this arrangement, must, it

---

[1] The extraordinary number of flag-officers in this fleet arose from the recent promotions.

was considered, from their situation, have fallen had the attack met with success.

In the mean time the French had landed some of their guns, and erected strong batteries on shore, for the protection of their ships. Still, hopes were entertained of destroying the squadron, and, for this purpose, two or three fire-ships were fitted, and intrusted to the command of two able officers, Lieutenants Ralph Willet Miller and Charles Brisbane; the latter of whom, it appears, had suggested the enterprise. But, on approaching the bay, these officers found the French so well prepared, and so strongly posted, that this plan also was given up. Both plans of attack having thus proved abortive, Lord Hood, taking with him, besides the Victory, the Princess Royal and two 74s, proceeded off Calvi, to resume the operations against Corsica; leaving Vice-admiral Hotham, in the Britannia, with the remaining eight line-of-battle ships, and the four frigates, to watch the French ships in Gourjean bay. These afterwards succeeded, owing, in a great degree, to the stormy state of the weather, in eluding the blockading force, and reached in safety the road of Toulon. Early in the succeeding November Lord Hood returned home in the Victory, leaving the command of the fleet to Vice-admiral Hotham.

On the 10th of November, soon after Lord Hood had quitted the station, a most alarming mutiny broke out on board the 98-gun ship Windsor Castle, Captain William Shield, bearing the flag of Rear-admiral Robert Linzee, and lying at anchor in San-Fiorenzo bay. The reason assigned by the mutineers was, a dislike to their admiral, captain, first-lieutenant, and boatswain; all of whom they declared should be changed. Vice-admiral Hotham, Rear-admiral Sir Hyde Parker, and several captains of the fleet, went on board the Windsor Castle, in the hope of prevailing on the men to return to their duty without the necessity of resorting to extremities. This the men positively refused. Captain Shield demanded a court-martial, in order that his conduct might be inquired into. The investigation took place; and nothing appearing to criminate the captain in the slightest degree, he was honourably acquitted. Notwithstanding the result of this trial, the commander-in-chief sent to the Windsor Castle another captain (John Gore), another first-lieutenant, and another boatswain; and as a still further lenity, pardoned the mutineers.

Light Squadrons and Single Ships.

On the 3rd of January, the British 12-pounder 32-gun frigate Juno, Captain Samuel Hood, quitted the island of Malta, with 150 supernumeraries (46 of them the Romney's marines, the remainder Maltese), for the use of the British Mediterranean fleet; which Captain Hood, being unapprised of the evacuation of Toulon, expected to find at anchor in that port. A strong lee current and a succession of foul winds prevented the Juno from arriving abreast of the harbour's mouth, until about 10 P.M. on the 11th; when Captain Hood, not wishing to run the risk of being again thrown to leeward, especially with so many men on board, determined to get into Toulon as quickly as possible. The Juno not having a pilot, nor any person on board acquainted with the port, two midshipmen, with night-glasses, were stationed forward, to look out for the fleet.

No ships making their appearance in the outer road of Toulon, Captain Hood concluded that the strong easterly gales had driven the fleet for shelter into the inner one: on entering which he saw a vessel, as well as the lights of several others, and he had now no doubt upon the subject. The Juno proceeded under her topsails, until, finding she could not weather a brig that lay off Pointe Grand-Tour, she set her foresail and driver, in order to be ready to tack. Presently the brig hailed; but no one in the Juno could understand what was said. Captain Hood, however, supposing they wanted to know what ship she was, told them her name and nation. They replied *Viva*, and, after seemingly not understanding several questions put to them, both in French and English, called out, as the Juno passed under their stern, *Luff*. The dread of shoal water caused the helm to be instantly put a-lee; but the Juno grounded before she got head to wind. The wind being light, and the water perfectly smooth, the sails were clewed up and handed.

About this time a boat was seen to pull from the brig towards the town, for what purpose was not then suspected. Before the Juno's people were all off the yards, a sudden flaw of wind drove the ship astern. To encourage this, and if possible get clear of the shoal, the driver and mizenstaysail was hoisted, and their sheets kept to windward. The instant the ship lost her way, the best bower-anchor was let go; on which she tended head to wind, but the after-part of her keel was still aground, and the rudder, in consequence, motionless. The launch and cutter were now hoisted out, and the kedge anchor, with two hawsers, put in them, in order to warp the ship clear.

Just before the Juno's boats returned from this service, a boat appeared alongside, and, on being hailed, answered as if an officer was in her. The people hurried out of her up the side; and one of two persons, apparently officers, told Captain Hood he came to inform him, that it was the regulation of the port and the commanding officer's orders, that the ship should go into another branch of the harbour, to perform ten days' quarantine. Captain Hood replied, by asking where Lord Hood's ship lay. An unsatisfactory answer excited some suspicion; and the exclamation of a midshipman, "They are national cockades," induced the captain to look at the French hats more stedfastly; when, by the light of the moon, the three colours were distinctly visible. To a second question about Lord Hood, one of the officers, seeing they were now suspected, replied, "Make yourself easy: the English are good people; we will treat them kindly; the English admiral has departed some time."[1]

Captain Hood's feelings at this moment can better be conceived than described. The words, "We are prisoners," ran through the ship like wildfire; and some of the officers soon came to the captain to learn the truth. A flaw of wind at this moment coming down the harbour, Lieutenant Webley, the third of the ship, said, "I believe, Sir, we shall be able to fetch out, if we can get her under sail." There did, indeed, appear a chance of saving the ship: at all events, the Juno was not to be given up without some contention. The men were ordered to their stations, and the Frenchmen to be sent below. Some of these began to draw their sabres; but the half-pikes of the Juno's marines were presented to them, and they submitted.

Never was seen such a change in people: every officer and man was already at his post; and, in about three minutes, all the sails in the ship were set, and the yards braced ready for casting. On the cable's being cut, the head-sails filled, and the ship started from the shore. A favourable flaw of wind, coming at the same time, gave her additional way; and the Juno, if the forts should not disable her, had every prospect of getting out. The launch and cutter, as well as the Frenchman's boat, that they might not retard the ship, were cut adrift. No sooner had the British ship begun to loose her sails, than the French brig made some stir, and lights appeared on all the batteries. The

---

[1] "Soyez tranquille: les Anglais sont de braves gens; nous les traitrons bien; l'amiral anglais est sorti il y a quelque tems."

brig now opened a fire upon the Juno, and so did a fort a little on the starboard bow; and presently all the forts fired, as their guns could be brought to bear. At one time it was feared a tack would be necessary, but the ship came up a little; and finally, about half an hour after midnight, after having sustained a heavy fire from the different batteries she had to pass, but not without answering several of them with seeming good effect, the Juno got clear off, without the loss of a man. Her rigging and sails, however, were much damaged, and two 36-pound shot had struck her hull.

An enterprise more happily conceived, or more ably executed, has seldom been witnessed, than that by which the officers and men of the British frigate Juno thus extricated their ship from withinside of an enemy's port, filled with armed vessels, and flanked by land-batteries of the most formidable description. On the 13th, the Juno joined the fleet of Lord Hood, at anchor in the bay of Hyères.

Rear-admiral Cornwallis, soon after the surrender of Pondicherry, in August 1793, having quitted the East India station with the whole of his squadron, except a 20-gun ship (by orders, it is presumed, as no inquiry apparently followed), the valuable interests of the Company became exposed to the ravages of the enemy; who, besides two frigates (the Cybèle already mentioned, and the 36-gun frigate Prudente, captain and senior officer, Jean-Marie Renaud, and two or three corvettes), possessed some very formidable privateers, which had recently been fitted out at the Isle of France. On the 27th of September, 1793, the outward-bound China ship, Princess Royal, mounting upwards of 30 guns, and commanded by Captain James Horncastle, being in the straits of Sunda, off Anjier point, island of Java, was attacked; and, after a long and brave defence, captured by three French ship-rigged privateers, each nearly equal in force to a British 28-gun frigate.

In this unprotected state of East India commerce, the governor-general of Bengal acted prudently in despatching a squadron, composed of four or five of the heaviest and best-appointed Indiamen, to the China seas, the favourite cruising ground of the enemy's frigates and privateers. On the 2nd of January this squadron, then consisting of the William Pitt, Commodore Charles Mitchell; Britannia, Captain Thomas Cheap; Nonsuch, Captain John Canning, and the Company's brig tender Nautilus, Captain Roper, arrived off Barbucet-hill, in the eastern entrance of the straits of Sincapore. Here Commodore Mitchell received intelligence that a French "60-gun ship," with another ship of 40, and a third of 26 guns, had been seen off Palambang, in the straits of Banca; but, by the time he had reached the island of Lingen on his way thither, the commodore ascertained the fallacy of the information, and, steering for the straits of Sunda, anchored on the 13th in Anjier bay. On the 21st the squadron was joined by the Houghton Indiaman, Captain Hudson, and soon afterwards got under way. Early the next morning, the 22nd, while the William Pitt was examining a detained ship, two strangers in the south-west were descried and chased by the Britannia and Nonsuch The strange ships were two French privateers, the Vengeur, Captain Corosin mounting 34 guns (French 8 and 6 pounders), with a crew of 250 men, and the Résolu, Captain Jallineaux, mounting 26 guns (six of them French 12-pounders, the remainder 8s and 6s), with a crew of 230 men; both ships from the Isle of France.

At about 11 A.M., the two privateers being then off the Shown rock, near the Zuften isles, the Britannia began engaging the Vengeur; and shortly afterwards the Nonsuch commenced firing at the Résolu. In about three-quarters of an hour both privateers, the William Pitt and Houghton then fast coming up, struck their colours; the Vengeur with the loss of 11 killed and 26 wounded, including among the latter Captain Corosin, who died after the amputation of his leg. The loss on board the Résolu does not appear. The Britannia had one man killed, and two wounded; but the Nonsuch, it is believed, not any.

These two French privateers had, five days before, made a vigorous but unsuccessful attack upon the Pigot Indiaman, Captain George Ballantyne, as she lay refitting in Rat island basin, near Bencoolen. The entrance of the basin was so narrow that one ship only could approach at a time. The Vengeur began the attack at 8 h. 15 m. A.M., on the 17th; at times within 150, and seldom beyond 350 yards. After fighting in this manner nearly an hour and three-quarters, the Vengeur cut her hawsers and made sail, and the Résolu advanced to fill her consort's place; but in 20 minutes she also was obliged to cut and run, and both privateers anchored about two miles off to repair their damages. Their loss, which was supposed to be tolerably severe, could not be ascertained. The Pigot mounted 32 guns, with a crew of 102 men and boys, and was very much damaged in her masts, sails, and rigging, but sustained no greater loss than one man mortally wounded. This persevering defence of their ship was very creditable to Captain Ballantyne, his officers, and crew.

In the afternoon of the 23rd, the William Pitt, Britannia, Houghton, and Nautilus, chasing in the north-east, parted company; and, the same evening, the Nonsuch and the two prizes came to an anchor a little to the northward of the Zuften isles. The remainder of the squadron also anchored unseen by, and at the distance of about six miles from, their companions, abreast of the entrance of Bantam bay, between the small islands of Pulo-Panjan and Toenda, or Pulo-Baby. On the 24th, at 6 A.M. three ships and a brig, being the French frigates Prudente and Cybèle, the late Indiaman, Princess Royal, now named the Duguay-Trouin, and the 14-gun brig-corvette, Vulcain, under the command of Captain Renaud, of the Prudente, were seen by the Nonsuch and prizes near Dwars in de Weg, or Thwart the Way island, working up in chase, with the wind from north-west by north. Finding, by their not answering the private signal, that these vessels were enemies, Captain Canning, at 1 P.M., weighed with the Nonsuch, and, directing the two prizes to follow, made sail upon a wind to the north-east. During the squally weather of the ensuing night the Résolu parted company, and had great difficulty in escaping from the Duguay-Trouin, who at one time was nearly on board of her. On the 25th, at daylight, the Houghton joined the Nonsuch and Vengeur, and informed Captain Canning of the situation of the commodore; towards whom all three ships immediately bore up. At 6 h. 30 m. A.M. the Houghton, Nonsuch, and Vangeur discovered the William Pitt, Britannia, and Nautilus brig at their anchorage, and at the same moment saw the French squadron getting under way from off Saint-Nicholas point, Java; also a ship, which proved to be the Résolu, trying her utmost to get from them.

At about 8 h. 30 m. A.M. the William Pitt, Britannia, and Nautilus, on the near approach of the French squadron, cut their cables, and prepared to engage. By this time the shot of the Prudente and Cybèle were passing over the Résolu: the latter, however, continued her course, and ran for protection between the William Pitt and Britannia, who now opened their fire upon the enemy. At 9 h. 30 m., just as the Cybèle, the rearmost French ship, was tacking to the southward, the Houghton commenced firing into her stern. The Nonsuch, also, in a very gallant manner, hauling up her mainsail, and backing her mizentopsail, luffed up as close as she could and poured into the Cybèle an acknowledged destructive fire, losing one man by a shot from the latter.[1]

After the firing had lasted in the whole about 18 minutes, the French squadron stood away out of gun-shot, and, weathering the small island of Pulo-Baby, anchored close to the northward of it. Commodore Mitchell having distributed among his ships a greater number of French prisoners than the amount of their united crews, and each ship, from assisting to man the prizes, having scarcely hands enough to work her guns, considered it best to make no attempts to renew the action. Nor did the French commodore seem more hostilely disposed.

The squadron of Indiamen afterwards proceeded to Batavia, to get a supply of guns and men, and, being reinforced by the Dutch 36-gun frigate, Amazone, Captain Kerwal, and an armed Dutch Indiaman, cruised without effect until the 8th of February. Commodore Mitchell then steered for Bencoolen, but did not arrive in time to save the Pigot, which ship, on the 9th, while at anchor in Rat-island basin, repairing her damages received in action with the two French privateers, was attacked and captured by the squadron of M. Renaud. While getting the Pigot out of the basin, the French commodore sent an officer, with a flag of truce, to demand the surrender and treat for the ransom of Fort-Marlborough; but the British commandant rejected both proposals, and, by assuring the French officer that the British squadron (meaning Commodore Mitchell's) was hourly expected, induced M. Renaud to put to sea immediately with his prize. The government of Batavia afterwards despatched the Amazone frigate to Sourabaya, at the east end of Java, to take possession of two French corvettes, which had long since arrived there in search of M. de la Peyrouse, and had been hospitably received by the Dutch; but the officers and crews of which had since turned republicans, and were about to cruise against Dutch property. Captain Kervan,

---

[1] The following was the exact gun-force of the Houghton and Nonsuch; and it is probable that the Britannia and William Pitt, and indeed all the larger Indiamen, at this time, were armed much in the same manner:—

HOUGHTON.				NONSUCH.		
	No.		Pdrs.	No.		Pdrs.
Lower deck	24	long	9	4	long brass	18
,,	..	..	..	13	,, iron	9
Upper deck	8	brass	6	10	,, ,,	6
,,	2	iron	6	2	,, (chasers)	12
,,	4	light carronades				
	38	guns.		34	guns.	

it seems, secured the two vessels, and the Batavian government sent them as cartels to France.

In the course of the present year several French frigates, chiefly in squadrons of three or four, cruised about the British Channel, and were very annoying and destructive to commerce. The success that attended this description of force led to its speedy augmentation; and, from the single port of Havre, six heavy frigates were launched and equipped.

To endeavour to put a check to a warfare that was as profitable to one party as it was hurtful and discreditable to the other, two or three British frigate-squadrons were ordered to sea. One of these was commanded by Sir John Borlase Warren, and consisted of the

Gun-frigate.
38		Arethusa.	Captain	Sir Edward Pellew.
36	(C)	Flora.	Commod.	Sir John Borlase Warren, bart.
		Melampus	Captain	Thomas Wells.
,,	(D)	Concorde	,,	Sir John Richard Strachan.
		Nymphe.	,,	George Murray.

On the 23rd of April, at 4 A.M., rock Douvre bearing east by south four or five leagues, the Seven islands south-south-west four or five leagues, and Guernsey north-east half-east seven or eight leagues, Sir John's squadron, having just hauled round on the starboard tack with the wind at south-south-west, descried and gave chase to four strange ships approaching on the opposite tack from the south-east. These were a French squadron, composed of the 36-gun frigate, Engageante, Commodore Desgareaux; 44-gun frigate Pomone, Captain Etienne Pevrieux; 36-gun frigate Résolue, Captain (we believe) Antoine-Marie-François Montalan; and 20-gun corvette Babet, Lieutenant Pierre-Joseph-Paul Belhomme.

Daylight discovered the national character of these ships; which shortly afterwards formed in line of battle in the following order; Engageante, Résolue, Pomone, and Babet. The Flora, which was the leading British ship, as soon as she had reached the wake of the enemy's squadron, tacked, and was followed by the Arethusa, Melampus, and Concorde, in succession; but the Nymphe was too far astern to be in a situation to change tacks. Fortunately for the British, a change of wind about this time, from south-south-west to south, enabled them to fetch to windward of their opponents.

At 6 h. 30 m. A.M. the Flora, being abreast of the rearmost French ship, opened her fire, and, running on, received the fire of the Babet, Pomone, and Résolue in succession, but particularly of the two former. At 7 h. 30 m. A.M. the Flora's maintopmast was shot away, the maintop was cut to pieces, and her foremast and all her yards much damaged. In this state, with her standing and running rigging greatly injured by the enemy's shot, the Flora dropped astern, and was succeeded by the Arethusa, who had previously been engaging the Babet.

The French now set every yard of canvas they could spread; but the Arethusa, Melampus, and Concorde, being less injured in their sails and rigging than the rearmost French ships, soon approached them, and the Arethusa and Melampus, who were the headmost, renewed the action with the Babet and Pomone. At 8 h. 30 m. A.M. the Babet, having lost her foretopmast, and being otherwise much damaged by shot, surrendered, and was taken possession of by the Flora. By this time the Engageante and Résolue had made sail, and the Pomone alone remained to sustain the fire of the Arethusa and Melampus. The consequence was, that the main and mizen masts of the Pomone, already much shattered by the Flora's broadsides, soon came down; and the wreck with the sails upon it, catching fire, destroyed a portion of the quick-work, and, for a while, endangered the ship.[1] In this state, at 9 h. 30 m. A.M., after a brave resistance, the Pomone hauled down her colours, and was taken possession of by the Arethusa.

The Concorde and Melampus, followed at some distance by the Nymphe, now, agreeably to a signal from the commodore, gave chase to the Résolue and Engageante. The Concorde, from her quick sailing, soon got near enough to the two French frigates to receive and return their fire. It was Sir Richard Strachan's intention to disable the sternmost ship, and then, leaving her to be taken possession of by his friends in the rear, to push after the leading one; but the latter, by bearing down and closing to support her second, frustrated that plan. This frigate, indeed, took so good a position across the bows of the Concorde, as to disable her in her sails and rigging, and compel her to drop astern.

Having partially refitted herself, the Concorde resumed the pursuit; yet Sir Richard had no hopes to effect more than to keep his two opponents in check until the arrival of either the Melampus or Nymphe. But as the day was advancing, and his companions in the chase rather losing ground than other-

[1] Some of the brass swivels mounted along the gangways were so hot, that they were obliged to be thrown overboard.

wise; and particularly as the Concorde's maintopmast, which had been shot through, was momentarily expected to fall, Sir Richard determined to secure the enemy's ship that was nearest to him. Accordingly, changing sides in the smoke, the Concorde was soon enabled to bring that frigate to close action. The latter, which was the Engageante, defended herself with great bravery, from noon until 1 h. 45 m. P.M.; when, the ship being silenced in her fire, and, owing to the state of her sails and rigging, totally unmanageable, her people called out that they surrendered. The other French frigate, after firing a few shot, stood on; and, as the Concorde, from the damaged state of her masts, sails, and rigging, was not in a condition to follow, and the Melampus and Nymphe were too far astern to be able to overtake her, the Résolue, Sir Richard's old opponent in India,[1] effected her escape into Morlaix.

The maindeck force of each of the five British frigates will be discovered by a reference to the letter of her class in the little table at p. 101. The guns on the quarter-deck and forecastle were: Arethusa, two long 9-pounders, and 14 carronades, 32-pounders, total 44 guns; Flora, 10 long 9-pounders, and six carronades, 18-pounders, total 42 guns; Melampus, two long 12, and six long 9-pounders, and eight carronades, 32-pounders, total 42 guns; Concorde, four long 6-pounders, and 10 carronades, 24-pounders, total 42 guns. The force of the Nymphe, 40 guns in all, has already appeared.[2] This makes the total guns on the British side 210.

Of the French frigates, the Pomone mounted 26 long 24-pounders French on her main deck, and 14 long 8-pounders, and four brass carronades, 36-pounders, on her quarter-deck and forecastle, total 44 guns; besides swivels along her gangways and in her tops. The Engageante and Résolue were armed according to the establishment of their class, as particularized at No. 7, in the small table at p. 59, except that the Engageante wanted two of her 6s; making the guns of the latter 38, and those of the Résolue 40. The Babet mounted 20 long 8-pounders on the main deck, and two brass 6 or 4 pounders on the quarter-deck; making the total guns on the French side 144.

The damages of the Flora we have already detailed. Those of the Arethusa, although not so heavy, were such as to disable her from becoming one of the chasing ships. The Melampus, also, suffered in her masts, sails, and rigging, and received some

[1] See p. 131.   [2] Ibid. 108.

shot between wind and water. The Concorde, being still more distantly engaged, suffered little or nothing until her engagement with the Engageante; and the Nymphe, to the great annoyance of her officers and crew, was unable to get up in time to partake of the action. The Flora out of a complement, if all were on board, of 267 men and boys, had one seaman killed and three wounded; the Arethusa, out of a complement of 277 men and boys, one master's mate (none of the killed or wounded officers are named in Sir John Warren's letter) and two seamen killed, and five seamen wounded; and the Melampus, out of a complement the same as the Flora's, had her master, three seamen, and one marine killed, one lieutenant of marines, three seamen, and one private marine wounded. The Concorde, out of a complement of 257 men and boys, appears to have sustained no loss until she closed the Engageante, and then had only one man killed and 12 wounded. The Concorde's three lieutenants in the action, and to whose good conduct Sir Richard bears testimony, were Charles Apthorp, Thomas Boys, and Andrew Fitzherbert Evans.

According to the loose statement that appears in the British official account, the Pomone lost between 80 and 100, and the Babet between 30 and 40 men, in killed and wounded; the latter, out of a crew of 178, and the former of 341. The loss on board the Engageante, from her damaged state (her masts having all fallen overboard a few hours after the action), must have been tolerably severe: but, singularly enough, no account of it appears in the British official account, and, at this late day, all other sources of information are shut.

Against so decided a disparity as, from the numbers and force on each side, evidently existed in this case, (for if the Nymphe did not, neither did the Résolue in more than a partial degree, participate in the action,) the French could never have succeeded. Great credit is therefore due to Captains Pevrieux and Belhomme; and the French commodore, although he made sail from his comrades before he had effected much in their behalf, defended his own ship manfully, when at length overtaken by the Concorde, as the state of the Engageante at her surrender places beyond a doubt.

Deceived by the statement at the foot of Sir John Warren's letter, that the Résolue and Engageante were 18-pounder frigates, and unacquainted, it is clear, with the particulars of this contest, none of which he gives, a contemporary adds a fifth ship to the enemy's force and then calls Sir John's performance "a very brilliant action."[1] The same writer has also committed a mistake, in stating that "the Melampus," instead of the Concodore, "was so fortunate as to capture a third ship."

Sir John Warren safely reached port with his prizes; all of which were added to the British navy; the Babet as a sloop, the Engageante, from her age and weakness, merely as a hospital-ship, but the Pomone as a cruising 40-gun frigate.

The Pomone was constructed on a new principle in naval architecture, her greatest breadth being at the gun abaft the mainmast. She proved an incomparable sailer, and possessed every good property of a ship of war; but, although quite a new vessel, her reign, as we shall by-and-by see, was a short one. A second French frigate, of the same force and construction, was, it is believed, built at Cherbourg in the year 1795, and named the Romaine. The principal dimensions of the Pomone were as follows:—

	Feet.	Inches.
Length of 'tween decks	159	2¾
Breadth extreme	41	11⅜
Depth in hold	12	4
Burthen	1239 tons	

Early in the present year the British 12-pounder 32-gun frigate Orpheus, Captain Henry Newcome, 50-gun ship Centurion, Captain Samuel Osborne, and 44-gun ship Resistance, Captain Edward Pakenham, arrived on the East India station. On the 5th of May, while this squadron was cruising off the Isle of France, two strange sail were discovered approaching before the wind. These were the French 34-gun ship Duguay-Trouin, late Princess Royal, Indiaman,[2] and, we believe, the Vulcan brig-corvette. As soon as it was thought that the British ships could lay up for the enemy, chase was given; and, at 11 h. 45 m. A.M., the Orpheus, from her superior sailing, got within long gun-shot of the Duguay-Trouin. In ten minutes afterwards a close action commenced, and, at a little after noon, the Orpheus obtained a position upon the Duguay-Trouin's starboard quarter. Here she kept pouring in her broadsides until 1 h. 5 m. P.M.; when the French ship, having had her bowsprit shot through, and three of the knees of her head cut away, and having sustained a considerable loss in killed and wounded, struck her colours: at which time the Centurion and Resistance were about three miles astern, crowding sail to get up. The brig-corvette, in the meanwhile, effected her escape.

[1] Brenton, vol. i., p. 240.   [2] See p. 216.

Having previously, out of her complement of 217, sent away in a prize one lieutenant, two midshipmen, and 20 seamen, the Orpheus commenced action with only 194 men and boys; of whom she had one midshipman (Mr. Singleton) killed, and one master's mate (Mr. Staines, badly) and eight seamen wounded. The Duguay-Trouin had on board, in all, as many as 403 persons; many of them sickly. It would be unfair to consider the whole number as her complement, when the absence of the idle passengers and the sick would have increased rather than diminished her effective strength. The Duguay-Trouin's loss in the action amounted to 21 officers, seamen, and marines killed, and 60 wounded. The ship is represented to have mounted 26 long 18-pounders on the main deck, and two 9 and six 4 pounders on the quarter-deck and forecastle; but it is more likely that the former were 12-pounders, the ship having mounted guns of that caliber when in the Company's service, and her ports not being adapted for 18-pounders.

The usual figure-statement of comparative force would, in this case, afford but a poor criterion of the relative strength of the parties, the British vessel being a regular ship of war, while the French vessel had recently been a merchant-ship, and was fitted out with such stores only as a foreign station, and that a very distant one, could supply. Her crew, also, were sickly, and, it is believed, short of water and provisions. Moreover, the action was fought in sight, and did not terminate till the near approach of a greatly superior force.

On the morning of the 5th of May, as the British 74-gun ship Swiftsure, Captain Charles Boyles, and 64-gun ship St. Albans, Captain James Vashon, were a few days out from Cork, with a convoy in charge, two strange sail, apparently frigates, hove in sight to the westward. Both British ships immediately went in chase. At 5 h. 45 m. P.M., the Swiftsure hoisted her colours, and fired three shot at the larger and rearmost of the two frigates; who thereupon fired a stern-chaser in return, and hoisted the republican ensign as did also her consort. The latter presently afterwards bore up, and was pursued by the St. Albans; while the Swiftsure continued in close chase of the former, which was the French 36-gun frigate, Atalante, Captain (de vais.) Charles-Alexandre-Léon Durand-Linois.

After dark, the St. Albans and her frigate, which ultimately escaped, were seen no more; but the Swiftsure kept sight of the Atalante during the night. At 4 A.M. on the 6th the Atalante bore from the Swiftsure west by north two or three miles, the wind at this time being about north-north-east. The pursuit was continued during the day; and at 5 h. 30 m. P. M. the Swiftsure commenced firing her bow-chasers. At 7 P. M. the latter ceased firing, the Atalante having increased her distance to about two miles. At midnight, vainly hoping that the manœuvre would be unseen by her persevering foe, the Atalante changed her course to the southward. On the 7th, at 2 A. M., the French frigate hauled yet more up, and the Swiftsure promptly did the same. At 2 h. 30 m. A. M. the latter commenced firing her starboard guns forward, and the action continued, at long range, until 3 h. 25 m.; when the Atalante, being crippled in her rigging and sails, and having sustained, out of her complement of 274 men and boys, the severe loss of 10 killed and 32 wounded, struck her colours. The Swiftsure had her rigging and sails also cut, and lost one man killed.

The endeavours of M. Linois to save his ship from capture, and to disable his enemy from pursuit, were highly meritorious, and prove that had he met, instead of a British 74, a British 12-pounder frigate, the Atalante, if conquered at all, would have been dearly purchased.

Scarcely had the prisoners been shifted, a prize crew placed on board the Atalante, and the rigging of both ships repaired, when, at 10 A.M., three French 74s, judged to be a part of M. Nielly's squadron, were discovered in chase of the Swiftsure and her prize. The two latter immediately separated, and steered different courses; but it was not until 10 P.M. that the Swiftsure lost sight of her pursuers. The Atalante, exerting the same powers for which she had been so long celebrated in the French navy, but which had failed to carry her clear of the Swiftsure's long-reached and well-directed shot, ran away from her ci-devant friends, and actually bent a new maintopsail while they were in pursuit of her.

The Atalante measured 986 tons, and was armed precisely as the Engageante. On being purchased for the use of the British navy, the prize became classed as a 12-pounder 36, but under the name of Espion, an Atalante sloop of war being already in the service.

On the 29th of May, in latitude 46° 38' north, longitude 9° 40' west, the British 28-gun frigate Carysfort, Captain Francis Laforey, fell in with the French (late British[1]) 32-gun frigate Castor, Captain L'Huillier, having in tow a Dutch merchant brig, in chase of which, five days before, she had parted from M. Nielly's squadron. The brig was cast off, and an action

[1] See p. 142.

commenced that lasted, without intermission, one hour and fifteen minutes; at the end of which time the Castor, who had on board her English guns, as specified at *H* in the table at p. 101, with four 24-pounder carronades in addition, hauled down the republican colours.

The Carysfort, whose armament was four 18-pounder carronades beyond her establishment at *I* in the same table, was very slightly injured in masts, rigging, or hull; and her loss in the action, out of a crew of 180 men and boys (she being 18 men short), amounted to no more than one seaman killed and three seamen and one marine wounded. The damages of the Castor, on the other hand, were tolerably severe, having had her main-topgallantmast shot away, her mainmast badly wounded, and her hull struck in several places. Her loss, out of a crew of 200 men, consisted of 16 officers, seamen, and marines, killed, and 9 wounded.

Comparative Force of the Combatants.

		Carysfort.	Castor.
Broadside-guns	No.	16	18
	lbs.	156	212
Crew	No.	180	200
Size	tons.	586	681

This statement shows that great credit was due to Captain Laforey, his two lieutenants (Richard Worsley and George Sayer), remaining officers, and a very new ship's company, for having captured the Castor. It is also due to the French officers and crew to state that the latter consisted of men very recently drafted from all the ships of Rear-admiral Nielly's squadron, and who of course did not find on board the Castor a rope or an article of any sort arranged in the manner to which they had been accustomed.

This recapture effected the release of one master's mate and 19 seamen, part of the Castor's original crew. The remainder with Captain Troubridge, had, as already has appeared, been removed on board the 80-gun ship Sans-Pareil.

Upon the arrival in port of the Carysfort and her prize, the principal officers and commissioners of the British navy claimed to have the latter restored to the service, on payment of the customary salvage, upon the principle that, as the Castor had not been into an enemy's fort for adjudication, she was not, in the contemplation of the act of parliament, a complete prize. This claim Captain Laforey and his officers resisted; and the cause came on to be heard before Sir James Marriot, the judge of the high court of admiralty. The French captain having deposed, in answer to the fourth standing interrogatory; that the admiral of the French squadron, by which the Castor had been taken, possessed full power and authority to condemn, arm, fit-out, and equip all such prizes as he might think calculated for the service of the French republic, and that the Castor was so armed and equipped, and himself duly appointed to the command of her, Sir James Marriot held that this was a sufficient "setting forth as a ship of war," according to the meaning of the prize-act, and thereupon adjudged that the whole value of his majesty's ship Castor, recaptured under the above circumstances, was lawful prize to the officers and crew of the Carysfort. The Castor was accordingly purchased by government, and restored to the rank she had formerly held in the service; and Lieutenant Richard Worsley, first of the Carysfort, was also made a commander as a reward for his good conduct.

On the 8th of June, at daylight, a British squadron, composed of the 36-gun frigate Crescent, Captain Sir James Saumarez, 12-pounder 32-gun frigate Druid, Captain Joseph Elliston, and 24-gun ship Eurydice, Captain Francis Cole, while cruising off the island of Jersey, fell in with a French squadron, consisting of the two cut-down 74s, or *rasées*, Scévola and Brutus,[1] the two 36-gun frigates Danaé and Félicite, and a 14-gun brig. Seeing the decided superiority of the French squadron, Sir James ordered the Eurydice, who was a dull sailer, to make the best of her way to Guernsey; while, with the Crescent and Druid following under easy sail, he gallantly engaged and kept at bay the French ships, until the Eurydice had reached a considerable distance ahead. The two British frigates then, finding it time to consult their own safety, carried a press of sail to get off. In a little while they approached Guernsey, closely pursued by the French ships, who made an attempt to cut off the Druid and Eurydice; but Sir James, by the following masterly manœuvre, extricated his friends from their perilous situation. The Crescent hauled her wind and stood along the French line, an evolution that immediately diverted the attention of the enemy from the Druid and Eurydice. The French commodore now made sure of capturing the Crescent; but the latter having on board an old and experienced pilot, pushed through an intricate passage, never before attempted by a king's ship, and effected her escape into Guernsey road, greatly to the surprise as well as disappointment of her pursuers. The lieutenant-governor of

[1] See p. 56.

the island, who, with the garrison and inhabitants generally, had been a spectator of the event, issued a general order, highly laudatory of the promptitude and professional skill displayed by the officers and men of the three ships, particularly of the Crescent, whose captain, as the general order set forth, was a native of the island in sight of which he had evinced so much presence of mind and nautical experience.

On the 17th of June, while the British 50-gun ship Romney, Captain the Honourable William Paget, having under her charge one British and seven Dutch merchant vessels, bound from Naples to Smyrna, was passing between the small islands of Tino and Miconi in the Archipelago, a frigate, with French national colours and a broad pendant, accompanied by three merchantmen, was discovered at anchor in-shore of Miconi. The British frigates Inconstant, Leda, and Tartar, from whom the Rodney had, on the preceding day, been detached, being still in sight from the mast-head, Captain Paget directed the convoy to join them; and the Romney, hauling to the wind, was presently at anchor in Miconi road, within a little more than a cable's length of the French 40-gun frigate Sibylle, chef de division, or commodore, Jacques-Mélanie Rondeau.

In the hope to save the effusion of blood, Captain Paget sent a message to the French commander, desiring him to surrender his ship. This Commodore Rondeau refused, alleging that he was well acquainted with the Romney's force, that he was fully prepared, both with men and ammunition, and that he had made oath never to strike his colours. By the time the Romney's officer had returned to his ship the Sibylle had placed herself between the Romney and the town of Miconi, which obliged Captain Paget to carry out another anchor, and warp the Romney farther ahead, in order that her guns might point clear of the town. At 1 P.M. the Romney, being abreast of the French frigate, and secured with springs on her cables, fired a broadside, which the Sibylle instantly returned. The action thus commenced lasted, without a moment's intermission, for one hour and ten minutes, when the Sibylle, being quite in a defenceless state, hauled down her colours, and, with the three merchantmen, was taken possession of by the Romney.

The Romney, when she commenced action, was 74 working men short of her established complement; consequently she had on board only 266 men and boys. Of these the Romney lost eight seamen killed and 30 (including two mortally) wounded. The Sibylle commenced action, as deposed to by three of her surviving officers, with a crew of 380; of which number she lost her second-lieutenant, captain of marines, and 44 seamen killed, and 112 officers, seamen, and marines (including nine mortally) wounded. The fact of the Romney's being so short of complement had, it appears, reached the ears of M. Rondeau; who, knowing, on the other hand, that his own ship could muster at quarters upwards of 100 men, and those effective hands, more than his adversary, was sanguine enough to hope for that success which his bravery so well merited.

The Sibylle, although she mounted but 26, had, like other 40-gun frigates, ports for 28 guns on her main deck, and actually fought through her aftmost port one of her guns from the opposite side, a measure which, from her stationary position, was not at all inconvenient. The force of that shifting-gun will accordingly be computed. On her quarter-deck and forecastle the Sibylle mounted 16 long 8-pounders and two brass carronades, 36-pounders, making her total number of guns 44. In the official letter the 8s and the carronades are called 9 and 42 pounders, but no such pounders are known in the French service. The mistake, which is a very frequent one, arises from adopting the denomination assigned to an English gun of the nearest apparent caliber in preference to that used by the French.

The Romney does not appear to have been supplied with carronades; consequently her 50 long guns, as particularised in the first annual abstract, were all that she mounted.

Comparative Force of the Combatants.

		Romney.	Sibylle.
Broadside-guns	No.	25	23
	lbs.	414	380
Crew	No.	266	380
Size	tons	1046	1091

From this statement it appears, that a British 50-gun ship of those days was not, in reality, a very decided overmatch for a French 40-gun frigate. Some allowance, however, is to be made for the advantage which a two-decker possesses over a one-decker in the power of concentrating her fire. Under all the circumstances of the case, had the French captain foreborne to communicate the oath he had taken, not to strike his ship's colours, this engagement would have been yet more creditable than it was to the officers and men of the Sibylle.

The Sibylle was built at Toulon in the year 1791, of the best materials, and is still, under the same name, one of the finest ships of her class in the British navy. The three lieutenants on board the Romney, in her action with the Sibylle, were William Henry Brisbane, Francis Ventris Field, and Edward O'Bryen; the first of whom was shortly afterwards promoted to the rank of commander.

On the 7th of August Captain Sir John Borlase Warren, K.B., put to sea from Falmouth, with, besides his own frigate, the Flora, the 38-gun frigates Arethusa, Captain Sir Edward Pellew, Diamond, Captain Sir William Sidney Smith, Artois, Captain Sir Edmund Nagle, and Diana, Captain Jonathan Faulknor, and 36-gun frigate Santa-Magarita, Captain Eliab Harvey, in quest of a squadron of French frigates reported to be cruising to the westward and northward of Scilly. On the 23rd, at 4 A.M., being off the Penmarck rocks, the British squadron discovered and chased the French 36-gun frigate Volontaire; and at 4 P.M. the Diamond, Artois, Santa-Margarita, and Diana, engaged and drove her on shore near the Penmarcks; where they left her, according to Sir John Warren's despatch, "disabled and irrecoverably lost."

In the mean time the Flora and Arethusa had gone in chase of two ship-corvettes to windward of Pointe du Raz; and which, on being pursued, had stood into the bay of Audierne, and come to an anchor off the Gamette rocks. Perceiving that the two British frigates intended still to close with them, the two corvettes, which were the Alert and Espion, both recently captured from the British, got under way, and ran aground " under cover of three batteries." The Flora and Diamond continued engaging the French batteries and grounded vessels until 6 h. 15 m. P.M.; when the masts of the latter went by the board, and a great proportion of their crews got on shore.

The boats of the two frigates were immediately despatched, under the orders of Captain Sir Edward Pellew, to destroy the two corvettes. This service, according to Sir John's letter, "was fully performed:" that is, Sir Edward Pellew, finding "there were from 20 to 30 killed and wounded in the Alert, and a greater number in L'Espion, and that it was impossible to remove the wounded to the two frigates," contented himself with bringing away 52 prisoners, and leaving the two corvettes to their fate; which fate, admitting that they were "bilged and scuttled," and "that the rocks appeared through their bottoms," was inevitable. So Sir John Warren appears to have reasoned, as he immediately stood to sea with the squadron.

The French ships of war, thus "destroyed," are officially represented as

	Guns.		Weight.		Men.
La Félicité	40		18-pounders		350
L'Espion	18		9 ditto		200
Alert	18		9 ditto.		200

And this ostensibly important service, notwithstanding the additional fire from three batteries, of what force, however, is not stated, was accomplished with so trifling a loss to the British as six men wounded.

We trust we shall not be charged with hypercriticism, if we examine a little strictly Sir John Warren's despatch, announcing the destruction of these three French ships. The misnomer of the frigate is of little consequence. The correction appears in Steel. But neither the Félicité nor the Volontaire carried 18-pounders: they were French 36-gun frigates, and mounted, like all the others, long 12s, with a crew of 280 or 300 men. It is not even quite clear that any French frigate was lost on this occasion; the French accounts, at all events, are silent on this subject. Neither of the two corvettes carried " 9-pounders:" their guns were 6-pounders, and their crews were not " 200," but about 140 men each. The Espion was not " destroyed," but was got off, and refitted by the French; and, to place the matter beyond a doubt, this small corvette (she measured only 275 tons), carrying " eighteen 6-pounders and 140 men," on the 2nd of March, 1795, was recaptured by the Lively frigate, Captain George Burlton, and afterwards restored to her rank in the British navy. There is also some reason to doubt, whether the asserted loss of the Alert was not equally a misstatement.

On the 24th of August the British 74-gun ship Impétueux, one of Lord Howe's prizes on the 1st of June, and, with the exception of the Sans-Pareil, the finest and most esteemed ship among them, caught fire, while lying moored in Portsmouth harbour. The flames spread with such rapidity as to threaten the destruction of the whole dockyard; the inhabitants of the town were so alarmed at the ship's nearness to the powder magazine, that they fled in every direction. The French prisoners at Porchester castle, amounting to nearly 5000, evinced feelings of quite an opposite kind; they shouted " Vive la république!" and sang " Ca-ira" and the " Marseillaise Hymn," all the while the flames were raging. To their disappointment, however, the proper precautions had been taken, and the Impétueux, after burning to the water's edge, drifted clear of the ships in ordinary, and of all other danger, and grounded upon the mud on the west side of the harbour.

On the 21st of October, at daybreak, the British 38-gun frigates Arethusa, Captain Sir Edward Pellew, Artois, Captain Edmund Nagle, and Diamond, Captain Sir William Sidney Smith, and the 18-pounder 32-gun frigate Galatea, Captain Richard Goodwin Keats, while cruising in company, at a distance of from eight to ten leagues west of Ushant, discovered a frigate under French national colours. Chase was immediately given, and the squadron, being to windward, succeeded in cutting her off from the land. The superior sailing of the Artois enabled that ship, singly, to bring to action the French 40-gun frigate Révolutionnaire, mounting the usual 44 guns of her class, Captain Henri-Alexandre Thèvenard. The latter defended herself with great spirit for 40 minutes; when, the Diamond having taken a position under her stern, and fired two shots as an earnest of what was presently to follow, and the two remaining British frigates being near at hand, the French crew refused any longer to defend their ship, which was already in a very crippled state from the fire of the Artois; whose force was also 44 guns, including 12 long 9-pounders and four 32-pounder carronades upon the quarter-deck and forecastle. The colours of the Révolutionnaire were accordingly struck.

Out of a crew, supposing her complement to have been on board, of 281 men and boys, the Artois had one lieutenant of marines (Mr. Craigy) and two seamen killed, and five seamen wounded. The Révolutionnaire, out of a crew, as certified by her officers, of 351, lost eight seamen killed, and her commander (slightly) and four seamen wounded.

Comparative Force of the Combatants.

		Artois.	Révolutionnaire.
Broadside-guns	No.	22	22
	lbs.	370	403
Crew	No.	281	351
Size	tons	996	1148

Here, considering the slight inferiority of force on the part of the British frigate as meeting a fair set-off in the officially-reported fact, that the French frigate had been launched but a few weeks, and out of port (Havre-de-Grace) but eight days, would have been a well-matched pair of combatants, had the Artois been alone; and the officers and crew of the latter no doubt regretted that their friends were near enough to interfere with, or even to be spectators of, the engagement. M. Thévenard cannot be accused of giving away his ship: he fought her bravely; and the very slight disparity in the loss renders it problematical which of the two frigates, had they been wholly by themselves, would have carried the day. Opposed, however, by a squadron, the contest unavoidably terminated against the French commander.

Shortly after the arrival in port of the Artois and her prize, "Captain Nagle," as his biographer tells us,[1] "for his gallant conduct on the occasion, received the honour of knighthood;" and the first-lieutenant of the Artois, Robert Dudley Oliver, was made a commander.

The Révolutionnaire was decidedly the finest frigate, except the Pomone, taken in the preceding April,[2] which had yet been captured from France; and, with that single exception, was larger by 50 tons than any captured, and by upwards of 140 tons than any home-built frigate at this time belonging to the British navy. On being received into the service, the Révolutionnaire was registered as a 38, and still continues to be one of the most esteemed vessels of her class.

On the 22nd of October, at 11 A.M., Isle-Ronde, off the northeast extremity of the Isle of France, bearing north-west by west nine or ten leagues, the British 50-gun ship Centurion, Captain Samuel Osborne, and 44-gun ship Diomede, Captain Matthew Smith, descried and gave chase to four strange sail in the west, steering to the northward with the wind easterly. These proved to be a French squadron, composed of the 40-gun frigate Cybèle, 36-gun frigate Prudente, 20-gun corvette Jean-Bart, and 14-gun brig-corvette Courier, under the orders of Commodore Jean-Marie Renaud, in the Prudente.

This officer, having put to sea from Port-Louis purposely, as was stated, to fight the two British ships, of whose names as well as force he was already apprised, suffered no long chase ere he hove to in line ahead; his own ship, the Prudente, leading, followed, at little more than a cable's length, by the Cybèle, Jean-Bart, and Courier. The British ships now edged down to take their stations; the Centurion placing herself abreast of the two frigates, with the greater part of her broadside bearing on the Prudente, while the Diomede took a similar position between the Cybèle and Jean-Bart, directing her chief attention to the Cybèle.

At 3 h. 29 m. P.M. the French commodore, having hoisted his broad pendant, and all his ships their colours, opened a fire within half musket-shot; and the cannonade presently became general. Having, from her close position, bore the brunt of this

---

[1] Marshall, vol. i., p. 277.   [2] See p. 226.

firing, the Centurion soon became very much damaged in her sails and rigging; whereupon the Prudente, at 4 P.M., with every spar standing, and with her sails and rigging not materially injured, bore up and ran to leeward out of gun-shot, signaling her comrades to do the same. According to the French commodore's account, this was, in order that the squadron might repair damages and be able to obtain the weathergage, an excuse, a contradiction in itself, for had his object been that which is stated, he would have fore-reached upon the disabled Centurion and then tacked; it certainly is something new in naval tactics, to *bear up* in order to get to windward.

The Cybèle made sail ahead, and, firing at the Centurion in passing, brought down the latter's mizentopmast and foretopgallantmast; but, being herself much cut up in sails and rigging, and being also retarded in her flight by the calm that, as usual, had succeeded the heavy firing, was compelled to sustain an action, broadside to broadside, with the British 50. The Diomede, whose signal to carry all possible sail was about this time ordered to be made, but the flags for which "could not be found," lay at some distance to windward, firing occasionally at the Cybèle, as well as at the Jean-Bart and Courier; but these ships, in obedience to their commodore's signal, soon bore up and joined the Prudente.

The Centurion and Cybèle continued closely engaged; and at about 5 h. 15 m. P.M., the latter's maintopgallantmast was shot away. Just at this moment a light air sprang up, and the Cybèle, taking advantage of it, edged down towards the Prudente; who, with the corvette and brig, had wore, and was fast approaching to her support. At 5 h. 45 m. P.M., just before she joined the Prudente, the Cybèle's wounded foretopmast fell. Both the Diomede and Centurion had wore in pursuit; but the latter had suffered so much in her masts, that Captain Osborne was compelled to put her head to the sea, to prevent them from falling overboard.

The Prudente, as soon as the Cybèle joined, took her in tow; and all four vessels, carrying as much sail as they could set, steered to the westward, followed and fired at, until dark, by the Diomede; whose shot, however, in reference to any visible effect produced by them, appear to have fallen short.

The Centurion lost three seamen killed, or mortally wounded the gunner and six seamen severely, and 17 seamen slightly wounded. The Diomede does not appear to have sustained any loss. The Prudente lost 15 men killed, and 20 wounded; the commodore among the latter, and his first and second lieutenants among the former. The Cybèle lost her first-lieutenant and 21 petty officers and seamen killed, and 62 wounded, 37 of them dangerously. The Jean-Bart had one man killed, and five men wounded. The Courier appears to have shared the good fortune of the Diomede.

In reviewing the conduct of this action, we might be disposed to blame the Prudente for having prudently withdrawn herself so early from the battle, were we not afraid that the French would retort, by referring us to that ship's return of loss; especially as contrasted with the entire state of impunity with which the Diomede had escaped. The backwardness to close and support her consort, so evident on the part of the latter, has been attributed to private pique and jealousy, and not to any want of courage, on the part of her commander. This feeling, in the breast of an officer towards his superior, is at all times reprehensible, and, in the present instance, appears to have been the principal reason that the Cybèle, at least, was not made a prize of by the British.

Captain Smith was afterwards brought to a court-martial for his conduct in this action, and broke; but, owing to an informality in the proceedings, or some other cause, was merely placed on the list of retired post-captains. Thus stands the statement in the first edition of this work. We now subjoin another account from the work of a contemporary. "The report made by Captain Osborne of the Centurion, of the action with the French squadron, in the preceding year, not being satisfactory to Captain Smith, he applied to that officer for an explanation. Captain Osborne, after more distinctly expressing his approbation of Captain Smith's conduct than he had done in his public letter, thought fit to demand a court-martial for inquiring into the conduct of the two ships, with a view of justifying his letter on service. The court sentenced Captain Smith to be dismissed the service; but, on his return to England in 1798, he appealed against their verdict; and his memorial being referred to the crown lawyers and the admiralty counsel, they reported their opinion that the sentence was unwarrantable, and not to be supported. Captain Smith was consequently restored to his rank in the navy, but never afterwards called into service."[1]

A writer in the "Victoires et Conquêtes," not satisfied with the share of credit gained on his side by this action, on the

[1] Marshall, vol. iii., p. 75.

other, declares that the Centurion and Diomede were "two ships of the line," "deux vaisseaux de ligne,"[1] leaving the French reader to fancy them first, second, or third rates, as the temperature of his patriotism, and the caliber of his credulity, may incline him. This caterer of "victories," regardless, also, of the account in his own newspaper, the Moniteur, substitutes the Courier for the Jean-Bart, and then assures his countrymen that two French frigates and a brig compelled two English "line-of-battle ships" to raise the blockade of a French colonial port; thereby enabling the French privateers to enter with their prizes, and to sail forth again when ready, in order to commit fresh depredations upon the eastern commerce. The departure of the British commodore to get his ship refitted renders the latter part of this statement probable enough; but the French are too politic to charge to the neglect or omission of an enemy that which, by a little skilful penmanship, they can make appear to have arisen from the bravery or good conduct of themselves.

Colonial Expeditions.—West Indies.

North America affording, this year, no occurrences of a nature to be noticed in these pages, we pass at once to the West Indies, where plans of magnitude and importance were on the eve of being brought into activity. In the latter end of January Vice-admiral Sir John Jervis, K.B.,[2] in the Boyne, arrived at Bar-

---

[1] Victoires et Conquêtes, tome v., p. 276.

[2] Invested with this honour, May 29, 1782, for having, says the author of the "Royal Naval Biography," fought one of the most brilliant actions which had occurred during the American war, namely, the capture of the Pégase, of 74 guns and 700 men, commanded by the Chevalier de Cillart. A part, and no inconsiderable part, of the plan of this work being to free historical statements from the dross of fiction, we may be allowed to step back a little, for the purpose of reducing Mr. Marshall's high-flown biographical, into plain matter-of-fact language. In April, 1782, the Foudroyant, a ship (formerly French) mounting 80 guns, 24-pounders on the main deck, manned with 700 men, and justly pronounced to be "one of the finest two-decked ships belonging to the British navy," was commanded by Captain John Jervis, and formed one of a fleet of 12 sail of the line and four frigates, under Vice-admiral Barrington, cruising in the Bay of Biscay. On the 20th, off Ushant, a fleet was discovered, consisting of an outward-bound East India convoy of 14 vessels, which had sailed from Brest the day before, under the protection of the two French 74-gun ships, Protecteur, Captain le Comte de Soulanges, and Pégase, Captain de Sillans, a frigate, and a 64 en flûte; and the vessels of which convoy, on discovering their danger, dispersed. The Foudroyant's superiority of sailing soon gave her the lead in the chase of one of the French 74s, the Pégase; and at dark the British 80 lost sight of her own fleet. At a little before 1 A.M. on the 21st the Foudroyant ran alongside of the Pégase, and, after an hour's fierce action, in which the latter had 80 men killed and wounded, and the Foudroyant none killed and very few wounded, the French ship hauled down her colours. "At this time," says Mr. M., "the sea was so rough, that it was with great difficulty Captain Jervis, with the loss of two boats, could put an officer and 80 men on board the prize. Soon after this was effected, the Foudroyant lost sight of the Pégase; but the Queen, fortunately coming up, took possession of her. In consequence of this gallant action, Captain Jervis was honoured with the insignia of a knight of the bath."—*Marshall*, vol. i., p. 16.

The writer of this article admits that the action lasted an hour at close quarters.

badoes, as the naval commander-in-chief on the station, accompanied by Lieutenant-general Sir Charles Grey, as commander of the troops, about 7000 in number (just half the number stated by the French writers), destined to act against the enemy's colonies. On the 2nd of February the expedition, with all the effective troops on board, amounting to less than 6100 men, sailed from Bridgetown, bound to Martinique, and on the 5th, when it arrived off the island, consisted of the following vessels of war :—

Gun-ship.

98	Boyne		Vice-admiral (b.) Sir John Jervis, K.B. Captain George Grey.
74	Vengeance		Commodore Charles Thompson. Captain Lord Henry Paulet.
	Irresistible		„ John Henry.
64	Asia		„ John Brown.
	Veteran		„ Charles Edmund Nugent.

Frigates, Beaulieu, Santa-Margarita, Blonde, Solebay, Quebec, Ceres, Winchelsea, and Rose.

Sloops, Nautilus, Rattlesnake, Zebra, and Avenger; *bomb*, Vesuvius.

Store-ships, Dromedary and Woolwich.

General Rochambeau was still governor of Martinique, and at the head of a force, if the French accounts are to be credited (and the small number of troops that ultimately surrendered rather confirms the statement), of no more than 600 men, of whom 400 were militia.[1] Whatever may have been the deficiency of troops for its defence, the island possessed many commanding positions and formidable batteries, upon which were mounted, according to the French accounts, as many as 90 pieces of cannon. The only ships of war at Martinique, except perhaps a privateer or two, were the French 28-gun

---

and yet is surprised that the Pégase, "considering the short time she was engaged," should have suffered so much. He adds: "Nothing could have afforded a more remarkable instance of the decided superiority of seamanship and discipline on the one side, and of the great effects which those qualifications produced on the other, than the circumstance of this gallant action." Does the writer, who avows himself a naval man, make no allowance for the difference in size and force between the two ships, one of which, as measuring 1977 tons, must have felt rather less inconvenience in action from the "rough sea," than the other, that was of no more than 1778 tons? Even had the Foudroyant been a 74 like the Pégase, the former, to use the words of her own captain, when on a subsequent occasion he gave an opinion upon the merits of the action between the Mars and Hercule, was, "an old commissioned, well-practised ship," with a crew inured to battle (the Foudroyant was Admiral Keppel's second in the action with M. d'Orvilliers, fought July 27, 1778); while the Pégase was just out of port, with her decks, as is too frequently the case with French ships, lumbered with stores for her long voyage. As M. de Sillans (not "Cillart") was evidently not un "chevalier" at the time of his capture by the Foudroyant, he probably was raised to that honour for his gallant defence of the Pégase.

[1] Victoires et Conquêtes, tome iii., p. 249.

frigate (mounting 30 or 32 guns) Bienvenue at Fort Royal, and an 18-gun corvette at St. Pierre. As the proceedings of the troops on each side properly belong to military history, and moreover, as the accounts cannot be rendered very intelligible without the aid of a map, we shall merely give a general sketch of the operations that led to the surrender of this important island.

For the purpose of dividing the force and attention of the enemy, the British troops were disembarked at three points, considerably distant from each other. The respective divisions, whose routes had been ably chosen, bore down all opposition; and, by the 16th of March, the whole island, except the forts Bourbon and Royal, was in the possession of the British. This was not effected, however, without a loss of 71 killed, 193 wounded, and three missing. The seamen of the fleet, employed on shore, exerted themselves with their usual promptitude and success, dragging the cannon and mortars for several miles, to heights that appeared almost impossible to reach; and a division of 200, armed with pikes and pistols, and headed by Lieutenants Thomas Rogers and William Gorden Rutherford, bore an unequalled part in storming the important post of Monte Mathurine.

Another detachment of about 300 seamen, with a small party of marines, was landed, under the command of Captain Eliab Harvey, of the Santa-Margarita, assisted by Captain William Hancock Kelly of the Solebay, and Lord Garlies of the Quebec, and by Lieutenants Isaac Wolley, Joshua Bowley Watson, Thomas Harrison, James Carthew, Alexander Wilmot Schomberg, and John W. Taylor Dixon; also Lieutenant Walter Tremenhere of the marines. This detachment, having in charge a 24-pounder gun and two mortars, began its march from the wharf in the Cul de sac Cohée towards the heights of Sourrière, a distance of five miles, and near to which Lieutenant-general Sir Charles Grey had established his head-quarters.

After cutting a road, nearly a mile in length, through a thick wood, making a passage across a river by filling it up with large stones and branches and trees, and levelling the banks of another river by the removal of immense fragments of rocks, this persevering party, before the night of the third day, to the astonishment of the whole army, got the 24-pounder on the heights of Sourrière, and the two mortars to the foot of the hill, from which the summit was about a mile distant. On the following day the howitzers and two additional 24-pounders were got to their places on the top of the hill; and this although the ascent was so steep that a loaded mule could not walk up in a direct manner.

On the 17th, at daybreak, a battery which had been erected on Pointe Carrière, forming the east side of the carénage, and some gun-boats, commanded, along with the guard-boats of the squadron, by Lieutenant Richard Bowen, of the Boyne, opened a fire upon Fort St. Louis: as did, at the same time, upon Fort Bourbon, the gun and mortar batteries recently erected on the heights of Sourrière; and which latter were most ably and effectively served by the seamen who, as we have seen, had laboured so hard in getting the guns to that position.

Perceiving a favourable moment, Lieutenant Bowen, with the rowing-boats only, pushed into the carénage, to attack the Bienvenue frigate, lying chain-moored within 50 yards of the shore, for the laudable purpose of rescuing a number of English prisoners supposed to be on board of her. The time was broad noon; and as soon as the British boats were seen entering the carénage, the walls of Fort Louis were covered with troops, who kept up an incessant fire of musketry upon the assailants; as did also the frigate, together with grape-shot from her great guns. In the face of all this, Lieutenant Bowen and his party dashed alongside the frigate, and boarded her with little opposition, the greater part of the crew having fled to the shore just as the British approached.

The French captain, one lieutenant, and 20 men were found in the Bienvenue, but no prisoners: these, it was now understood, were on board another vessel higher up the harbour. The wind blowing directly in, the frigate's sails being unbent, and the incessant fire still kept up from the forts, and to which the British were unable to bestow an adequate return from the frigate's 8-pounders, rendering it impracticable to send men aloft to bring the sails to the yards, Lieutenant Bowen was constrained to depart with his 22 prisoners, and leave his principal trophy behind. Considerable risk attended the return of the boats; but, at length, this intrepid young officer got clear, not, however, without a loss of three men killed, and four or five wounded.

The success of Lieutenant Bowen's attack upon the Bienvenue led to an immediate assault upon the town of Fort Royal. A number of scaling-ladders were made of long bamboos connected with strong line, and the Asia 64 and Zebra sloop, the latter commanded by Captain Robert Faulknor, were ordered to hold themselves in readiness to enter the carénage, for the purpose of battering the lower and more exposed part of Fort Louis, the walls of which were not high; also of covering the flat boats, barges, and pinnaces sent in under the direction of Commodore Thompson, and commanded by Captains Nugent of the Veteran, and Edward Riou of the Rose. Meanwhile, a detachment of the army was to advance, with field-pieces, along the side of the hill under Fort Bourbon, towards the bridge over the canal at the back of Fort Royal town.

On the 20th this plan of attack was put into execution, and succeeded in every point, except that the Asia was unable to get into her station, owing to the misconduct of M. de Tourelles, the former lieutenant of the port; and who, after having undertaken to pilot the ship in, refused to do so, from an alleged dread of shoals, but probably from a real dread of what he might justly expect, should any unforeseen event place him in the hands of General Rochambeau. Observing the Asia baffled in her attempt, Captain Faulknor dashed singly on; and, running the Zebra, in defiance of the showers of grape that poured upon her, close to the wall of the fort, "leaped overboard," says Sir John Jervis in his despatch, "at the head of his sloop's company, and assailed and took this important post before the boats could get on shore, although rowed with all the force and animation which characterize English seamen in the face of an enemy." This, however, was not strictly the case. The boats, already mentioned as commanded by Captains Nugent and Riou, and which boats contained as many as 1200 men, pushed across the carénage before the Zebra could get in, and stormed and took possession of Fort Royal. Captain Nugent, with the Veteran's people, hauled down the French colours, and hoisted the English in their stead. Even the admiral himself appears to have been subsequently aware that this was the case, as he appointed Captain Nugent, by the consent of the general, to the command of the captured fort.

Before we proceed further in the narrative, justice to the memory of a slandered British officer requires that we should do our best to refute a statement which appears in the work of a contemporary. "As soon as the Asia," says Captain Brenton, "was within reach of grape, she put her helm up and came out. The vice-admiral, supposing that Captain Brown was killed, or that some very serious accident had happened, sent Captain Grey to ascertain the cause of this extraordinary proceeding. Captain Grey returned and informed the admiral that not a man was hurt on board the Asia, and she again stood in, and again came out. This unusual act of a British ship of war was attributed to the pilot, and, being admitted, was no palliation, since the ship had actually got within reach of grape, whence her lower deck guns must quickly have driven the enemy from the fort. It was the duty of the captain to have anchored, and to have remained there till the service was completed, or until recalled by his superior officer, who was present."[1] The best answer that can be given to the above statement is an extract from the public letter of Sir John Jervis himself. "This combination," says the vice-admiral, "succeeded in every part, except the entrance of the Asia, which failed for the want of precision in the ancient lieutenant of the port, Monsieur de Tourelles, who had undertaken to pilot the Asia." As a further proof of the vice-admiral's opinion of the conduct of the captain of the Asia in this attack, "Captain Brown," is the first in the list of officers, to whom Sir John, at the end of the same public letter, declares that he is "greatly indebted."

The unparalleled exploit of Captain Faulknor produced an immediate effect upon M. Rochambeau at Fort Bourbon, and he requested that commissioners might be appointed to discuss the terms of surrender. These were presently arranged; and, on the 22nd, the British colours were hoisted on Fort Bourbon, the name of which was changed to Fort George, and that of Fort Louis to Fort Edward.

The gallant defence made by General Rochambeau and his garrison, amounting at first, as the British were led to believe, to 1200 men, but, as the French themselves say, to only half that number, and reduced at the surrender to about 200 men, including the wounded, was strongly manifested on entering the fort, there being scarcely an inch of ground untouched by the shot and shells of the British.[2]

The loss of the latter, between the 16th and 21st, was, on the part of the army, three rank and file killed, and one captain, 11 rank and file wounded; on that of the navy, one captain (James Milne, of the Avenger) and 13 seamen killed, and one captain (Sandford Tatham, of the Dromedary), two lieutenants (Thomas

---

[1] Brenton, vol. ii., p. 23.
[2] In his details of the military operations at this island, Captain Brenton (vol. iii. p. 19) says: "General Bellegarde moved his whole force upon our position at Cohée, but Sir Charles Grey, perceiving his design, attacked him with great fury and compelled him to retreat." Who the "general" was, and of what description his "whole force," may be pretty well imagined from the following account of both: "Un colon nommé Bellegarde, à la tête d'un corps de chasseurs volontaires, après plusieurs actes de lâcheté, finit par trahir ses concitoyens, en les menant aux Anglais, sous la prétexte de faire une sortie. Ce félon passa ensuite à l'Amérique septentrionale, sur un bâtiment Anglais."— *Victories et Conquêtes*, tome iii., p. 251

Henry Wilson and Thomas Clarke), one surgeon, and 24 seamen wounded. The Bienvenue was added to the navy, upon the establishment of a 28-gun frigate, by the (as significant of the manner in which she had been attacked and carried) very appropriate name of Undaunted; and Captain Faulknor, by whom she had been so gallantly won, was appointed to the command of her: Lieutenant Bowen, also, as no less justly his due, was made a commander into the Zebra.

Martinique being reduced, the forts garrisoned with British, under the command of Lieutenant-general Prescott, who was appointed governor of the island, and a small squadron, under Commodore Thompson, being left to co-operate, if necessary, in its defence, a detachment of troops was embarked at Fort Royal bay, on the 31st, to attack the island of Sainte Lucie. On the next day, the 1st of April, the ships of war and transports arrived there; and, on the same evening, the troops were landed at three different points, with little resistance and no loss. The same good fortune had attended the ships in their passage along the shore, although compelled to pass within gunshot of the numerous batteries that lined it. Their hulls, masts, yards, sails, and rigging, received many shots; but, crowded as they were with troops and seamen, yet not a man on board was hurt. Between the 1st and 3rd of April the troops assaulted and carried the enemy's outposts; and, on the 4th, General Ricard, commanding the works on Morne Fortunée, surrendered on terms of capitulation.

Thus did Great Britain become possessed of a valuable sugar-island, without the loss, on her part, of a single life; and with no greater loss, on the part of the enemy, than two officers and about 30 men, killed at the storming of a redoubt. The garrison of this redoubt consisted but of 33 men: consequently one prisoner only was taken; and how he happened to escape the customary massacre on such occasions is not stated in the gazette account. Colonel Eyre Coote appears to have been the commanding officer of the storming party. A garrison being left at Sainte Lucie, under the command of Colonel Sir Charles Gordon, the remainder of the troops returned on the 5th to Martinique. The two following days were occupied in shifting the troops, and making arrangements· and, on the 8th, Sir John Jervis, in the Boyne, with two other ships of the line, besides frigates and the necessary transports, set sail for the reduction of Guadeloupe.

On the 10th the ships of war and a few of the transports

anchored in Gosier bay in that island; but the remainder, being driven to leeward by the strong wind and lee current, did not all arrive before the 12th. On the 11th, at 1 A.M., a part of the troops that had then arrived, and a detachment of seamen and marines, effected their landing in the Anse de Gosier, under cover of the 32-gun frigate Winchelsea: whose commander, Lord Garlies, placed his ship within half musket-shot of the batteries, and, by her well-directed fire, soon silenced the enemy's guns. On this occasion, Lord Garlies was the only person wounded, and that by a bad contusion. On the 12th, early in the morning, the strong post of Fleur-d'Epée was stormed by a detachment of the army, composed of the first and second battalions of light infantry, under Major-general Dundas, assisted by a detachment of seamen, commanded by Captain Robert Faulknor. The seamen had been directed to use their pikes and swords only, and the soldiers their bayonets. The side of the mountain which the seamen had to ascend, under a tremendous fire of grape-shot and musketry, was almost perpendicular: they, however, surmounted every difficulty, gained the parapet, dashed into the fort, and fought their way to the gates. Here the seamen joined the military; and their united efforts, although opposed in the most gallant manner, carried the post. In this desperate service the seamen are represented to have borne a conspicuous part. Fort Saint Louis, the town of Pointe-à-Pitre, and the new battery upon Islot-à-Cochon, were soon afterwards abandoned, and many of the inhabitants escaped in boats to Basse-terre.

This completed the conquest of Grande-terre. The loss sustained by the British was, on the part of the army, 15 rank and file killed, two captains, three lieutenants, one sergeant, and 39 rank and file wounded, and two rank and file missing; and, on the part of the navy, two midshipmen and 11 seamen wounded. The enemy lost, in defending Fleur-d'Epée, 67 killed, 55 wounded, and 110 prisoners. We should hope, and we rather think, that nearly the whole of this heavy loss was sustained previously to its surrender; and that, therefore, the statement of a contemporary, that "most of the garrison of Fleur-d'Epée were put to the sword,"[1] is incorrect.

Previously to his quitting Martinique, the vice-admiral had detached Captain Josias Rogers, with the 32-gun frigates Quebec and Ceres, the latter commanded by Captain Richard Incledon, 28-gun frigate Rose, Captain Matthew Henry Scott,

[1] Brenton, vol. ii., p. 26.

and a sloop of war, to attack the three small islands adjacent to Guadeloupe, called the Saintes. They were carried on the morning of the 10th, without the slightest loss, by a party of seamen and marines disembarked from those ships.

The 43rd regiment being left to garrison Fort Fleur-d'Epée (its new name, Prince of Wales, was, as we shall presently see, retained for so short a time, that it will be unnecessary to use it), the town of Pointe-à-Pitre, and other neighbouring posts, the remainder of the troops, on the 14th, quitted Grande-terre, in transports; and, dropping down opposite to Petit-Bourg on Basse-terre, landed there, on the same afternoon, without opposition. On the 20th, after two or three batteries, including the famous post of Palmiste, had been carried, with some resistance, and no great loss, General Collot, commanding at Fort Saint-Charles, capitulated on honourable terms; surrendering to Great Britain Guadeloupe, and all its dependencies, comprehending the Islands of Marie-Galante, Désirade, and the Saintes.

The loss on the part of the British amounted to two rank and file killed, four rank and file wounded, and five missing. The loss of the republicans is not stated; but, according to a return found among General Collot's papers, the number of men capable of bearing arms in Guadeloupe, was 5877, and the number of fire-arms actually delivered out to them, 4044. The number of pieces of cannon upon the different batteries in Basse-terre amounted, including fifty-eight 24, and thirty-five 18 pounders and 15 heavy mortars, to 182. A French 16-gun brig-corvette, the Guadeloupe, was captured in the road of Bailiff, but was not deemed fit for the service. Having placed Major-general Dundas in the command of Guadeloupe, with what was considered to be a sufficient garrison, Sir Charles Grey quitted the island, in company with the admiral and squadron.

Matters remained in the same state until the morning of the 3rd of June; when a squadron of nine ships, bearing the national colours of France, was seen off the town of Saint François, passing along the coast towards Pointe-à-Pitre. At 4 P.M. the French squadron, consisting of two frigates (probably the Thétis and Pique), one corvette, two large ships armed en flûte, and five transports, and which appear to have stolen out of Lorient or Rochefort about the middle or latter end of April, anchored off the village of Gosier, and commenced disembarking troops, at the head of which was the famous, or rather infamous, Victor Hugues, with the title of civil commissary, " commissaire civil," having, as his colleagues, Chretien (died soon after he landed) and Lelsas. On the same evening, and on the following day, the 11th, the republican troops, impatient to gratify their chief's taste, employed themselves in burning and pillaging some estates near Gosier. The delay occasioned by this species of amusement enabled Lieutenant-colonel Drummond, commanding at Fleur-d'Epée, to assemble within the fort 310 officers and men, consisting of 180 French royalists, and 130 of the 43rd regiment and Royal Irish artillery. The enemy's force being estimated at no more than 300 men, and they fatigued with their voyage and subsequent excesses, Colonel Drummond assented to the repeated solicitations of the royalists to be permitted to attack them.

Accordingly, at 8 P.M., 180 royalists, with Captain M'Dowall of the 43rd at their head, marched from the fort on this service. While proceeding along the road leading to Gosier, a few shots were fired, probably from a piquet of the enemy: instantly the most shameful panic prevailed throughout the royalist party. A general discharge of musketry took place. Many of the men threw away their arms and deserted; and about 30 returned to the fort with Captain M'Dowall. Three of the royalists were killed, and four wounded on this unfortunate occasion.

On the 6th, at 1 A.M., the republicans, amounting, as was supposed, to between 1200 and 1500 men, commenced their march against the fort of Fleur-d'Epée, now garrisoned with about 160 men. These made a resolute defence, but, being at length overpowered, were obliged to retreat, with the loss of one lieutenant, one ensign, four sergeants, and 48 rank and file missing, including several killed and wounded. Finding on his arrival at the next post, Fort Saint Louis, that he could muster only 40 men, Colonel Drummond collected the detachment (33 in number) that was at Fort Government, and embarked at Petit-Canal, in two boats, for Grande-terre; which place, on the morning of the 10th, the colonel and his men reached in safety. Besides the missing at Fort Fleur-d'Epée, (some of whom had since escaped and joined the colonel), there were left sick at Pointe-à-Pitre, one captain, one ensign, seven sergeants, and 94 rank and file.

On the 5th, early in the morning, the arrival of the French squadron became known to the British admiral, who, with the Boyne, Veteran, Winchelsea, and Nautilus, was then at the island of St. Christopher; and who did not lose a moment in forwarding reinforcements. On the same afternoon Sir John Jervis, with the Boyne, having on board Sir Charles Grey, and

Veteran, made sail for Guadeloupe, having previously despatched the Winchelsea to Antigua, and the Nautilus to Martinique, to collect troops.

On the 7th, in the afternoon, the admiral and general arrived off Guadeloupe, and were there joined by commodore Thompson's two 74s, the Vanguard and Vengeance: the first, commanded by Captain Charles Sawyer, had recently joined, in lieu of the Irresistible, sent down to Jamaica, and now bore the commodore's pendant. Sir Charles Grey immediately landed at Basse-terre; while Sir John Jervis, with the Boyne, Vanguard, Vengeance, and Veteran, proceeded direct to Pointe-à-Pitre. On the 8th, at noon, the vice-admiral anchored off the harbour, and discovered the French squadron moored within the carénage. It was not until the morning of the 19th, that a sufficient number of troops was assembled, to attempt a recapture of Grande-terre. Early on that morning a landing was effected, under cover of the 32-gun frigates, Solebay and Winchelsea, without loss or opposition, at Anse-à-Canot. On the same afternoon the troops, joined by two battalions of seamen under the command of Captain Lewis Robertson of the Veteran, and Captain Charles Sawyer, of the Vanguard, took possession of the village of Gosier.

From the 25th to the end of June, several skirmishes occurred between the republicans and British; ending with much loss and some credit to each, but with no solid advantage to either. On the morning of the 2nd of July an unsuccessful attempt was made upon the town of Pointe-à-Pitre; the failure of which led to the abandonment of an intended assault upon the post of Fleur-d'Epée, and to a withdrawal, on the 3rd, of the British forces from Grande-terre.

The British loss, between the 10th of June, and 3rd of July, amounted, on the part of the army, to one lieutenant-colonel, four captains, seven lieutenants, and 93 non-commissioned officers and privates killed, one major, three captains, seven lieutenants, and 319 non-commissioned officers and privates wounded, and 56 non-commissioned officers and privates missing; total, 105 killed, 330 wounded, and 56 missing. On the part of the navy, the loss was, one captain (Lewis Robertson of the Veteran), four seamen, and two private marines killed, one lieutenant (Isaac Wolley), one lieutenant of marines (John Mercer), 24 seamen, and three private marines wounded, and 16 seamen missing; total, seven killed, 29 wounded, and 16 missing.

The French troops remained in quietness at Grande-terre until the 27th of September; when, having received from France, by means of some frigates whose names we are unable to give, a considerable reinforcement, they proceeded to Basse-terre, landing at Goyanne and Lamentin. From these points, the French immediately marched to the attack of the British camp at Berville, commanded by Brigadier-general Graham. The latter defended his position until the 6th of October; when, finding his provisions nearly exhausted, his communication with the shipping cut off, his hopes of relief at an end, and his effective force reduced to 125 rank and file, he surrendered to the French commander, or commissary, Victor Hugues, on honourable terms. The British, during the siege, had sustained a loss, as far as could be ascertained, of two officers, and 25 non-commissioned officers and privates killed, and five officers and 51 non-commissioned officers and privates wounded; total, 27 killed and 56 wounded. Thus were the French again masters of the whole island of Guadeloupe, except Fort Matilda.

Against this post, which was commanded by Lieutenant-general Prescott, and was extremely weak both in point of position and masonry, the republican forces commenced operations on the 14th of October. It took them until the 10th of December to render the works completely untenable; and at 10 p.m. the garrison, amounting to 621 officers and men, under the judicious management of Captain Richard Bowen, recently promoted to the Terpsichore frigate, got safe off, without even the knowledge of the French commander, who continued firing at the fort until 3 a.m. on the 11th.

The British loss, between the 14th of October and 10th of December, was, to the army, 13 killed and 60 wounded, and, to the navy, three killed and 18 wounded; including, among the badly wounded of the latter, Captain Bowen, who was unfortunately struck by a musket-ball in the face, while bringing off, in his own boat, the last man of the garrison. The behaviour of this officer, as well during the two months' siege as at the time of embarkation, gave such entire satisfaction to General Prescott, that the latter addressed a letter to Vice-admiral Caldwell (the successor of Sir John Jervis, who had sailed for England in November), expressly to acquaint him with the essential benefit which the garrison of Fort Matilda had derived from the zeal, vigilance, and great professional experience of Captain Bowen.

At the close of the preceding year we left Commodore Ford, in the 50-gun ship Europa, with a few frigates and sloops, and a detachment of British troops under Lieutenant-colonel Dansey, in possession of Jérémie, Cape Nicolas-Mole, the province of

Léogane on the south side of the island, and several small places, including Boncassin on the north side.[1]

The newly surrendered post of Boncassin being within 12 or 14 miles of Port-au-Prince, and the Spaniards, from their side of the island, having taken possession of Borgue, Gonaïves, Petite-Rivière, and Verette, Commodore Ford, on the 2nd of January, detached the 32-gun frigate Penelope, Captain Bartholomew Samuel Rowley, with a flag of truce, to Port-au-Prince; offering to the civil commissary, Santhonax, the same capitulation which had been voluntarily accepted by so many of the parishes. The offer was refused; and the port in consequence was closely blockaded by some ships of the commodore's squadron.

On the 2nd of February, the strong and highly important post at Cape Tiburon, mounting 22 pieces of heavy cannon, was taken by the British, after a slight resistance, and the loss of three privates killed, and one captain, one lieutenant, and nine non-commissioned officers and privates wounded. On the 18th the post of Aoul, about six miles from Léogane, was also attacked, and after a sharp resistance carried, with the loss of one captain and four privates killed, and one captain, four lieutenants, and 27 non-commissioned officers and privates wounded.

On the 31st of May, early in the morning, an expedition, composed of the 74-gun ship Irresistible, Captain James Richard Dacres, 64s Belliqueux and Sceptre, Captains Richard Dacres and Augustus Brine, 50-gun ship Europa, Captain Gregory, three frigates, and three sloops, the whole under the command of Commodore Ford, whose pendant was still flying on board the Europa, and of 1465 effective troops, commanded by Brigadier-general White, which had sailed from Cape Nicolas-Mole, arrived in the bay of Port-au-Prince. An officer with a flag of truce was sent in, but was not allowed to land.

The possession of Fort Brissoton being an object of the first consideration, the Belliqueux and Sceptre, on the 1st of June, at 11 h. 30 m. A.M., by signal from the Europa, got under way, and placed themselves, with the utmost precision, against the fort; as did also the Penelope, so as to flank a ravine to the eastward. All three ships then commenced a well-directed and very brisk fire upon the enemy. In the mean time the Europa and Irresistible remained under sail, throwing in their broadsides whenever it could be done with effect, and keeping in check a body of the enemy's horse and some brigands, that appeared disposed to interrupt the troops in their landing. By 5 P.M. the detach-

[1] See p. 131.

ment was wholly disembarked, under the direction of Captain Thomas Affleck, of the Fly sloop. The fort had fired but at intervals from the time the ships were placed, yet the colours were still flying. A stop, however, was put to all firing at 6 P.M., by a most tremendous thunder-storm and deluge of rain. This was taken advantage of by Captain Daniel of the 41st regiment, at the head of an advanced party then marching towards the fort. He and his 60 men, rushing forward with their bayonets, carried the place by assault, and were soon afterwards joined by the main body under Major Spencer.

On the following morning, the 2nd, the British colours were hoisted on Fort Brissoton. On the same evening a party of 200 British, under Colonel Hampfield, landed at Pointe Saline; and, on the morning of the 3rd, the 32-gun frigates Hermione, Captain John Hills, and Iphigenia, Captain Patrick Sinclair, got under way, and cannonaded an advanced post of the enemy at Bernadon, in order to divert their attention from Colonel Hampfield's detachment. The badness of the weather prevented any further operations until the morning of the 4th, when the principal posts, which had been abandoned in the night, were taken possession of by the troops. The inhabitants of Port-au-Prince requested that the British colours should be hoisted, which was accordingly done. Thus did the capital of the French part of St. Domingo fall into the same hands as Tiburon, Cape Nicolas-Mole, and Jérémie

The loss sustained by the British, and which was incurred wholly at the storming of Fort Brissoton, was, one captain of infantry and eight privates killed, and one captain of infantry and two privates wounded; also, on board the Hermione, five seamen killed and six wounded, and on board the Belliqueux, ten seamen and marines wounded. In the harbour of Port-au-Prince were found 16 ships and brigs, richly laden with colonial produce, and 16 others in ballast, two of which were of 600 and one of 700 tons.

The British post at Cape Tiburon was garrisoned by 450 men, chiefly colonial troops, under the command of Lieutenant George Bradford, of the 23rd regiment of infantry. A small battery, mounting three long 18-pounders, scarcely in a serviceable state, and an armed merchant-ship, the King George ("King Grey" in the Gazette), moored with springs on her cable at the entrance of the harbour, were the principal sea-defences of the place.

On the 25th of December, at daylight, a body of French and colonial troops from Aux-Cayes, amounting as supposed to 3000, including 800 regulars and artillery, and assisted by three armed vessels, commenced an attack upon the King George, whose crew defended the harbour with much spirit. Finding more resistance from the ship than they expected, the French landed their artillery; and having erected a battery of one long 18 and one 8 pounder, with three smaller pieces and an 8-inch mortar, they opened a heavy fire upon the King George; which, however, she still continued to return. At the end of a 48 hours' incessant cannonade, during which, at intervals of ten minutes, a 50 lb. shell was thrown from the mortar, the King George, from the shot-holes in her hull, had sunk nearly up to her battery; when a red-hot shot striking the magazine, the ship blew up, and all on board, as far as we know, perished.

Having accomplished this their first object, the French turned their guns upon the lower battery, and very soon dismounted the two remaining 18-pounders, the third having burst on its first discharge. As soon as this battery was silenced, the French attacked the upper fort; and, having thrown into it several shells, and killed and wounded about 100 of the garrison, they compelled the remainder to abandon their works and retire to Cape Donna Maria.

Coast of Africa.

On the 28th of September a French squadron from Brest, consisting of the 50-gun frigate, or cut-down 74, Expériment, Captain and senior officer Zacharie-Jacques-Théodore Allemand, frigates Vengeance and Félicité, brig-corvettes Mutine and Epervier, and two Guinea ships that had been captured in the passage, approached the town of Sierra-Léone under English colours, and, unmolested, drew up before it in such a manner as to command every street.[1] The ships then exchanged their colours to French, and commenced a heavy cannonade upon the inhabitants; who, being without any naval or other force to protect them, hauled down the British ensign from the flagstaff on which, out of compliment to their supposed friends, they had previously hoisted it.

Regardless of this unequivocal symbol of submission, the Vengeance and Félicité continued, for nearly two hours, raking the streets with grape-shot, and thereby killed two and wounded five men.[2]

[1] Mr. James has given a vast importance to Sierra-Leone, by speaking of its *streets*. In 1810 it had but one; and no poetical imagination could sufficiently picture the misery of this insignificant, unimportant, and unworthily denominated *town*—ED.

[2] The population of this sink of wretchedness must have retired to the woods (not their log-built houses), or the slaughter occasioned by two hours' firing from large frigates must have been very ineffectual.—ED.

At length the French landed from the ships, and immediately proceeded to plunder such houses as remained standing, and which the owners had very wisely abandoned. Just as the relentless invaders were preparing to involve the whole town in one blaze, several of the maroon settlers from Jamaica and Nova-Scotia returned to it, and solicited the preservation of their dwellings. The French commander granted their request, observing, that his vengeance should be confined to the British settlers: he then caused the church, the company's warehouses, and the houses of all the English residents, to be set on fire and destroyed.

After the performance of this most cruel act, by which 1500 poor settlers were left destitute, one of the frigates proceeded up the river to the island of Banca; which, for two days, the French ship cannonaded without success, the garrison of the small fort at the town making a resolute defence. On the third day the second frigate arrived to reinforce her consort; when, the inhabitants having withdrawn their property, the garrison retired from the fort, leaving their colours flying: a well-planned ruse, as it imposed upon the enemy the idea of resistance, and gave to the few troops and inhabitants a full hour's unmolested retreat.

The French continued at Sierra-Léone until the 23rd of October; during which time they wooded and watered, but never proceeded into the country, nor injured the plantations. The crews, indeed, were already so weakened by the disease of the climate, that two well-manned British 38-gun frigates, and one 20-gun ship would, in all probability, have made prizes of the whole squadron. After having captured or destroyed eleven vessels belonging to the company, the squadron of M. Allemand made sail along the coast, in company with the Harpy, of London, a fine ship of 400 tons, mounting 12 guns, and very richly laden.

On the 7th of November the French arrived at Cape Mount; where, and at other places along the coast between Sénégal and Bonny, they destroyed about 27 Guineamen; having previously, as they had done at Sierra-Léone, taken out everything valuable, and landed the seamen and slaves, detaining only the captains. Thus freighted with spoils, the squadron made sail homewards, and succeeded in reaching the port of their departure, after having, according to the French accounts, destroyed 210 English, Spanish, and Portuguese vessels.

BRITISH AND FRENCH FLEETS.

The abstract of the British navy, for the commencement of the present, advances but slowly upon that of the preceding year. In the line-total there is a decrease of three cruisers; but the commission column shows an increase of six, and the increase of cruisers, line and under-line, amounts to 63.[1] The number of French national ships captured by the British during the year 1794 amounts to 36, of which number 27 (and of these 24 only as cruisers) were added to the British navy.[2] The latter lost during the same period 17 vessels, of which nine, including one of the line, fell into the hands of the enemy.[3]

Of the 15 ships that remained of those building at the commencement of the war, four had been launched, also 20 of the 24 ordered in the year 1793, and 16, all of a small description, out of the 31[4] ordered in 1794. Among the latter was a first-rate, originally intended to be a 100-gun ship, but subsequently ordered to be made large enough to carry 120 guns, besides poop-carronades. Of this ship we shall say more when we come to the abstract of the year succeeding that in which she is launched.

During the year 1794 an admiralty order was issued directing that all frigates, down to the 18-pounder class of 32s inclusive, should in future be constructed with four instead of three-inch bottoms; whereby it was considered the ships would be more strong and durable, and, in the event of grounding, be able to bear the shock with less injury to their frames.

---

[1] See Appendix, Annual Abstract, No. 3.
[2] See Appendix, No. 15.
[3] Ibid. No. 16.
[4] The deduction of the 16 is already made in the "ordered" column of the abstract; as, indeed, is the case in every similar instance. All ships, in either of the "launched" columns of one abstract, that are not to be found in the "building" column of the preceding one, must have been ordered to have been built since the date of the latter.

But improvement was not confined to the strength of the ships. It had long been an imputation upon the British that their ships of war were, generally speaking, very indifferent sailers. As one means of obviating this, it was determined to give to the ships greater length, in proportion to their breadth, than had hitherto been customary in the English dockyards. The raising of the lower batteries of the two and three-decked ships, with a due regard to their proper stability, was also an improvement, and no slight one, in the higher rates that were constructing.

Towards the end of November, 1794, a new scale was drawn up, by order of the board of admiralty, for arming the navy with carronades; and this establishment, unlike that of 1779,[1] was made compulsory on the part of the ships coming forward to be fitted. But still, as a captain might generally, on a special application, have the whole or any less number of his long guns exchanged for an equal number of additional carronades; and, as many ships, from continuing at sea, underwent no change in their armament until long subsequent to the date of the order, little use can be made of it in the way of a general guide. A whole, although a small class of vessels, had been armed throughout, except for chase-guns, with 18-pounder carronades; a great accession of force, undoubtedly, as vessels of the size in question could only have borne an equal number of 3, or at most of 4 pounders. Two instances occur in the year 1794 where carronades of the highest caliber were employed; the 74-gun ship Albion and 64 Nonsuch, on being fitted as floating batteries, were armed, the one with twenty-eight the other with twenty 68-pounders.[2]

During the year 1794 an alteration took place in the established complements of British ships of war. The order in council directing it bears date on the 16th of April; but as the alteration could scarcely take effect throughout the navy before the end of the year, we have deferred any notice of it till now. The order purports to direct a reduction in the complement of every ship in the British navy; complements, as we have elsewhere observed, already much lower than those allowed in any other naval establishment. But the reduction, in truth, was merely nominal; as few, if any, of the "servants" forming so large a proportion of the old complements were ever on board the ship to which they were attached. They were nearly as much men of straw as the widow's men that, even now, are

[1] See p. 38. [2] See notes f*, and u*, Annual Abstract, No. 3.

absurdly reckoned as part of the complement of a British ship of war. These servants were to be replaced by about three-fourths as many boys, who were to be actually on board. A fifth of these boys was to consist of young gentlemen volunteers, intended for officers, and who were not to be under 11 years of age. The second class was to consist of three-fourths boys between 15 and 17 years of age, and who were to keep watch with the seamen. The remainder of the boys were to be between 13 and 15 years of age, and were intended chiefly to wait upon the lieutenants and other officers.

The greatest proportion in which these boys are to the complement is a seventh, the smallest about a twentieth, and even the latter far exceeds what is customary in the complements of the ships of war belonging to any other nation. The additional carronades and the complement, as altered, of every class of British ship, will be found annexed to the abstract for the year 1795.

The number of commissioned officers and masters belonging to the British navy at the commencement of the year 1795 was,

Admirals	21
Vice-admirals	36
Rear-admirals	31
,, superannuated	28
Post-captains	425
,, superannuated	27
Commanders, or sloop-captains	230
Lieutenants	1623
,, superannuated	26
Masters	361

and the number of seamen and marines voted for the service of the same year was 100,000.[1]

Several circumstances conspired to diminish the effect which the defeat of the 1st of June might be supposed to have produced on the French navy. The exaggerated accounts, which alone were permitted to be read, rather heightened than depressed the national confidence; and the arrival of the great American convoy furnished supplies, if not of provisions to any great extent on account of the amazing consumption of so populous a country as France, of seamen at least; and these became increased owing to another cause, the languishing state of privateering during the year 1794 (three French privateers only were captured), occasioned chiefly by the little encouragement

[1] See Appendix, No. 17

which the government, for the very purpose perhaps of manning the navy, held out to the merchants.

The navy of France was still very strong. In the road of Brest there were, including the new 74 Fougueux on her way from Rochefort, 35 sail of the line, besides the Invincible three-decker and two 74s repairing, and the immense Vengeur and one 74 building (the latter nearly ready) in the arsenal. At Lorient there were on the stocks one 80 and two 74-gun ships, and at Rochefort one three-decker, one 80, and one 74, making a total, without reckoning the ships in Toulon, of 46 sail of the line.

Three distinct expeditions appear to have been in the contemplation of the French government at the close of the year 1794. One squadron of six sail of the line and a few frigates and corvettes under the orders of Rear-admiral Renaudin, the late Vengeur's gallant captain, was to hasten to the Mediterranean, to reinforce the Toulon fleet. With a second squadron of six sail of the line, four frigates, four corvettes, and a sufficiency of transports to contain 6000 troops, Rear-admiral Kerguelen, an officer of the old French marine, and one of the most active and experienced at this time in the service, was to make his way to India, for the purpose of placing the Isle of France in a proper state of defence. A third squadron, composed of two or three sail of the line and smaller vessels, including transports with troops, was destined for Saint Domingo, in order, if possible, to restore the French authority in that ill-fated island.

Such, however, was the state of penury, both in the arsenals and the storehouses of Brest, that there was not timber and cordage enough properly to repair the ships disabled on the 1st of June, nor a sufficiency of provisions to supply the fleet with sea-stores, flour and biscuit in particular, for even a much shorter voyage than either of those in contemplation by the French minister, or commissary, M. d'Albarade. To increase the evil of waiting for the expected convoy of 50 or 60 vessels north-about from the Baltic, the number of mouths daily to be fed in the port amounted to 72,000.[1]

The reinforcement to the Toulon fleet being considered of more immediate consequence than the other expeditions, the squadron allotted for that service was with great difficulty provisioned for six months; and the remainder of the Brest fleet, many of the ships with only a 15 days' stock on board, and a few others with fished masts, and with hulls, from the hard battering they had received, scarcely seaworthy, were to quit port, and escort

[1] Relations des Combats, &c. par Y. I. Kerguelen, ancien contre amiral. p. 369.

those six sail of the line beyond the probable cruising ground of the British Channel fleet, reported to consist, including the Portuguese squadron, of 33 sail of the line.

Everything being in readiness, or as much so at least as circumstances would permit, a gale of wind from a fair quarter was considered a favourable opportunity; and on or about the 24th of December, 1794, the Brest fleet, consisting of 35 ships of the line (five three-deckers, three 80s, and the remainder 74s),[1] 13 frigates, and 16 corvettes, avisos, and tenders, making in the whole 63 vessels of war, got under way, and stood for the harbour's mouth or goulet. The commander-in-chief of this, for France, immense armament, was Vice-admiral Villaret-Joyeuse, having under him the Rear-admirals Bouvet, Nielly, Vanstabel, and Renaudin, and, as his colleagues and supervisors, the conventional deputies Faure and Tréhouart.

The folly of attempting to move so numerous and ill-provided a fleet in the midst of a peculiarly severe winter, and, above all, during the prevalence of a violent gale of wind, very soon showed its effects. The Républicain three-decker struck on the Mingan rock, which stands nearly in the centre of the goulet, and was entirely lost; and the Redoubtable 74, but for the skill and presence of mind of her captain, M. Moncousu, would have shared the same fate; as it was, the latter ship lost all her anchors and boats.

In consequence of these disasters the remaining ships of M. Villaret's fleet came again to an anchor, and did not make a second attempt until the 31st of December. On this day the fleet, now by the loss of the Républicain reduced to 34 sail of the line and frigates, weighed and stood out to sea, where we will leave the French ships to make the best of their way, while we recount a very dashing exploit in the reconnoitring way, which occurred during their absence.

On the 2nd of January, early in the morning, an indistinct account of the sailing of the Brest fleet having reached Falmouth, a squadron of British frigates, consisting of the Flora, Captain Sir John Borlase Warren; Arethusa, Captain Sir Edward Pellew; and Diamond, Captain Sir William Sidney Smith, was despatched to the Bay of Brest to ascertain the truth of the prevailing rumour.

On the 3rd the squadron arrived off the port, and Sir John immediately sent the Diamond to look well into the harbour.

---

[1] As no action occurred with these ships thus united as a fleet, their names need not appear.

With the wind at east the frigate commenced beating up towards the entrance. At 2 P.M. Sir Sidney observed, also working in, three sail, evidently French ships-of-war. At 5 P.M., in order to be ready to take advantage of the next flood-tide, the Diamond cast anchor between Pointe Saint Mathieu and Bec-du-Raz, and found lying, within about a mile from Saint Mathieu and scarcely two from herself, a large ship, judged to be one of the three which had been seen beating to windward. At 11 P.M. the Diamond got under way, and continued working up under all sail.

On the 4th, at 2 A.M., Sir Sidney made out the vessel at anchor to be a ship of the line, and at 2 h. 30 m. A.M. passed close to windward of a frigate at anchor within Basse-Buzée. The ebb-tide had now made; but the Diamond, that she might not drift to leeward or create suspicion, continued under sail, tacking between the roads of Bertheaume and Camaret.

The appearance of daylight at 7 A.M. brought to her view two ships coming through the goulet de Brest, 15 sail of small vessels at anchor in Camaret road, and a ship without her fore and mizenmasts aground, as it appeared, on Petit-Menou point. This ship there can be very little doubt was the Républicain, Pointe du Petit Menou lying directly in a line with the Mingan rock and with Pointe de Bertheaume, near to which at that time was the Diamond.

At 7 h. 40 m. A.M., not observing any ships in Brest road, the Diamond bore up towards Saint Mathieu. At 8 A.M. the Château de Bertheaume made several signals, on which the Diamond hoisted French national colours. In ten minutes afterwards a corvette, which had been running along Bertheaume bay to the westward, shortened sail, and evinced her suspicion of the Diamond by hoisting several signals, and hauling close under the lee of the castle. The British frigate, nevertheless, stood on, and soon passed within hail of the line-of-battle ship; which, with jury-yards and topmasts, was still at anchor, apparently without any main-deck guns, and very leaky. Sir Sidney asked the French commander, if he wanted any assistance. The latter is stated to have replied "No," and to have readily informed Sir Sidney, that the ship's name was the Nestor, that she had been dismasted in a gale of wind, and had parted from the fleet three days before. With this intelligence, the Diamond, whose disguised appearance, aided by Sir Sidney's excellent French, had completely deceived the French captain and his officers, crowded sail to rejoin her consorts.

While the French 74 and British frigate were speaking each other, a French frigate, with topgallantyards across, lay at anchor a short distance to windward. It appears that this was the new 40-gun frigate Virginie, Captain Jacques Bergeret, and that the remaining French ship of the three which were beating up when the Diamond first saw them, was the 74-gun ship Fougueux, recently launched at Rochefort, and which, with the Virginie, had escorted from Bordeaux the 15 sail of vessels at anchor in Camaret bay. The Diamond, notwithstanding her perilous situation, got clear off, and at 10 h. 30 m. joined the Arethusa, which frigate the commodore stationed in-shore, on the look-out for her venturous companion.

Scarcely had the French fleet got well to sea before it encountered a gale of wind, in which several of the ships were damaged, and the Nestor, with the loss of some of her masts, put back, as has already been stated. The probability of the fleet's being kept at sea beyond the 15 days, for which the majority of the ships had been provisioned, rendered it necessary for the six Toulon ships to divide their six months' stock among their companions, and defer their voyage to another opportunity. In a day or two after the gale had abated a thick fog came on, in which the whole of Rear-admiral Vanstabel's division, of eight sail of the line and some frigates, separated and returned to Brest.

On the 28th of January, when the remainder of the fleet, continuing their cruise, had reached 150 leagues from Brest, a second and a much more tremendous gale overtook them. The Neuf-Thermidor (late Jacobin), Scipion, and Superbe, being old ships, foundered. Nearly the whole of the Neuf-Thermidor's crew perished, many of them on account of the fore and main masts falling on the quarter-deck. The crews of the other two ships, except 21 men in the Superbe, were fortunately saved The latter ship overset before all her people had quitted her. The Neptune ran on shore and was wrecked at Péros, a bay about 12 leagues from Brest, between Bréhet and Morlaix. The Téméraire and Convention reached with great difficulty, the one Port Malo, the other Lorient. The remainder of the fleet returned to Brest on the 1st and 2nd days of February, in a very crippled state. The Majestueux three-decker was so leaky, that she could hardly be kept afloat, even at her moorings.

As some slight compensation for these disasters to his fleet, M. Villaret captured and destroyed, during his 34 days' cruise, about 100 sail of enemy's vessels, great and small, including the British 20-gun ship, or, as from her real mounted force the French were warranted in designating her, 30-gun frigate Daphne.

On the 14th of February, after several days' detention in Torbay by a heavy gale at south-east, in which nine of the 36 sail of the line in company parted their cables, but fortunately brought up again, Admiral Earl Howe, although in a state of health that would have justified retirement from the command, put to sea with the Channel fleet, and on the following day was joined, off Plymouth, by the Raisonable 64, Rear-admiral Parker, and the already-named five Portuguese line-of-battle ships under Admiral-de-Valle ;[1] making his lordship's whole force 42 sail of the line, exclusive of about an equal number of frigates and sloops. Having seen the East and West India and other convoys safe out of the Channel, and parted company with the detachments that had been ordered to attend them to their respective destinations; and having also gained certain intelligence that the French fleet was again in Brest harbour, Lord Howe, with the remainder of his fleet, reanchored at Spithead.

The moment the Brest fleet, with so serious a reduction of its numbers, had regained their port, the utmost exertions were used, in the first instance, to requip and reprovision the six sail of the line and frigates intended for Toulon. By great exertion, and not without some difficulty, that was accomplished, and on the 22nd of February Rear-admiral Renaudin sailed for his destination, and, as we shall hereafter show, arrived there in safety.

In a week or two after the departure of M. Renaudin, 12 of the remaining ships of the Brest fleet, with the whole of the frigates, were at anchor in the road ready for sea; and early in May Rear-admiral Jean-Gaspar Vence, with three 74s and six or seven frigates, was detached to the southward, to escort a convoy of coasters from Bordeaux.

On the 30th of May the following squadron sailed from Spithead on a cruise off Ushant:—

Gun-ship.			
100	Royal Sovereign	{	Vice-adm. (b.) Hon. Wm. Cornwallis. Captain John Whitby.
74	{ Mars	,,	Sir Charles Cotton.
	Triumph	,,	Sir Erasmus Gower.
	Brunswick	,,	Lord Charles Fitzgerald.
	Bellerophon	,,	Lord Cranstoun.
Gun-frigate.			
38	Phaëton	,,	Hon. Robert Stopford.
32	Pallas	,,	Hon. Henry Curzon.
G.-brg.slp.			
18	Kingfisher	,,	Thos. Le Marchant Gosselyn.

See p. 202.

On the 8th of June, at 10 A.M., the squadron made the land about the Penmarcks; and at 10 h. 30 m. A.M. the Triumph threw out the signal for six sail east by north. These, and the other vessels seen about the same time, composed the squadron of Rear-admiral Vence; who, with a numerous convoy in charge, was on his return to Brest. Having lain to until he discovered that the vessels in chase of him were enemy's cruisers, the French admiral, at about noon, stood away for Belle-Isle, under a press of sail.

At 2 P.M. the Kingfisher, Phaëton, and Triumph, then considerably ahead of their companions, one of whom, the Brunswick, was hull-down astern, commenced firing at the enemy; but, finding it impossible for the rest of the squadron to arrive up in time to prevent the French from getting under the island, within the southmost point of which the leading British ships then were, the vice-admiral made the signal to close. At 4 P.M. two French frigates were chased in the south-west, one with a large ship in tow, which she abandoned to the British, as they approached: and then the two crowded away to join their admiral, who was about coming to an anchor. Several shots were now interchanged between the batteries of Belle-Isle and the advanced British ships, until the Triumph and Phaëton, shoaling their water, made the signal for danger.

The vice-admiral thereupon recalled his ships from chase, and stood off with eight French vessels, laden with wine and brandy, which the squadron had captured out of a fleet, that was still plying to windward under the land, to gain the anchorage in Palais road. On the next day, the 9th, it was calm until 8 P.M., when, a breeze springing up, the British squadron took the prizes in tow, and steered for the Channel. On the 11th, when a few leagues to the southward of Scilly, the vice-admiral ordered the Kingfisher into port with the prizes, and stood back to the southward and eastward, to look after M. Vence and his squadron.

When the news reached Brest, that Rear-admiral Vence had been chased into, and, as the account added, was blockaded at, Belle-Isle, the nine ships of the line at anchor in Brest road were still waiting for a supply of provisions, before they could attempt to sail upon their distant missions. All other considerations were now to give way to the relief of this squadron, supposed to be in jeopardy at Belle-Isle: supposed, we say, because it was known to the more experienced among the French officers, that no blockading force could prevent Rear-admiral Vence from reaching Lorient; and, in fact, the French admiral was not blockaded at all, Vice-admiral Cornwallis, as has been shown, having sailed for the mouth of the Channel to protect his prizes. However, the French minister was resolved; and, accordingly, on the 12th of June, nine sail of the line, two 50-gun rasés, seven other frigates, and four corvettes, under the orders of Vice-admiral Villaret-Joyeuse in the Peuple (late Montagne), attended by the two deputies Palasne-Champeaux and Topsent, and by Rear-admirals Kerguelen and Bruix, got under way and stood out, the ships still having on board, as it appears, only a 15 days' stock of provisions.

On the 10th, when a few leagues from Isle Groix, M. Villaret's squadron fell in with M. Vence; who, in verification of what Rear-admiral Kerguelen and others had stated to be practicable, had quitted his anchorage at Belle-Isle without difficulty or molestation, and was now on his return from Brest. The French fleet, thus united, was composed of the following line-of-battle ships and frigates :—

Gun-ship.		Gun-ship.		Gun-ship.	
120	Peuple.		Fougueux.		Redoutable.
74	Alexandre.	74	Jean-Bart.	74	Tigre
	Droits-de-l'Homme.		Mucius.		Wattigny.
	Formidable.		Nestor.		Zelé.

Frigates.

Brave, *rasé*.	Insurgente.	Cocarde.
Scévola, ,,	Driade.	Régénérée.
Virginie.	Fraternité.	Name unknown.
Proserpine.	Fidelle.	

There were also three large ship and two brig corvettes, and two cutters; making in all, 30 vessels.

On the 16th, at about 10 h. 30 m. A.M., while working off the land near the Penmarcks on his return to Brest, with the wind at west-north-west, M. Villaret discovered, directly to windward, the squadron of Vice-admiral Cornwallis, then making the best of his way towards Belle-Isle, to reconnoitre the road in which he had left M. Vence and his squadron.

As the Phaëton, when as the look-out frigate of the British squadron she first discovered the French fleet, did not, after making the signal that the enemy was of superior force, haul her wind and return to the squadron, the vice-admiral concluded that the signal had reference to the number, rather than to the apparent strength of the French ships, and accordingly stood on nearer than he otherwise would. At 11 A.M., however, being too weak to offer battle to a force now so evidently superior, the British squadron hauled to the wind on the starboard tack under all sail, formed in line ahead thus: Brunswick, Royal Sovereign, Bellerophon, Triumph, Mars.

At 2 P.M. the French fleet, then on the same tack as the British squadron, separated into two divisions; one of which tacked and stood to the northward, in order to take advantage of the land-wind, while the other continued its course to the southward. At 4 P.M. the British squadron tacked, and did so again at 5 P.M. At 6 P.M. the French north division tacked to the southward. Soon afterwards, as the French admiral appears to have expected, the wind shifted to the northward, and thus enabled the north division to weather, and the south division to lie well up for the British squadron; from the centre ship of which, the Bellerophon, the first division bore east by north, or upon her starboard quarter, distant eight or nine miles, and the second division south-east, or upon her larboard quarter, distant about ten miles.

The Bellerophon and Brunswick, the former in particular, had always been considered as excellent sailers; but, owing to some error in their stowage, they were now quite out of trim. The consequence was, that, in the course of the night, to improve their sailing, these ships were obliged to cut away their anchors and launches and start a portion of their water and provisions; and the Bellerophon had also to throw overboard her four poop-carronades, with their carriages, and a great quantity of shot.

Notwithstanding they had thus lightened themselves, the Bellerophon and Brunswick very much retarded the squadron in its progress: so much so, indeed, that at daylight on the 17th the French fleet was discovered coming up very fast, formed in three divisions. The weather division consisted of three ships of the line and five frigates, and was nearly abreast of the British rear. The centre division consisted of five ships of the line and four frigates; and the lee division, of four sail of the line, five frigates, two brigs, and two cutters.

At about 9 A.M. the French van-ship, believed to have been the Zélé, Captain Magnae, opened her fire upon the rearmost English ship, the Mars; who, hoisting her colours, as did the rest of the squadron, promptly returned it with her stern-chasers. One of the French frigates from the centre division, since known to have been the Virginie, Captain Bergeret, gallantly ran up on the larboard or lee quarter of the Mars, and, yawing, fired repeatedly into her. At 9 h. 30 m. A.M., wishing to cover the Bellerophon from the effects of the enemy's fire, neither that ship nor the Triumph being able to spare the loss of a sail, the vice-admiral ordered the former to go ahead.

The Bellerophon, accordingly, passed close under the lee of the Royal Sovereign, the latter having shortened sail for that purpose, and took her station next in line to the Brunswick. At a few minutes before noon the cannonade became general on the part of the British ships, each firing her stern or quarter guns as she could bring them to bear. At 1 P.M. the second ship of the French van opened her fire on the British rear; and at 1 h. 30 m. P.M. the first ship, having had her main topgallant-masts shot away, and being otherwise damaged by the fire of the Mars, sheered off, and dropped astern. The supposed Zélé's late second astern, the present van-ship, now opened a brisk cannonade on the larboard quarter of the Mars.

A harassing fire continued to be kept up at intervals by the leading French ships in succession, during the next three or four hours; at the end of which Vice-admiral Cornwallis, observing that the Mars, from the crippled state of her rigging and sails, had fallen to leeward, and was likely to be overpowered, threw out the signal for her to alter her course to starboard, or from the ships that were most annoying her.

Immediately afterwards the Royal Sovereign bore round up in the direction of the Mars, and, opening her powerful broadside on the enemy, ran down, in company with the Triumph, to the support of her gallant but crippled friend; who was thereby soon brought into close order of battle, and saved from further molestation. The commencement of this bold and well-executed manœuvre, we have endeavoured to illustrate by the diagram opposite.

Four of the French van-ships had, in the mean time, bore up to secure the crippled ship; but, seeing the approach of the British three-decker, they again hauled to the wind. A partial firing continued until about 6 h 10 m. P.M., when it entirely ceased. In another half-hour the French ships shortened sail, and gave over the pursuit. Soon afterwards they tacked and stood to the eastward, and at sunset were nearly hull-down in the north-east.

The brunt of the action having been borne by the Mars and Triumph, those ships, particularly the former, were the only sufferers by the enemy's shot. The Triumph had some of her sails and running rigging cut, but escaped without the loss of a man. The Mars had her mainmast, and fore and maintopsail yards damaged, besides standing and running rigging; she had also 12 men wounded, but none killed. Owing to the comparatively flimsy structure of their stern-frames, and the want of proper port-holes, all the British ships were great sufferers from the protracted stern-fire which they were obliged to maintain. In the Triumph, who from her position in the line had the most occasion to keep up a stern-fire, the stern-galleries, bulkheads, and every part of the stern of the ward-room except the timbers, were cut away, and, from her three stern-batteries (first deck, second deck, and quarter-deck), that ship expended, in single shots, nearly 5000 lbs. of powder.

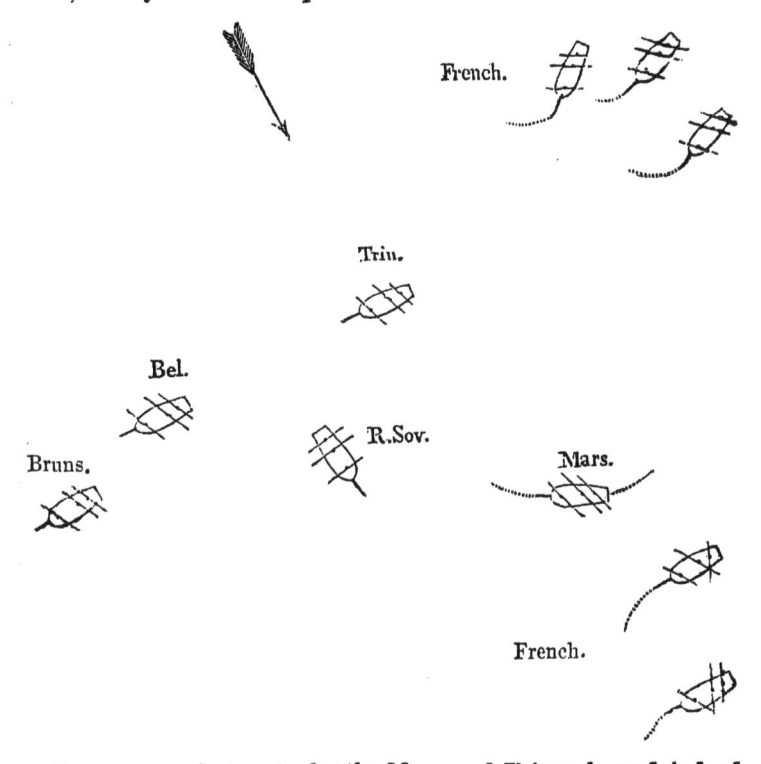

It was very fortunate for the Mars and Triumph, and indeed for the whole British squadron (for their admiral does not appear to have been one who would have abandoned any of his ships), that there were no Captains Bergeret among those who commanded the headmost line-of-battle ships of the chasing fleet.

But, after all, what could have induced the French admiral to withdraw his 12 sail of the line and 14 or 15 frigates, at a time when they had almost surrounded five British sail of the line and two frigates? The French accounts admit that M. Villaret, with a force such as we have described it, surrounded Vice-admiral Cornwallis's squadron, consisting of not a ship more than it really contained; and the reason they allege why the former did not make a prize of that squadron is, that several of the leading French ships disobeyed signals and were badly manœuvred.

This is not doing the French admiral justice. We can better explain the cause of M. Villaret's extraordinary forbearance. On the 17th, in the morning, the British frigate Phaëton was detached ahead of her squadron, to try the effect of a *ruse-de-guerre*, which we will proceed to describe.

Having got to the distance of some miles, the frigate made the signal for a strange sail west-north-west; soon afterwards, for four sail; and finally, the well-known signal for a fleet, by letting fly the topgallantsheets, and firing two guns in quick succession. At 3 P.M., being then very far ahead, the Phaëton made the private signal to the supposed fleet; and then, by the tabular signals, with which the French were well acquainted, she communicated to her own admiral that the fleet seen were friends, and, at 4 h. 30 m., that they were ships of the line. The Phaëton then repeated the signal, as from the admiral to call in the strange fleet, by hoisting the Dutch ensign, and shortly afterwards shortened sail.

At 6 P.M., as a singular coincidence, there actually appeared, in the direction to which the Phaëton's signals had been pointing, several small sail. The British frigate immediately wore to rejoin her squadron; and very soon afterwards, as has already been stated, Vice-admiral Villaret, to whom the strange sails must just then have discovered themselves, gave over the chase and tacked to the eastward.

So far from the French officers denying this, several of them, when afterwards in company with British officers, strenuously insisted that it was Lord Bridport's fleet, which they knew was at sea, that they saw, and that that, and that alone, was the cause of their not following up their advantage. Let, however, M. Villaret's reasons for his conduct have been what they may, the masterly retreat of Vice-admiral Cornwallis excited general admiration; and the spirit manifested by the different ships' companies of his little squadron, while pressed upon by a force from its threefold superiority so capable of crushing them, was just such as ought always to animate British seamen when in the presence of an enemy.

Among the merits of the British admiral on this occasion, must not be forgotten the handsome manner in which, in his official letter, he mentions his officers and men; nor the modest manner in which he refers to his own gallant act of bearing up, in the face of so formidable a fleet, to support one of his crippled ships. After extolling the behaviour of every captain by name, the vice-admiral proceeds thus: "Indeed, I shall ever feel the impression which the good conduct of the captains, officers, seamen, marines, and soldiers in the squadron, has made on my mind; and it was the greatest pleasure I ever received to see the spirit manifested by the men, who, instead of being cast down at seeing 30 sail of the enemy's ships attacking our little squadron, were in the highest spirits imaginable. I do not mean the Royal Sovereign alone: the same spirits was shown in all the ships as they came near me; and although, circumstanced as we were, we had no great reason to complain of the conduct of the enemy, yet our men could not help repeatedly expressing their contempt of them. Could common prudence have allowed me to let loose their valour, I hardly know what might not have been accomplished by such men." Of the Royal Sovereign's individual share he merely says: "In the evening they made a show of a more serious attack upon the Mars, and obliged me to bear up for her support." Such good conduct in all concerned met its reward; and both houses of parliament unanimously voted their thanks to Vice-admiral Cornwallis and his companions in arms on this memorable occasion.

Two English naval writers of respectability, and, indeed, of no slight influence, both being professional men, seem to attribute the successful issue of Vice-admiral Cornwallis's retreat to the manner, the peculiar manner, in which he formed his squadron. One says: "He retreated with his ships in the form of a wedge, of which the Royal Sovereign was the apex; and whenever the enemy approached sufficiently near, they were soon taught to keep at a safer distance."[1]

The other writer, upon two of his plates, actually represents the British squadron in this wedge-like form, with "the flagship at the angular point." He is afterwards obliged to admit, that "a distinguished officer, who was present on this occasion, has observed that these figures are not wholly correct."[2]

[1] Brenton, vol i., p. 374. [2] Ekins's Naval Battles, p. 210.

Admiral Ekins, then, in a third and fourth plate, represents the Brunswick and Bellerophon in extended line abreast, the first on the weather, and the last on the lee bow of the Royal Sovereign; who has, in a well-formed line astern of her, the Triumph and Mars.

That the Bellerophon was not on the lee bow of the Royal Sovereign is clear from the following extract from the former ship's log, referring to the period when the Mars compelled the supposed Zélé to sheer off: "The admiral hailed the Bellerophon, and desired her to keep her station a little on his weather bow." As it appears to us, the Brunswick, Bellerophon, and Royal Sovereign should have been represented nearly in line ahead, and the Triumph and Mars, from the latter's accidental fall to leeward, nearly in line abreast, and bearing on each quarter (as the Brunswick and Bellerophon are represented in the above plate on each bow) of the Royal Sovereign; who, in consequence, was able occasionally to fire from her stern-chasers between them.

Vice-admiral Cornwallis proceeded straight to Plymouth, with the intelligence of the fleet from which he had had so narrow an escape, and Vice-admiral Villaret Joyeuse made the best of his way back to Brest, to give an account of the disaster that had attended him. Just as the French fleet, having rounded the point of Penmarck, was about to enter the bay of Andierne, a violent gale of wind from the northward, that lasted 27 hours, separated the ships, and drove them for shelter to the anchorage of Belle-Isle.

Here all the ships assembled, and the fleet soon afterwards weighed, and made sail; when, on the 22nd of June, 3 h. 3 m. A.M., the British Channel fleet made its appearance in the north-west. This fleet, on account of the continued indisposition of Earl Howe, under the command of Lord Bridport, had sailed from Spithead on the same day that the French fleet had quitted Brest, and consisted of the

Gun-ship.

100	Royal George	Admiral (w.) Lord Bridport. Captain William Domett.
	Queen Charlotte	„ Sir Andrew Snape Douglas.
98	Queen	Vice-adm. (b.) Sir Alan Gardiner. Captain William Bedford.
	London	Vice-adm. (b.) John Colpoys. Captain Edward Griffith.
	Prince of Wales	Rear-adm. (r.) Henry Harvey. Captain John Bazely.

Gun-ship.		
98	Prince.	Captain Charles Powell Hamilton.
	Barfleur	,, James Richard Dacres.
	Prince George.	,, William Edge.
80	Sans-Pareil	{ Rear-adm. (r.) Lord Hugh Seymour. Captain William Browell.
74	Valiant	,, Christopher Parker.
	Orion	,, Sir James Saumarez.
	Irresistible	,, Richard Grindall.
	Russel	,, Thomas Larcom.
	Colossus	,, John Monkton.

Frigates, Révolutionnaire, Thalia, Nymphe, Aquilon, Astrea, and 20-gun ship Babet; Mægera and Incendiary fireships, Charon hospital-ship, and Argus and Dolly luggers.

The object of the departure of the Channel fleet appears to have been to give protection to an expedition under the command of Commodore Sir John Borlase Warren, in the 40-gun frigate Pomone, bound to Quiberon bay; and of which expedition we shall presently say more. Lord Bridport continued in company with Sir John Warren and his charge until the 19th; when, being near Belle-Isle, and the wind blowing fair for Quiberon, the admiral, with the Channel fleet, stood out from the coast, in order to keep an offing and be ready to receive the Brest fleet, should the latter quit port (its departure being then unknown) and attempt to molest the expedition.

The Arethusa, Sir John's advanced frigate, just as she had made the land of Belle-Isle, descried the fleet of M. Villaret coming from under it, and immediately made the signal for "16 sail of the line and 10 frigates." The squadron and transports thereupon altered their course, so as to avoid the French fleet, and Sir John despatched a fast-sailing vessel with the intelligence to Lord Bridport.

Either the expedition was not seen by the Brest fleet, or was considered to be the Channel fleet, and of superior force. At all events, M. Villaret missed a very fine opportunity of benefiting his country; and early on the next morning, the 20th, Sir John Warren came in sight of Lord Bridport. The latter, meanwhile, had despatched a lugger to Sir John, with directions to send to him his three line-of-battle ships, the Robust and Thunderer 74s, Captains Edward Thornborough and Albemarle Bertie, and the Standard 64, Captain Joseph Ellison, in order that the British fleet might be more upon an equality with the French fleet, according to the account of its numbers, as first represented by the Arethusa, and since communicated to the admiral by the commodore's despatch-vessel.

Lord Bridport, with his 14 sail of the line exclusive of the three in sight in the north-west and endeavouring to join him, kept between the expedition and the French fleet, composed, it will be recollected, of 12 sail of the line; but he was prevented, by a sudden change in the wind, from gaining a sight of the latter until 3 h. 30 m. A.M. on the 22nd, as has already been stated. At this time the British fleet was in latitude 47° 4' north, longitude 4° 16' west, Belle-Isle bearing east by north half-north, distant about 14 leagues, standing upon the starboard tack, with a light air of wind from about south by east.

Finding that the French admiral, by his manœuvres, had no intention to offer battle, Lord Bridport, at 6 h. 30 m. A.M., directed, by signal, the Sans-Pareil, Orion, Colossus, Irresistible, Valiant, and Russel, as being the best sailing ships, to chase; and at 6 h. 45 m. P.M. signalled the whole fleet to do the same. Every sail that could be carried on a wind was now set on all the ships; and at noon the centre of the French fleet, then standing in for the land, bore east-south-east, distant about 12 miles. During the afternoon it became nearly calm, but the little wind there was had drawn rather more aft.

At 7 P.M. the British admiral made the signal to harass the enemy's rear, and at 7 h. 25 m. P.M. to engage as the ships came up, and to take stations for mutual support. By sunset the British fleet, notwithstanding the unfavourable state of the weather, had advanced considerably upon that of the French. At about 10 h. 30 m. P.M. the ships were all taken aback, and soon afterwards it again fell nearly calm. At 3 A.M. on the 23rd, however, a fine light breeze sprang up from the south-west by south; and, with the daylight, appeared the French fleet, right ahead, all in a cluster, except three or four ships, the rearmost of which was a long way astern of her companions, and at no greater distance from the van of the British fleet than three miles.

At this time the British ships were very much scattered, and all astern of the Queen Charlotte, except the Irresistible, who was within hail on her larboard bow. The Queen Charlotte had attained this advanced, and for a three-decker rather extraordinary, station in the chase, by the nicest attention in trimming her sails, so as to meet the light and variable airs of the preceding night, and by constantly keeping her head in the direction of the enemy. The ships which, besides the Irresistible, were the nearest to the Queen Charlotte, were the Orion, Sans-Pareil, Colossus, and Russel.

At 4 A.M. the isle of Groix, or Belle-Isle, as the Royal George and one or two other British ships appear to have considered it, bore on the Queen Charlotte's lee bow, or nearly east, distant about eight miles. At 5 A.M. one of the French frigates took in tow the Alexandre, Captain François-Charles Guillemet; which ship, not having improved in the quality that had, in the preceding year, deprived the British navy of her services, was now the sternmost of M. Villaret's fleet. At a few minutes before 6 A.M. this ship, and one or two ahead of her, began firing their stern-chasers at the Irresistible. At 6 A.M. the latter opened her fire upon the Alexandre, whom the frigate, for her own safety, had by this time abandoned; and in a minute or two afterwards, the Orion commenced firing at the same ship.

At about 6 h. 15 m. A.M. the next ship ahead of the Alexandre, the Formidable, Captain Charles-Alexandre Durand-Linois, received the starboard guns of the Queen Charlotte, and immediately discharged her larboard guns in return. At 6 h. 30 m. A.M. the Formidable, at whom the Sans-Pareil had just commenced a cannonade, caught fire on the poop, and soon being, in hull, masts, rigging, and sails, very much cut up by the well-directed broadsides of two such antagonists, particularly of the Queen Charlotte (the Sans-Pareil having passed ahead in search of a better-conditioned opponent), dropped astern. Shortly afterwards, on her mizenmast falling over the side, the Formidable bore up and struck her colours.

The Colossus, Russel, London, and Queen, on the part of the British, and the Peuple, Mucius, Redoutable, Wattigny, and Nestor, on the part of the French, now participated more or less in the action. The remaining four French ships, the Zélé, Fougueux, Jean-Bart, and Droits de l'Homme, kept too far ahead to be engaged; and all the British ships, except the eight already named, notwithstanding the quantity of sail they carried, were far astern.

The rigging and sails of the Queen Charlotte soon exhibited proofs of the destructive fire which the French rear-ships had been pouring upon her, and she became in consequence quite unmanageable. At 7 h. 14 m. A.M., finding herself, as she dropped astern, annoyed very much by the fire of a ship on her larboard beam, the Queen Charlotte opened her broadside upon this antagonist, and at once compelled the Alexandre, already in a very crippled state from the gallant resistance she had previously made, to haul down her colours. As the Queen

Charlotte had edged away to close the Alexandre, the Tigre, Captain Jacques Bedout, with whom, as well as partially with the Peuple, the former had been engaged on the larboard side, ranged ahead, pursued and cannonaded by the Sans-Pareil. A freshening breeze from the south-south-east now brought up the Queen and London; and, on receiving their fire, the Tigre hauled down her colours.

At about 7 h. 57 m. A.M. the Royal George passed the Queen Charlotte on the starboard and weather side, as the latter lay repairing her damaged rigging. Having knotted her ropes in the best manner the time would allow, the Queen Charlotte hauled on board her fore and main tacks, to afford every possible assistance to the admiral. At 8 h. 15 m. Lord Bridport threw out a signal for the Colossus, who was about a mile and a half on the Queen Charlotte's weather bow, to discontinue the action; and, in five minutes afterwards, made the same signal to the Sans-Pareil, who was about a mile and a-half on the Queen Charlotte's lee bow, and then receiving a fire from the larboard quarter guns of the Peuple. The Royal George, when about half a mile from the west point of Isle-Groix, bore up and fired her starboard broadside into the stern and larboard quarter of the Peuple and her larboard broadside (not knowing that she had struck) into the starboard bow of the Tigre; who immediately bore up, and a second time made the signal of submission.

Immediately after she had done firing at the Tigre, which was about 8 h. 37 m. A.M., the Royal George wore round from the land and from the French fleet; and the other British ships followed the motions of their admiral. The Prince, Barfleur, and Prince George were now directed, by signal, to take in tow the prizes; and they and the fleet stood away to the south-west. The weathermost French ships, when Lord Bridport discontinued the action, did not, it appears, point higher than the mouth of the river Quimperlay, and could therefore have been weathered by the Royal George and the other fresh ships that were coming up. Finding himself thus unexpectedly relieved, the French admiral kept his wind, and, after making several tacks, sheltered his fleet between Isle-Groix and the entrance to the Lorient.

None of the British ships appear to have had any spars shot away; but the ships that were near enough to get into action suffered more or less damage in their masts, rigging, and sails. The fore and main masts of the Queen Charlotte, who, as we have seen, particularly distinguished herself, were badly wounded.

So were the main masts of the Sans Pareil and Irresistible; as well as the main yard of the latter and the foretopsail yard of the former.

Taking the ships in the order in which they appear to have been engaged, the Irresistible had three seamen killed, her captain, master (Thomas Troughton), and nine seamen and marines wounded; the Orion, six seamen and marines killed, and 18 wounded; the Queen Charlotte, four seamen killed, and one master's mate (David Coutts), one midshipman (Hornsby Charles), and 30 seamen, marines, and soldiers wounded; the Sans-Pareil, her second-lieutenant (Charles M. Stocker), second-lieutenant of marines (William Jephcott), and eight seamen and marines or soldiers killed, and, as far as the official returns show, only two midshipmen (Francis John Nott and Richard Spencer) wounded; the Colossus, five seamen, marines, and soldiers killed, and one lieutenant (Robert Mends), one midshipman (John Whyley), and 28 seamen, marines, and soldiers wounded; the Russel, three seamen killed, and Captain Bacon of the 118th regiment, and nine seamen, marines, and soldiers wounded; and the London and Royal George, one three, and the other seven seamen and marines wounded: total, 31 killed and 113 wounded.[1]

The three prizes were much shattered in their hulls, the Alexandre in particular. The loss sustained by the French ships, either separately or in the gross, has been omitted in the official account; but it otherwise appears that the three respectively lost as follows: Tigre, out of a complement, as deposed by her officers, of 726 men and boys, 130 in killed and wounded together; the Alexandre, out of a complement, owing to her greatly inferior size, of only 666, as many as 220; and the Formidable, out of a complement of 717, the still greater number of 320. Each ship's loss contained, doubtless, a large proportion of officers; but we are unable to particularize further than that the Formidable had three lieutenants killed; Captain Linois (in the eye), her second captain, and three (being

[1] The following statement shows the total numerical loss sustained by each of the eight ships that were fortunate enough to get into action:—

	killed	wounded
Irresistible	3	11
Orion	6	18
Queen Charlotte	4	32
Sans-Pareil	10	2
Colossus	5	30
Russel	3	10
London	0	3
Royal George	0	7
Total	31	113

the remainder of her) lieutenants wounded. Nor can the slightest doubt remain, that the officers and men of all three French ships conducted themselves in the bravest manner.

Had the whole of the ships on each side been able to engage, the opposing forces would have stood thus: British, 14 sail of the line (including eight three-deckers), five frigates; French, 12 sail of the line (including one three-decker), 11 frigates. Two of these frigates were superior in size, and nearly equal in force, to almost any two of Lord Bridport's 74s. Still the disparity here shown excuses M. Villaret for declining to engage.

With respect to three-decked ships of war, we may be allowed to remark that, unless of the first class in size and force, they are not so desirable in a fleet, particularly a chasing fleet, as first-class two-deckers. It is impossible to disguise their appearance, and their commanding height and three tiers of cannon frequently occasion an enemy, as in the case of the British 98s, for instance, to overrate their force and fly before them, a mode of escape seldom very difficult, owing to their usual slowness of sailing; whereas, a two-decked ship, like the Sans-Pareil, although larger every way but in height, and throwing full as heavy a broadside, is still only a two-decker, and is therefore permitted to approach until the enemy finds it too late to get beyond the reach of her guns.

As soon as M. Villaret had recovered from his surprise at the unaccountable forbearance of Lord Bridport, he called a council of his admirals on board the Proserpine frigate, in which his flag was flying, to consult with them upon the propriety of anchoring on the coast so as best to resist the attack which he still conjectured would be renewed against him, as soon as the British admiral had made the necessary arrangements for the purpose.

Rear-admirals Kerguelen and Bruix both assured Admiral Villaret, that, if he adopted the measure, the whole of his fleet would be lost; that the anchorage was very bad all along that coast; that his cables would be cut by the rocks; and that the British, having the weathergage, would cannonade his ships when they pleased, or probably send fireships to destroy them. These experienced officers advised the admiral to wait until the tide suited, and then enter the port of Lorient. Vice-admiral Villaret attended to these wise suggestions, and by 8 P.M. was at anchor in Lorient with the whole of his fleet except the three captured ships.

One of the two officers, to whom the preservation of the French fleet was thus owing, expresses himself very pointedly on the manner in which Lord Bridport had terminated the action of the morning. "Le combat cessa avant neuf heures du matin; nous étions à une demie-lieue de Groix, lorsque les ennemis levèrent la chasse. S'ils avaient bien manœuvré, ils auraient pu, ou prendre tous nos vaisseaux, ou les faire périr à la côte."[1] However, the affair was viewed differently in England, and Lord Bridport, Sir Alan Gardner, and Lord Hugh Seymour, three out of the five flag-officers present, received the thanks of parliament.

We are at a loss to discover the reason of this selection. If it was meant to include the flag-officers of the ships which had the good fortune to get into action, why was the London's flag-officer, Sir John Colpoys, omitted? This appears almost as extraordinary as that the accidental absence of Rear-admiral Sir Roger Curtis (he was attending Captain Molloy's court-martial at Portsmouth) should have occasioned the Queen Charlotte, who, under Captain Sir Andrew Snape Douglas, had distinguished herself beyond any ship in the fleet, not only to be unrewarded by the thanks of parliament, but, a much less pardonable omission, to be unmentioned in Lord Bridport's official despatch. The letter, indeed, is peculiarly meagre of thanks to any officers but those belonging to the Royal George; the very ship on board of which the signal was made that eventually saved the French fleet, or the greater part of it, from capture. Lord Bridport applies the term "fleet," properly enough, to the enemy's "12 sail of the line," but actually uses the diminutive term "squadron," when he refers to his own force; and that, too, with seeming propriety, as he names no more than 10 out of his 14 line-of-battle ships.

The French fleet being disposed of in the manner we have related, the expedition to Quiberon proceeded fearlessly to its destination; and Lord Bridport prepared to follow it as soon as he had despatched home the trophies of his victory. Of his three prizes, the Alexandre, or Alexander, as now again entitled to be called, was scarcely worth anything; but the Tigre and Formidable were fine new 74s, similar in size to the Impétueux and America, captured by Earl Howe. The Tigre was allowed to retain her name; but there being a Formidable 98 already in the service, the name of the Formidable 74, as if to perpetuate an acknowledged discreditable mistake, was changed to that of the island, close to which, instead of to Groix, the action was supposed to have been fought; and both the Belle-Isle and her

[1] Histoire des Evènemens &c par contr' amiral Kerguelen, p. 381.

classmate the Tigre, as British ships of war, we shall frequently have to name amidst the details that are to follow. We will now return to Sir John Warren's expedition; of the success of which, since Lord Bridport's affair especially, the most sanguine hopes were entertained.

On the 25th of June this famous expedition, consisting of the three line-of-battle ships already named, Robust, Thunderer, and Standard, also of the frigates Pomone, bearing Sir John's broad pendant, Anson, Artois, Arethusa, Concorde, and Galatea, and 50 sail of transports, with about 2500 French emigrants on board, commanded by the Comte de Puisaye, and assisted by the Comtes d'Hervilly and de Sombreuil, entered the bay of Quiberon, considered to be one of the finest on the coast of France for landing an army. It possesses a capacious and secure anchorage of nearly six miles in extent, beyond the reach of shot or shell, and is protected from westerly and south-west gales by the peninsula of Quiberon, the small but fruitful islands of Hoedic and Houat, and the Cardinal rocks.

On the 27th, at daybreak, the troops were landed near the village of Cramac, without the loss of a man; and without being opposed, except by about 200 republicans, who were driven back with some slaughter. Arms and ammunition for 16,000 royalists, who had joined the emigrants, were now landed from the ships; and the troops were cantoned among the inhabitants.

An attack on the peninsula of Quiberon having been projected, Sir John Warren disembarked 2000 royalists and 500 emigrants, together with 300 British marines. Fort Penthièvre, situated on a commanding eminence on the northern extremity of the peninsula, being invested on the other side by the Comte d'Hervilly, at the head of about 8000 royalists and emigrants, and having a garrison of only 600 men, surrendered. Stores and provisions were here landed in abundance; and the emigrants, royalists, and Chouans, fared sumptuously.

On the night of the 16th of July the Comte d'Hervilly, at the head of about 5000 men, including 200 British marines, made an unsuccessful attack on the right flank of General Hoche's army, strongly posted on the heights of St. Barbe. In this affair the comte, a brave and active officer, was badly wounded, and the emigrant troops were only enabled to make good their retreat to the fort in consequence of the unremitting fire kept up by five British launches, armed each with an 18 or 24 pounder carronade, and stationed close to the beach.

Desertion now daily thinned the royalist ranks, and treachery was at work in every quarter of the garrison. Matters continued growing worse until the night of the 20th, when, amidst the howling of the storm and the pelting of the rain, and amidst a darkness, too, as black as the deeds that were agitating, a party of emigrant soldiers who were on guard deserted, and quickly conducted back to the fort a large body of republican troops. In an instant all within was confusion. While the faithful were staining the ground with their blood, the timorous laid down their arms and joined the assailants in the cry of *Vive la république!* and the traitorous turned round and massacred their officers, and such of their comrades, too, as did not at once re-echo the republican war-whoop. About 1100 troops, led by Puisaye, hastened to the shore, and there awaited the return of daylight to escape to the shipping. Others, headed by the brave Sombreuil, resisted to the last, and finally obtained terms of capitulation.

In direct violation of those terms, however, the whole of the officers and men that had surrendered were marched as prisoners to Nantes. There, after being tried by a military tribunal, the young and amiable Comte de Sombreuil, the Bishop of Dol, and several other emigrants of distinction, were shot: the remainder, being chiefly privates, sought refuge in the ranks of the inhuman General le Moine.

Early on the morning (the 21st) succeeding the reduction of the fort, the British frigates, which on account of the gale and extreme darkness had been unable to approach the shore during the night, worked up to the south-east point of the peninsula, and there received on board, by means of the boats of the squadron, under the able direction of Captain Richard Goodwin Keats of the Galatea, the Comte de Puisaye and his 1100 troops, besides about 2400 royalist inhabitants; leaving behind, however, for the use of the republicans, 10,000 stands of arms, 150,000 pairs of shoes, and magazines and clothing for an army of 40,000 men.

To add to the mishaps of this ill-fated expedition, six transports that had arrived the evening previous to the disgraceful treachery at the fort, laden with rum, brandy, and provisions, fell also into the hands of the republicans. What was the extent of the loss in men sustained by the detachment of British marines that was landed does not appear to have been made public.

Sir John Warren next proceeded to the small islands oi

Hoedic and Houat, of which he took quiet possession. He afterwards disembarked near to Lorient, at their own request, 2000 of the Chouans brought from Quiberon. He also detached the Standard 64 and a frigate or two to summon the governor of Belle-Isle, which lies about five leagues to the westward, to deliver up the island for the use of Louis XVIII. Captain Ellison, to his very long letter on the subject, received from General Boucret a very laconic reply, the purport of which was, that, being well supplied with provisions and artillery, he, the general, was ready for the English fleet whenever it chose to come.

Sir John himself, in the meanwhile, having left a few frigates to keep the command of the anchorage at the islands of Hoedic and Houat, and cover, if necessary, the retreat of the garrisons, had proceeded to the island of Noirmoutier at the mouth of the Loire; but the republicans, who had recently dispossessed of that island the royalist General Charette, were too well prepared to warrant an attack by so inferior a force. After destroying two or three small armed vessels, the commodore contented himself with taking possession of Isle d'Yeu, a small island about five leagues to the southward of Noirmoutier.

In the beginning of October Sir John was joined at Isle d'Yeu by the 38-gun frigate Jason, Captain Charles Stirling, escorting a fleet of transports, containing 4000 British troops under the command of Major-general Doyle. On board of the Jason had also arrived the Comte d'Artois, the Duc de Bourbon, and several other French noblemen. The troops were landed on the island, along with a great quantity of military stores, clothing, and provisions; but no use was, or, in the desperate situation of the royalist cause, could be, made of this force. Accordingly, at the close of the year, Isle d'Yeu was evacuated, and the troops, after remaining in a state of inactivity for nearly three months, were re-embarked on board the transports and carried back to England.

Lord Bridport continued at sea hovering off the coast where the unfortunate Quiberon expedition was frittering away its strength, until the 20th September, when the admiral returned to Spithead with two or three of his ships, leaving Rear-admiral Harvey, with the remainder of the Channel fleet, to watch the motions of the French at Brest and Lorient. The ships in the latter port, having, as stated before, quitted Brest with only 15 days' provisions on board, had been compelled, owing to the poverty of the place, to discharge the principal part of their crews; disease and desertion had gradually thinned the remainder. Towards the end of the year, when the severity of the season obliged the blockading ships to keep farther in the offing, several of the ships at Lorient made an effort to escape from so ill-provided a port, and, by coasting it at favourable opportunities, contrived to reach Brest in safety: two or three others, we believe, shifted their quarters to Rochefort.

On the 17th and 18th of November the English Channel was visited by a westerly gale of such extraordinary violence, as scarcely to fall short of a West Indian hurricane. Rear-admiral Christian, with a squadron of eight sail of the line, having in charge a fleet of 200 transports and West Indiamen with upwards of 16,000 troops on board, was compelled to return to Spithead, after having had the ships of his convoy, with which he had quitted St. Helen's only a day or two before, scattered in every direction. Several of the transports and merchantmen foundered, and others went on shore and were wrecked. Above 200 dead bodies were taken up between Portland and Bridport. While the gale was at its height the shock of an earthquake was felt in several parts of the kingdom. The repairs of the squadron and remaining ships of the convoy made it the 5th of December before the rear-admiral could again put to sea; but the fleet was again separated in a dreadful storm, which continued for two or three weeks.

Among the ships that nearly became the grave of her crew in the first of these disasters was the late French three-decker Commerce-de-Marseille. Having been found so badly timbered and so greatly out of order as not to be worth the cost of a thorough repair, she remained at anchor at Spithead until the autumn of the present year; she then underwent a partial repair and was armed and equipped for sea. Shortly afterwards, however, the guns on her first and second decks were sent on shore again, and the ports caulked up; and, fitted as a storeship, the Commerce-de-Marseille, drawing at the time 29 feet water, formed part of Rear-admiral Christian's expedition to the West Indies. In the gale, the partial effects of which we have just described, this castle of a store-ship was driven back to Portsmouth; and, from the rickety state of her upper works, and the great weight of her lading, it was considered a miracle that she escaped foundering. The Commerce-de-Marseille relanded her immense cargo, and never went out of harbour again; but the ship was not taken to pieces, and consequently remained on the lists of the navy until the month of August, 1802.

On the 16th of January, while the British Mediterranean fleet of 15 sail of the line and frigates, still under the command of Vice-admiral Hotham, was riding at anchor in San Fiorenzo bay (island of Corsica), in a heavy cross swell, the effect of a recent gale of wind, the 74-gun ship Berwick, Captain William Smith, then under refit, with her lower masts stripped of their rigging, rolled all three over the side. The captain, first-lieutenant, and master were immediately tried by a court-martial; and it appearing that the proper precaution had not been taken in securing the masts, all three officers were dismissed the ship. Having appointed Captain Adam Littlejohn to command the Berwick, and directed him to follow as soon as he had rigged his ship with jury-masts, Vice-admiral Hotham made sail for Leghorn road, a step, we must be permitted to pronounce, not quite so prudent as if the vice-admiral had deferred his departure until the disabled ship was able to accompany the fleet; a delay which, considering that it was only necessary to place the Berwick in a state to be taken in tow, could not, with the accustomed alacrity of British seamen, have extended much beyond the period of a day.

By great exertions during the winter in repairing the old ships and in expediting the new 74, the Barras, left on the stocks by the British at their evacuation of the port in December, 1793, the French in Toulon got ready for sea, by the latter end of February, the following fifteen sail of the line:—

Gun-ship.		Gun-ship.		Gun-ship.	
120	Sans-Culotte.		Barras.		Guerrier.
	Ca-Ira.		Censeur.		Heureux.
80	Tonnant.	74	Conquérant.	74	Mercure.
	Victoire.		Duquesne.		Peuple-Souverain.
74	Alcide.		Généreux.		Timoléon.

Frigates, Minerve, Alceste, Artémise, Courageuse, Friponne, and Vestale, and two brig-corvettes.

With the four first-named frigates and the two 28-gun frigates Badine and Brune, chef de division Perrée, had on the 7th of January returned from a very successful cruise in the Mediterranean. He is represented to have captured a frigate (not from the British, certainly) and two corvettes, forming a part of those taken from Toulon (untrue: the Scout and Speedy brigs were the only British "corvettes" captured in the Mediterranean in the year 1794), also 25 merchant vessels richly laden, and to have brought into port as many as 600 prisoners.

As soon as intelligence reached Toulon that the British fleet had quitted the shores of Corsica and retired to the road of Leghorn, the utmost exertions were made to get ready the long-meditated expedition for attempting the recovery of that island. The troops, about 5000 in number, being at length embarked in due proportions on board the different ships. On board the Sans-Culotte there was embarked what in those days was considered the necessary appendage to a French fleet, a spy or deputy from the National Convention, and Rear-admiral Martin on the 3rd of March weighed and put to sea with his 15 sail of the line and six frigates. On the 7th at daybreak, after a succession of north-easterly gales, which had partially dismasted two of the ships, the fleet gained a sight of the island to which it was bound. At 7 A.M., when within five leagues of Cape Corse, the advanced frigates discovered to leeward, standing out of the Bay of San-Fiorenzo, where she had been detained by foul winds until the preceding morning, the jury-rigged Berwick, making the best of her way to Leghorn.

All sail was immediately set, on the part of the French, for pursuit, and the moment Captain Littlejohn, by the usual mode of signalling, had ascertained that the strange fleet was not, what by its colours it purported to be, Spanish, he used every means to effect his escape. The crippled state of the Berwick greatly retarded her progress; and at 11 A.M., when close off Cape Corse, the Alceste frigate, Captain Lejoille, passed to leeward, under Spanish colours, but changed them to French as she opened her fire, within musket-shot, on the 74's lee bow. The Minerve and Vestale presently took their stations on the Berwick's quarter; and it was not long, according to the British account, before one or two of the headmost line-of-battle ships joined in the carronade.

In the hope that Vice-admiral Hotham's fleet might have put to sea, the Berwick kept a steady course for Leghorn; but, before noon, her rigging was cut to pieces, and every sail in ribands. Just as the Berwick had punished the temerity of the Alceste by a broadside that is represented to have disabled her, a bar-shot took off Captain Littlejohn's head. The command then devolved upon Lieutenant Nesbit Palmer; who, considering all further resistance useless, and having, it is said, obtained the concurrence of his officers, ordered the Berwick's colours to be struck.

On board the Berwick four seamen were wounded, but the captain was the only person killed. So small a loss was attributed to the high firing of the French; who, making sure of the Berwick's capture, and wanting such a ship entire in their fleet, were wise enough to do as little injury as possible to her hull. The Alceste lost, by the Berwick's fire, her captain, another officer, and six seamen wounded, but none killed. It does not appear that the two other frigates sustained any loss. According to the French accounts, the three frigates were all that engaged the Berwick, and the action continued from first to last very little more than a quarter of an hour.

The Berwick's officers and crew were distributed among the different ships, without being allowed to take any clothes except those on their backs, and were, in every other respect, most shamefully treated. On their subsequent enlargement and return home, they were tried by a court-martial for the loss of their ship, and honourably acquitted.

On the 8th Vice-admiral Hotham, who with the British fleet composed of the

Gun-ship.		
100	Britannia	Vice-adm. (r.) William Hotham, Captain John Holloway,
98	Princess Royal	Vice-adm. (w.) Sam. Cranst. Goodall, Captain John Child Purvis,
	St. George	Vice-adm. (b.) Sir Hyde Parker, Captain Thomas Foley,
	Windsor Castle	Rear-adm. (r.) Robert Linzee, Captain John Gore,
74	Tancredi	,, Chevalier Caraccioji, *Neapolitan*,
	Captain	,, Samuel Reeve,
	Fortitude	,, William Young,
	Illustrious	,, Thomas Lennox Frederick,
	Terrible	,, George Campbell,
	Courageux	,, Augustus Montgomery,
	Bedford	,, Davidge Gould,
64	Agamemnon	,, Horatio Nelson,
	Diadem	,, Charles Tyler,

Frigates, Pilade and Minerva, *Neapolitan*, and Inconstant, Lowestoffe, Meleager, and Romulus, also two sloops, and one cutter, *British*,

was lying in Leghorn roads, received intelligence, by express from Genoa, that the French fleet, composed of fifteen sail of the line, besides frigates, had two days before been seen off the islands of Sainte-Marguerite. Shortly afterwards the British ship-sloop Moselle appeared in the offing, with the signal for a fleet in the north-west; which fleet, according to the report of the Moselle when she entered the road, was steering to the southward. The British fleet instantly unmoored; and at daybreak on the following day, the 9th, weighed and put to sea with a strong breeze from the east-north-east.

Having no doubt that the strange fleet was from Toulon, and judging, from its alleged course when seen by the Moselle on the 6th, its destination to be Corsica, Vice-admiral Hotham shaped his course for that island; having previously despatched the Tarleton brig to San-Fiorenzo, with orders for the Berwick to join him off Cape Corse. In the course of the night the brig returned to the fleet, with the unwelcome intelligence of the Berwick's capture; and, as we conjecture, with some information that led the vice-admiral to steer to the north-west, instead of towards Corsica as he had at first intended. This alteration in the course soon began to show its beneficial effects; for on the very next day, the 10th, the advanced British frigates gained a distant sight of the French fleet, standing towards the land in the direction of Cape Noli; that is, working its way back to Toulon against a south-west wind, to avoid an encounter with the British fleet, which, the Berwick's people had doubtless informed the French admiral and deputy, was likely to have put to sea from Leghorn road. Yet the "committee of public safety," in its report to the National Convention, insisted that the only object (it being the policy of the French government to conceal the intended attack upon Corsica) of the fleet's sailing was, "to seek the enemy, fight the English wherever they could be found, drive them out of the Mediterranean, and restore for that sea a free navigation."

On the 11th, in the afternoon, the French fleet, counted at 15 sail of the line, six frigates, and two brigs, was descried in the south or windward quarter by the Princess Royal and several ships then near her, and which ships were distant between five and six miles from their main body. On the 12th, at daylight, the French fleet again made its appearance, and presently bore up as if to reconnoitre. On arriving within about three miles of the Princess Royal, the French van-ship hauled to the wind on the larboard tack, and was followed, in succession, by her companions astern. At this time, owing to the lightness of the wind and a heavy swell from the westward, none of the ships could make much progress. Towards evening, however, a fresh breeze sprung up from the south-west, and the British ships took advantage of it to close each other and form in order of battle, with their heads to the westward. At sunset the extremes of the French fleet bore from the British van west and south-west by south.

During the night, which was very squally, the French 74 Mercure carried away her maintopmast, and was permitted to part company, attended by a frigate. Subsequently the two ships reached in safety the anchorage in Gourjean bay, and found lying there the prize-ship Berwick, attended also by a frigate, and then on her way to Toulon to get refitted.

On the 13th, at daylight, or soon after, the French admiral evincing no intention of bearing down to engage, Vice-admiral Hotham threw out the signal for a general chase, which was promptly complied with, the wind at this time blowing very fresh, attended with frequent squalls. At 8 A.M. the French 80-gun ship Ca-Ira, the third ship from the rear, accidentally ran foul of her second ahead, the Victoire, also of 80 guns, and, besides doing some damage to the latter, carried away her own fore and main topmasts.

So fine an opportunity was not lost upon Captain Thomas Francis Freemantle, then, with the 36-gun frigate Inconstant, far advanced in the chase. At about 9 A.M. this frigate, ranging up within musket-shot on the larboard quarter of the French 80, gave her a broadside and stood on. The French frigate Vestale presently bore down, and, after firing several distant broadsides at the Inconstant as she ran by her, took the Ca Ira in tow. Having tacked, the Inconstant again passed under the lee of the two-decker, and fired into her. The latter, however, having by this time cleared the wreck of her topmasts from her larboard side, opened a heavy fire from her lowerdeck guns; which killed three, and wounded 14, of the Inconstant's men. One of the shots, a 36-pounder, struck the frigate between wind and water, and compelled her to bear up.

At 10 h. 45 m. A.M. the Agamemnon got upon the quarter of the Ca-Ira, still in tow by the Vestale, and, aided for a short time by the Captain, continued a distant engagement with the crippled 80, until about 2 h. 15 m. P.M.; when, several of the French ships bearing down to the protection of their disabled companion, the Agamemnon ceased firing, and dropped into her station in the line. In the mean time a partial firing had been kept up, by the Bedford and Egmont on one side, and, on the other, by the three rearmost French ships, one of which was the Timoléon of 74, and another the Sans-Culotte of 120 guns; but the action terminated, for that day, after the Agamemnon had bore up.

Rear-admiral Martin and Deputy Letourneur, who, for the alleged purpose of better directing the manœuvres of the fleet, had removed from the regular flag-ship, the Sans-Culotte, to the frigate Friponne, not considering, probably, their one three, and 13 two deckers able to cope with Vice-admiral Hotham's four three, and 11 two deckers, put about on the larboard tack, and kept close to the wind, which now blew moderately from the south-south-east, under all sail, followed by the British fleet on the larboard line of bearing, as fast as four or five heavy working ships would permit. By some accident, or, as the French accounts allege, by some mismanagement on her part, the Sans-Culotte, in the course of the night, separated from her companions. The French were thus left without a single three-decked ship in their fleet, to oppose to the four plainly visible in the fleet that was chasing them.

On the 14th, at daybreak, Genoa bearing north-east, distant about seven leagues, the French fleet was again descried to the westward, standing as before, on the larboard tack, with a moderate breeze from the southward. During the night the Vestale had given up the charge of the Ca-Ira to the Censeur 74; and the latter, with her dismasted companion in tow, was a considerable distance astern and to leeward of the French line.

At about 5 h. 30 m. A.M. a breeze sprang up from the northwest, which brought the British fleet to windward. At 6 h. 30 m. A.M. the Captain and Bedford, having been ordered by signal, stood for and engaged the two separated French ships; both of whom opened their fire as the two British 74s bore down to attack them.

Being some distance ahead of the Bedford, the Captain had to sustain the united broadsides of the French 80 and 74 for the space of 15 minutes ere she was in a situation to return a shot with effect. The consequence was that, when the firing, including that period, had lasted one hour and 20 minutes, the Captain had all her sails cut to pieces, her fore and main stay, topmast stays, three fourths of the shrouds, and all the running rigging, shot away, her fore and mizen yards, and fore and main topmasts, disabled, some shot in the mainmast, and several in the hull, a lowerdeck gun split, several carriages broken, and all her boats rendered unserviceable. Being thus reduced to an unmanageable state, the Captain made a signal for assistance, and was towed clear of her opponents.

The Bedford, also, having had her standing and running rigging and sails much cut, her foremast, fore-yard, bowsprit, maintopsail yard, and mizen topmast shot through, and the poles of the fore and main topgallantmasts shot entirely away, was equally obliged to discontinue the engagement and suffer herself to be towed out of the line.

In this smart affair with the Ca-Ira and Censeur, the Captain had three men killed, her first-lieutenant (Wilson Rathbone), master (William Hunter), and seven seamen wounded, two of them mortally; and the Bedford had six seamen and one marine killed, her first-lieutenant (Thomas Miles), 14 seamen, and three marines wounded. The two French ships also suffered considerably in hull, masts, and men, and were both reduced to nearly a defenceless state.

Since the beginning of this partial engagement with his rear, the French admiral had made a signal for the fleet to wear in succession and form the line upon his van-ship, the Duquesne; intending to pass, on the starboard tack, to leeward of the British line then on the contrary tack, and to windward of the Ca-Ira and Censeur, so as to cover the latter from the fire of the Illustrious and Courageux, who, having made sail to support the Captain and Bedford, were now far ahead and rather to leeward of their line.

Owing to the lightness of the wind, the Duquesne was some time in coming round on the starboard tack. It was about this time, when almost every ship in the two fleets was in an ungovernable state for the want of wind, that the Lowestoffe found herself lying with her starboard quarter and stern exposed, at a long-gun range, to the larboard broadside of the Duquesne; who, opening her lowerdeck ports, commenced a fire upon the British frigate. Not being in a position to discharge a gun in return, Captain Hallowell judiciously ordered all his crew, except the officers and the man at the wheel, to go below; so that, when the large and beautiful Neapolitan frigate Minerva, as she drifted near to the Duquesne, took off the attention of the French crew from the Lowestoffe, the latter had not a man hurt: her stern and sails, however, were a good deal cut, by the 74's shot. At length the Duquesne got round on the starboard tack, and then, instead of leading her line, as she had been ordered by the signal, to leeward, the French 74 passed to windward, of the British van-ships.

At 8 A.M. the Illustrious began, within about 600 yards, to engage the Duquesne and Victoire in succession, when a third ship, the Tonnant, joined against her; and with the three French ships, two of which were 80s, the Illustrious and Courageux kept up a warm cannonade. At 9 A.M. the foretopmast of the Illustrious went over the starboard bow; and at 9 h. 15 m.

A.M. her mainmast fell aft on the poop, carrying away the mizenmast, and breaking the beams of the poop deck. Her foremast and bowsprit were also dangerously wounded, and her hull pierced with shot in every direction. The Courageux, also, had her main and mizen masts shot away, and her hull much shattered.

The three French ships, at length, passing ahead, and, in consequence of the calm state of the weather, not being closely followed by the remainder of their line, the Illustrious and Courageux were fortunate enough (their friends having, in like manner, been retarded by the want of wind) to be no longer assailed by a force, the decided superiority of which must soon either have sunk or subdued them; as, coupled with their damages, the following account of their loss will testify:—The Illustrious had 15 seamen and five marines killed, one midshipman (Mr. Moore), 68 seamen, and one marine wounded; the Courageux, one midshipman (Mr. Coleman), eight seamen, and six marines killed; her master (Mr. Blackburn), 21 seamen, and 11 marines wounded.

The Duquesne, Victoire, and Tonnant, after exchanging a few shots with the British ships astern of their two crippled opponents, abandoned the Ca-Ira and Censeur to their fate, and, followed by the ships astern, which a light air of wind was now bringing up, stood away to the westward under all sail. The firing, which, as we have shown, had commenced at 6 h. 20 m. A.M., ceased altogether about 2 P.M.; at which time Vice-admiral Hotham, considering that his van-ships were not in a condition to renew the action, and still impressed, we suppose, with the idea that the French fleet consisted of 15 sail of the line, did not tack in pursuit: hence, the two fleets, steering in opposite directions, were soon so far separated as to be mutually out of sight.

None of the British ships sustained any damage or loss equal in extent to the Captain, Bedford, Illustrious, and Courageux; and the greater part of the Egmont's loss, which, except that of the Windsor Castle, was the most severe of any suffered by the remaining British ships, arose from the bursting of one of her lowerdeck guns. The Neapolitan 74 Tancredi received several shots between wind and water, and had her foremast injured: her loss amounted to one killed and five wounded. The frigate Minerva, belonging to the same power, was struck by three of the Ca-Ira's shots: one entered the cabin-window, and wounded four men, the only loss the frigate suffered; another lodged in the counter between wind and water; and the third cut away a considerable quantity of lower rigging.

The Windsor Castle had six seamen killed, one lieutenant (Thomas Hawker), and 30 seamen and marines wounded; Egmont, seven killed and 21 wounded; Saint George, four killed and 13, including Lieutenant Robert Honeyman, wounded; Princess Royal, three killed and eight wounded; Diadem, three killed and seven wounded; Britannia, one killed and 18 wounded; Fortitude, one killed and four wounded; Terrible, six, and Agamemnon, 13, including her master, John Wilson, wounded: making, with the loss of the Inconstant, Captain, Bedford, Illustrious, Courageux, Tancredi, and Minerva frigate, already given, a total of 74 killed, and 284 wounded.[1]

Of the French ships, the Ca-Ira and Censeur made a most gallant resistance; not surrendering until the latter had her mainmast, and the former (from the first, as we have seen, without topmasts) her fore and main masts shot away. Their captains, Jean-Félix Benoît, and Louis-Marie Coudé, merited every praise; and so did their officers and crews. Having, in addition to their regular complements, a quantity of troops on board, the united loss of these ships in the action was about 400 men. The Duquesne, Victoire, Tonnant, and Timoléon, also

---

[1] The following statement will exhibit the separate loss of each ship, and other particulars, including the order of battle, as laid down in the official letter:—

Division.	Squadron.	Ships of the Line.	Tons.	Men and Boys.	K.	W.
Starboard or Weather.	Van.	Captain	1639	584	3	19
		Bedford	1605	584	7	18
		Tancredi (Neapolitan)	1800	600	1	5
		Princess Royal (flag)	1973	753	3	8
		Agamemnon	1384	485	0	13
		Illustrious	1616	584	20	70
		Courageux	1721	634	15	33
	Centre.	Britannia (flag)	2091	850	1	18
		Egmont	1643	584	7	21
Larboard or Lee.		Windsor Castle (flag)	1874	746	6	31
		Diadem	1376	485	3	7
	Rear.	Saint George (flag)	1950	753	4	13
		Terrible	1678	584	0	6
		Fortitude	1645	584	1	4
			23996	8810		
		Frigates.				
		Inconstant	...	267	3	
		Minerva	...	...	0	

sustained some loss, particularly the second and last ships; but we are unable to specify its amount. Much damage was likewise done to the Timoléon and Victoire, to the latter in particular; and the credit of inflicting it, as well as what the Tonnant and Duquesne may have suffered, belonged almost exclusively to the Illustrious and Courageux.

This not being an action of a very decisive or important nature, it will be unnecessary to enter minutely into the force on either side. A general view, however, may be desirable, and that we can readily present. None of the British ships appearing to have been ordered any carronades, their long-gun force, as specified in the First Annual Abstract, will suffice. With respect to the Neapolitan 74 Tancredi, we shall consider her to have been armed with the same nominal calibers, as the French 74, No. 4, in the table at p. 59; and, in reducing the weight into English pounds, shall apply the rule (see p. 48) laid down for Spanish guns. Hence, the Tancredi's broadside weight of shot will be 849 pounds English: her number of tons we shall consider to be 1800. The Britannia mounted 42-pounders on her lower deck: her broadside weight of metal consequently amounts to 280 pounds more than what stands as the force of her class at E in the First Annual Abstract.

The French Toulon ships do not appear to have mounted, as yet, any carronades. Their force is therefore readily obtained by a reference to the establishment of each class, as shown in the small table to which we have before referred. The French fleet, in this instance, had troops on board, in number, according to the British official account, 4220. As, however, the principal officers of the Ca-Ira and Censeur swore, on their examination in the prize-court, that the total number of persons on board their respective ships, at the commencement of the action, amounted, instead of, as in the official account, 1300 for each ship of 80, and 1000 for each ship of 74 guns, in the Ca-Ira to 1060, and in the Censeur to 921, the probability is, that the troops did not much exceed 3400; and there can be no doubt that the French naval officers, on going into action, wished the troops and the baggage out of the ships. It will be to the advantage of the British not to notice the troops at all, but to consider the French ships as having had on board their full complements of men, and no more. These complements appear also to be overrated in the British admiral's letter: the establishment of a French 120 is, in round numbers, 1100 men, of an 80, 840 men, and of a 74, 700 men; and not 1200, 950, and 730.

The tonnages of the French ships may be stated, at 2600 for the 120, an estimate that makes her 147 tons less than her reputed sister-ship, the Commerce-de-Marseille; at 2210 tons, as the actual measurement of one, and a moderate average for another 80; at 2281, as the actual measurement of the third 80; and at 19,711 tons, for the eleven 74s, part of them by actual measurement, the remainder upon a fair average. These points settled, the following statement will exhibit a tolerably correct view of the

Comparative Force of the Two Fleets.

		BRITISH. March. 12, 13, & 14.	FRENCH. March. 12.	FRENCH. March. 13.	FRENCH. March. 14.
Ships	No.	14	15	14	13
Broadside-guns	No.	557	587	550	490
	lbs.	12711	14587	13680	12307
Crews	Agg. No.	8810	11320	10620	9520
Size	,, tons	23996	29012	27212	24612

Those who recollect the boasting of the French Republic, at this particular time, may be surprised that Rear-admiral Martin and M. Deputy Letourneur did not bear down to engage on the first day, whatever they may have done on the second, when the French had lost one ship by parting company, and another, it may be said, by getting dismasted; or, on the third day, when they had lost the weather-gage, and a third ship, by far the most powerful in the fleet.

It may here be remarked, that, according to a list in the British official account, the Sans-Culotte and Mercure were both present on the 14th of March; yet not only are the French accounts clear on that point, but no notice is taken in the log of any one of the British ships of the sight of an enemy's three-decked ship after the evening of the 13th. Yet a periodical naval work of some notoriety contains the following statement: "The Sans-Culotte was so severely handled by him (Captain Frederick of the Courageux) and others, that it was the principal cause of her quitting her own fleet, and (she) with difficulty reached Genoa, during a heavy gale that succeeded the action.[1]

To enumerate the instances of want of precision discoverable in Vice-admiral Hotham's letter would be to enter again into

[1] Naval Chronicle, vol. xxxvii., p. 354.

the details of an action of which enough has already appeared. Suffice it, that one English writer, finding nothing but confusion in the gazette account, and not knowing, seemingly, where else to search for particulars, has drawn up a very brief, but not the less obscure account of the battle; and another writer, although obliged to confess himself unable to comprehend on which tack either fleet was formed, has persisted in giving three sets of figures descriptive of the evolutions of the two.[1]

The French naval writers, very naturally, lay all the blame of what befel their fleet to the conventional deputy who was on board of it; and one writer makes M. Letourneur's surname "de la Manche," or "of the Channel," the butt of his wit, in saying, that it "appeared to be a pledge of knowledge in the direction of a fleet, but now seems only to denote a countryman of the hero of Cervantes."[2] One thing is clear, that there was no landman to control the movements of the British fleet; and yet who, from a review of all the circumstances, will say that the commander-in-chief of it did all that was practicable? However, the capture of two line-of-battle ships, and the superiority of force against the British in the statement at the foot of the gazette letter, occasioned Vice admiral Hotham's action off Genoa to rank, in public opinion, as a sort of second-rate victory.

Taking in tow his dismasted ships, including the two prizes, the British admiral bore away for Spezia bay. On the night of the 17th the Illustrious, and the Meleager frigate that had her in tow, separated from the fleet in a violent gale of wind from the south-east. Shortly afterwards the hawser parted, and being unable, on account of the heavy sea and increasing gale, to send a fresh tow-rope to the frigate, the Illustrious hove to. The ship now laboured very much, and shipped a great deal of water through the lowerdeck ports, many of the lids of which had been damaged or destroyed in the action: her jury mizen-mast also went by the board, and most of her sails blew to pieces. At daylight on the 18th land was seen ahead, but it could not be made out. To avoid the threatened danger, the two ships put their head to the eastward, which brought them on the starboard tack.

---

[1] Ekins's Naval Battles, p. 196 and plate.

[2] "La convention nomma à ce poste Letourneur *de la Manche*, dont le surnom parut un gage de science dans la direction d'une armée navale, et semble aujourd'hui ne désigner qu'un compatriote du héros de Cervantes."—*Principes Organiques de la Marine Militaire, et Causes de sa Décadence dans la dernière Guerre*, par Pinière.

At about noon the Meleager parted company; and at 1 h. 30 m. P.M. the third gun from forward on the larboard side of the lower deck of the Illustrious went off, from the friction of the shot in the gun, blew off the port-lid, and carried away the upper port-sill. Unable to continue on this tack, owing to the rush of water through the open port, or to put about on the other on account of the proximity of breakers in that direction, the Illustrious wore until the port was secured, and then, hauling up again, as well as the want of aftersail would permit, and laid up north.

At about 2 P.M. the Illustrious made the land to the eastward of the gulf of Spezia, and at 2 h. 30 m., Captain Frederick gave charge of the ship to a man on board, who declared himself a pilot for that part of the coast, and promised to anchor the Illustrious in safety. At 7 h. 30 m. P.M., shoaling the water unexpectedly, Captain Frederick ordered the anchor to be let go, and veered to a whole cable : the ship was then in Valence bay, situated between Spezia and Leghorn. Just as this was done, the Illustrious struck the ground abaft, and the cable by which she had till then been held, and another employed to supply its place, parted successively. The previously damaged state of the stocks of the sheet and spare anchors rendering it impossible to let go a third anchor, the ship paid round off inshore, and, although the wind had moderated since 6 P.M., the sea made a fair breach over her. At 10 P.M. it began to blow hard from the west-south-west, and at 10 h. 30 m. P.M., owing to the heavy shocks which the ship received, the rudder was carried away.

Soon after daylight on the 19th attempts were made to get a hawser on shore, then only half a mile distant, with the view of saving the people by a raft, but without success. In the evening the brig-sloop Tarleton, Captain Charles Brisbane, arrived, and anchored near the wreck, but the weather would not admit the passage of boats. On the 20th, in the morning, the Lowestoffe frigate, Captain Benjamin Hallowell, arrived; and shortly afterwards the Romulus, Captain George Hope, together with the launches of the British fleet, then at anchor in Spezia bay. At length, the crew and principal part of the stores having been removed to the vessels in company, the hull of the Illustrious was set on fire and destroyed.

On the 25th, after some partial repairs done to the disabled ships, the fleet weighed from Spezia bay, and on the 26th cast anchor in the bay of San-Fiorenzo. Here the British fleet lay refitting until the 18th of April; when Admiral Hotham (promoted on the 16th to be admiral of the blue), leaving behind the two prizes, to one of which, the Ca-Ira, Captain Henry Dudley Pater had been appointed, and to the other, the Censeur, Captain John Gore, proceeded to Leghorn, and on the 27th anchored with his fleet in the road.

The French, after their disaster, proceeded straight to the bay of Hyères, where the fleet was soon afterwards joined by the Mercure and Berwick from Gourjean bay, and on the 23rd by the Sans-Culotte from Genoa; which port the French three-decker had entered on the morning of the 16th, after having been chased by five ships of war, supposed to be British, but in all probability Spanish. The French admiral despatched the Victoire, Timoléon, and Berwick, and the frigates Alceste and Minerve, to Toulon, to get repaired, and, with his fleet, now reduced to 11 sail of the line and about four frigates, remained at anchor in Hyères bay.

On the 4th of April Rear-admiral Renaudin, whose departure from Brest we formerly noticed, anchored in Toulon road with the 80-gun ship Formidable, 74s Jupiter, Mont Blanc, Jemmappes, Révolution, and Tyrannicide, frigates Embuscade, Félicité, and another, and two or three corvettes. This squadron was a great acquisition to Vice-admiral Martin (promoted to that rank on the 22nd of March); as, not only were the ships, except perhaps the Formidable recently launched at Lorient, prime sailers, but, among the captains in command of them were the two enterprising officers, Richery and Ganteaume. We are in doubt whether Rear-admiral Jean Louis Delmotte, and chef de division Villeneuve, arrived with this reinforcement, or had previously belonged to Vice-admiral Martin's force, now augmented, without reckoning the three ships ordered for repair, to 17 sail of the line.

About the time that Rear admiral Renaudin arrived, Vice-admiral Martin removed from Hyères bay to the road of Toulon; where, some time in May, a spirit of disaffection broke out among the crews of the Toulon ships, but not, it appears, among those from Brest. The latter were moored across the entrance of the road, to defend the harbour and shipping from any attempt that might be made upon them by the British; but such precautions were unnecessary, the British fleet lying inactive at Leghorn. At length, by the great exertions of the new conventional deputy M. Niou, a man either belonging or that had belonged to the navy, order was restored in the fleet, and the seamen pledged themselves, in the most solemn manner, "to wash their crime in the blood of the enemies of the republic."

To keep alive this laudable feeling and profit by its effects, Vice-admiral Martin, or rather, as the French accounts say, M. deputy Niou, on the 7th of June, put to sea with the fleet, consisting, as already mentioned, of 17 sail of the line (one 120, two 80s, remainder 74s), besides six frigates and two or three corvettes.

On the 8th of May the British fleet sailed from Leghorn on a cruise off Cape Mola, the south-west extremity of the island of Minorca; and on the 14th of June, while close to the cape, was joined by a squadron of nine sail of the line, under Rear-admiral Mann, from Gibraltar and England. Admiral Hotham continued cruising off Minorca until the morning of the 24th; then bore up and made sail to the eastward, and on the 29th, in the afternoon, anchored in the bay of San-Fiorenzo.

On the 4th of July Admiral Hotham detached Commodore Nelson, with the Agamemnon 64, Meleager frigate, 20-gun ship Ariadne, Moselle sloop, and Mutine cutter, with directions to proceed, in the first instance, off Genoa, and then cruise along the coast to the westward. On the 7th, at 4 p.m., Cape del Melle bearing north by west, distant six or seven leagues, the Agamemnon discovered the Toulon fleet, about five leagues off in the north-west. In the evening the French fleet went in chase; and, during the night, some of the leading ships came fast up with the Moselle. On the 8th, at 7 h. 20 m. a.m., Cape Corse bearing south-east by south, distant five leagues, the Agamemnon began firing guns as signals to the fleet in San-Fiorenzo bay; and at 9 h. 30 m. a.m., the French ships discovering the British fleet of 22 sail of the line and several frigates, at anchor, left off chase and turned their heads to the westward.

The state of the wind, which blew right into the bay, was not the only obstacle that prevented the British fleet from immediately proceeding in chase. Most of the ships were in the midst of watering and refitting. Owing, however, to the extraordinary exertions of their crews, Admiral Hotham was enabled at 9 p.m. to take advantage of the land-wind, and get under way with the fleet. That fleet, on being joined by Commodore Nelson's squadron, consisted of the

1795.] ADMIRAL HOTHAM OFF HYÈRES. 297

Gun-ship.			
100	Britannia	Admiral (b.) William Hotham. Captain John Holloway.	1
	Victory[1]	Rear-admiral (b.) Robert Mann.[2] Captain John Knight.	5
98	Princess Royal	Vice-admiral (r.) Sam. Cranston Goodall. Captain John Child Purvis.	2
	St. George	Vice-admiral (r.) Sir Hyde Parker. Captain Thomas Foley.	3
	Windsor Castle	Vice-admiral (w.) Robert Linzee. Captain John Gore.	4
80	Barfleur[1]	,, John Bazeley.	
	Gibraltar[1]	,, John Pakenham.	
74	Captain	,, Samuel Reeve.	
	Fortitude	,, William Young.	
	Bombay Castle[1]	,, Charles Chamberlayne.	
	Saturn[1]	,, James Douglas.	
	Cumberland[1]	,, Barth. Samuel Rowley.	
	Terrible	,, George Campbell.	
	Defence[1]	,, Thomas Wells.	
	Egmont	,, John Sutton.	
	Culloden[1]	,, Thomas Troubridge.	
	Bedford	,, David Gould.	
	Courageux	,, Benjamin Hallowell.	
	Audacious[1]	,, William Shield.	
	Guiscardo. Samnito	} Portuguese ships, captains unknown.	
64	Agamemnon	Commodore Horatio Nelson.	
	Diadem	Captain Charles Tyler.	

Frigates, Meleager and Cyclops, 20-gun ship Ariadne; *sloops*, Comet Eclair, and Flêche; and *cutter* Resolution.

On the 8th, at noon, the British fleet, having cleared San-Fiorenzo bay, steered to the westward under all sail, with the wind from the south-south-west. On the 12th, in the evening, Levant island bearing from the van of the British fleet west, distant eight leagues, two vessels, spoken by the Cyclops, Captain William Hotham, and Flêche, Captain Thomas Boys, gave information that a few hours before they had seen the French fleet to the southward of the Hyères. The admiral immediately threw out the signal to prepare for battle, and the fleet made all sail to the south-west.

During the night a heavy gale from the west-north-west split the maintopsails of six of the British ships; and on the 13th, at daybreak, the wind still blowing fresh, attended by a heavy swell, while different ships were bending new topsails, the French

---

[1] The ships thus marked were those that joined the admiral on the 14th of the preceding month.

[2] Had shifted his flag from the Cumberland a few hours only before the fleet got under way.

fleet was discovered about five miles off upon the lee beam; standing on the larboard tack and very much scattered was the British fleet then on the opposite tack, standing to the southward. At 3 h. 45 m. A.M. Admiral Hotham made the signal for his fleet to form the starboard, and in about an hour afterwards the larboard line of bearing, and to make all possible sail, preserving that order. This was done for the alleged purpose of keeping the wind of the enemy and cutting him off from the shore, then only five leagues distant.

At 8 A.M., finding that the French admiral, whose fleet formed now in a compact line on the larboard tack, was steering about two points off the wind, which at this time blew from the westward, had no other view than that of endeavouring to escape, Admiral Hotham made the signal for a general chase, and for the ships to take suitable stations for mutual support, and to engage the enemy on arriving up with him in succession. The signal was obeyed with alacrity, and the ships were soon under all the sail that their masts would bear. In the course of the forenoon the wind moderated and drew more to the southward, and at noon the rear of the French fleet bore from the British van north-north-east, distant three-quarters of a mile; but the rearmost ship of the British fleet, as a proof of its disunited state, was nearly eight miles off in the west-south-west.

At half-past noon the wind suddenly changed from south-west-by-west to north, and thus brought the starboard and lee broadsides of the three rearmost French ships to bear upon the British van; the three leading ships of which were the Victory, Culloden, and Cumberland. The fire thus opened upon them was quickly returned with interest, especially upon the sternmost French ship, the Alcide, which in less than an hour became greatly disabled. At about 1 h. 30 m. P.M. the Culloden had her maintopmast shot away, but nevertheless was using every effort, by crowding sail upon her fore and mizenmasts, to get again alongside of the enemy.

At a few minutes before 2 P.M. the Alcide, after a noble defence, struck her colours to the Cumberland, who, without stopping to take possession, passed on to the second French ship in the rear. In the mean time the French frigates Justice and Alceste had approached the Alcide to take her in tow, and the Alceste actually sent her boat for that purpose; but a shot from the Victory sank the boat, and the two French frigates were compelled to retreat. The Agamemnon, Blenheim, Captain, and Defence were now becoming distantly engaged.

At 2 h. 42 m. P.M., just as the Cumberland having fired several shots at the Justice, and received great annoyance from the stern guns of one of the French line-of-battle ships, had attained a position alongside of the latter, the signal was thrown out to discontinue the action. Once, if not twice, had the Victory to repeat the signal with the Cumberland's pendants before that ship would, or we suppose we must say could, see it. When this signal was made by Admiral Hotham, the Blenheim, Gibraltar, Captain, and a few other ships were closing with the enemy's rear; and the Defence, from her known good sailing, would probably have been in advance of them had she not, while lying upon the larboard quarter of the Victory, kept her mizentopsail aback after repeated hails from that ship to fill and stand on.

At the time the action ended in this indecisive manner Cape Roux bore from the Victory, then among the ships that were nearest the shore, north-west half-west, distant four leagues. The French fleet, however, by a sudden change of wind to the eastward, had gained the weathergage on the starboard tack, and while the centre and rear of the British fleet lay nearly becalmed in the offing, was standing, with a light air, towards the bay of Fréjus; but we believe that Vice-admiral Martin, having about 7 P.M. been headed by a breeze from the south-west, did not reach an anchorage until very late.[1]

[1] The following statement of this miserable action is from the note-book of as gallant an admiral as the service can boast—he was an eye-witness, and a lieutenant on board the Victory:—

"On the 12th of July, 1795, the English fleet, of 21 sail of the line, six of them being three-deckers, in company with two Neapolitan (Mr. James calls them Portuguese) seventy-fours, were a very few leagues to the eastward of Toulon. The wind blowing strong from the Gulf of Lyons from W.N.W. to N.W. In the evening the look-out frigates signalled 'the French fleet out, and at no great distance.' The admiral made the signal to prepare for battle.

"At 4 o'clock on the morning of the 13th July, it being my morning watch, on going on deck I saw the whole French fleet under our lee, at about the distance of from two to four leagues, consisting of 17 sail of the line, irregularly formed, and sailing large on the larboard tack, standing in for the land about Frejus bay. The English fleet, more collected, although six ships had split topsails in the night during the gale, which was still blowing at 4 o'clock, were on the starboard tack standing off the shore, which must have been at least 13 leagues distant. We thus continued to stand on opposite tacks, separately from each other, until about 6 o'clock, when the signal was made to wear, and soon afterwards that for 'a general chase.' At this time the French fleet were six or seven leagues from us, and had got in shore, leaving us little hope of our nearing them before they reached the land. However, by carrying a press of sail, and the wind dying away as the French drew in shore, and the English carrying the strong breeze up with them, we were enabled, with six of the fastest and best-managed ships of the van, to close with the rear of the French line, and the action commenced at noon with the three or four rearmost ships of the enemy.

"At this time, or very shortly afterwards, the wind having fallen away, a breeze sprung up from the eastward, which brought the French to windward of us on the starboard tack, our ships in the rear coming up with a fresh breeze at N.W., about 1 P.M. Our six ships before mentioned were joined by the Blenheim and Princess Royal, the Bombay Castle, and

Of the six or seven ships that were enabled to take any part in this action, if such it can be called, the Culloden was the only one that lost any mast; but the Victory was a considerable sufferer, having had all her stays except the fore stay shot away, as well as her maintopgallant, foretopsail, and spritsail yards. Her bowsprit and all three of her lower masts were also wounded in several places. The Cumberland likewise suffered considerably, having had her main stay, maintopmast stay, shrouds, and running rigging much cut.

The loss sustained in the action was as follows: Culloden, two seamen killed, her first-lieutenant (Tristram Whitter) and four seamen wounded; the Victory, two midshipmen (James Beale and William Willison, neither of whom are named in the Gazette), and three marines killed, one lieutenant (John Hinton),

---

one or two more, being not far astern. It was about this time that the Alcide caught fire in the foretop, and was soon in flames: she was the second in the rear of the enemy. The Victory, which ship ought to have pushed on and been foremost on such a day, hailed several of the ships to pass ahead of her; and she positively backed her maintopsail to allow others to get in advance of her; whereas, had she carried sail at first, before the wind chopped round, she might easily have passed through the rear of the enemy's line, between the third and fourth ships, have secured three, and brought on a general action. At 2 o'clock the commander-in-chief, being eight or nine miles astern, not knowing the actual state of affairs, and fearing his van to be too near the coast, made the signal to discontinue the action, and recalled his van.

"It was not too late at this hour of the day to have done much, had the admiral, whose flag was flying on board the Victory (Rear-admiral Robert Mann), stated by signal 'that the enemy could have been attacked with advantage,' for we were at least three leagues off the land, and had nine ships up, three of three decks, and others coming. At this time three or four more ships might have been captured with ease; but, no! the signal to discontinue the action was obeyed without remonstrance, or stating what could be done. The Cumberland, however, was some time before she obeyed the signal, and followed the enemy; then, firing her broadside, she wore round and rejoined her fleet. The enemy were very badly manœuvred, and fired without doing any execution of consequence for two hours.

"Had the English fleet only put their heads the same way as the enemy's, and stood in-shore at 4 o'clock, the whole of the French line might have been cut off from the land, taken, or destroyed; and even afterwards they might have been followed into Frejus bay, and *wholly destroyed*.

"There was a most beautiful manœuvre performed by the captain of the French frigate, the Alceste, stationed to windward of the enemy's line. Seeing the second ship from the rear (the Alcide) in distress, and dropping astern into our fire, she bore down right athwart the bows, lowered a boat, and attempted to send her on board the Alcide with a hawser, in order to tow her clear of us; but before the boat accomplished the object, a shot from the Cumberland cut her in two, and she disappeared in an instant, with all her brave and unfortunate crew. The frigate perceiving the calamity, immediately made all sail in a masterly manner, as such a clever officer would naturally do, and soon got out of danger.

"On this frigate coming down to take the Alcide in tow, the captain of the Victory, of 100 guns, came down below with orders to reserve our fire for the frigate which had bore away to rescue the French 74, then abreast of us, and not half a mile distant; and although the Victory did fire, and many other ships also at this gallant vessel, she had the good fortune to escape any serious accident, having only some of the running rigging cut, which was soon replaced by her daring crew. She got off most beautifully, to the astonishment and wonder of all our fleet, and I pronounce this to be the best executed (although unsuccessful) and most daring manœuvre I ever witnessed in the presence of so very superior a force."

one midshipman (William Irwin), one major and one lieutenant of marines (Frederick Hill Flight and William Darley), and 11 seamen wounded; the Blenheim, two seamen killed and two wounded; the Captain and Defence each one seaman killed, and the latter six wounded. Owing to the high firing of her opponents, the Cumberland sustained no loss whatever. The total loss in the British fleet amounted, therefore, to no more than 11 killed and 27 wounded.[1]

About a quarter of an hour after her surrender the Alcide caught fire in the foretop, owing, it is believed, to some grenades or other combustible missiles placed there for use; and notwithstanding every exertion by the people on board of her, the ship was soon in a blaze fore and aft. About 300 out of the 615 deposed to by her officers as the number of her crew were saved by the boats of the nearest British ships; but the remainder unfortunately perished in the awful explosion which took place about an hour and a half after the fire had broken out.

Upon the merits of the affair off Hyères we are relieved from the task of commenting, by the scientific remarks of a professional contemporary; who, however, has left the action, in the way of detail, quite as brief and unsatisfactory as it stands in the official account.

"In this action," says Captain Brenton, "there was a total misapplication of tactic, neither recommended by a Clerk[2] nor justified by experience. The French fleet should have been attacked by a general chase as soon as discovered: the bending new topsails, when the enemy was dead to leeward, was at best a useless measure; and it is much to be regretted that time was lost in forming a line of bearing, which could not be preserved with any effect; as the admiral observes in his despatches, 'the calms and shifts of wind in that country rendering all naval operations peculiarly uncertain.' With this knowledge it was incumbent on him to have dashed upon his enemy, who he knew would not wait for him, and who must have been in a great measure unprepared: by an immediate chase he would have compelled them to engage, or have increased their distance from the land, which would in a great degree have insured their capture or destruction. The delay of making the signal gave them time to recover from their confusion; and when, after a lapse of four hours, the

---

[1] In Admiral Hotham's letter in the Gazette, the total stated is 10 killed and 25 wounded; but there appears to have been a mistake in the return of the Victory's loss, no officer being mentioned except one midshipman, and he is not named.

[2] Mr. Clerk of Eldon.

British admiral made sail in chase, the wind failed, and the opportunity was irrecoverably lost."[1]

To this it may be added, that the British admiral, had he persevered in the chase for a few hours longer, would have regained the wind of his opponent, as appears by the following entry in the log of the Victory: "At half-past 7 bore up; enemy turning into Fréjus; wind south-west." On the other hand, great allowance must be made for the locomotive disqualifications of the chasing fleet, or rather of the single ship, by whose rate of going the speed of the fleet was in a great measure to be regulated. To talk of making a "dash," where such ships as the old Britannia and St. George are present, is enough to raise a smile. Had the first been a private ship, the two might have been left behind to join the next day; but, as carrying on board of her the commander-in-chief of the fleet, the Britannia, who was by far the worst sailer of the two, could not be left entirely out of sight.

The decided inferiority of the French, who, besides having but 17 ships to oppose to 23, had but one three-decker to oppose to six, is a sufficient excuse for their declining to engage. The French writers admit that Vice-admiral Martin did his utmost to avoid an engagement, on account of the odds against him; but they wish to have it believed that the Alcide caught fire and blew up in the act of defending herself, instead of after she had struck. The interval between the hauling down of the colours and the first appearance of the fire in the foretop is, however, clearly marked in the logs of the adjacent British ships. It will be enough to say that the captain of the Alcide did his duty like a brave officer; and we wish we knew both his name and the name of the officer who commanded the ship next ahead of him in the line, that ship having in the most gallant manner backed her maintopsail to cover, however ineffectually, her disabled companion from the irresistible force by which she was assailed.[2]

The French fleet soon afterwards returned to Toulon, and the British fleet proceeded first to San-Fiorenzo and then to Leghorn. On the 6th of August Admiral Hotham again put to sea, with 20 English and three Neapolitan sail of the line, and, arriv-

---

[1] Brenton, vol. ii., p. 74.

[2] The contempt with which the officers of the present day speak of this action, considering the superiority of the English, both in three-deckers and in general numbers, sufficiently bears out Brenton in any remarks he may have made on the subject. The relinquishing pursuit, at the moment the Victory bore up, is perfectly incomprehensible, and the results of the action are as trivial as the list of killed and wounded.—*Editor*

ing off Cape Sepet on the 8th, saw the French fleet at anchor in Toulon road. The British admiral then stood away to the eastward, having first detached Captain Nelson, in the Agamemnon, with the frigates Inconstant, Meleagar, Tartar, and Southampton, 20-gun ship Ariadne, and brig-sloop Speedy, on a cruise along the coast of Italy, for the purpose of co-operating with the Austrian and Sardinian armies in an attempt to expel the republicans from the Genoese territories.

On the 26th, the boats of this squadron, under the personal direction of the commodore, boarded and cut out of the bays of Allassio and Langueglia, in the vicinity of Vado, and then in the possession of a French republican army, two French gun-brigs, the Résolu of ten, and another of six guns, two 5-gun galleys, and five merchant vessels laden with provisions. Captain Nelson also destroyed two other vessels, and performed the whole service without the loss of a man.

After the capture of the Tigre, Formidable, and Alexandre, off Isle-Groix, the French government deemed it necessary to restore to the Brest fleet, as many ships from Toulon as had previously been detached thither; and accordingly, on the 14th of September, Rear admiral Richery, with the 80-gun ship Victoire, 74s Barras, Jupiter, Berwick, Résolution, and Duquesne, and frigates Embuscade, Félicité, and Friponne, put to sea from the road. The orders of M. Richery, it appears, were not to proceed straight to Brest, but to cruise for a few months on the coast of Newfoundland; and, fortunately for the rear-admiral, no conventional deputy divided with him the command of the squadron.

On the 22nd a cartel brought to Admiral Hotham, who two days before had anchored in San-Fiorenzo bay, the first intelligence of the escape of this French squadron from Toulon. On the 5th of October, and not before, Rear-admiral Mann, with a squadron of six sail of the line, composed of the Windsor Castle 98 (his flag-ship), Cumberland, Defence, Terrible, Audacious, and Saturn, 74s, and frigates Blonde and Castor, was detached in pursuit; too late, however, to be of any service, as the sequel will show.

On the 25th of September the British 74-gun ships Fortitude, Captain Thomas Taylor, Bedford, Captain Augustus Montgomery, and Censeur (jury-rigged and armed en flûte), Captain John Gore, which had been detached from Admiral Hotham's fleet a few weeks before, sailed from Gibraltar for England, with a valuable convoy from the Levant, numbering 63 sail; and with, for its additional protection, the 44-gun ship Argo, Captain Richard Randell Burgess, 12-pounder, 32-gun frigates Juno, Captain Lord Amelius Beauclerk, and Lutine, Captain William Haggitt, and fireship Tisiphone, Captain Joseph Turner.

On the same night, in passing through the gut, the Argo and Juno, with 32 sail of the convoy, parted company. The remaining ships kept with the commodore until the 7th of October; when, at about 9 h. 30 m. A.M., Cape. St. Vincent, by account, bearing east half-south distant 48 leagues, a squadron, which proved to be that of Rear-admiral Richery, was descried in the north-east. As soon as the character of the strangers became known, the commodore made the signal for the convoy to disperse, and, with the Bedford, Censeur, and Fortitude, formed the line, determined, if the French meditated an attack, to give them battle, and save as many as possible of the convoy.

At 1 P.M., just as the three ships had formed in line, the Censeur rolled away her foretopmast, and having only a frigate's mainmast, was compelled to drop astern. On observing that the French ships now fast approached, Captain Taylor judged it proper, with the concurrence of his officers and of Captain Montgomery, to bear up. The British immediately did so, the two efficient 74s keeping close together for mutual support.

At 1 h. 50 m. P.M. the leading French ship opened her fire on the Censeur; who, in about five minutes, returned it with spirit, and was assisted occasionally by the stern chasers of the Fortitude and Bedford: to fire which they had been obliged to cut down a great part of the stern. Meanwhile the three French frigates, as they came up, brought to the merchant vessels, and the French line-of-battle ships pressed hard upon all five of the English ships of war. At 2 h. 30 m. P.M., having had her two remaining topmasts shot away, and having expended nearly all the small quantity of powder with which she had originally been supplied, the Censeur struck her colours to three of the French 74s. Shortly afterwards the latter commenced firing at the Lutine. The frigate returned their fire smartly, and, in the end, effected her escape; as did also the Fortitude, Bedford, and Tisiphone.

The 32 merchant vessels, in charge of the Argo and her consort, arrived safe at their destination, but those with Captain Taylor were not so fortunate. Thirty out of 31 sail of them fell into the hands of M. Richery; who on the 13th with his squadron, the recaptured Censeur, and his fleet of prizes, entered in triumph the port of Cadiz: where, however, he was compelled to remain longer than suited his wishes, or the interests of his government.

But M. Richery's was not the only squadron which escaped from Toulon in the autumn of 1795. Towards the latter end of September chef de division Honoré Ganteaume, with the Mont Blanc 74, frigates Junon and Justice of 40, Artémise and Sérieuse of 36, and Badine of 28 guns, and the 16-gun brig-corvette Hasard, sailed from the road on a cruise in the Levant, expressly to intercept, previously to its departure from that sea, the very convoy, which afterwards, by accident as it were, fell into the hands of M. Richery.

While contending with contrary winds between Sardinia and Minorca, M. Ganteaume passed barely out of sight of Rear-admiral Mann's squadron on its way to Gibraltar. A French writer, in the "Victories et Conquêtes," declares that M. Ganteaume chased, and very nearly captured, the Agamemnon 64, Captain Horatio Nelson, and that subsequently he himself was chased by a squadron of five sail of the line under Vice-admiral Sir Hyde Parker, and only saved from capture by the fall of the topmasts of the two advanced ships. Although it is certain that several detachments from Admiral Hotham's fleet were at this time traversing the Mediterranean, we cannot discover, on inspecting the log-books of the British ships, that M. Ganteaume's squadron was seen by any of them.

Having, in spite of the chances against him, accomplished his passage to the Levant, M. Ganteaume there captured a great many English, Russian, and Neapolitan merchant vessels, and, by his appearance off the port of Smyrna, released the 36-gun frigate Sensible, Commodore Jacques-Mélanie Rondeau, and corvette Sardine; which, with their prize, the late British 28-gun frigate Nemesis, Captain Samuel Hood Linzee, had, until the proximity of Commodore Ganteaume's squadron became known, been blockaded by the British 38-gun frigate Aigle, Captain Samuel Hood, and 28-gun frigate Cyclops, Captain William Hotham. We may remark, in passing, that the Nemesis had been captured on the 9th of December, while at anchor in the neutral port of Smyrna, by the Sensible and Sardine, without, as it appears, any opposition on the part of the British frigate beyond a fierce remonstrance at the illegality of the measure.

While cruising in the northern quarter of the Archipelago the French squadron encountered a violent gale of wind, in which, besides some inconsiderable damage done to two or three of the ships, the Justice lost all her masts. Ordering the Junon to take the latter in tow, M. Ganteaume steered for the road of the Dardanelles. In a few days after he had reached this anchorage, intelligence arrived from Constantinople, that two British sail of the line and three or four frigates had been detached to intercept him.

Leaving the Justice to follow as soon as she could be got ready, the French commodore, with the remainder of his ships, weighed and set sail, in the hope to be able to quit the Archipelago before the British squadron could enter it; M. Ganteaume being well aware that, from the little respect which, in the case of the Nemesis, Captain Rondeau and the Turks had shown to the neutrality of a port, the British commanding officer would be justified in attacking him in any Turkish road or port in which he might be lying. That the French commodore did not take his departure a day too soon is clear from the fact, that on the 27th of December Captain Troubridge's squadron, consisting of the 74-gun ship Culloden, Diadem 64, and Inconstant, Flora, and Lowestoffe frigates, when seven or eight leagues to the south-east of Cape Matapan, standing into the Archipelago, chased the Badine, which had just been detached by M. Ganteaume, purposely, as he states, to draw the British squadron away from his own.

Running into the gulf of Coron, the Badine anchored close off the town; and on the next day the Lowestoffe cast anchor alongside of her, in order to watch her motions. On the 31st of December Commodore Troubridge, with the remainder of his squadron, anchored in the harbour of Milo, and subsequently steered for Smyrna. Meanwhile, Commodore Ganteaume was bending his course for Toulon, and on the 5th of February, 1796, reached the road in safety.

Having detached Rear-admiral Mann and Vice-admiral Sir Hyde Parker, as already stated, Admiral Hotham sailed on the 12th of October, for Leghorn, where he arrived on the next day. On the 1st of November, Admiral Hotham struck his flag,[1] and was immediately succeeded in the command by Vice-admiral Sir Hyde Parker, who had the day before rejoined the fleet with his squadron. On the 11th, the fleet sailed for Leghorn, and on the 20th, anchored in the bay of San-Fiorenzo; where, on the 30th, the 32-gun frigate, Lively, Captain Lord Garlies, arrived from Portsmouth, having on board Admiral Sir John Jervis, appointed the commander-in-chief on the station.

[1] The admiral soon afterwards returned to England, and, by dint of sheer interest, got himself made an Irish peer.

On the 3rd of December, Sir John shifted his flag from the Lively to the Victory, and on the 13th, sailed with the fleet for Toulon; between which port and the Isle of Minorca, the admiral was cruising at the close of the year.

War between England and Holland.

The extraordinary success which had attended the French arms throughout the year 1794, operating upon the revolutionary spirit by which Holland was overrun, rendered the conquest of that country, especially after the fall of the Netherlands, no difficult task. France, in her policy, permitted Holland to retain the nominal dignity of an independent state, under the style of the Batavian Republic; as, while it flattered the vanity of the Dutch, it gave to the conquerors every advantage to be derived from possessing Holland as a province, without the expense of maintaining her as an integral part of the French empire.

England now found it her duty not to let slip the opportunity of weakening the maritime power of this new ally in her enemy's cause. Accordingly, on the 19th of January, orders were issued to seize all Dutch vessels in British ports; in consequence of which, the 64-gun ship, Zeeland, 54-gun ship, Braakel, 40-gun frigate, Thulen, and two brig-corvettes, together with seven homeward and two outward bound Dutch Indiamen, and from 50 to 60 merchant vessels, all lying in Plymouth Sound, were detained by the port-admiral, Vice-admiral Sir Richard Onslow. It was understood at the time, that the ships were not to be considered as prizes, but were to be held in trust for the stadtholder, who had recently arrived at Harwich from Scheveling, in an open boat, with only three men and a boy to navigate her, should he ever regain his supremacy over the Dutch people. The ships were ordered round to Hamoaze; where, after landing their powder, they were allowed, for the present, at least, to keep their colours flying.

On the 9th of February, instead of the customary letters of marque and reprisal, the British government issued a proclamation, authorizing the detention of all Dutch vessels, as well as of all neutral vessels bound to or from Dutch ports. Measures were at the same time taken to gain possession of the islands and settlements belonging to Holland, both in the west and in the east; and, in the course of the month, a small British squadron, under the orders of Vice-admiral Adam Duncan, in the 74-gun ship Venerable, was despatched to the North Sea, to watch the motions of the Dutch fleet lying in the Texel, or rather squadron, for the ships ready for sea did not, at this time, amount to more than three or four sail of the line, and about as many frigates.

Early in August a fleet of Russian ships, consisting of 12 crazy sail of the line and seven frigates, associated itself with that under Vice-admiral Duncan; but the combined fleets, during the remainder of the year, had no enemy to encounter, save the perils of a winter's cruise in that favourite region for storms and shoals, the North Sea. Besides having Holland for an enemy, against whom letters of marque and reprisal issued on the 15th of September, England lost Prussia as a friend, that power having, since the 30th of April, concluded a separate peace with France.

Light Squadrons and Single Ships.

On the 30th of December, 1794, at 11 A.M., the British 12-pounder 32-gun frigate Blanche, Captain Robert Faulknor, cruising off the island of Desirade, one of the dependencies of Guadeloupe, and, like the latter, again in French possession, chased a large French armed schooner under a fort at the bottom of a bay in the first-named island. At 2 P.M. the Blanche stood into the bay after the schooner, which had come to an anchor, with springs on her cables. At 2 h. 30 m. the fort and schooner, as well as some troops drawn up on the shore, opened a fire upon the Blanche, then about 700 yards distant, working up to a nearer and more effectual position.

At 3 h. 45 m. P.M., having got close abreast of the fort, the Blanche dropped her anchor, and commenced a heavy fire, as well upon the fort as upon the schooner and some troops drawn up on the shore to assist in defending her. At 4 P.M., having silenced the fort, Captain Faulknor despatched the boats of the frigate to capture the schooner. This the boats very soon effected; and the Blanche weighed and stood out with her prize, which was a national schooner mounting eight guns, and commanded by a lieutenant de vaisseau, recently from Pointe-à-Pitre in the island of Guadeloupe. The loss sustained by the Blanche in this spirited enterprise was rather severe, amounting to one midshipman (Mr. Fitzgibbon) and one marine killed, and four seamen wounded: that on the part of the French schooner could not be ascertained, as the crew, previously to her being boarded, had escaped to the shore.

Having manned his prize and despatched her to the harbour of the Saintes, two small islands close to Guadeloupe, and still in British possession, Captain Faulknor proceeded on a cruise off Pointe-à-Pitre, a harbour in Grande-terre, Guadeloupe, and in which lay, ready for sea, the French 36-gun frigate Pique, Captain Conseil. On the 2nd of January the Blanche was joined by the 12-pounder 32-gun frigate Quebec, Captain James Carpenter; but, the next afternoon, the latter parted company, and, bearing up to the westward under all sail, was soon out of sight.

Thus left alone, the Blanche at about 6 P.M. steered straight for Pointe-à-Pitre, and, on arriving within four miles of the port, lay to for the night. On the next day, the 4th, at daybreak, the Blanche discovered the Pique lying at anchor just outside of the harbour. At 7 A.M. the French frigate got under way, and began working into the offing under her topsails, backing her mizentopsail occasionally, to keep company with a schooner which had weighed with her. At about 8 h. 30 m. the Blanche made sail to meet the French ship and schooner, until nearly within gun-shot of Fort Fleur-d'Epée; when, finding the Pique apparently disinclined to come out from the batteries, the Blanche, who had hove to, made sail to board a schooner running down along Grande-terre. At this time Pointe-à-Pitre bore from the Blanche north-west, distant two leagues, and the French frigate north-north-west, distant three miles.

At half-past noon the Pique filled and made sail towards the Blanche. At 1 P.M. the latter brought-to an American schooner from Bordeaux to Pointe-à-Pitre with wine and brandy, and taking her in tow, steered towards the Saintes. At 2 P.M. the Pique crossed the Blanche on the opposite tack, and, hoisting French colours, fired four shots at her. This challenge, as it might be considered, the British frigate answered, by firing a shot to windward. The battery at Gosier also fired two shots; but they, like those of the frigate, fell short. At 2 h. 30 m. P.M., finding that the Pique had tacked and was standing towards her, the Blanche shortened sail for the French frigate to come up; but at 3 h. 30 m. P.M. the latter tacked and stood away.

In the hope to induce the Pique to follow her, the Blanche, under topsails and courses, stood towards Marie Galante. At 7 P.M., observing the Pique still under Grande-terre, Captain Faulknor took out the American crew from the schooner, and sent on board a petty officer and a party of men. The Blanche then wore, and stood towards the island of Dominique, with the schooner in tow. At about 8 P.M. the French frigate was descried astern, about two leagues distant, standing after the Blanche. The latter immediately cast off the schooner, and tacking, made all sail in chase.

At about a quarter-past midnight the Blanche, on the starboard tack, passed under the lee of the Pique on the larboard tack, and returned the distant broadside which the Pique had fired at her. At half-past midnight, having got nearly in the wake of her opponent, the Blanche tacked; and, at a few minutes before 1 A.M. on the 5th, just as she had arrived within musket-shot upon the starboard quarter of the Pique, the latter wore, with the intention of crossing her opponent's hawse and raking her ahead. To frustrate this manœuvre, the Blanche wore also; and the two frigates became closely engaged, broadside to broadside.

At about 2 h. 30 m. A.M. the Blanche, having shot ahead, was in the act of luffing up to port to rake the Pique ahead, when the former's wounded mizen and main masts, in succession, fell over the side. Almost immediately after this, the Pique ran foul of the Blanche on her larboard quarter, and made several attempts to board. These attempts the British crew successfully resisted, and the larboard quarter-deck guns, and such of the main-deck ones as would bear, were fired with destructive effect into the Pique's starboard bow; she returning the fire from her tops, as well as from some of her quarter-deck guns run in amidships fore and aft. At a few minutes before 3 A.M., while assisting his second-lieutenant, Mr. David Milne, and one or two others of his crew, in lashing, with such ropes as were handy, the bowsprit of the Pique to the capstan of the Blanche, preparatory to a more secure fastening by means of a hawser which was getting up from below, the young and gallant Captain Faulknor fell by a musket-ball through his heart.

At this moment, or very soon afterwards, the lashings broke loose; and the Pique, crossing the stern of the Blanche, who had now begun to pay off for the want of after-sail, fell on board the latter, a second time, upon the starboard quarter. In an instant the British crew, with the hawser which had just before been got on deck, lashed the bowsprit of the Pique to the stump of their own mainmast. In this manner the Blanche commanded now by Lieutenant Frederick Watkins, towed before the wind her resolute opponent: whose repeated attempts to cut away this second lashing were defeated by the quick and well-directed fire of the British marines. In the meanwhile, the constant stream of musketry poured upon the quarter-deck of the Blanche from the forecastle and tops of the Pique, and a well-directed fire from the latter's quarter-deck guns pointed forward, gave great annoyance to the former; particularly, as having, like many other ships in the British navy at this period, no stern-ports on the main deck, the cannonade on the part of the Blanche was confined to two quarter-deck 6-pounders. The carpenters having in vain tried to cut down the upper transom beam, no alternative remained but to blow away a part of it on each side. As soon, therefore, as the firemen with their buckets were assembled in the cabin, the two after guns were pointed against the stern-frame. Their discharge made a clear breach on both sides, and the activity of the bucket-men quickly extinguished the fire it had occasioned in the wood-work. The two 12-pounders of the Blanche, thus brought into use, soon made considerable havoc upon the Pique's decks.

At about 3 h. 15 m. A.M. the mainmast of the French frigate (her fore and mizen masts having previously fallen) fell over the side. In this utterly defenceless state, without a gun which, on account of the wreck of her masts, she could now bring to bear, the Pique sustained the raking fire of the Blanche until 5 h. 15 m. A.M.; when some of the French crew, from the bowsprit end, called aloud for quarter. The Blanche immediately ceased her fire; and, every boat in both vessels having been destroyed by shot, Lieutenant Milne, followed by ten seamen, endeavoured to reach the prize by means of the hawser that still held her; but, their weight bringing the bight of the rope down in the water, they had to swim a part of the distance.

The following diagram will assist in explaining the manner in which this gallantly-fought action was brought to a termination.

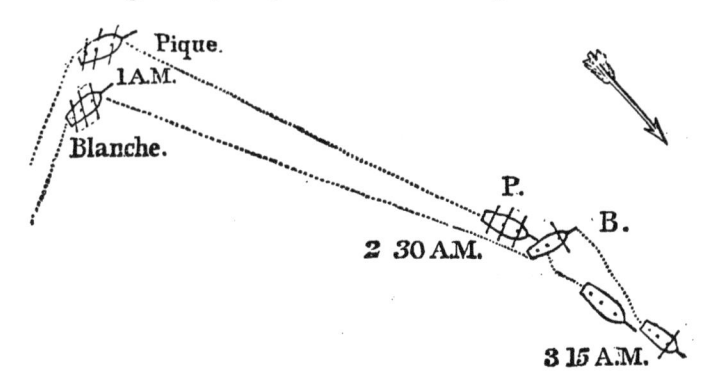

The Blanche, besides her 32 long 12 and 6 pounders, mounted six 18-pounder carronades, total 38 guns; and, having sent away in prizes two master's mates and 12 seamen, she had on board no more than 198 men and boys. Of these, the Blanche lost her commander, one midshipman (William Bolton) five seamen, and one private marine killed, one midshipman (Charles Herbert), two quartermasters, the armourer, one sergeant of marines, 12 seamen, and four private marines wounded; total, eight killed and 21 wounded.

The Pique was armed with two carriage-guns, 6-pounders, less than her establishment, or 38 in all; but she mounted along her gunwale on each side, several brass swivels. Respecting the number composing the crew of the Pique, the accounts are very contradictory. Lieutenant Watkins, in his official letter, states the number at 360; and Vice-admiral Caldwell, at Martinique, when enclosing that letter to the Admiralty, says, "many more than 360." On the other hand, the three French officers, examined before the surrogate of the colonial vice-admiralty court, subsequently deposed, two of them to "between 260 and 270 men," and the third to "about 270 men," as the total number on board their ship when the action commenced. Upon these certificates, head-money was paid for 265 men; but, according to the documents transmitted along with those certificates, the actual number of men on board was 279. Among the documents is a letter, with Admiral Caldwell's signature, stating that the number of killed, wounded, and prisoners, the amount of which, however, is not shown, accords exactly with the number, 279, alleged to be on board the Pique; yet, in the admiral's letter in the Gazette, the total of killed, wounded, and prisoners, amounts to 360. Schomberg makes the number 460;[1] and another writer considers the Pique's men to have nearly doubled those of the Blanche. We are satisfied, however, that 279 is the full amount of the French crew. Of this number the Pique had, it appears, 76 officers and men killed, and 110 wounded; a loss unparalleled in its proportion.

Comparative Force of the Combatants.

		Blanche.	Pique.
Broadside-guns	No.	19	19
	lbs.	228	273
Crew	No.	198	279
Size	tons	710	906

A difference there is, but scarcely sufficient, except perhaps in

[1] Schomberg, vol. ii., p. 403.

point of crew, to entitle the action to be considered otherwise than as an equal match. The French officers and crew fought the Pique in a most gallant manner; surrendering only when their ship was a defenceless hulk, and themselves reduced to a third of their original number.

Nor must we omit to do a further act of justice to Captain Conseil, or to his memory rather, for, although not stated, he was, we believe, among the mortally wounded in the action, and express it as our conviction, that he evinced a laudable caution in not going out to meet the Blanche, until he was certain that the frigate, so recently seen in her company, had retired to a safe distance. On the part of the British officers and crew, consummate intrepidity was displayed, from the beginning to the end of this long and sanguinary battle. Indeed, a spirit of chivalry seems to have animated both parties; and the action of the Blanche and Pique may be referred to with credit by either.

At 8 A.M. the 64-gun ship Veteran, Captain William Hancock Kelly, joined the Blanche and her prize, and assisted in exchanging the prisoners. The 64 then took the Pique in tow, and carried her, in company with the Blanche, to the Saintes. The approach of the Veteran to perform this service occasioned the French officers to declare, that that ship must have witnessed the combat, and they refused, at first, to sign the usual head-money certificates, unless the Veteran was named as one of their captors. The fact is, the Veteran, at 3 A.M., while beating up from the Saintes, did see the flashes of the guns, bearing from her east-north-east, but did not gain a sight of the combatants themselves until daylight, which was about a quarter of an hour after the action had terminated; and, even then, the Veteran was upwards of two hours in endeavouring to reach the spot.

The Pique became afterwards added to the British navy as a 12-pounder 36; and Lieutenants Watkins and Milne were both deservedly made commanders. The third-lieutenant, and who, on the promotion of these two officers, succeeded to be first of the Blanche, was John Prickett, since dead, as a commander.

On the 13th of March, at 7 A.M., Ushant bearing south halfwest, distant 13 leagues, the British 18-pounder 32-gun frigate Lively, Captain George Burlton, acting in the absence of Lord Garlies, sick on shore, while standing down Channel on the starboard tack, discovered three strange sail on the same tack, steering for the coast of France. Chase was given by the Lively; and soon afterwards, the largest of the three strangers, which was the French 28-gun corvette, or frigate, Tourterelle, Captain Guillaume S. A. Montalan, tacked and stood towards the British frigate.

At 10 h. 30 m. A.M. the two ships having approached within gun-shot on opposite tacks, commenced firing at each other. As soon as she had got abaft the Lively's beam, the Tourterelle wore; and a close action ensued, which continued until 1 h. 30 m. P.M.; when the French ship, having had her three topmasts shot away, her remaining masts, rigging, and sails entirely disabled, and her hull greatly shattered, hauled down her colours. Shortly afterwards the Tourterelle's mainmast fell over the side.

The damages of the Lively were chiefly confined to her rigging and sails. The latter were much burnt by red-hot shot fired from her opponent; on whose lower or berth deck, until it was thrown overboard just previously to surrender, had been a regular furnace for heating them. Notwithstanding the use of this additional means of resistance, the Lively, out of her complement of 251 men and boys, escaped with only two, Lieutenant Loftus Otway Bland and one seaman, wounded; whereas the Tourterelle, out of her crew, as deposed by her officers, of 230 in number, had 16 officers and men killed and 25 wounded.

The Lively's guns were those of her class at F in the table at p. 101, with six brass 24-pounder carronades, or 38 guns in all. The Tourterelle mounted two sixes fewer than No. 9 in the small table at p. 59, or 30 guns in all.

Comparative Force of the Combatants.

		Lively.	Tourterelle.
Broadside-guns	No.	19	15
	lbs.	324	188
Crew	No.	251	230
Size	tons	806	581

Captain Montalan, in commencing the attack, either mistook the Lively for a less formidable ship, or relied too much upon the effects of his red-hot shot. In either case, he showed himself an enterprising officer; and the Tourterelle's three hours' resistance, disabled state, and heavy loss, afforded ample proofs of his bravery and determination. The employment of hot shot is not usually deemed honourable warfare; but the blame, if any, rested with those who had equipped the ship for sea.

The two other vessels in sight, when the action began, were prizes to the resuscitated[1] French corvette Espion. These, a

[1] See p. 335.

few days afterwards, were retaken by the Lively. The Tourterelle, on her arrival in port, was purchased for the British navy, and, although called by the French a corvette, became classed as a British 28-gun frigate. The Tourterelle did not, however, long continue as a cruiser: in the year 1799 she was converted into a troop or store ship.

The near approach to equality in the nominal force of the Lively and Tourterelle—that is, in the rated number of guns on board one ship, and the mounted number on board the other—has been made the basis of an attempt to raise this action far above its proper level. For instance, a naval writer says: "The Lively, of 32 guns, captured the Tourterelle, of 30 guns."[1] Now, as "of" can mean nothing else than "mounting," what is the uninformed reader to infer, but that these ships differed in force by only a 16th? Suppose the writer not to have known that the Lively mounted six 24-pounder carronades in addition to her "32 guns," he still, from his professional experience, must have been aware, that the English ship carried long 18-pounders, the French ship long 8, or, putting them into English, long 9 pounders; a difference itself of one-half in the weight of metal. Many similar instances might be quoted from the same work; but the case of the Lively and Tourterelle will be sufficient to expose the absurdity and unfairness of such a manner of stating the force between contending ships.

On the 10th of April, at 10 A.M., a British squadron, composed of five ships of the line and three frigates, under the command of Rear-admiral John Colpoys, while cruising to the westward, with the wind at east by north, discovered three strange sail in the north-west quarter. Chase was immediately given; and, at noon, the strangers were discovered to be three French frigates. The 74-gun ship Colossus, Captain John Monkton, having got within gun-shot of one of them, opened her fire; which the frigate returned with her stern-chasers. The three French frigates, soon afterwards, took different courses. The two that pointed to the westward were pursued by the 74-gun ships Robust and Hannibal; while the one that steered a north-westerly course, and which was the 36-gun frigate Gloire, Captain Beens, was followed, closely by the 12-pounder 32-gun frigate Astræa, Captain Lord Henry Paulet, and, at a great distance, by one or more of the other ships.

[1] Brenton, vol. i., p. 367.

At 6 P.M., having far outstripped her consorts, the Astræa got within gun-shot of, and fired several of her quarter-deck guns at, the Gloire; who, in return, kept up an incessant fire from her stern-chasers. Advancing gradually up, the Astræa, at 10 h. 30 m. P.M., brought the Gloire to close action, and, after a 58 minutes' spirited cannonade, compelled the French frigate to haul down her colours. The three topmasts of the Astræa were so wounded by the Gloire's shot, that her maintopmast fell over the side in two hours after the action, and the fore and mizen topmasts were obliged to be shifted. The masts and yards of the Gloire, and the rigging and sails of both ships, were also much cut.

The Astræa mounted, it appears, no more than the 32 long guns of her class, and, out of her 212 men and boys, did not lose a man killed, but had one mortally, two dangerously, and five slightly wounded. The Gloire, who appears to have mounted two more sixes than the establishment of her class, or 42 guns in all, lost, according to the representation of her officers, 40 in killed and wounded together.

Comparative Force of the Combatants.

		Astræa.	Gloire.
Broadside-guns	No.	16	21
	lbs.	174	286
Crew	No.	212	275
Size	tons.	703	877

Nothing was wanted but a meeting less likely to be interrupted, to render the capture of the Gloire a very gallant performance on the part of the Astræa. Nor did the officers and men of the French frigate by any means give away their ship. Much credit is also due to Lord Henry Paulet individually, both for the fairness of his account, and the feeling manner in which he speaks of his antagonist. He expresses sorrow at the Gloire's loss of men, and describes Captain Beens as "an able, humane, and intelligent officer." The first-lieutenant of the Astræa, Mr. John Talbot, was sent to take charge of the Gloire, and, soon after his arrival at Portsmouth with the prize, was deservedly made a commander.

The Gloire's two consorts were the Gentille and Fraternité, each of the same force as herself. The Gentille was captured, on the following morning, by the Hannibal; but the Fraternité effected her escape. The Gloire was purchased for the use of the British navy, and registered as a 12-pounder 36; but, being old and nearly worn out, she did not long continue as a cruising-ship.

On the 1st of May, at 11 A.M., a fire broke out on board the 98-gun ship Boyne, Captain George Grey, bearing the flag of Vice-admiral Sir John Jervis, as she lay at her anchors at Spithead. The flames had burst through the poop before the fire was discovered; and they now spread so rapidly that, in less than half an hour, this fine ship, in spite of every exertion of her officers and crew, was in a blaze fore and aft. As soon as the fire was discovered by the fleet, all the boats of the ships proceeded to the Boyne's assistance; and the whole of her numerous crew, except eleven, were thereby saved. The port-admiral, Sir Peter Parker, went on board the Royal William, and made the signal for all ships most in danger to get under way; which order, although both wind and tide were unfavourable, was executed with promptness and judgment, and the ships lying to the eastward of the Boyne, and from the direction of the wind unsafely situated, dropped down to St. Helen's.

The Boyne's guns, being loaded, went off as they became heated, discharging their shot among the shipping; whereby two men were killed and one wounded on board the Queen Charlotte. Some of the shot even reached the shore in Stoke's bay. At about 1 h. 30 m. P.M. the Boyne broke from her cables, and drifted slowly to the eastward, till she grounded on the Spit, opposite South Sea castle. Here the ship continued to burn until near 6 P.M.; when, the flames having reached the magazine, she blew up with a dreadful explosion. "The blowing up of her fore-magazine," says Captain Brenton, "offered one of the most magnificent sights that can be conceived. The afternoon was perfectly calm, and the sky clear: the flames which darted from her in a perpendicular column of great height, were terminated by an opaque white cloud like a round cap, while the air was filled with fragments of wreck in every direction, and the stump of the foremast was seen far above the smoke descending to the water."[1]

It has never been correctly ascertained how the fire on board the Boyne originated. One account is, that a part of the lighted paper from the cartridges of the marines, who were exercising and firing on the windward side of the poop, flew through the quarter-gallery into the admiral's cabin, and communicated with the papers and other inflammable materials. Captain Brenton thinks, that the overheating of the funnel of the ward-room

[1] Brenton, vol. i., p. 372.

stove, which passed through the decks, was the cause of the accident.

Among the British light squadrons cruising on the coast of France in the summer of this year, was one commanded by Captain Sir Richard John Strachan of the Melampus, having under him the 38-gun frigates Diamond and Hébé, Captains Sir William Sidney Smith and Paul Minchin, and 32-gun frigates Niger and Syren, Captains Edward James Foote and Graham Moore.

On the 9th of May, at 3 A.M., while these frigates were lying at an anchor in Gourville bay, island of Jersey, 13 sail of French vessels were discovered running along the French shore to the southward. The squadron instantly weighed and gave chase, with the wind off the land. At 6 A.M. the Melampus got near enough to fire upon the headmost vessels; but the whole convoy, except a cutter which escaped round Cape Carteret, ran close in shore, under the protection of two gun-vessels, the Eclair and Crache-Feu, aided by a small battery on the beach. The boats of the frigates having assembled on board the Melampus, proceeded, under cover of that ship and the other frigates, to attack the convoy; between whose armed vessels and battery, and the British frigates, as they came up in succession, a smart fire was maintained.

Opposed to so formidable a force, the French soon abandoned their vessels; and the boats boarded and took possession of the whole convoy, including the two gun-vessels, each of which was armed with three long 18-pounders. One small sloop, on account of the tide having left her, was burnt; the remaining 10, composed chiefly of ships and brigs, were brought safe off. One of the vessels measured 397 tons, and. the average of the whole was about 180 tons. They were laden with ship-timber, powder, cannon, cordage, and other articles of naval stores.

In performing this service, the Melampus lost one petty officer, and seven seamen wounded; the Diamond two seamen wounded; the Hébé, her surgeon (John Leggett) and two seamen wounded; the Niger, her second-lieutenant (Charles Long) and one seaman wounded; and the Syren, one midshipman (John M'Guffock) and one marine killed, and two seamen wounded; total, 2 killed and 17 wounded.

Subsequently, on the 3rd of July, when Sir Richard had with him the Hébé only, this enterprising officer captured, off St. Malo, six out of 13 French vessels, laden with military stores, and convoyed by a ship of 26 guns, two brigs, and a lugger: he also succeeded in taking one of the brigs, the Vésuve, armed with four 18 or 24 pounders, and 60 men.

The British 36-gun frigate Thetis, Captain the Honourable Alexander Inglis Cochrane, and 28-gun frigate Hussar, Captain John Poer Beresford, being stationed off Chesapeake bay, United States of America, in order to intercept three French store-ships lying in Hampton roads, discovered, at daybreak on the 17th of May, Cape Henry bearing west by south, distant 20 leagues, five sail on the larboard tack, standing to the northwest. These ships, which, although large, were evidently armed en flûte, drew up in line, and awaited the approach of the two British frigates. At 10 h. 30 m. A.M. the strangers hoisted French colours, and the second ship from the van, a broad pendant. The names of the five ships were Normand, Trajan, Prévoyante, Hernoux, and Raison; but what stations the ships severally held in the line (except that the Prévoyante is rightly placed), or which ship was the French commodore's, cannot now be ascertained, and is, indeed, of no great consequence.

The Hussar, by signal, hauled up and placed herself opposite to the two van-ships; and the Thetis, following in line, opened her broadside upon the centre-ship, which was the largest. By 11 A.M. the Hussar had compelled the commodore and his second ahead to quit the line, and make sail to the east-south-east. The fire of both frigates now fell upon the centre-ship and the two ships in her rear; all three of which, at 11 h. 45 m. A.M., hauled down their colours; but the two rear-ships, notwithstanding they had surrendered, crowded sail to get away. One of them, the Raison, was soon overtaken by the Hussar; but the other effected her escape.

The large ship was the Prévoyante, pierced for 36, but mounting 24 guns only, believed to have been 8-pounders. As a proof how resolutely she had been defended, her fore and main masts went over the side in half an hour after her surrender. What was her complement at the commencement of, or her loss during, the action, does not appear in Captain Cochrane's letter. The Raison mounted, according to the journal of one of the officers of the Hussar, her principal opponent, 14 guns, but Captain Cochrane, in his letter, says 18; in either case probably 6-pounders, with a complement, as it appears, of 125 men, of whom between 20 and 30 were too sick to go to quarters. Her loss in the action is nowhere stated.

The Thetis, whose long guns were 18 and 9 pounders, besides

as many 18 or 24 pounder carronades on the quarter-deck and forecastle as gave her 42 or 44 guns in the whole, with a complement of 261 men and boys, lost eight men killed, and nine wounded, some of them badly. The Hussar, whose 24 maindeck guns were long 9-pounders, exclusive of six 18-pounder carronades and four long sixes on the quarter-deck and forecastle, total 34 guns, with a complement of 193 men and boys, lost only three men wounded. With respect to damages, the latter ship had her standing and running rigging much cut, and three shot-holes in the fore, and one in the main mast.

The Hussar alone, as a regular man of war, was more than a match for the two captured store-ships; and they and their three consorts were of no greater force, however formidable in appearance, than a British 18-pounder 36 and a 28-gun frigate would, at any time, have gladly encountered.

The Prévoyante and Raison were purchased by government, and fitted out at Halifax, Nova Scotia. They only remained, however, as cruising-ships until their arrival in England in 1799. The Prévoyante measured 803 tons, and, until subsequently restored to her original employment of a store-ship, was registered as a 36-gun frigate; not in Steel, for he classes her as a 40, but in the books of the navy. If we look, for a moment, at the Prévoyante's establishment of guns, as by Admiralty-order of August 17, 1795, we shall find that this "36-gun frigate" was, in more than one instance, an anomaly of her day.

	No.	Pdrs.
First, or berth deck	10 carrs.	24
Second, or main deck	30 long	12
Quarter-deck and forecastle	6 ,,	9
,,	10 carrs.	18
Carriage-guns	56	
Men and boys	281	

Suppose the captain of the Prévoyante, having taken a French frigate, were to state, as others had done before him, that his ship was "of 36 guns," would not the French officers consider the discrepancy as too gross to be other than a typographical error—a substitution of a 3 for a 5?

On the 25th of May the British 16-gun ship-sloop Thorn, Captain Robert Waller Otway, being on the Windward Island station, fell in with, and, after a spirited action of 35 minutes, during which the enemy was repulsed in two attempts to board, captured the 18-gun ship-corvette, Courier-National, commanded by a lieutenant de vaisseau.

The Thorn, whose guns were 6 pounders, with a crew on board of 80 men and boys, had only five men wounded; while the loss of the Courier-National, whose guns were 8 and 6 pounders, with a crew of 119 men and boys, amounted to seven killed and 20 wounded.

This was a well-contested match; and, while every credit is due to Captain Otway and his numerically inferior crew, for so promptly deciding it, the loss sustained by the French ship shows that her officers and men were by no means deficient in bravery.

In the month of June Admiral Hotham, while cruising with the British fleet off the Island of Minorca, received intelligence that the French fleet was at sea. To ascertain the fact, the admiral, on the evening of the 23rd, detached the 28-gun frigate Dido, Captain George Henry Towry, and 12-pounder 32-gun frigate Lowestoffe, Captain Robert Gambier Middleton, to reconnoitre the road of Toulon. On the 24th, at 4 A.M., latitude 41° 8′ north, longitude 5° 30′ east, these frigates, standing close hauled on the larboard tack, with the wind at north-north-west, descried approaching them, nearly ahead, the French 40-gun frigate Minerve, Captain Perrée, and 36-gun frigate Artémise, Captain Charbonnier, which frigates, by a singular coincidence, had been ordered by the French admiral to proceed off Minorca, and ascertain the truth of a rumour that the British fleet was at sea.

As soon as the private signal made by the Dido, who was ahead of her consort, discovered the relation of the parties to each other, the French frigates wore round on the other tack and stood away. The Dido and Lowestoffe immediately made sail in chase. At 7 A.M. it was evident that the French frigates were leaving their pursuers; but at 8 A.M. the Minerve and Artémise, as a proof that they were not disposed to decline a combat with two ships, whose inferior force must now have betrayed itself, again wore round, and, with French colours flying, stood on under easy sail to meet the Dido and Lowestoffe; who, with colours hoisted, and all clear for action, kept their course to hasten the junction.

On arriving within about a mile of the Dido's larboard and weather bow, the Minerve, who was at some distance ahead of her consort, wore round on the same tack as the Dido, and at 8 h. 30 m. A.M. opened her fire upon the latter. The Dido, however, reserved her fire until 8 h. 45 m.; when, having got close under the Minerve's starboard and lee beam, the British frigate commenced a steady and well-directed cannonade. In about five minutes the Minerve, suddenly bearing up, with yards square, attempted to decide the contest at once by running down the little ship that was presuming to contend with her. Just as the Minerve's flying jib-boom was about to touch the Dido's main yard, the latter put her helm aport, to avoid receiving directly upon her beam, a shock which, with the weight and impetus of the French frigate, must have sent her to the bottom. Owing to this well-planned movement, the Dido received the blow obliquely, the luff of the Minerve's starboard bow taking her on the larboard quarter. But so heavy, notwithstanding Captain Towry's precaution, was the shock, that it drove the Dido nearly athwart the hawse of the Minerve; and, the latter's jib-boom being carried away by the former's main rigging, the bowsprit of the Minerve became locked in the mizen rigging of the Dido.

From the bowsprit, thus favourably placed, the Frenchmen, under cover of the Minerve's foremost guns and a heavy fire of musketry, attempted to board, but were prevented, as well by the pikemen on the Dido's quarter-deck, as by the violence with which the ships, owing to a great swell and hollow sea, were striking against each other. After about a quarter of an hour's contest in this situation, and when the Dido was literally hanging by her mizen rigging on the Minerve's bowsprit, the latter snapped short in two, carrying overboard with it, besides eight or ten of the French boarders, the Dido's badly wounded mizenmast. The wreck was quickly cleared; and, the colours of the Dido having fallen into the sea with the gaff, the signal-man, Henry Barling, with characteristic bravery, nailed a union jack to the stump of the mast.

As soon as she had thus cleared herself, the Minerve passed along the Dido's larboard beam, rubbing sides the whole way, and the mutual cannonade recommenced with vigour. Presently, however, the lower yards of the Minerve, hooking the leeches of the Dido's two remaining topsails, tore them out of the bolt-ropes; and the French frigate, continuing to range ahead, left the Dido almost a wreck upon her larboard quarter.

Having, owing to the Dido's position ahead of the Minerve, been prevented from firing into the latter's stern as she passed under it to assist her consort, the Lowestoffe now placed herself on the Minerve's larboard bow, about a ship's length from her;

and at 9 A.M. opened her fire, which, in six or eight minutes, brought down by the board the French frigate's unsupported foremast, also her main and mizen topmasts. About this time the Artémise, who, in running past, had fired an ineffectual broadside into each of the British frigates, hauled her wind and made all sail.

At 9 h. 15 m. A.M., the escape of the Minerve being rendered impossible, Captain Towry caused the signal to chase to be spread over the Dido's quarter. The Lowestoffe thereupon quitted the Minerve, and made all sail in pursuit of the Artémise; and the Dido, setting her only serviceable sail, the foresail, stretched ahead to repair her damages. The Artémise and Lowestoffe soon began exchanging their chase-guns; but the latter, having unfortunately received a shot through her mizenmast, could not carry her mizentopsail. In consequence of this, the Artémise gained upon the Lowestoffe so much, that Captain Towry, at 10 h. 30 m. A.M., made the latter's signal of recal.

At 11 h. 30 m. the Lowestoffe again closed with the Minerve on the starboard quarter, and soon opened upon her a heavy raking fire. In the mean time the Dido, having bent new fore and main topsails, and partially repaired her damaged rigging, had wore and made sail in the direction of the Minerve; who, at 11 h. 45 m., on her mizenmast being shot away by the board, and with it her colours, hailed the Lowestoffe to send a boat and take possession. At this time the Artémise was nearly hull down to windward; and the Minerve, certainly, if not in a defenceless, was in an utterly unmanageable state.

The Dido, out of her complement of 193 men and boys, had her boatswain (Cuthbert Douglas) and five seamen killed, her first-lieutenant (Richard Buckoll, who, however, did not quit the deck), captain's clerk (Richard Willan), and 13 seamen wounded. The Lowestoffe, out of her complement of 212, had none killed and only three wounded. Each of these frigates carried the guns of her class, as described at G, H, and I of the table at p. 101, with four 18-pounder carronades in addition; making the Lowestoffe's guns 36, and those of the Dido 32.

The Minerve mounted two carronades less than her establishment at p. 59, or 42 guns in all, with a complement on board of 318 men and boys, and is represented to have lost upwards of 20 in killed and wounded (among the latter her captain), exclusive of those that were drowned by the falling of the bowsprit. The loss sustained by the Artémise, a regular 36, mounting 40 guns, out of a complement amounting at least to 300, could not of course be ascertained, but, from her small share in the action, was probably of very slight amount.

In every point of view, this was a gallantly-fought action on the part of the British. The Minerve alone was superior in broadside weight of shot to the Dido and Lowestoffe together, and the Artémise was rather more than a match for the Lowestoffe. The conduct of Captain Towry was noble in the extreme. His senior rank gave him, although commanding the smaller ship, the right of choosing his antagonist, and he did not hesitate a moment in laying the Dido alongside a ship of nearly double her size and force. A ship of 1102 tons, and 318 men, coming stem-on upon a ship of 595 tons, and 193 men, was indeed a critical situation for the latter; and, had the Minerve's consort not behaved in a most dastardly manner, the Dido at least must have become the prize of the French commodore.

It was well for the Dido that the Lowestoffe's captain possessed none of the backwardness of the captain of the Artémise; and, indeed, so ready is Captain Towry to admit the benefit he derived from his consort's aid; so far is he from wishing to monopolize the credit of the victory, that in his official letter he says, "By Captain Middleton's good conduct the business of the day was, in a great measure, brought to a fortunate issue."

The Minerve was conducted in safety to Port Mahon, and afterwards to Ajaccio, and was added to the British navy, under the command of Captain Towry, as a 38-gun frigate; to which class, from her fine qualifications, the Minerve became a valuable acquisition. The Dido's first-lieutenant, already named, was justly promoted to the rank of commander; as was also Mr. Joshua Sydney Horton, the first-lieutenant of the Lowestoffe.

On the 22nd of August, at 1 P.M., as a British squadron under the orders of Captain James Alms of the 36-gun frigate Réunion, composed of, besides that frigate, the 50-gun ship Isis, Captain Robert Watson, 18-pounder 32-gun frigate Stag, Captain Joseph Sydney York, and 28-gun frigate Vestal, Captain Charles White, was cruising in the North Sea, off the coast of Norway, the two Dutch 36-gun frigates Alliance and Argo, and the 16-gun cutter Vlugheld (Nelly, in the Gazette account), were discovered to windward, standing towards the shore on the larboard tack. Chase was given, and a change of wind enabled the Stag, at about 4 h. 15 m. P.M., to close with the Alliance, the sternmost vessel. The remaining British ships, meanwhile, devoted their attention to the Argo and Vlugheld, in the hope to cut them off from the harbour of Egeroe, towards which they were directing their course. After about an hour's action with the Stag, the Alliance hauled down her colours; but under what circumstances, as to damage or loss, the official account does not inform us, and, at this late day, we have no means of ascertaining.

The Stag, armed and manned like her sister frigate, the Lively, had four men killed and 13 wounded. The Alliance, whose 36 guns consisted of 26 long 12-pounders, six long 6s, and four brass 24-pounder carronades, with a crew of 240 men and boys, undoubtedly sustained a loss, and, in all probability, to a much greater amount than that of her superior opponent, the Stag; but, as above stated, no notice is taken of it in Captain Alms's letter: a piece of neglect of which we have already pointed out the injustice. One circumstance is clear, that the Alliance, from the first, had no chance of success, the Réunion alone being quite a match for the Argo, who was armed precisely the same as the Alliance; and then a 50-gun ship and a 28-gun frigate were ready, if necessary, to assist the Stag.

After a running fight, in which the Réunion lost one man killed and three wounded, the Isis, two men wounded, and the Argo, two killed and 15 wounded, besides being hulled with thirty 24-pound shot, and having her sails and rigging much cut, the Argo, with the cutter, got safe into Egeroe.

Having blamed Captain Alms for an omission, we are bound to show where he has acted in a manner highly laudable and worthy of imitation. "I have," he says in his letter, "thought proper, for their lordships' information, to send in the Alliance with my despatches by Lieutenant William Huggell, of his majesty's ship under my command, whom I recommend to their favour, who will inform their lordships with every proceeding of the chase and action; but, as the Alliance struck to the Stag, have put Mr. Patrick Tonyn, her first-lieutenant, to take charge of her, with orders to proceed to the Nore."

In the beginning of the month of September the 12-pounder 32-gun frigate Southampton, Captain James Macnamara, had been left, in company with the 18-gun ship-sloop Moselle, Captain Charles Brisbane, to watch the port of Genoa, in which lay, waiting for an opportunity to return to Toulon, the French 36-gun frigate Vestale, 28-gun frigate or "corvette" Brune, and 14-gun brig-corvettes Alerte and Scout. On the 28th Captain Macnamara detached the Moselle on service to Vado; and, on the 29th, in the afternoon, while standing in towards Genoa, the Southampton discovered several sail steering to the westward. The British frigate immediately crowded sail after the largest ship, which was no other than the Vestale, who, with her little squadron, and several small privateers, had taken advantage of the Moselle's temporary absence to effect her own and their escape.

At 10 P.M. the Southampton arrived within hail of the Vestale, and receiving no satisfactory answer, fired her starboard broadside into the French frigate's larboard quarter. The Vestale returned the fire, but, wishing to avoid an action, at 10 h. 25 m. P.M. tacked, and was promptly followed by the Southampton, who soon brought her larboard guns to bear. The Vestale now crowded all sail to get away, as did also the Brune, who was at a short distance ahead of her. The Southampton, after having partially repaired her damaged rigging, as she stood on in chase, discovered the Alerte and Scout brigs close to her, endeavouring to effect their escape by steering different courses. At 11 P.M., just as the Southampton was getting within point-blank range of the Vestale, the former's mizenmast, from a severe wound it had received and the press of sail now carried, fell over the side. Although the wreck was cleared, a jury-mast erected, and fresh sails bent and set, with surprising alacrity, the time lost could not be regained; and the Vestale, in chase of whom the Moselle joined about midnight, effected her escape, with the loss, as it afterwards appeared, of eight men killed and nine wounded.

Thus ended an affair, in which a different line of conduct on the part of the French commander might, on a fair calculation of the odds in his favour, have enabled him to capture a British frigate. All that can now be said is, that the gallantry of the Southampton's captain afforded a remarkable contrast to the pusillanimity (for it would be wrong to call it by any other name) of the captain of the Vestale.[1]

On the 28th of September, at 4 h. 30 m. A.M., the British hired cutter Rose, Lieutenant William Walker, of eight 4-pounders and only 13 men and one boy on board, being near to the island of Capraria on her passage from Leghorn to Bastia in Corsica, discovered three French lateen-rigged privateers to

[1] Mr. Marshall, in his biographical work (vol. i., p. 686), states that the Southampton ran the Vestale on board, and "soon compelled her to surrender," but that, when about to take possession, the former lost her mizenmast, and the Vestale "rehoisted her colours," and went off before the wind. Not a word of this is to be found in the Southampton's log; it is therefore, in all probability, incorrect.

leeward. At this time almost the only man on deck was the steersman, but the alarm soon brought up from their beds the remainder of the cutter's small crew; and, although he had on board a king's messenger, Mr. Mason, and two ladies, as passengers, and 10,000*l.* in specie, Lieutenant Walker formed the bold resolve of attacking the three vessels, either of which, in point of men at least, was known, from the complement they usually carried, to be more than treble the force of the Rose.

The cutter was quickly cleared for action, and bore down with a moderate breeze and smooth sea directly for the largest of the privateers, which was at some distance to leeward of the other two. It was the intention of Lieutenant Walker to give this privateer the cutter's stem, and for that purpose he himself attended to the steering; but, the Rose getting near, the lieutenant rushed forward to be among the foremost of the boarders, when the man whom he had left at the helm either misunderstood or neglected his orders, and permitted the privateer to shoot too far ahead.

The consequence was, that instead of striking the privateer amidships, the cutter with her bowsprit merely carried away the former's mizenmast and the projecting part of her stern. While passing to leeward, however, the Rose poured in a destructive raking fire with three round shot in every gun. She then luffed up, with the intention of placing herself on the bows of her antagonist, but became becalmed by the latter's sails. At length the Rose moved ahead, and, in tacking, carried away with her main boom the privateer's foreyard. On coming round upon the other tack, the Rose discharged a second broadside into her antagonist, and set fire to her foresail and mizen. The privateer instantly called for quarter and struck.

After threatening the French captain to sink his vessel if he attempted to make sail, Lieutenant Walker, who could have ill spared any hands to take possession, stood after the nearest of the two other privateers, and, by a well-directed broadside between wind and water, sent the second privateer to the bottom; nor, circumstanced as he was, and knowing the unprincipled character of these sea banditti, could that officer be blamed for not staying to pick up the drowning crew. The Rose left them to their fate, and, finding the third privateer making off to windward, stood towards, and with great difficulty secured the one that had struck to her.

This privateer mounted one brass long 6-pounder and four 1-pound swivels on her bow, and 12 brass blunderbusses, or musketoons, on her sides, and had on board when taken, exclusive of 13 reported as killed, 29 men. The privateer that was sunk was stated to have had on board 56 men, and the one that escaped, 48; making a total of 146 opposed to 14. Of this her small crew the Rose was so fortunate as to have only one man hurt, and that was by having his foot accidentally crushed by one of the gun-carriages. This intrepid fellow, William Brown by name, although so painfully wounded, could not be persuaded to go below, saying to his commander, "Indeed, sir, you cannot spare a man; I can sit here and use a musket as well as any of them."[1] Notwithstanding her crew had escaped so surprisingly, the Rose had her hull struck with shot in every direction, her mast and main boom badly wounded, and her sails riddled like a sieve.

Battening down the privateer's men in their vessel and then taking her in tow, the Rose steered with her prize for Bastia, where, in a day or two, they both arrived. Lieutenant Walker soon afterwards, for his very gallant behaviour, received a most flattering letter from the Viceroy of Corsica, Sir Gilbert Elliot, as well as from Admiral Hotham, the British commander-in-chief on the station. But, owing to some unexplained cause, the official letter addressed to Admiral Hotham never found its way into the Gazette: hence the affair, although long a topic of admiration among the officers of the British navy serving in the Mediterranean, produced no beneficial result to the party who had so nobly sustained the honour of the British flag.

On the 10th of October, at 9 h. 30 m. A.M., the British 12-pounder 32-gun frigate Mermaid, Captain Henry Warre, cruising off the island of Grenada, discovered a ship and brig at anchor off La-Baye, and made all sail towards them. At 10 h. 30 m. A.M. the two vessels, which were the French ship-corvette République, of 18 guns, and the brig-corvette Brutus, of 10 guns, got under way and made sail to the southward, with the wind easterly.

Finding that the Mermaid was gaining fast upon her, the Brutus bore up and steered for the land, anchoring, at 10 h. 50m., in the bay of Requain. The frigate bore up also, and at noon anchored close to the brig; who soon began landing her crew, consisting of 50 sailors and 70 soldiers. After firing several broadsides at the Brutus and at the people landing from her, Captain Warre sent his boats, manned and armed, and took

---

[1] The men, in these cases, being hired with the vessel, receive no allowance for wounds.

possession of the brig. It now appeared that two men, left on board for that purpose, had just set the brig on fire in the forehold, and the British were obliged to scuttle the decks to extinguish the flames. This done, the Mermaid and her prize, at 3 P.M., weighed and made sail out of the bay.

On the 13th, in the evening, having seen the Brutus safe into St. George's, the Mermaid came to an anchor off one of the small islands close to the northward of Grenada; and on the 14th, at daybreak, weighed in chase of a ship in the west by north, or leeward quarter. At 10 h. 45 m. A.M. the Républicaine, as the ship proved to be, put before the wind under all sail; and at 3 h. 50 m. P.M., after a running fight since noon, and a close action of ten minutes, struck her colours, with a loss, out of a crew, including a French general (intended to command at Grenada) and his suite and several other passengers, amounting to 250 men, of nearly 20 killed and several wounded. On board the Mermaid one seaman only was killed, and three wounded.

On the 14th of October, at 1 P.M., while the British frigates Melampus, Captain Sir Richard John Strachan, and Latona, Captain the Honourable Arthur Kaye Legge, were running before a fresh south-south-east wind, between the island of Groix and the main land of France, the batteries on each side of the channel opened upon them a heavy but ineffectual fire; and which the frigates, as they passed rapidly on, returned with one or two broadsides each. At 6 P.M. the south point of the island of Groix bore from them east, distant seven leagues.

On the 15th, at 6 h. 15 m. A.M., as these two frigates were standing close-hauled on the starboard tack, with the wind at west by north, two ships were descried in the south-west, and a brig in the north-west. The latter was the French 16-gun brig-corvette Eveillé, and the two former the French 40-gun frigate Tortue and 36-gun frigate Néréide, making the best of their way to Rochefort, after a 60 days' tolerably successful cruise in company with the new 44-gun frigate Forte, who appears to have got safe in during the preceding night.

The Latona, as soon as she had signalled the two strange frigates to her consort, edged away towards them, and was quickly followed, under all sail, by the Melampus. At 11 A.M. the 74-gun ship Orion, Captain Sir James Saumarez, and 36-gun frigate Thalia, Captain Lord Henry Paulet, made their appearance in the north-east, and joined in the chase. At three-quarters past noon the Latona, who was at some distance ahead of her consort, began firing her bow-chasers at the rearmost French frigate; and the latter, shortly afterwards, returned the fire from her stern-chasers. At 3 P.M. the Orion, having badly sprung her main topmast, wore and discontinued the chase, hauling up for two sail in the north-north-west; which proved to be the 40-gun frigate Pomone, Commodore Sir John Borlase Warren, and 36-gun frigate Concorde, Captain Anthony Hunt.

In the mean time the Latona and Melampus, followed by the Thalia, continued the chase under all sail, with a fresh breeze from south-west by west. At 4 P.M. the Latona had gained considerably upon the sternmost French frigate; when, the Barges d'Olonne bearing east half-north distant only two miles, and the wind blowing dead upon the shore with a heavy sea, the pilot refused to take further charge of the ship. The Latona thereupon shortened sail, and hauled her wind to the north-west; as did, about the same time, the Melampus, and other chasing ships. The two French frigates, thus unavoidably left to themselves, ran through the Pertuis-Breton, and were soon at anchor in the waters at Rochefort.

The brig-corvette was not so fortunate. At 2 P.M., Isle d'Yeu bearing south-east by south distant three leagues, the British 74-gun ship Thunderer, Captain Albermarle Bertie, discovered the Eveillé standing to the south-east, and made all sail in chase. At 4 h. 30 m. P.M. Sir John Warren, with his ships, appeared to leeward. Both the Thunderer and Pomone soon opened their fire upon the Eveillé; and at 6 P.M., having previously thrown all her guns overboard, the brig struck her colours, and was taken possession of by an officer from the Pomone. The latter, shortly afterwards, accompanied by the Thunderer, Concorde, and prize, anchored in the road of Isle d'Yeu.

As the commanding officer on this occasion, Sir John Borlase Warren possessed the right to do, what he was always fond of doing, pen the official letter to the Admiralty. Whether any one of the captains under him would not have given a more correct account of the occurrences he reports, will appear by a slight analysis of his letter, as it stands in the London Gazette. Sir John says: "The Aquilon, who was the headmost, being within gun-shot of the enemy, they doubled the Baleine bank, and proceeded up the Pertuis d'Antioche to Rochefort." Now, the Aquilon, if she was in chase at all, got scarcely any nearer than the Pomone herself. Admitting a mistake in the name.

and that Sir John meant the Latona, did he also mistake the Pertuis-Breton for the Pertuis-d'Antioche? So far from the Latona having "doubled the Baleine bank," she found herself, on shortening sail, much within it, and had to beat out at a considerable risk.

But, let us see what Sir John says about the capture of the Eveillé:—" I hauled to the wind directly, and discovered two other sail in the north-west, steering in for the land; the whole squadron chased, and on our nearer approach found them to be a line-of-battle ship and a corvette-brig; I endeavoured to cut them off from the land, and, after several shots had been fired, the corvette brought to, and proved to be, &c." What is the inference here, but that Sir John, in a frigate, endeavoured to cut off from the land a French line-of-battle ship and corvette-brig? Will it be credited, that neither the Thunderer nor the captain of her is named in Sir John Warren's letter? It was the accidental discovery of the following words in the Orion's log, "An English line-of-battle ship in chase of a corvette, brig," that induced us to investigate the subject. In the chase of the two frigates, Sir John might have alleged as an excuse, the distance of the Pomone from them; but how happened he to forget the Thunderer, when that ship actually accompanied the Pomone and their joint prize to the anchorage at Isle d'Yeu?

Colonial Expeditions.—West Indies.

As soon as news reached France of the success of the republicans at Guadeloupe, every exertion was used to send out supplies to Victor Hugues. On the 17th of November, 1794, the 50-gun frigate, or rasé, Hercule, 36-gun frigate Astrée, two corvettes, an armed ship or two, and eight or ten sail of transports, having on board about 3000 troops, with warlike stores of every description, sailed from Brest bound to the Antilles.

On the 5th of January, 1795, at 8 A.M., latitude 16° 30' north, Désirade bearing west, distant 12 leagues, the British 74-gun ship Bellona, Captain George Wilson, cruising in company with the 32-gun frigate Alarm, Captain Charles Carpenter, descried two ships of that very French convoy standing towards her; but which, on discovering their mistake, tacked and stood away. The British ships went immediately in chase, with light winds and very hazy weather. At noon 10 sail, lying to, were discovered to leeward.

Supposing these ships and the two first seen to be a squadron of French men of war, the British 74 and frigate discontinued the chase until 1 P.M.; when the strangers gave a decided proof of their unwarlike character by bearing up. Observing this, the Bellona and Alarm again stood after them, the weather very squally and still hazy. At 5 P.M. the Bellona made the Alarm's signal to attack the convoy, while she prepared to engage the five ships, or, as Captain Wilson calls them, "frigates," which had formed in the rear of the convoy.

The Bellona, who was one of the fastest and handiest 74s in the British navy, soon overtook, and, after the discharge of a few shot, compelled the sternmost of these to strike. On taking possession, at 8 A.M., of the "frigate," as Captain Wilson in his journal still calls her, she was found to be "the Duras, of 20 guns, 400 troops, and 70 seamen." The crew reported their ship in a sinking state; "during which time," says Captain Wilson, "I lay to, expecting the other frigates to fetch me on the same tack, when Captain Carpenter hailed me to observe the same." At 8 h. 30 m. P.M., continues Captain Wilson, "I saw the frigates had bore up." On this, after directing the Alarm to take charge of the prize and follow with all expedition, the Bellona, a third time, made sail in chase; but, favoured as well by a dark and squally night as by the awkwardness, to use no harsher term, of the British 74 and frigate, the whole of the French ships, except the one which appears to have been thrown out as a bait or decoy, effected their escape.

While the Bellona was making the best of her way to Martinique, the Hercule and her charge steered for the island of their destination, Guadeloupe, and on the following day, the 6th, reached Pointe-à-Pitre in safety, and, after such an escape, it may be added, in triumph. A second piece of good fortune, indeed, appears to have attended the French commodore; for, on the preceding morning, the British 64-gun ship Veteran, Captain William Hancock Kelly, when within only a few hours' sail of her appointed station in Gosier bay, had put back to the southward, to attend the crippled Blanche and Pique to the Saintes.

The arrival of this important reinforcement inspired Victor Hugues with designs against the other ceded islands. Having not only troops, but transports to convey, and ships of war to protect them, this demon of republicanism, whose barbarity, as fully accredited on several occasions, was of the most revolting description, readily contrived to land soldiers at Sainte Lucie, St. Vincent, Grenada, and Dominique. Artful emissaries accompanied the troops, and soon succeeded in raising a ferment in the islands which they visited. The negroes, charibs, and many of the old French inhabitants, revolted; and dreadful were the atrocities perpetrated upon the well-affected. Neither age nor sex was spared; and plantations, in every direction, were seen mouldering beneath the firebrands of the insurgents.

The British troops, thinly distributed from the first, and since reduced by fatigue and sickness, could offer, in general, but a feeble resistance to the numbers of different enemies opposed to them. The garrison of Sainte Lucie, numbering 2000 men, evacuated that island on the 19th of June, and were embarked on board the armed store-ship Experiment, Lieutenant John Barrett, and a transport in company: they had suffered greatly, both by the climate and the enemy. By the 27th of the month, the rebellion in Dominique had been completely quelled by the few British troops stationed there, assisted by the bulk of the inhabitants. The island of St. Vincent and a part of Grenada were, at the close of the year, still in a revolted state.

In landing troops at the commencement, co-operating with them in the prosecution, or withdrawing them at the abandonment, of an attack, the officers and seamen of the British navy evinced their customary zeal and activity, and freely obtained, from those with whom they acted on shore, their commendations and thanks. Our researches have enabled us to name the following as among the officers, who, on the occasions alluded to, particularly distinguished themselves:—Captain Charles Sawyer of the Blanche, Captain Frederick Watkins of the Resource, Captain Josias Rogers of the Quebec (pre-eminently so, at Grenada especially), and Lieutenant John Barrett of the Experiment.

Early in the month of August, a British squadron, under the orders of Vice-admiral Sir George Keith Elphinstone, and composed of the

Gun-ship
74	Monarch	.	Vice-admiral (b.) Sir George Keith Elphinstone, K.B., Captain John Elphinstone,
	Victorious	.	,, William Clark,
	Arrogant	.	,, Richard Lucas,
64	America	.	,, John Blankett,
	Stately	. .	,, Billy Douglas,

g.-sh.-slps.
16	Echo	. .	,. Temple Hardy,
	Rattlesnake	.	,, John William Spranger,

having on board a detachment of the 78th regiment, commanded by Major-general Craig, anchored in Simon's bay, Cape of Good Hope.

Proposals were immediately made to the Dutch governor, General Sluysken, to the effect that he should place the settlement under the protection of his Britannic majesty. This the governor refused, and, preparatory to his intention to set fire to Simon's town, sent away the inhabitants. On the 14th, before this could be accomplished, 450 men of the 78th, and 350 marines from the squadron, were landed and took possession of the town. The Dutch militia and Hottentots, meanwhile, had taken post on the adjacent heights, and occupied the pass of Muyzenburg, distant six miles from Cape Town, well furnished with cannon, having a steep mountain on its right, and the sea on its left, but difficult of approach on account of shallow water and a high surf on the shore. From this strong position, the enemy fired occasionally on the British patroles; who, agreeably to their instructions, had forborne to commence the slightest act of hostility. The British now determined on offensive operations; and accordingly, a detachment of 1000 seamen, formed into two battalions, under the command of Captains Hardy of the Echo and Spranger of the Rattlesnake, were disembarked, making, with the soldiers and marines already on shore, a force of about 1800 men. To facilitate the attack, the vice-admiral equipped a gun-boat, and armed the launches of the ships with 24 and 18 pounder carronades.

On the 7th of August, at noon, everything being ready, and the wind favourable, the America 64 got under way, and, with the Stately of the same force, and the two sloops, the Echo, commanded, in the absence of her captain, by Lieutenant Andrew Todd of the Monarch, leading, stood in-shore, as close as the shallowness of the water would admit. The ships then, aided by the gun-boats and launches, which latter were of course enabled to get much closer, covered the line of march of the troops. At 1 P.M. the ships having arrived abreast of an advanced post, on which two 24-pounders were mounted, drove the enemy from it by the discharge of a few shots. A second position, defended by one gun and one howitzer, was similarly abandoned. Soon afterwards the ships arrived opposite the enemy's camp: and being judiciously posted by Commodore Blankett, opened so brisk and well-directed a fire, as to compel the Dutch to fly, long ere Major-general Craig and the troops could co-operate. The fire from the enemy's three field-pieces, killed two and wounded four men, besides disabling a gun, on board of the America, and wounded one man in the Stately. Some shots, also, passed through both ships, but did not materially injure either of them. At 4 P.M. Major-general Craig, after a fatiguing march over heavy, sandy ground, arrived at and took possession of the abandoned Dutch camp.

The Dutch, who after retiring had taken post on an advantageous ridge of rocky heights at a short distance off, were the same evening driven from that position also, by the advanced guard of the 78th, supported by the battalion, with the loss of only one British officer, Captain Scott of the 78th, wounded. On the day following, the 8th, having augmented their force from Cape Town, the Dutch advanced with eight field-pieces, to regain the position they had lost; but, after some slight skirmishing, in which great steadiness was displayed by the first battalion of seamen under Captain Hardy, the former were compelled to retire. The last-named officer had crossed the water with his battalion of seamen, as had also Major Hill, with the marines, and both seamen and marines received the enemy's fire without returning a shot. "They" (the seamen) "manœuvred," says Major-general Craig, "with a regularity which would not have discredited veteran troops." The general also compliments the marines for their steady resolution on the same occasion. On the 18th five Dutch Indiamen, lying in Simon's bay, were detained by the rear-admiral's orders. Among them was the Willemstadt en Boetzlaar; which was afterwards named the Princess, and fitted out by the British at the Cape as a 20-gun ship.

Some partial successes, gained on the 1st and 2nd of September, encouraged the Dutch, on the 3rd, to meditate a general attack on the British camp. The former advanced in the night with all the force they could muster, and with a train of not less than 18 field-pieces. But, just at this critical moment, the long-expected English fleet, with reinforcements, appeared in the offing. On the following morning 14 sail of East India ships, having on board a considerable quantity of troops, under the command of General Alured Clarke, with guns, ammunition, and stores of every sort, including an ample supply of provisions, came to anchor in Simon's bay.

With this accession of strength, the admiral and general determined on an immediate attack upon Cape Town. The disembarkation of the troops, artillery, and stores, occupied until the morning of the 14th; when the army began its march, each man carrying with him four days' provisions. The seamen with their usual alacrity and cheerfulness, dragged the cannon through a deep sand, although annoyed accasionally by a galling fire. In the mean time the America, the two sloops, and the Bombay Castle Indiaman, Captain Acland, whose men had volunteered and greatly assisted in the removal of the cannon, proceeded round to Table Bay, to make a diversion on that side. This so alarmed the Dutch governor, whose troops had been retiring before those of General Clarke, that the former, on the same night, sent in a flag of truce, asking a cessation of arms for 48 hours, in order to settle the terms of capitulation. General Clarke refused to grant more than 24 hours; and, at the termination of that period, the town and colony fell into the possession of Great Britain. The regular troops that surrendered amounted to about 1000. The ship Castor, and armed-brig Star, both belonging to the Dutch East India Company, were here seized. The latter was taken into the British service, and named the Hope.

In our account of the proceedings of Lord Howe's fleet in the year 1794, we mentioned that the Suffolk 74, Captain Peter Rainier, and a few other vessels of war, parted company from his lordship off the Lizard on the 4th of May, bound with convoy to the East Indies. By the able management of Commodore Rainier, that convoy, and a very numerous one it was, arrived in the succeeding November at Madras, without a missing ship, and what is still more extraordinary, without having touched anywhere on the voyage. The commodore remained on the East India station as the British commander-in-chief, and in June, 1795, obtained his flag.

On the 21st of July, in pursuance of orders from the government of Fort George, Rear-admiral Rainier, with the Suffolk, Captain Robert Lambert, and 50-gun ship Centurion, Captain Samuel Osborn, sailed from Madras road, having in charge some transports containing a detachment of troops, under the command of Colonel James Stuart, destined to act against the Dutch possessions in the island of Ceylon, particularly against the important posts of Trincomalé and Oostenburg.

At the same time the 44-gun ship Resistance, Captain Edward Pakenham, accompanied by the tender of the Suffolk, and a transport having on board a small party of troops, was detached to assist in an expedition that had previously sailed, escorted by the 32-gun frigate Orpheus, Captain Henry Newcome, for the reduction of Malacca. On the 23rd the Suffolk and convoy, then off Negapatnam, were joined by the 44-gun ship Diomede, Captain Matthew Smith (who had not yet been tried by the court-martial noticed at p. 238), and a transport or two, with some additional troops.

Thus strengthened, the expedition again set sail on the 25th, and on the 1st of August cast anchor in Back bay, in company with the 32-gun frigate Heroine, Captain Alan Hyde Gardner, who had joined the day previous. On board the Heroine was Major Agnew, deputy-adjutant-general, who had been sent to Fort Columbo, by Lord Hobart at Madras, ostensibly to explain to the Governor-general of Ceylon, M. Van, Angelbeck, the object of the expedition, but really to obtain from him an order to the commandant at Trincomalé, to admit 300 British troops to garrison Fort Oostenburg, situated within the harbour. This order Major Agnew had brought with him, but to which the commandant of Trincomalé refused obedience.

Nearly two days were occupied in useless remonstrances, when it was resolved to land the troops. Unfortunately, on that afternoon, the Diomede, in working into the bay against a strong land wind, with a transport in tow, struck on a sunken rock, not laid down in the charts; and, scarcely allowing time for the people to save themselves, went down with all her stores on board. The delay occasioned by this accident made it the following morning, the 3rd, before the troops could be landed. The disembarkation then took place, at a spot about four miles to the northward of the fort of Trincomalé, without the slightest opposition. Owing, in part, to an extraordinary high surf and the violence of the wind, it took as many as ten days to land the whole of the stores and provisions. The carriage of these and of the artillery to the camp, a distance of about three miles, over a heavy sand, was cheerfully executed by the seamen.

On the 18th the troops broke ground, and still remained unmolested by the Dutch. On the 23rd the English batteries, consisting of 8 18-pounders (three of them from the Suffolk), besides some guns of smaller caliber, opened their fire on the fort of Trincomalé, and, by the 26th effected a practicable breach. A summons to the commandant was then sent in; and, while that was being discussed within, every preparation for the assault was making without. The garrison demanded such terms as could not be granted. Others were forwarded. The non-acceptance of these occasioned a recommencement of the firing; but, before it had continued many minutes, a white flag was suspended from the walls, and the Dutch commandant agreed to the terms which had been offered. The garrison consisted of 679 officers and men, and the serviceable ordnance, of nearly 100 pieces, including a large proportion of 18 and 24-pounders. The loss sustained by the British in gaining this post amounted, in king's and in company's troops, to 15 killed and 54 wounded, and in seamen to one killed and six wounded.

On the 27th the fort of Oostenburg was summoned, and on the 31st surrendered upon the same terms as had been granted to Trincomalé. On the 18th of September the fort of Batticaloe surrendered to a detachment of troops under the command of Major Fraser, of the 22nd regiment.

On the 24th General Stuart embarked from Trincomalé, with a considerable detachment of troops and artillery, on board of the Centurion, Captain Samuel Osborn, company's frigate Bombay, Bombay store-ship, and Swallow and John packets, and on the 27th disembarked the whole at Point Pedro, island of Ceylon, about 24 miles from Jaffnapatam; of which important post, on the 28th, the general took quiet possession.

On the 1st of October the British 18-gun ship-sloop Hobart, Captain Benjamin William Page (late one of Rear-admiral Ranier's lieutenants and an officer of considerable experience in East Indian navigation), having on board a detachment of the 52nd regiment, under the command of Captain the Honourable Charles Monson, took quiet possession of Molletive, another Dutch factory and military post on the island of Ceylon. On the 5th the fort and small island of Manar, situated a short distance to the north-west of Ceylon, surrendered to Captain Barbutt, whom General Stuart, immediately after taking possession of Jaffnapatam, had detached on that service.

The settlement of Malacca had also, since the 17th of August, surrendered by capitulation to the force under the orders of Major Brown, and of Captain Newcome of the Orpheus frigate, Chinsura and its dependencies likewise surrendered; as, before the close of the year, did Cochin and all the remaining Dutch settlements on the continent of India.

BRITISH AND FRENCH FLEETS.

The abstract of the British navy for the commencement of this year[1] differs so slightly, in its more important totals, from that of the preceding year, as to require few if any additional observations. The first commission-column shows an increase of 14 ships of the line, and of 50 ships altogether; a sufficient proof that the dockyards had not slackened in their exertions. The number of ships and vessels added to the British, from the French navy, since the date of the last abstract, amounts to 28, exclusive of five from the Dutch navy,[2] and two captured Dutch East India Company's vessels, which we have considered as privateers. The 15 purchased vessels in the abstract, or the greater part of them, had been in the English merchant service. The loss sustained by the British navy, during the year 1795, amounted to 12 ships,[3] including four of the line; two of which, under circumstances that have been related, were captured by the French.

Of the 11 ships which, at the date of the last, or third year's abstract, remained on hand out of the 20 that were building at the date of the first, one ship only, the Ville-de-Paris, had been launched. Although the largest vessel hitherto built in an English dockyard, this 110-gun ship was rather exceeded, in length, by each of the French 80-gun ships captured by Lord Howe. For instance :—

		ft.	in.
Ville-de-Paris	length of lower deck,	190	2
Sans-Pareil	,,	193	0
Juste	,,	193	4

[1] See Appendix, Annual Abstract, No. 3.   [3] Ibid. No. 20
[2] See Appendix, Nos. 18 and 19.

Not, however, to be outdone by the French in the size of the 74-gun ship, the Admiralty had ordered ten to be laid down, nine of which, with the two 24-pounder 74s already on the stocks, averaged 1914 tons

The old 50-gun ship, it will be seen, has been displaced from the head of the under-line division, to make room for two new classes, composed of ships purchased from the East India Company. These ships are described in a note subjoined to the abstract:[1] it may therefore suffice to say of them, that they proved, on trial, to be far fitter for their old than their new occupation. The 14 newly-built 18-gun brig sloops at Y and Z, with another, the Despatch, referred to in a note in that abstract,[2] were the first British men of war constructed of fir since the year 1757.[3]

Carronades were rapidly spreading through the navy. Scarcely a ship was now without them. A tier of 32-pounders was mounted upon the second-deck of the nine purchased ships at R and S; and there were individuals in several classes whose armament was principally, if not wholly, composed of them. The 32-pounder had been assigned as the main battery of a whole class,[4] which otherwise would have had only 6-pounder long guns. A new use had been found for the smaller calibers: every ship in the navy, down to the 18-gun brig inclusive, was ordered to be supplied with a carronade for her launch;[5] to assist in carrying into execution the desperate service of cutting out vessels, an employment in which British seamen have so often distinguished themselves.

The number of commissioned officers and masters belonging to the British navy, at the commencement of this year, was,

Admirals	29
Vice-admirals	40
Rear-admirals	36
,, superannuated	31
Post-captains	466
,, superannuated	26
Commanders, or sloop-captains	241
Lieutenants	1878
,, superannuated	29
Masters	404

and the number of seamen and marines, voted for the year 1796, was 110,000.[6]

[1] See note R* to Annual Abstract, No. 4.
[2] See note Y* ibid.
[3] See p. 31.
[4] See note Y* to Annual Abstract, No. 4.
[5] First-rates, as well as 80s and 76s (or 24-pdr. 74s), were allowed 24-pounders; 98s, 90s, 74s, and 64s, 18-pounders; and from 50s (or 56s) to large sloops inclusive 12-pounders. Order dated August 28, 1795
[6] See Appendix, No. 21.

Towards the latter end of the year 1795, after having been long torn by domestic factions of the usual sanguinary character, France effected a change in her constitution. Instead of a national convention, the ruling power in the republic was vested in an executive directory of five members, and a legislative body composed of two chambers, namely, a council of ancients consisting of 250 members, and a " council of five hundred ;" one third of each to be annually renewed. This, in a great degree, restored peace at home, but produced no such beneficial effects abroad. France, indeed, having no internal commotions to suppress, could now devote her sole attention to her favourite pastime, that of attacking, overrunning, and oppressing the nations around her. With most of these she succeeded; but there was one nation, whose humiliation would have gratified her more than that of all the others, which still opposed her with success. Against England a blow was at length to be struck, that, all good republicans hoped, and many expected, would number her eventually among the conquests of France.

Although the summer and autumn passed without the Brest fleet's making any attempt to put to sea, yet the English government knew that an expedition upon a very extensive scale was maturing in the port. The destination of that armament, however, much to the credit of the French government, was kept a profound secret. The British were left to conjecture, whether it was Ireland, Portugal, or Gibraltar ; the latter was considered as by far the most likely. To be prepared for either case, the Channel fleet had been divided into three squadrons; one, under Rear-admiral Sir Roger Curtis, in the Formidable 98, was ordered to cruise to the westward ; another, under Rear-admiral Thompson, in the London 98, was stationed off Brest : and the third, under Admiral Lord Bridport, in the Royal George 100, remained at Spithead, to be despatched wherever the intelligence received by government might lead. On the 29th of October Vice-admiral Colpoys, in the Niger frigate, joined the squadron off Brest, and exchanged ships with Rear-admiral Thompson; who immediately departed for England, leaving the vice-admiral with ten sail of the line. On the 7th of November, Sir John having then 12 sail, was joined by Rear-admiral Sir Roger Curtis with seven ; but the latter shortly afterwards parted company, and on the 17th anchored with his squadron at St. Helen's.

The expedition, so long preparing at Brest, did certainly sail in this year ; but as it was quite at the latter end of it, we shall postpone our account of its proceedings until the next year's events arrive in order of detail.

On the morning of the 23rd of February, during the temporary absence of the British squadron from before the Texel, a Dutch squadron, consisting of two 64, and two 54-gun ships, and several frigates and sloops, escaped to sea; not unobserved, however, by the British 16-gun brig-sloop Espiègle, Captain Benjamin Roberts, and a cutter, both of which had been detached by the British admiral purposely to reconnoitre the port. The Dutch ships steered to the northward, with the wind fresh at north-east, and, while the cutter hastened home with the intelligence, were followed by the Espiègle, until the succeeding day, the 24th; when, being 40 leagues to the north eastward of Yarmouth, Captain Roberts quitted them. In a day or two afterwards this squadron fell in with the 54-gun ship Glatton, Captain Henry Trollope, and three or four smaller vessels, belonging to Rear-admiral Pringle's division. The Dutch formed in line, but did not follow the Glatton on her making sail to get off. In a short time afterwards Admiral Duncan resumed his cruising-ground, and prevented any other Dutch squadron from quitting the Texel during the remainder of the year.

At the commencement of the present year the fleet, under Sir John Jervis, who, it will be recollected, had, at the close of the last, succeeded Admiral Hotham in the chief command upon the Mediterranean station, amounted to 18 sail of the line, exclusive of a very numerous train of frigates and sloops. The fleet in Toulon, now, we believe, under the command of Rear-admiral Eustache Brueys, amounted to 15 sail of the line, exclusive of three ships building; one, an 80, nearly ready to be launched, and the remaining two, an 80 and a 74, in a very forward state. There was, at anchor in the port of Carthagena, a squadron of seven sail of the line, which, in the present equivocal state of Spanish politics, required also to have its motions occasionally watched.

In the latter end of February, or beginning of March, Sir John Jervis detached Vice-admiral the Honourable William Waldegrave, with the Barfleur 98, and four 74s, on a "particular mission" to Tunis; or, in plain words, to bring out, either by fair means or by foul, the late British 28-gun frigate Nemesis, and one of her captors, the French ship-corvette Sardine, which, with the French brig-corvette Postillon, had taken refuge in the harbour. On the night of the 9th of March the service was executed, with scarcely any opposition and no loss, by the boats of the squadron placed under the orders of Captain John Sutton of the Egmont, and covered in their approach by that ship and the Bombay Castle. On the next day the vice-admiral quitted Tunis, and in a few days afterwards rejoined the commander-in-chief off Toulon.

Among the separate squadrons employed by Sir John Jervis, was one under Commodore Nelson, consisting of the Agamemnon and Diadem 64s, the latter commanded by Captain George Henry Towry, the 32-gun frigate Meleager, Captain George Cockburn, and ship-sloop Peterel, Captain John Temple, detached on the 23rd of April, when the fleet was cruising off Vado, with orders to the commodore to harass the coast of Genoa, and blockade the port. On the 25th, in the afternoon, the squadron steered for Laöna bay, the commodore having received intelligence that a large convoy, laden with stores for the French army, had cast anchor off the coast of Finale at the bottom of the bay. On arriving in sight of the anchorage, however, four vessels only made their appearance, and these were moored under some batteries which opened on the Peterel as she was leading the boats of the squadron to the attack. The animated fire kept up from the ships in return effectually secured the boats, as they advanced to board and bring off the enemy's vessels; a service which the British gallantly executed, notwithstanding a heavy fire opened upon them from the shore, close to which the vessels were lying. The detachments were commanded by Lieutenant Maurice W. Suckling, assisted by Lieutenants James Noble, Henry Compton, John Culverhouse, and Charles Ryder, all of whom distinguished themselves Lieutenant Noble was badly wounded by a musket-ball in the head, and two seamen of the Meleager, one of them the cockswain of her barge, were also wounded, but not dangerously.

On the 31st the commodore, then with his little squadron, to which the 32-gun frigate Blanche, Captain d'Arcy Preston, and 16-gun brig-sloop Speedy, Captain Thomas Elphinstone, had recently been added, cruising off Oneglia, chased six French vessels running along shore, until they anchored close under a battery. At 3 p.m. the Agamemnon, preceded by the Meleager and followed by the Peterel and Speedy, anchored in less than four fathoms' water. The Diadem and Blanche, meanwhile, to the regret of their officers and crews, were too far to leeward to co-operate. The smart cannonade of the three ships and brig soon silenced the batteries; whereupon the boats of the squadron, in the face of the fire still kept up from three 18-pounders in a national ketch, the Génie, and one 18-pounder in a gun-boat, carried both vessels. The four transports in company had, in the mean time, run on shore; but these, notwithstanding the musketry of the crews stationed on the beach, were finally brought off. The transports were laden with cannon, ordnance-stores, intrenching tools, and provisions; which had been brought from Toulon, and were to have been landed at St. Pierre d'Acæne, to be employed in the siege of Mantua. To the want of the artillery on board these vessels was attributed, in a great degree, the failure of the attack upon that city. The loss sustained by the British, in the important service just detailed, amounted to only one man killed and three wounded.

In the latter end of June the near approach of the French troops to Leghorn rendered the speedy removal of the British residents and their property, as well as of the stores and provisions lying there for the use of the British fleet, an object of immediate importance. Accordingly, the 36-gun frigate Inconstant, Captain Thomas Francis Fremantle, then with two or three store-ships in company at anchor in the road, succeeded, on the morning of the 27th, in bringing away the English and emigrants, or such of them as were desirous to quit Tuscany; also 23 merchant ships and brigs, and 14 tartans, lying in the mole; the chief part of the valuable effects in the warehouses, and 240 oxen which had been purchased for the use of Sir John Jervis's fleet. At noon the French entered the town; and at 1 P.M. the batteries opened on the Inconstant, who immediately got under way, and with the only vessel that remained, a brig laden with ship-timber, escaped without any damage or loss. Commodore Nelson, in the 74-gun ship Captain, to which he had just been promoted, anchored off the Malora, to be ready to stop any ships that might be uninformed of the change that had taken place. The remainder of the British squadron in this quarter, under the orders of Captain John Garlies, in the 32-gun frigate Lively, proceeded, with the merchants and emigrants, to San-Fiorenzo bay, where the British fleet was then lying.

It being well understood that one of the objects of France, in taking forcible possession of the neutral city of Leghorn, was to afford her the additional means of recovering possession of Corsica, no doubt could exist as to her intentions upon the neutral fortress of Porto-Ferrajo, in the Isle of Elba, also belonging to the Grand Duke of Tuscany. To frustrate the attempt Sir Gilbert Elliot, the Viceroy of Corsica, in conjunction with

Sir John Jervis, made proposals to the governor of the town; and on the 10th of July, in the morning, Commodore Nelson, with the Captain 74 and a small frigate-squadron, on board of which was Major Duncan of the engineers, with a detachment of troops, took quiet possession of Porto-Ferrajo, a place mounted with 100 pieces of cannon, and garrisoned by 400 regulars, exclusive of militia. Every preparation had been made to storm the town, had the governor refused the terms offered, among which was an assurance that the Tuscans should receive no injury whatever in their persons or property.

On the 19th of August a treaty of alliance, offensive and defensive, between France and Spain, was signed at Madrid; in one of the articles of which it was stipulated, that, within the space of three months, reckoning from the moment of the requisition, the power called on should hold in readiness, and place at the disposal of the power calling, 15 sail of the line, and 10 heavy frigates and corvettes, properly manned, armed, and victualled. It might easily have been guessed which would be the "calling" power; and France did not even wait until the negotiation had produced its result ere she demanded a Spanish fleet to escort the squadron of M. Richery clear of that of Rear-admiral Mann, which was supposed to be hovering off Cadiz to intercept it.

On the 4th of August the French squadron in question, consisting of the 80-gun ship Victoire, and 74s Barras, Berwick, Censeur, Duquesne, Jupiter, and Révolution, with the frigates Embuscade, Félicité, and Friponne, sailed from the bay of Cadiz, under the protection of a Spanish fleet of 20 ships of the line and 14 frigates and corvettes, commanded by Admiral Don Juan de Langara; a service which M. Richery might have performed alone, as Rear-admiral Mann, with his seven sail of the line, had quitted the bay since the 29th of the preceding month. Almost as soon as the Spanish fleet had got out to sea, Admiral Langara detached Rear-admiral Solano, with 10 sail of the line and six frigates, to escort M. Richery to a spot distant 100 leagues to the westward. Having complied with his orders, the Spanish rear-admiral put about on his return, and the French rear-admiral, in pursuance of the instructions he had received, continued his route towards the coast of North America.

This treaty between France and Spain was ratified at Paris on the 12th of September; and in three days afterwards, which was immediately on the receipt of the intelligence, England laid an embargo on all Spanish ships at anchor in her ports

Next followed, bearing date the 5th day of October, a declaration of war by Spain against England. In this declaration, as is customary, the most plausible story is told to justify the resort to arms; but the real origin of the war was to be found in the mean subserviency of Spain to France, which country was now straining every nerve to overwhelm a power that would neither be corrupted by intrigue nor intimidated by threats.

About a week before the Spanish manifesto issued from Madrid, a fleet of 19 sail of the line and 10 frigates and corvettes, under the command of Admiral Don Juan de Langara, put to sea from Cadiz, bound through the Straits. On the 1st of October, at sunset, Cape de Gata bearing west by north distant three or four leagues, the squadron of Rear-admiral Mann, then lying nearly becalmed on its way from San-Fiorenzo bay to England with three transports and a brig under convoy, discovered the Spanish fleet in the south-east quarter. At 11 P.M., on a breeze springing up from the eastward, the Spaniards bore up in chase, and on the morning of the 3rd captured the merchant brig and one of the transports; but the squadron and remaining transports succeeded, the same evening, in reaching the anchorage in Rosia bay near the mole of Gibraltar.

Foiled in his principal object, Admiral Langara stood back to the eastward, and calling off Carthagena, was joined by seven line-of-battle ships out of that port; which made his whole force 26 sail of the line besides frigates. With this formidable fleet the Spanish admiral cruised as far up the Mediterranean as Cape Corse: in the neighbourhood of which he was seen on the 15th by some of the cruisers of Sir John Jervis, then, with his fleet numbering only 14 sail of the line (the Ca-Ira having been burnt by accident, the Princess Royal and Agamemnon sent to England, and the Captain detached off Bastia), lying at anchor in Mortella bay. Notwithstanding the opportunity thus afforded him, of striking a decisive blow against the British naval power in the Mediterranean, Admiral Langara steered for the road of Toulon; where, on or about the 26th of the month, he anchored, in company with 12 French sail of the line and several frigates ready for sea; forming, in the aggregate, a force of 38 sail of the line and 18 or 20 frigates, the largest fleet of men of war, we believe, ever seen in that port.

The rapid and extraordinary successes of General Buonaparte in Italy had greatly reduced the weight and influence of England along the northern and eastern shores of the Mediterrancan. The King of Sardinia, since the 15th of May, had been compelled to sign a treaty with France, by which he yielded up Savoy, the patrimony of his ancestors for many ages, together with the city and territory of Nice, and a large tract of land, which the conquerors entitled the Department of the maritime Alps. The King of the Two Sicilies, being also unable to stand against the victorious army of Buonaparte, solicited and obtained, on the 5th of June, a cessation of hostilities, and on the 10th of November signed with France a treaty of peace equally humiliating. With these powers as neutrals, or vassals rather, and with Spain as an ally in the war, France was on the eve of attaining what had long been her wish, the sole dominion of the Mediterranean sea.

One island, however, that had only a year or two before belonged to the republic, was still in the hands of the English. Precarious, indeed, was the tenure of the latter. The report of the continual victories of their countrymen had encouraged the Franco-Corsicans to renew their endeavours to undermine the interest of the British. Discontent soon prevailed all over the island, and a communication was established between the exiles at Leghorn and elsewhere with their partisans in Corsica. It soon became manifest to the viceroy, that an insurrection was preparing, of such a magnitude, that the comparatively small British force on the island would be insufficient to put it down. On becoming acquainted with this state of things, and actuated also by the daily expected rupture with Spain, the British government sent out orders for Corsica to be evacuated, and the troops and stores removed to Porto-Ferrajo. Just as this measure was beginning to be carried into effect, the island was invaded, and the departure of the British, to say no worse of it, rather prematurely urged.

No English detailed account of the evacuation of Corsica having, that we know of, been published, not even in a contemporary work, written chiefly to blazon the deeds of the admiral who superintended the operations, we must either pass over the subject as beneath our comprehension, or trust to the French accounts for particulars. In doing the latter we shall keep our discrimination to its duty, and not admit a fact but such as circumstances may seem to warrant.

Leghorn, after its possession by the French, became, as Buonaparte had intended it should be, the chief seat of preparation for the invasion of Corsica. General Gentili, a countryman of Buonaparte's, was placed at the head of the enterprise. Not having vessels enough to transport the whole of his troops at once, General Gentili detached General Casalta, another Corsican, with a small division, which, having embarked on board 14 feluccas and other small craft, sailed out of the port of Leghorn, and on the 19th of October landed on the island; unobserved, we believe, by a single British cruiser, although a contemporary informs us, that, at this very time, "Cockburn in the Minerve blockaded Leghorn."[1]

Casalta was soon joined by a considerable number of patriotic Corsicans, and, thus reinforced, marched against Bastia, near which he arrived on the 21st. Master of the heights that command the city, and certain of the support of the inhabitants, the general summoned the garrison of Bastia to surrender in an hour. "The English troops amounted to very near 3000 men."[2] Here we must be allowed to express a doubt, and yet we have no means of showing how the fact really was. In the port lay the Captain and Egmont 74s, with some other vessels, and on board of these, it appears, under the personal direction of Commodore Nelson, the British troops embarked.

The following is an English account, which describes in very creditable, and, we have no doubt, in very just terms, the exertions of the British officers in performing this important service. "The great body of Corsicans were perfectly satisfied, as they had good reason to be, with the British government, sensible of its advantages, and attached to it; but when they found that the English intended to evacuate the island, they naturally and necessarily sent to make their peace with the French. The partisans of France found none to oppose them. A committee of thirty took upon themselves the government of Bastia, and sequestered all the British property; armed Corsicans mounted guard at every place, and a plan was laid for seizing the viceroy. Commodore Nelson, who was appointed to superintend the evacuation, frustrated these projects. On the 14th of October, 1796, he sent word to the committee, that, if the slightest opposition was made to the embarkation and removal of British property, he would batter the town down. A privateer, moored across the mole head, pointed her guns at the officer who carried this message, and muskets were levelled against him from the shore. Hereupon Captain Sutton, pulling out his watch, gave them a quarter of an hour to deliberate upon their answer. In five minutes after the expiration of that time, the ships, he said, would open their fire. Upon this, the very sentinels scampered

[1] Brenton, vol. ii., p. 130.   [2] Victoires et Conquêtes, tome vii., p. 158.

off, and every vessel came out of the mole. During the five following days, the work of embarkation was carried on: the property of individuals and public stores to the amount of 200,000*l*. was saved.[1]

On the 22nd, after having, as the French accounts say, taken the British rear-guard, consisting of 700 or 800 men of Dillon's regiment, prisoners, General Casalta quitted Bastia for the town of San-Fiorenzo. He found the gorges of San-Germano strongly guarded; but, after a smart brush, his troops forced the passage. The republicans then marched on towards the town, and, in the face of a constant and very destructive discharge of grape from two British 74s moored off the beach, made themselves masters of it, taking prisoners a part of the garrison. On the 22nd, in the evening, Bonifacio was occupied by the French, and the garrison also, as it appears, made prisoners. In the meanwhile General Gentili, like General Casalta, had found the means, with the remainder of his troops, to get across from the "blockaded" port, and immediately marched upon Ajaccio, the birthplace of Buonaparte; the capture of which port restored the whole island to the dominion of the republic.

On the 2nd of November, having completed, as far as was deemed practicable, the evacuation of Corsica, and ascertained that the fleet of Admiral Langara had come to an anchor in Toulon, Sir John Jervis set sail from Mortella bay, with a fleet of 15 ships of the line and some frigates, having on board the troops and stores embarked at Bastia, and under his convoy 10 or 12 merchant vessels, which his cruisers had brought down from Smyrna. On the 11th of December the whole of this fleet anchored in safety in Rosia bay; and thus was the Mediterranean left without a single British line-of-battle ship cruising upon its waters.

On the day preceding that on which Sir John arrived at Gibraltar, the Spanish fleet, accompanied by the French Rearadmiral Villeneuve, with the 80-gun ship Formidable, the JeanJacques, Jemmappes, Mont Blanc, and Tyrannicide 74s, and the Alceste, Diana, and Vestale frigates, put to sea from Toulon. On the 5th or 6th of December the Spanish admiral, with his fleet numbering, as already mentioned, 26 sail of the line, besides 12 or 13 frigates, entered the port of Carthagena; leaving M. Villeneuve, with his five sail of the line and three frigates, to make the best of his way to Brest unattended. On the 10th, in the afternoon, the French admiral passed the rock of Gibraltar,

[1] Marshall, vol. i., p. 255.

and was of course seen by a part of the fleet at anchor in the bay; but a heavy gale of wind from the east-south-east, while it drove the French rapidly through the gut, rendered it impracticable for the British to make any movement in pursuit, any, at all events, that was likely to succeed. Supposing the destination of this squadron to be the West Indies, Sir John Jervis, on the following day, the 11th, despatched a sloop of war with the intelligence to the commanders in chief at Barbadoes and Jamaica.

Figurative language, however much to be admired in poetry, ill suits the sober page of history: it is indeed so foreign to the subject, that the reader is apt to overlook the hyperbole, and either to treasure up in his memory the literal meaning, or wholly to reject it as too extravagant for his credence. A contemporary, feeling himself called upon to explain why Sir John Jervis quitted the Mediterranean with his fleet, says thus: "We now begin to perceive the full force of our mistaken lenity to the Toulonese, whose half-burnt fleet was, in conjunction with that of Spain, driving before them the most intrepid admiral and the bravest captains Britain had ever seen: Jervis, Nelson, Troubridge, Hood, Hallowell, and many others were compelled to fly before the united forces of France and Spain."[1]

Can this allude to Sir John Jervis's voyage from Corsica to Gibraltar? Who was "driving" him? Surely not Don Juan de Langara, who did not quit Toulon until the British admiral had been a month on his passage; nay, not until he was in the very act of sheltering himself under the guns of an impregnable fortress? It appears to us that the writer would have better served the cause of his patron by endeavouring to reconcile Sir John's proceedings to the pledge which, within a fortnight of the commencement of his retreat, he gave to the King of the Two Sicilies, in the following words, part of a letter copied at full length into the same writer's work: "The gracious condescension your majesty has been pleased to show to me, in deprecating under your royal hand the dreadful effect which the retreat of the fleet of the king, my master, from these seas, would have on your majesty's dominions, and upon all Italy in the present crisis, has prompted me to exert every nerve to give all the support in my power to the cause of religion and humanity in which we are engaged; and I have, in consequence thereof, and conformably to the instructions I have recently received, concerted with the Viceroy of Corsica to take post in

[1] Brenton, vol. ii., p. 138.

the island of Elba, and to face the enemy as long as the subsistence of the fleet and the army will admit."[1]

The gale of wind, which came so opportunely for M. Villeneuve's passage through the Straits of Gibraltar, fell heavily, and in one instance fatally, upon the British ships at anchor in the bay. The 74-gun ship Courageux, commanded by Lieutenant John Burrows, in the absence of Captain Benjamin Hallowell, who was on shore attending a court-martial, parted from her anchors, and drove nearly under the Spanish batteries on the opposite side of the bay before she could be brought up. It being necessary to retire from this dangerous situation, the Courageux weighed, and under close-reefed topsails, stood over towards the Barbary coast, Lieutenant Burrows feeling averse, as it has since appeared, to run through the gut, lest he should fall in with M. Villeneuve's squadron.[2] Towards evening the wind increased to a perfect hurricane, and the weather became very thick. The rain, also, poured down in torrents, and there came on a tremendous storm of thunder and lightning. Soon after 8 P.M. the crew, who had been harassed the whole day, were suffered to go to dinner, and the officers, except a lieutenant of the watch, also retired below to take some refreshment. At 9 P.M., while stretching across under her courses, to get well to windward of her port, the Courageux struck on the rocks at the foot of Ape's hill (Mons Abyla), on the coast of Barbary, and in a very few minutes was a complete wreck. Of about 593 officers and men that were on board, 129 only effected their escape; five by means of the launch that was towing astern, and the remainder by passing along the fallen mainmast to the rugged shore. Many perished in the attempt, and those who did reach the shore were compelled to undergo very severe privations ere they got back to Gibraltar.[3]

The same gale of wind in which the Courageux was lost nearly proved fatal to the 80-gun ship Gibraltar, Captain John Pakenham, and the Culloden 74, Captain Thomas Troubridge. The latter drove from her anchors, and narrowly escaped being cast away on the Pearl rock; and the former was obliged to cut from her anchors, and struck several times on the bank off Cabrita point. The critical situation of the Gibraltar merits being

[1] Brenton, vol. ii., p. 135.
[2] Captain Brenton (vol. ii., p. 139) says, "the combined fleet," not knowing, seemingly, that Admiral Langara had stopped at Carthagena.
[3] In the first edition, the date of this melancholy accident was stated to be the 17th. Steel makes it the 18th, and Marshall (Royal Nav. Biog., vol. i., p. 468) the 19th; but it really happened on the night of the 10th. Captain Brenton enumerates the number

recorded. On cutting her cable, which she did at 9 P.M., the ship set her foresail and staysails, and at 9 h. 30 m. P.M., in order to haul up clear of Cabrita point, her mainsail and main-topsail. The latter sail split almost as soon as it was set. At 10 P.M., owing to the increased violence of the gale, the Gibraltar carried away her foretopmast, and split her foresail, mainsail, maintopmast staysail, and mizen staysail. At 10 h. 30 m. P.M. the ship, thus deprived of the means of clearing the land, struck several times on a bank off Cabrita point, but in five minutes drove over it, and, being a remarkably strong ship, made no water. At midnight the Gibraltar hove to, and at noon on the 11th let go her only remaining anchor in Tangier bay.

This is the substance of what is noted down in the Gibraltar's log; but an account somewhat different appears at p. 140, vol. ii. of Captain Brenton's work. "Driven by the violence of the gale down upon Cabrito point, the topgallant yard stowed in, the main rigging caught the lee-clew of the mainsail, and prevented their setting that sail, in consequence of which she caught upon the Pearl rock, which lies about three-quarters of a mile from the shore off the western point of the bay: here in a dark night, with a tremendous sea breaking over her, the crew assembled on the deck, and testified by their screams and actions every symptom of despair, and madly proposed, as a last resource, cutting away the masts and saving themselves on the wreck. The axes were brought, and preparations made for this purpose, but strongly opposed by the first-lieutenant, who, moving the wheel, assured the captain that the rudder was free and uninjured; a

---

saved from the wreck, "by jumping from the side of the ship to the shore," at 160. That the account, as we have stated it, is correct, will appear by the following abstract taken from the ship's pay-book at the Navy Office:—

Established complement, exclusive of widows' men.		633
In the barge with Captain Hallowell	12	
In the pinnace with Lieut. Tucker, assisting a transport under the Spanish batteries	9	
At work in Gibraltar dockyard	4	
In prizes at Porto-Ferrajo	9	
On board the Utile sloop of war	5	
Absent	39	
Saved { in the launch	5	
{ from the wreck	124	
	129	
		168
Number that perished, admitting the ship to have been fully manned		465

wave at the same time struck the ship forward with such force as to upset a forecastle gun, and the shock carried away the foretopmast; the next sea lifted her off the rock; being fortunately one of the strongest-built ships in the service, she made no water. Sufficient sail was set to enable her to weather Cabrito point, and in the morning she got into Tangier bay, and soon after rejoined the fleet; she was however considered to have sustained so much injury, that it was judged necessary to send her to England in order to have her taken into dock: here it was discovered that a very large fragment of the rock had pierced her bottom and remained there—had it disengaged itself, the consequence might have been fatal to all on board."

Now, the log states, that the mainsail *was* set, and shows clearly that the ship struck on the bank, rock, or whatever it may be, in consequence of the loss of her foretopmast (half an hour before) and the splitting of nearly all her sails. These manifest inaccuracies in the account lead us to hope that there is equal untruth in the alleged behaviour of the crew, behaviour more characteristic of timid females than of hardy British seamen. The Pearl rock lies about a mile and a half due south, and Cape Malabata, the north-east point of Tangier bay (on the opposite side of the strait), about 22 miles south-west of Cabrita point: how then, with the wind at east-south-east could the Gibraltar want "to weather Cabrito point" to get into Tangier bay?

The Gibraltar did not sail for England until five weeks after the accident; but, when taken into dock at Plymouth, in March 1797, a large piece of rock was undoubtedly found sticking in her bottom. Had the Gibraltar, on her way home, encountered a resolute enemy, the concussion of a few broadsides might have dislodged the rock and proved fatal to the ship. Of such a circumstance, too, the enemy would have taken due advantage, and have declared, with some show of reason, that he had sunk his opponent.

Having intrusted the command of the naval force at Porto-Ferrajo to commodore Nelson, who forthwith shifted his broad pendant from the Captain to the Minerve frigate, Sir John Jervis, on the 16th of December, got under way with his fleet and steered for the Tagus, where he expected to be joined by a reinforcement from England. Very soon after his departure, the Zealous struck on a sunken rock in Tangier bay, and, although she presently got off, was greatly damaged. On the 21st Sir John entered the river of Lisbon; and here another sad accident befel his fleet. The Bombay Castle 74, Captain Thomas Sotheby, having put her helm a-port to avoid running foul of the Camel store-ship, was swept from her course by the tide, and obliged to let go an anchor. Before, however, the ship could swing, she struck on the sand-bank at the river's mouth. Here the Bombay Castle remained beating from the 21st until 8 h. 30 m. P.M. on the 28th, when every officer and man of her crew was safe out of her. In the first instance some delay occurred in the arrival of boats to her assistance; and afterwards the increased violence of the weather rendered unavailing all the efforts that were made to get the ship afloat. The Camel also grounded on the bar, but got off without any material damage.

This last accident reduced Sir John Jervis's fleet in force, but not in number, as the St. Albans 64, bearing the flag of Vice-admiral Vandeput, was lying in the Tagus when the admiral arrived: consequently, the latter had still under his command 14 sail of the line, including one ship, however, the Zealous, not in a condition for immediate service. A contemporary states, that Sir John sailed from Gibraltar with only ten, and had now but nine sail of the line, "to contend against the French and Spanish fleets."[1] As a proof that our account is correct, here follow the names of the ships: Victory, Britannia, Barfleur, Blenheim, St. George, Gibraltar, Captain, Culloden, Egmont, Excellent, Goliath, Zealous, Diadem, and St. Albans. As to the danger of a contention with the French and Spanish fleets, that was surely over-rated, when one lay at Toulon, the other at Carthagena, and neither had evinced the least disposition to act on the offensive.

Light Squadrons and Single Ships.

Captain Sir William Sidney Smith, of the 38-gun frigate Diamond, having sounded the entrance to the port of Herqui, near Cape Fréhel on the coast of France, determined notwithstanding its narrowness and intricacy, to make an attempt upon a French corvette and six smaller vessels, which had previously been chased into it. Accordingly, on the 18th of March, at noon, the Diamond, accompanied by the 14-gun brig Liberty, Lieutenant George M'Kinley, and hired lugger Aristocrat, Lieutenant Abraham Gossett, stood for the port; the entrance to which was defended by two batteries, one of one, the other of two 24-pounders, erected on a high and rocky promontory, and, on this occasion, by a fourth gun mounted on a commanding

---

[1] Brenton, vol. ii., p. 141.

point. This gun opened upon the Diamond as she passed, but in eleven minutes was completely silenced. On rounding the point, the Diamond became exposed to a very galling fire from the three guns on the height, the only practicable way of silencing these guns being to storm them, Lieutenant Horace Pine, first of the Diamond, and Lieutenant Edmund Carter of the marines, were sent with a detachment of men, to effect that object.

The French troops from the batteries having in the mean time formed on the beach, checked by their fire the approach of the boats; whereupon Lieutenant Pine, proceeding to a spot, pointed out by Sir Sidney, landed in front of the guns; then, climbing the steep precipice, reached the heights before the troops from below could regain them. After spiking the guns, the lieutenant and his party descended the hill, and re-embarked, with the loss of only one wounded; but that one was Lieutenant Carter, mortally. The Diamond, Liberty, and Aristocrat, then proceeded, without further annoyance from the shore, to attack the corvette and the other armed vessels lying near her. Lieutenant M'Kinley, profiting by the Liberty's light draught of water, followed the corvette closely, and engaged her in a very gallant and judicious manner.

Finally, in spite of the fire kept up, as well from the vessels, as from the troops that had mustered on the beach and rock to protect them, the Etourdie corvette, of sixteen 12 (as represented, but more probably 8) pounders on the main deck, four brigs, two sloops, and one out of the two armed luggers, were set on fire and effectually destroyed. At 10 P.M., the wind and tide suiting, the little squadron weighed and repassed the point of Herqui, receiving a few shots from a gun which the enemy had succeeded in restoring to use. The loss of the British in these several attacks amounted to two seamen killed, Lieutenants Pine and Carter, the latter mortally as already stated, and five seamen wounded.

On the 20th of March, at 6 A.M., Bec du Raz bearing north by east distant four miles, a squadron under Sir John Borlase Warren, composed of the 44-gun frigate Anson, Captain Philip Charles Durham, 40-gun frigate Pomone, Captain Sir John Borlase Warren, 38-gun frigate Artois, Captain Sir Edmund Nagle, and 32-gun frigate Galatea, Captain Richard Goodwin Keats, having just tacked from the Saintes with the wind at east by south, discovered five strange sail in the south-south-east. The squadron immediately gave chase; and at 8 A.M.,

39 sail of French vessels appeared in sight. At 10 A.M. the two leewardmost, two merchant brigs, were brought to by the Pomone and Artois; as, in about half an hour afterwards, were a ship and a brig. The enemy's vessels of war were now drawn up in line to leeward of their convoy, counted at 60 sail, and about three miles to windward of the British squadron; and which vessels of war consisted of the

Gun-frigate
40	Proserpine . . .	Commodore Franç.-Hen.-Eugène Daugier,
36	Unité	Captain Ch.-Alex.-Léon Durand-Linois,
	Coquille . . .	,, Pierre-Paul Gourrege,
	Tamise	,, Jean-Bap.-Alexis Fradin,

Gun-corvette
20	Cigogne . . .	Lieutenant Louis-Gabriel Pillet,

together with the armed store-ship Etoile, Lieutenant Mathurin-Théodore Berthelin, and gun-brig Mouche.

At 45 minutes past noon, having formed his four frigates in line on the larboard tack, Sir John made sail in chase, leaving the Valiant lugger in charge of the four prizes to leeward. At 3 P.M., the British having gained so much in the chase as to point toward the rear of the French, the latter's van-ships bore down to support their rear, and the two squadrons except the corvette, which remained on the starboard tack to windward, engaged as they passed on opposite tacks. The Galatea, which was the rearmost as well as smallest of the British frigates, bore the brunt of this encounter. She had her rigging a good deal cut, and one main-deck gun dismounted; also a midshipman (Mr. Evans) killed, and four seamen wounded. The Artois, which was next ahead of her, had her maintopmast stay and some of her rigging cut away, but sustained no loss. At 5 h. 50 m. P.M. the British squadron tacked, and again at 4 h. 20 m. P.M.; when a battery on shore fired two shots, but neither of which reached.

By making short boards, the British ships had now got to windward of their adversaries; and at 4 h. 45 m. P.M. the Galatea was hailed by the commodore, and directed to lead through the enemy's line. At 5 P.M., by which time all the British ships had put about, the Galatea bore down, followed by her companions in line of battle; and the French squadron, thus determinedly pursued, made all sail towards the entrance of the passage du Raz. At 5 h. 30 m. P.M. the rearmost French ship, the Etoile store-ship, of 28 long 8-pounders and 159 men, after exchanging a few shots with the Galatea, struck her colours. Night coming on, the four French frigates and ship-corvette effected their escape through the narrow and intricate passage which they had entered. Meanwhile the bulk of the convoy, left under the charge of the Mouche, two other gun-brigs, and a lugger, had taken shelter among the Penmarck rocks, and were protected also by batteries to the eastward.

One seaman killed, and an acting lieutenant (Henry Burke, and one seaman wounded, on board the Galatea, making her total loss two killed and six wounded, was the only additional loss sustained by the British. It does not appear that the Etoile sustained any loss; nor could the casualties, if any, on board the remaining French ships be ascertained.

It is not worth while, in this slight skirmish, to make any display of the comparative force of the parties. It is clear, however, that the British, with two very powerful 24-pounder and two 18-pounder frigates, to oppose to one French 18-pounder and three 12-pounder frigates, a corvette and an armed store-ship, had the odds greatly in their favour. This is as the fact really was, and not according to the statement of force at the foot of Sir John Warren's letter. There the Unité and Coquille are described as 18-pounder frigates, and the Etoile as mounting 30, and the Cigogne 22, long 12-pounders. The complements of the frigates are even more exaggerated than their guns. The Proserpine is assigned 500 men, although, when captured three months afterwards, she had only 346; and the Unité and Coquille 400 each, although the first, at her capture in less than a month afterwards, had only 255.

On the 13th of April, at 4 P.M., a squadron under the command of Captain Sir Edward Pellew in the 44-gun frigate Indefatigable, consisting, besides that ship, of the 44-gun ship Argo, Captain Richard Rundell Burgess, 38-gun frigate Révolutionnaire, Captain Francis Cole, and 36-gun frigates Amazon and Concorde, Captains Robert Carthew Reynolds and Anthony Hunt, while cruising off Ushant, discovered and chased an enemy's frigate at some distance to windward. The Révolutionnaire, being the nearest to the stranger, was directed to tack and endeavour to cut her off from the land. Just as it grew dark, the Révolutionnaire compelled the French frigate to go about, but, owing to the haze and darkness of the night, lost sight of her until 9 P.M.; when, being discovered in the act of bearing up, she was followed under all sail. At 11 h. 30 m. the Révolutionnaire closed with the stranger; and Captain Cole, very much to his credit, hailed, and endeavoured to persuade the

French commander to surrender his ship to the powerful force then coming up.

This being refused, the Révolutionnaire was compelled to open her fire, which the French frigate feebly returned with her stern-chase guns. After the discharge of the second broadside, and just as the Révolutionnaire, then going 10 knots an hour and fast nearing the land, had put her helm a-port, in order to run her opponent on board, the crew of the latter called out that they surrendered. The prize proved to be the French 36-gun frigate Unité, armed precisely as the Engageante, Captain (de vais.) Charles-Alexandre-Léon Durand-Linois, from Lorient bound to Rochefort. The Révolutionnaire, who appears to have mounted eight 32-pounder carronades in addition to her 38 long guns, had not a man of her 287 hurt. The Unité, on the other hand, out of a complement, as sworn to by her officers, and stated in Captain Cole's letter, of 255, had nine men killed and 11 wounded.

Comparative Force of the Combatants.

		Révolutionnaire.	Unité.
Broadside-guns	No.	23	19
	lbs.	425	240
Crew	No.	287	255
Size	tons	1148	893

Here are two "38-gun frigates;" and yet, in broadside weight of metal, one of them is almost twice the force of the other. Even had she met the Révolutionnaire single-handed, the Unité would have engaged with scarcely a chance of success. As a man of war, too, the ship of Captain Linois was not a little incommoded by the presence of Madame le Large, wife to the governor of Rochefort, with the whole of her family and domestics. These, including the lady's son, an officer belonging to the ship, Captain Pellew, very considerately, allowed to proceed to Brest in a neutral vessel; taking the young man's parole not to serve again during the war until exchanged. The Unité was a fine little frigate, about seven years old, and became added to the British navy as a 12-pounder 36.

On the 17th of April, in the morning, the 38-gun frigate Diamond, Captain Sir William Sidney Smith, then cruising alone, came to an anchor in the outer road of Havre, and immediately discovered, at anchor in the inner road, ready for sea, a French armed lugger, known, from the recapture of one of her prizes, to be the Vengeur, of ten 3-pounders and 45 men, an exceedingly swift-sailing privateer, that had been several times chased in vain, and whose commander was a very enterprising and experienced seaman. Conceiving it an object to stop the career of such a pest to commerce, Sir Sidney resolved to attempt cutting her out.

The expedition for that purpose, when all was ready, consisted of the Diamond's launch, armed with an 18-pounder carronade and muskets, and four other boats, one of which was a two-oared wherry, armed with muskets only. In the boats were embarked nine officers (six of them from 12 to 16 years of age), three servants, and 40 seamen; total 52. As is rather unusual on such occasions, the captain himself took the command of the boats. Circumstanced as the Diamond then was, there appears to have been no alternative. Her first-lieutenant had been sent to England with despatches, the second-lieutenant was sick in his cot, and the third so indisposed as to be unequal to any exertion. There was also an acting-lieutenant, but although possessed of all the requisite courage, he was too young to have the entire charge of such an enterprise; and the services of the master, who was an excellent pilot for the French coast, were wanted on board the frigate.

At 10 P.M. Sir Sidney, having embarked in the two-oared wherry, pushed off from the Diamond at the head of his boats. On arriving within sight of the lugger, the boats lay upon their oars to reconnoitre her position, and to receive from their commanding officer his definitive orders. This done, the boats took a broad sheer between the Vengeur and the shore, in order to assume the appearance of fishing-boats coming out of the harbour, and thereby protract the moment of alarm. The plan appeared to succeed, and the boats, unsuspected if not unobserved, pulled straight towards the object of attack; intending to reserve their fire until the lugger herself should open upon them. This the latter did as soon as they arrived within half pistol shot. The boats instantly returned the fire, and in less than ten minutes, without the slightest casualty, were in possession of the Vengeur.

Now it was that the British discovered the difficulties of their situation. During the short struggle between them and the privateer's men, the latter, very wisely, had cut the cable of their vessel; which, in consequence, had been, and still was, drifting with the tide towards the shore. Search was in vain made for an anchor heavy enough to hold the vessel against the strength of a rapid tide that rushed into the Seine. All the boats were sent ahead to tow, and every sail was set on the lugger, but all was in vain. After these fruitless efforts, a small kedge was let go, with scarcely a hope of its holding. The vessel dragged it a long way, but at length brought up nearly abreast of Harfleur, on the northern shore of the river.

Sir Sidney now quitted the prize in his boat, to proceed to the Diamond; but observing, as daylight approached, several vessels coming out of Havre to attempt her recapture, he returned to the lugger, with the determination of defending her till the north-east tide made, or a propitious breeze sprang up, by which his brave companions in arms might be extricated from their perilous situation; perilous, indeed, for the lugger was at anchor nearly two miles higher up the river than the town of Havre.

Every preparation was now made for an obstinate resistance, as far as the scanty means possessed by the vessel would allow. There was not a round of grape-shot on board, and the match was so bad that it would with difficulty fire the powder. Almost the first step taken by Sir Sidney on his return to the lugger, was to discharge his prisoners, by sending them upon their parole to Honfleur, on the southern bank of the river. The launch that carried them, and another boat, it is believed, then pulled towards and reached the Diamond, still at anchor in the outer road of Havre, and anxiously awaiting the return of her commander.

While the prisoners were embarking in the boats, several shot from the shore reached the Vengeur; and shortly afterwards a large armed lugger advanced to attack her. To receive the latter to the best advantage, the Vengeur got under way, and eventually beat her off, but not without sustaining a loss of several men wounded, including a young midshipman, Charles Beecroft. A variety of small craft, filled with troops, now surrounded the Vengeur; and a furious action commenced, chiefly with musketry. No breeze springing up, and the force opposed to him every moment increasing, Sir Sidney was compelled to surrender, with a loss of four of his party killed and seven wounded.

The prisoners thus made, consisting, in consequence of the return of some of the boats, of not more than 20 or 30 officers and men, were landed at Havre, and marched thence to Rouen; where they were imprisoned. On the 21st Sir Sidney Smith and midshipman John Westley Wright quitted Rouen under an escort, and arrived the next day at Paris. Here, upon a principle that would equally apply to any zealous and enterprising officer belonging to the navy of any belligerent nation, Sir Sidney Smith and Mr. Wright were considered not as prisoners of war, but as prisoners of state. Under the scandalous *régime secret,* they, on the 3rd of July, were removed to the tower of the temple at Paris, and there confined in separate cells. At the end of two years, however, Sir Sidney and his young friend effected their escape (by the connivance, as is thought, of the French government), and arrived in London in the month of May, 1798.

On the 20th of April, in the morning, as Sir Edward Pellew, having despatched home the Révolutionnaire and her prize, was lying to, while the latter weathered the Lizard, a suspicious sail appeared coming in from the seaward. Her not answering the private signal, when she tacked from the squadron, marked her out as an enemy; and Sir Edward, having ordered the Argo to Plymouth, made all sail in chase, accompanied by the frigates Amazon and Concorde.

After a chase of 15 hours, and a run of 168 miles, the Indefatigable, from her superior sailing, was enabled to come up with the strange frigate; whom the wind had prevented from steering for Ushant, otherwise she must have escaped. At a little past midnight the action commenced, and continued, at close quarters, both ships under a crowd of sail, during one hour and 45 minutes. The French frigate, by this time, had lost her mizenmast and maintopmast, and was otherwise greatly crippled; nor was the Indefatigable much less disabled, having lost her gaff and mizentopmast, as well as the use of her maintopsail, both leech-ropes having been shot away.

Having no after-sail to back, the Indefatigible unavoidably shot past her opponent; and owing to the latter's masterly manœuvres, had some difficulty, in this dilemma, to avoid being raked. While the Indefatigable lay ahead, reeving new braces, in order to come to the wind and renew the action, the Concorde (the Amazon not far behind) got up, and took a commanding position under the stern of the French ship. Whereupon the latter, having four feet water in the hold, and being greatly damaged in hull, masts, and rigging, fired a lee-gun and struck her light, as a signal of surrender.

The prize proved to be the French 40-gun frigate Virginie, Captain Jacques Bergeret, a remarkably fine ship, and armed precisely according to the establishment of her class. The Indefatigable was a cut-down 64-gun ship, and mounted twenty-six long 24-pounders on the main deck, and two long 12-pounders and eighteen 42-pounder carronades on the quarter-deck and forecastle, total 46 guns, with a complement of 330 men and boys. Of these the Indefatigable, like the Artoise in the last action, did not lose a man. The Virginie, on the contrary, out of her crew of 339 men and boys, as deposed to by her officers, had only one less than is stated in Captain Pellew's letter, lost 14 or 15 men killed and 27 wounded, 10 of them badly.

Comparative Force of the Combatants.

		Indefatigable.	Virginie.
Broadside-guns	No.	23	22
	lbs.	702	342
Crew	No.	327	339
Size	tons	1384	1066

This statement shows that the French frigate, except in number of men, was greatly inferior to the ship with which she fought; yet Captain Bergeret did not surrender until a second frigate was preparing to rake him, and a third approaching under all sail to join in the action. No one was more ready than Sir Edward Pellew himself to do justice to his enemy on this occasion.

The Virginie, as we have already stated, was a remarkably fine frigate, and became in consequence, a valuable acquisition to the class of British 38s. Sir Edward, however, had been misinformed when in his official letter he stated, that the Virginie was "158 feet long and 43 broad." On the contrary, the Virginie measured but 151 feet $3\frac{3}{4}$ inches on the lower deck, and her extreme breadth was only 39 feet 10 inches. In fact, she was a ship considerably shorter and narrower than the Indefatigable, and was exceeded in size by several of the French 40-gun frigates which had previously been captured.

On the 27th of April the British 12-pounder 32-gun frigate Niger, Captain Edward James Foot, was detached by Vice-admiral Colpoys, cruising with his fleet off Brest, in pursuit of a large French armed lugger, which, at sunset, anchored for shelter among the rocks off the Penmarcks. Having approached as near as the depth of water would allow, the Niger anchored, with a spring on her cable, and kept up a brisk, but, owing to the distance, ineffectual fire on the lugger, until 9 P.M.; when Captain Foote despatched the barge and cutters, with the Niger's first and third lieutenants, George Long and Thomas Thompson, master's mate, Jeremiah Morgan, and midshipman James Patton, with a party of seamen and six marines, to bring away or destroy the vessel.

The tide having ebbed considerably, it was not without great difficulty that the boats got alongside the object of attack. After an obstinate resistance on the part of the French, in which many of them were killed and wounded, the national lugger Ecureuil, of eighteen 4-pounders and 105 men, commanded by Lieutenant Jean-Baptiste-Augustin Rousseau, who with the survivors of his crew excepting 28 taken prisoners, escaped to the shore, was set on fire and destroyed ; with the loss, on the part of the British, of Lieutenant Long, wounded severely on the head and hand, and one midshipman (Mr. Patton), three seamen, and two marines, wounded slightly.

On the 4th of May, at noon, latitude 28° north, and longitude 69° west, the British ship-sloop Spencer, of fourteen 12-pounder carronades and two long fours, with 80 men and boys, Captain Andrew Fitzherbert Evans, after a long chase came up with the French gun-brig Volcan, of twelve 4-pounders, and between 80 and 90 men. A close action ensued, which, owing to the upsetting of three of the Spencer's carronades on the side engaged, was protracted to an hour and a quarter; at the end of which time the Volcan, having had both topmasts shot away, and her standing and running rigging cut to pieces, hauled down her colours.

The Spencer had her mizenmast badly wounded, and some of her running rigging rendered useless, but sustained no greater loss than one seaman killed and one wounded. The loss on board the Volcan was known to be considerable, but could not be ascertained, and arose in a great degree from the explosion of some powder-flasks and combustibles which the crew had prepared to assist them in boarding the British vessel. Several of the Frenchmen, to avoid the effects of the explosion, leaped overboard and were drowned, and others were miserably burnt; of which latter number some died shortly after their removal. Notwithstanding these losses, the surviving prisoners are stated to have far exceeded in number the crew of the Spencer, who probably had not her full complement on board. Captain Evans speaks in the highest terms of his officers and ship's company, and names among the former Lieutenant Joseph Lenox and Mr. Harriden the master.

Intelligence having reached Admiral Duncan, the British commander-in-chief in the North Sea, and then cruising off the Texel with a squadron of nine sail of the line, besides 50-gun ships, frigates, and sloops, that the Dutch 36-gun frigate Argo and three national brigs were on their way from Flickerve, in Norway to the first-named port, Captain Lawrence, William Halsted, in the 36-gun frigate Phœnix, accompanied by the

50 gun ship Leopard, 28-gun frigate Pegasus and brig-sloop Sylph, was despatched to intercept them.

On the 12th of May, at 5 A.M., just as these ships, in pursuance of their orders, had made sail from the squadron, with the wind at west-north-west, the Argo, the three brigs, and a cutter, all standing upon a wind on the starboard tack, hove in sight in the south-east. Chase was immediately given, both by the detached ships, and by the squadron in the rear. At the approach of the former, the three brigs bore up, and were pursued by the Pegasus and Sylph; while the Phœnix and Leopard, the latter far astern, directed their attention to the Argo.

As if undetermined whether to go large or keep by the wind, the latter frequently changed her position, but, at length, kept with the wind a-beam. At 8 A.M., the Phœnix having got close to her weather quarter, the Argo hoisted Dutch colours; whereupon the former fired a shot across her. A few minutes placed the Phœnix alongside of her opponent to windward, and a smart action commenced on both sides, which continued for about 20 minutes; when, having sustained some damage in her masts, rigging, and sails, and seeing no prospect of escaping from the numerous foes surrounding her, the Argo struck her flag.

The Phœnix appears to have mounted eight 32-pounder carronades beyond her establishment as an 18-pounder 36, or 44 guns in all, with a net complement of 271 men and boys. The only damage she sustained was in her rigging and sails, and her only loss was one man killed and three wounded; while the Argo, whose armament was precisely the same as that of the Alliance,[1] with a crew of 237 men and boys, lost six men killed and 28 wounded—a proof that her officers and crew were not deterred from doing their duty by the superiority of the force opposed to them.

On the 27th of May, early in the morning, the Lizard bearing north-north-east distant 15 leagues, the British 14-gun brig-sloop Suffisante, Captain Nicholas Tomlinson, discovered a strange sail about six mile to windward. After a chase of 11 hours, the Suffisante came up with the French brig-corvette Revanche, of twelve long 4-pounders and 85 men, commanded by Lieutenant George-Henri Draveman, an old and experienced seaman, and who was now endeavouring to escape into Brest by the Passage du Four. After a close engagement of half an hour, amidst the rocks between the island of Ushant and the main, the Revanche

[1] See p. 324.

struck her colours, having sustained a loss of two men killed and seven wounded, and inflicted no greater loss upon the Suffisante than one seaman wounded.

The action having been fought close upon a lee-shore, the greatest exertions were required, as well to avoid the numerous rocks by which the British brig was surrounded, as to prevent the French brig from effecting her escape by her better acquaintance with the intricate navigation of this part of the coast. Captain Tomlinson, however, had previously distinguished himself by his skill and activity in operations upon the French coast, and, we believe, was made a commander, chiefly on account of his praiseworthy conduct in the Pelter gun-brig, when, in the summer and autumn of 1795, that vessel formed a part of Sir John Warren's unfortunate expedition to Quiberon.

On the 8th of June, at 2 A.M., Scilly bearing east half-south distant 17 leagues, the British 18-pounder 32-gun frigate Unicorn, Captain Thomas Williams, and 12-pounder 36-gun frigate Santa-Margarita, Captain Thomas Byam Martin, discovered, about three miles on their lee beam, three strange ships of war; which, on being neared in chase, were ascertained to be two frigates and a ship-corvette. They were, in fact, the French 36-gun frigates Tribune, Commodore Jean Moulston, and Tamise (late British Thames[1]), Captain Jean-Baptiste-Alexis Fradin, and 18-gun corvette Légère, Lieutenant Jean-Martin-Michel Carpentier. These ships had sailed from Brest on the 4th, in company with the 40-gun frigate Proserpine, Captain Etienne Pevrieux, who had since parted from them in a fog.

At 9 A.M. the three French ships formed in a close bow and quarter line, and continued to run from the two British frigates in that position, the Tribune keeping under easy sail for the support of the others. The Légère, as the two British frigates approached, hauled out to windward, passing the latter at long gun-shot; but she afterwards continued the same course as her two companions, apparently to be in readiness to lend her aid to the one that should most need it. At 1 P.M. the Tribune and Tamise, having hoisted French colours, and the former a broad pendant, commenced with their stern-chasers a quick and well-directed fire, and which, from its destructive effects on the sails and rigging of the Unicorn and Santa-Margarita, greatly retarded their progress.

At 4 P.M. the Tamise bore round up, both to avoid the fire of the Unicorn, and to pour a broadside into the bow of the Santa-

[1] See p. 118.

Margarita; but the latter judiciously evaded the salute, by laying herself close alongside her opponent. This pair of combatants now went off by themselves, engaging with great spirit during 20 minutes; at the end of which the Tamise, having sustained considerable damage in hull, sails, and rigging, struck her colours.

The Santa-Margarita, whose force was 40 guns, including four 32-pounder carronades, with a complement of 237 men and boys, had only two seamen killed, and her boatswain and two seamen wounded. The Tamise was armed precisely as No. 7 in the table at p. 59, with two additional brass 36-pounder carronades for her maindeck bow-ports, and is represented to have lost, out of a complement of 306 men and boys, 32 killed and 19 wounded, several of them mortally, and the rest badly.

Comparative Force of the Combatants.

		Santa-Margarita.	Tamise.
Broadside-guns	No.	20	20
	lbs.	250	279
Crew	No.	237	306
Size	tons	993	656

Were it not for the preponderance in the size of the two ships, an undisturbed meeting between the Santa-Margarita and Tamise would have fallen within the line of well-matched cases. Nothing appears that can in any way reflect on the professional character of Captain Fradin and the officers and crew of the French frigate.

As a proof of the modesty with which the captain of the Santa-Margarita communicated the account of his action, the prize is described as "mounting 36 guns," Captain Martin, apparently, deeming it unfair to enumerate the Tamise's carronades, and omit those of the Santa-Margarita. In every prize-list of the time the mounted force of the Tamise is stated at "36 guns." We are therefore happy in having it in our power to correct a mistake that must, in every way, enhance the merit of the officer by whose skill and gallantry the Tamise was captured. In addition to the assistance which he derived from his first-lieutenant, Mr. George Harison, Captain Martin speaks highly of the services of Captain Joseph Bullen, a volunteer on board the frigate; and who, shortly afterwards, was promoted to post-rank, as was Lieutenant Harison to the rank of commander.

During the 20 months she had belonged to the French, the Tamise had been a very active cruiser. The Moniteur of the month preceding her capture boasted, that she had sent into Brest and the neighbouring ports upwards of 20 prizes, many of them valuable. The recapture of the Tamise, therefore, was a fortunate occurrence. She was reinstated, under her English name, as a 12-pounder 32 in the British navy.

Seeing the fate of her companion, the Tribune crowded sail to effect her escape. The parity of sailing in the British and French frigates, aided by the judgment of Commodore Moulston (represented as a native of the United States of America), kept the two ships in a running fight for ten hours; during which the Unicorn suffered greatly in her sails and rigging, and was at one time deprived of the use of her maintopsail. But the wind falling soon after dark, the British frigate was enabled to use her light sails, and by that means gradually approached so near to the Tribune's weather quarter as to take the wind out of her sails; when, at 10 h. 30 m. P.M., after having run in the pursuit 210 miles, the Unicorn ranged up alongside of her antagonist.

The British crew instantly gave three cheers, and a close action commenced, which continued, each ship being in the same position, with great spirit, for 35 minutes; when, on the smoke clearing away, the Tribune was observed to have dropped in the rear, and to be attempting, close hauled, to cross the Unicorn's stern and gain the wind of her. To frustrate this manœuvre, the sails of the Unicorn, in the most masterly manner, were thrown aback: she then dropped astern, passed the Tribune's weather bow, regained her station, and renewed the attack. A few well-directed broadsides brought down the fore and main masts and mizen topmast of the Tribune, and not only put an end to all further manœuvring on the part of the French frigate, but silenced her fire and compelled her to surrender. The corvette, which was the Légère of 18 long 6-pounders, had long since disappeared.

The Unicorn, besides her thirty-two long 18 and 6 pounders, mounted six 32-pounder carronades, or 38 guns in all. Although the Unicorn's established complement was 251 men and boys, Captain Williams mentions that his third-lieutenant, two master's mates, and some of his best seamen, had, on the evening previous to the action, been put on board a prize. The absentees could not well have been fewer than 11; making the crew of the Unicorn, when she commenced the action, amount to 240. Of this number the Unicorn, like the Révolutionnaire and Indefatigable, had not a man hurt. The Tribune mounted.

in all, 44 guns (six more 6-pounders than the Tamise, and two brass 36-pounder carronades), and is represented to have lost, out of a complement of 339 men and boys, 37 men killed, and her commander and 14 men wounded.

Comparative Force of the Combatants.

		Unicorn.	Tribune.
Broadside-guns	No.	19	22
	lbs.	348	260
Crew	No.	240	339
Size	tons	791	916

That the Unicorn should have captured the Tribune must now appear far less extraordinary, than that the latter should have expended her powder and shot so uselessly, as, in a running fight of several hours and a close combat of more than half an hour, not to have shed one drop of blood on board the former. Commodore Moulston, notwithstanding, fought his ship most bravely, and manœuvred her to admiration. The Santa-Margarita, although nominally superior to the Unicorn, would have been a more suitable match for the Tribune, whose broadside weight of metal, be it observed, even without computing the pair of 36-pounder carronades in the bow-ports, is a trifle inferior to that of the Tamise.

Soon after the Unicorn's return into port, Captain Williams received the honour of knighthood; and the frigate's first-lieutenant, Thomas Palmer, was promoted to the rank of commander. The Tribune, also, was added to the British navy as a 12-pounder 36, under the name by which she had been captured.

A contemporary says, that Captain Williams obtained his reward because he had captured a ship "of superior force."[1] This mistake, in all probability, arose from the writer's unacquaintance with the real force of the Unicorn. Nor is the force of the Tribune very explicitly stated in the official letter; for, notwithstanding she is described as "mounting 44 guns, though pierced for 48," the details of her force make the guns but 42, the number (twenty-six 12s, eight 6s, and eight 32-pounder carronades) afterwards established upon the Tribune in the British service, and quite as many as the ship could mount with effect. Although, perhaps, rather too much stress has been laid upon the superiority of force against the Unicorn and Santa-Margarita, in having opposed to them two French 12-pounder frigates, besides an 18-gun corvette which abandoned her consorts before a shot was fired, the whole affair, in its success-

[1] Brenton, vol. i., p. 398.

ful result, reflects great credit upon the officers and crews of the British frigates.

On the 13th of June, at 1 A.M., Cape Clear bearing west by north distant 12 leagues, the British 18-pounder 36-gun frigate Dryad, Captain Lord Amelius Beauclerk, standing close hauled on the starboard tack, with the wind a fresh breeze from north-west by west, discovered a sail in the south-west by west, or right ahead, standing towards her; but which, on nearing the Dryad, hauled her wind, and then tacked. This was the French frigate Proserpine, in search of her consorts, and who, now that she had discovered the ship approaching to be an enemy, was endeavouring to effect her escape.

Chase was immediately given by the Dryad, both ships on a wind upon the starboard tack. At 8 P.M. the Proserpine hoisted her colours; and immediately afterwards the Dryad did the same. The Proserpine then fired her stern-chasers, several of the shot from which went through the Dryad's sails and cut away her rigging. At 9 P.M., having reached her opponent's lee or larboard quarter, the Dryad commenced a close action, and maintained it with so much spirit and effect that, at 9 h. 45 m. P.M., the Proserpine hauled down the French ensign.

The Dryad, whose guns, 44 in number, were the same as those of the Phœnix, with a complement of 251 men and boys, had two seamen killed and seven wounded. The Proserpine was armed the same as the 40-gun frigate in the table at p. 59, except in having two 18-pounders less (although pierced for them) on the main deck, making her total number of guns 42; with a complement, as deposed to by her officers, of 348 men and boys: of whom she is represented to have lost 30 killed and 45 wounded.

Neither frigate lost a spar. The Dryad's foretopsail was much cut, as well as the greater part of her running, and some of her standing rigging, and her jib and peak halliards were shot away, but her colours, which had fallen with the gaff, were quickly rehoisted at the mizentopgallantmast head. The Proserpine suffered even less in her rigging and sails than the Dryad; but her hull, on the larboard or engaged side especially, showed clearly where the Dryad's shot had been directed.

Comparative Force of the Combatants.

		Dryad.	Proserpine.
Broadside-guns	No.	22	21
	lbs.	407	363
Crew	No.	254	346
Size	tons	924	1059

Were it not for the slight preponderance occasioned by the Dryad's carronades, the British frigate would have been inferior in guns, as well as in crew and size, to the French frigate. But, as what little the latter wanted in broadside weight of metal was amply made up to her in number of men, the action of the Dryad and Proserpine may be pronounced at least an equal match. Captain Pevrieux appears to have thought otherwise. Hence, the Proserpine fled, and by flying, not only sustained a very serious loss, but was unable to bring guns enough to bear upon her antagonist, to do any more injury to her than a single shot has often inflicted.

Had the French captain, instead of trying to escape, brought his frigate to, he might have manœuvred her to some advantage, and even, if eventually compelled to yield, would have surrendered without discredit. As it was, after capturing the Proserpine, the Dryad, owing solely to her opponent's forbearance, was able to fight another frigate of the same force; and, could he have secured his prisoners without diminishing his crew, the Dryad's captain would no doubt have rejoiced at such an opportunity. Lord Amelius, in his official letter, speaks highly of his first-lieutenant, Mr. Edward Durnford King, and the latter, most deservedly, was promoted to the rank of commander.

The only remaining ship of Commodore Moulston's squadron, the Légère, was captured, on the 22nd, in latitude 48° 30′ north, and longitude 8° 28′ west, after the exchange of a few shot, by the British frigates Apollo and Doris, Captains John Manley and the Honourable Charles Jones.

The Proserpine, under the name of Amelia (a Proserpine being already in the service), was admitted into the British navy as a cruising frigate, and, from her size and sailing properties, became a valuable acquisition to her class. The distinction between a British 38 and 36, as remarked elsewhere, is simply in the latter's having a pair of ports less on the main deck. The late Proserpine's two foremost ports (vacant when captured) were considered to be sufficiently aft to admit two guns; hence, the Amelia fell into the class of 38-gun frigates. The Légère, a frigate-built corvette of 453 tons, capable of carrying eighteen 6-pounders, with six 18-pounder carronades on the quarter-deck, was also added to the British navy under the same name.

On the 9th of June, about noon, while the British Mediterranean fleet was cruising before Toulon, a French corvette was descried working up towards the road of Hyères, situated within the islands so named. Sir John Jervis immediately called on board the Victory, by signal, Captain James Macnamara of the 12-pounder 32-gun frigate Southampton; and, pointing out the object of his wishes, said, "Bring out the enemy's ship if you can. I'll give you no written order; but I direct you to take care of the king's ship under your command."[1] Captain Macnamara, hastening back to his ship, reached her about 5 h. 30 m. P.M.; and the Southampton was presently under all sail steering for the Grande Passe, or passage between the islands of Porquerolles and Portcros. At 6 P.M. the Southampton discovered the corvette to the northward, at no great distance from the shore; and hauling up, under easy sail, close under the batteries on the north-east side of Porquerolles, was apparently mistaken, as had been hoped would be the case, for either a French or a neutral frigate.

Profiting by her stratagem, the Southampton stood boldly across Hyères road, and at 8 h. 30 m. P.M. got within pistol-shot of the French ship-corvette Utile, of 24-guns (eighteen 6-pounders and six pieces of smaller caliber), with a crew of 130 men, commanded by Lieutenant de vaisseau François Vega, 14 days from Toulon on a cruise. Captain Macnamara, taking the trumpet, cautioned the French commander not to make a fruitless resistance; but the latter instantly snapped his pistol at the speaker, and the Utile fired her broadside at the Southampton. The frigate, backing her main topsail, promptly returned the salute. At the end of the third broadside, the Southampton, finding herself very near to the heavy battery of Fort Bregançon, hauled athwart the bows of the Utile, and lashed the corvette's bowsprit to her main rigging. Lieutenant Charles Lydiard, at the head of a party of seamen, then sprang on board, and, after a ten minutes' spirited resistance, during which the French captain gallantly fell at his post, carried the corvette. This dashing service was executed with the trifling loss to the Southampton of only one marine killed by a pistol-shot while standing near the captain upon the quarter-deck; but the loss sustained by the Utile was of far greater amount, being eight officers and men killed and 17 wounded.

Captain Macnamara's next difficulty was to get clear of the batteries on the coast, particularly of Fort Bregançon, which immediately opened a fire upon the Southampton and her prize. At 10 P.M. the lashings that had held the two ships together were cut away, and they made all sail on a wind. At 10 h. 30 m.

[1] Marshall, vol. i., p. 686.

p.m. the Southampton was obliged to take the Utile in tow, and succeeded after a while in getting out of range of the batteries, without any loss, or any greater damage than a shot through the centre of her mizenmast. The state of the wind and intricacy of the navigation, however, made it 1 h. 30 m. a.m. on the 10th, before the two ships could clear the passage and effect their junction with Sir John Jervis's fleet. The Utile was immediately commissioned as a British sloop of war, and Lieutenant Lydiard, with the necessary step in his rank, became her commander.

In the year 1795 the British government purchased nine East India ships, measuring from 1165 to 1434 tons, and armed them with 28 (some of the smaller with 26) long 18-pounders on the first, and 28 carronades, 32-pounders, on the second and only remaining deck. Subsequently the Glatton, of 1256 tons, at the suggestion of Captain Henry Trollope, appointed to command her, was fitted on the lower deck with 28 carronades of his favourite caliber, the 68-pounder;[1] making her total of guns 56.

These 56 guns were more, by six at least, than the Glatton, although pierced for that number, could advantageously mount; her ports, as was the case, more or less, with all the other purchased Indiamen, being too small to allow even a long 18-pounder properly to traverse. With respect, also, to the 68-pounder carronade, its muzzle was almost of equal diameter with the port: hence it could scarcely be pointed in any other direction than right a-beam. Moreover, as these carronades were all fixed guns, the Glatton was without a bow or stern chaser. Her net complement was established at 320 men and boys; too few by 30 at the least.

On the 13th of July, 1796, the Glatton sailed from Sheerness, where she had been just refitted, for the purpose of reinforcing the North Sea fleet under Admiral Duncan; and, arriving soon afterwards in Yarmouth roads, sailed thence on the afternoon of the 14th, by the orders of Rear-admiral Macbride, to join a squadron of two sail of the line and some frigates, commanded by Captain Henry Savage of the Albion 64, and supposed to be cruising off Helvoetsluys.

On the 15th, at 1 a.m., the Glatton made the coast of Flanders, and discovered four large ships under the land. The weather was now calm; but at 8 p.m., Goree steeple bearing south by east, a breeze sprang up from the north-west, and at the same time two other ships were observed to join the four already in view. The Glatton now made all sail towards the strangers,

[1] See p. 40.

and, on closing within signal distance, ascertained that they were an enemy's squadron of four frigates, two ship-corvettes, with a large brig-corvette and an armed cutter, hastening to join from to-leeward.

Having cleared for action, the Glatton stood on with a light breeze in her favour; and, so far from being daunted at the formidable appearance of the enemy, Captain Trollope was rejoiced at the opportunity thus afforded him of trying the effect of the heavy carronades in his ship. At 6 P.M. the wind freshened, and the four ships formed in close line of battle with their heads to the north-east. At 8 P.M., as a proof how confident they were of success, the strangers shortened sail, backing their mizentopsails occasionally to keep in their stations.

At about 9 h. 45 m. P.M. the Glatton, having hoisted the St. George's ensign, arrived abreast of the three smaller and rearmost ships, but reserved her fire for the next ship, the latter from her superior size appearing to be the commodore; and which ship was now the second in the line, the ship next ahead of her having fallen to leeward. At a few minutes before 10 P.M., as the Glatton ranged up close alongside of the supposed commodore, Captain Trollope, hailing the ship, desired her commander to surrender to a British man of war. In an instant French colours and a broad pendant were displayed, and the commodore, and immediately afterwards all the other ships commenced firing at the Glatton.

The Glatton was not slow in returning the compliment, and poured into the French commodore, at the distance of not more than 20 yards, a broadside such as perhaps no single-decked ship ever before received. While the Glatton and the French commodore were continuing to go ahead and mutually engaging, the French van-ship tacked, in the expectation of being followed by her squadron, and thereby driving the Glatton upon the Brill shoal, which was close to leeward. The French van-ship soon arrived within hail on the Glatton's weather beam, and received a fire from her larboard guns, the effects of which were heard in the cries and groans of the wounded, and partially seen in the shattered state of the ship's side. This quickly elicited the cheers of the British crew, and the discomfited enemy passed on to the southward; leaving the Glatton still engaged with the French commodore upon her lee bow, another large frigate (the latter's second ahead when the action commenced) upon her lee quarter.

The action had now lasted about 20 minutes; when the Glatton's pilot called out, that the ship, if she did not tack in five minutes, would be on the shoal. Captain Trollope replied: "When the French commodore strikes the ground, do you put the helm a-lee." Almost immediately afterwards the French commodore tacked to avoid the shoal, and, while in stays, received a heavy raking fire that much disabled him. The other French ships had previously gone about; and the Glatton, as well to continue the action as to escape running on the shoal, prepared to do the same, but, owing to the damaged state of her sails and rigging, experienced a great difficulty in getting her head round.

The combatants were now all on the starboard tack; and, although the three large and hitherto principally engaged frigates had fallen to leeward, the three smaller ones still kept up a harassing long-shot fire; to which the Glatton, on account of the distance, could not make a very effectual return. The wounded state of the topmasts and the increasing power of the wind rendering it necessary to take a reef in the topsails of the Glatton, her men unhesitatingly flew upon the yards, which were also wounded by shot, and performed their task in the face of a smart cannonade from the nearest of the three ships to leeward left in a state to continue the action; and which ship, mistaking the cause of the cessation of the Glatton's fire, was seemingly advancing to reap the fruits of her prowess. The British crew, however, were soon at their guns again, and the fall of a topsail yard belonging to one of the French ships, coupled with some other damage, convinced the Frenchmen on board that the victory was not yet to them, and very soon induced these three ships to follow the example of their three more powerful companions, and withdraw themselves from the combat.

The six French ships, thus beaten, were not, however, the only opponents that had been assailing the Glatton. Towards the close of the action the brig and cutter, the first mounting 16, and the other eight or ten guns, had stationed themselves under her stern, and opened a smart fire; a fire which the Glatton, from the defects in her equipment already noticed, could only answer by musketry. After receiving a few well-directed volleys, the brig and cutter made sail after their companions; and at 11 P.M. all firing ceased between the Glatton and her many opponents.

The dismantled state of the Glatton rendered pursuit on her part out of the question. Every brace, and every stay except the mizen, had been cut away or rendered useless; and so had all the running and the greater part of the standing rigging. The principal part of the enemy's fire had passed between her tops and gunwale, so that the lower sails of the Glatton were cut nearly from the yards: the jib and mainsail, indeed, were in ribands. The mainmast, and the fore and main yards, were also badly wounded, and ready to fall. Scarcely half a dozen shot had struck the hull; and, in consequence, no men were killed, and, except a few bruises and scratches, two only wounded. One of the latter was Captain Henry Ludlow Strangeways, of the marines; the other, a corporal of the same corps. The first-named gallant officer, although badly wounded by a musket-ball in the thigh, and compelled in consequence to have a tourniquet applied, insisted on returning to his quarters; where he remained until, being faint with loss of blood, he was carried off the deck: he died shortly afterwards.

The Glatton, during the night, used every exertion to put herself in a state to renew the action by morning, with the assistance, it was hoped, of one or two ships of Captain Savage's squadron. On the 16th, at daybreak, the French squadron, drawn up in a close head-and-stern line, was still in sight, with the advantage, by a shift of wind during the night to south-west, of the weather-gage. At 8 A.M., having knotted and spliced her rigging, bent new sails, and otherwise refitted herself, the Glatton offered battle to her opponents; but these, having felt too sensibly the effects of her 68 lb. shot, declined a renewal of the engagement, and about noon bore away for Flushing, followed by the Glatton. Having thus compelled a whole squadron of French ships to take shelter in port, the Glatton turned her head to the northward, and, standing in need of great repairs, steered for Yarmouth roads; where, on the 21st, she came to an anchor.

The Glatton's affair, like many other drawn battles, is imperfect in its details, for the want of any correct information as to the names, force, damage, and loss of the ships which she had engaged. One French frigate was known to be the Brutus, a 74-gun ship cut down, mounting from 46 to 50 guns; 24-pounders on the first or main deck,[1] and 12-pounders, with 36-pounder carronades, on the quarter-deck and forecastle. A second ship is stated to have been the 38-gun frigate Incorruptible;[2] and a third, the 36-gun frigate Magicienne. A Flushing paper, of July 5, 1796, states that the French frigate Incorruptible, with another frigate, a 36, not named, the 28-gun

[1] See p. 56.   [2] See table at p. 59.

frigate Républicaine, two ship-corvettes of 22 guns each, and an armed brig or snow, were lying in the road waiting an opportunity to get to France. These then, with the Brutus, were probably the squadron which the Glatton had engaged.

That the French ships sustained considerable damage in their hulls may reasonably be inferred, from the size of the Glatton's shot, the closeness of the action, and the shyness which they ultimately evinced. Moreover, on the morning succeeding the action, the Glatton's people plainly saw men, on stages, over the sides of the French ships, stopping shot-holes. In further corroboration, several of the Flushing fishermen afterwards reported, that considerable damage had been sustained by three or four of the frigates, so much so, indeed, that one of them had sunk in the harbour; that either that or one of the others had lost 70 men in killed and wounded, and that the French were astonished at finding the decks of their ships so ripped up by the Glatton's shot.

Viewed in every light, the action between the Glatton and this French frigate-squadron was highly honourable to the officers and crew of the former. The prompt decision of Captain Trollope to become the assailant, when one of the six opponent ships, admitting her to have been the Brutus, was 300 or 400 tons larger than the Glatton, coupled with the latter's conduct throughout the engagement, well entitled her commander to the honour of knighthood subsequently conferred upon him by his sovereign. The merchants of London, too, with their usual liberality, presented Captain Trollope with an elegant piece of plate. The three lieutenants of the Glatton on this memorable occasion were Robert Williams, Alexander Wilmot Schomberg, and William Pringle.

The crew of the Glatton not being sufficiently numerous to man her guns on both sides, the following expedient was resorted to: The allotment of men for each gun upon either broadside was divided into two gangs; one of which, having loaded and run out the gun, left it to be pointed and fired by the other, composed of picked hands, and then ran across and did the same to the gun on the opposite side. And how well the British crew plied their guns has already been shown in the result of the engagement.

The most formidable objection to the use of carronades, of the larger calibers, is their alleged liability to overset on becoming heated. It appears, however, that, notwithstanding the long and incessant fire kept up by them, none of the 68, and two only of the 32 pounders, were dismounted. These facts certainly enhance the merit of large-sized carronades: at the same time it should be remarked, that no ship of war ought to be sent to sea, as the Glatton was, without the power of using bow and stern chasers; and no other than a swift-sailing ship, who can choose her distance, ought to be wholly armed with carronades. The Glatton, had she been of that description, might have succeeded in cutting off one, if not two of her opponents; and the smallest ship among them would have served to identify the whole of her companions.

On the 22nd of July, at 5 P.M., the British 12-pounder 32-gun frigate Aimable, Captain Jemmet Mainwaring, being on a cruise off the island of Guadeloupe, discovered the French 36-gun frigate Pensée coming round the point of land named Englishman's Head. The Aimable immediately hauled to the wind in chase, stretching close in shore, to prevent the Pensée from getting into Anse-la-Barque. At 6 h. 35 m. P.M., the weather nearly calm, the two frigates, being then about three miles south of the Hayes and about half that distance from the shore, met and came to action on opposite tacks, but not very closely. At 7 h. 45 m. a breeze sprang up from the eastward, and the Aimable ran down for the purpose of boarding her adversary; but, just as she had got within half a cable's length of the Pensée's starboard bow, the Aimable was taken aback by the wind from the southward. The Pensée immediately made sail to the northward, and was followed by the Aimable, who succeeded in raking her with the starboard broadside. At 8 h. 10 m. P.M. the firing, which, owing to the distance maintained by the Pensée, had been rather ineffective, ceased; and the latter, whom the trade-wind had just reached, crowded sail to the west-north-west.

The Aimable continued in chase during the night, and at daylight the next morning, the 23rd, discovered the Pensée about seven miles off right ahead. Every effort was now used by Captain Mainwaring to increase the sailing of his ship: the stays were slackened, the wedges of the masts eased, and the guns shifted, to give the vessel her proper trim; but still the Pensée was getting ahead. At 7 A.M., however, the French frigate shortened sail, and hauled up on the starboard tack under her topsails. The Aimable immediately steered down for her opponent; who, as if determined this time to fight, backed her mizen topsail occasionally for the former to come up.

At 8 h. 35 m. the Aimable advanced near to the Pensée's

weather quarter; and the two captains, in the true spirit of chivalry, exchanged salutes with the hat. But, in another five minutes, the Pensée, as if desirous to evade coming to close action, filled her mizentopsail, and hauled on board her fore and main tacks. Whereupon the Aimable, bearing round up, discharged her starboard broadside into her opponent; who then bore up also, and the firing became mutual. At 8 h. 50 m. A.M. the Pensée, having ranged ahead, hauled up on the larboard tack, with the intention of raking the Aimable; but the latter, putting her helm a-port, poured a raking broadside into the former. At 8 h. 55 m. A.M. the Pensée, pursued by the Aimable, made sail: at first she hauled close up, then kept gradually going off the wind, until her stern-chasers would bear; from which the Pensée maintained, until 10 A.M., an unremitting though ineffectual fire. By this time the Aimable, in spite of every effort, had fallen so far astern as to be out of gun-shot. After running two hours longer and still increasing her distance, the Aimable discontinued the chase, and hauled her wind to the southward. That her opponent was the French frigate Pensée, there could be no doubt, the name having been plainly seen on her stern.

The Aimable had the good fortune to escape with only two men wounded; while the Pensée, as related upon her arrival soon afterwards at St. Thomas's, where, for a short time, she was blockaded by the 12-pounder 32-gun frigate Mermaid, Captain Robert Waller Otway, lost 90 men in killed and wounded.

The two frigates were armed precisely as their respective class-mates in the two tables already given.[1] Surely, then, there was nothing to alarm the French captain; nothing to excuse him for having disappointed the wishes of Captain Mainwaring and his crew; unless the severity of the Pensée's loss may be considered as a justification for her taking to flight while she had sails to carry herself off.

On the 8th of August, at 9 h. 30 m. A.M., Rear-admiral Pole, then with the 74-gun ship Carnatic, and two or three other British ships, lying at the Saintes near Guadeloupe, directed Captain Otway to proceed in chase of a strange ship, seen at a great distance in the offing. The Mermaid accordingly made all sail; and, on getting through the passage formed by the two islands, hauled to the northward, when a strange sail hove in sight under the land of Basse-terre. At 11 h. 30 m. A.M., as

[1] See pp. 59 and 101.

the Mermaid advanced nearer, the stranger was seen to be a frigate with French colours flying. Captain Otway, as directed, immediately made the signal for an enemy, and fired a gun. At 11 h. 45 m. A.M. the batteries on shore opened a fire upon the Mermaid, and many shots went over her. At about noon a shift of wind brought the strange ship, which was the 40-gun frigate Vengeance, on the beam of the Mermaid, who thereupon opened her broadside; one of the shots from the Mermaid sank a boat that was towing astern of the Vengeance, in which an aide-de-camp of Victor Hugues, then standing on the beach at Basse-terre, with orders to the French captain to take or sink the British frigate, had embarked.

In a few minutes the Mermaid wore round, and hove to on the starboard tack; in which position she exchanged several broadsides with the Vengeance. At 30 minutes past noon the latter's larboard topgallant sheet and mizentopsail tie were shot away. At 1 P.M. the Vengeance filled her main topsail, and bore down a little. At 1 h. 10 m. P.M., finding that her opponent had shot ahead, the Mermaid filled also, and kept close to the wind, still engaging. At 1 h. 30 m. P.M. the Vengeance endeavoured to stay, but missed, and in this state received a heavy broadside from the Mermaid. Again the Vengeance tried to stay; again she missed, and again lay exposed to a destructive raking fire. At 2 P.M. the Vengeance set her foresail, and soon afterwards succeeded in tacking. The Mermaid, on getting into her opponent's wake, tacked also. At 2 h. 30 m. P.M. the wind, coming more northerly, prevented the Mermaid from fetching the Vengeance; whereupon the Mermaid, at whom the batteries on shore were still occasionally firing, wore round, fired a broadside into her opponent's stern, and hove to on the larboard tack. The Vengeance then filled and stood on, followed by the Mermaid; the two ships still firing at each other.

At 3 P.M. the Mermaid had her fore topgallantmast shot away. About this time the Vengeance tacked; as, presently afterwards, did the Mermaid, with her courses set, in close pursuit. At 3 h. 4 m. P.M. the Vengeance stood close in under the batteries and lay to, nearly becalmed. The Mermaid then, as she ran past the latter's stern, fired two distant broadsides, and afterwards wore and stood off. During all this time the batteries continued firing at the British frigates, but without effect. Presently a breeze sprang up from the east-north-east, and the Vengeance made sail for Basse-terre. The British 40-gun frigate Beaulieu, Captain Francis Laforey, was now seen coming down before the wind, under all sail; but, before she could get near, the Vengeance was safe at an anchor in the road of Basse-terre.

Besides losing her fore topgallantmast, the Mermaid had her sails pierced with shot-holes, and her standing and running rigging a good deal cut; but, fortunately, without a man killed or wounded. The Vengeance, on the other hand, suffered considerably in sails, rigging, and hull; and, according to the report of Victor Hugues, as communicated to some British dragoon officers, prisoners at Basse-terre, and who witnessed the whole of the combat, lost 12 men killed and 26 wounded.

When it is known that the Mermaid was a small 12-pounder 32-gun frigate, and the Vengeance one of the largest 18-pounder frigates out of France, mounting 52 guns, the disparity in point of force may be readily conceived. The French frigate was unfortunate in twice missing stays within short gun-shot of an active enemy; and the Vengeance, no doubt, sustained the chief of her loss at those critical periods. Her ultimately retiring from the contest became an imperative duty, considering what ship was approaching to have a share in it. The Beaulieu having a tier of 18 pounders, with some heavy carronades, had she been alone, would have been a much fairer match for the Vengeance than the Mermaid.

On the 6th of July, at 7 p.m., the British 12-pounder 32-gun frigate Quebec, Captain John Cooke, being about seven leagues to the westward of the island of Porto Rico, steering for Cape Nicolas Mole, St. Domingo, with four transports and one merchant vessel under her convoy, which she had brought from Martinique, perceived two strange sail, one to the westward and the other to the southward. At 9 p.m. the strangers were made out to be frigates, and were, as we conjecture, the French frigates Thétis and Pensée on a cruise. The Quebec immediately hauled her wind to the northward, and made the necessary signals to keep her convoy together for the night.

On the 7th, at daylight, the nearest frigate was seen with Spanish colours flying. These, at noon, she hauled down. At 1 h. 15 m. p.m. the Quebec, having been standing to the southeast on the larboard tack, hoisted her colours, and edged away to protect two of her convoy to leeward; whereupon the frigate on her lee bow hoisted French colours and fired a gun to windward. Having made the signal for her convoy to disperse, the Quebec kept her wind, and at 1 h. 30 m. p.m. exchanged broadsides with the French frigate; but without effect on either side, the shot from the lee-guns of the British frigate falling short, while those from the weather-guns of the French frigate passed over the Quebec.

In the mean time the second French frigate was employed in taking possession of the convoy; and never did English vessels so give themselves away, so court capture apparently, as the five ships and brigs in charge of the Quebec. Their masters had previously disobeyed all the signals made to them, and now crowned their misconduct by yielding up their vessels without an effort. Some of them did not wait to be fired at, or even approached within two or three miles, but shortened sail and hauled down their colours the moment they saw the head of the French frigate directed towards them. To give the names of these transports and their masters at this late day would be useless, otherwise we would most willingly expose them to the indignation of their countrymen.

Having now nothing but her own safety to consult, the Quebec made all sail, and soon outstripped the French frigate that was in chase of her. The following account of this occurrence appears in the work of a contemporary: "After capturing a French national cutter, Captain Cooke (previously mentioned to have joined the Quebec, January 1, 1796) was again ordered to the West Indies; where, by his conduct in a rencontre with two frigates of far superior force, he obtained the commendations of his commodore, the late Sir John T. Duckworth."[1] At least, we can discover no other case than that we have just recorded, to which this account can apply; and, assuredly, Captain Duckworth, at the period referred to, was the commanding officer at Cape Nicolas Mole, the port to which, after the capture of her convoy, the Quebec proceeded.

On the 22nd of August, at 10 A.M., as the squadron of British frigates under Commodore Sir Borlase Warren in the Pomone, consisting, besides that ship, of the 44-gun frigate Anson, Captain Philip Charles Durham, 38-gun frigate Artois, Captain Sir Edmund Nagle, 32-gun frigate Galatea, Captain Richard Goodwin Keats, and 18-gun brig-sloop Sylph, Captain John Chambers White, were cruising off the mouth of the river Gironde with the wind from the north-north-west, the French 36-gun frigate Andromaque made her appearance in the south-south-west, standing in towards the entrance of the river. This frigate had been cruising, and successfully, in company with the

[1] Marshall, vol. ii., p. 21.

Néréide and Décade of the same force, and the 28-gun frigate (or 24-gun corvette, as the French would call her) Baïonnaise.

The Galatea, who, with the Sylph brig, was close in shore and considerably ahead of her consorts, crowded sail to cut off the French frigate from the Gironde, and, by making several French signals, induced the Andromaque to come to an anchor near the entrance of the Grave channel. In a few minutes, however, the Andromaque, discovering her mistake, cut her cable, and made all sail to the southward, pursued by the Galatea; who, having stood into the channel between the lighthouse and the Chevrier bank, now hauled to windward of and rounded the latter into four fathoms water. Having cleared this danger, the Galatea made all sail before the wind, followed by the Pomone and Anson. Meanwhile, the Artois and Sylph had been detached to examine two suspicious ships away in the south-west.

At 8 P.M. the Galatea was not more than two miles astern of the Andromaque. At 9 P.M. a violent squall, attended with heavy rain, thunder, and lightning, obliged the chasing ships to shorten sails; whereby the French frigate was suddenly lost sight of, owing to the extreme darkness of the night. At 10 P.M. the weather moderated; and, while the Pomone and Anson stood to the northward, on the supposition that the Andromaque had hauled her wind in that direction, the Galatea continued her course along the French coast to the southward.

At 11 P.M., the weather clearing, the Galatea regained a sight of the French frigate in the south-south-wes , and made all sail in chase. At midnight the Galatea was only a mile off shore, and, at 4 A.M. on the 23rd, not above two miles astern of the Andromaque. At daybreak the Artois and Sylph, who had found the two ships they had been sent to examine to be Americans from Bordeaux bound to Boston, were seen nearly hull-down in the north-west. At about 5 h. 30 m. A.M. the Andromaque hauled up for the land, and at 6 A.M. ran on shore within five leagues of Arcasson, successively cutting away her mizen, main, and fore masts.

As the Andromaque had not hoisted either ensign or pendant, Captain Keats concluded she did not intend to make resistance, and therefore fired no more than three shots before he sent the boats, under the command of Lieutenant Henry Lloyd, first of the Galatea, to effect her destruction. At a few minutes before 7 A.M. the Artois and Sylph came up, and joined their boats, with Lieutenant Benjamin Carter, first of the Artois, in command, to those already despatched by the Galatea. Notwithstanding the height of the surf, and the consequent danger of any attempt to reach the shore, the French crew seemed much more desirous to encounter the risk than to surrender themselves as prisoners to the few boats which the heavy breakers would permit to approach the vessel. Several prisoners, however, including the captain, some of his principal officers, and a few Portuguese seamen, taken out of two Brazil ships, were at length brought away; and the remainder of the frigate's crew, whom the ebbing of the tide had now enabled to walk to the shore, were humanely apprised by the British that it was the intention of the latter to destroy the ship.

At 8 A.M. the boats with the prisoners reached the Sylph, and, having placed them on board, took the brig in tow. On getting close abreast of the Andromaque the Sylph anchored with a spring on her cable, and commenced firing into the frigate's bottom, in order to prevent the possibility of her floating at the return of high water. At noon the Sylph, having accomplished her object, ceased firing, and sent the boats to their proper ships; the two nearest of which, the Artois and Galatea, were about two miles outside of her, and the remaining two, the Pomone and Anson, away in the offing.

Finding it impossible to board the frigate until the tide flowed, the Sylph weighed, and stood off and on until 3 P.M.; then again stood in towards the frigate. The French crew were now assembled among the sand-hills near their ship, as if they intended to prevent her being boarded; but a few well-directed shot from the brig soon dispersed them. At 4 P.M., when it was nearly high water, the Sylph ran within 700 yards of the shore, and, having again anchored, sent her boats to complete the destruction of the frigate; the crew of which made some resistance, but were kept in check by the fire of the brig. At 4h. 30 m. P.M. the boats returned, having set the frigate on fire. At 5 P.M. the Andromaque being in a total blaze fore and aft, and having blown up forward, the Sylph weighed and made sail towards her squadron; which, at 6h. 30m. P.M., she rejoined.

We regret to be obliged to observe, that very few of these particulars, so creditable to the respective officers and crews of the Galatea and Sylph, are contained in Sir John Warren's letter in the Gazette. The account of the destruction of the Andromaque French frigate ought to have been written by the captain of the Galatea. Under the peculiar circumstances of this case, almost any commanding officer would either have written such a letter as should have transferred the credit to the party by whose exertions (Sir John Warren was not even in sight during the critical point of this enterprise) the service was executed, or would have allowed that party to render his own account of the transaction; thereby enabling him, not merely to do justice to himself, but to recommend for promotion his deserving subordinates.

This latter consideration alone should induce an officer to try to conquer that modesty, that dread of being thought an egotist, which generally characterizes the man of true spirit. How many a lieutenant or commander, having missed a recommendation from his captain or superior officer, has never found a second opportunity of distinguishing himself. How many a one has remained ever afterwards in the back-ground of the service, soured against a profession of which he might have been one of the brightest ornaments, and disposed, from a misconception of the cause of the neglect with which he is treated, to attach blame to a wrong quarter.

On the 25th of August, at 1 A.M., latitude 41° 39′ north, and longitude 66° 24′ west, the British 20-gun ship Raison, Captain John Poer Berseford, steering north-east by north, with a light breeze at south-east by east, discovered a large ship coming down under a press of sail. The stranger, not answering signals, betrayed herself to be an enemy, and was such a one, in point of apparent force, as the Raison did well to fly from with all the canvas she could spread. The chasing ship, which was no other than the Vengeance, the Mermaid's late opponent, now hoisted French colours, and commenced firing her bow-guns at the Raison. Having cut away her jolly-boat to make room for four stern-chasers, the Raison opened a fire from them, as soon as the Vengeance, whose shot were passing over her, got fairly within range. A thick fog intervening put an end, for the present, to all offensive operations.

In order to have the weather-gage in case of a second meeting, the Raison, at about noon, hauled her wind to the eastward. At 7 P.M. she again saw, close on the larboard quarter, her powerful opponent; who, hailing, ordered the British ship to strike. To this the latter replied by a broadside. A running fight now commenced, and lasted until nearly 9 P.M.; when, after receiving a well-directed broadside from the Raison, the Vengeance dropped to leeward, and, owing to the density of the fog, was almost immediately out of sight. The Raison, in this rencontre, suffered greatly in her rigging and sails, and lost three men killed and six wounded.

Of the identity of the frigate from which the Raison had so fortunately escaped, not a doubt can remain, as an American vessel, the Martha-Brand, Captain Henry Stratton, on her arrival at Plymouth on the 26th of September, reported that, on the 25th of August, in latitude 41°, longitude 63°, she fell in with the French national frigate Vengeance, who, on the preceding evening, had been fired into by an English sloop of war of 24 guns, which got under her stern and gave her a broadside; whereby the Vengeance was considerably damaged, and had six of her crew killed; and that the sloop of war then stood away under a press of sail, and escaped. It was not until 10 or 12 days afterwards that any account reached England of Captain Beresford's action.

Of what description of frigate, in point of force, the Vengeance was, has already been stated. She measured 1180 tons; while the Raison, whose armament was 20 long 9-pounders, and two 18-pounder carronades in the bridle-ports, on the main-deck, and six long 6-pounders and two 12-pounder carronades on the quarter-deck and forecastle, total 30 guns, with a complement of 195 men and boys, measured only 472 tons.

On the 28th of August, at 5 A.M., as a British squadron, composed of the

Gun-ship.
| 74 | Resolution | { Vice-admiral (w.) George Murray, Captain Francis Pender, |
| 50 | Assistance | ,, Henry Mowat, |

Gun-frigate.
38	Thetis	,, Hon. Alex. F. Cochrane,
36	Topaze	,, Stephen G. Church,
28	Thisbe	,, John Oakes Hardy,

Gun-brig-slp.
| 14 | Bermuda | ,, Thomas Maxtone, |

was lying becalmed about four leagues east-south-east from Cape Henry, three strange ships made their appearance in the east-north-east quarter. The signal was made for a general chase, but the British ships were unable to steer before noon. At 5 h. 30 m. P.M. the Topaze, who was considerably ahead of the remainder of her squadron, brought the sternmost of the enemy's ships to action. This ship, which was the French frigate Elizabet, of 36 guns (twenty-four 12-pounders on the main deck, and twelve 8-pounders on the quarter-deck and forecastle) and 297 men, fired a broadside and hauled down her colours.

The Assistance and Bermuda were directed to take charge of

the prize; and the admiral, with the rest of the squadron, continued in pursuit of the Elizabet's consorts, now seen to be two frigates, until dark, when the latter disappeared. The Elizabet was taken to Halifax, Nova-Scotia, but, having been an Indiaman bought into the French service, and a very indifferent sailor, was not purchased for the use of the British navy.

In the beginning of the year 1794, if not still earlier in the war, the French government contemplated sending out an expedition to India, to supply the isles of France and Bourbon with troops and munitions of war; and, that accomplished, to play havoc with the valuable commerce of their enemies in those far distant, and, at this time, ill-protected seas. In the summer of the ensuing year, we find Rear-admiral Kerguelen appointed to command this expedition; which was to consist of the three 74-gun ships Redoubtable, Wattigny, and Droits-de-l'Homme, three rasés or 50-gun frigates, and a proportion of smaller vessels and transports. It was afterwards discovered that the rasés, having been worn out before they were reduced, and very slightly repaired while undergoing the alteration, were rotten and leaky. As a substitute for these, it was planned that three 74s should remove their lower-deck guns into the hold, so as to carry about 700 troops each; thus making the whole expedition consist of six sail of the line, four frigates, six corvettes, and transports enough to carry, including those on board the ships of war, about 6000 troops.

The loss of the three ships off the Isle of Groix, and the subsequent blockade of the French fleet in Lorient, with all the attendant evils of sickness, desertion, and dearth of provisions, having rendered it impracticable to equip an expedition upon the enlarged scale at first contemplated, in conjunction, especially, with the plans then forming for the invasion of Ireland, the Indian expedition was to consist of two 74s only, one armed wholly, the other en flûte, carrying, between them, no more than about 800 troops. In the mean time, the 36-gun frigate Preneuse, Commodore Charles Magon, and corvettes Brûle-Gueule, and, we believe, Moineau, sailed from one of the ports of France for the East India station.

After a delay, partly attributable, no doubt, to the unsettled state of the French government and its vacillating councils, it was resolved that the expedition to India should be composed of some frigates lying in Rochefort, and that Rear-admiral Sercey should have the command of it. While the expedition, consisting of four frigates and two corvettes, was lying at anchor in the road of the isle of Aix, waiting for a fair wind, the 36-gun frigate Cocarde got upon the rocks, and was so damaged that she could not proceed on the voyage. The 40-gun frigate Vertu, then repairing at Rochefort, was designed as a substitute for the Cocarde; but Rear-admiral Sercey did not feel justified in waiting until she could be got ready.

Accordingly, on the 4th of March, 1796, the rear-admiral weighed and put to sea with the 44-gun frigate Forte, bearing his flag, 36-gun frigate Régénérée, Captain (de vais.) Jean-Baptiste-Philibert Willaumez, Seine frigate, armed en flûte and commanded by Lieutenant Julien-Gabriel Bigot, ship-corvette Bonne-Citoyenne, and brig-corvette Mutine. On board the squadron were 800 troops under General Magalon, two companies of artillery, and a quantity of munitions of war; and on board the Forte were the two agents from the Directory, Baco and Burnel, sent out to the Isles of France and Bourbon, to give freedom to the slaves, in compliance with the regulations of the new constitution of September, 1795.

Encountering bad weather in the Bay of Biscay, the Bonne-Citoyenne on the 7th parted company; and on the 10th was captured by a squadron of British frigates under Captain the Honourable Robert Stopford of the Phaëton. This corvette was a beautiful ship of 511 tons, and would not have been caught but for the damage she had suffered in the gale. The Bonne-Citoyenne mounted twenty long 8-pounders with a crew of 145 men, and became a great acquisition to the British navy as a first-class sloop of war. On the 8th the Mutine, having lost a topmast, was allowed also to part company, and eventually shared the fate of the Bonne-Citoyenne. The Seine, in the same gale, carried away her maintopmast, but replaced it on the 10th. On the same day the squadron captured an English brig, which had formed part of a numerous convoy bound to the West Indies, under the protection of three sail of the line and several frigates.

On the 14th Rear-admiral Sercey passed Madeira and Porto-Santo, and on the 17th anchored off Santa Cruz, the principal city of the isle of Palma, one of the Canaries, and the rendezvous fixed for the junction of the Vertu. On the 29th that frigate arrived, after a ten days' passage, under the command of Captain (de vais.) Jean-Marthe-Adrien l'Hermite. This officer commanded the Cocarde when she struck on the rocks, and had previously commanded the Seine during a long and successful cruise in the North Sea.

Setting sail from Santa Cruz with his four frigates, the rear-admiral met with nothing remarkable until the 15th of May, in latitude about 32° south, and longitude from Paris 3° east, when he captured an English whaler. On the night of the 24th, also, when just abreast of Cape Aiguïlles, a strange ship came into the midst of the squadron. This was a large Portuguese Indiaman, richly laden from Calcutta. On the 25th, at 7 A.M., two other ships made their appearance under the land to the northward. One of these vessels was the British 20-gun ship Sphynx, Captain George Brisac; the other, an American ship, from Batavia bound to the Isle of France with provisions, and on that account detained by the former. While the Vertu was bringing to the American ship, the Régénérée, as the best sailer of the French squadron, went in chase of the Sphynx; who, the moment she discovered that her pursuers were not friends, spread all her canvas and steered for the land, then about four leagues distant. After a chase that lasted nearly the whole of the day, and during which the Sphynx was obliged to throw overboard the greater part of her guns, to keep ahead of the Régénérée, the latter was recalled to the squadron.

On the 3rd of June the French admiral captured a British Indiaman from Bengal, and sent her to the Isle of France; where, on the 18th, the four French frigates, with the captured Portuguese and American ships, also cast anchor. A small British squadron, which had been blockading the two French frigates Prudente and Cybèle, Captains (de vais.) Charles Magon and Pierre-Julien Thréouart, had a few days before sailed from the coast; thus affording to the French admiral the wished-for opportunity to enter Port Louis unobserved, as well as unmolested.

It appears that MM. Baco and Burnel, the agents from the Directory, as soon as the nature of their mission was known, were very ill-received by the colonists of the Isle of France. In short, an insurrection ensued; and the governor, General Malartic, was obliged to order the two deputies to embark on board the corvette Moineau, whose commander had received instructions to carry them to Manilla. On the day after their departure, however, the two deputies, dressed in full costume, appeared on the deck of the vessel, and, in the presence of the crew, ordered the captain to carry them to Europe. The latter obeyed, and the Moineau, with the two rejected deputies, arrived safe in a port of France.

On the 14th of **July**, the Seine having remounted her guns and taken on board Captain Latour as her commander, and all the ships having been thoroughly refitted and stored, Rear-admiral Sercey put to sea with his six frigates, accompanied, for an aviso to the squadron, by the privateer-schooner Alerte. On the 18th the Forte and Vertu anchored in the road of St. Denis, and the four remaining frigates and schooner in the road of St. Paul, Isle of Bourbon. On the 22nd the rear-admiral again got under way, and steered towards the coast of Coromandel. On making the land, the schooner, which from her bad sailing had greatly retarded the squadron, was detached to gain information respecting, as well the state of the British naval force in this quarter, as the number of merchant vessels at anchor in the different ports, their times of departure, and a few other necessary particulars. The captain of the privateer, corsair-like, preferred a cruise on his own account to the mission upon which he had been ordered. He accordingly, on the night of the 19th of August, ran down upon a supposed Indiaman, to carry her by boarding, and was himself taken by the British 28-gun frigate Carysfort, Captain James Alexander; with such precipitation, too, that his papers containing the plan and route of the French admiral's intended cruise fell into the hands of the captors.

Unacquainted with this disaster, Rear-admiral Sercey, on the 14th of August, made the south-east point of the island of Ceylon. Here he cruised four days and made a few prizes: he then ascended to the northward, and stood along the Coromandel coast between Pondicherry and Madras; making there and at Tranquebar, whither the Prudente and Régénérée had previously been detached, a few more prizes, but, like the others, of no great value. As the British force off this coast was far too weak to prevent Rear-admiral Sercey from capturing a number of richly-laden ships about to sail for Europe, the French squadron would have made a fine harvest; but the British officer, who had captured the Alerte, and thus become acquainted with the schemes of the rear-admiral, practised upon the latter a very successful ruse. By false information, adroitly conveyed, he induced the French admiral to believe that his squadron was far inferior to that which was cruising to intercept him.

Rear-admiral Sercey, accordingly, made sail for the straits of Malacca, with the intention of destroying the British factory at Pulo Penang. On the 1st of September the squadron made Pulo Way, and Point Pedro, island of Sumatra, and afterwards captured two or three vessels in the road of Acheen. On the 7th, when cruising off the north coast of Sumatra, the squadron captured the country ship Favourite, laden with rum and rice; and on the 8th, at daybreak, while occupied in transferring several useful articles of stores from the prize to the frigates preparatory to the former's departure for the Isle of France, the squadron descried two large ships to leeward.

It was just at 6 A.M., Point Pedro bearing west distant about eight leagues, that the two British 74-gun ships Arrogant, Captain Richard Lucas, and Victorious, Captain William Clark, descried the French squadron, bearing about south-west by west. At 10 A.M., Rear-admiral Sercey, having formed his squadron in line of battle astern of the Forte, tacked, with a light air from west by north, to reconnoitre the strangers. At noon the French ships hoisted their colours; and shortly afterwards the prize parted company and stood in under the high land of Pulo Way. At 1 P.M. the Arrogant, who was considerably ahead of her consort, tacked to speak her; and, on arriving within hail about 2 P.M., Captain Lucas stated to Captain Clark, that he considered the strangers to be six large French frigates, and the seventh ship, the Triton Indiaman, their prize. Captain Clark, in reply, gave it as his opinion, that two of the ships were of the line. Captain Lucas subsequently went on board the Victorious; and it was agreed between the two captains, that they should dog the six French frigates, and bring them to action whenever it could be done with advantage.

The leading French frigate, the Forte, had, in the mean time, approached near enough to count the ports in both British ships, and to ascertain precisely their force. Having done so, the French admiral, at 2 h. 30 m. P.M., tacked and stood away, as if to seek a less troublesome enemy. That Rear-admiral Sercey did not intend to be the assailant, is acknowledged by a French naval writer; who maintains, also, that the principle is a correct one, and ought to be, and indeed is, the general practice of the French navy. As this last assertion, if true, will tend to elucidate much that is recorded in these pages, we may be allowed to digress so far as to give the French writer's words on the subject:—

"In the weak state of the French marine, the greatest of all follies is to send ships to sea to seek and offer battle to those of the enemy. It was done, however, at the commencement of the war, and we have witnessed the ill consequences arising from it. This fatal experience, moreover, was unnecessary to prove that such are not the proper tactics of the weaker party. To deceive the vigilance of the stronger, escape his pursuit, strike unawares upon a point which he has left unprotected (and it is impossible for him to protect all), is the proper way to compensate for great inequality of force: even were the forces of two enemies equal, he who acted thus would soon triumph over the other. In naval matters, an engagement is not always the aim to be proposed, unless a party possesses a force so superior, that he may hope very soon to annihilate his enemy. Ships of war have thus always an object, other than that of fighting the ships of an enemy; and it often happens that, whatever may be the issue of the combat, this first and principal object fails to be fulfilled. The important point to the state is, that a naval commander should execute the mission with which he is charged, and not neglect to do so, in order to afford a proof of his courage and acquire a trophiless glory for his country. According to these principles, the different governments which succeed each other in France during the war of the revolution, have, almost all of them, and very wisely, given a formal order to their flag-officers and captains, to avoid an action, except in case of absolute necessity, and to devote the whole of their energies towards the accomplishment of their mission.[1]

Soon after M. Sercey and his frigates had tacked, the Arrogant and Victorious did the same, and at 4 h. 30 m. P.M. bore up in chase of the former, who were still stretching in towards Pedro in the following order: Cybèle, Forte, Seine, and Vertu, as the four heaviest frigates in one line, and, a little to windward of them, to act as a light squadron, and, if an action ensued, to double upon the enemy, the Prudente and Régénérée. At 6 P.M. the two 74s hoisted their colours; and at 9 h. 30 m., getting very near the land, they tacked and stood off; just previous to which the rearmost French ship bore about three miles ahead of the Arrogant. At about 10 P.M., having sounded in 20 fathoms, the Forte made the signal to tack in succession; and she and her consorts, favoured by the land-wind, then steered about east-south-east.

On the 9th, at daybreak, the French frigates were again ahead of the two British 74s, steering to the eastward with very light airs; and the two rearmost frigates, being nearly within gun-shot, were carrying a press of sail to close their companions. The Arrogant and Victorious now edged away a little, to endeavour to cut off these two frigates, but did not succeed, owing chiefly to the calm state of the weather. At a few minutes

[1] As our translation is more according to the spirit than the letter of the original, we have copied the original passage into the Appendix, for which see No 22.

past 6 A.M., finding an action inevitable, Rear-admiral Sercey signalled his squadron to put about together, intending to try or the weather-gage. The frigates were soon reformed on the larboard tack, and, with the Vertu now as the van-ship, stretched on to windward of their opponents.

At 7 h. 25 m. A.M. the Arrogant, still with her consort on the starboard tack, opened her fire on the Vertu, at the distance of about 700 yards, and succeeded in discharging two broadsides before the French frigate, owing to her position, could bring any guns to bear. The first broadside, however, which the Vertu did fire, brought down the Arrogant's ensign. It was immediately replaced by a union-jack. The frigates were formed thus: Vertu, Seine, Forte, Régénérée, the latter a little to windward of her second ahead and astern, Cybèle, Prudente, the last on a line with the Régénérée. As they slowly passed in succession, the frigates kept up a brisk cannonade upon the two 74s; the fire from one of which cut away the foretopsail yard of, and otherwise greatly damaged, the Vertu. At 8 h. 30 m. A.M., the rearmost French frigate, the Prudente, having got so far on the starboard quarter of the Arrogant as to be out of gun-shot from her, the latter ceased firing.

Since ten minutes after the commencement of the action a calm had prevailed; and the Arrogant, even had she been in perfect order, would have found it difficult to wear. As it was, her foretopsail yard had been shot away; and so had the larboard arm of the maintopsail and cross-jack yards, starboard arm of the spritsail yard, and the mizen topgallantmast. The main topgallantmast had also been shot through, and the main yard, mainmast, and bowsprit much wounded. Three of her boats had been rendered useless by shot; and all the larboard main rigging and stays were cut away, with the whole of the starboard or weather braces and yard tackles. Her sails, also, were in a shattered condition. Thus situated, the Arrogant was quite in an unmanageable state.

The Victorious, who lay about a cable's length astern, and rather to leeward, of the Arrogant, opened her fire, as the French frigates, after having discharged their broadsides at the latter, successively got abreast of her. At about 8 A.M. Captain Clark was wounded in the thigh and carried below, and Lieut. William Waller took command of the ship. At 8 h. 40 m. A.M., which was soon after the Arrogant had, as already stated, ceased firing, the Victorious wore round on the same tack as the enemy, and brought her larboard guns to bear. At

9 A.M. she perceived a signal at the Arrogant's foretopmast head; but, owing to the smoke and to the flags not blowing out, did not understand it. The signal, which was for the Victorious to come to again on the starboard tack, remained up about ten minutes, and was then hauled down without having been answered.

The two leading frigates had now stationed themselves on the larboard bow of the Victorious; and the remaining four lay from the beam to the quarter, at the distance of about 900 yards. The 74 sustained and returned the united fire of the six French frigates until 10 h. 15 m. A.M.; when, having received several shot in her hull, upwards of 40 of them between wind and water, had her three lower masts and bowsprit, as well as her yards and topmasts, badly wounded, and her rigging and sails very much cut; and finding that the Arrogant, whose distance already was nearly a mile and a half, still continued to stand on upon the opposite tack, the Victorious attempted, with a light air of wind, to wear and rejoin her consort.

No sooner was the stern of the Victorious, in wearing, exposed to the enemy, than three of the frigates advanced to rake her, and, it falling a dead calm, continued pouring a destructive fire until 10 h. 45 m. A.M.; when, fortunately for the Victorious, a breeze sprang up from the northward, and enabled the latter to bring her starboard broadside to bear. At this time the Vertu, from the loss of her foretopsail yard, had dropped astern, and lay in the south quarter, and another frigate was observed to be sweeping and towing with boats in that direction. The latter was the Cybèle, proceeding, by signal, to take the crippled Vertu in tow. At 10 h. 55 m. A.M., this service having been executed, the French squadron bore up and steered west by north, under a crowd of sail; and at 11 h. 15 m. A.M. the Victorious ceased firing, the last of the frigates being out of gunshot.

The condition of the two British ships at the close of this long and tedious contest, as far as it respects their masts, yards, rigging, and hulls, has already been described. It remains to show what loss in men they each of them sustained. The Arrogant, out of a crew of 584, or thereabouts, lost one midshipman and six seamen killed, and 27 men wounded. Among this ship's damages should have been noticed, the disabling of one second-deck, and two lowerdeck guns, and the dismounting of one gun on the quarter-deck. The loss of the Victorious, whose established complement was the same as the Arrogant's, but who had sent away in prizes her first-lieutenant and 90 seamen, amounted to 15 seamen and two marines killed, her captain, one midshipman, 48 seamen, and seven marines, wounded: making the total of loss on board the two ships 24 killed, and 84 wounded.

With respect to the damage sustained by the squadron of Rear-admiral Sercey, we can only gather, that three of the frigates, including the Vertu and Seine, were much cut up in hull, masts, yards, and rigging. That the remaining three frigates also suffered in some degree, will be evident from the following account of the loss incurred in the action :—The Vertu had nine officers and men killed, and 15 wounded; the Seine, 18, including Captain Latour her commander, killed, and 44 wounded; the Forte, six killed and 17 wounded; the Cybèle, four killed and 13 wounded; and the Prudente, three killed and nine wounded: making a total of 42 killed and 104 wounded.

Of the force opposed in this action it may be sufficient to state, that the two British 74s were of the common or 18-pounder class; the Forte, a frigate of 1400 tons, mounting 52 guns, including thirty long 24-pounders; the Seine, Vertu, and Cybèle, all large 18-pounder frigates, armed like the Virginie; and the Régénérée and Prudente, frigates of the 12-pounder or 36-gun class. Consequently, the superiority of force, especially in men, the numbers there being about as 10 to 19, was on the side of M. Sercey. Judging, however, from the relative loss of the combatants, we should say that, had the state of the weather, and other circumstances to which we need scarcely advert, permitted the two 74s to manœuvre and act in concert, they would, in all probability, have captured two, at least, of the six frigates opposed to them; unless, indeed, the French admiral had put in practice a well-concerted plan of boarding, in which case, undoubtedly, his decided numerical superiority would have placed the two line-of-battle ships in great jeopardy.

After the action the Arrogant and Victorious, the latter in tow of the former, proceeded straight to Madras, and on the 6th of October anchored in the road. The French squadron steered for Isle-du-Roi, in the Archipelago of Margui, and anchored there on the 15th. Here the frigates got themselves thoroughly stored and refitted, even to the renewal of their damaged lower masts. They sailed thence in the early part of October, steering first towards the coast of Golconda, and afterwards to the eastern coast of Ceylon.

Having, while on this station, been led to believe that he

should get all the wants of his squadron supplied at Batavia, Rear-admiral Sercey proceeded thither; particularly as the Vertu, Seine, and another of the frigates required large repairs in their hulls. The delay occasioned by this step detained M. Sercey in port at a very critical season; and so far the action between his squadron and the two British 74s contributed to preserve from spoliation much valuable property in the eastern hemisphere.

Plymouth was this year visited by a calamity which will long be remembered by its inhabitants. On the 22nd of September, at about 4 h. 30 m. P.M., the 32-gun frigate Amphion, Captain Israel Pellew, while lashed to the sheer-hulk on one side and almost touching the Yarmouth receiving-ship on the other, both of which lay close to the dockyard jetty, unfortunately blew up. Two parties were on board at dinner, one in the cabin, the other in the gun-room; and, owing to its being known that the Amphion would put to sea on the following day, nearly 100 men, women, and children, over and above the ship's complement, were on board, taking leave of their kindred and townsfolk. Captain Pellew, his first-lieutenant, and a visitor, Captain William Swaffield of the Overyssel, were sitting at table, when the first shock threw them all from their seats against the carlings of the main deck. The first two, although much bruised, retained their self-possession, and, running to the cabin windows, threw themselves out and were saved. Captain Swaffield, stunned probably by the blow against the deck, shared the fate of the ship, and of 300 out of her 310 or 312 unfortunate inmates. The mangled bodies, limbless trunks, and disunited arms, legs, and heads, that everywhere presented themselves, made humanity shudder. The Amphion having been chiefly manned from the town, these black and scorched pieces of flesh had to be scrutinized by the sorrowful inhabitants, in order that they might ascertain, if they could, which had belonged to a father, a son, a brother, a husband, or a friend.

Three or four of the survivors had been among the men engaged in the tops. Another, the boatswain, was standing on the cat-head, superintending the rigging of the jib-boom: after being lifted up by the shock, he fell into the sea, and escaped with the loss of an arm. The sentinel at the cabin-door happened to be looking at his watch, when he felt it suddenly dashed out of his hand: beyond that he knew nothing, and yet was but little hurt. The cause of this dreadful disaster has never been satisfactorily explained. If by design, the incendiary, and, if by accident, the defaulter, probably fell a victim to his crime or his carelessness. Early in October an attempt was made to weigh the Amphion, and two frigates, the Castor and Iphigenia, were moored on each side of her. It only served to harrow up afresh the feelings of the inhabitants, by dislodging the putrid bodies, and casting them on shore all along the beach. In November, however, Mr. Hemmings, the master-attendant at Plymouth, succeeded in dragging the wreck to the jetty to be broken up. As one means of preventing the repetition of such an accident so near to the town, it was ordered that every ship should land her powder previously to entering the harbour.

On the 23rd of September, at daybreak, the island of Désirade bearing south-east by south distant six or seven leagues, the British 18-gun brig-sloop Pelican, Captain John Clarke Searle, mounting sixteen 32-pounder carronades and two long sixes, found herself close on the lee beam of an enemy's frigate. Not over-desirous of engaging where the odds were so decidedly against him, Captain Searle made sail to the north-west, and was followed by the frigate; who, having the weather-gage, and sailing remarkably fast in the prevailing fresh breeze, rapidly approached the Pelican.

Having away in prizes her master and several of her petty-officers and seamen, the brig could not muster, at this time, more than 97, out of her established complement of 121, men and boys; and some of the seamen appeared to hesitate about engaging a ship of such evident superiority of force. But, when Captain Searle called to their recollection the frequent occasions on which they had distinguished themselves while under his command, and expressed a hope that they would not sully their well-earned reputation, nor place less confidence in him than they had been accustomed to do, the fine fellows gave three cheers, and at once declared their resolution, rather to sink with their commander than forfeit his good opinion.

As soon as she had made all ready, the Pelican, to the great surprise, no doubt, of all on board the frigate, shortened sail: and at 7 A.M. the French 36-gun frigate Médée, having arrived within gun-shot, opened her fire. The brig reserved hers until her carronades could reach with effect. Having at length got within the proper distance, the Pelican commenced a very brisk fire, and kept it up until 8 h. 53 m. A.M.; when the Médée, whose crew appeared to be in some confusion, hauled on board her maintack, and made off to the northward under all possible sail. Having had every brace and bowline, all the after backstays, the main-stay, several of the lower shrouds, the topsail ties, and other parts of her rigging, shot away, her sails very much torn, and her mainmast, maintopsail yard, and fore-yard a good deal injured, the Pelican was not in a condition for an immediate pursuit; and the Médée, being thus left to herself, soon ran out of sight. With all her heavy damage, the Pelican had no person killed, and only one slightly wounded.

At 10 A.M., while the Pelican was repairing her damages, the man at the mast-head discovered a large ship on the lee beam. At 11 A.M., having got her rigging and sails in tolerable order, the Pelican gave chase; and at 3 P.M., Englishman's Head, Guadeloupe, bearing south-south-east, distant a mile and a half, succeeded, after firing several shot, in cutting away the stranger's maintopsail yard. Upon this the latter brought to, and proved to be the Alcyon, late a British army-victualler, but then a prize in the possession of the Médée; who had captured her on the 9th, about 100 leagues to windward of Barbadoes. Having put on board the Alcyon acting-lieutenant Thomas Ussher and a party of men, the Pelican, at 4 P.M., made sail to the southward with the prize in tow; but at midnight, owing to a calm and a heavy westerly swell which caused the Alcyon three times to fall on board the Pelican, the latter was obliged to cast her off.

At daybreak on the 24th the Alcyon was found to have drifted very near to the shore at Anse-la-Barque; and, at about a gunshot within her, was seen the Médée herself, having a light air from the land, while the Pelican and her prize lay quite becalmed. The Médée's boats soon regained possession of the Alcyon; and Captain Searle, knowing that the Thétis and another French frigate, either the Pensée or Concorde, were at anchor in Anse-la-Barque, thought it the most prudent course to abandon his prize. Scarcely had the Pelican taken advantage of the breeze which had just sprung up, and set sail from the spot, ere one of the frigates came out and joined the Médée; but neither frigate evinced any further disposition to molest the Pelican, and she proceeded to the Saintes to refit.

Soon after the Médée, in company with the Alcyon, had anchored at Anse-la-Barque, Victor Hugues, the governor of Guadeloupe, sent for Lieutenant Ussher who had been taken prisoner in the prize, to ascertain from him, whether or not there was any truth in the statement made by the captain of the Médée, that the English vessel, which he had engaged on the 23rd, was a frigate with her mizenmast out. The mistake was soon cleared up, to the evident mortification of the French governor.

On the day after the Pelican had anchored at the Saintes, an aide-de-camp of Victor Hugues arrived with a flag of truce; and the French officer, appearing to entertain a doubt about the force of the vessel which had beaten off the Médée, was allowed to go on board the Pelican to count her guns. About the same time arrived an officer of the 60th regiment, who had been a prisoner on board the Médée, during the action, and got released on her arrival at Guadeloupe. He confirmed every statement respecting the proceedings of the Médée; adding, that she mounted 40 guns, with a complement of 300 men, and sustained much damage, besides a loss, in killed and wounded together, of 33 men.

It was afterwards ascertained from Lieutenant Ussher, that the Pelican's first broadside killed the man at the wheel, wounded three men, and disabled a gun; and that the last raking broadside, which the Pelican poured into the stern of the Médée, killed and wounded from 10 to 12 men upon the main deck. Great as was the noise which this truly gallant exploit of the Pelican made in the West Indies, we have searched in vain for any account of it in the "Victoires et Conquêtes," and in some other French works to which we have had occasion to refer.

On the 13th of October, at daybreak, the British 12-pounder 32-gun frigate Terpischore, Captain Richard Bowen, while cruising off the port of Carthagena, with a light air at west-south-west, observed a strange frigate to windward, standing towards her. The former's situation was such, that an engagement with an enemy, of the apparent force of the ship approaching, was not very desirable. The Terpsichore had left 30 of her men sick at the hospital in Gibraltar, and her sick and convalescent lists showed more than that number still on board; many of whom were dangerously ill, and none strong enough to be useful at quarters. Moreover, she was then in sight of the very spot on which the Spanish fleet had been cruising only two days previous; and a small Spanish vessel, apparently a tender, was at this very time passing in the direction of Carthagena, the port to which the fleet belonged. Under all the circumstances, therefore, Captain Bowen could hardly flatter himself with bringing off, either the enemy's frigate if captured, or his own if disabled. To fly, however, was not to be borne; and the Terpsichore continued standing on, without any alteration in her course.

At 9 h. 30 m. the Spanish 12-pounder 34-gun frigate Mahonesa, Captain Don Tomas Ayaldi, having approached within hail of the Terpsichore, hauled to the wind on the latter's weather beam. This being apparently done in order to place herself to advantage, the Terpsichore, whose position was then tolerably good, fired one gun as a trier of her opponent's intention. It was instantaneously returned by a whole broadside, and the action proceeded with mutual spirit. After a while the Spanish crew began to slacken their exertions; and at the end of one hour and 20 minutes, the Mahonesa tried to make off. By this time the Terpsichore had had her three lower masts and bowsprit wounded, her spare spars and boats shot through, two of her anchors disabled, and her rigging and sails much cut. In the course of 20 minutes, however, by characteristic alacrity in refitting and making sail, the British frigate was again close alongside of her antagonist, with every gun well charged and pointed; when the Mahonesa, whose booms had fallen down and disabled her waist-guns, and who was altogether in a crippled and defenceless state, hauled down her colours.

Out of her 182 men and boys, the Terpsichore lost none in killed, and but four in wounded: whereas the Mahonesa, out of her 275 in complement, had 30 killed, and the same number wounded, a portion of them mortally.

Both frigates mounted guns of the same nominal caliber, and of the number, 32 and 34, expressed by their respective rates. Admitting, therefore, the Terpsichore to have had her full complement at quarters, we should pronounce this to be as fair a match as an English officer would wish to fight, or an English writer to record. Nothing is more truly characteristic of a brave man, than promptitude in doing justice to the efforts of an unsuccessful enemy. Captain Bowen, in his official letter, dwells with emphasis on the zeal, courage, and good conduct of Don Tomas Ayaldi, the commander of the Mahonesa. He declares that this officer, although, towards the last, he could rally but few of his men, persevered to defend his ship, longer almost than was justifiable.

Notwithstanding the crippled state of the Mahonesa's masts, which had been left with scarcely a shroud to support them, Captain Bowen succeeded in carrying his prize to Lisbon. But the fine contour of the Mahonesa, boasted of as it was by the Spaniards, had been so disfigured by the Terpsichore's shot, that the ship, although, setting aside what she had suffered in the action, a remarkably fine frigate of 921 tons (239 more than the

Terpsichore), was considered not worth the cost of a thorough repair; hence, the Mahonesa had little more than a nominal existence among the 36-gun frigates of the British navy.

The following is the account given of this action by a contemporary: "The first Spanish ship captured after the declaration of war was the Mahonesa of 36 guns, by Captain Richard Bowen, of the Terpsichore. The action took place off Malaga. The Mahonesa had between 50 and 60 of her people killed and wounded; the Terpsichore had no one hurt on board. There is little credit to be gained in conquering such antagonists."[1] Passing over the slight mistake, that "the Terpsichore had no one hurt on board," we shall extract another passage from the same work, if only to show how differently the writer could reason in (as he has made it appear) a similar case. "This instance," that of the Crescent and Réunion, "may be fairly adduced in support of the proposition, that a long list of killed and wounded is not always a certain criterion of the merit of an action."[2]

On the 24th of October the British 12-pounder 36-gun frigate Santa-Margarita, Captain Thomas Byam Martin, cruising at the entrance of the Channel, captured the ship-privateer Buonaparte of 16 guns and 137 men; and on the next morning discovered two ships approaching her, which came nearly within hail before they discovered the Santa-Margarita to be a frigate. They now made all sail from her, and, to secure the retreat of one or the other, stood on different tacks.

The Santa-Margarita followed the larger ship, with little prospect of taking the other; but Lieutenant William Birchall, first of the frigate, gallantly volunteered to attack the latter in a boat. At this time the shot from the frigate had so disabled this ship, as to enable the boat to get alongside, and Lieutenant Birchall took possession, without resistance, of the merchant ship Potomak, from Poole bound to Newfoundland, with a cargo, a prize to the Vengeur, of 16 guns and 120 men, from Brest, the ship of which the Santa-Margarita was in pursuit; and which, on receiving a few shot from the latter, hauled down her colours. Having now nearly as many prisoners on board as equalled his crew in number, Captain Martin was obliged to return into port to get rid of them.

An express from the island of Anguilla having reached St. Kitt's on the 25th of November, bringing an account that two French ships of war, with smaller vessels and a body of troops,

[1] Brenton, vol. ii., p. 142. [2] Idid. vol. i., p. 248.

were attacking the island, the British 28-gun frigate Lapwing, Captain Robert Barton, lying at anchor at St. Kitt's, immediately weighed and made sail, in the hope of reaching Anguilla in time to save the inhabitants from the dreadful consequences that invariably attended one of Victor Hugues's pillaging visitations.

A northerly wind made it the following evening ere the Lapwing reached Anguilla; too late, as was evident, to prevent the enemy from setting fire to the houses. The very appearance of the frigate, however, freed the inhabitants from the further presence of the invaders; who, that very afternoon, to the number of nearly 300, embarked on board the French 20-gun ship Décius and brig Vaillante, which had transported them thither. These vessels, one of which mounted 26 guns, 18 of them long 6, and two brass 8 pounders, with six English 18-pounder carronades, and the other six, two long 24s and four brass 36-pounder carronades, then stood out of the bay of Anguilla, and were immediately chased by the Lapwing; who, at about 10 P.M., brought them to close action. At the end of an hour's mutual cannonade the brig bore away; and, in less than half an hour, the Décius, after making a vain attempt to escape, struck her colours. As soon as he had secured the ship, Captain Barton directed his attention to the brig; but, in the mean time, the latter had run on shore on the neighbouring island of St. Martin: she was, however, soon destroyed by the fire of the Lapwing.

The Lapwing, whose damages were chiefly confined to her sails and rigging, had but one man, the pilot, killed, and six seamen wounded. The Décius is represented to have lost, out of a complement, including troops, of 336 men, as many as 80 killed and 40 wounded. It is probable that the Décius had some of her masts shot away; but, although the Gazette contains two letters on the subject of the action, not a word appears about any damage sustained by either ship: nor, in short, are any details given. The loss sustained by the brig, whose complement, including troops, was about 135, was doubtless severe, but could not be ascertained.

The promptitude and vigour of the Lapwing's attack upon these French vessels reflect great credit upon Captain Barton, his officers and crew. A slight degree of less decision in the business might have encouraged the French commodore to try the effects of boarding, in the hope, by his overwhelming numbers, to have carried the British ship. With respect to the immediate effect of Captain Barton's success, it was most salutary and cheering; inasmuch as it routed a nest of hornets, and relieved a suffering people from further pillage, and, not improbably, from massacre.

On the following day, the 27th, the Lapwing having her prize in tow, was chased by the French frigates Thétis and Pensée. Their near approach compelled Captain Barton, after removing his men and the prisoners from the Décius, to set the vessel on fire. Thus unencumbered, the Lapwing escaped from her pursuers, and reached St. Kitt's in safety. Soon after his return to this island, Captain Barton was presented by a deputation of the inhabitants with a very flattering address, lauding as well his gallantry in the action we have just detailed, as his subsequent humanity towards the crew of the Décius. To this address a suitable reply was returned.

Having repaired at Gibraltar the damages which she had sustained in her action with the Mahonesa, the Terpsichore frigate was again at sea in search of an opponent; when, on the 12th of December, at daybreak, while lying to about 20 leagues to the westward of Cadiz, Captain Bowen descried an enemy's frigate also lying to, distant about four miles on his weather quarter. Owing to the stormy weather of the preceding night, and the fresh south-easterly wind which, with a short uneasy sea, still prevailed, the Terpsichore was under a close-reefed maintopsail, and had her topgallantmasts struck. Quickly replacing these, and spreading as much sail as the state of the weather would permit, the Terpsichore tacked and stood after the stranger; whom we may at once introduce as the French 36-gun frigate Vestale, Captain Foucaud, who had parted company a few days before, in a gale, from the squadron of Rear-admiral Villeneuve, already mentioned as on its way from Toulon to Brest.

As if desirous to avoid an action, the Vestale made sail, tacked, and stood to windward. The Terpsichore, owing to the breeze getting more ahead, was unable to fetch within gun-shot, but continued working up until past 2 P.M.; when the Vestale wore, and stood to the east-north-east. This brought the two ships nearer together; but a change in the wind again baffled one and favoured the other, and its increased violence sprang the Terpsichore's fore and main topmasts. The chase was nevertheless persevered in, each ship under her courses, until 2 A.M. on the 13th; when, being close in with the land about Cape Marcus, the Terpsichore wore and brought to with her head off shore.

At about 8 A.M. the Vestale was again seen from the masthead; and, a shift of wind to the south-west having now given the British frigate the weather-gage, the latter again wore and made sail in chase. The sprung state of the Terpsichore's masts rendered it likely that the Vestale, carrying the sail she did, would soon reach Cadiz, the port towards which she was seemingly directing her course, and then but a few miles distant. However, at 9 h. 30 m. P.M., to the great joy of the Terpsichore's officers and men, the Vestale hauled up her courses and hove to. In this state, without firing a shot, or even hoisting her colours, the latter waited until the Terpsichore had reached her weather quarter.

Having there in vain hailed the Vestale several times, the Terpsichore, at 10 P.M., ranged alongside of her opponent within 10 yards, and opened her fire. The Vestale, as she promptly returned this warm salute, ran up the tri-coloured flag with lights, and a most determined action ensued; during which the Terpsichore, owing to her braces getting foul, was compelled for several minutes to receive her adversary's fire without the power of returning it. At length, when the action had lasted with mutual spirit until 11 h. 40 m. P.M., the French frigate, having all her three masts and bowsprit in a tottering state, and her captain and a great proportion of her crew killed and wounded, struck her colours. Immediately afterwards the Vestale's mizenmast fell over the side; and, almost at the same instant, unintentionally, it is supposed, a double-shotted gun belonging to her went off, and killed a boy, and wounded dangerously in the shoulder (by which his arm was ever afterwards rendered nearly useless) the only lieutenant on board the Terpsichore, George Bowen, brother to the captain, besides four of her seamen.

The Terpsichore had received several shots between wind and water, and between the guns on the main and quarter decks. All her boats, except the small cutter, were much damaged; and so were her bowsprit, fore and main masts, maintopmast, spare spars, sails, and standing and running rigging.

It appears that, at the time of this action, the British frigate had away in prizes and sick at the hospital, two lieutenants, three midshipmen, the boatswain, and 40 men; which therefore reduced her complement to 166 men and boys. Of these the Terpsichore lost four seamen killed, her second and only lieutenant, and 17 petty-officers, seamen, and marines wounded. The Vestale, out of a complement, according to one English account, of 300, and to another, of 270, lost her captain, two officers, and 27 men killed, and 37 officers and men, including her first-lieutenant, wounded.

Had the Terpsichore's 46 absentees, including two of her three lieutenants, three midshipmen, and the boatswain, been where their wishes would have led them, still the Vestale, as will sufficiently appear by a reference to the comparative statement in the action of the Astræa and Gloire, would have had a preponderance of force in her favour. It cannot be said, however, that the French frigate yielded without a struggle, and a manful one too. In addition to the loss of her mizenmast, the fore and main masts and bowsprit of the Vestale fell, just as the Terpsichore's boat got alongside. Of what avail, then, would have been a longer resistance; especially against an adversary whose masts, although much wounded, were still standing?

Having possessed the Terpsichore of her well-earned prize, our next business is to show what became of her. Such had been the ardour of the conquerors in this long night-action, that their near approach to a treacherous shore had been entirely overlooked. Both ships, in fact, were close to windward of the shoals that lie between Cape Trafalgar and Cadiz. The Vestale in particular, to whom Captain Bowen, in the reduced state of his crew, and the critical situation of the Terpsichore's masts, yards, and rigging, had been able to send only his master, one midshipman, and seven seamen, had drifted into four fathoms' water, and was without an anchor clear for letting go. The Vestale's surviving crew, too, or the greater part of them, lay drunk about the decks, and were incapable, even if they were willing, to assist in saving the lives of those on board: of whom, in all probability, the whole would have perished, had the ship gone on shore. By great exertions on the part of Mr. James Elder and his handful of men, the prize was brought up in little less than three fathoms' water. The Terpsichore, with great difficulty, weathered the rocks of St. Sebastian, and gained an offing.

On the following morning, the 13th, the Terpsichore stood back in search of her prize, and at 10 A.M. cast anchor in 20 fathoms' water, about four miles south-west of the island of San-Pedro. Hitherto no opportunity had offered for removing any more of the prisoners than the Vestale's second-lieutenant; and the shattered state of the boats belonging to both frigates, added to the loss of the Terpsichore's cutter by swamping alongside the prize in the troubled state of the sea, rendered even the passing of a tow-rope to the Vestale a hazardous and tedious operation. At length a stream-cable was got on board the latter; and, at about 4 P.M., a favourable slant of wind enabled the two ships to cut the cables by which they rode, and make sail. But, while the Terpsichore's people were heaving in the bend of the stream-cable, to which a hawser had been made fast, the cable got foul of a rock, and the Terpsichore was compelled to cut herself free. The Vestale, meantime, rode by the stream-cable as it clung to the rock, and, owing to the master's provident care, had a second anchor ready to let go. Darkness coming on, the Terpsichore again stood off for the night; and, it falling calm about midnight, was drifted by the current into the Straits. Towards daylight on the 14th the wind changed to the south-east; and Captain Bowen, having chased and spoken a Swedish ship that had hove in sight, again steered towards the spot on which he had left his prize; but he and his officers and crew had the mortification to see the Vestale, with some spars erected and sails set, and with French colours flying, towing, within the shoals, straight towards Cadiz. The Terpsichore gave chase, but, in her crippled state, was quite unable to overtake the Vestale; who, in a few minutes more, was safe moored in port.

The fact is, that, as soon as the Terpsichore had sailed out of sight on the preceding evening, the French crew, recovering from their inebriated stupor, dispossessed the master of his charge, and anchored the ship in five fathoms' water. They then got up a pair of sheers for hoisting out the launch, in order that some of them might proceed to the shore. By this time the wind, as already mentioned, had drawn round to the south-east, and blew fair for Cadiz. Soon afterwards, some Spanish boats coming alongside, the French crew hove up the anchor, and, setting a few sails on the sheers, allowed the Spaniards to tow the Vestale out of the reach of those, by whom she had been so honourably fought and so fairly won.

Captain Bowen afterwards sent into Cadiz a letter addressed to the Vestale's late first-lieutenant, then her commanding officer, demanding the restitution of his prize; but the Frenchman, feeling his head shake at the bare thought, returned no answer.

Thus had the brave crew of the Terpsichore no second trophy to carry home; but what, it may be asked, is the worth of a shattered hulk, compared with the glory acquired in gaining a victory over, at the least, an equal opponent? This mode of estimating the merits of the case was not, however, that adopted in the proper quarter. Hence Captain Bowen's letter to Sir John Jervis, describing the action, never made its appearance in the London Gazette; nor, that preliminary omitted, did the Terpsichore's captain receive the honour of knighthood: an honour, as we have seen, frequently conferred, even where a British 18-pounder frigate had captured a French frigate of the class of the Vestale.

Captain Bowen's vigilance in protecting the trade equalled his ardour in vindicating the honour of his country; and, in order to show their sense of both, the merchants of London presented him with an elegant piece of plate: that, too, while Captain Bowen was in command of the same Terpsichore in which he had thus captured, in succession, two frigates of the enemy, each of equal, if not superior force, to his own.

On the 19th of December, at 10 P.M., Commodore Nelson, in the 38-gun frigate Minerve, Captain George Cockburn, accompanied by the 12-pounder 32-gun frigate Blanche, Captain d'Arcy Preston, being on his way from Gibraltar to Porto-Ferrajo, to bring away the stores left there, fell in with two Spanish frigates. While the Blanche, agreeably to the commodore's directions, wore to attack the frigate to leeward, the Minerve hauled up, and at 10 h. 40 m. A.M. brought to close action the larger frigate, or that to windward. After a brave resistance of two hours and 50 minutes, during which she lost her mizenmast, and had her fore and main masts shot through in several places, the Spanish 40-gun frigate Sabina, Captain Don Jacobo Steuart, struck her colours to the Minerve; whose masts, although none of them had been shot away, were, as well as her rigging and sails, much wounded.

Out of her complement, consisting with a few supernumeraries of 286 men and boys, the Minerve had one midshipman and six seamen killed, one lieutenant (James Noble, who had quitted the Captain 74, to serve under Commodore Nelson), the boatswain, and 32 petty-officers, seamen, and marines, or soldiers (a detachment from the 18th regiment), wounded. The Sabina had commenced the action also with 286 men and boys; of whom she lost, in killed and wounded together, according to Commodore Nelson's letter, 164, but, according to a Spanish account of the action published at Carthagena, 10 men killed and 45 wounded, two of them mortally.

The Minerve mounted her 42 French guns,[1] and the Sabina, 40 guns, 18 and 8 pounders Spanish. The loss and damages of

[1] See p. 323.

the former show, that the Spaniards pointed the Sabina's guns with more than their accustomed precision. The British, on the other hand, must have felt some disadvantage from the French armament of the Minerve. Upon the whole, the action was very gallantly maintained on both sides; and it is scarcely necessary to state, that Commodore Nelson, in his official letter, pays the full tribute of praise to his Spanish opponent.

The first and second lieutenants of the Minerve, John Culverhouse and Thomas Masterman Hardy, with 40 petty-officers and seamen, having been placed on board the Sabina, the latter was taken in tow, when, at 4 P.M., a frigate, known by her signals to be Spanish, was seen coming up. The Minerve cast off the prize, which immediately stood to the southward; and at 4 h. 30 m. P.M., the former came to action with the 34-gun frigate Matilda. In half an hour the Minerve compelled this her second antagonist to wear and haul off, and would, most probably, have captured her, had not three other Spanish ships, the Principe-de-Asturias of 112 guns, and the frigates Ceres of 40, and Perla of 34 guns, hove in sight. At daylight on the 20th these three ships were joined by the Matilda; and the Blanche also made her appearance far to windward. The Minerve had now her own safety to look to; and crippled as she was, it required the greatest exertions to get clear. The squadron chased all day, but at dark gave up the pursuit; leaving the Minerve with much additional damage to her rigging and sails, and with the additional loss of 10 men, including the gunner, wounded.

Lieutenant Culverhouse, now the commander of the Sabina, purposely to draw the attention of the Spaniards from what, on more than one account, would have been by far the more valuable prize of the two, hoisted English over Spanish colours; and the lieutenant and his few hands, although greatly inconvenienced in having the whole surviving Spanish crew, except the captain, in their custody, manœuvred the prize with the utmost skill and steadiness, not surrendering the Sabina until her two remaining masts went over the side, and left her a mere wreck upon the water.

In three or four minutes after the Minerve had poured her first broadside into the Sabina, the Blanche was close alongside the frigate to leeward. Eight or nine broadsides, very feebly returned, silenced her; and, calling for quarter, the Ceres hauled down her colours, with a loss, as subsequently ascertained, of seven men killed, and 15 wounded. But the consummation of the victory was impracticable; the Matilda and Perla, who were almost within gun-shot when the action commenced, being at this time so near that the Blanche was obliged to wear and make sail in the direction of her consort the Minerve. As, however, the Matilda and Perla did not close immediately with the Ceres, who, although damaged in her rigging and sails, had now got her foresail, fore topsail, and fore topgallantsail set, the Blanche again stood towards the latter. But the Ceres outsailed the Blanche before the wind, and, moreover, was presently joined by the Principe-de-Asturias three-decker, from near the land. Captain Preston, therefore, although his ship had sustained neither damage nor loss, was obliged to content himself with a trophiless triumph.

The Minerve, in the mean time, had proceeded upon her destination, and on the 26th anchored in the harbour of Porto-Ferrajo. Here the commodore remained, embarking the troops and stores, until the morning of the 29th of January, 1797; when the Minerve, accompanied by the Romulus, Southampton, and Dido frigates, Dolphin and Dromedary store-ships, two sloops, and 12 transports, set sail upon her return. On the same evening, the Minerve and Romulus parted company from the squadron, and stood towards the French coast. On the 1st of February these two frigates reconnoitred the road of Toulon, and successively the ports of Barcelona and Carthagena, and on the 10th rejoined their companions at Gibraltar.

Colonial Expeditions.—North America.

Rear-admiral Richery, with his seven sail of the line and three frigates, as soon as the kind friends, who had released him from his long thraldom at Cadiz, parted company on their return home, steered straight for North America, and on the 28th of August arrived on the grand bank of Newfoundland. The British naval commander-in-chief on the station was Vice-admiral Sir James Wallace, who had under his command only the 50-gun ship Romney and three or four 12-pounder frigates; and all of these were out on a cruise, except the 32-gun frigate Venus, Captain Thomas Graves, lying at an anchor in the harbour of St. John. As soon as it became known that the French squadron was off the coast, Captain Graves, with the greater part of his crew, was ordered on shore to assist in manning the batteries, one of which, called the Chain Rock, is but a few feet above the level of the sea; the frigate, meanwhile, under the command of the second-lieutenant, was moored across the entrance of the harbour, which is only 160 yards wide. Rear-admiral Richery stood close in, with a fresh breeze, but, not liking the appearance of the defence, bore away to the southward.

On the 4th of September the French squadron entered the bay of Bulls: here M. Richery plundered and set fire to the huts of the poor fishermen, and destroyed their vessels and fishing-stages. On the 5th he detached chef de division Zacharie-Jacques-Théodore Allemand, with the Duquesne and Censeur 74s and frigate Friponne, to the bay of Castles on the coast of Labrador; while he himself, with the Victoire, Barras, Jupiter, Berwick, and Révolution 74s, and frigates Embuscade, and Félicité, set sail for the islands of Saint-Pierre and Miquelon; where on his arrival, he destroyed all the buildings, vessels, and fishing-stages of the inhabitants, as he had previously done at the bay of Bulls.

Delayed by head winds and fogs, M. Allemand did not enter the bay of Castles until the 22nd of September; by which time the greater part of the vessels had departed for Europe. The French commodore then sent an officer with a flag of truce, demanding the surrender of the town. This was refused, but the approach of the squadron compelled the British commanding officer to destroy the fishing-stages. Finding this to be the case, M. Allemand stood away from the coast, and, as M. Richery had done, steered homewards. On the 5th of November, the latter, with his division, entered the port of Rochefort: and on the 15th M. Allemand, with his, was equally fortunate, in reaching Lorient. The two divisions, between them, had destroyed upwards of 100 merchant vessels, and made a great many prisoners; part of whom were sent in a cartel to Halifax, and the remainder about 300 in number, were carried into France.

On the 15th of April Captain John Parr of the 54-gun ship Malabar, having under his orders a few frigates and transports with a detachment of troops amounting to 1200 men, commanded by Major-general John Whyte, was detached by Admiral Sir John Laforey, who, since June of the preceding year, had been reappointed the commander-in-chief on the Leeward-island station in the room of Vice-admiral Caldwell, to take possession of the Dutch settlements of Demerara, Essequibo, and Berbice, in Dutch Guayana, on the continent of South America. On the 22nd of April the first two, and on the 2nd of May, the last of those settlements surrendered peaceably to the British arms. A

Dutch 24-gun ship, the Thetis, and a 12-gun cutter, along with several richly-laden merchant vessels, were captured at Demerara.

On the 21st of April the long-delayed expedition under Rear-admiral Sir Hugh Cloberry Christian, consisting of two sail of the line and five smaller vessels of war, having in charge a numerous fleet of transports, arrived in Carlisle bay, Barbadoes. After the squadron and convoy had sailed on the 9th of December, the greater part of the ships were again, in the course of January, driven back by tempestuous weather, and did not finally quit Spithead until the 20th of March. The recapture of Sainte Lucie was the first object to be attended to. Accordingly, on the following day, the 22nd, Sir John Laforey proceeded, with the squadron (now greatly augmented) and transports, to Marin bay, Martinique; where, on the 23rd, the whole expedition came to an anchor. On the 24th the admiral resigned the command to Rear-admiral Christian, and sailed for England in the 74-gun ship Majestic.

On the 26th, in the evening, Rear-admiral Christian, with the squadron and transports, on board of which was a large body of troops, under the command of Lieutenant-general Sir Ralph Abercromby, quitted the bay and stood across to Saint Lucie; off which, by the morning of the 27th, the whole had arrived. The three intended points of debarkation were, Anse-du-Cap and Anse-Béquêne in Longueville bay, Choc bay and Anse-la-Raye, some distance south of the Cul-de-Sac. The first point in Longueville bay, Anse-du-Cap, was protected by a 5-gun battery on Pigeon island. To keep this battery in check the 38-gun frigate Hebe, Captain Matthew Henry Scott, led into the anse, or creek. The 74-gun ship Ganges, Captain Robert M'Doual, supported her; and the 18-gun brig-sloop Pelican, Captain John Clarke Searle, anchoring in Anse-Béquêne, covered the troops in their approach. Other able dispositions were made; and the fire of the ships, dismounting one and silencing the remainder of the guns at the Pigeon island battery, enabled the first division of troops to make good its landing.

The 74-gun ship Alfred, Captain John Totty, was to have led the second division into Choc bay, and the 54-gun ship Madras, Captain John Dilkes, supported by the 40-gun frigate Beaulieu, Captain Lancelot Skynner, the third, into the anchorage at Anse-la-Raye. A strong lee current, which had set the transports considerably to leeward, rendered it necessary to defer both attempts. However, on the next morning, the 28th, the landing at Choc bay was effected without the slightest opposition; as, on the following day, the 29th, was that at Anse-la-Raye. Eight hundred seamen, under the command of Captain Richard Lane of the 32-gun frigate Astræa, and George Frederick Ryves, of the bomb-vessel Bull-dog, were then landed, to co-operate with the troops in the intended attack upon Morne-Fortunée.

Morne-Chabot, the first post attacked, was, on the night of the 28th, carried by one division only of the force that had marched against it, with the loss of 13 officers and privates killed, 49 wounded, and nine missing. The failure of an attempt, on the 3rd of May, to dislodge the republicans from their batteries on the base of the mountain, near the Grand Cul-de-Sac, occasioned a loss of 12 officers and privates killed, 56 wounded, and 34 missing. An attempt, made in the night of the 17th, to get possession of a post named the Vigie, although conducted with the utmost bravery, and partially successful, failed also in the main object, and was attended with the loss of one lieutenant killed, 114 officers and privates wounded, and 65 missing. After a few attacks of outposts, the enemy, annoyed by the guns brought by the ships and planted by the seamen, retired to the fortress of Morne-Fortunée. At length, on the evening of the 24th, the enemy desired a suspension of arms until noon the next day. It was granted until eight in the morning, when the whole island surrendered by capitulation. On the 26th the garrison, to the number of 2000 men, marched out and laid down their arms. A great quantity of ordnance, besides stores of every description, was found in the different forts; and one or two small privateers and some merchant vessels were taken in the carénage. The total loss sustained by the British army, in the reduction of this valuable island, amounted to 56 officers and privates killed, 378 wounded, and 122 missing.

Exclusive of 800 seamen, 320 marines had been landed from the ships of war; and both departments exerted themselves with their usual promptitude and gallantry. In establishing batteries, especially on commanding eminences deemed almost inaccessible, the ready resources of the sailors astonished their land-associates, and mainly contributed to the successful result of the expedition. An acknowledgment to this effect, made in the handsomest terms by Lieutenant-general Sir Ralph Abercromby, was communicated to the navy through the channel of a general order issued for the purpose; and in which, besides Captains Lane and Ryves, Captain James Stevenson, of the Charon armed store-ship, is named.

The islands of St. Vincent and Grenada were the next to be subdued. On the 8th of June, in the evening, the troops destined for the attack of the former island were safely disembarked, under cover of the 38-gun frigate Arethusa, Captain Thomas Wolley; who also sent a detachment of seamen to serve on shore with the troops. After some skirmishing and an obstinate resistance, the enemy, composed chiefly of people of colour and Charibs, capitulated on the terms proposed by General Abercromby; who, on the 11th, took possession of the island. The loss sustained by the British on the occasion amounted to 38 officers and privates killed, and 145 wounded.

In a few days afterwards Grenada followed the example of St. Vincent; but the monster Fedon, after having, in the very face of the British troops, butchered several Europeans (twenty white people of Morne-Quaquo were laid out, stripped, pinioned, and murdered, all in full view of the British on the plain below), had withdrawn with his banditti into the wood. Here, being closely pursued by a detachment of German riflemen, many of the villains paid the forfeit of their crimes. The loss of the British, in the several attacks that led to the reduction of this island, amounted to nine privates killed, and 60 officers and privates wounded. The 32-gun frigate Mermaid, Captain Robert Waller Otway, while co-operating with the Hebe frigate, and Pelican and Beaver sloops, in covering the landing of the troops, unfortunately had a main-deck gun burst, whereby seven of her seamen were killed and five badly wounded.

On the 17th and 18th of March a detachment of British and colonial troops from the garrison of Port-au-Prince in the island of St. Domingo, under the command of Major-general Forbes, was embarked to proceed against the town and fort of Léogane, in the same island. On the 21st the troops landed, in two divisions, the western division covered by the 32-gun frigate Ceres and sloop Lark, Captains James Newman Newman and William Ogilvy; and the eastern, by the 32-gun frigate Iphigenia, Captain Francis F. Gardner, and sloops Cormorant and Sirène, Captain Francis Collingwood and Daniel Guerin; with the Leviathan 74, Captain John Thomas Duckworth, and Africa 64, Captain Roddam Home, to cannonade the fort, and the Swiftsure 74, Captain Richard Parker, the town.

In the course of half an hour the fire of the Swiftsure was interrupted by the march of the troops, but the Leviathan and Africa continued to play upon the fort for nearly four hours; when, it growing dark, the ships took advantage of the land-wind, and moved off to an anchorage. The town and fort being much stronger, and the enemy more numerous, than had been expected, the troops were withdrawn in the course of the following day and night, with the loss of a few men. The ships, however, were the principal sufferers on this occasion. The Leviathan had five men killed, and 12 (two of them mortally) wounded; and the Africa, one killed and seven wounded. Both ships, too, had been so seriously damaged in their masts and yards, that they were compelled to proceed to Jamaica to refit.

A more successful attack was afterwards made upon the fort and parish of Bombarde. The fort was at a distance of 15 miles; and the only road by which cannon could be transported had been blocked up by felled trees, and even, in some places, by stone walls built across it. Besides these impediments, the weather was excessively hot, and not a drop of water could be procured. Finally, however, the troops reached and surrounded the fort; when the garrison, consisting of 300 whites, and who had in vain attempted to check the advance of the troops, surrendered on capitulation. The possession of the place cost the British eight officers and privates killed, 18 wounded, and four missing.

On or about the 12th of May a French squadron arrived at Cape-François, having on board about 1200 troops, 20,000 muskets, 400,000 lbs. weight of powder, and 12 field-pieces, besides the agents from the directory, Santhonax, Giraud, Raymond and Leblanc, General Rochambeau, and several military and civil officers. This squadron had quitted France in two divisions; one, commanded by Commodore Henri-Alexandre Thévenard, and consisting of the 74-gun ships Fougueux and Wattigny, 40-gun frigate Vengeance, and, we believe, 20-gun ship-corvette Berceau sailed from Rochefort; the other, consisting of the 40-gun frigate Méduse, 36-gun frigate Insurgente, 20-gun ship-corvette Doucereuse, and eight transports, under Captain Guillaume Thomas, had escaped from Brest. The most extraordinary circumstance is that, in spite of the numerous British cruisers afloat, all these ships got safe back to France.

East Indies.

On the 5th of February an expedition, composed of the British 12-pounder 32-gun frigate Heroine, Captain Alan Hyde Gardner, 16-gun ship-sloops Rattlesnake, Echo, and Swift, Captains Edward Ramage, Andrew Todd, and James Sprat

Rainier, and five armed ships belonging to the East India Company, with a body of troops on board, under the command of Colonel Stuart, from the Cape of Good Hope, anchored off Negombo, a settlement and roadsted distant about 18 miles from the object of the expedition, the important fortress of Columbo in the island of Ceylon. The fort at Negombo, having been abandoned by the enemy, was immediately taken possession of; and, in the course of the 6th, the whole of the troops were safely disembarked.

While the troops proceeded over land to Columbo, meeting on their march with little opposition, the Heroine and squadron had stationed themselves close to the fortress, to be ready to land the artillery. On the 14th, everything being prepared for commencing the attack, the garrison was summoned to surrender, and, on the next day, the 15th, agreed to the terms of capitulation proposed. Thus was this valuable and highly important settlement and its dependencies, with a very trifling loss, transferred to the possession of Great Britain. The pepper, cinnamon, and other merchandise, independent of the ships and the military and naval stores, were valued at 25 lacks of rupees, or about 300,000*l.* sterling.

On the 16th of February an expedition under Rear-admiral Peter Rainier, composed of the 74-gun ship Suffolk, Captain Robert Lambert, 50-gun ship Centurion, Captain Samuel Osborne, 44-gun ship Resistance, Captain Edward Pakenham, 32-gun frigate Orpheus, Captain Henry Newcome, and 16-gun ship-sloop Swift, Captain James Sprat Rainier, with one or two armed ships belonging to the East India Company, and three transports containing a body of troops, arrived off the Dutch island of Amboyna, the capital of the Molucca islands, and the principal settlement of the Dutch in this quarter. On the same afternoon the troops were landed and possession taken, without resistance, of this important island and its dependencies. In the treasury were found 81,112 rix-dollars, and in the warehouses 515,940 lbs. weight of cloves.

On the 5th of March, the rear-admiral and squadron got under way, and made sail for the Banda or Nutmeg islands. On the 7th, in the evening, the expedition arrived off Great-Banda, or Banda-Neira, and on the 8th, early in the afternoon, the troops, along with a detachment of marines from the squadron, were disembarked on the north side of the island, under cover of the Orpheus frigate, and Harling armed East India ship; between which ships and two batteries of two guns each, some firing was interchanged. The batteries, however, were soon silenced, and the troops took possession of them. All further hostility ceased; and on the same evening the settlement of Fort Nassau on Banda-Neira, with that and all the other islands, its dependencies surrendered to the British arms, upon nearly the same terms as had been granted at Amboyna. In the treasury at Banda-Neira were found 66,675 rix-dollars, and in the warehouses 84,777 lbs. of nutmegs, 19,587 lbs. of mace, exclusive of a great quantity of valuable merchandise and other stores.

In a military point of view, captures effected like those of Amboyna and Banda, can excite very little interest; and their principal political importance is of a negative character, resting on the loss of property sustained by the despoiled enemy. We must, however, except the enrichment of the captors. That is a positive, although an individual advantage; and we believe that the five captains of the navy, present at the surrender of Amboyna and Banda, received each about 15,000*l.* sterling. Aware, from our researches, that Captain Benjamin William Page, of the 18-gun ship-sloop Hobart, owing to his local experience, had been employed by Rear-admiral Rainier to lead the squadron through the straits of Malacca, Sincapore, and Banca, we had hoped that an officer who had been so instrumental to the success of the expedition would also have been one of the fortunate sharers of the prize-money that flowed from it. We find, however, that on the capture, towards the end of January, of the Dutch brig of war Haerlem, with important despatches, the Hobart was sent back by Rear-admiral Rainier with those despatches to Madras and Bengal, and that Captain Page, being necessarily absent at the time of surrender, was not allowed by his brother-captains to participate in the fruits of the conquest.

Misled as to the amount of the British naval force at the Cape of Good Hope, or, more probably, cajoled by the proffers of co-operation made by their allies the French, the Dutch had actually sent the small squadron which we formerly noticed as having pursued the Glatton and other ships in February, to regain possession of that important settlement; and which squadron consisted of the

Gun-ship.			
66	Dordrecht	Rear-adm.	Engelburtus Lucas.
		Captain	————
	Revolutie	,,	Rhubende.
54	Van Tromp.	,,	Valkenburg.

Gun-frigate.

40	Casthor	Captain	Clariffe.
	Braave.	,,	Zoetmans.
26	Sirène.	,,	De Cerf.
24	Bellona	,,	Valk.

Gun-sloop.

18	Havik	,,	Bezemer.

On the 3rd of August intelligence was received at Cape Town, of the appearance of nine sail of Dutch ships, which was the squadron in question, off Saldanha bay. At this time Vice-admiral Sir George Keith Elphinstone was lying in Simon's bay, with the

Gun-ship.

74	Monarch	Vice-adm. (b.) Sir Geo. Keith Elphinstone. Captain John Elphinstone.
	Tremendous	Rear-adm. (r.) Thomas Pringle. Captain John Aylmer.
64	America	,, John Blankett.
	Ruby	,, Henry Edwin Stanhope.
	Stately	,, Billy Douglas.
	Sceptre	,, William Essington.
	Trident	,, Edward Oliver Osborn.
50	Jupiter	,, George Losack.

Frigates, Crescent and (20-gun ship) Sphynx.
Sloops, Moselle, Rattlesnake, Echo, and Hope.

Owing to the Monarch's being without her mainmast, and to the tempestuous state of the weather during the 3rd, 4th, 5th, it was not until the 6th of August, that the British squadron was enabled to put to sea. Information now arriving that several sail had, the preceding night, been seen in the offing near False bay, the vice-admiral steered to the southward and westward. The storm soon afterwards increased in violence, so as to damage several of the ships, and compel the squadron, on the 12th, to re-enter Simon's bay. Here the vice-admiral learnt that nine sail of ships had, since the 6th, put into Saldanha bay. The British squadron remained weather-bound until the 15th, when it put to sea, and on the following evening at sunset, arrived off Simon's bay. The Crescent frigate then stood in, and plainly descried the Dutch squadron, consisting of two 66-gun ships, one 54-gun ship, five frigates and sloops, and one store-ship, as already named, lying at anchor. The British ships, formed in line, soon afterwards anchored within gun-shot of the Dutch; to whose commanding officer, Sir George immediately sent a message, inviting him to surrender without attempting any resistance, which, in the great disparity between the forces, could not be otherwise than unavailing. On the 17th a capitulation was agreed to, and Rear-admiral Lucas surrendered his nine ships to the British admiral. The highest complement among the Dutch ships was that of the Revolutie, 400 men. The Van-Tromp had but 280 men; the Havik sloop only 76; and the whole of the "seamen and troops" on board the nine Dutch ships amounted to no more than 1972. The aggregate number of men in the British squadron, according to Sir George's letter, was, without reckoning the crew of the Hope brig, 4291. No imputation, therefore, could attach to Admiral Lucas or his officers, for having refrained from engaging a British force more than treble their own. In the month of October, Vice-admiral Sir George K. Elphinstone, in the Monarch, sailed for England, leaving the command of the fleet to Rear-admiral Pringle.

On the 2nd of December, Captain John William Spranger, in the 36-gun frigate Crescent, accompanied by the Braave, late Dutch frigate, of the same force, and Sphynx 20-gun ship, took possession of and destroyed the French settlement on Foul Point in the island of Madagascar; bringing away with him five merchant vessels that were lying in the road.

APPENDIX.

No. 1.—AN ABSTRACT OF THE

At the commencement of the year 1677, with the exact force, in Guns and Men

| | | | \multicolumn{8}{c}{"WAR AT HOME," OR MAXIMUM} |
| No. | Rate. | Class. | First or Main Deck. | | Second Deck. | | Third Deck. | | Quarter-Deck. | |
			No.	Nature.	No.	Nature.	No.	Nature.	No.	Nature.
1	First	Gun-ship 100	26	Canon VII.	28	24-pounders	28	Demi-culv.	10	Lt. sakers.
2	,,	,,	,,	,,	,,	Whole cul.	,,	,,	,,	,,
3	,,	,,	,,	,,	,,	,,	,,	Sakers.	12	,,
4	,,	96	,,	,,	,,	,,	26	Demi-culv.	10	,,
5	,,	,,	,,	,,	,,	,,	,,	,,	,,	,,
6	,,	90	,,	Demi-cann.	26	,,	,,	,,	,,	,,
7	Second	,,	,,	,,	,,	,,	,,	Sakers.	,,	,,
8	,,	84	,,	,,	,,	,,	24	,,	6	,,
9	,,	82	24	,,	,,	,,	,,	,,	,,	,,
10	,,	80	,,	,,	24	,,	,,	,,	,,	,,
11	,,	70	22	,,	22	,,	20	,,	6	,,
12	,,	64	,,	,,	,,	Demi-culv.	14	,,	,,	,,
13	Third	74	28	,,	28	Whole cul.	—	— —	12	,,
14	,,	72	26	,,	26	,,	—	— —	,,	,,
15	,,	70	,,	,,	,,	12-pounders	—	— —	,,	,,
16	,,	,,	24	,,	24	,,	—	— —	14	,,
17	,,	,,	26	,,	26	,,	—	— —	10	,,
18	,,	66	,,	24-pounders	24	,,	—	— —	,,	,,
19	,,	64	24	,,	26	,,	—	— —	,,	,,
20	,,	,,	,,	Demi-cann.	24	,,	—	— —	,,	,,
21	,,	62	,,	24-pounders	,,	,,	—	— —	,,	,,
22	,,	60	,,	,,	,,	,,	—	— —	8	,,
23	Fourth	54	,,	,,	22	Sakers.	—	— —	,,	,,
24	,,	,,	22	,,	,,	,,	—	— —	10	,,
25	,,	50	,,	Whole cul.	,,	,,	—	— —	6	,,
26	,,	48	,,	,,	20	,,	—	— —	,,	,,
27	,,	46	,,	,,	,,	,,	—	— —	4	,,
28	,,	,,	,,	,,	,,	,,	—	— —	,,	,,
29	,,	44	,,	Demi-culv.	18	Demi-culv.	—	— —	,,	,,
30	,,	42	20	,,	,,	,,	—	— —	,,	,,
31	,,	32	6	,,	22	,,	—	— —	,,	3 pounders
32	,,	30	4	,,	,,	,,	—	— —	,,	,,
33	Fifth	32	18	,,	10	Sakers.	—	— —	,,	Minions.
34	,,	,,	,,	,,	,,	,,	—	— —	,,	,,
35	,,	30	,,	,,	8	,,	—	— —	,,	,,
36	,,	28	16	,,	—	—	—	— —	,,	,,
37	Sixth	18	16	Sakers.	—	— —	—	— —	2	,,
38	,,	16	16	,,	—	— —	—	— —	—	— —
39	,,	10	10	,,	—	— —	—	— —	—	— —
40	,,	4	4	,,	—	— —	—	— —	—	— —
41	Sloops	,,	,,	3-pounders.	—	— —	—	— —	—	— —

ITISH ROYAL NAVY—See p. 7,

every class of Ship; also the gross weight of the Guns, the Tonnage, &c.

TABLISHMENT OF GUNS.							Ships in each Class.	Highest and Lowest Tonnages.	When first and last Built.	RATE.	No.
Forecastle.		Poop.		No.	Gross Weight.	Com-ple-ment.					
o.	Nature.	No.	Nature.								
					Tons.	No.	No.	Tons.	Years.		
4	L. sakers.	4	3-pdrs.	100	177	815	1	1543	1637	First	1
,,	,,	,,	,,	,,	173	780	3	1400–1441	1670–75	,,	2
,,	,,	2	,,	,,	187¾	,,	1	1703	Building.	,,	3
2	,,	4	,,	96	157	710	1	1227	1668	,,	4
,,	,,	,,	,,	,,	166	730	2	1313–1328	1670	,,	5
—	— —	2	,,	90	138½	600	1	1107	1669	,,	6
—	— —	,,	,,	,,	159½	660	9	1376–1462	Building.	Second	7
—	— —	—	— —	84	131½	540	1	1664	1050	,,	8
—	— —	—	— —	82	129	530	2	1020–1029	1656–65	,,	9
—	— —	—	— —	80	120	520	1	968	1666	,,	10
—	— —	—	— —	70	112½	460	2	898–900	1622–23	,,	11
—	— —	—	— —	64	104	460	2	817–845	1617–33	,,	12
4	L. sakers.	2	3-pdrs.	74	128	470	1	1107	1674	Third	13
,,	,,	4	,,	72	116½	445	1	998	1668	,,	14
,,	,,	2	,,	70	104	420	3	885–941	1666–67	,,	15
,,	,,	4	,,	,,	112	,,	2	978–987	1673–74	,,	16
,,	,,	,,	,,	,,	— —	460	20	1055–1116	Building.	,,	17
,,	,,	2	,,	66	96	400	2	813–880	1665–66	,,	18
2	,,	,,	,,	64	92	365	1	795	1649	,,	19
4	,,	,,	,,	,,	103½	,,	1	902	1674	,,	20
2	,,	,,	,,	62	88	355	4	735–809	1654	,,	21
,,	,,	,,	,,	60	83	340	6	697–760	1640–54	,,	22
—	— —	—	— —	54	77	280	8	620–677	1653–69	Fourth	23
—	— —	—	— —	,,	82	,,	1	716	1674	,,	24
—	— —	—	— —	50	67½	240	1	588	1649	,,	25
—	— —	—	— —	48	62	230	16	510–576	1650–69	,,	26
—	— —	—	— —	46	53	220	3	408–479	1647–53	,,	27
—	— —	—	— —	,,	56½	,,	1	664	1675	,,	28
—	— —	—	— —	44	50	190	2	432–457	1646–47	,,	29
—	— —	—	— —	42	42	180	6	345–376	1646–68	,,	30
—	— —	—	— —	32	30	220	1	526	1676	,,	31
—	— —	—	— —	30	25	200	1	433	1676	,,	32
—	— —	—	— —	32	— —	135	4	265–305	1651–69	Fifth	33
—	— —	—	— —	,,	— —	,,	2	305–346	1673–75	,,	34
—	— —	—	— —	30	— —	130	4	255–265	1651–69	,,	35
—	— —	—	— —	28	— —	125	2	223–234	1655–74	,,	36
—	— —	—	— —	18	— —	85	1	199	1675	Sixth	37
—	— —	—	— —	16	— —	75	5	144–180	1653–72	,,	38
—	— —	—	— —	10	— —	50	3	79–80	1666–73	,,	39
—	— —	—	— —	4	— —	30	1	33		,,	40
—	— —	—	— —	,,	— —	10	3			Sloops	41

No. 2.—See p. 9.

The following List of the ancient Sea-service Ordnance, as used in England, is taken from Sir William Monson's "*Naval Tracts*," for which see *Archæologia*, vol. vi., p. 192.

NAMES.	Bore of Cannon.	Weight of Cannon.	Weight of Shot.	Weight of Powder.
	Inches.	lbs.	lbs.	lbs.
Cannon-royal . . .	8½	8000	66	30
Cannon	8	6000	60	27
Cannon-serpentine .	7	5500	53½	25
Bastard-cannon . .	7	4500	41	20
Demi-cannon . . .	6¾	4000	33½	18
Canon-petro . . .	6	4000	24½	14
Culverin	5½	4500	17½	12
Basilisk	5	4000	15	10
Demi-culverin . . .	4	3400	9½	8
Bastard-culverin . .	4	3000	5	5¾
Sacar	3½	1400	5½	5½
Minion	3½	1000	4	4
Falcon	2½	660	2	3½
Falconet	2	500	1½	3
Serpentine	1½	400	¾	1¾
Rabinet	1	300	½	½

[NOTE.—This List of Sir Wm. Monson's is so incorrect as to be almost beneath criticism. He represents two balls of the *same* size as weighing 12 lbs. different, and two others as 4½ lbs. different! Perhaps, cannon serpentine was 7½-inch bore instead of 7, and demi-culverin 4½ instead of 4.—H. Y. POWELL.]

APPENDIX.

No. 3.—See p. 40.

The following is a List of such of the Ships, down to 20-gun Ships inclusive, so ordered to mount Carronades, as were in existence on the 1st of January, 1793.

Gun-ship.		Third and Second Deck.	Quarter-Deck.	Forecastle.	Poop.	Total of Long Guns and Carronades.
100	Victory	— —	2 32-pdrs.	2 32-pdrs.	6 18-pdrs.	110
90 {	Duke	— —	,,	— —	— —	92
	Prince George	2 32-pdrs.	4 18-pdrs.	— —	— —	96
80	Gibraltar	— —	— —	— —	6 12-pdrs.	86
74 {	Alcide	— —	— —	2 12-pdrs.	6 ,,	82
	Alfred	— —	— —	— —	4 ,,	78
	Bellona	— —	— —	— —	6 ,,	80
	Edgar	— —	— —	2 12-pdrs.	6 ,,	82
	Fortitude	— —	— —	— —	6 ,,	80
	Monarch	— —	— —	— —	4 ,,	78
	Ramillies	— —	— —	2 18-pdrs.	6 ,,	82
64 {	Magnanime	— —	— —	— —	6 ,,	} 70
	St. Alban's	— —	— —	— —	6 ,,	
50 {	Adamant	— —	2 18-pdrs.	2 18-pdrs.	8 ,,	62
	Isis	— —	— —	— —	6 ,,	56
	Jupiter	— —	2 18-pdrs.	— —	— —	52
	Leander	— —	2 24-pdrs.	— —	6 12-pdrs.	58
44 {	Assurance	— —	6 18-pdrs.	2 18 pdrs.	— —	52
	Ulysses	— —	8 12-pdrs.	2 ,,	— —	54
38	Minerva	— —	4 18-pdrs.	— —	— —	42
36	Flora	— —	4 ,,	— —	— —	40
32 {	Active	— —	4 ,,	2 18-pdrs.	— —	
	Alarm	— —	6 ,,	— —	— —	} 38
	Ambuscade	— —	4 ,,	2 18-pdrs.	— —	
	Boston	— —	4 ,,	2 ,,	— —	
	Fox	— —	6 ,,	2 ,,	— —	40
	Juno	— —	4 ,,	— —	— —	} 36
	Orpheus	— —	4 ,,	— —	— —	
	Pearl	— —	6 ,,	— —	— —	38
28 {	Aurora	— —	4 ,,	2 18-pdrs.	— —	
	Carysfort	— —	4 ,,	2 ,,	— —	} 34
	Hussar	— —	4 ,,	2 ,,	— —	
	Mercury	— —	4 ,,	— —	— —	} 32
	Vestal	— —	4 ,,	— —	— —	
24 {	Amphitrite	— —	4 12-pdrs.	2 12-pdrs.	— —	30
	Champion	— —	6 ,,	2 ,,	— —	
	Hyæna	— —	8 ,,	2 ,,	— —	34
20 {	Ariadne	— —	6 ,,	2 ,,	— —	
	Daphne	— —	6 ,,	2 ,,	— —	} 28
	Perseus	— —	6 ,,	2 ,,	— —	

No. 4.—See p. 50.

State of the French Navy, October 1st, 1792, both Afloat and on the Stocks.

	Ships of the Line.					Frigates.				Corvettes and Avisos.	Gun-vessels.	Flûtes and Armed Store-ships.
	gs. 120	gs. 110	gs. 80	gs. 74	gs. 64	gs. 40	gs. 38	gs. 36	gs. 32			
Squadron of Brest	1	5	7	26	—	10	—	24	—	23	7	16
,, Lorient	—	—	—	10	—	1	—	5	—	—	—	—
,, Rochefort	—	—	—	12	1	2	—	14	—	11	—	10
,, Toulon	2	—	3	19	—	5	2	13	2	13	—	2
	3	5	10	67	1	18	2	56	2	47	7	28

86   78

Total . . . . 246 vessels.

	gs. 120	gs. 110	gs. 80	gs. 74	gs. 64	gs. 40	gs. 38	gs. 36	gs. 32			
In ordinary at the different ports	1	3	3	38	1	10	2	32	2	25	7	18
On the stocks to be launched in { 1791	—	—	1	5	—	1	—	1	—	—	—	2
{ 1792	—	—	1	3	—	2	—	4	—	—	—	—
In the Antilles	—	—	—	3	—	—	—	6	—	9	—	—
Asiatic Sea	—	—	—	—	—	3	—	2	—	—	—	1
Levant	—	—	—	—	—	1	—	—	—	6	—	—
Coasts of France and Corsica	—	—	—	—	—	—	—	1	—	2	—	6
Seeking M. de la Peyrouse	—	—	—	—	—	—	—	2	—	—	—	—
In port { about to put to sea	—	—	—	—	—	—	—	4	—	5	—	1
{ in commission	2	2	5	18	—	1	—	4	—	—	—	—
	3	5	10	67	1	18	2	56	2	47	7	28

Total . . . . 246 vessels.

No. 5.—See p. 53.

The following were the Sea-service Supplies for the year 1793:—

	£.	s.	d.
For the pay and maintenance of 20,000 seamen and 5000 marines	1,300,000	0	0
,, 16,000 seamen and 4000 marines, in addition	1,040,000	0	0
,, the ordinary expenses of the navy, including half-pay to sea and marine officers	669,205	5	10
,, the extraordinaries, including the building and repairing of ships, and other extra work	387,710	0	0
,, ordnance not provided for in 1791	32,068	15	4
Towards paying off the navy debt	575,000	0	0
Total supplies granted for the sea-service	£4,003,984	1	2

APPENDIX. 425

No. 6.—See p. 56.

A List of the Line-of-battle Ships and Frigates belonging to France at or about the commencement of the year 1793, drawn up with as much accuracy as the confusion thrown into the French Accounts by the practice of changing the Names of Ships will admit.

LINE-OF-BATTLE SHIPS.

Port belonging to.	Gun-ship.		New Names, &c.	State.
BREST.	110	Royal Louis	Républicain	
	80	Languedoc	Anti-fédéraliste, Victoire	
	74	Entreprenant		
	,,	Eole		
	,,	Jupiter	Batave, Jupiter	
	,,	Léopard		Ready for sea.
	,,	Patriote		
	,,	Phocion	Ferme	
	,,	Thémistocle		
	,,	Tourville		
	,,	Trajan	Gaulois	
	,,	Vengeur		
	120	Etats-de-Bourgogne	Cote-d'Or, Montagne, Peuple, Océan	
	110	Majestueux		
	80	Indomptable*		
	,,	Juste		Fitting for sea.
	,,	Résolution	doubtful	
	74	Borée	Agricole, *rasé*, as supposed	
	,,	Duguay-Trouin		
	80	Sans-Pareil*		
	74	Achille		
	,,	America*		
	,,	Audacieux*		
	,,	Brave		
	,,	Jean-Bart*		In good condition.
	,,	Fougueux*		
	,,	Suffren*	Redoubtable	
	,,	Superbe		
	,,	Téméraire		
	,,	Tigre*		
	,,	Zélé	made a *rasé*, as supposed	
	110	Bretagne	Révolutionnaire	
	,,	Invincible		
	,,	Terrible		
	80	Auguste	Jacobin, Neuf-Thermidor	
	,,	St.-Esprit	Scipion	
	74	Argonaute	made a *rasé*, as supposed	
	,,	Diadême	Brutus, *rasé*	In want of repair.
	,,	Hercule	made a *rasé*, as supposed	
	,,	Illustre	ditto	

No. 6—*continued.*

LINE-OF-BATTLE SHIPS.

Port belonging to.	Gun-ship.		New Names, &c.	State.
BREST.—*cont.*	74	Magnanime		In want of repair.—*cont.*
	,,	Neptune		
	,,	Northumberland		
	,,	Pluton		
	,,	Sceptre	Convention	
	,,	Victoire	made a *rasé*, as supposed	
	,,	Citoyen		Unserviceable.
ROCHEFORT.	,,	Généreux		
	,,	Apollon	Gasparin	Ready for sea.
	,,	Orion	Trente-un-Mai	
	,,	Séduisant		Fitting for sea.
	,,	Aquilon*		
	,,	Jemmappes		
	,,	Impétueux*		
	,,	Lion	doubtful. Perhaps Formidable.[a]	In good condition.
	,,	Mont Blanc*		
	,,	Révolution*		
	,,	Sphynx	doubtful.	
	,,	Marseillois		Unserviceable.
TOULON.	120	Dauphin-Royal	Sans-Culotte, Orient	
	80	Tonnant		
	74	Centaure		
	,,	Commerce-de-Bordeaux	Timoléon	Ready for sea.
	,,	Lys	Tricolor	
	,,	Scipion		
	80	Triomphant		
	74	Destin		
	,,	Dictateur	Liberté	
	,,	Duquesne		Fitting for sea.
	,,	Héros		
	,,	Heureux		
	,,	Pompée		
	120	Commerce-de-Marseille		In good condition.
	80	Couronne	Ca-Ira	
	74	Censeur		
	,,	Mercure		
	,,	Alcide		
	,,	Conquérant		In want of repair.
	,,	Guerrier		
	,,	Puissant		
	,,	Souverain	Souverain-Peuple	
	,,	Suffisant		

APPENDIX.

No. 6—*continued*.

FRIGATES.

Gun-frig.		Gun-frig.		Gun-frig.	
44	Pomone,*	40	Thétis,		Calypso,
			Sibylle,		Capricieuse,
	Aréthuse,		Uranie,		Cléopâtre,
	Carmagnole,*	38	Impérieuse,		Confiante,
	Concorde,*		Minerve,		Courageuse,
	Cybèle,		Aigle,	36	Danaë,
	Driade,		Alceste,		Embuscade,
40	Junon,		Althée,		Engageante,
	Méduse,	36	Andromaque,		Fée,
	Melpomène,		Aurore,		Félicité,*
	Nymphe,		Bellone,		Fidelle,
	Perle,		Boudeuse,		Fine,
	Proserpine,		Prudente,		Iris,
	Fortunée,		Railleuse,	32	Montréal,
	Friponne,		Résolue		Richmond,
	Galathée,*		Réunion,		Badine,
	Gloire,		Sémillante,*		Baïonnaise,
	Gracieuse,		Sensible,		Belette,
	Hélène,	36	Sérieuse,		Bienvenue,
	Hermione,		Sultane,		Blonde,
36	Inconstante,		Surveillante,	28	Brune,
	Insurgente,*		Topaze,		Calliope
	Iphigénie,		Tribune,*		Fauvette,
	Lutine,		Unité,		Mignonne,
	Médée,		Vestale,		Républicaine,
	Modeste,		Victorieuse,		Tourterelle.
	Précieuse,				
	Preneuse,				

The ships marked with an asterisk were all new; but none, it is believed, were upon the stocks on the 1st of January, except the Jemmappes launched on the 22nd of the month, the Sans-Pareil in June, and the Lion (or rather Formidable, as it is believed she was then named) and Mont-Blanc in the course of the summer. There were also, doubtless, four or five more 74s on the stocks, but not sufficiently advanced to be named; although four were afterwards, as we conjecture, named Wattigny, Droits-de-l'Homme, Cassard, and Marat. Among the new frigates, the Carmagnole was launched on the 21st of May, and all the remainder within a week or two of that period.

No. 6—*continued.*

An Abstract of the French Navy as it stood at the commencement of the year 1793, down to 28-gun Frigates, or "Corvettes," inclusive.

Class.	Ready for Sea.	Fitting for Sea.	In good Condition.	In want of Repair.	Unserviceable.	Total.	Port Belonging to Brest.	Rochefort.	Toulon.
120-gun ships	1	1	1	—	—	3	1	—	2
110 ,,	1	1	—	3	—	5	5	—	—
80 ,,	2	4	2	2	—	10	7	—	3
74 ,,	17	9	20	16	2	64	34	12	18
Line	21	15	23	21	2	82	47	12	23
44-gun frigates	—	—	—	—	—	1			
40 ,,	—	—	—	—	—	14			
38 ,,	—	—	—	—	—	2			
36 ,,	—	—	—	—	—	48			
32 ,,	—	—	—	—	—	3			
28 ,,	—	—	—	—	—	11			
Frigates	—	—	—	—	—	79			
Total	—	—	—	—	—	161			

No. 7.—See p. 102.

Copie d'une Lettre du Citoyen Vincent, Ordonnateur de la Marine au port de Bordeaux, au Ministre de la Marine, en date du 6 Juin. Mon. 12 Juillet 1793.

Je vous rends compte de la rentrée dans notre rivière, depuis hier, du corsaire la Citoyenne-Française, de Bordeaux, capitaine Dubedat, de 26 canons de huit et de douze en batterie, et de six sur les gaillards, après un glorieux combat, qu'il a soutenu de 13 du mois dernier, depuis 6 heures jusqu'à 8 heures et demie du soir, contre une frégate anglaise, de 40 canons, par la latitude de 42 degrés 24 m. nord, et 15 degrés de longitude de Paris.

Le capitaine Dubedat a été tué dans le combat par un boulet qui lui a donné dans la poitrine; le citoyen Rigal, son second, a pris le commandement; mais l'Anglais ayant fait vent arrière, étant désemparé de son beaupré et de son mât de misaine, la Citoyenne-Française le poursuivait; mais obligée de réparer sa manœuvre toute hachée, et de jumeller ses bas mâts qu'elle s'apperçut être prêts à tomber, elle a perdu l'ennemi de vue dans la nuit, sans le retrover le lendemain, n'ayant pu forcer de voile pour le conserver. Elle a eu 16 hommes de tués et 37 blessés: elle avait fait une prise peu de jours après sa sortie. On ne sait pas qu'elle soit arrivée dans nos ports: elle doit envoyer à terre seize prisonniers anglais que je ferai mettre au château du Ha.

Le capitaine Rigal rapporte que l'Anglais avait des troupes à bord en grande quantité. Cette forte mousqueterie leur a tué et blessé beaucoup de monde: ayant le vent sur l'ennemi qu'il a conservé, malgre ses tentatives pour le lui gagner, il s'est battu bord à bord. Il fait le plus grand éloge de la fermeté et de la bravoure de son équipage, et si sa manœuvre et sa mâture n'avaient pas été si délabrées, il ne doute pas que, dans l'état de détresse où était l'Anglais, il ne l'eût enlevé à l'abordage, quoique d'une force inférieure à l'ennemi.

No. 8.—See p. 104.

Lettre du Commandant d'Armées au Ministre de la Marine, datée de Brest, le 3 Juin 1793.

J'ai l'honneur de vous rendre compte que la frégate la Sémillante, qui avait été croisée sur Finistre, est rentrée hier ici. Le citoyen Garreau, enseigne non-entretenu, qui la commande aujourd'hui, fait rapport que le 27 Mai, par la latitude nord de 46 degrés 12 minutes, et 16 degrés 13 de longitude occidentale, ils ont vu à une heure du matin, vent de E.N.E. un bâtiment sous le vent courant à bord opposé vers S.E. La Sémillante, que courait N. a viré de bord pour l'observer. L'ayant reconnu frégate anglaise de 40 canons, le lieutenant Gaillard l'attaqua à six heures, et après trois quart d'heure de feu, cet officier (Gaillard) a été tué d'un coup dans la poitrine. L'officier en second, Belleisle, pris alors le commandement, et après quelques minutes, il fut tué aussi. Garreau, ayant pris le commandement, et voyant que plusieurs coups de ses canons se perdaient inutilement, s'approcha à portée du pistolet; alors le feu devint plus vif jusqu'à neuf heures et demie, où la Sémillante tenta d'aborder l'Anglaise, qui s'y refusa en serrant au vent en ralingue; mais les boulines de la Sémillante venant d'être coupées, elle ne put serrer assez près l'ennemi dans cet instant, et n'a pu exécuté l'abordage auquel la frégate ennemie se refusa net, en faisant servir ce qu'elle avait de voiles pour courir vers l'est, et quitter le combat, bien maltraitée sans doute, trois de ses sabords ne paraissant qu'en faire une, et son gaillard d'arrière très fricassé.

La Sémillante alors songea à se réparer, et, pour y procéder hors de la portée des croiseurs qu'elle aurait pu rencontrer en force, elle courut un peu à l'ouest, d'où la situation de ses mâts l'ont obligée de revenir à Brest pour s'y réparer. Cette frégate, dont l'équipage a bravement fait son devoir, sans se rebuter de perte des deux premiers chefs, a eu 12 hommes tués et 20 blessés, sa mâture et sa haubanne endommagée.

APPENDIX.

No. 9.—See p. 134.

The ships in the following List, and in every similar one throughout the work, are classed, with the exception presently to be noticed, not as the British, but as the French class them. Without the adoption of this plan, much confusion would ensue; and, indeed, the rated force of a French ship of war seldom differs more from the mounted force (see p. 59) than in the addition of four brass 36-pounder carronades. The same description of ship which the British denominate a "28-gun frigate," the French call a "24-gun corvette;" but, for the sake of consistency, we shall designate as frigates such large and powerful "corvettes." The alphabetical letter in front of the name shows to what class in the Annual Abstracts the ship, on being transferred to the British navy, belongs. The vessels in italics had been captured from the British.

A List of Ships of the Line and Frigates, late belonging to the French Navy, Captured, Destroyed, Wrecked, Foundered, or Accidentally Burnt during the year 1793.

Gun-ship.			How, when, and where Lost.
120	(A)	Commerce-de-Marseille	Captured, August 29, by the British, at Toulon.
80		Triomphant	
74		Centaure	
		Destin	
		Duguay-Trouin	Destroyed, December 18, at the evacuation of Toulon.
		Héros	
		Liberté	
		Suffisant	
		Thémistocle	
		Tricolor	
		Léopard	Foundered, February 15, in the Bay of Cagliari.
		Name unknown	Wrecked near Ajaccio, in Corsica. Some accounts name her the Vengeur.
	(L)	Pompée	
	(M)	Puissant	
	"	Scipion	Captured with the Commerce-de-Marseille.
Gun-frigate			
40	(Z)	Aréthuse	
	(A)	Perle	
38	"	Impérieuse	Captured, October 11, by the Captain 74, near Genoa.
36	(D)	Cléopâtre	Captured, June 18, by the British frigate Nymphe off the Start.
	"	Réunion	Captured, October 20, by the British frigate Crescent off Cape Barfleur.
	"	Modeste	Captured, October 17, by the Bedford and Captain 74s, at Genoa.

432 APPENDIX.

No. 9—*continued.*

Gun-frigate   How, when, and where Lost.

36	.. Alceste (D) Topaze ,, Lutine (G) Aurore ,, Prosélyte	}	Captured with Commerce-de-Marseille. Alceste was delivered up to the Sardinians.
	,, Inconstante	{	Captured, October 29, by the British frigates Penelope and Iphigenia, off St. Domingo.
	.. Name unknown	{	Destroyed, May 21, by the Spanish fleet, under Admiral Borja, at St. Piétro.
32	.. Victorieuse .. *Montréal* .. *Iris*	}	Destroyed with Triomphant, &c.
28	.. Blonde	{	Captured, November 27, by the Brit. frigs. Latona and Phaëton, off Ushant.
	(I) Belette		Captured with Commerce-de-Marseille.

ABSTRACT.

	Lost through the Enemy.		Lost through Accident.			Total lost to the French Navy.	Total added to the British Navy.
	Capt.	Dest.	Wrecked.	Foundered.	Burnt.		
Ships of the line	4	9	1	1	..	15	4
Frigates	14	4	..	..	..	18	12
Total	18	13	1	1	..	33	16

APPENDIX.

No. 10.—See p. 134.

In the following and every similar List, the alphabetical letter refers to the vessel's class in the Annual Abstracts, and the names in italics point out which of the vessels had been captured from the enemy.

A List of Ships and Vessels, late belonging to the British Navy, Captured, Destroyed, Wrecked, Foundered, or Accidentally Burnt, during the year 1793.

Gun-ship
  74 (M) *Scipion* . Captain Degoy . { Accidentally burnt, Nov. 20, in Leghorn roads: crew saved.
Gun-frigate
  32 (*H*) Thames . „ Jas. Cotes { Captured Oct. 4, by a squadron of French frigates.
G. p. sh.
  24 (*K*) Hyæna . „ W. Hargood { Captured, May 27, by the French frigate Concorde.
Gun-brig-slp.
  14 (b) *Alerte*. (not in commission) { Captured December 18, by the French on retaking Toulon.

F.S. (e) { Conflagration, Capt. J. Loring { Destroyed, Dec. 18, by the British at Toulon, to prevent capture.
         { Vulcan   . „ Charles Hare { Destroyed, ditto, ditto, in firing the French ships.

Gun-cnt.
  14 (i) Pigmy . Lieut. A. Pullibank { Wrecked in Dec. on the Mother-bank: crew, except seven, saved.

4 (o) { Advice . „ Edward Tyrrel { Wrecked in Dec. to leeward of Key-Bokell, Honduras: crew saved.
      { *Vipère* . (name unknown) { Wrecked in Dec. in Hèires bay: crew saved.
      { *Vigilante* . (ditto) . . . Captured as *Alerte*.

ABSTRACT.

	Lost through the Enemy.		Lost through Accident.			Total.
	Capt.	Dest.	Wrecked.	Foundered.	Burnt.	
Ships of the line . .	..	..	..	..	1	1
„ under the line .	4	2	3	..	..	9
Total . .	4	2	3	..	1	10

No. 11.—See p. 135.

	£	s.	d.
For the pay and maintenance of 72,885 seamen and 12,115 marines	4,420,000	0	0
,, the ordinary expenses of the navy, including the half-pay to sea and marine officers	558,021	11	9
,, the extraordinaries; including the building and repairing of ships, and other extra works	547,310	0	0
Total supplies granted for the sea-service	£5,525,331	11	9

No. 12.—See p. 169.

The following Statement will show, with other particulars, the loss sustained by each ship (as far as it can be ascertained) on each of the three days of action. Where the loss on the first day is doubtful or unknown, it will be found included in that of the last.

Ships.	Burden in Tons.	Men and Boys.	May 28. K.	May 28. W.	May 29. K.	May 29. W.	June 1. K.	June 1. W.	Total. K.	Total. W.
Queen Charlotte	2286	891	–	–	1	–	13	29	14	29
Royal George	2286	866	–	–	15	23	5	49	20	72
Royal Sovereign	2175	866	–	–	8	22	6	22	14	44
Barfleur	1947	758	–	–	–	–	9	25	9	25
Glory	1944	743	–	–	–	–	13	39	13	39
Impregnable	1887	758	–	–	–	–	7	24	7	24
Queen	1876	758	–	–	22	27	14	40	36	67
Cæsar	2003	724	–	–	3	19	15	52	18	71
Gibraltar	2185	644	–	–	–	–	2	12	2	12
Brunswick	1836	634	–	–	–	–	44	114	44	114
Valiant	1799	634	–	–	–	–	2	9	2	9
Leviathan	1707	634	–	–	–	–	10	33	10	33
Alfred	1638	594	–	–	–	–	–	8	–	8
Audacious	1624	594	3	19	–	–	–	–	6	16
Bellerophon	1613	609	–	–	–	–	4	27	4	27
Culloden	1683	594	–	–	–	–	2	5	2	5
Defence	1603	594	–	–	1	3	17	36	18	39
Invincible	1631	594	–	–	–	–	14	31	14	31
Majestic	1642	594	–	–	1	13	2	5	3	18
Marlborough	1642	594	–	–	–	–	29	90	29	90
Montague	1631	594	–	–	–	–	4	13	4	13
Orion	1646	594	–	–	3	–	2	24	5	24
Ramillies	1677	594	–	..	3	–	2	7	2	7
Russell	1642	594	–	–	–	–	8	26	8	26
Thunderer	1679	594	–	–	–	–	–	–	–	–
Tremendous	1680	594	–	–	–	–	3	8	3	8
Phaeton, frigate	–	–	–	–	–	–	3	4	3	4
Total	46962	17241	3	19	57	107	230	698	290	858

The total of killed and wounded, as carried out in this table, exceeds that in the official return by 50; namely, three killed on board the Ramillies, and 13 wounded on board the Majestic, on May 29, as extracted from their respective logs, and 34 additional wounded men on board the Cæsar, on June 1st, as deposed to by her surgeon, at Captain Molloy's court-martial. Moreover, the official amount, by lumping the loss of the several ships, makes it appear as if the whole had been incurred on the 1st of June.

No. 13.—See p. 193.

Barrère actually succeeded in getting the national convention to pass the following decree:—

"Art. 1ier. Une forme du vaisseau de ligne le Vengeur sera suspendue à la voûte du Panthéon, et les noms des braves républicains composant l'équipage de ce vaisseau, seront inscrits sur la colonne du Panthéon.

"2. A cet effet les agens maritimes des ports de Brest en Rochefort enverront sans délai la rôle d'équipage du vaisseau le Vengeur.

"Le vaisseau à trois ponts, qui est en construction dans le bassin couvert de Brest, portera le nom de Vengeur. Le commissaire de la marine donnera les ordres les plus prompts pour accélérer la construction de ce vaisseau.

"4. La convention nationale appele les artistes, peintres, sculpteurs, et poëtes, à concourir pour transmettre à la postérité le trait sublime du dévoûment républicain des citoyens formant l'équipage de Vengeur. Il sera décerné dans une fête nationale, des recompenses aux peintres, et aux poëtes, qui auront le plus dignement célébré la gloire de ces républicains."

No. 14.—See p. 195.

"Le combat s'engagea très-vivement de part et d'autre. Les capitaines anglais, plus accoutumés que les nôtres à manier des vaisseaux de guerre, coupèrent notre ligne en plusieurs points. Cependant les républicains se battirent avec un courage infini. Plusieurs vaisseaux furent démâtés ou désemparés dans les deux armées, et le combat cessa sans que la victoire se décidât. Un de nos vaisseaux seulement, le Vengeur, désemparé et coulant bas, avait été amariné par les ennemis. Mais ce qui est incompréhensible, c'est l'abandon que nous fîmes sur le champ de bataille, de six vaisseaux français désemparés, mais non vaincus, qui formant un groupe, faisaient briller le pavillon tricolore, en tendant les bras, pour ainsi dire, à l'armée, pour la prier de les secourir. Il suffisait, pour les railler et pour prendre deux vaisseaux Anglais démâtés, qui étaient peu éloignés de nos six vaisseaux; il suffisait, dis-je, de virer simplement de bord. Il serait à désirer que l'on pût passer l'éponge sur un si honteux événement.

"On a donc sacrifié inutilement des hommes, des vaisseaux, et les intérêts de la république. Mais l'ignorance et la présomption présidaient alors à ses destinées sur l'océan; et la plus honteuse défaite fut transformée en un véritable triomphe. En effet, on annonça une victoire après avoir perdu sept beaux vaisseaux qui avaient plus de 500 pièces de canons. On donna au commandant en chef le grade de vice-amiral, et l'on jeta des fleurs sur le passage du preprésentant embarqué dans l'armée, à son retour à Brest."

APPENDIX. 437

No. 15.—See p. 255.

A List of Ships of the Line and Frigates, late belonging to the French Navy, Captured, Destroyed, Wrecked, Foundered, or Accidentally Burnt during the year 1794.

	Name.	How, when, and where Lost.
Gun-ship.		
110	. . Républicain . . .	Wrecked, December 27, on the Mingan rock, having drifted from her anchors in a gale.
80	(K) Sans-Pareil . . . ,, Juste	
74	(M) América . . . . ,, Impétueux . . . ,, Achille . . . . ,, Northumberland . . . . Vengeur	Captured, June 1, by the British fleet under Earl Howe. The Vengeur sank soon after she was taken possession of.
Gun-frig.		
44	(X) Pomone	Captured, April 23, by Sir J. B. Warren's squadron, off the isle of Bas.
40	(Z) Révolutionnaire . .	Captured, October 21, by Sir Edw. Pellew's squadron, off Brest.
	,, Sibylle	Captured, June 17, by the Romney 50, at Miconi, Mediterranean.
	(A) Melpomène . . .	Captured, August 10, by Lord Hood, at Calvi, Corsica.
38	(B) Minerve	Captured, February 19, by the British, at San-Fiorenzo, Corsica.
36	Volontaire . . .	Destroyed, August 23, after being run on shore on the Penmarcks by Sir J. B. Warren's squadron.
	. . Fortunée . . .	Destroyed when Minerve was captured.
36	(D) Engageante . . .	Captured, April 23, by the Concorde 36, in the Channel.
	,, Atalante	Captured, May, by the Swiftsure 74, in the Channel.
32	(H) Castor	Captured, May 29, by the Carysfort 28, off the Land's End.
28	(I) Bienvenue . . .	Captured, March 17, by Sir John Jervis's squadron, at Martinique.
	,, Mignonne	Captured along with the Minerve.
	. . Duguay-Trouin . .	Captured, May 5, by the Orpheus 32, in the East Indies.

VOL. I 2 G

	Lost through the Enemy.	
	Capt.	Dest.
Ships of the line	7	..
Frigates	11	2
Total	18	2

No. 16.—See p. 255.

A List of Ships and Vessels late belonging to the British Navy, Captured, Destroyed, Wrecked, Foundered, or Accidentally Burnt, during the year 1794.

	Name.	Commander.	How, when, and where Lost.
Gun-ship.			
74	(M) *Impétueux* (in ordinary)		Burnt by accident and blown up, Aug. 24, in Portsmouth harbour: crew saved.
	(O) Alexander	R. Rodney Bligh	Captured, Nov. 6, by a French squadron of five 74s and three frigates off Sicily.
64	(P) Ardent	R. Manners Sutton	Burnt by accident and blown up, sometime in April, with all the crew, off Corsica.
Gun-frig.			
32	(G) *Convert*	John Lawford	Wrecked, March 8, on the Grand Caymanes, West Indies: crew saved.
	(H) Castor	T. Troubridge	Captured, May 9, by Admiral Nielly's squadron, off Cape Clear.
28	(I) Rose	Matt. H. Scott	Wrecked, June 28, on Rocky-Point, Jamaica: crew saved.
G. p. ship.			
18	(K) Amphitrite	Anthony Hunt	Wrecked, Jan. 30, by striking on a sunken rock in the Mediterranean: crew saved.
G. sh slp.			
24	(R) *Moselle*	H. A. Bennett	Captured, January 7, by the French in Toulon, having entered by mistake.
	(T) Alert	Charles Smith	Captured, in May, by the French frigate Unité, off the coast of Ireland.
16	,, Pylades	Thos. Twysden	Wrecked, Nov. 26, in Heraldswick bay, isle of Nest, Shetland: crew saved.
	(U) Hound	R. Piercy	Captured, July 24, by the French frigates Seine and Galathée, on her passage from the West Indies.
	(V) *Espion*	W. Hugh Kittoe	Captured, date unknown, by three French frigates.
G. bg. slp.			
16	(a) Scout	Charles Robinson	Captured, in August, by two ditto, off Bona.
14	(b) Speedy	George Eyre	Captured, in June, by a French squadron, off Nice.

No 16—continued.

Name.	Commander.	How, when, and where Lost.
G. gun-brig 10 (b) *Actif*	John Harvey	Foundered, November 26, off Bermuda: crew saved.
G cut. 14 (i) *Ranger*	Isaac Cotgrave	Captured, in June, by a French squadron, off Brest.
6 (n) *Spitfire*	J. W. Rich	Foundered or overset, in Feb. off St. Domingo: crew perished.
Float.-bat. (v) *Prosélyte*	Walter Serocold	Destroyed, April 11, by the fire from the French batteries at Bastia.

ABSTRACT.

	Lost through the Enemy		Lost through Accident.			
	Capt.	Dest.	Wrecked.	Foundered.	Burnt.	Total.
Ships of the line	1	..	..	..	2	3
„ under the line	8	1	4	2	..	15
Total	9	1	4	2	2	18

No. 17.—See p. 157.

	£	s.	d.
For the pay and maintenance of 85,000 seamen and 15,000 marines	5,200,000	0	0
„ the ordinary expenses of the navy, including the half-pay to the sea and marine officers	589,683	3	9
„ the extraordinaries; including the building and repairing of ships, and other extra works	525,840	0	0
Total supplies granted for the sea-service, exclusive of ordnance	6,315,523	8	9

APPENDIX. 441

No. 18.—See p. 339.

A List of Ships of the Line and Frigates, late belonging to the French Navy, Captured, Destroyed, Wrecked, Foundered, or Accidentally Burnt during the year 1795.

	Name.	How, when, and where Lost.
Gun-ship. 80	(K) Ca-Ira	Captured, March 14, by Vice-admiral Hotham's fleet, off Genoa.
	.. Scipion .. Neuf-Thermidor	Foundered in a gale of wind, in January.
74	.. Superbe	
	.. Neptune	Wrecked, some time in January, in the bay of Audierne, coast of France.
	(M) Censeur	Captured along with the Ca-Ira.
	(L) Formidable (M) Tigre (O) *Alexandre*	Captured, June 23, by Lord Bridport's fleet, off L'Orient.
	.. Alcide	Captured, July 13, by Vice-admiral Hotham's fleet, but immediately afterwards caught fire, and blew up: about half of the crew perished.
Gun-frig. 40	(Z) Minerve	Captured, June 24, by the Lowestoffe and Dido frigates, in the Mediterranean.
36	.. Galathée	Wrecked, April 23, near the Penmarcks.
	.. Duquesne	Captured, January 5, by the Bellona 74, in the West Indies.
	(D) Gloire	Captured, April 10, by the Astræa 32, in the Channel.
	,, Gentille	Captured, April 11, by the Hannibal 74, in the Channel.
	,, Pique	Captured, January 6, by the Blanche 32, in the West Indies.
	.. Iphigénie	Captured, Feb. 10, by a Spanish squadron under Admiral Langara, Mediterranean.
	.. Droits-du-Peuple	Wrecked, in November, off Drentheim, coast of Norway.
28	(*I*) Tourterelle	Captured, March 13, by the Lively 32, off Ushant.

No. 19.—See p. 339.

A List of Ships of the Line and Frigates, late belonging to the Dutch Navy, Captured, Destroyed, Wrecked, Foundered, or Accidentally Burnt, during the year 1795.

Name.	How, when, and where Lost.
Gun-ship. 64 (Q) Overyssel	Captured, October 22, by the Polyphemus 64, in Cork Harbour.
Gun-frig. 36 (H) Alliance	Captured, Aug. 22, by a British squadron, off the coast of Norway.

An Abstract of French and Dutch Ships of the Line and Frigates, Captured, &c., during the year 1795.

		Lost through the Enemy.		Lost through Accident.			Total lost to the French and Dutch Navies.	Total added to the British Navy.
		Capt.	Dest.	Wrecked.	Foundered.	Burnt.		
Ships of the line.	Fr.	6	..	1	3	..	10	5
	Du.	1	..	..	..	..	1	1
Frigates.	Fr.	7	..	2	..	..	9	5
	Du.	1	..	..	..	..	1	1
Total		15	..	3	3	..	21	12

APPENDIX.

No. 20.—See p. 339.

A List of Ships and Vessels, late belonging to the British Navy, Captured, Destroyed, Wrecked, Foundered, or Accidentally Burnt, during the year 1795.

	Name.	Commander.	How, when, and where Lost.
Gun-ship. 98 (H)	Boyne	George Grey	Accidentally burnt, May 1, at Spithead: crew saved.
74 (M)	*Censeur*	John Gore	Captured, Oct. 7, by a French squadron, off Cape St. Vincent.
74 (O)	Berwick	Adam Littlejohn	Captured, March 7, by the French fleet in the Mediterranean.
,,	Illustrious	T. L. Frederick	Wrecked, March 14, in a gale, on the rocks near Avenga: crew saved.
44 (V)	Diomede	Matthew Smith	Wrecked, Aug. 2, by striking on a sunken rock off Trincomalé, island of Ceylon: crew saved.
Gun-frig. 38 (A)	*Amethyst*	Thomas Affleck	Wrecked, Dec. 29, at Alderney: crew saved.
28 (I)	Nemesis	Samuel H. Linzee	Captured, December 9, by the French frigate Sensible and corvette Sardine, in the road of Smyrna.
Gun p. sh. 20 (O)	Daphne	Wm. E. Cracraft	Captured, Feb. 12, by a detachment of the Brest fleet.
G. b. slp. 14 (b)	*Flèche*	Charles Came	Wrecked, Nov. 12, in San-Fiorenzo bay: crew saved.
G. sch. 6 (n)	*Flying-fish*	—— Seton	Captured, in June, by two French privateers.
Float. bat. .. (v)	Musquito	—— M'Carty	Wrecked, exact time unknown, on the coast of France, near Jersey: crew perished.
G. Dutch hoy. 4 (w)	Shark	—— Watson	Captured, Dec. 11, by being run away with into La Hogue by her own crew.

ABSTRACT.

	Lost through the Enemy.		Lost through Accident.			
	Capt.	Dest.	Wrecked.	Foundered.	Burnt.	Total.
Ships of the line.	2	..	1	..	1	4
,, under the line.	4	..	4	..	..	8
Total	6	..	5	..	1	12

No. 21.—See p. 340.

	£	s.	d.
For the pay and maintenance of 92,000 seamen and 18,000 marines	5,720,000	0	0
„ the ordinary expenses of the navy, including the half-pay to sea and marine officers	624,152	1	8
„ the extraordinaries; including the building and repairing of ships, and other extra work	708,400	0	0
Ordnance	61,000	8	9
Towards discharging the navy-debt	500,000	0	0
Total supplies granted for the sea-service	£7,613,552	10	5

No. 22.—See p. 391.

"Dans l'état de faiblesse de la marine française, la plus grande de toutes les follies était de faire sortir des vaisseaux pour chercher ceux de l'ennemi et leur livrer bataille. On la fit pourtant au commencement de la guerre, et nous en avons vu les tristes résultats. Cette funeste expérience, au surplus, n'était pas nécessaire pour convaincre que ce n'est pas là la tactique du plus faible. Tromper la vigilance du plus fort, échapper à ses poursuites, se présenter à l'improviste sur un point qu'il n'a pas gardé, et il est impossible qu'il les garde tous, voilà le vrai moyen de compenser une trop grande inégalité de forces; celles des deux ennemis, fussent-elles égales même, celui des deux qui agirait ainsi triompherait bientôt de l'autre. En marine, le combat n'est donc jamais le but qu'on doit se proposer, à moins qu'on ne possède une telle supériorité de forces sur son ennemi, qu'on puisse espérer parvenir à anéantir bientôt les siennes. Les bâtimens de guerre ont ainsi toujours une destination autre que de combattre ceux de l'ennemi; et il arrive souvent que, quelle que soit l'issue du combat, cette destination première et principale ne peut plus être remplie. L'important pour l'Etat est qu'un commandant de forces navales s'acquitte de la mission dont il est chargé, et non qu'il la manque pour faire preuve de courage et acquérir une gloire stérile pour son pays. D'après ces principes, les divers gouvernemens qui se sont succédé en France pendant la guerre de la révolution, ont presque tous, et très-sagement, donné l'ordre formel aux généraux et capitaines de bâtimens de guerre d'éviter toute espèce d'engagement, de ne livrer combat qu'en cas de nécessité absolue, et de tourner tous leurs efforts vers l'accomplissement de leur mission."—*Victoires et Conquêtes*, tome vii., p. 251.

An ABSTRACT of the Ships and Vessels belonging to the British Navy at the commencement of the Year 17—

| Letters of reference. | RATE. | CLASS.† | CRUISERS. ||||||| Stationary Harbour-ships, &c. |||||
| | | | In Commission. || In Ordinary, under or for Repair. || TOTAL. || No. || In Commission. || Not in Commission. || |
			No.	Tons.	No.	Tons.	No.	Tons.	British Built.	Foreign Built.	No.	Tons.	No.	Tons.	British Built.
A	Three-deckers. First.	120-gun ship	—	—	—	—	—	—	—	—	—	—	—	—	—
B	,,	112 ,,	—	—	—	—	—	—	—	—	—	—	—	—	—
D*	,,	100 ,, 18-pounder	—	—	2	4572	2	4572	2	—	—	—	—	—	—
E	,,	,, 12 ,,	1	2091	2	4337	3	6428	3	—	—	—	—	—	—
F*	Second.	98 ,, 18 ,, large	—	—	—	—	—	—	—	—	—	—	—	—	—
G	,,	,, ,, small	—	—	—	—	—	—	—	—	—	—	—	—	—
H	,,	,, 12 ,,	4	7877	11	20970	15	28847	15	—	1	1869	—	—	1
I*	,,	90 ,,	—	—	1	1814	1	1814	1	—	2	3699	—	—	2
	Two-deckers.														
K*	Third.	80 ,,	—	—	1	2185	1	2185	—	1	—	—	—	—	—
L*	,,	74 ,, 24-pounder	—	—	—	—	—	—	—	—	—	—	—	—	—
M*	,,	,, 18 ,, large	1	1836	2	3624	3	5460	3	—	—	—	—	—	—
N	,,	,, ,, middl.	1	1721	3	5144	4	6865	3	1	—	—	1	1778	—
O	,,	,, ,, small	17	27833	37	60422	54	88255	54	—	—	—	8	12864	8
P	,,	64 ,,	2	2758	28	38802	30	41560	29	1	—	—	13	18003	12
Q	Fourth.	60 ,,	—	—	—	—	—	—	—	—	—	—	3	3718	3
		Line	26	44116	87	141870	113	185986	110	3	3	5568	25	36363	26
T		50 ,,	7	7249	5	5280	12	12529	12	—	—	—	7	7413	6
V	Fifth.	44 ,,	3	2670	15	13488	18	16158	18	—	—	—	3	2575	2
	One-deckers.	38-gun frigate large	—	—	1	1063	1	1063	—	1	—	—	—	—	—
Z*	,,	,, ,, small	—	—	2	1892	2	1892	—	—	—	—	—	—	—
A	,,	36 ,, 18-pounder	5	4861	2	1892	7	6753	6	1	—	—	—	—	—
C	,,	,, ,, 12 ,,	6	5297	3	2704	9	8001	9	—	—	—	—	—	—
D	,,	32 ,, 18 ,,	2	1906	2	1882	4	3788	—	4	—	—	3	2752	—
F	,,	,, ,, 12 ,, large	1	779	1	782	2	1561	1	1	—	—	—	—	—
G*	,,	,, ,, ,, small	18	12555	20	13719	38	26274	38	—	—	—	5	3499	4
H	Sixth.	28 ,,	10	5990	13	7760	23	13750	23	—	—	—	4	2418	4
I	,,	24-gun post-ship	3	1606	3	1553	6	3159	6	—	—	—	1	528	—
K*	,,	20 ,,	2	864	4	1723	6	2587	6	—	1	481	—	—	—
O	Sloops.	18-gun ship-sloop, flush	—	—	1	342	1	342	1	—	—	—	1	340	1
S*	,,	16 ,, quarter-deck large	7	2656	1	342	8	2998	8	—	—	—	2	718	2
T*	,,	,, ,, ,, small	6	1938	2	631	8	2569	8	—	—	—	1	319	1
U	,,	14 ,, ,,	7	2118	1	306	8	2424	8	—	—	—	2	605	2
W	,,	18-gun brig-sloop	2	737	—	—	2	737	1	1	—	—	—	—	—
Y*	,,	16 ,,	5	1320	—	—	5	1320	4	1	—	—	—	—	—
a	,,	14 ,,	7	1460	2	409	9	1869	9	—	—	—	1	209	1
b		Bombs, of 8 guns and 2 mortars	—	—	2	609	2	609	2	—	—	—	—	—	—
d*		Fireships, 14 guns	—	—	5	2124	5	2124	5	—	—	—	1	423	1
e		Cutters, &c.	11	2160	—	—	11	2140	9	2	—	—	1	199	1
i		,, 12 ,,	6	895	—	—	6	895	4	2	—	—	1	123	1
k		,, 4 ,,	1	95	—	—	1	95	1	—	—	—	3	270	—
o		Fifth-rates. 24 ,,	—	—	—	—	—	—	—	—	1	880	3	2658	4
s*		Sloops on Discovery	—	—	—	—	—	—	—	—	2	743	—	—	—
y		Armed Transports	—	—	—	—	—	—	—	—	—	—	5	1294	5
z		Yachts royal, or large	—	—	—	—	—	—	—	—	6	1083	—	—	6
b*		,, small	—	—	—	—	—	—	—	—	1	66	3	213	4
		*Grand Total	135	101272	169	198137	304	299409	288	16	14	8821	72	62849	77

VOL. I.

An ACCOUNT of the Carriage Long-guns‖ and Complement of Men and Boys, as mounted and borne by the several Classes of Ships, down to Sloops inclusive, at the date of the preceding Abstract.§

lding, or Ordered to e Built.		GRAND TOTAL.		Carriage Long-guns.										Complement.				
			First, or Main-deck.		Second-deck.		Third-deck.		Quarter-deck.		Forecastle.		Total No.	Broadside weight of Metal in lbs.	Officers, Seamen, and Marines.	Servants, including 3-4ths Boys.	Widows' Men.††	Men and Boys on Board.
Tons.	No.	Tons.	No.	Nature.	No.	Nature.	No.	Nature.	No.	Nature.	No.	Nature.						
2508	1	2508	30	32-pdrs.	32	24-pdrs.	32	18-pdrs.	14	12-pdrs.	4	12-pdrs.	112	1248	788	53	9	841
2351	1	2351	,,	,, ,,	28	,, ,,	30	,, ,,	10	,, ,,	2	,, ,,	100	1158	,,	,,	,,	,,
— —	2	4572	28	,, ,,	,,	,, ,,	28	12 ,,	12	,, ,,	4	,, ,,	,,	1048	,,	,,	,,	,,
— —	3	6428																
2276	1	2276																
6363	3	6363	,,	,, ,,	30	18 ,,	30	18 ,,	8	,, ,,	2	,, ,,	98	1048	694	49	7	743
2024	17	32740	,,	,, ,,	,,	,, ,,	,,	12 ,,	,,	,, ,,	,,	,, ,,	,,	958	,,	,,	,,	,,
— —	3	5513	26	,, ,,	26	,, ,,	26	,, ,,	10	,, ,,	,,	,, ,,	90	878	,,	,,	,,	,,
4065	3	6250	30	,, ,,	32	24 ,,	—	—	14	,, ,,	4	,, ,,	80	972	676	47	6	724
3695	2	3695	28	,, ,,	30	,, ,,	—	—	,,	9 ,,	2	9 ,,	74	880	602	42	,,	644
— —	3	5460	,,	,, ,,	,,	18 ,,	—	—	,,	,, ,,	,,	,, ,,	,,	790	,,	,,	,,	,,
1718	6	10361	}, ,,	,, ,,	28	,, ,,	—	—	,,	,, ,,	4	,, ,,	,,	781	554	40	,,	594
— —	62	101119	26	24 ,,	26	,, ,,	—	—	10	,, ,,	2	,, ,,	64	600	458	36	,,	494
— —	43	59563																
— —	3	3718																
25000	153	252917																
3344	22	23286	22	,, ,,	22	12 ,,	—	—	4	6 ,,	2	6 ,,	50	414	316	29	5	345
— —	21	18733	20	18 ,,	,,	,, ,,	—	—	—	—	,,	,, ,,	44	318	271	26	3	297
— —	1	1063	}28	,, ,,	—	—	—	—	8	9 ,,	2	12 ,,	38	300	251	,,	,,	277
— —	7	6753	26	,, ,,	—	—	—	—	,,	6 ,,	,,	6 ,,	36	282	232	25	,,	257
— —	9	8001	,,	12 ,,	—	—	—	—	,,	,, ,,	,,	,, ,,	,,	186	223	24	,,	24"
— —	7	6540	,,	18 ,,	—	—	—	—	4	,, ,,	,,	,, ,,	32	252	232	25	,,	257
2375	2	2375	}, ,,	12 ,,	—	—	—	—	,,	,, ,,	,,	,, ,,	,,	174	194	23	,,	217
— —	48	29703	24	9 ,,	—	—	—	—	2	,, ,,	—	—	28	120	176	22	2	198
— —	27	16168	22	,, ,,	—	—	—	—	,,	,, ,,	—	—	24	105	138	20	,,	158
— —	7	3687	20	,, ,,	—	—	—	—	—	—	—	—	20	90	119	19	,,	138
— —	7	3068	18	6 ,,	—	—	—	—	—	—	—	—	18	54	107	17	1	124
— —	1	340	}16	,, ,,	—	—	—	—	—	—	—	—	16	48	,,	,,	,,	,,
2 664	10	3716	14	,, ,,	—	—	—	—	—	—	—	—	14	42	,,	,,	,,	,,
— —	11	3552	18	,, ,,	—	—	—	—	—	—	—	—	18	54	,,	,,	,,	,,
— —	10	3029	16	4 ,,	—	—	—	—	—	—	—	—	16	32	67	12	,,	79
— —	2	737	14	,, ,,	—	—	—	—	—	—	—	—	14	28	57	,,	,,	69
— —	5	1320																
— —	10	2078																
— —	2	609																
— —	6	2547																
— —	12	2359																
— —	7	1018																
— —	4	365																
— —	4	3538																
— —	2	743																
— —	5	1294																
— —	6	1083																
1 93	5	372																
21 31476	411	402555																

2 H

No.

An ABSTRACT of the Ships and Vessels belonging to the British Navy at the commencement of the Year 1794.

| Letters of Reference. | RATE. | CLASS.† | CRUISERS. ||||| Stationary Harbour-ships, &c. |||||| Building Ordered to be Bu ||
| | | | In Commission. || In Ordinary, under or for Repair. || TOTAL. || No. || In Commission. || Not in Commission. || No. || | |
			No.	Tons.	No.	Tons.	No.	Tons.	British Built.	Foreign Built.	No.	Tons.	No.	Tons.	British Built.	Foreign Built.	No.	To
A	Three-deckers. First.	120-gun ship	–	–	1	2747	1	2747	–	1	–	–	–	–	–	–	1	2
B	,,	112 ,,	–	–	–	–	–	–	–	–	–	–	–	–	–	–	1	
D	,,	100 ,, 18-pounder	2	4572	–	–	2	4572	2	–	–	–	–	–	–	–	–	2
E	,,	,, 12 ,,	3	6428	–	–	3	6428	3	–	–	–	–	–	–	–	–	
F	Second.	98 ,, 18 ,, – large	–	–	–	–	–	–	–	–	–	–	–	–	–	–	1	
G	,,	,, ,, ,, – small	–	–	–	–	–	–	–	–	–	–	–	–	–	–	3	6
H	,,	,, 12 ,,	9	17356	6	11491	15	28847	15	–	1	1869	–	–	1	–	–	2
I	,,	90 ,,	–	–	1	1814	1	1814	1	–	2	3699	–	–	2	–	–	
	Two-deckers.																	
K*	Third.	80 ,,	2	4188	–	–	2	4188	1	1	–	–	–	–	–	–	1	2
L	,,	74 ,, 24-pounder	1	1901	–	–	1	1901	–	1	–	–	–	–	–	–	2	3
M	,,	,, 18 ,, – large	3	5434	1	1825	4	7259	3	1	–	–	–	–	–	–	–	
N	,,	,, ,, ,, – middl.	4	6863	1	1720	5	8583	4	1	1	1778	–	–	–	–	–	
O	,,	,, ,, ,, – small	43	70374	11	17881	54	88255	54	–	2	3189	6	9075	8	–	–	
P	,,	,, 64 ,,	18	24977	11	15197	29	40174	28	1	–	–	13	18003	9	4	–	
Q	Fourth.	60 ,,	–	–	–	–	–	–	–	–	–	–	3	3718	3	–	–	
		Line	85	142093	32	52675	117	194768	111	6	6	10535	22	31396	23	5	10	21
T	,,	50 ,,	8	8314	4	4215	12	12529	12	–	1	1052	6	6361	6	1	3	3
V	Fifth.	44 ,,	12	10769	3	2702	15	13471	15	–	1	882	2	1693	2	1	–	
	One-deckers.																	
Z	,,	38-gun frigate – large	2	2127	–	–	2	2127	–	2	–	–	–	–	–	–	–	
A	,,	,, ,, small	9	8822	–	–	9	8822	6	3	–	–	–	–	–	–	6	5
C	,,	36 ,, 18-pounder	8	7119	–	–	8	7119	8	–	–	–	1	882	1	–	–	
D	,,	,, 12 ,,	10	9298	–	–	10	9298	–	10	–	–	3	2752	–	3	–	
F	,,	32 ,, 18 ,,	1	792	–	–	1	792	1	–	–	–	–	–	–	–	6	4
G	,,	,, 12 ,, – large	2	1561	–	–	2	1561	1	1	–	–	–	–	–	–	–	
H	,,	,, ,, ,, small	34	23541	3	2077	37	25618	37	–	–	–	3	2080	2	1	–	
I	Sixth	28 ,,	22	13126	2	1204	24	14330	23	1	1	594	3	1824	4	–	–	
K	,,	24-gun post-ship	4	2118	1	519	5	2637	4	1	–	–	1	528	1	–	–	
L	,,	20 ,,	6	2663	1	433	7	3096	6	1	1	481	–	–	1	–	–	
R	Sloops.	18-gun ship-sloop, quarter-decked flush	4	1890	–	–	4	1890	–	4	–	–	–	–	–	–	6	2
S	,,	,, ,, quarter-decked, large	10	3727	1	342	11	4069	10	1	–	–	1	340	1	–	–	
T	,,	16 ,, ,, ,, small	10	3233	–	–	10	3233	10	–	–	–	2	718	2	–	4	1
U	,,	14 ,, ,, ,, ,,	8	2424	–	–	8	2424	8	–	–	–	1	319	1	–	–	
W	,,	18-gun brig-sloop	2	737	–	–	2	737	1	1	–	–	2	605	2	–	–	
Y	,,	16 ,,	7	1858	1	273	8	2131	4	4	–	–	–	–	–	–	–	
a	,,	14 ,,	9	1942	1	207	10	2149	9	1	–	–	1	209	1	–	–	
b	Bombs, of	8 guns and 2 mortars	2	609	–	–	2	609	2	–	1	–	–	–	1	–	–	
d	Fireships,	14 ,,	3	1273	–	–	3	1273	3	–	–	–	1	423	1	–	–	
e	Cutters, &c.	12 ,,	8	1580	–	–	8	1580	6	2	–	–	2	380	2	–	–	
i	,,	10 ,,	6	895	–	–	6	895	4	2	–	–	1	123	1	–	–	
k	,,	8 ,,	2	298	–	–	2	298	1	2	–	–	–	–	–	–	–	
l	,,	6 ,,	3	212	–	–	3	212	–	3	–	–	–	–	–	–	–	
m	,,	4 ,,	–	–	–	–	–	–	–	–	–	–	1	88	1	–	–	
n	Third rates,	36 ,,	–	–	–	–	–	–	–	–	1	1386	–	–	1	–	–	
o	Fifth ,,	24 ,,	–	–	–	–	–	–	–	–	6	5338	1	887	7	–	–	
q	,,	18 ,,	–	–	–	–	–	–	–	–	1	932	–	–	–	1	–	
s	Float. Batt.	20 ,,	–	–	–	–	–	–	–	–	2	1336	–	–	1	1	–	
t	Sloops on Discovery		–	–	–	–	–	–	–	–	2	743	–	–	2	–	–	
v	Armed Transports		–	–	–	–	–	–	–	–	6	1388	1	688	7	–	–	
y	Yachts	– – – royal, or large	–	–	–	–	–	–	–	–	3	494	3	589	6	–	2	
z	,,	,, small	–	–	–	–	–	–	–	–	1	66	2	135	3	–	–	
		Grand Total	279	253262	49	64647	328	317909	282	46	32	25227	60	53620	78	14	37	39

VOL. I.

Increase and Decrease in the Classes since the date of the last Year's Abstract.

GRAND TOTAL.	Launched. King's Yards.		Launched. Merchants' Yards.		Purchased.		Captured.		Converted from other Classes.		Ordered to be Built.		TOTAL of Increase.		Loss by Capture, &c.		Converted to other Classes.		Sold, or taken to Pieces.		TOTAL of Decrease.	
Tons.	No.	Tons.	No.	Tons.	No.	Tons.	No.	Tons.	No.	Tons.	No.	Tons.	No.	Tons.	No.	Tons.	No.	Tons.	No.	Tons.	No.	Tons.
5255	-	-	-	-	-	-	1	2747	-	-	-	-	1	2747								
2351																						
4572																						
6428																						
2276																						
6363																						
32740																						
5513																						
6250	1	2003	-	-	-	-	-	-	-	-	-	-	1	2003								
5596	-	-	-	-	-	-	1	1901	-	-	-	-	1	1901								
7259	-	-	-	-	-	-	2	3609	-	-	-	-	2	3609	1	1810	-	-	-	-	1	1810
10361	1	1718	-	-	-	-	-	-	-	-	-	-	1	1718								
101119																						
58177	-	-	-	-	-	-	-	-	-	-	-	-	-	-	-	-	1	1386	-	-	1	1386
3718																						
257978	2	3721	-	-	-	-	4	8257	-	-	-	-	6	11978	1	1810	1	1386	-	-	2	3196
23286															-	-	3	2687	-	-	3	2687
16046																						
2127	-	-	-	-	-	-	1	1064	-	-	-	-	1	1064								
14804	-	-	-	-	-	-	2	2069	-	-	6	5982	8	8051								
8001																						
12050	-	-	-	-	-	-	8	7392	-	-	-	-	8	7392	-	-	2	1882	-	-	2	1882
5608	1	792	-	-	-	-	-	-	-	-	4	3233	5	4025								
1561																						
27698	-	-	-	-	-	-	-	-	-	-	-	-	-	-	1	656	-	-	2	1349	3	2005
16748	-	-	-	-	-	-	1	580	-	-	-	-	1	580								
3165	-	-	-	-	-	-	1	509	-	-	-	-	1	509	1	522	-	-	-	-	1	522
3577	-	-	-	-	-	-	-	-	-	-	-	-	-	-								
4448	-	-	-	-	-	-	4	1890	-	-	6	2558	10	4448								
340																						
6256	-	-	2	731	-	-	1	340	-	-	4	1469	7	2540								
3552	-	-	2	664	-	-	-	-	-	-	-	-	2	664								
3029																						
737																						
2131	-	-	-	-	-	-	3	811	-	-	-	-	3	811								
2358	-	-	-	-	-	-	2	528	-	-	-	-	2	528	1	248	-	-	-	-	1	248
609															2	851	-	-	-	-	2	851
1696	-	-	-	-	-	-	-	-	-	-	-	-	-	-	1	181	-	-	1	218	2	399
1960	-	-	-	-	-	-	-	-	-	-	-	-	-	-								
1018																						
298	-	-	1	111	-	-	1	187	-	-	-	-	2	298								
241	-	-	-	-	-	-	2	241	-	-	-	-	2	241								
212	-	-	-	-	-	-	3	212	-	-	-	-	3	212								
88	-	-	-	-	-	-	3	181	-	-	-	-	3	181	3	181	-	-	3	277	6	458
1386	-	-	-	-	-	-	-	-	1	1386	-	-	1	1386								
6225	-	-	-	-	-	-	-	-	3	2687	-	-	3	2687								
932	-	-	-	-	-	-	-	-	1	932	-	-	1	932								
1336	-	-	-	-	1	386	-	-	1	950	-	-	2	1336								
743																						
2076	-	-	-	-	2	782	-	-	-	-	-	-	2	782								
1083																						
399	1	93	-	-	-	-	-	-	-	-	2	198	3	291	-	-	-	-	2	171	2	171
435802	4	4606	5	1506	3	1168	36	24261	6	5955	22	13440	76	50936	10	4449	6	5955	8	2015	24	12419

2 I

An ABSTRACT of the Ships and Vessels belonging to the British Navy at the commencement of the Year 1795.

Letters of Reference	RATE	CLASS	Cruisers - In Commission No.	Cruisers - In Commission Tons	Cruisers - In Ordinary, under or for Repair No.	Cruisers - In Ordinary, under or for Repair Tons	Cruisers - Total No.	Cruisers - Total Tons	No. British Built	No. Foreign Built	Stationary - In Commission No.	Stationary - In Commission Tons	Stationary - Not in Commission No.	Stationary - Not in Commission Tons	No. British Built	No. Foreign Built	Building, or Ordered to be Built No.	Building, or Ordered to be Built Tons	Grand Total No.	Grand Total Tons	Launched King's Yards No.	Launched King's Yards Tons	Merchant Yards No.
A	First	Three-deckers. 120-gun ship	—	—	1	2747	1	2747	—	1	—	—	—	—	—	—	2	5124	3	7871	—	—	—
B	,,	112 ,,	—	—	—	—	—	—	—	—	—	—	—	—	—	—	1	2351	1	2351	—	—	—
C	,,	100 ,, 18-pounder	2	4572	—	—	2	4572	2	—	—	—	—	—	—	—	—	—	2	4572	—	—	—
D	,,	98 ,, 12 ,,	3	6428	—	—	3	6428	3	—	—	—	—	—	—	—	—	—	3	6428	—	—	—
E	Second	98 ,, 18 ,, large	—	—	—	—	—	—	—	—	—	—	—	—	—	—	1	2276	1	2276	—	—	—
F	,,	,, ,, ,, small	—	—	—	—	—	—	—	—	—	—	—	—	—	—	3	6363	3	6363	—	—	—
G	,,	90 ,, 12 ,,	14	26976	2	3895	16	30871	16	—	1	1869	—	—	1	—	—	—	17	32740	1	2024	—
H	,,	90 ,,	—	—	1	1814	1	1814	1	—	2	3699	—	—	2	—	—	—	3	5513	—	—	—
		Two-deckers.																					
K	Third	80 ,,	2	4188	2	4385	4	8573	1	3	—	—	—	—	—	—	1	2062	5	10635	—	—	—
L	,,	74 ,, 24-pounder	2	3754	—	—	2	3754	2	—	—	—	—	—	—	—	2	3782	4	7536	1	1853	—
M	,,	,, ,, 18 ,, large	3	5460	1	1884	4	7344	3	1	—	—	3	5411	—	3	—	—	7	12755	—	—	—
N	,,	,, ,, ,, middl.	4	6863	1	1720	5	8583	4	1	1	1778	—	—	—	1	2	3549	8	13910	—	—	—
O	,,	,, ,, ,, small	43	70415	9	14557	52	84972	52	—	3	4803	4	6455	7	—	—	—	59	96230	—	—	—
P	,,	64 ,,	18	25013	6	8262	24	33275	23	1	3	4194	10	13869	9	4	—	—	37	51278	—	—	—
Q	Fourth	60 ,,	—	—	—	—	—	—	—	—	—	—	3	3178	3	—	—	—	3	3178	—	—	—
		Line	91	153659	23	39264	114	192933	106	8	10	16283	20	29453	22	8	12	25507	156	264176	2	3877	—
T	Fifth	50 ,,	10	10426	2	2103	12	12529	12	—	2	2101	3	3192	4	1	3	3344	20	21166	—	—	—
V	,,	44 ,,	9	8083	3	2699	12	10782	12	—	1	882	2	1693	2	1	—	—	15	13357	—	—	—
		One-deckers.																					
W	,,	44-gun frigate	2	2759	1	1370	3	4129	3	—	—	—	—	—	—	—	—	—	3	4129	—	—	—
X	,,	40 ,,	1	1239	—	—	1	1239	1	—	—	—	—	—	—	—	—	—	1	1239	—	—	—
Y	,,	38 ,,	4	4366	—	—	4	4366	4	—	—	—	—	—	—	—	2	2129	6	6495	—	—	—
Z	,,	,, ,, small	16	15618	—	—	16	15618	14	2	—	—	—	—	—	—	1	1024	17	16642	—	—	6
A	,,	36 ,, 18-pounder large	1	1032	—	—	1	1032	1	—	—	—	—	—	—	—	—	—	1	1032	—	—	—
B	,,	,, ,, ,, small	8	7119	—	—	8	7119	8	—	1	882	1	—	—	—	6	5557	15	13558	—	—	—
C	,,	,, ,, 12 ,,	9	8494	—	—	9	8494	—	9	1	931	3	2660	—	4	—	—	13	12085	—	—	—
D	,,	32 ,, 18 ,,	7	5608	—	—	7	5608	7	—	—	—	—	—	—	—	—	—	7	5608	2	1583	4
E	,,	,, ,, 12 ,, large	2	1561	—	—	2	1561	—	2	—	—	—	—	—	—	—	—	2	1561	—	—	—
F	Sixth	,, ,,	38	26322	1	679	39	27001	37	2	2	1393	1	—	1	1	—	—	41	28394	—	—	—
G	,,	24-gun post-ship	22	18109	1	605	23	18714	21	2	1	594	3	1826	4	—	—	—	27	16134	—	—	—
H	,,	20 ,,	1	1605	1	519	2	2124	4	—	—	—	1	528	1	—	—	—	5	2652	—	—	—
I	Sloops	18-gun ship-sloop, quarter-decked	6	2745	2	862	8	3607	6	2	1	481	—	—	—	1	—	—	9	4088	—	—	—
K	,,	,, flush	10	4448	—	—	10	4448	6	4	—	—	1	340	1	—	2	849	12	5297	—	—	6
L	,,	16 ,, quarter-decked, large	12	4464	1	342	13	4806	12	1	—	—	2	718	2	—	—	—	15	5524	—	—	—
M	,,	,, ,, ,, small	8	2590	1	322	9	2912	9	—	—	—	1	319	2	—	—	—	10	3231	—	—	4
N	,,	14 ,, flush	1	355	—	—	1	355	—	1	—	—	—	—	—	—	—	—	1	355	—	—	—
O	,,	,, quarter-decked	8	2424	—	—	8	2424	8	—	—	—	2	605	2	—	—	—	10	3029	—	—	—
P	,,	18-gun brig-sloop	2	737	—	—	2	737	1	1	—	—	—	—	—	—	—	—	2	737	—	—	—
Q	,,	16 ,,	10	2807	—	—	10	2807	3	7	—	—	—	—	—	—	—	—	10	2807	—	—	—
R	,,	,,	8	1681	1	207	9	1888	8	1	—	—	1	209	1	—	—	—	10	2097	—	—	—
S	Bombs, of	8 guns and 2 mortars	3	609	—	—	3	609	2	—	—	—	—	—	—	—	—	—	2	609	—	—	—
T	Fireships	14 ,,	3	1273	—	—	3	1273	2	1	—	—	1	423	1	—	—	—	4	1696	—	—	—
U	Gun-brigs	12 ,,	3	613	—	—	3	613	2	1	—	—	—	—	—	—	—	—	3	613	—	—	—
W	,,	10 ,,	13	1947	—	—	13	1947	13	—	—	—	—	—	—	—	—	—	13	1947	—	—	12
X	Cutters, &c.	16 ,,	1	185	—	—	1	185	1	—	—	—	—	—	—	—	—	—	1	185	—	—	—
Y	,,	14 ,,	5	772	—	—	5	772	5	—	—	—	2	181	1	—	—	—	7	953	—	—	—
Z	,,	12 ,,	4	743	—	—	4	743	4	—	—	—	1	275	2	—	—	—	7	1018	—	—	—
a	,,	10 ,,	2	298	—	—	2	298	—	2	—	—	—	—	—	—	—	—	2	298	—	—	—
b	,,	8 ,,	2	241	—	—	2	241	—	2	—	—	—	—	—	—	—	—	2	241	—	—	—
c	,,	6 ,,	1	151	—	—	1	151	—	—	—	—	—	—	—	—	—	—	2	151	—	—	—
d	,,	,,	1	47	—	—	1	47	1	—	1	88	1	—	—	—	—	—	2	135	—	—	—
e	Third-rate	36 ,,	—	—	—	—	—	—	—	—	1	1386	—	—	1	—	—	—	1	1386	—	—	—
f	Fifth	24 ,,	—	—	—	—	—	—	—	—	10	8914	—	—	10	—	—	—	10	8914	—	—	—
g	,,	18 ,,	—	—	—	—	—	—	—	—	1	932	—	—	1	—	—	—	1	932	—	—	—
h	Float. Batt.	56 and 46 guns	—	—	—	—	—	—	—	—	2	3035	—	—	2	—	—	—	2	3035	—	—	—
i	,,	20 guns and under	—	—	—	—	—	—	—	—	5	1798	—	—	5	—	—	—	5	1798	2	794	2
k	Gun-vessels	from 1 to 3 guns	—	—	—	—	—	—	—	—	19	1250	—	—	19	—	—	—	19	1250	—	—	—
l	Sloops on Discovery		—	—	—	—	—	—	—	—	2	743	—	—	—	—	—	—	2	743	—	—	—
m	Armed Transports		—	—	—	—	—	—	—	—	7	2307	—	—	6	1	—	—	7	2307	—	—	—
n	Yachts	royal, or large	—	—	—	—	—	—	—	—	3	494	3	589	6	—	1	102	7	1083	—	—	—
o	,,	small	—	—	—	—	—	—	—	—	3	255	1	42	4	—	—	—	5	399	1	96	—
		*Grand Total	326	290290	37	48972	363	339262	306	57	69	42386	51	45416	83	37	27	38512	510	465576	7	6350	34

VOL. I

Increase and Decrease in the Classes since the date of the last Year's Abstract.

Pur-chased.	Captured.		Converted from other Classes.		Ordered to be Built.		TOTAL of Increase.		Loss by Capture, &c.		Converted to other Classes.		Sold, or taken to Pieces.		TOTAL of Decrease.		CARRONADES, as established by an Admiralty-Order of Nov. 19, 1794.						Total of Carriage-Guns.	Complement, exclusive of Widows' Men, according to an Order of Council of April 16, 1794.		
																	Quarter-deck.		Forecastle.		Poop.						
Tons.	No.	Tons.	No.	Tons.	No.	Tons.	No.	Tons.	No.	Tons.	No.	Tons.	No.	Tons.	No.	Tons.	No.	Nature.	No.	Nature.	No.	Nature.		Men.	Boys.	Total.
-	-	-	-	-	1	2616	1	2616	-	-	-	-	-	-	-	-	-	-	2	32-prs.†	6	24-prs.	118	788	40	828
-	-	-	-	-	-	-	-	-	-	-	-	-	-	-	-	-	-	-	,,	,, ,,	,,	,, ,,	108	,,	,,	,,
-	-	-	-	-	1	2024	1	2024	} -	-	-	-	-	-	-	-	-	-	,,	,, ,,	,,	18 ,,	106	694	37	731
-	-	-	-	-	-	-	-	-	-	-	-	-	-	-	-	-	-	,,	,, ,,	,,	,, ,,	98	,,	,,	,,
-	2	4385	-	-	-	-	2	4385	-	-	-	-	-	-	-	-	-	-	,,	,, ,,	,,	,, ,,	88	677	36	713
-	4	7374	-	-	1	1940	4	7374	-	-	-	-	1	1878	1	1878	-	-	,,	,, ,,	,,	,, ,,	82	604	32	636
-	-	-	-	-	2	3549	2	3549	-	-	1	1621	1	1662	1	1606	5	4889	-	-	,,	,, ,,	,,	556	30	586
-	-	-	-	-	-	-	-	-	1	1397	4	5502	-	-	3	6899	-	-	,,	24	,,	,, ,,	72	458	27	485
-	6	11759	-	-	4	8105	12	23741	3	4896	5	7164	1	1606	9	13666										
-	-	-	-	-	-	-	-	-	-	-	3	2689	2	2120	2	2120	4	24-prs.	,,	18 ,,	,,	12 ,,	62	317	21	338
-	-	-	-	-	-	-	-	-	-	-	-	-	-	-	3	2689	6	18 ,,	,,	18 ,,	-	-	52	271	20	291
-	1	1239	3	4129	-	-	3	4129	-	-	-	-	-	-	-	-	,,	32 ,,	,,	32 ,,	-	-	46	251	20	271
-	2	2239	-	-	2	2129	4	4368	} -	-	-	-	-	-	-	-	,,	,, ,,	,,	,, ,,	-	-	44	232	19	251
-	1	1014	-	-	1	1024	8	8020																		
-	1	1032	-	-	-	-	1	1032																		
-	2	1917	-	-	6	5557	6	5557	1	930	-	-	1	952	2	1882	4	24 ,,	,,	24 ,,	-	-	38	223	18	241
-	-	-	-	-	-	-	2	1917	-	-	-	-	-	-	-	-	,,	,, ,,	,,	,, ,,	-	-	,,	194	,,	212
-	3	2064	-	-	-	-	6	4816	1	681	-	-	1	687	2	1368	} ,,	,, ,,	,,	,, ,,	-	-	34	176	17	193
-	1	573	-	-	-	-	3	2064	1	594	-	-	1	593	2	1187	6	18 ,,	,,	18 ,,	-	-	32	137	15	152
-	1	511	-	-	-	-	1	573	1	513	-	-	-	-	1	513	,,	12 ,,	,,	12 ,,	-	-	28	118	14	132
-	1	486	-	-	2	849	1	511	1	486	-	-	-	-	1	486	,,	,, ,,	,,	,, ,,	-	-	26	108	12	120
							9	3893																		
-	-	-	-	-	-	-	4	1469	2	732	-	-	-	-	2	732	,,	,, ,,	,,	,, ,,	-	-	22	,,	,,	,,
-	2	630	-	-	-	-	2	630	1	321	-	-	-	-	1	321										
									1	275	-	-	-	-	-	275	,,	,, ,,	,,	,, ,,	-	-	20	,,	,,	,,
-	3	952	-	-	-	-	3	952	1	276	-	-	-	-	1	276										
-	1	227	-	-	-	-	1	227	1	208	-	-	1	180	2	488										
172	-	-	3	613	-	-	3	613																		
							13	1947																		
-	2	300	-	-	-	-	2	300	1	165	-	-	1	199	1	165										
									1	195	3	613			5	1007										
47	-	-	-	-	-	-	1	47	1	61	-	-	-	-	1	61										
-	-	-	3	2689	-	-	3	2689																		
-	-	-	2	3035	-	-	2	3035																		
							4	1412	1	950	-	-	-	-	1	950										
1308	-	-	-	-	-	-	20	1308	-	-	-	-	1	58	1	58										
919	-	-	-	-	-	-	1	919	-	-	-	-	1	688	1	688										
							1	96																		
2446	27	24943	11	10466	15	17664	117	77504	18	11283	11	10466	10	7183	39	28932										

2 K

No. 4.

An ABSTRACT of the Ships and Vessels belonging to the British Navy at the commencement of the Year 1796.

Letters of Reference	RATE	CLASS			Cruisers – In Commission No.	Tons	In Ordinary, under or for Repair No.	Tons	Total No.	Tons	No. British Built	No. Foreign Built	Stationary Harbour-ships, &c. – In Commission No.	Tons	Not in Commission No.	Tons	No. British Built	No. Foreign Built	Building, or Ordered to be Built No.	Tons	Grand Total No.	Tons
A	First. Three-deckers.	120-gun ship			1	2351	–	–	1	2351	1	–	–	–	–	–	–	–	2	5124	2	
B*	,,	112 ,,			–	–	–	–	–	–	–	–	–	–	–	–	–	–	–	–	2	
C	,,	100 ,, 18-pounder			2	4572	–	–	2	4572	2	–	–	–	–	–	–	–	–	–	2	
D	,,	,, 12 ,,			3	6428	–	–	3	6428	3	–	–	–	–	–	–	–	–	–	3	
E	Second.	98 ,, 18 ,, – large			–	–	–	–	–	–	–	–	–	–	–	–	–	–	1	2276	1	
F	,,	,, ,, ,, – small			–	–	–	–	–	–	–	–	–	–	–	–	–	–	3	6363	3	
G	,,	,, 12 ,,			15	28860	–	–	15	28860	15	–	1	1869	–	–	1	–	–	–	16	30
H	,,	90 ,,			1	1814	–	–	1	1814	1	–	2	3699	–	–	2	–	–	–	3	5
I	Third. Two-deckers.	80 ,,			5	10783	–	–	5	10783	1	4	–	–	–	–	–	–	1	2062	6	12
K	,,	74 ,, 24-pounder			2	3754	1	1889	3	5643	1	2	–	–	–	–	–	–	8	15339	11	20
L	,,	,, ,, 18 ,, – large			4	7347	1	1884	5	9231	3	2	–	–	2	3600	–	2	4	7538	11	20
M	,,	,, ,, ,, – middl			5	8583	–	–	5	8583	4	1	1	1778	–	–	–	–	2	3549	8	13
N	,,	,, ,, ,, – small			43	70357	8	12997	51	83354	51	–	3	4803	4	6455	7	–	–	–	58	95
O	,,	64 ,,			24	33282	1	1379	25	34661	24	1	3	4134	10	13869	9	4	–	–	38	55
P	Fourth.	60 ,,			–	–	–	–	–	–	–	–	–	–	4	4944	3	1	–	–	4	
Q	,,		Line		105	178131	11	18149	116	196280	106	10	10	16283	20	28868	22	8	21	42251	167	283
R*	,,	56 ,, flush			3	4022	1	1434	4	5456	4	–	–	–	–	–	–	–	–	–	4	5
S*	,,	54 ,, ,,			4	4848	1	1176	5	6024	5	–	–	–	–	–	–	–	–	–	5	
T	,,	50 ,, quarter-decked			10	10562	2	1967	12	12529	12	–	2	2101	3	3192	4	1	3	3344	20	21
V	Fifth.	44 ,, ,,			8	7205	1	898	9	8103	9	–	1	882	2	1693	2	1	–	–	12	10
W	One-deckers.	44-gun frigate			3	4129	–	–	3	4129	3	–	–	–	–	–	–	–	–	–	3	4
X	,,	40 ,, 24-pounder			1	1239	–	–	1	1239	–	1	–	–	–	–	–	–	1	1277	2	4
Y	,,	38 ,, 18 ,,			5	5468	–	–	5	5468	–	5	–	–	–	–	–	–	2	2302	2	
Z	,,	,, ,, ,, – large			15	14789	–	–	15	14789	14	1	–	–	–	–	–	–	6	6075	21	20
A	,,	36 ,, ,, – small			1	1032	–	–	1	1032	–	1	–	–	–	–	–	–	2	1049	2	2
B	,,	,, ,, 12 ,, – large			14	12676	–	–	14	12676	14	–	–	–	1	882	1	–	2	1852	17	15
C	,,	,, ,, ,, – small			8	7394	3	2810	11	10204	11	–	1	931	5	4398	–	6	–	–	17	15
D	,,	32 ,, 18 ,,			7	5608	–	–	7	5608	7	–	–	–	–	–	–	–	–	–	7	5
E	,,	,, ,, 12 ,, – large			2	1561	–	–	2	1561	1	–	–	–	–	–	–	–	3	2463	5	4
F	,,	,, ,, ,, – small			35	24251	3	2051	38	26302	37	1	–	–	2	1393	1	1	–	–	40	27
G	Sixth.	28 ,, ,,			22	13098	1	599	23	13697	20	3	1	594	3	1826	4	–	–	–	27	16
H	,,	24-gun post-ship			3	1605	1	519	4	2124	4	–	–	–	2	1147	–	2	–	–	6	3
I	,,	22 ,, flush			1	524	–	–	1	524	–	1	–	–	–	–	–	–	–	–	1	
K	,,	20 ,, quarter-decked			7	3218	1	432	8	3650	5	3	1	481	–	–	–	1	–	–	8	4
L	,,	,, ,, flush			1	424	–	–	1	424	–	1	–	–	–	–	–	–	–	–	1	
M	Sloops.	Arrow and Dart			–	–	–	–	–	–	–	–	–	–	–	–	–	–	2	772	2	
N	,,	18-gun ship-sloop, quarter-decked			10	4448	–	–	10	4448	6	4	–	–	2	648	2	–	6	2544	16	6
O*	,,	,, ,, flush			–	–	–	–	–	–	–	–	–	–	–	–	–	–	2	801	2	
P	,,	16 ,, quarter-decked, large			13	4797	–	–	13	4797	11	2	–	–	2	694	2	–	3	1146	18	10
Q	,,	,, ,, ,, small			9	2912	–	–	9	2912	9	–	–	–	1	319	1	–	–	–	10	4
R	,,	,, ,, flush			3	915	–	–	3	915	–	3	–	–	1	355	1	–	–	–	4	5
S	,,	14 ,, quarter-decked			9	2693	–	–	9	2693	9	–	–	–	2	605	2	–	–	–	11	7
T	,,	,, ,, flush			1	200	–	–	1	200	1	–	–	–	–	–	–	–	–	–	1	
U	,,	18-gun brig-sloop – large			6	3319	–	–	6	3319	8	1	–	–	–	–	–	–	–	–	9	
V	,,	,, ,, ,, small			6	1906	–	–	6	1906	6	–	–	–	–	–	–	–	2	631	8	9
W	,,	16 ,, ,,			11	3147	1	275	12	3422	9	2	–	–	1	202	1	–	–	–	13	12
X	,,	14 ,, ,,			9	2037	3	612	12	2649	9	3	–	–	1	423	1	–	–	–	13	13
Y	Bombs, of	8 guns and 2 mortars			2	609	–	–	2	609	2	–	–	–	–	–	–	–	–	–	2	2
Z	Fireships,	14 guns			3	1273	–	–	3	1273	3	–	–	–	–	–	–	–	–	–	3	4
b	Gun-brigs,	,,			3	613	–	–	3	613	3	–	–	–	–	–	–	–	–	–	3	
c	,,	12 ,,			16	2368	–	–	16	2368	16	–	–	–	–	–	–	–	–	–	16	
d	Cutters, &c.	14 ,,			4	300	–	–	4	300	–	2	–	–	1	181	1	–	–	–	5	
e	,,	12 ,,			5	773	–	–	5	773	4	–	–	–	2	275	2	–	–	–	7	
f	,,	10 ,,			2	743	–	–	2	743	4	–	–	–	–	–	–	–	–	–	2	
g	,,	8 ,,			2	298	–	–	2	298	–	2	–	–	–	–	–	–	–	–	2	
h	,,	6 ,,			2	241	–	–	2	241	–	2	–	–	–	–	–	–	–	–	2	
i	,,	4 ,,			1	71	–	–	1	71	–	–	–	–	–	–	–	–	–	–	1	
k	First-rate,	50 ,,			1	47	–	–	1	47	1	–	1	2747	1	88	1	1	–	–	1	2
l	Third ,,	36 ,,			–	–	–	–	–	–	–	–	12	10706	–	–	12	–	–	–	12	10
m	Fifth ,,	24 ,,			–	–	–	–	–	–	–	–	2	1629	–	–	2	2	–	–	2	
n	,,	18 ,,			–	–	–	–	–	–	–	–	2	3035	–	–	2	–	–	–	2	
o	Float. Batt.	58 and 46 guns			–	–	–	–	–	–	–	–	4	1489	–	–	4	–	–	–	4	
p		20 guns and under			–	–	–	–	–	–	–	–	18	1419	4	273	22	–	–	–	22	
q	Gun-vessels, from 1 to 4 guns				–	–	–	–	–	–	–	–	1	406	2	337	6	2	–	–	2	
r	Sloops on Discovery				–	–	–	–	–	–	–	–	8	2984	–	–	8	–	–	–	8	2
s	Armed Transports				–	–	–	–	–	–	–	–	4	679	2	404	6	–	–	–	6	
t	Yachts		– – – royal, or large		–	–	–	–	–	–	–	–	2	162	4	135	4	–	1	102	6	5
u	,,		– – – – – small		–	–	–	–	–	–	–	–	–	–	–	–	–	–	–	–	–	

*Grand Total – – 376 335493 29 30922 405 366415 333 72 70 46528 59 47690 83 46 58 69790 592 53

VOL. I.

Increase and Decrease in the Classes since the date of the last Year's Abstract.

Launched.				Pur-chased.		Captured.		Converted from other Classes.		Ordered to be Built.		TOTAL of Increase.		Loss by Capture, &c.		Converted to other Classes.		Sold, or taken to Pieces.		TOTAL of Decrease.	
King's Yards.		Merchants' Yards.																			
No.	Tons.	No.	Tons.	No.	Tons.	No.	Tons.	No.	Tons.	No.	Tons.	No.	Tons.	No.	Tons.	No.	Tons.	No.	Tons.	No.	Tons.
1	2351	–	–	–	–	–	–	–	–	–	–	1	2351	–	–	1	2747	–	–	1	2747
–	–	–	–	–	–	–	–	–	–	–	–	1	2011	–	–	–	–	–	–	1	2011
–	–	–	–	–	–	1	2210	–	–	–	–	1	2210	–	–	–	–	–	–	–	–
–	–	–	–	–	–	1	1889	–	–	6	11557	7	13446	–	–	–	–	–	–	–	–
–	–	–	–	–	–	2	3707	–	–	4	7538	6	11245	1	1820	–	–	1	1811	2	3631
–	–	–	–	–	–	1	1621	–	–	–	–	1	1621	2	3239	–	...	–	–	2	3239
–	–	–	–	–	–	–	–	1	1386	–	–	1	1386								
–	–	–	–	–	–	1	1226	–	–	–	–	1	1226								
1	2351	–	–	–	–	6	10653	1	1386	10	19095	18	33485	4	7070	1	2747	1	1811	6	11628
–	–	–	–	4	5456	–	–	–	–	–	–	4	5456								
–	–	–	–	5	6024	–	–	–	–	–	–	5	6024								
–	–	–	–	–	–	–	–	–	–	–	–	–	–	1	887	2	1792	–	–	3	2679
–	–	–	–	–	–	–	–	–	–	1	1277	1	1277								
–	–	–	–	–	–	–	–	–	–	2	2302	2	2302								
–	–	–	–	–	–	1	1102	–	–	1	1052	2	2154								
–	–	–	–	–	–	–	–	–	–	5	5051	5	5051	1	1029	–	–	–	–	1	1029
–	–	–	–	–	–	–	–	–	–	1	1049	1	1049								
–	–	6	5557	–	–	–	–	–	–	2	1852	8	7409								
–	–	–	–	–	–	4	3448	–	–	–	–	4	3448								
–	–	–	–	–	–	–	–	–	–	3	2463	3	2463								
–	–	–	–	–	–	1	697	–	–	–	–	1	697	–	–	1	697	1	699	2	1396
–	–	–	–	–	–	1	581	–	–	–	–	1	581	1	598	–	–	–	–	1	598
–	–	–	–	–	–	1	619	–	–	–	–	1	619								
–	–	–	–	–	–	1	524	–	–	–	–	1	524								
–	–	–	–	–	–	1	472	–	–	–	–	1	472	1	429	–	–	–	–	1	429
–	–	–	–	–	–	1	424	–	–	–	–	1	424								
–	–	–	–	–	–	–	–	–	–	2	772	2	772								
–	–	–	–	–	–	–	–	–	–	4	1695	4	1695								
–	–	–	–	–	–	–	–	–	–	2	801	2	801	–	–	–	–	1	340	1	340
–	–	–	–	–	–	1	345	–	–	3	1146	4	1491							1	378
–	–	–	–	–	–	3	915	–	–	–	–	3	915								
–	–	–	–	1	269	–	–	–	–	–	–	1	269								
–	–	–	–	1	200	–	–	–	–	–	–	1	200					1	365	1	365
–	–	8	2947	–	–	–	–	–	–	–	–	8	2947								
–	–	6	1906	–	–	–	–	–	–	2	631	8	2537					1	262	1	262
–	–	–	–	–	–	3	877	–	–	–	–	3	877	1	227	–	–	1	209	2	436
–	–	–	–	1	243	4	947	–	–	–	–	5	1190								
–	–	–	–	3	421	–	–	–	–	–	–	3	421								
–	–	–	–	–	–	1	165	–	–	–	–	1	165								
–	–	–	–	–	–	–	–	–	–	–	–	–	–	1	80	–	–	–	–	1	80
–	–	–	–	–	–	–	–	1	2747	–	–	1	2747	–	–	1	1386	–	–	1	1386
–	–	–	–	–	–	–	–	2	1792	–	–	2	1792								
–	–	–	–	–	–	–	–	1	697	–	–	1	697								
–	–	–	–	–	–	4	505	–	–	–	–	4	505	1	309	–	–	–	–	1	309
–	–	–	–	–	–	1	677	–	–	–	–	1	677								63
1	2351	20	10410	15	12613	34	22951	5	6622	38	39186	113	94133	12	10692	5	6622	7	4064	24	21378

2 L

NOTES TO ANNUAL ABSTRACTS.

NOTES TO ABSTRACT, No. 1.

† The official navy-list contains four classes not to be found in this Abstract; the 110, 76, 52, and 22 gun ship. The 110, a building class, consisted of the Hibernia and Ville-de-Paris. The latter ship, on being launched, was fitted with thirty-two instead of thirty 24-pounders, but was not registered as a 112 until many years afterwards. The Hibernia was made 11 feet longer than originally intended, and became pierced, in consequence, for a pair of additional ports upon each deck; but, although mounting at first 118, and afterwards 120 guns, exclusive of poop-carronades, the Hibernia still classed as a 110-gun ship. The 76-gun class was filled by one ship only, the Canada; her captain, the late Sir George Collier, having applied for and obtained two additional 18-pounders (making the number 30 instead of 28) for her second deck. The Canada, one of the smallest 74s in the navy, is here restored to her proper class. The 52 and 22 gun classes also contain each but one individual; the former, the Leander, because she had exchanged two of her carronades for two long 6-pounders; the latter, the Myrmidon, because she had received on board two 3-pounders for her quarter-deck. Both ships are here re-instated among their former class-mates; the one as a 50, the other as a 20 gun ship. The above four classes, together with "Hospital and Receiving ships" (here added to their respective classes in the "Stationary" columns), "Hoys, Lighters, and Transports," and "Hulks" (both for their insignificance omitted), are the only classes in the official list of the year 1793 not to be found in this Abstract. But the latter is, in other respects, much more copious than the former. For instance, the numerous sub-classes, or varieties of the primary *gun*-class, appear nowhere but in this series of Abstracts. A difference in the nature is often as important as a difference in the number of the guns mounted. That forms one distinction. Another distinction lies in the difference of the tonnage, or size, especially among the British-built ships. In the official register, sloops, without any regard to their guns, are divided into "Sloops rigged as ships," "Sloops rigged as brigs." Here, each of those classes is sub-divided according to the gun-force of the vessels; and the ship-sloops are further distinguished, as they are "quarter-decked," with room to mount six or eight additional guns, or "flush," with every, except occasionally the bow, port already filled.

Captured ships, especially when commissioned and retained in service on a foreign station, were frequently mis-registered. These are placed in their proper stations, or where they would have classed had they been British-built ships. Soon after the commencement of the year 1793, carronades became so extensively employed, sometimes in lieu of, and sometimes in addition to, the quarter-deck and forecastle long guns, that an exact enumeration of the ship's long guns, the alleged groundwork of the classification would have multiplied, without end, the number of classes, besides subjecting them to repeated fluctuations: in short, the object of any classification at all would thereby have been defeated. One instance, and that a real one, may suffice. A frigate receives on board as her equipment 38 long guns and eight carronades, and becomes, in consequence, a 38. She afterwards exchanges her 28 main-deck long guns for carronades, and is then, or, in strictness ought to be, a 10-gun frigate. She subsequently receives back her long 18s, and is restored to a 38; but presently parts with six of her long 9s for an equal number of carronades, and, in obedience to the rule laid down, ought then to be a 32. An enumeration of the carronades, as well as the long guns, would have continued her as a 46 through all these changes; but not only were carronades not considered as *guns* (see p. 40), but they were, as yet, too partially mounted to be of any great use in classification. The only way left to avoid any confusion of the kind is, to class the ships, other circumstances considered, in reference to their original establishment of long guns on the principal deck or decks. Thus, the frigate just instanced, mounting on the main deck, through every alteration in her armament, 28 guns (whether long guns or carronades), may continue to rank as a 38-gun frigate. It is true that the classes D and G or H agree in the number of their main-deck guns, and yet are separated. The ships of D are, however, considerably larger than those of G, and a full third larger than those of H; and besides, every ship of D, all through the Abstracts, is foreign-built. Due notice will be taken of any other exception that may hereafter occur.

‡ It is here that worn-out cruisers eke out the remnant of their days. Not to have separated them from their active class-mates, would have been doing an injustice to the latter. The "&c." comprehends all the classes below the cutters of four guns.

‖ Swivels, being mounted on stocks, are not *carriage*-guns. Carronades were not, at this time, officially considered even as *guns* (see p. 40), and are not considered anywhere as *long* guns. Both swivels and carronades were in use; but, as the latter gained ground, the former decreased, and finally disappeared.

§ Captured ships, and ships built or bought as experiments, were frequently armed somewhat differently from the regular establishment: also the rapid increase of carronades soon gave an entire change to the quarter-deck and forecastle armaments. Still the guns on the principal decks of all the classes, down to frigates inclusive, remained the same, with very few exceptions, beyond those remarked upon in the first note.

†† These are fictitious men, whose pay and maintenance, by a very ancient regulation in the navy, constitute a fund for pensioning the widows of officers,

Hence they are called "Widows' men," and are invariably included in the established complement of every ship, in the proportion assigned to her rate: so that a 112-gun ship's ostensible complement is 850 men and boys; but, as the statements in this work look to fighting, rather than fictitious men, we have thought fit to exclude the latter, and carry out the net complement only.

D*. The "18-pounder" and other "pounders" below it apply to the nature of the guns on the third deck (see p. 20) of three-deckers, second deck of two-deckers, and single or main deck of one-deckers. A reference to the gun-compartment of the Abstract will show, that on the other deck or decks there is always, among the subdivisions of the primary class, a uniformity of caliber.

F*. The usefulness of this division, into *large* and *small*, will be more apparent in some of the other classes, particularly in those of the 74-gun ship and frigate. It will exhibit, in a clear manner, the progressive increase in the size of the ships.

I*. The single cruising individual of this class is the Namur, built in 1756. Steel classes the Blenheim and Impregnable as 90s, but improperly, as both those ships, although nearly as small as the Namur, mounted 28, and not 26 guns, on each of their principal decks.

K*. The single cruiser of this class is the Gibraltar, a Spanish-built ship, and an exception, in point of armament (she mounted 24s on both her first and second decks), to the establishment of the class, that having reference to the two ships building, the Cæsar and Foudroyant. There had been two ships of this class; one, the Foudroyant, of 1977 tons, captured from the French in 1758, the other, the Formidable, of 2002 tons, captured also from the French in 1759. Both ships were established with the guns assigned to the class in this Abstract, excepting in having 9 instead of 12 pounders for the quarter-deck and forecastle.

L*. There had been a French-built ship of this class, the Magnanime, of 1836 tons, captured as long ago as 1748; at which time the British 90-gun ship scarcely exceeded 1730 tons. There had also been two British-built 24-pounder 74s, the Valiant, built in the year 1759, of 1799, and the Triumph, built in the year 1784, of 1825 tons; but both ships subsequently exchanged their 24 for 18 pounders, and consequently rank in the class next below.

M*. The first British-built 74-gun ship appears to have been the "Royall-Oake," launched in 1674. She is the single individual at No. 13 of the Abstract given at pp. 420, 421; and, although comparatively of so small a tonnage, the ship mounted on her first and second decks the same number and nature of guns as the 18-pounder 74 of the present day. Nothing can better demonstrate the improvement that has been effected in this highly-important line-of-battle class. The *large* division is made to descend to 1799 tons inclusive; the *middling*, to all below that and above 1699 tons; and the *small*, to the remainder.

Z*. The *large* class will descend to 1050 tons inclusive.

G*. And this to 740 tons.

452   APPENDIX.

K*. So designated, as being the lowest classes to which post-captains are appointed. They are frequently called frigates; but even the ships of the class next above them scarcely deserve that name, and would, in the French navy, class as corvettes.

S*. For an explanation of this term, see p. 17.

T*. The *large* descends to 340 tons.

Y*. As the official list makes a distinction between *ship-rigged* and *brig-rigged* sloops, we have done the same, and placed all the former ahead of the latter; although it is clear that the 18-gun brig-sloop deserves a higher rank than the 14, or even the 16-gun ship-sloop.

d*. The ships both of this and the class next below it usually cruise until required for the special purpose for which they were designed; and most of the vessels in question, the fire-ships in particular (three of which were made permanent sloops, and class at *T*), were very fast sailers.

s*. Although it may appear strange to class a 4-gun cutter of 95 above a 24-gun ship of 800 or 900 tons; yet it should be recollected, that store-ships and other *armées en flûte* do not cruise, but proceed straight to their destination, fighting only when attacked; while the smallest cutter goes to sea on purpose to harass the enemy's commerce: a service often very effectually performed by a British cruiser even of that insignificant class.

b*. Some of these class, in the official list, as second and third rates; simply because the captains and crews are paid in the same proportion as those rates. We long hesitated about introducing "Yachts" at all, but at all events, can assign to none of them any higher station than this. Steel usually classes them as post-ships, but it appears absurd to rank such toys among fighting vessels.

* The time necessarily occupied in transmitting information from the outports, and then in carrying it through the press to publication, renders Steel's January list a safer guide for the December than the January state and disposition of the British navy. A mean of the numbers in the January and February lists may come nearer the truth. The mean of those for the year 1793 gives 30, as the commissioned, and 159 as the whole line-total. This Abstract states the one to have been 29, and the other 153; which latter sum, added to Steel's five line "hulks," and one old 60 which we have classed as a 50, makes the 159. Steel's grand total is 423 for January and 424 for February. The 10 hulks added to our grand total makes it 421. The difference is accounted for by Steel's having inserted the Fortunée frigate and Ætna bomb, long previously struck out of the lists of the navy, as well as a tender which we have omitted. The official line-total, not including the 12 hospital and receiving ships, amounts to 141; and the grand total, including 50 hoys, lighters, and transports, 10 hulks, and 5 tenders and surveying vessels, amounts to 476.

It may be not out of place here to introduce a short table, showing the registered tonnage of the British navy at different epochs since the year 1521, which is as early as the tons of the ships appear to have been computed.

Year.	King's Reign.	Ships, including Hulks, &c.	
		No.	Tons.
1521	Henry VIII.	16	7260
1546	,,	58	12455
1558	Mary	26	7110
1578	Elizabeth	24	10506
1588	,,	34	12590
1603	,,	42	17055
1607	James I.	36	14710
1618	,,	39	15100
1633	Charles I.	50	23595
1641	,,	42	22411
1660	Charles II.	154	57463
1675	,,	151	70587
1685	,,	179	103558
1702	William	272	159020
1714	Anne	247	167219
1721	George I.	233	170862
1753	George II.	291	234924
1760	George III.	412	321104
1783	,,	617	500781
1789	,,	452	413667

NOTES TO ABSTRACT, No. 2.

* FOR observations upon the classes, and the general arrangement of the tabular matter, see notes † and ‡ to the first Annual Abstract.

‡ As captured vessels are also purchased of the captors before they can enter the service, this distinction may appear unnecessary. The term, however, is officially employed in contradistinction to *captured*. It means that the vessel, being deemed fit for the British navy, was purchased by the government from the British or foreign (but not enemy) owner, as the case might be.

|| The names and other particulars of such of these vessels as had belonged to the enemy's national navy, and did not rank below 24-gun corvettes in the latter, will be found in the prize-list for the year. The names of the few remaining vessels are of no importance.

§ The names and other particulars of all these vessels will be found in the proper list.

K*. The newly-launched ship of this class was the Cæsar, the first British-built 80 on two decks. The Cæsar began building at Plymouth yard, January 24, 1786, and was launched November 16, 1793. The last built three-decked 80 appears to have been the Princess Amelia, of 1579 tons, launched in 1757. It is rather surprising that the British, having in their possession the old French Formidable and Foudroyant (see note K* p. 451), should have waited 30 years before they set about building a similar class of ship.

* In comparing this total or the corresponding total in any of the succeeding Abstracts, with that in Steel's or any other list of the navy, care must be taken to allow for the excluded vessels, as explained in the last note to the first Abstract. Since March, 1793, a certain number of hired vessels had been attached to the British navy. They were chiefly employed in convoying the coasting trade; and, according to Steel, amounted, at the commencement of the present year, to 28 vessels, carrying from 8 to 24 guns.

NOTES TO ABSTRACT, No. 3.

† WHERE the established long guns of the line-of-battle ships are four on the forecastle; these may be considered as in substitution of two of them.

W*. The three ships of this class, the Anson, Indefatigable, and Magnanime, had been cut down from 64s. They were allowed to retain their 26 long 24s on their (first, but now) single or main deck, and were ordered to be fitted with twelve long 12-pounders and six 42-pounder carronades on the quarter-deck and forecastle; with a complement at first of 310, but afterwards of 330 men. They registered, in conformity to the number of their long guns, as 38-gun frigates; and this affords an opportunity of showing how little of a ship's actual force is to be known by taking her numerical force, either as the same is set down in the official navy-list, or found to be when carefully summed up. For instance, the Magnanime and Prudente, two British 38s, very near to each other in the alphabetical list, appear to have mounted as follows:—

	MAGNANIME.		PRUDENTE.	
	No.	Pdrs.	No.	Pdrs.
Main deck	26 long	24	26 long	12
Quarter-deck and forecastle	12 "	12	12 "	6
	6 carr.	42	6 carr.	18
	44 guns.		44 guns.	

While such a difference of force as this can exist between two ships of one and the same class, classification by *guns* becomes a nullity. To each of these ships we have assigned a different class. The Magnanime, and her two sister *rasés* rank, as they for some years did in Steel, as 44s; while the Prudente is one of the two stationary harbour-ships in class *D*, where she originally was registered, but, receiving on board, in the year 1779, two long 6s in lieu of two of her 18-pounder carronades, the Prudente became a 38. Not one of the three *rasés*, for all their class had been fixed from their number of long guns, went to sea with that number on board. The Indefatigable mounted but 28, and neither of the others probably more than 30 long guns: the deficiency, however, was amply made up in carronades. The French, about the same time, reduced some of their old and crank 74s in this way, calling them *vaisseaux rasés*.

B*. Of 1000 tons and upwards. The principal difference between a 38 and an 18 pounder 36, is that the latter has a pair of ports less on the main deck. Hence, a few inches of extra width to the ports and the intermediate spaces, and three or four feet of additional space before the foremost port (common in French ships, owing to the sharpness of their bows not admitting a broadside-gun so far forward), will easily occasion the longer and larger ship to mount the fewer guns upon her main deck.

c*. Twelve "fire-vessels" had been purchased in 1794; but which, as they mounted no guns, and were merely fitted up in readiness to be destroyed when the occasion suited, we have purposely omitted. Steel's list contains the whole of them.

f.* Whence this term originated is not very clear. A "gun-brig" is literally a brig armed with guns; and accordingly, the brig-sloop of 18 guns is also a gun-brig. The term is here meant to signify an armed brig commanded, not as usual by a master and commander, but by a lieutenant. The 12 new brigs at (g) were constructed to carry ten 18-pounder carronades and 2 long 18-pounders. The latter (24-pounders had been first ordered) were subsequently found too heavy and incommodious; and chase-guns of a lighter caliber were substituted. Some of these brigs, as well as of those afterwards built, mounted two guns, generally 3 or 4 pounders, in addition.

u*. The two individuals of this class were the Albion and Nonsuch, originally a 74 and 64. They were partially cut down and armed, the one with 30 long guns and twenty-eight 68-pounder carronades; the other with 26 long guns and twenty 68-pounder carronades.

v*. The first pair of the launched vessels were the Bravo and Firm, each constructed to carry sixteen long 18-pounders. The one was stationed at Jersey, the other in Leith roads. The next pair of launched vessels were the Mosquito and Sandfly, each constructed upon a plan of Sir Sidney Smith's, and fitted with two long 24-pounders and two 68-pounder carronades. One was stationed at Isle St. Marcou, the other at Jersey. Three of these vessels were registered as gun-vessels, and the Bravo as a sixth rate, to increase the pay of her captain. The whole, however, were no better than floating-batteries, and as such we have classed them. The Spanker floating-battery was built in 1794; but, as she was not measured, and resembled no other vessel in shape or appearance, we have omitted her. She mounted 24 heavy guns, and two large mortars.

w*. The 20 purchased vessels of this class had been "Dutch hoys," and were armed with from one to three guns for coast-defence. The same number of "river barges" had also been purchased and similarly armed, but the latter we have omitted. The names of the whole will be found in Steel.

* There were attached to the navy at the date of this Abstract about 54 hired vessels, mounting from 6 to 24 guns, and commanded by lieutenants.

NOTES TO ABSTRACT, No. 4.

B*. This ship is the Ville-de-Paris, the largest British-built ship of her day She began building at Chatham July 1, 1789, and was launched July 17 1795. See first note of Abstract No. 1, p. 449.

R* and S*. Had been East-Indiamen. Anomalous in their construction as two-decked ships of war, having the second or upper deck without an over-built quarter-deck and forecastle. On this account they mounted no more guns, except perhaps a pair or two of bow-chasers, than stands as the sign of their respective classes. These ships were fitted with 28 long 18-pounders on the first deck; the 56s with 28, and the 54s with 26, 32-pounder carronades on the second deck.

Q*. Two experimental vessels designed by Samuel Bentham, Esq., at that time inspector-general of his majesty's naval works. They were in shape much sharper than vessels of war in general, and projected or raked forward, at each end like a wherry. Their breadth increased from the water-line upwards; whereby it was considered that they would be stiffer and less liable to overset than ordinary vessels. The decks were straight fore and aft, and the frames or ribs of less curvature than usual. They were constructed to carry twenty-four 32-pounder carronades upon the main deck, and were afterwards fitted to receive two more carronades of the same nature on each of their two short decks, which we may call the quarter-deck and forecastle. All these carronades were fitted upon the non-recoil principle. It is believed that both the Arrow and Dart subsequently took on board, for their quarter-decks, two additional 32s. They proved to be stiff vessels and swift sailers, but it was found necessary to add some dead wood to their bottoms, in order to make them stay better. Not knowing exactly what characteristic designation to give the Arrow and Dart, we have merely named them: they must be considered, especially when their force is compared with that of the two or three classes next above them, as extraordinary vessels for *sloops of war*, but as such only they ranked. Three or four schooners were afterwards built upon a similar plan.

Y*. The *large* are of 340 tons and upwards. The new brigs of this and the next class were built of fir, and intended to carry long 6s, but by an admiralty-order of April 22, 1795, they were directed to be prepared for, and afterwards mounted, sixteen 32-pounder carronades and two long 6s. This armament, owing to the additional weight of the carronade-carriages and slides (the 32-pounder carronade and six feet 6-pounder weigh nearly alike), proved rather too much for the small class; and, in consequence, the carronades of many of the brigs were exchanged for 24s. The brig in the "Sold or taken to Pieces" column, was one of the larger description, the Despatch, which, as soon as launched, was transferred to the Russian admiral at Portsmouth.

* The hired vessels numbered about 60. See the last notes of Abstracts Nos. 1 and 2, pp. 452 and 453.

END OF VOL. I.

PRINTED BY WILLIAM CLOWES AND SONS, LIMITED, LONDON AND BECCLES.